Sweet Blue Flowers

Part Three

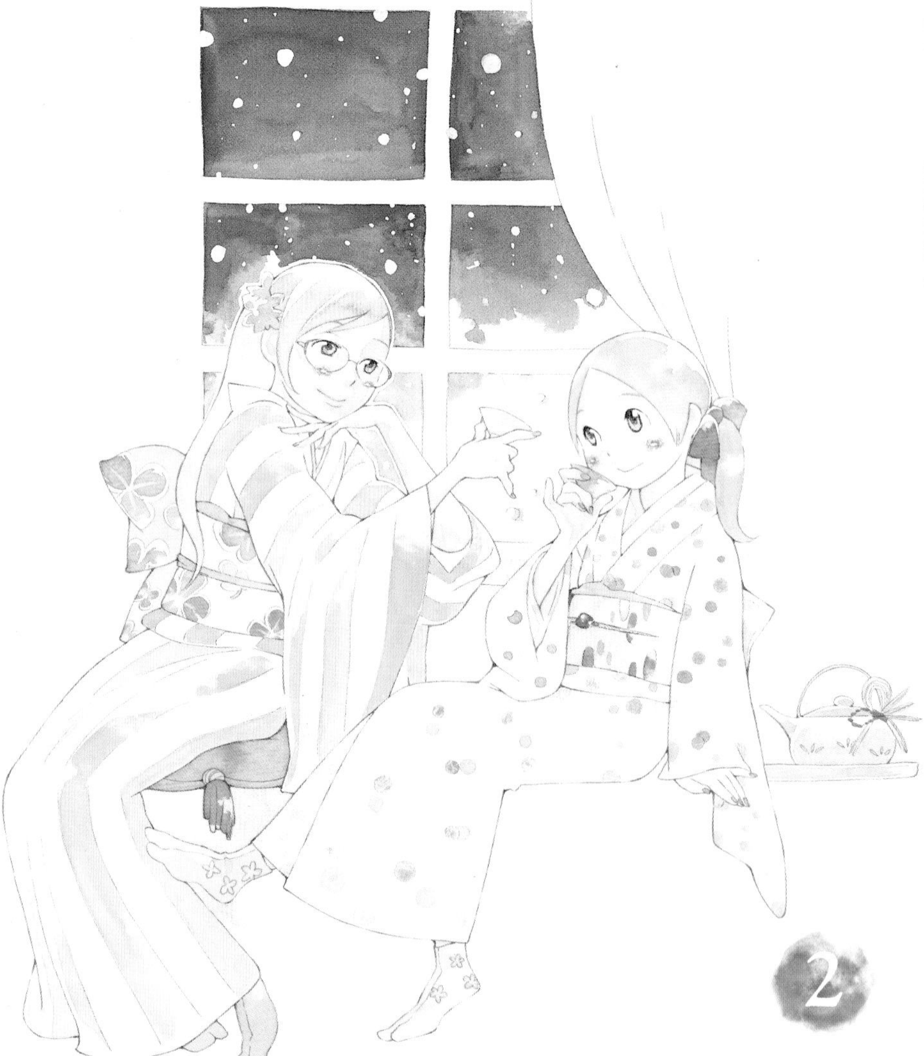

2

Story and Art by
Takako Shimura

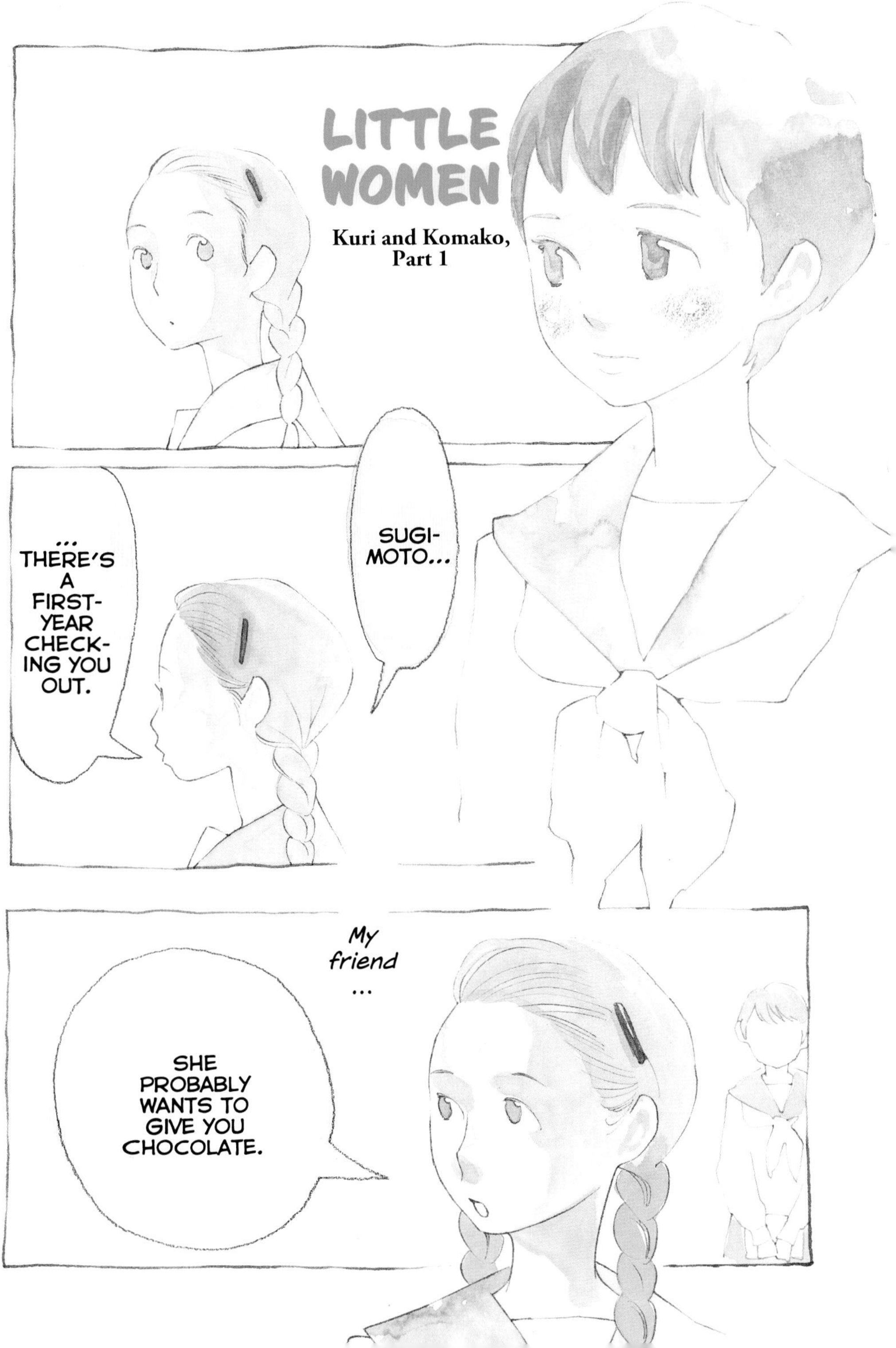
LITTLE WOMEN
Kuri and Komako, Part 1
SUGI-MOTO...
...THERE'S A FIRST-YEAR CHECKING YOU OUT.
My friend...
SHE PROBABLY WANTS TO GIVE YOU CHOCOLATE.

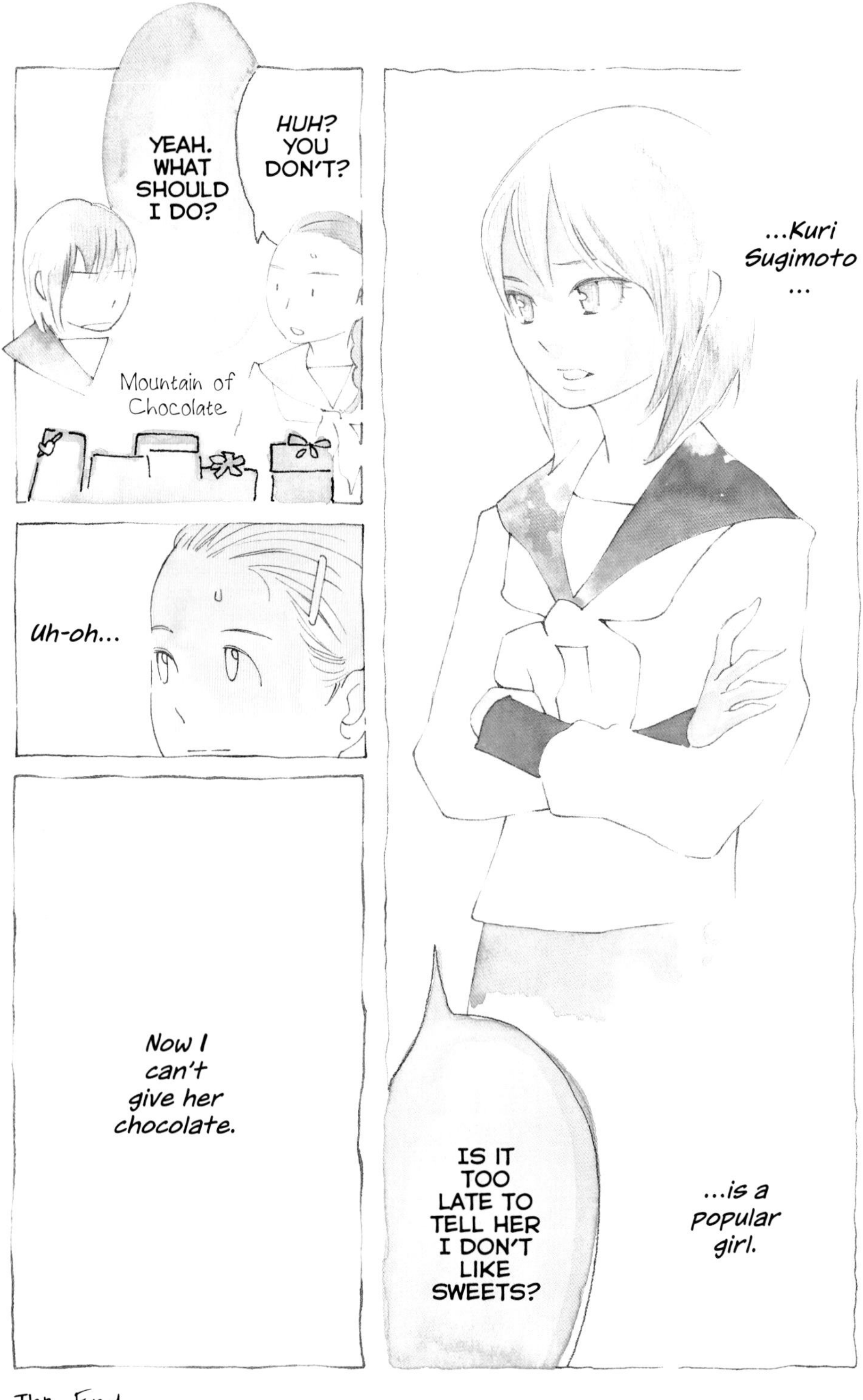
...Kuri Sugimoto ...
...is a popular girl.
IS IT TOO LATE TO TELL HER I DON'T LIKE SWEETS?
HUH? YOU DON'T?
YEAH. WHAT SHOULD I DO?
Mountain of Chocolate
Uh-oh...
Now I can't give her chocolate.

The End

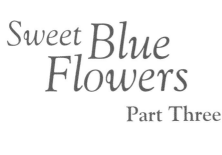

Sweet Blue Flowers

Part Three

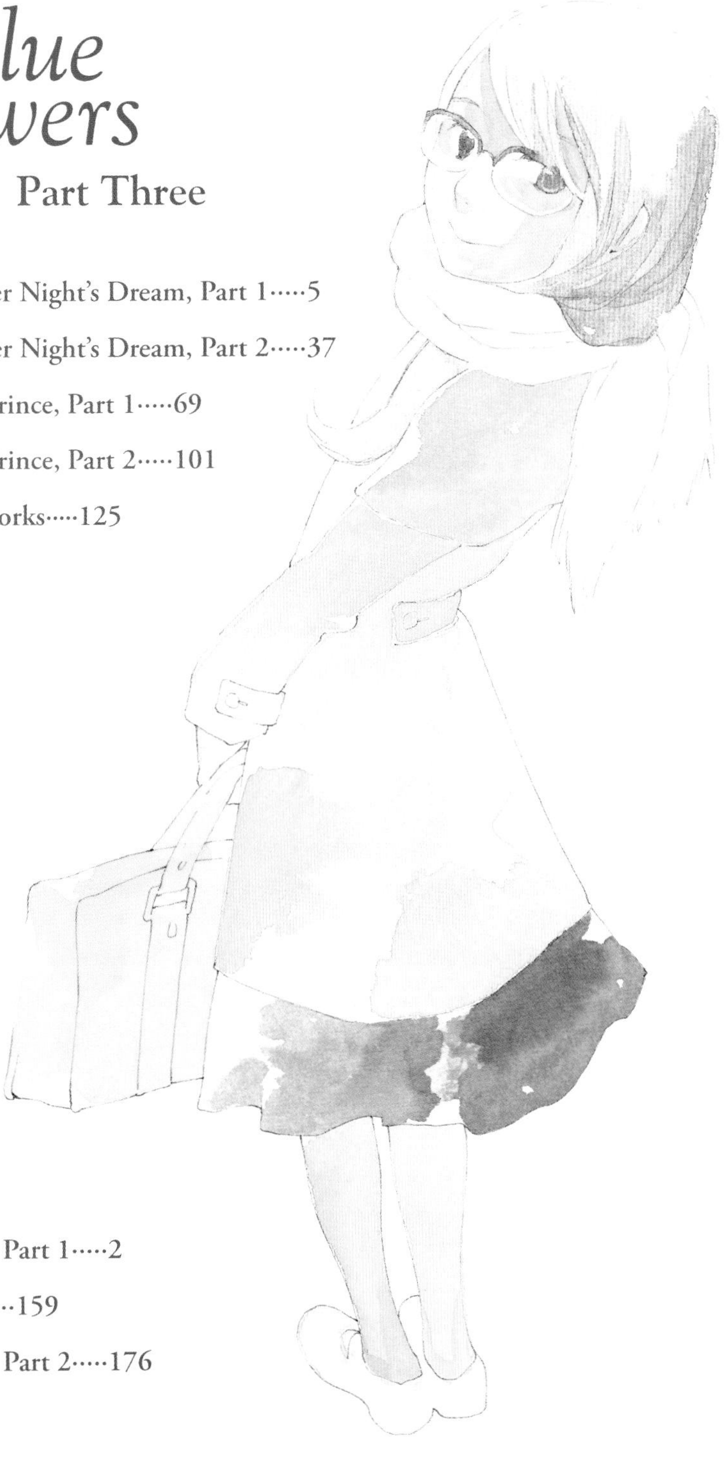

Little Women

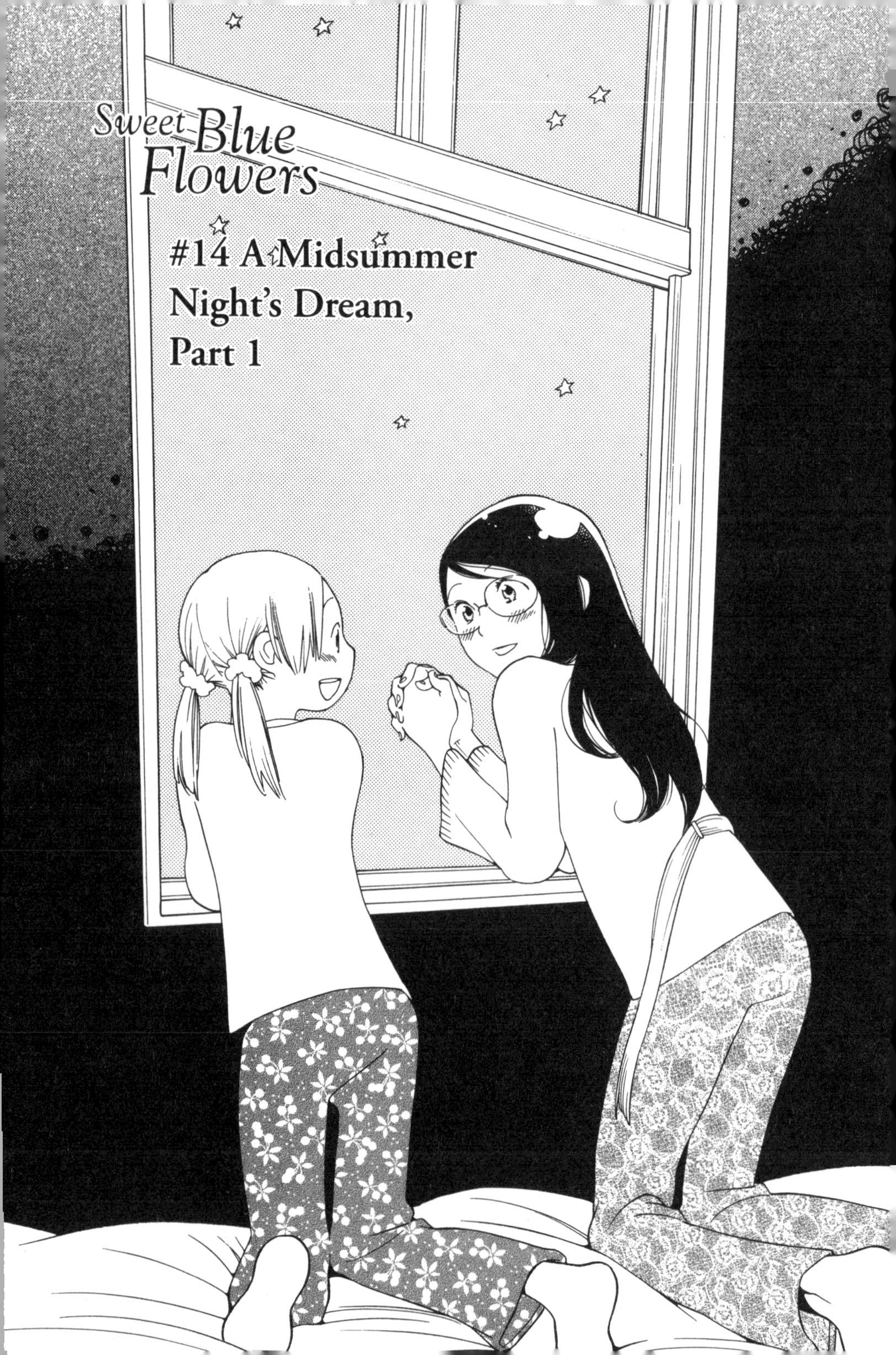
Sweet Blue Flowers
#14 A Midsummer Night's Dream, Part 1

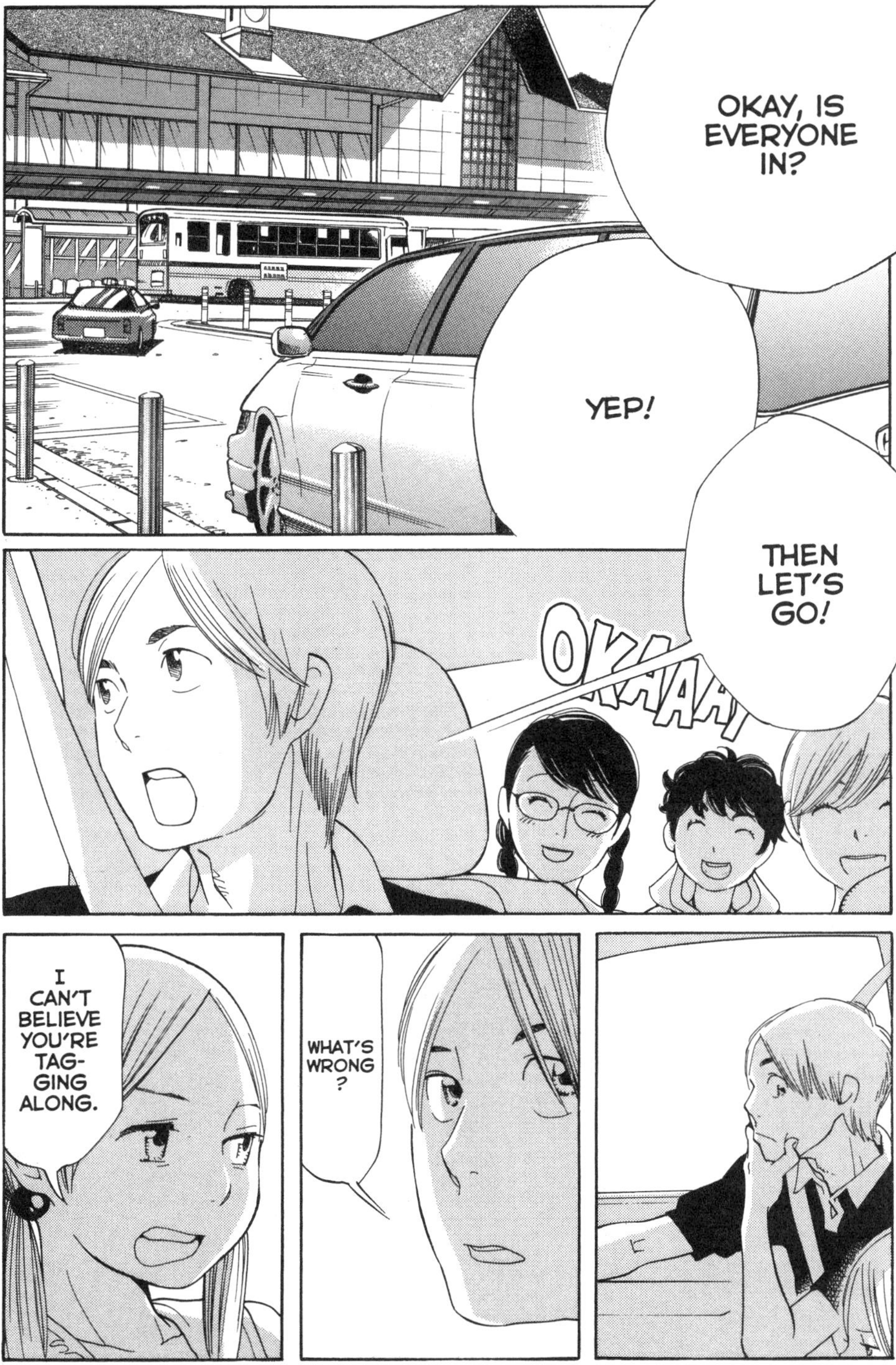
OKAY, IS EVERYONE IN?
YEP!
THEN LET'S GO!
OKAAAY
WHAT'S WRONG?
I CAN'T BELIEVE YOU'RE TAG-GING ALONG.

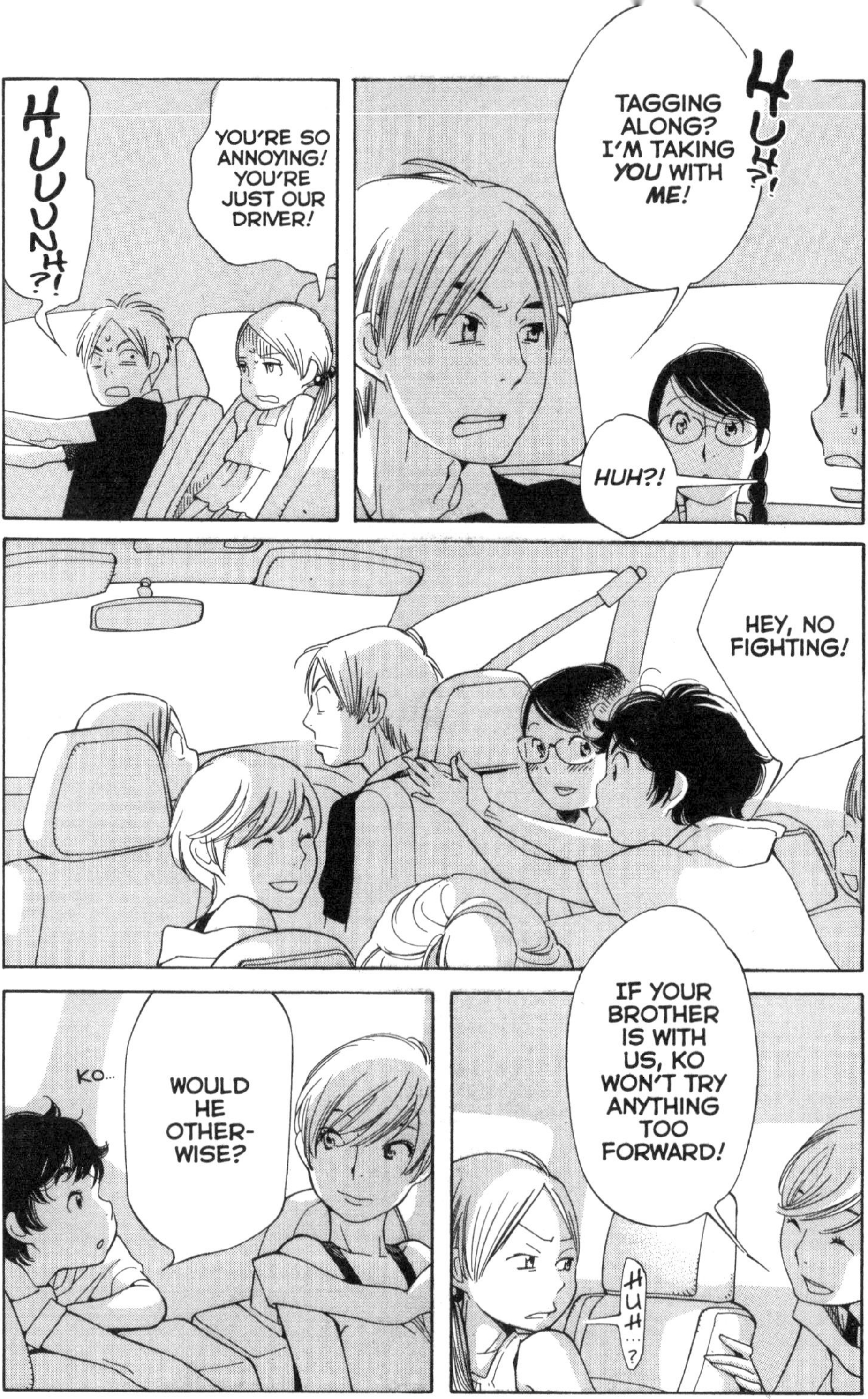
HUH?!
TAGGING ALONG? I'M TAKING *YOU* WITH *ME*!
HUH?!
YOU'RE SO ANNOYING! YOU'RE JUST OUR DRIVER!
HUUUNH?!
HEY, NO FIGHTING!
IF YOUR BROTHER IS WITH US, KO WON'T TRY ANYTHING TOO FORWARD!
HUH...?
WOULD HE OTHER-WISE?
KO...

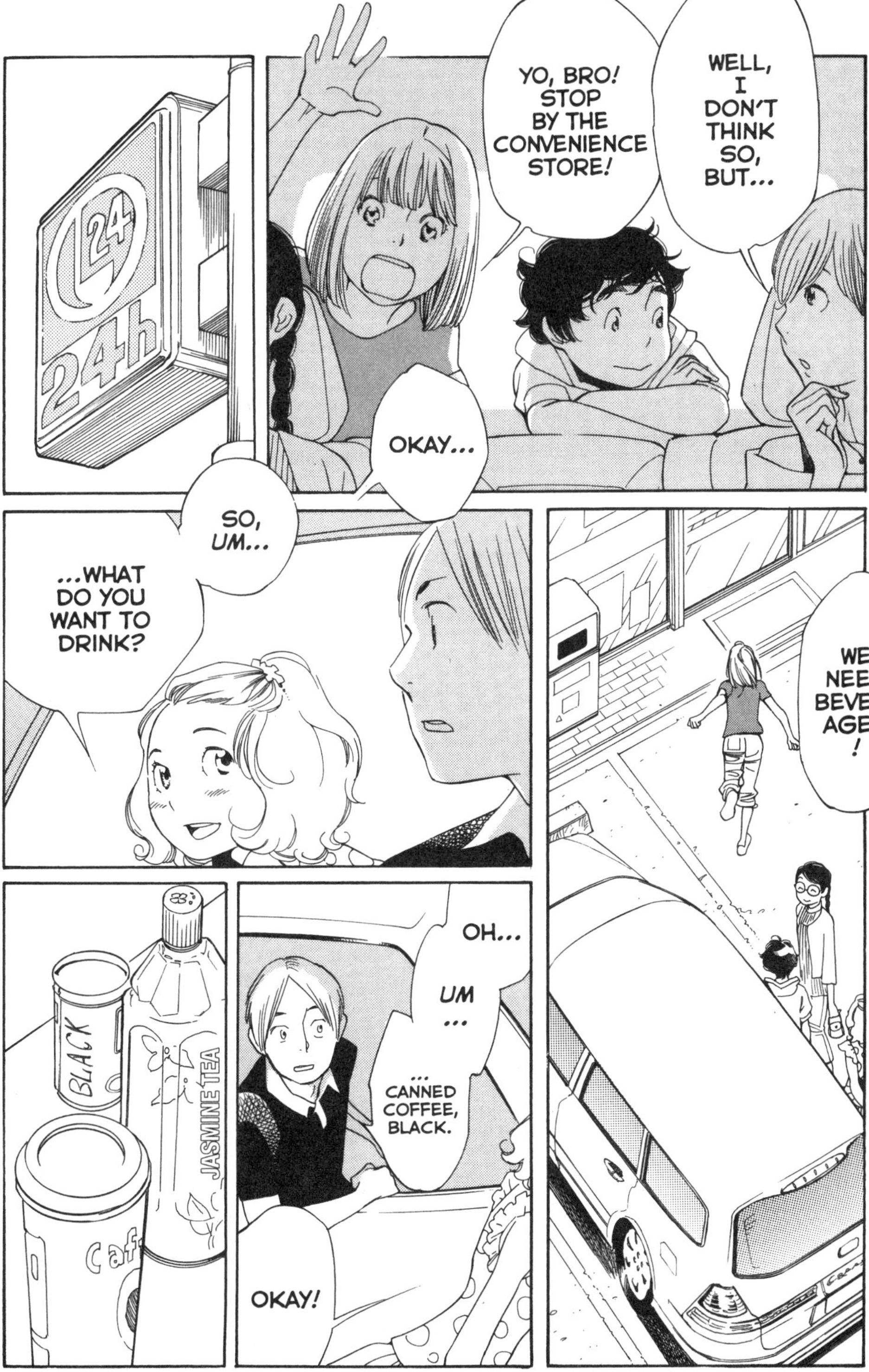
WELL, I DON'T THINK SO, BUT...
YO, BRO! STOP BY THE CONVENIENCE STORE!
OKAY...
L24
24h
WE NEED BEVERAGES!
SO, UM...
...WHAT DO YOU WANT TO DRINK?
OH...
UM...
...CANNED COFFEE, BLACK.
OKAY!
BLACK
JASMINE TEA

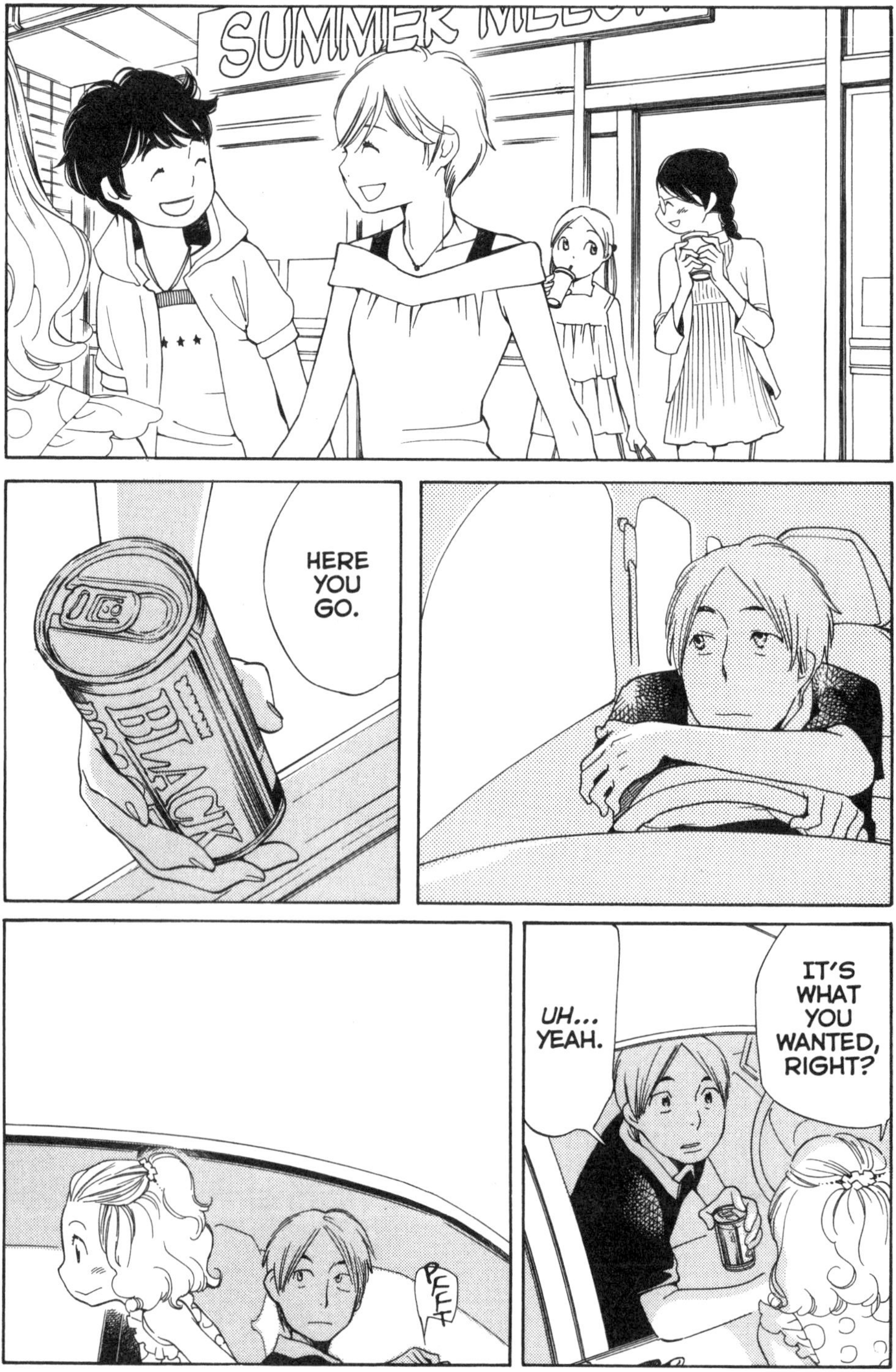

SUMMER
HERE YOU GO.
BLACK
IT'S WHAT YOU WANTED, RIGHT?
UH... YEAH.
PFFT

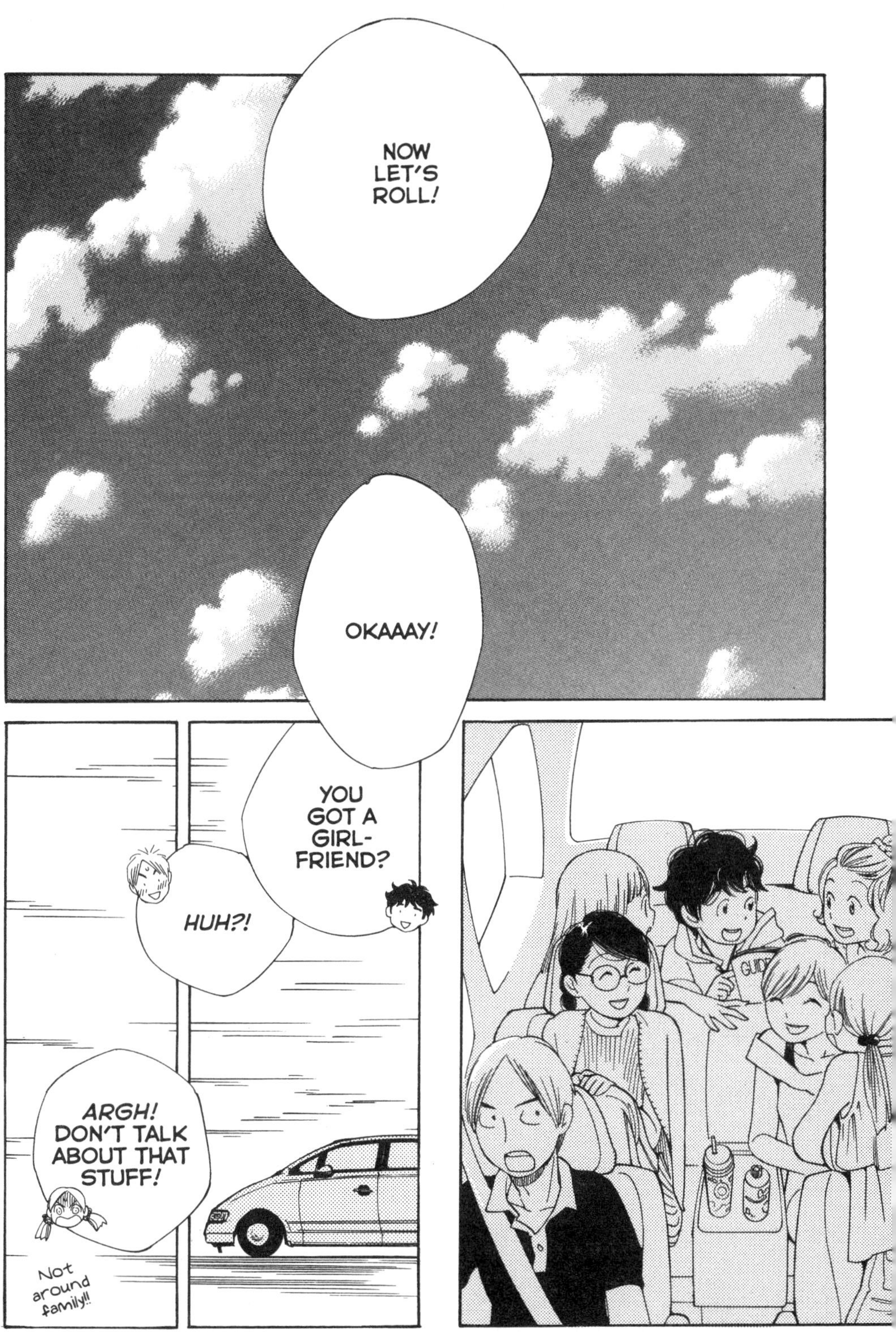
NOW LET'S ROLL!
OKAAAY!
YOU GOT A GIRL-FRIEND?
HUH?!
ARGH! DON'T TALK ABOUT THAT STUFF!
Not around family!!

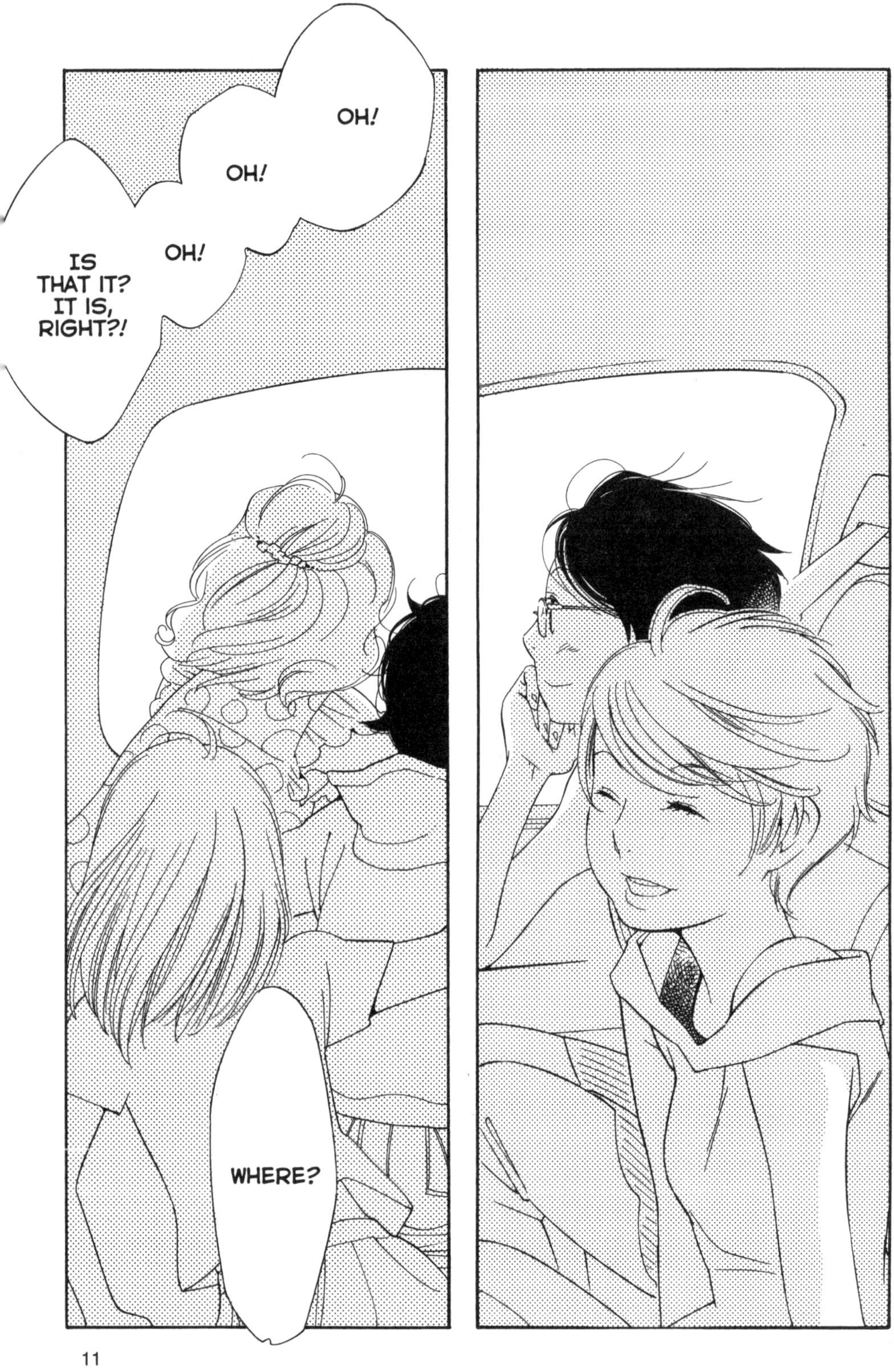
OH!
OH!
OH!
IS THAT IT? IT IS, RIGHT?!
WHERE?

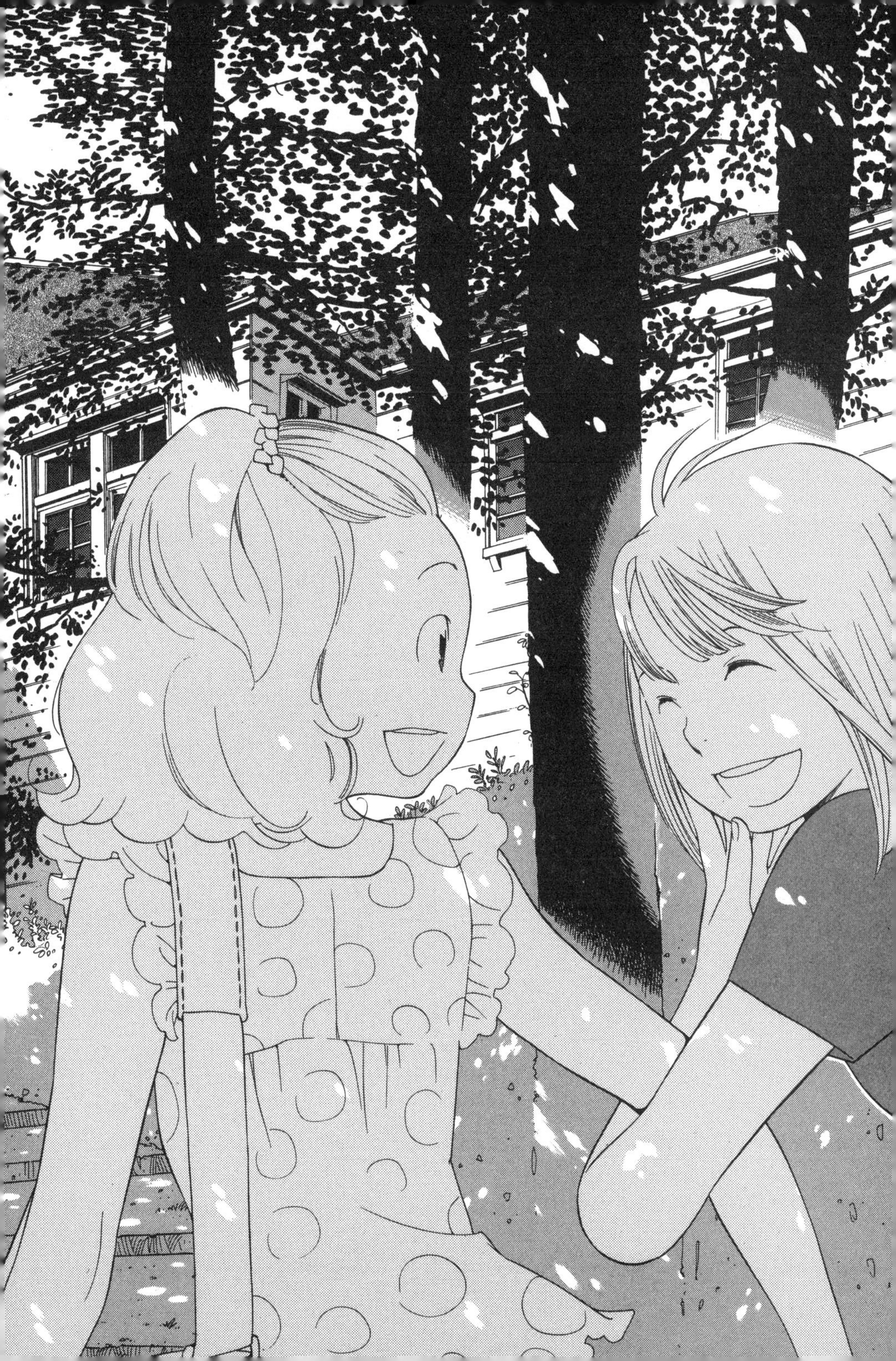

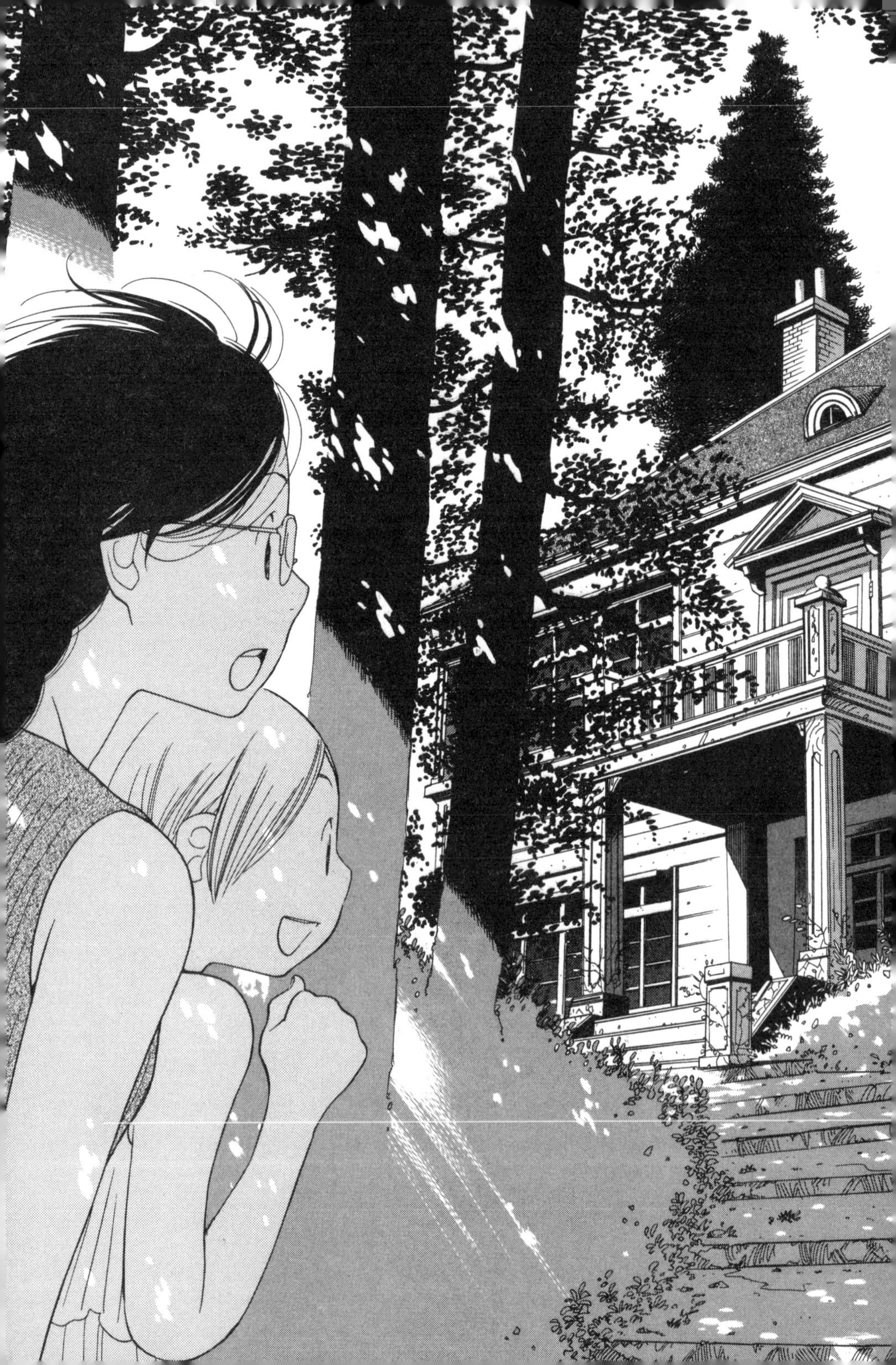

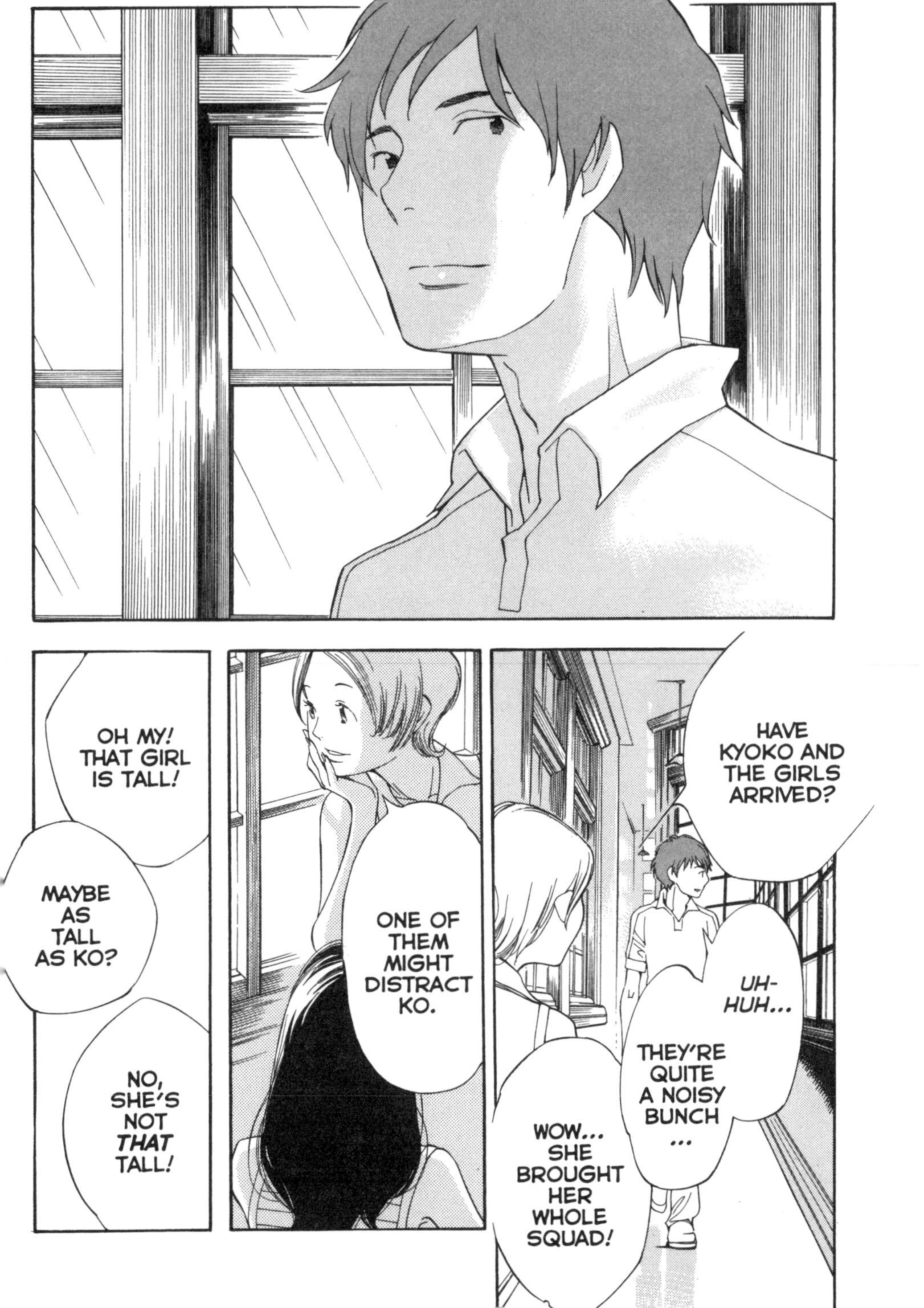
HAVE KYOKO AND THE GIRLS ARRIVED?
UH-HUH...
THEY'RE QUITE A NOISY BUNCH...
WOW... SHE BROUGHT HER WHOLE SQUAD!
ONE OF THEM MIGHT DISTRACT KO.
OH MY! THAT GIRL IS TALL!
MAYBE AS TALL AS KO?
NO, SHE'S NOT *THAT* TALL!

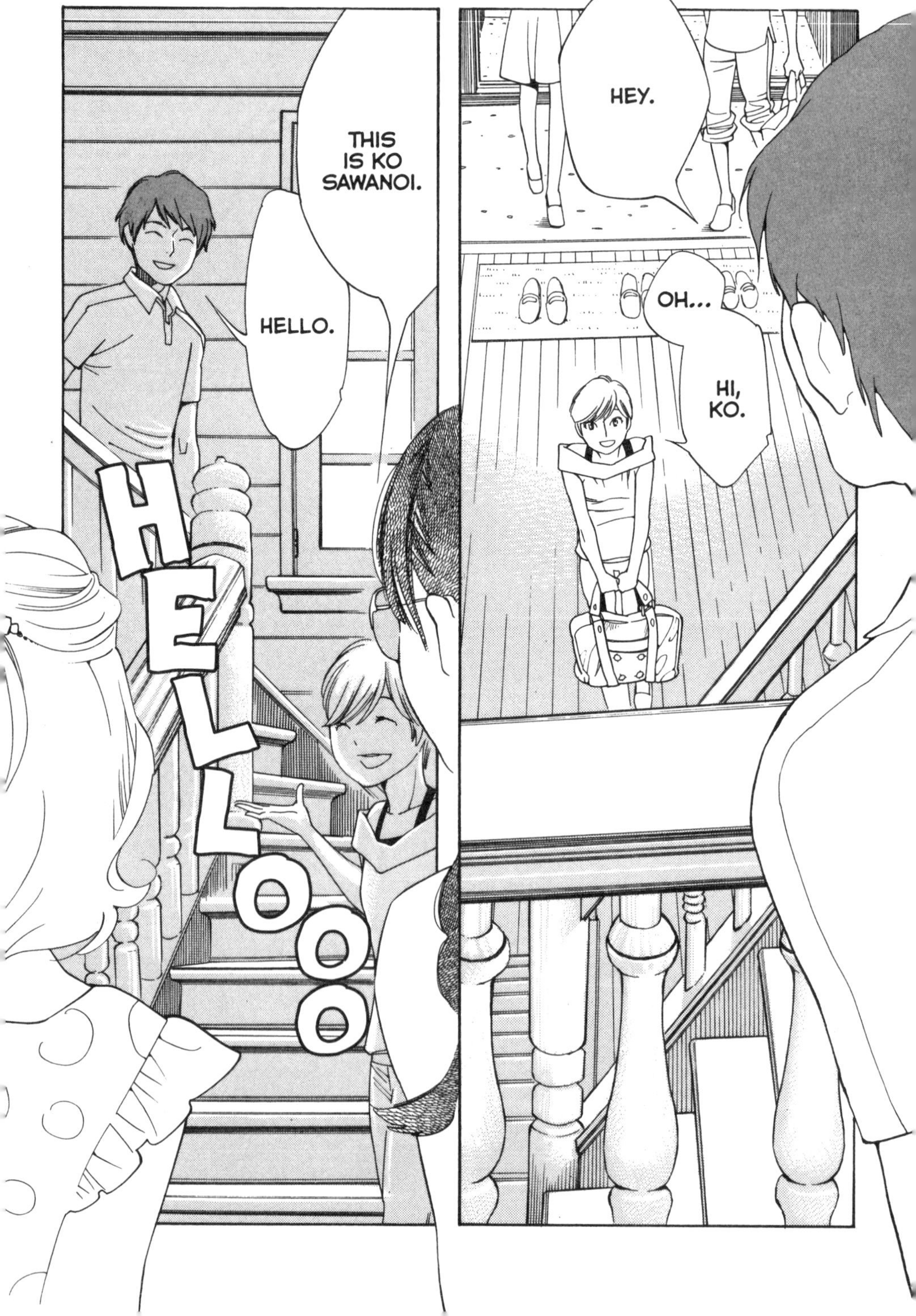
HEY.
OH...
HI, KO.
THIS IS KO SAWANOI.
HELLO.
HELLOOO

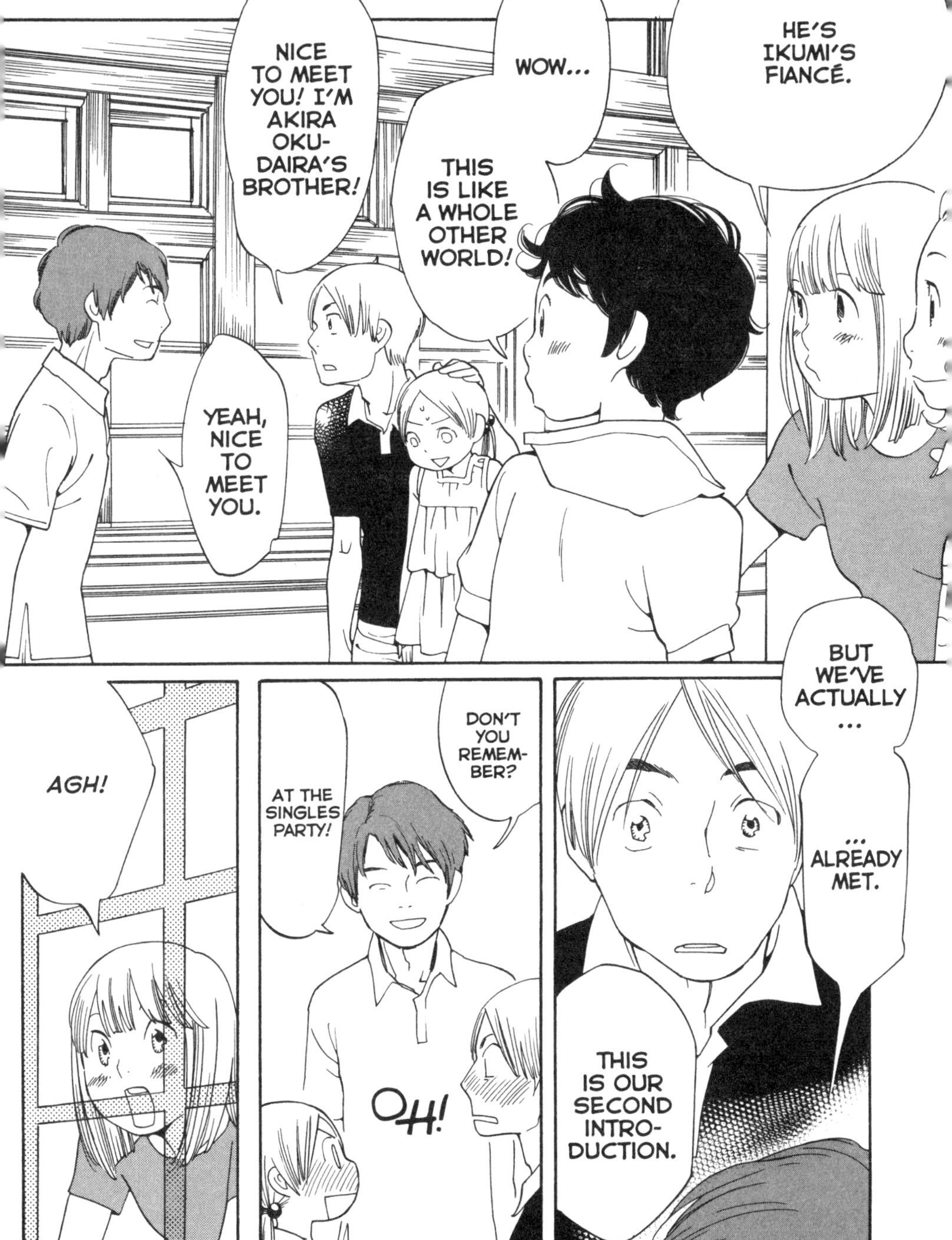
HE'S IKUMI'S FIANCÉ.
WOW...
THIS IS LIKE A WHOLE OTHER WORLD!
NICE TO MEET YOU! I'M AKIRA OKU-DAIRA'S BROTHER!
YEAH, NICE TO MEET YOU.
BUT WE'VE ACTUALLY ...
... ALREADY MET.
THIS IS OUR SECOND INTRO-DUCTION.
DON'T YOU REMEM-BER?
AT THE SINGLES PARTY!
OH!
AGH!

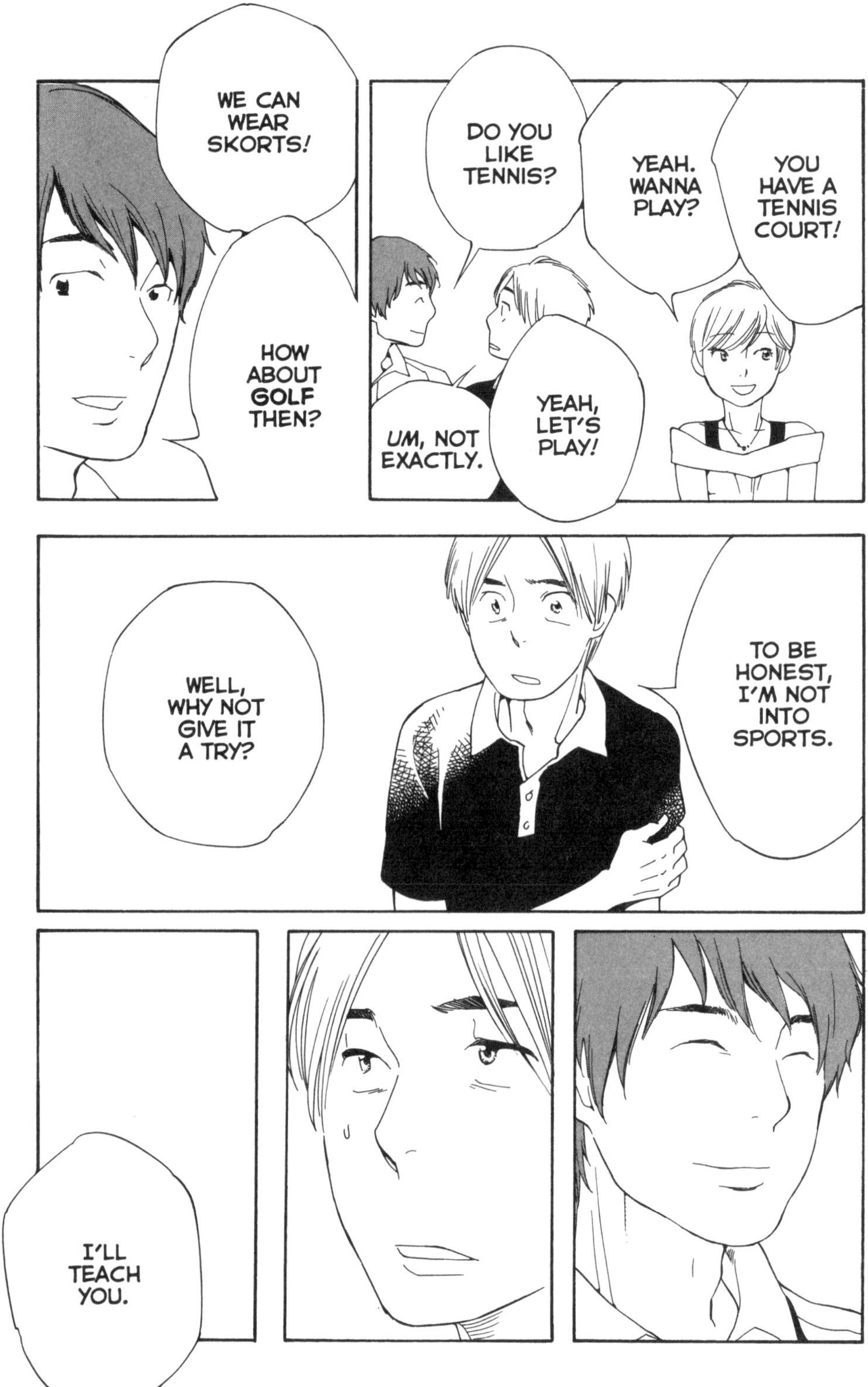
YOU HAVE A TENNIS COURT!
YEAH. WANNA PLAY?
DO YOU LIKE TENNIS?
YEAH, LET'S PLAY!
UM, NOT EXACTLY.
WE CAN WEAR SKORTS!
HOW ABOUT GOLF THEN?
TO BE HONEST, I'M NOT INTO SPORTS.
WELL, WHY NOT GIVE IT A TRY?
I'LL TEACH YOU.

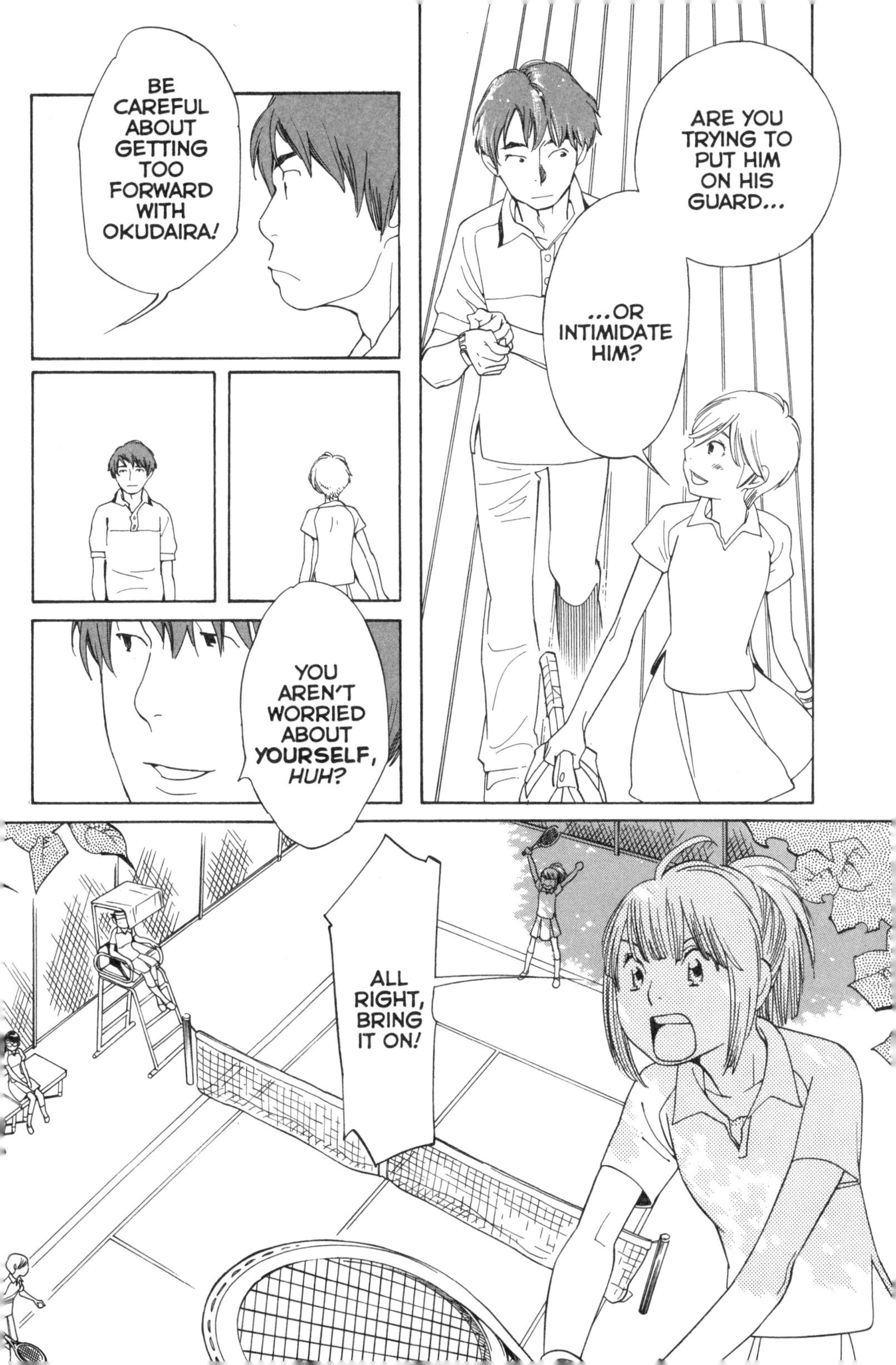
ARE YOU TRYING TO PUT HIM ON HIS GUARD...
...OR INTIMIDATE HIM?
BE CAREFUL ABOUT GETTING TOO FORWARD WITH OKUDAIRA!
YOU AREN'T WORRIED ABOUT YOURSELF, *HUH?*
ALL RIGHT, BRING IT ON!

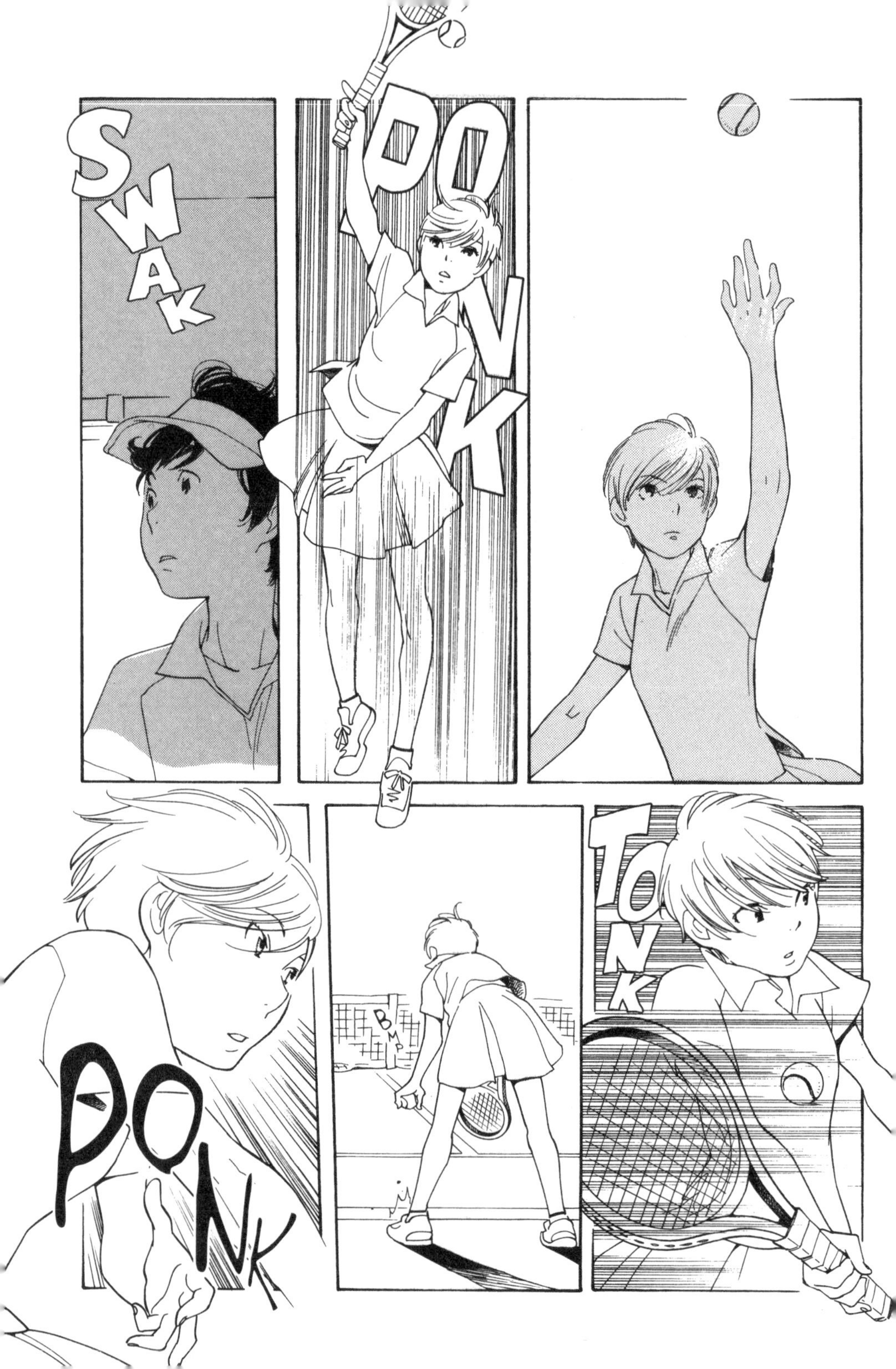
DONK
SWAK
TONK
BMP
PONK

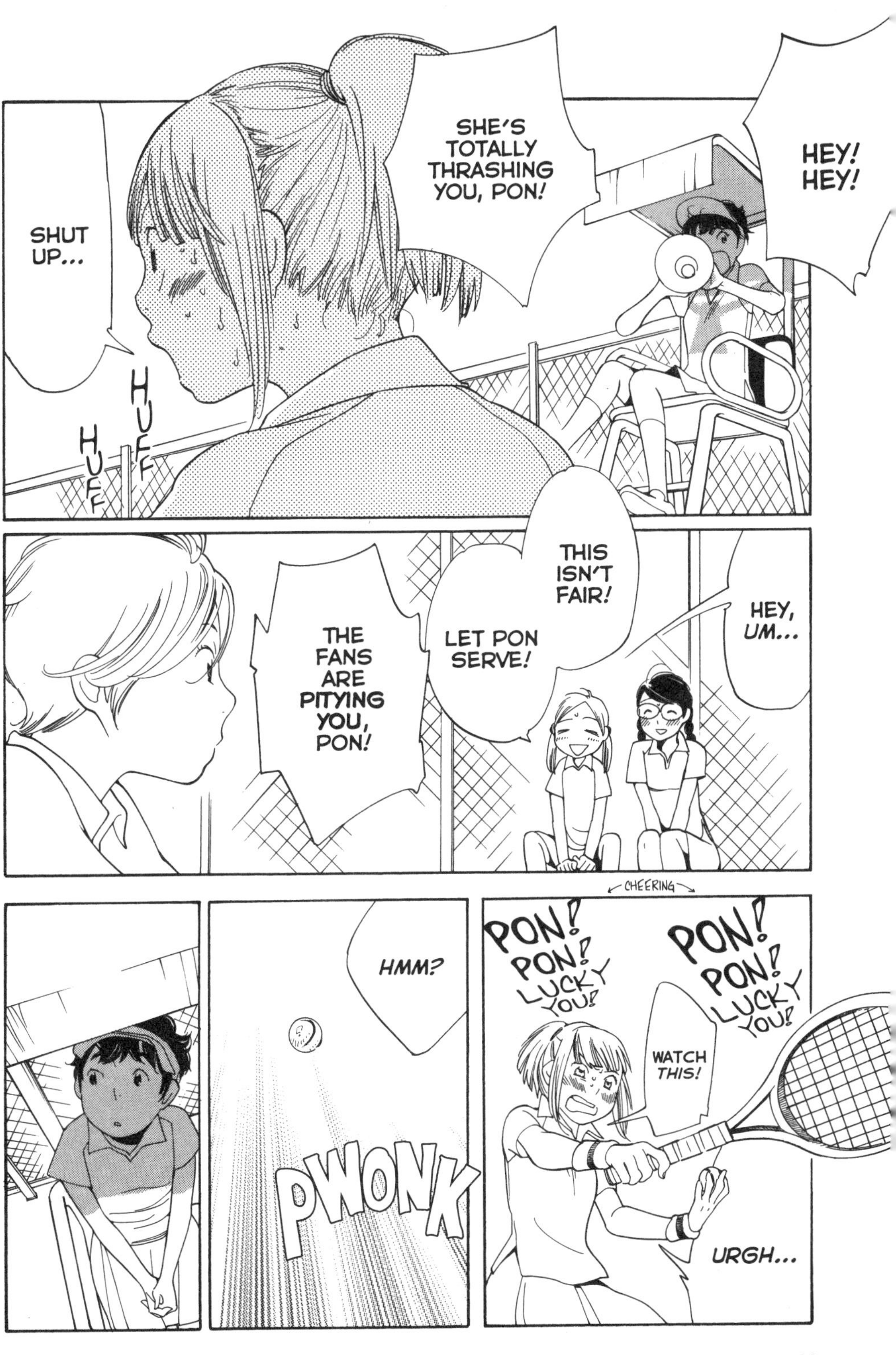
HEY! HEY!
SHE'S TOTALLY THRASHING YOU, PON!
SHUT UP...
HUFF
HUFF
HEY, UM...
THIS ISN'T FAIR!
LET PON SERVE!
THE FANS ARE PITYING YOU, PON!
CHEERING
PON! PON! LUCKY YOU!
PON! PON! LUCKY YOU!
WATCH THIS!
URGH...
HMM?
PWONK

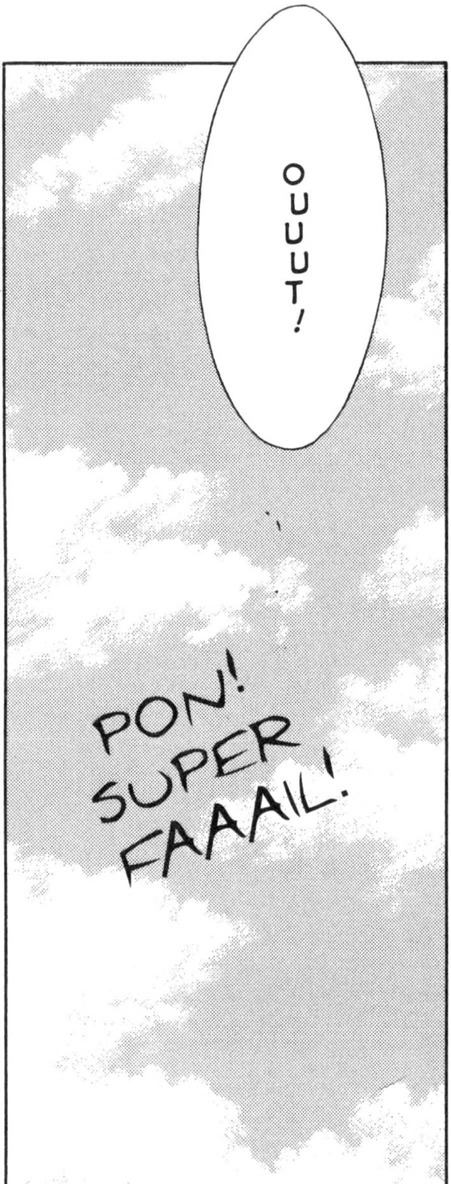
OUUUT!
PON! SUPER FAAAIL!
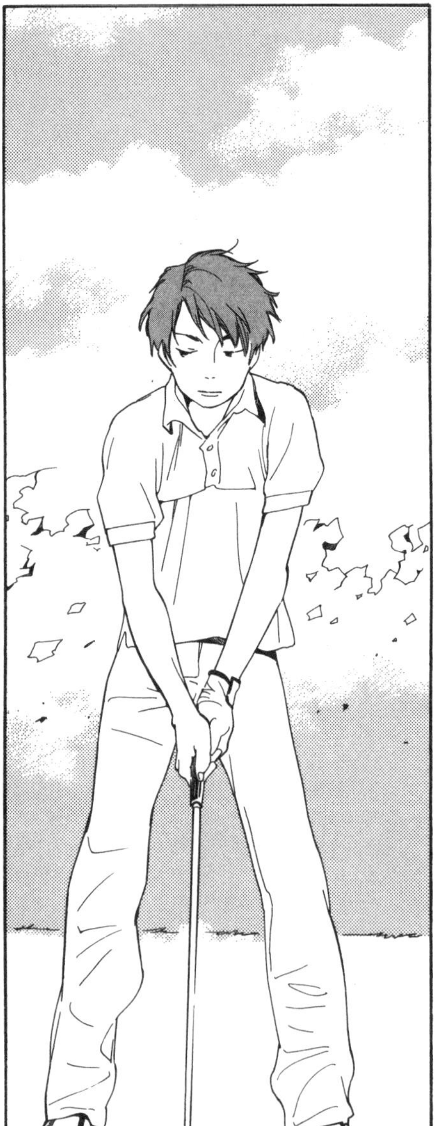

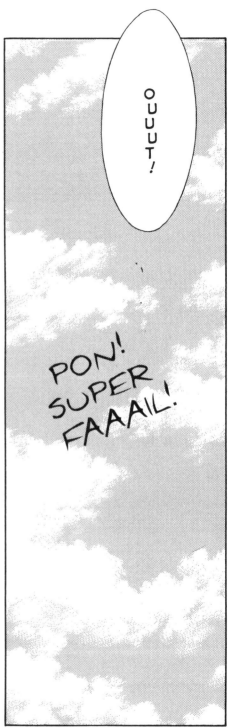

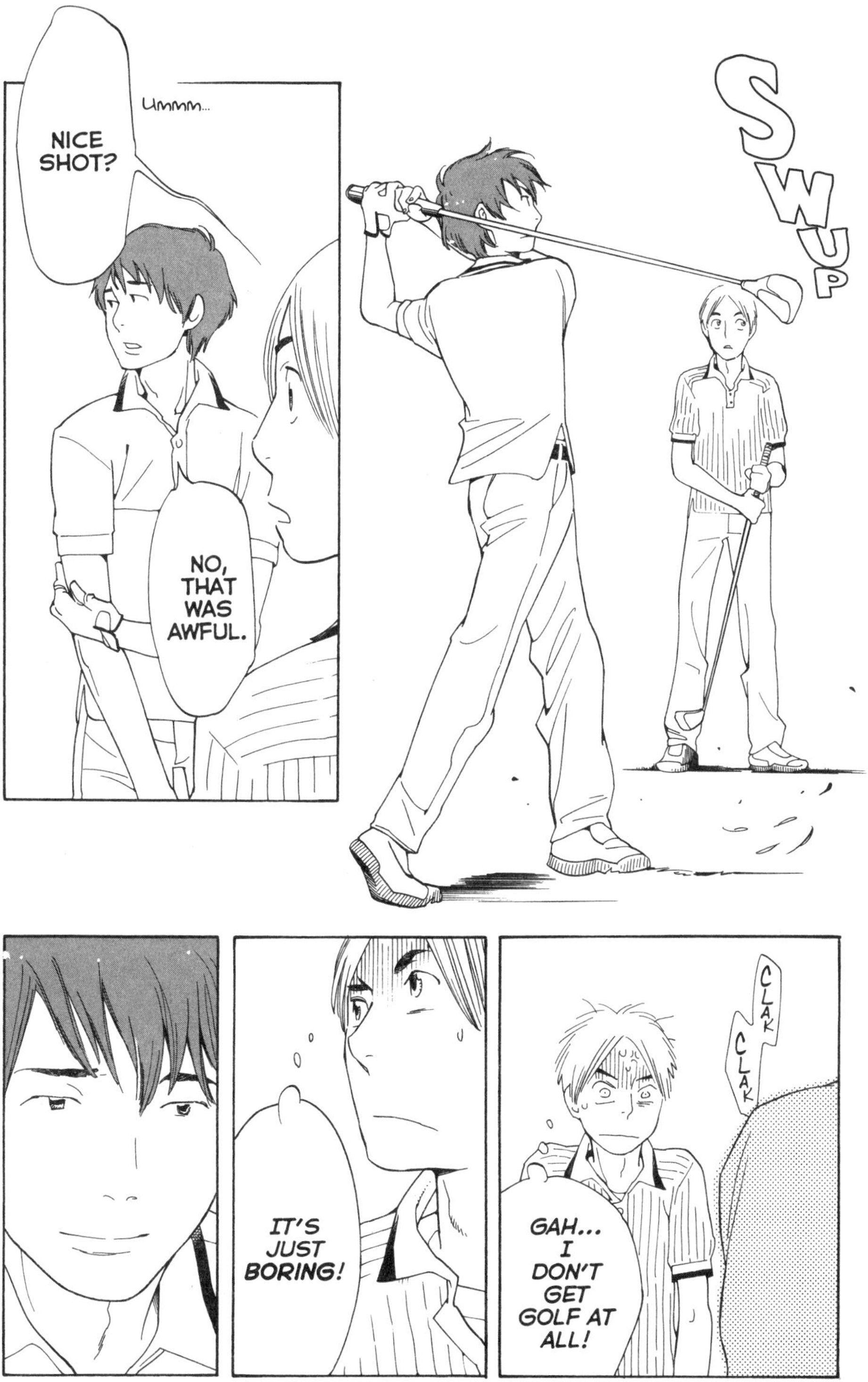
SWUP
Ummm...
NICE SHOT?
NO, THAT WAS AWFUL.
CLAK CLAK
GAH... I DON'T GET GOLF AT ALL!
IT'S JUST BORING!

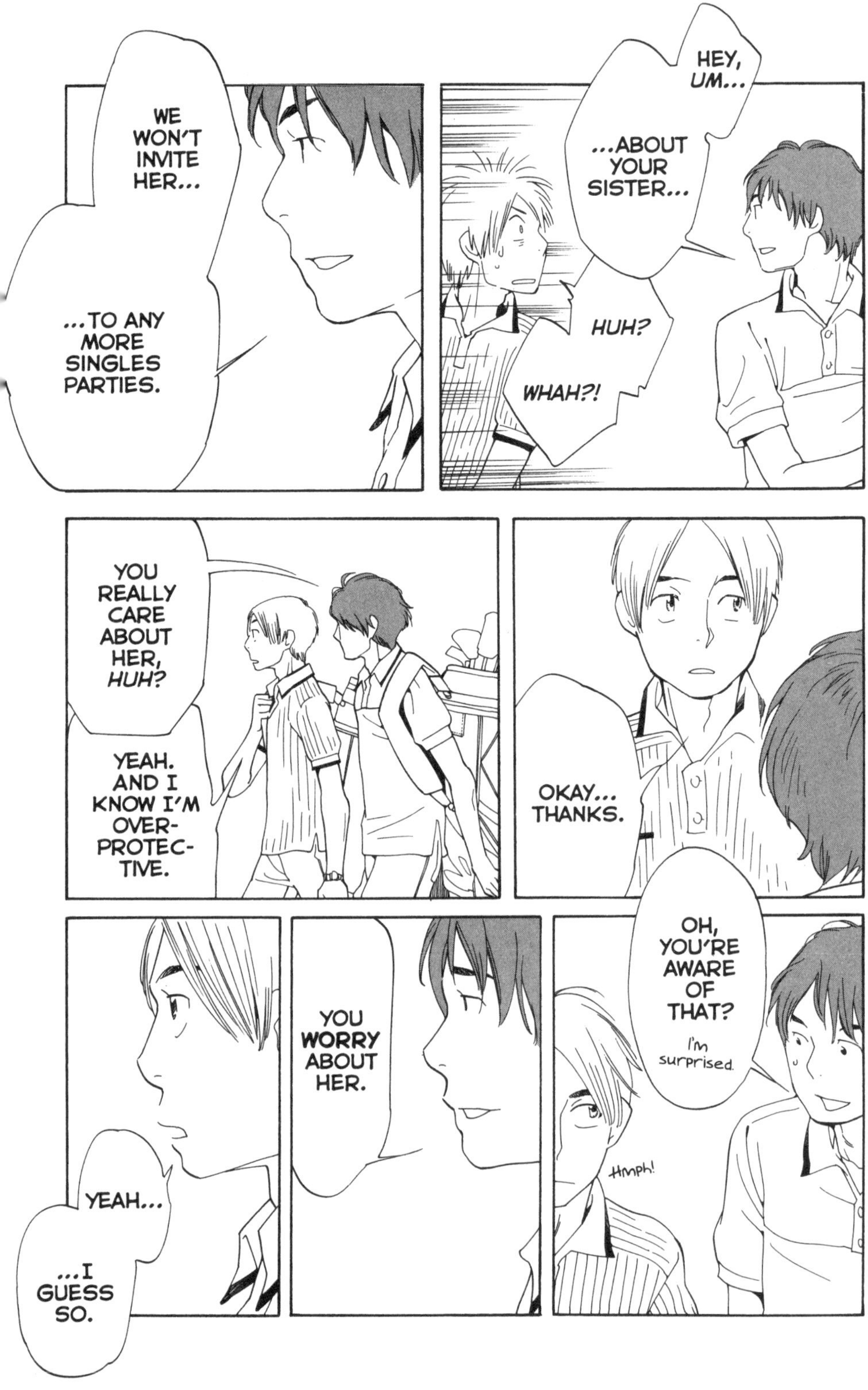
HEY, UM...
...ABOUT YOUR SISTER...
HUH?
WHAH?!
WE WON'T INVITE HER...
...TO ANY MORE SINGLES PARTIES.
OKAY... THANKS.
YOU REALLY CARE ABOUT HER, HUH?
YEAH. AND I KNOW I'M OVER-PROTECTIVE.
OH, YOU'RE AWARE OF THAT?
I'm surprised.
Hmph!
YOU WORRY ABOUT HER.
YEAH...
...I GUESS SO.

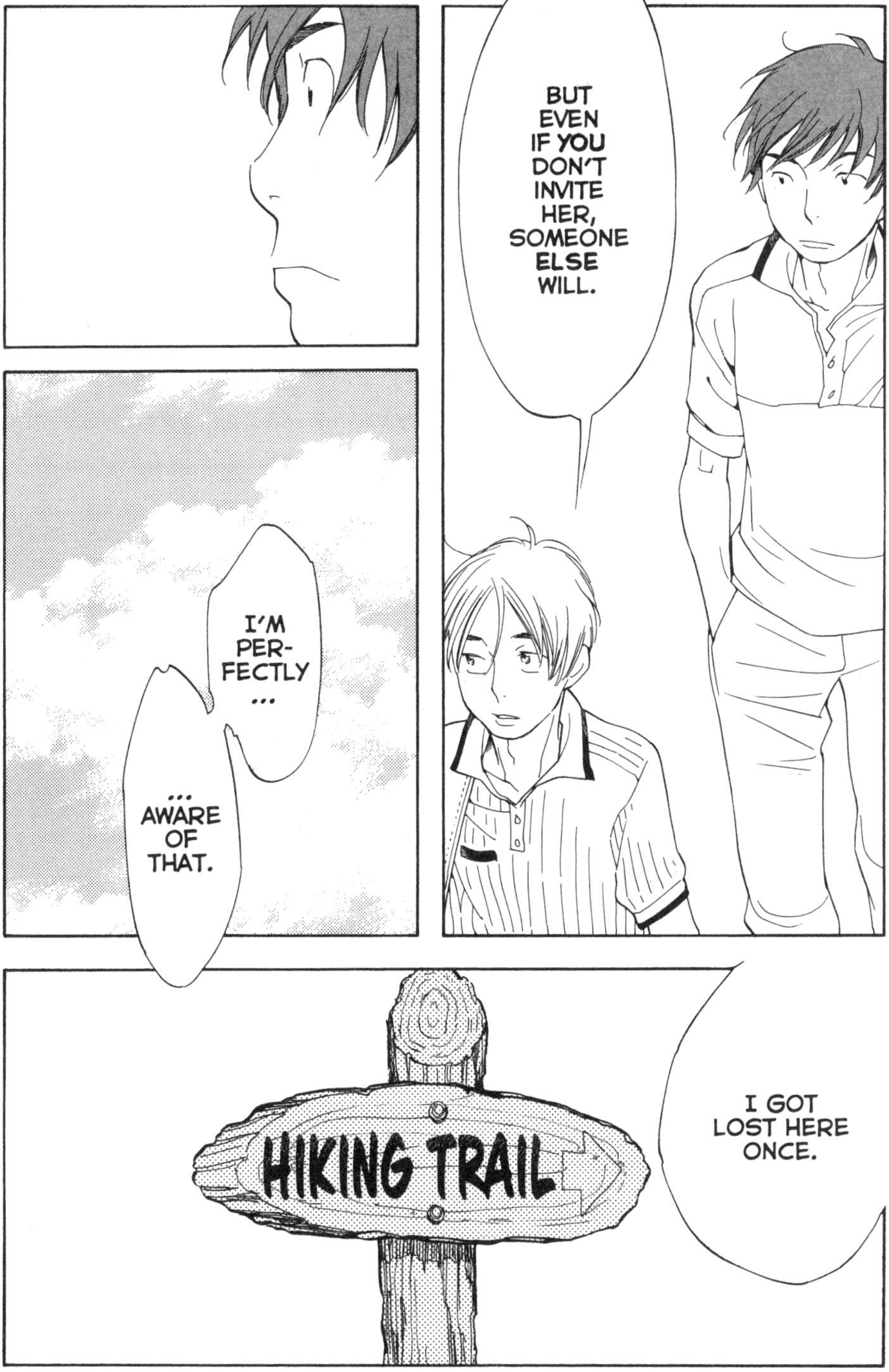
BUT EVEN IF YOU DON'T INVITE HER, SOMEONE ELSE WILL.
I'M PER-FECTLY...
...AWARE OF THAT.
HIKING TRAIL
I GOT LOST HERE ONCE.

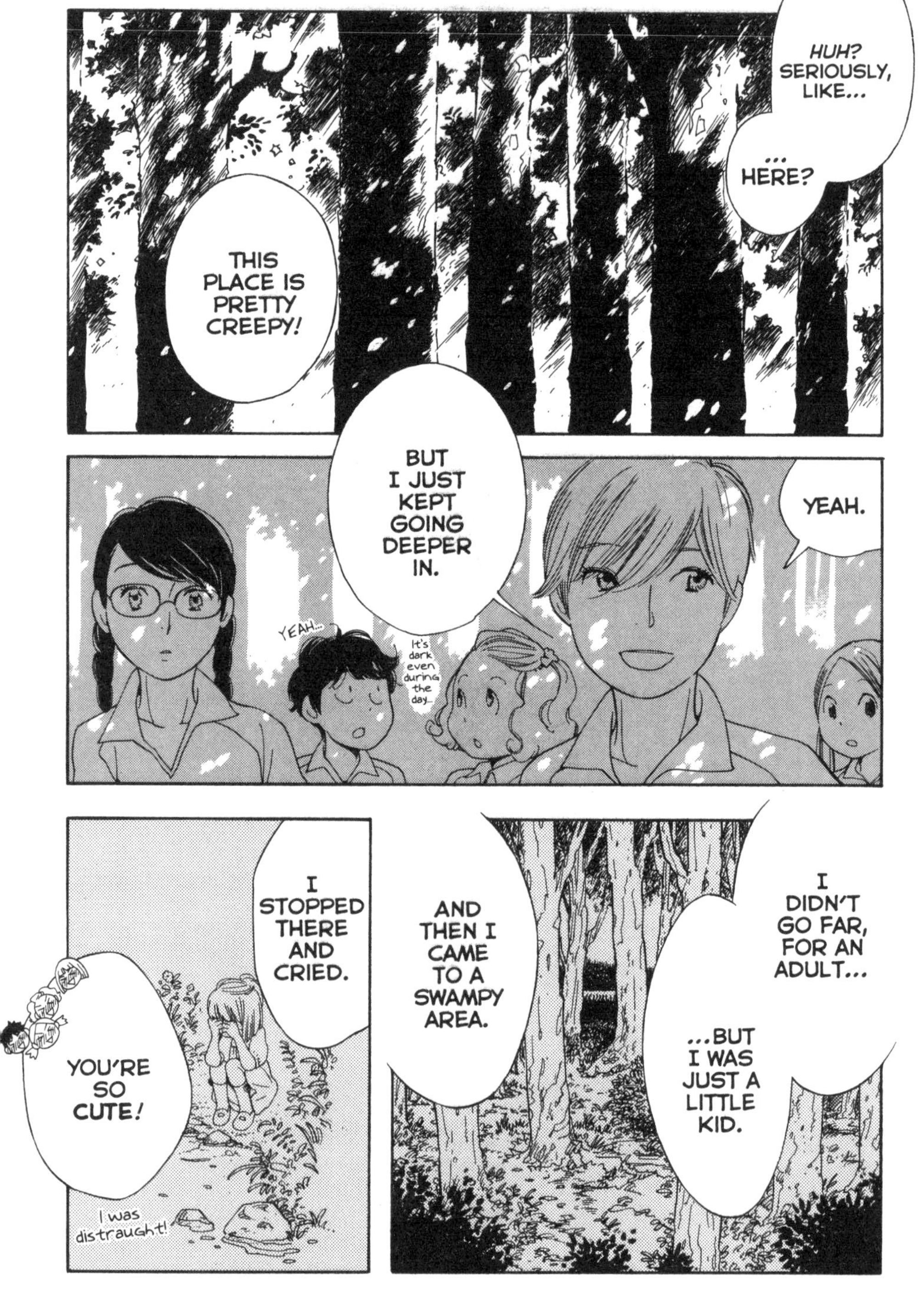
HUH? SERIOUSLY, LIKE...
... HERE?
THIS PLACE IS PRETTY CREEPY!
YEAH.
BUT I JUST KEPT GOING DEEPER IN.
It's dark even during the day...
YEAH...
I DIDN'T GO FAR, FOR AN ADULT...
...BUT I WAS JUST A LITTLE KID.
AND THEN I CAME TO A SWAMPY AREA.
I STOPPED THERE AND CRIED.
YOU'RE SO CUTE!
I was distraught!

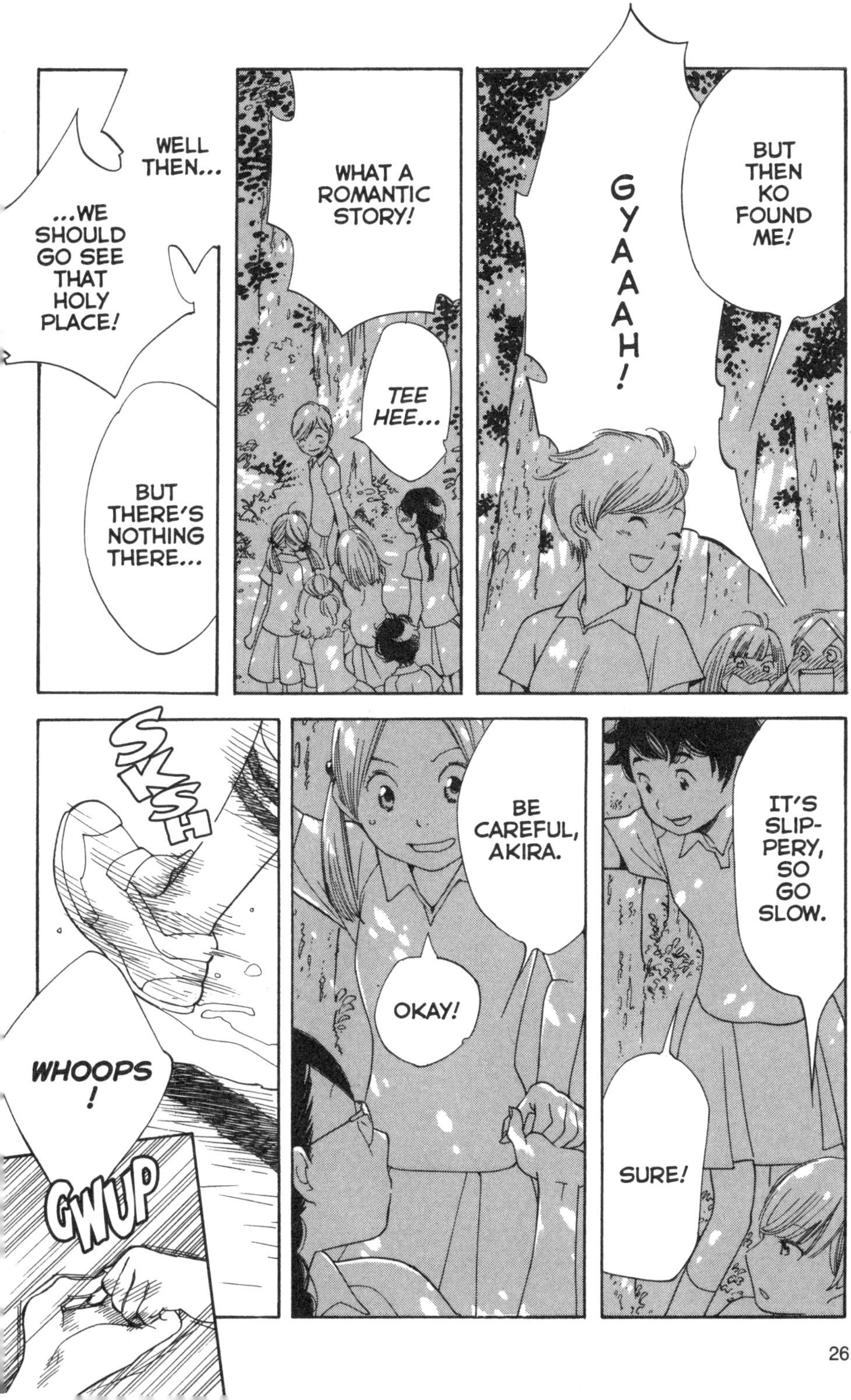
BUT THEN KO FOUND ME!
GYAAAH!
WHAT A ROMANTIC STORY!
TEE HEE...
WELL THEN...
...WE SHOULD GO SEE THAT HOLY PLACE!
BUT THERE'S NOTHING THERE...
IT'S SLIPPERY, SO GO SLOW.
SURE!
BE CAREFUL, AKIRA.
OKAY!
SWSH
WHOOPS!
GWUP

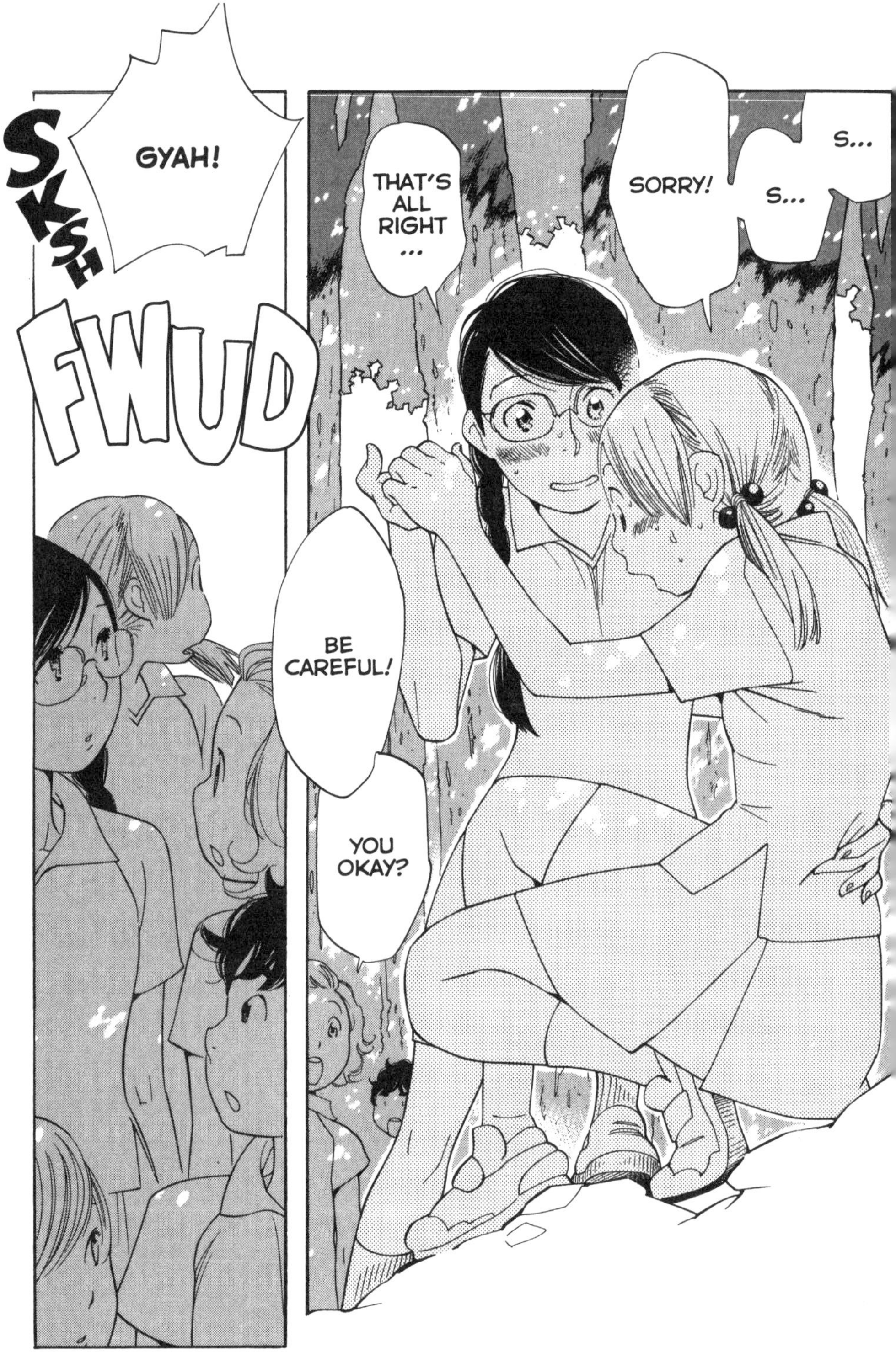

S...
S...
SORRY!
THAT'S ALL RIGHT ...
BE CAREFUL!
YOU OKAY?
GYAH!
SKSH
FWUD

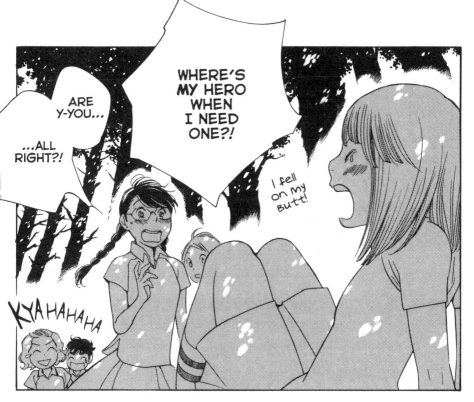

WHERE'S MY HERO WHEN I NEED ONE?!

ARE Y-YOU...

...ALL RIGHT?!

I fell on my butt!

KYAHAHAHA

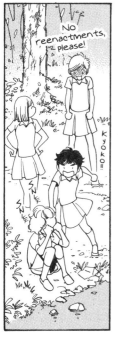

No reenactments, please!

KYOKO!!

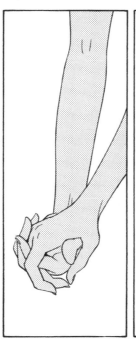

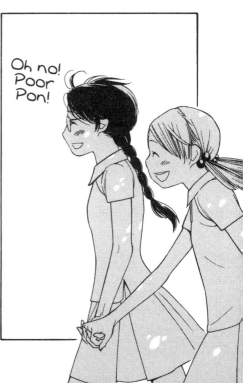

Oh no! Poor Pon!

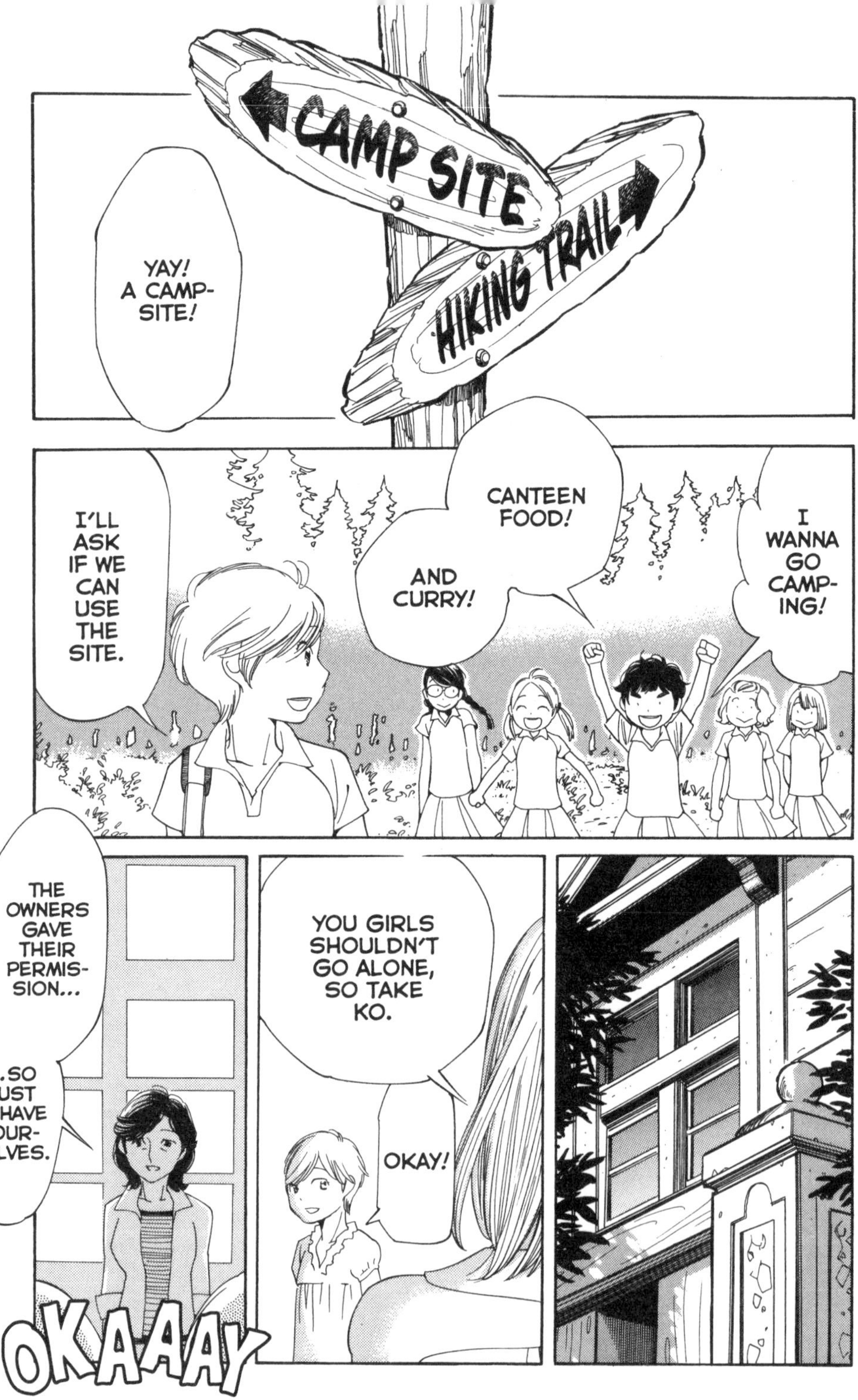
CAMP SITE
HIKING TRAIL
YAY! A CAMP-SITE!
I WANNA GO CAMP-ING!
CANTEEN FOOD!
AND CURRY!
I'LL ASK IF WE CAN USE THE SITE.
YOU GIRLS SHOULDN'T GO ALONE, SO TAKE KO.
OKAY!
THE OWNERS GAVE THEIR PERMIS-SION...
...SO JUST BEHAVE YOUR-SELVES.
OKAAAY

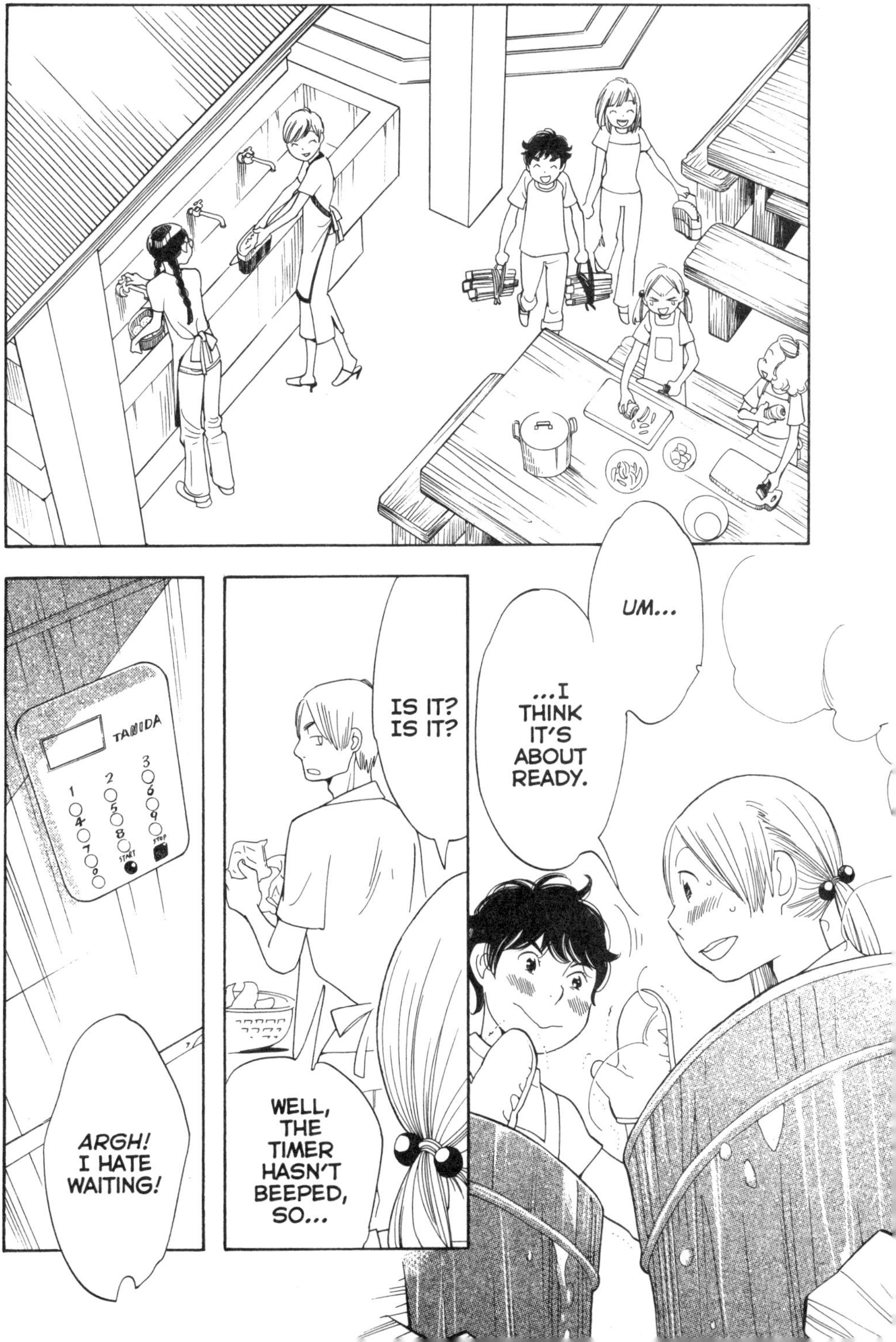
UM...
...I THINK IT'S ABOUT READY.
IS IT? IS IT?
WELL, THE TIMER HASN'T BEEPED, SO...
TANIDA
START
STOP
ARGH! I HATE WAITING!

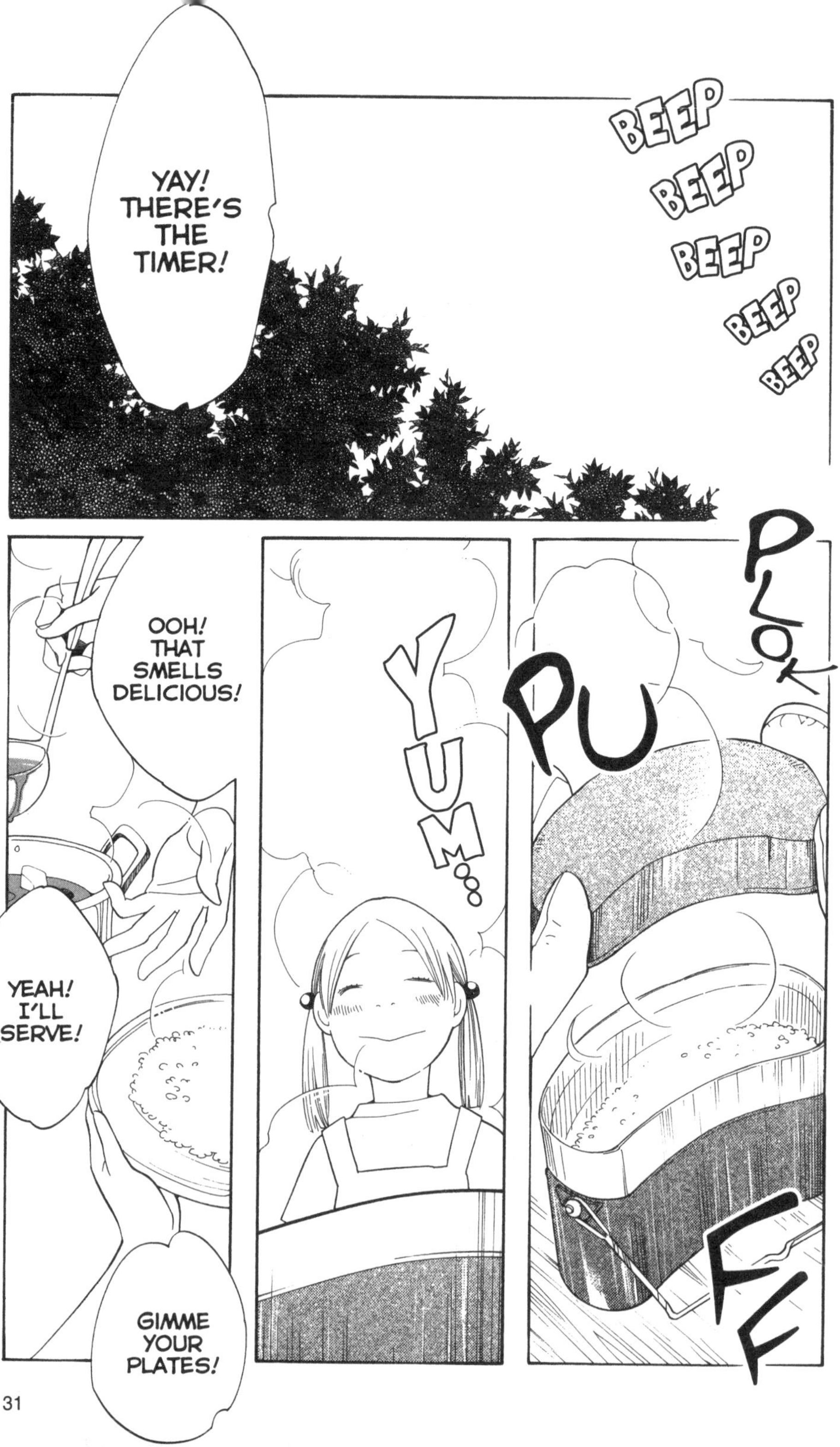
BEEP BEEP BEEP BEEP BEEP
YAY! THERE'S THE TIMER!
PLOK
PU
FF
YUM...
OOH! THAT SMELLS DELICIOUS!
YEAH! I'LL SERVE!
GIMME YOUR PLATES!

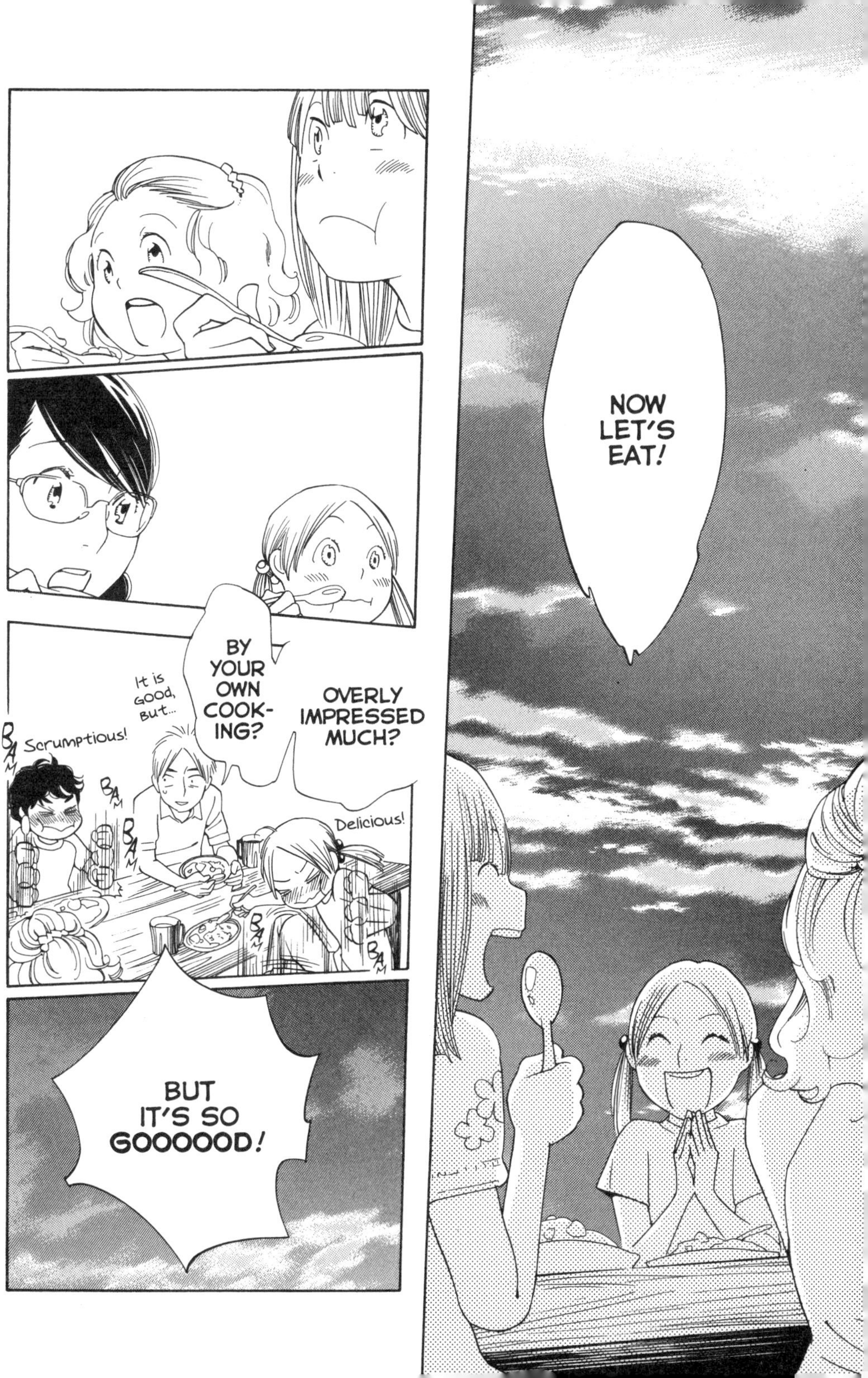
NOW LET'S EAT!
BY YOUR OWN COOKING?
OVERLY IMPRESSED MUCH?
Delicious!
It is good, but...
Scrumptious!
BAM
BAM
BAM
BAM
BAM
BUT IT'S SO GOOOOOD!

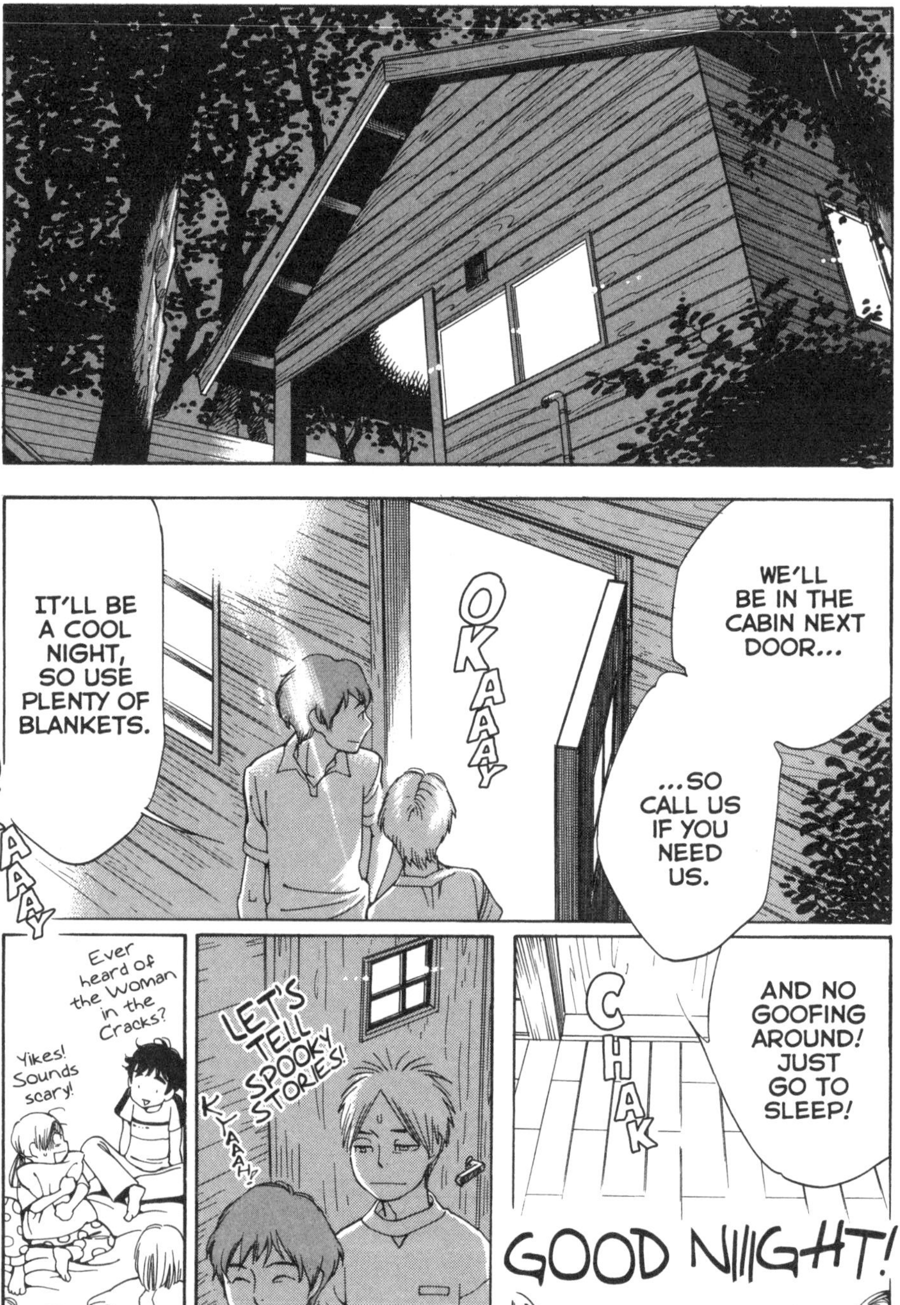
WE'LL BE IN THE CABIN NEXT DOOR...
...SO CALL US IF YOU NEED US.
OKAAAY
IT'LL BE A COOL NIGHT, SO USE PLENTY OF BLANKETS.
OKAAAY
AND NO GOOFING AROUND! JUST GO TO SLEEP!
CHAK
GOOD NIIIGHT!
LET'S TELL SPOOKY STORIES!
KYAAAH!
Ever heard of the Woman in the Cracks?
Yikes! Sounds scary!

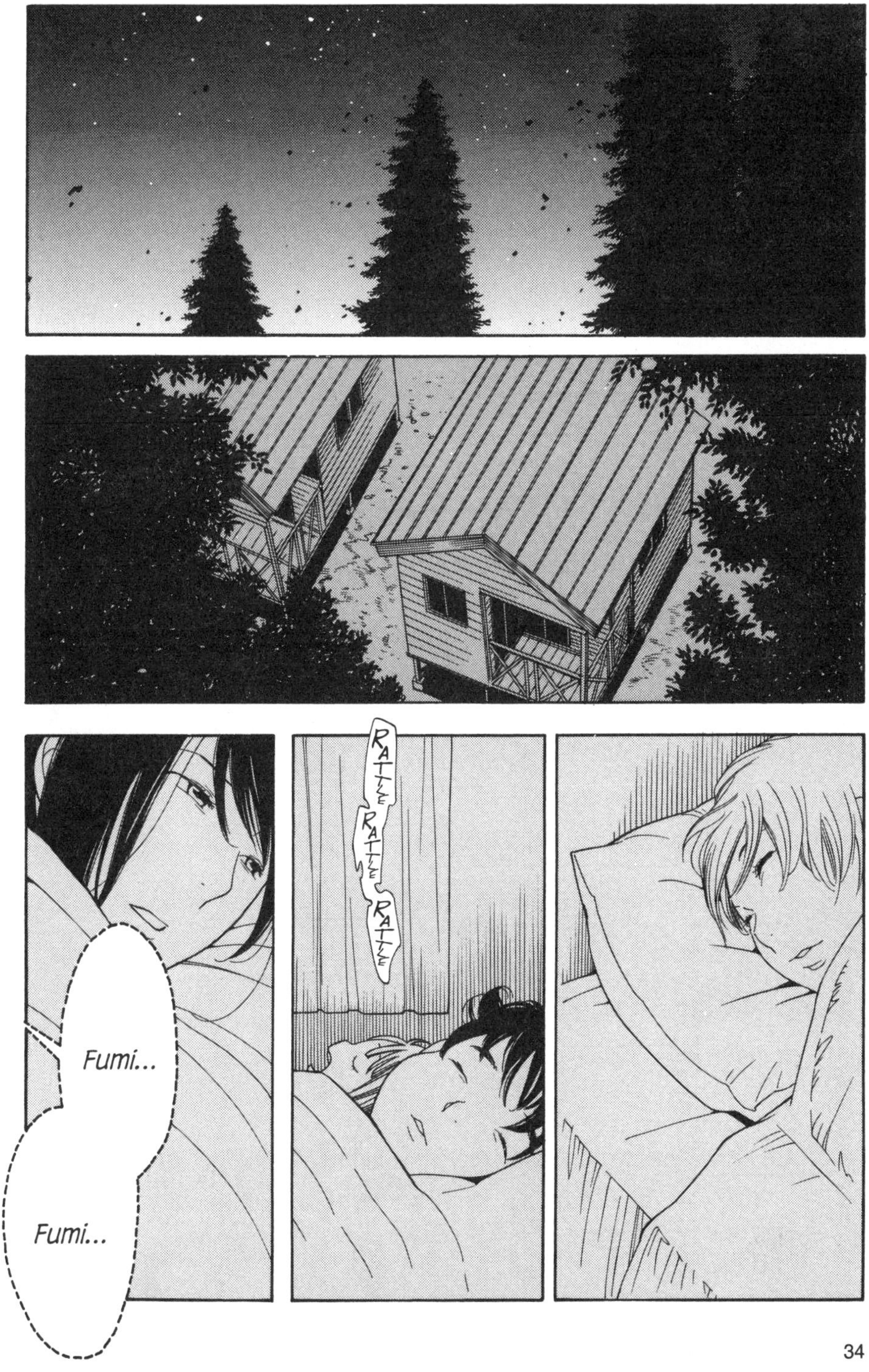
RATTLE RATTLE RATTLE
Fumi...
Fumi...

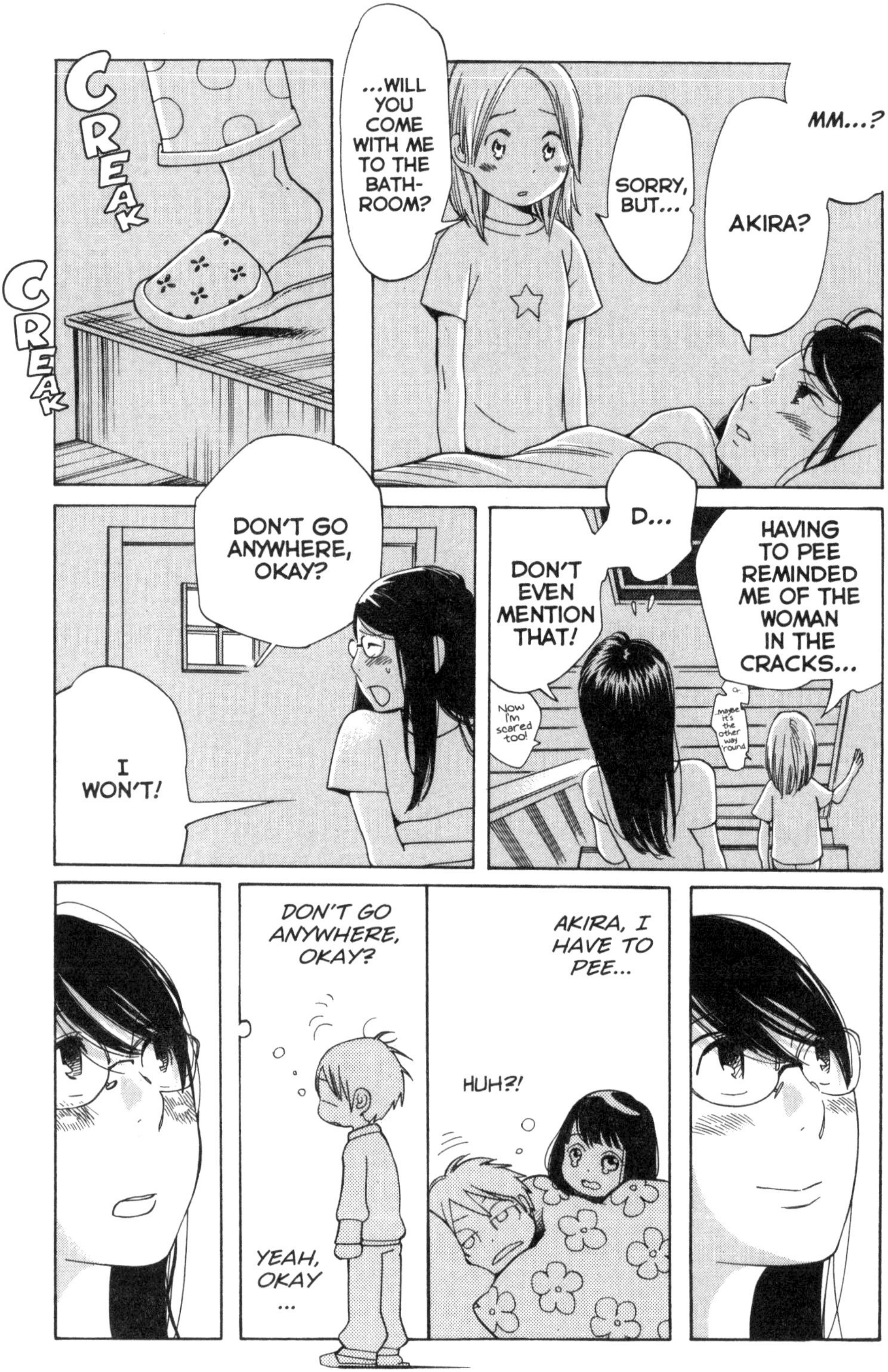
MM...?
AKIRA?
SORRY, BUT...
...WILL YOU COME WITH ME TO THE BATH-ROOM?
CREAK
CREAK
HAVING TO PEE REMINDED ME OF THE WOMAN IN THE CRACKS...
D...
DON'T EVEN MENTION THAT!
O-... MAYBE IT'S THE OTHER WAY 'ROUND
NOW I'M SCARED TOO!
DON'T GO ANYWHERE, OKAY?
I WON'T!
AKIRA, I HAVE TO PEE...
HUH?!
DON'T GO ANYWHERE, OKAY?
YEAH, OKAY ...

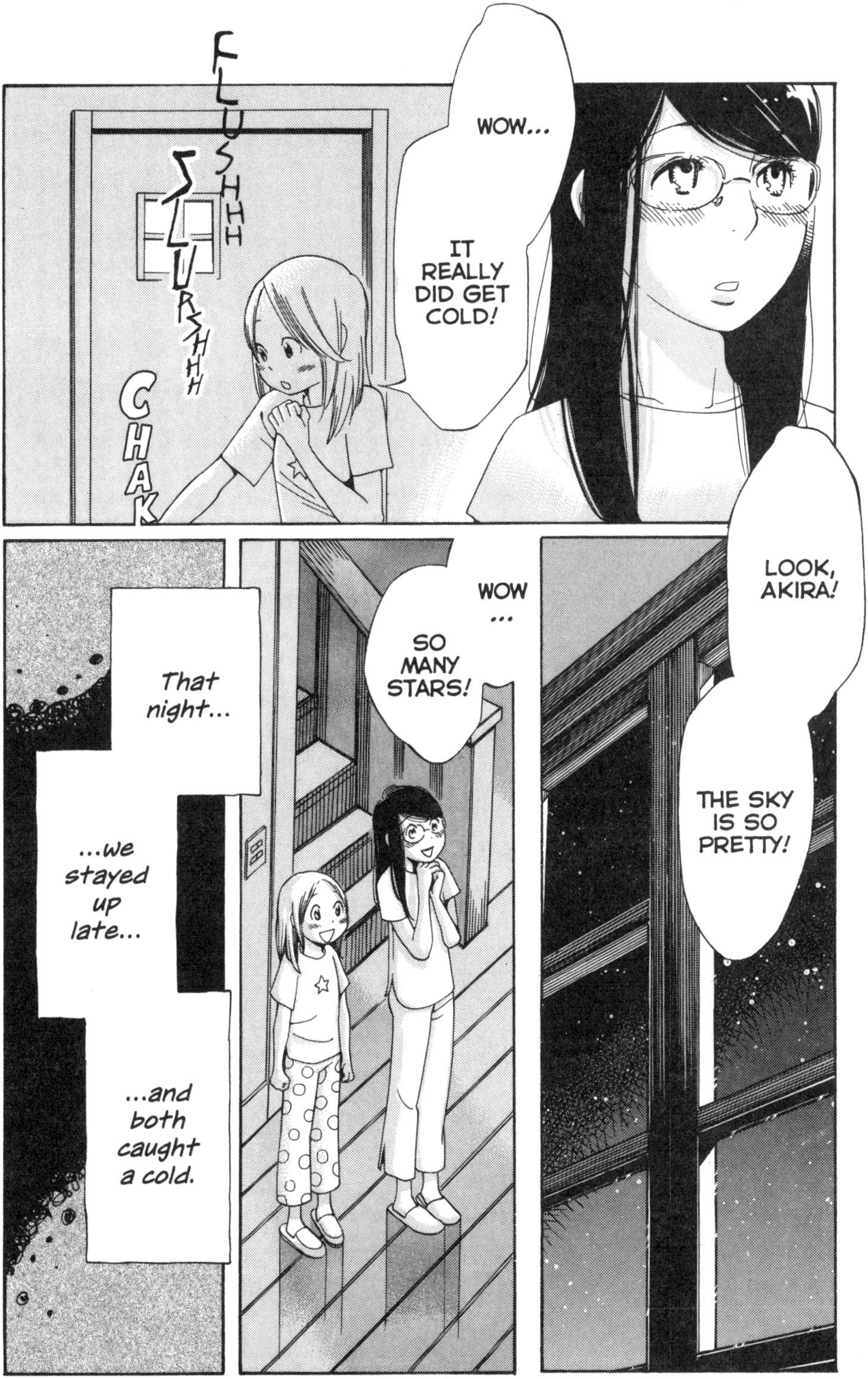
WOW...
IT REALLY DID GET COLD!
FLUSHHH
SLURSHHH
CHAK
LOOK, AKIRA!
THE SKY IS SO PRETTY!
WOW...
SO MANY STARS!
That night...
...we stayed up late...
...and both caught a cold.

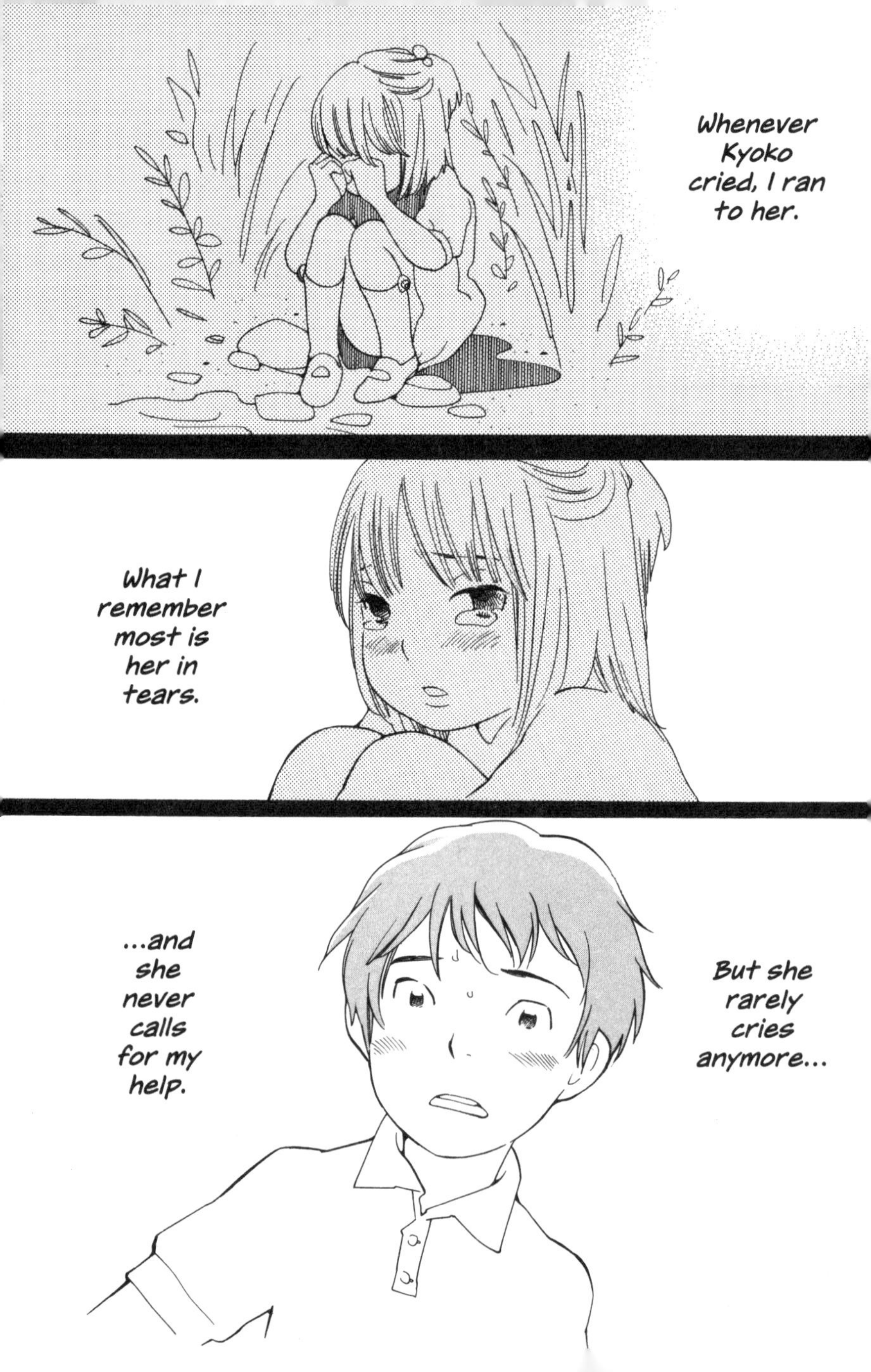
Whenever Kyoko cried, I ran to her.
What I remember most is her in tears.
But she rarely cries anymore...
...and she never calls for my help.

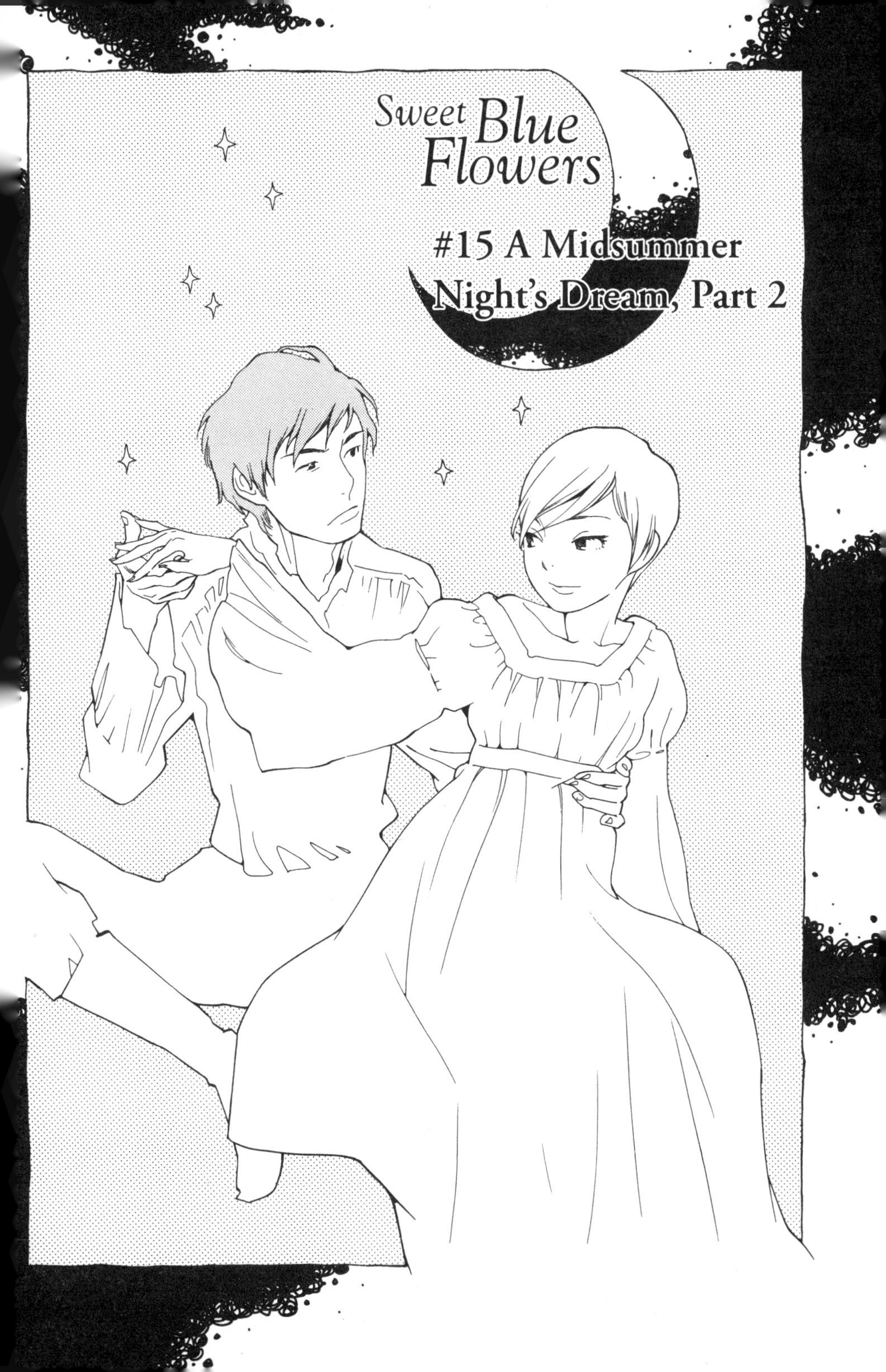
Sweet Blue Flowers
#15 A Midsummer Night's Dream, Part 2

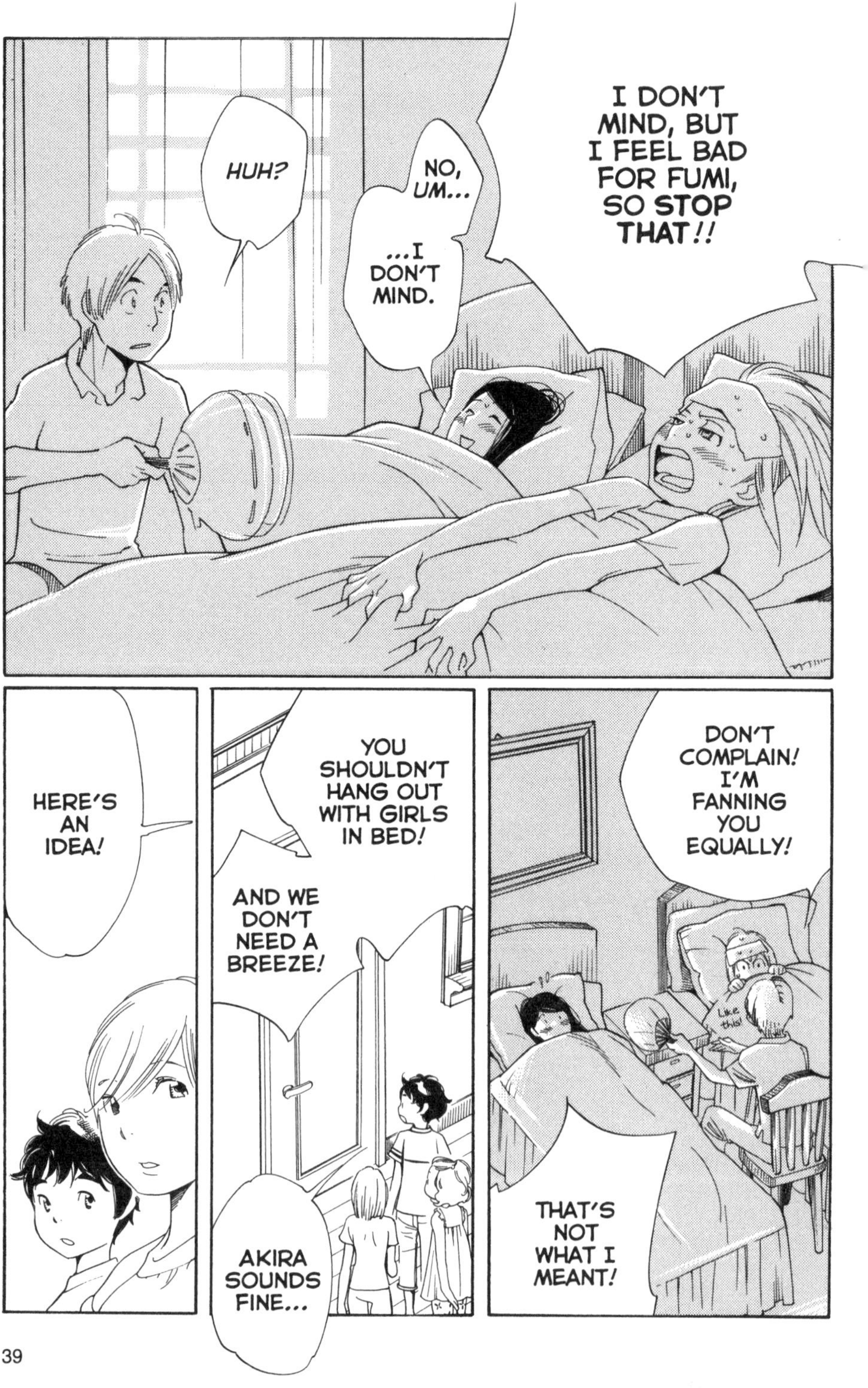
I DON'T MIND, BUT I FEEL BAD FOR FUMI, SO STOP THAT!!
NO, UM...
...I DON'T MIND.
HUH?
DON'T COMPLAIN! I'M FANNING YOU EQUALLY!
Like this!
THAT'S NOT WHAT I MEANT!
YOU SHOULDN'T HANG OUT WITH GIRLS IN BED!
AND WE DON'T NEED A BREEZE!
AKIRA SOUNDS FINE...
HERE'S AN IDEA!

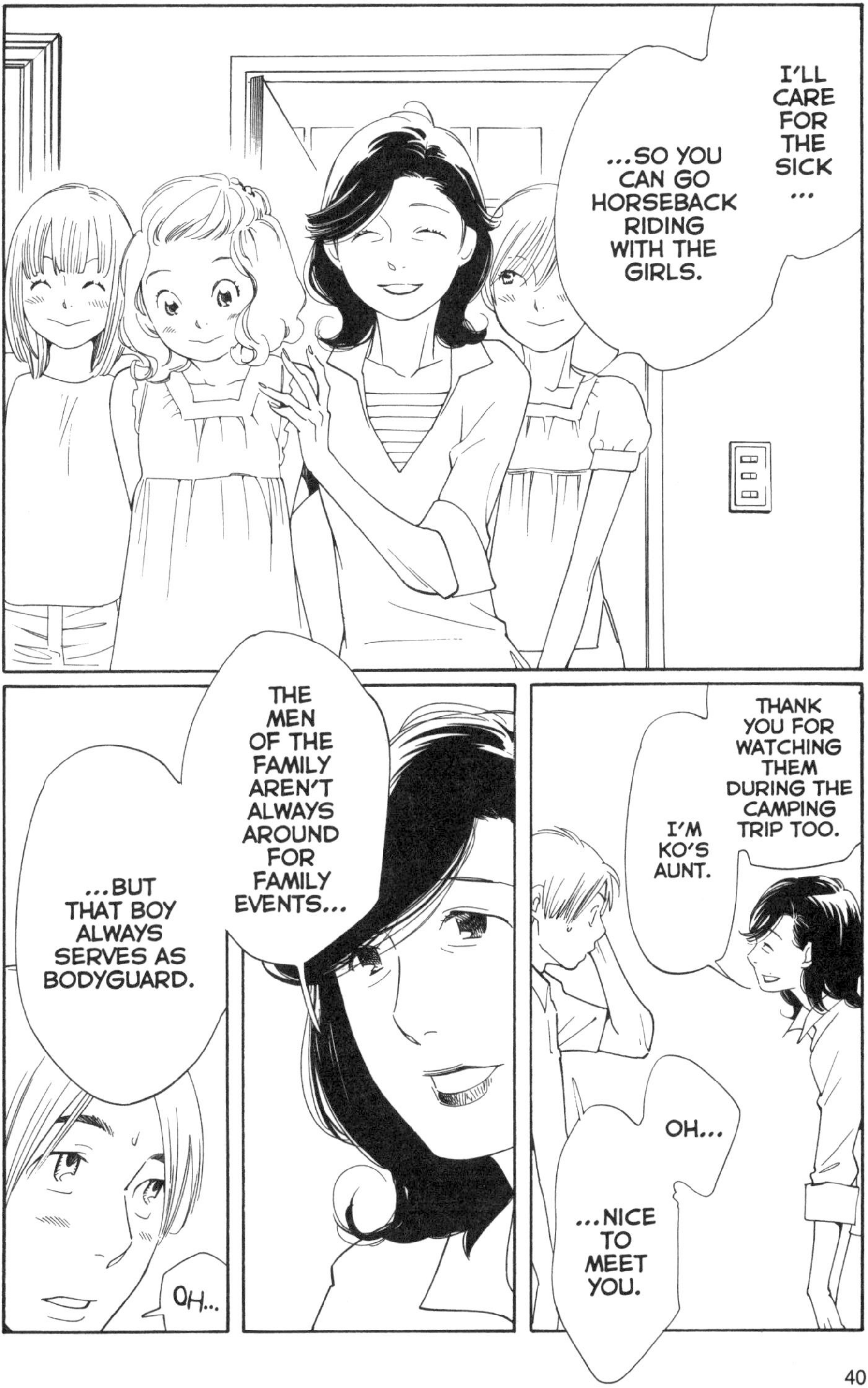
I'LL CARE FOR THE SICK...
...SO YOU CAN GO HORSEBACK RIDING WITH THE GIRLS.
THANK YOU FOR WATCHING THEM DURING THE CAMPING TRIP TOO.
I'M KO'S AUNT.
OH...
...NICE TO MEET YOU.
THE MEN OF THE FAMILY AREN'T ALWAYS AROUND FOR FAMILY EVENTS...
...BUT THAT BOY ALWAYS SERVES AS BODYGUARD.
OH...

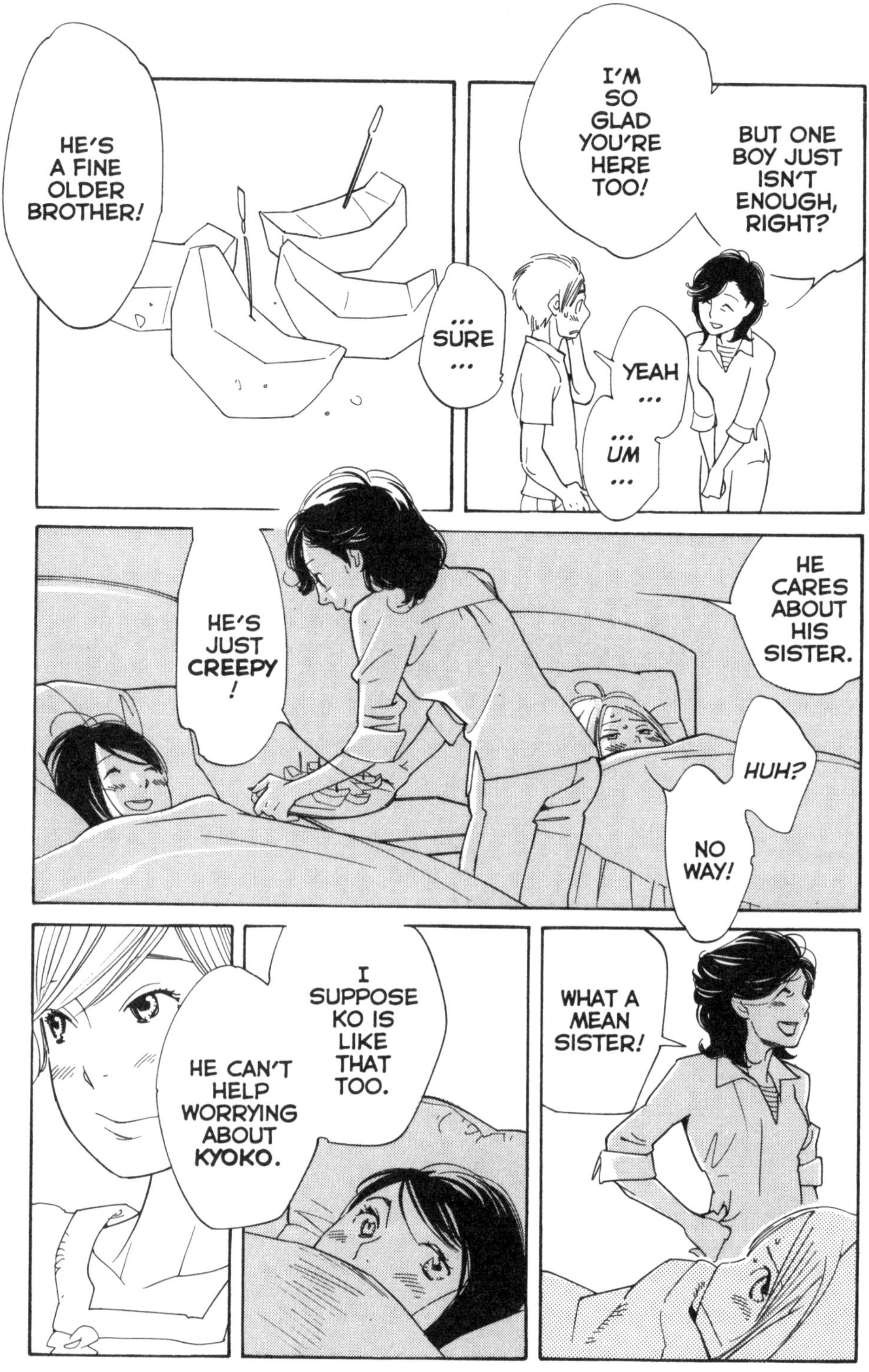
I'M SO GLAD YOU'RE HERE TOO!
BUT ONE BOY JUST ISN'T ENOUGH, RIGHT?
YEAH...
...SURE...
...UM...
HE'S A FINE OLDER BROTHER!
HE CARES ABOUT HIS SISTER.
HE'S JUST CREEPY!
HUH?
NO WAY!
WHAT A MEAN SISTER!
I SUPPOSE KO IS LIKE THAT TOO.
HE CAN'T HELP WORRYING ABOUT KYOKO.

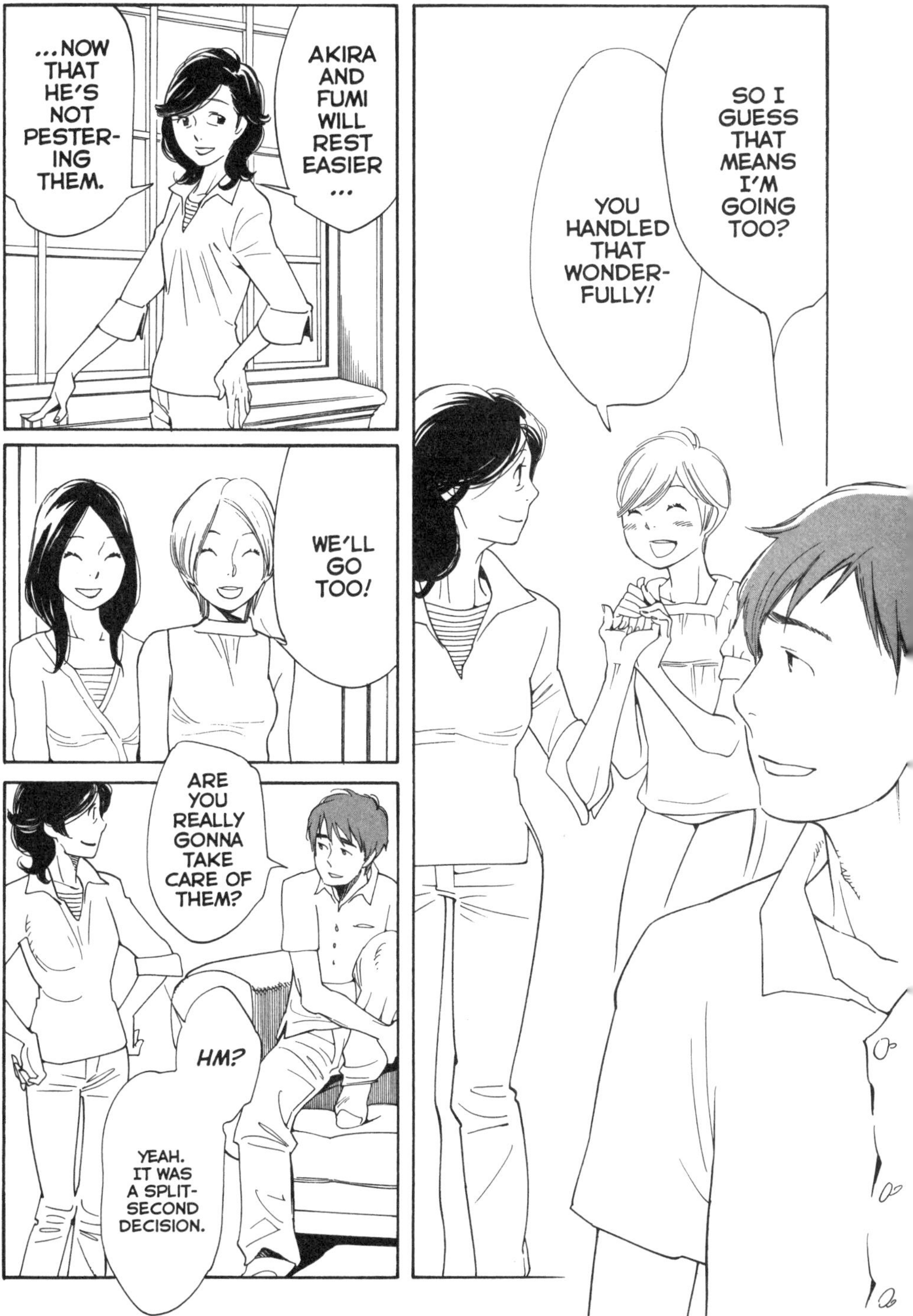
SO I GUESS THAT MEANS I'M GOING TOO?
YOU HANDLED THAT WONDERFULLY!
AKIRA AND FUMI WILL REST EASIER...
...NOW THAT HE'S NOT PESTERING THEM.
WE'LL GO TOO!
ARE YOU REALLY GONNA TAKE CARE OF THEM?
HM?
YEAH. IT WAS A SPLIT-SECOND DECISION.

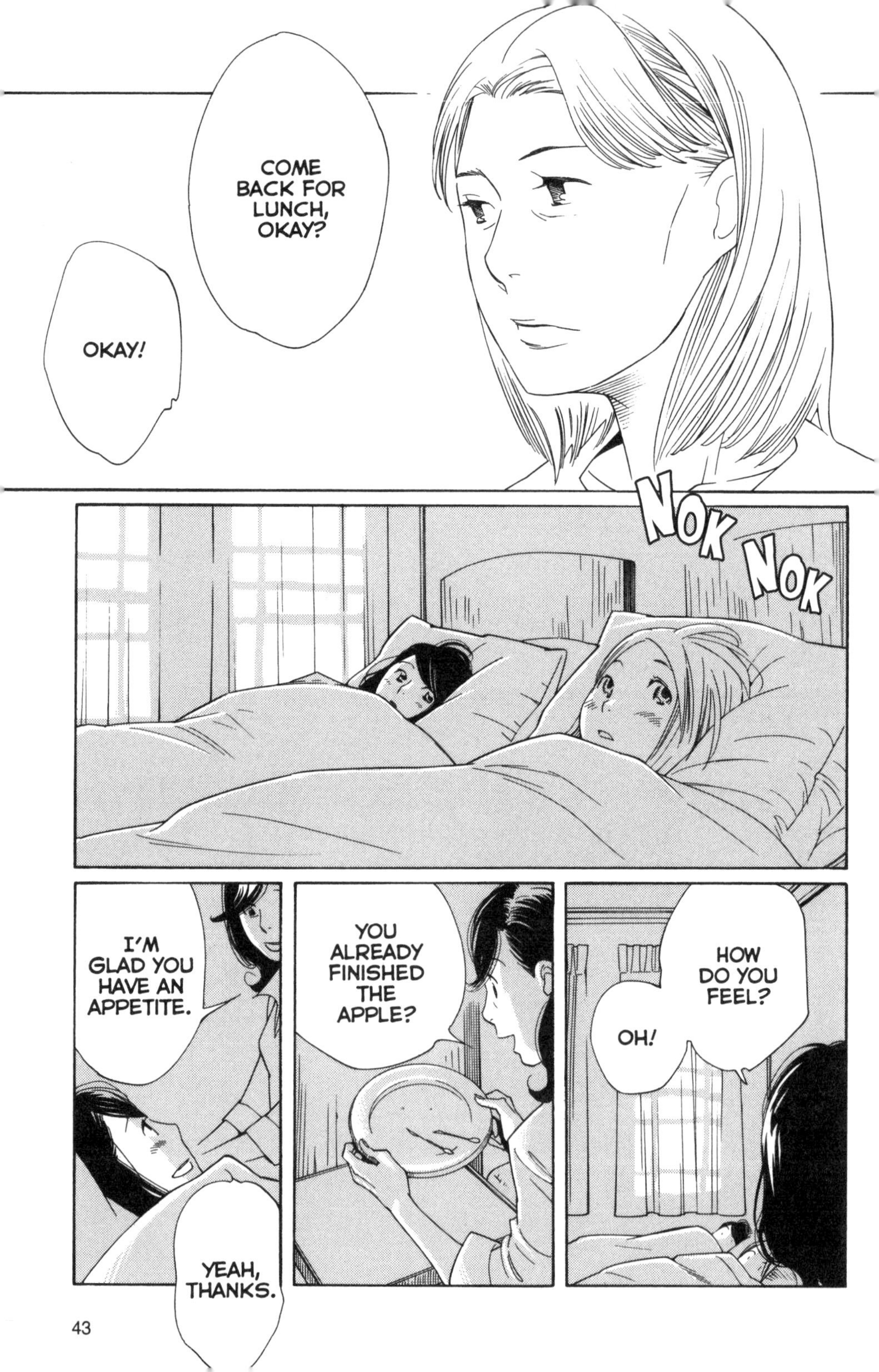
COME BACK FOR LUNCH, OKAY?
OKAY!
NOK NOK
HOW DO YOU FEEL?
OH!
YOU ALREADY FINISHED THE APPLE?
I'M GLAD YOU HAVE AN APPETITE.
YEAH, THANKS.

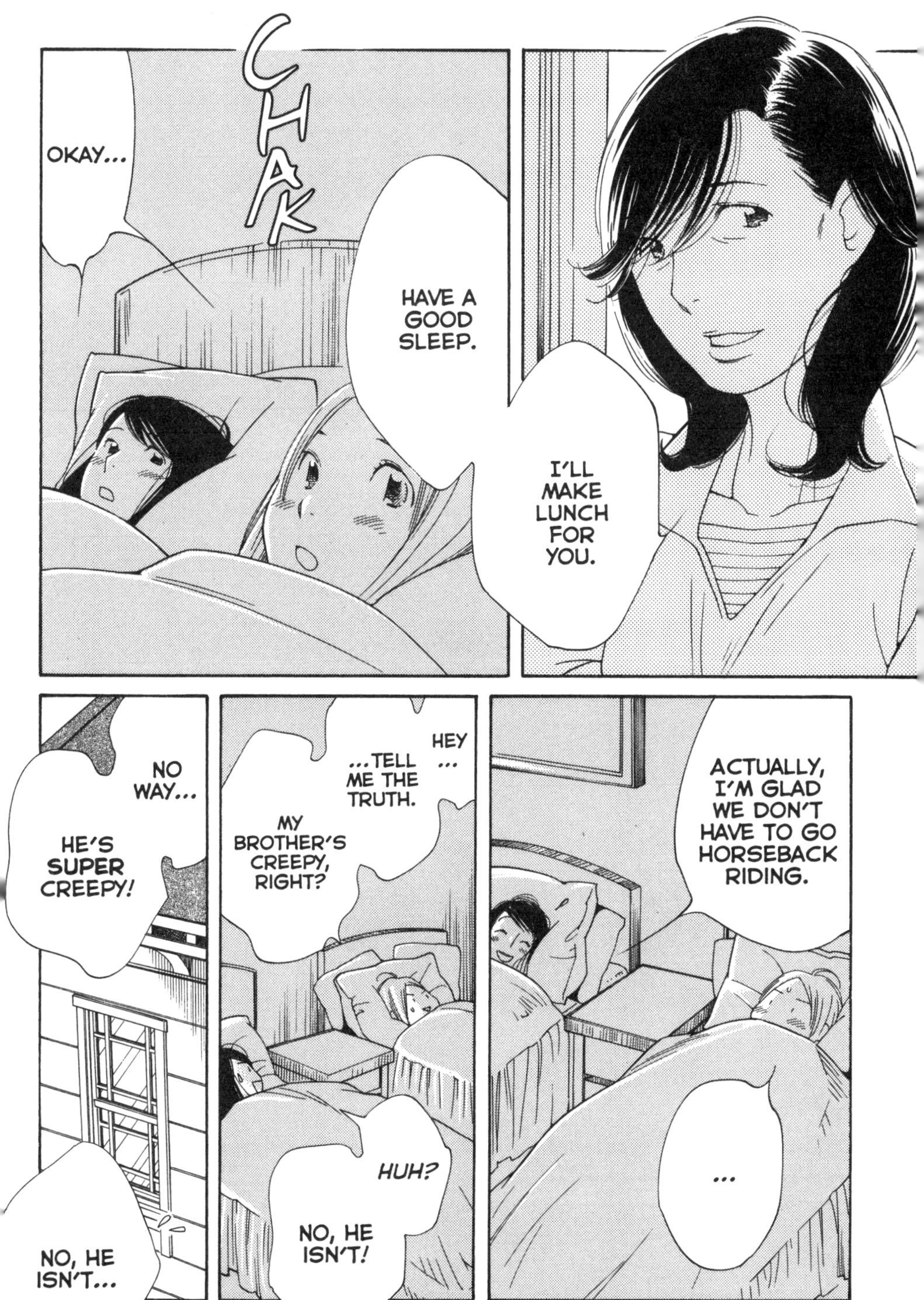
I'LL MAKE LUNCH FOR YOU.
CHAK
HAVE A GOOD SLEEP.
OKAY...
ACTUALLY, I'M GLAD WE DON'T HAVE TO GO HORSEBACK RIDING.
...
HEY...
...TELL ME THE TRUTH.
MY BROTHER'S CREEPY, RIGHT?
HUH?
NO, HE ISN'T!
NO WAY...
HE'S SUPER CREEPY!
NO, HE ISN'T...

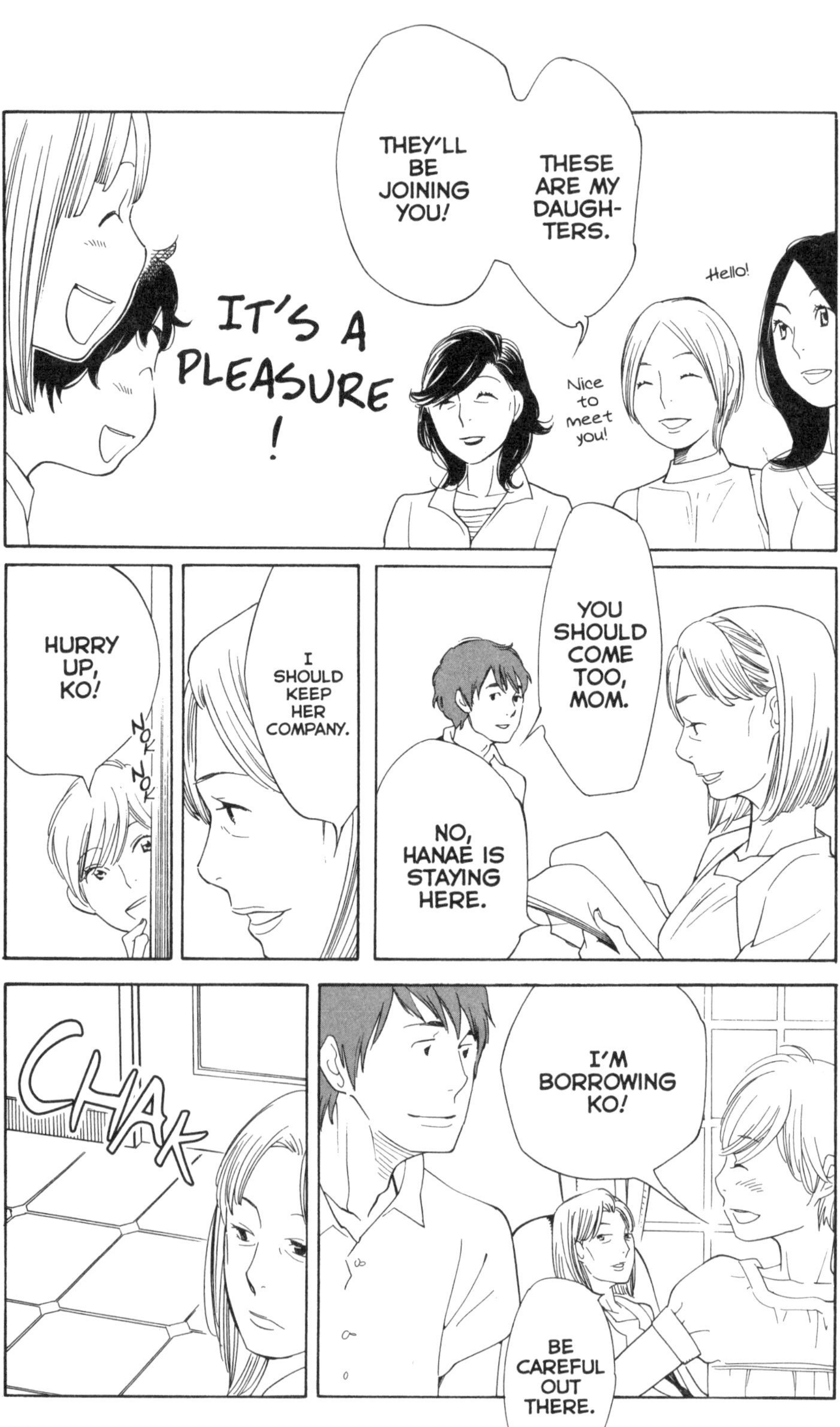
THESE ARE MY DAUGHTERS.
THEY'LL BE JOINING YOU!
Hello!
Nice to meet you!
IT'S A PLEASURE!
YOU SHOULD COME TOO, MOM.
NO, HANAE IS STAYING HERE.
I SHOULD KEEP HER COMPANY.
HURRY UP, KO!
NOK NOK
I'M BORROWING KO!
BE CAREFUL OUT THERE.
CHAK

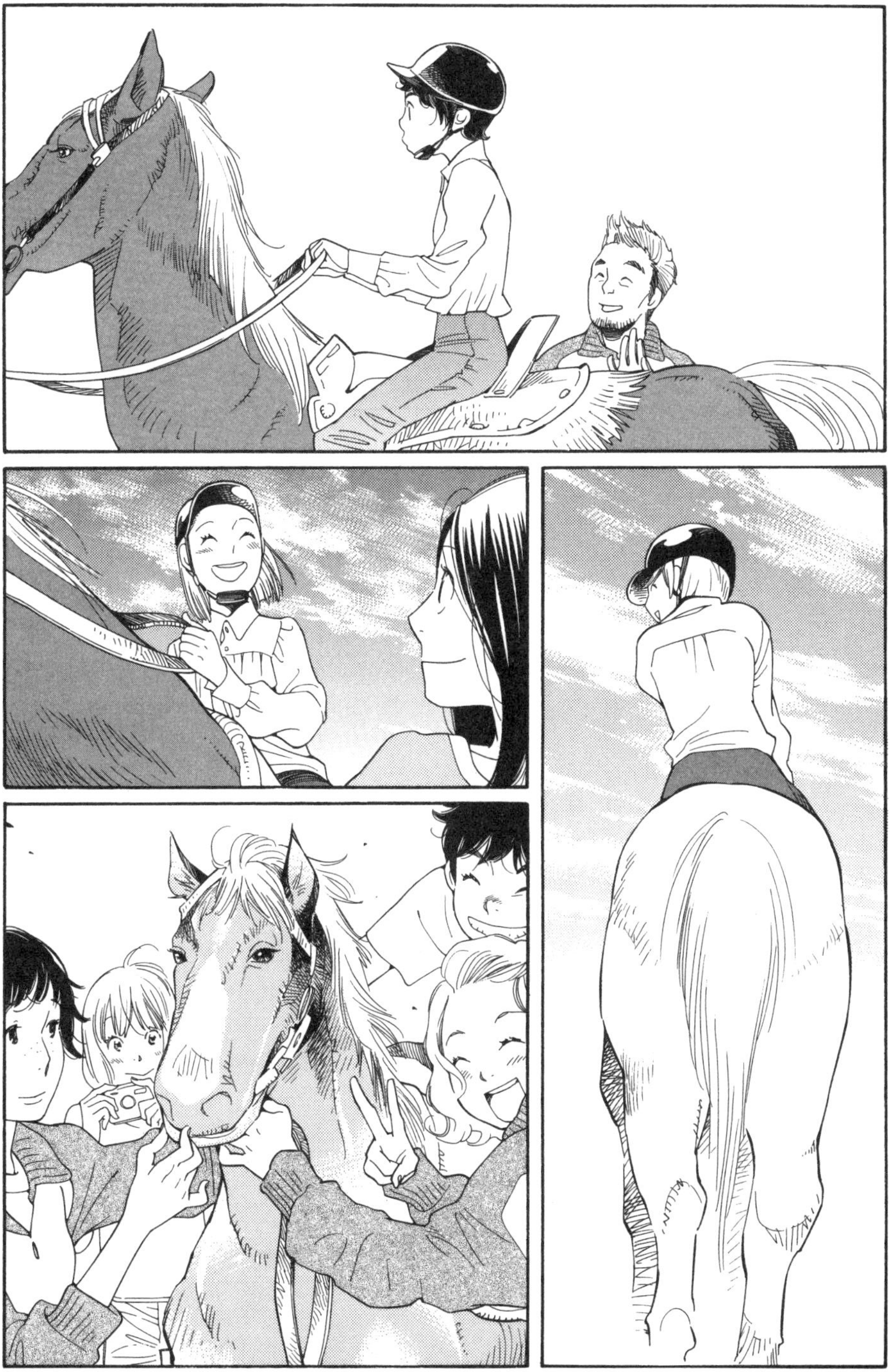

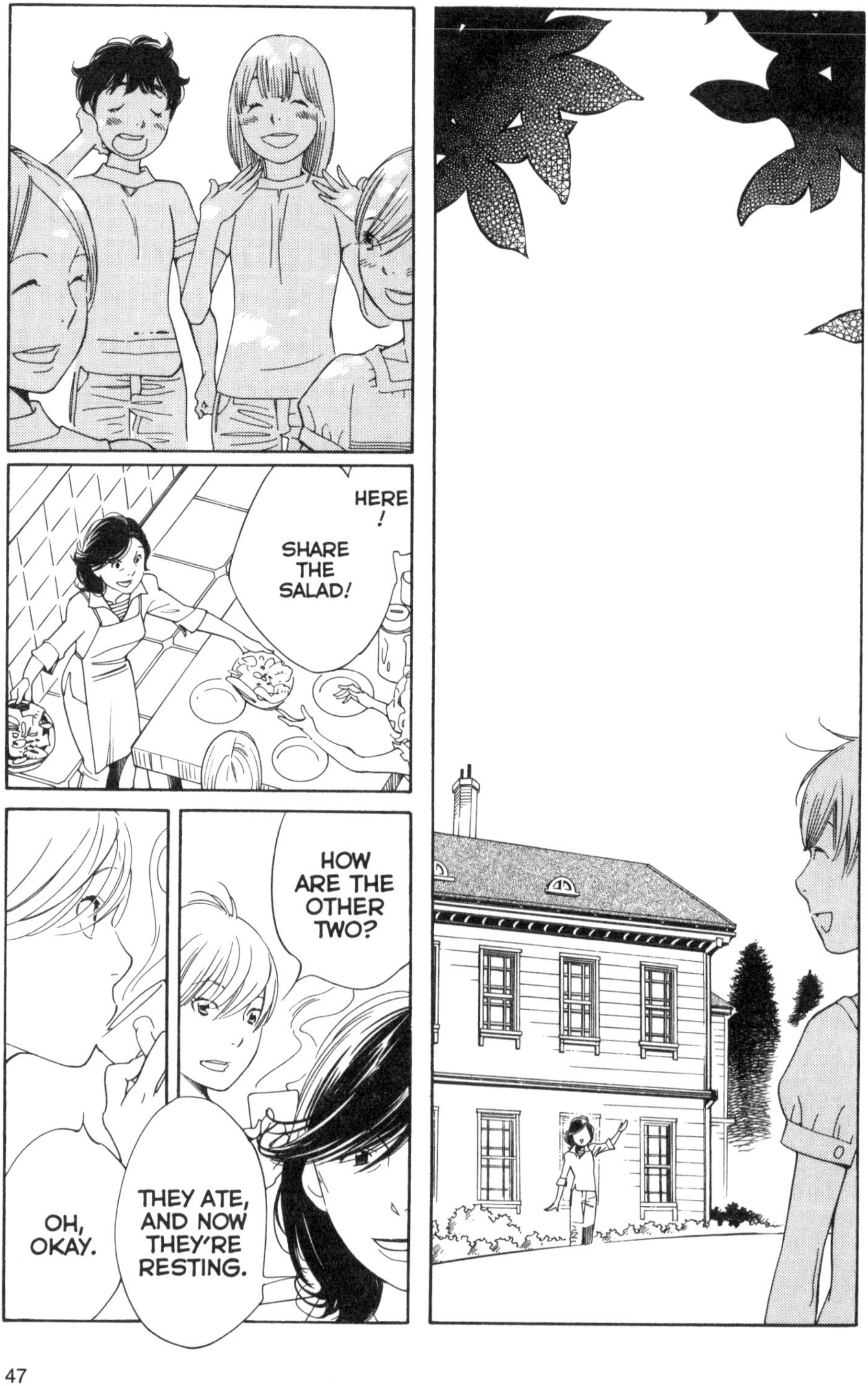
HERE!
SHARE THE SALAD!
HOW ARE THE OTHER TWO?
THEY ATE, AND NOW THEY'RE RESTING.
OH, OKAY.

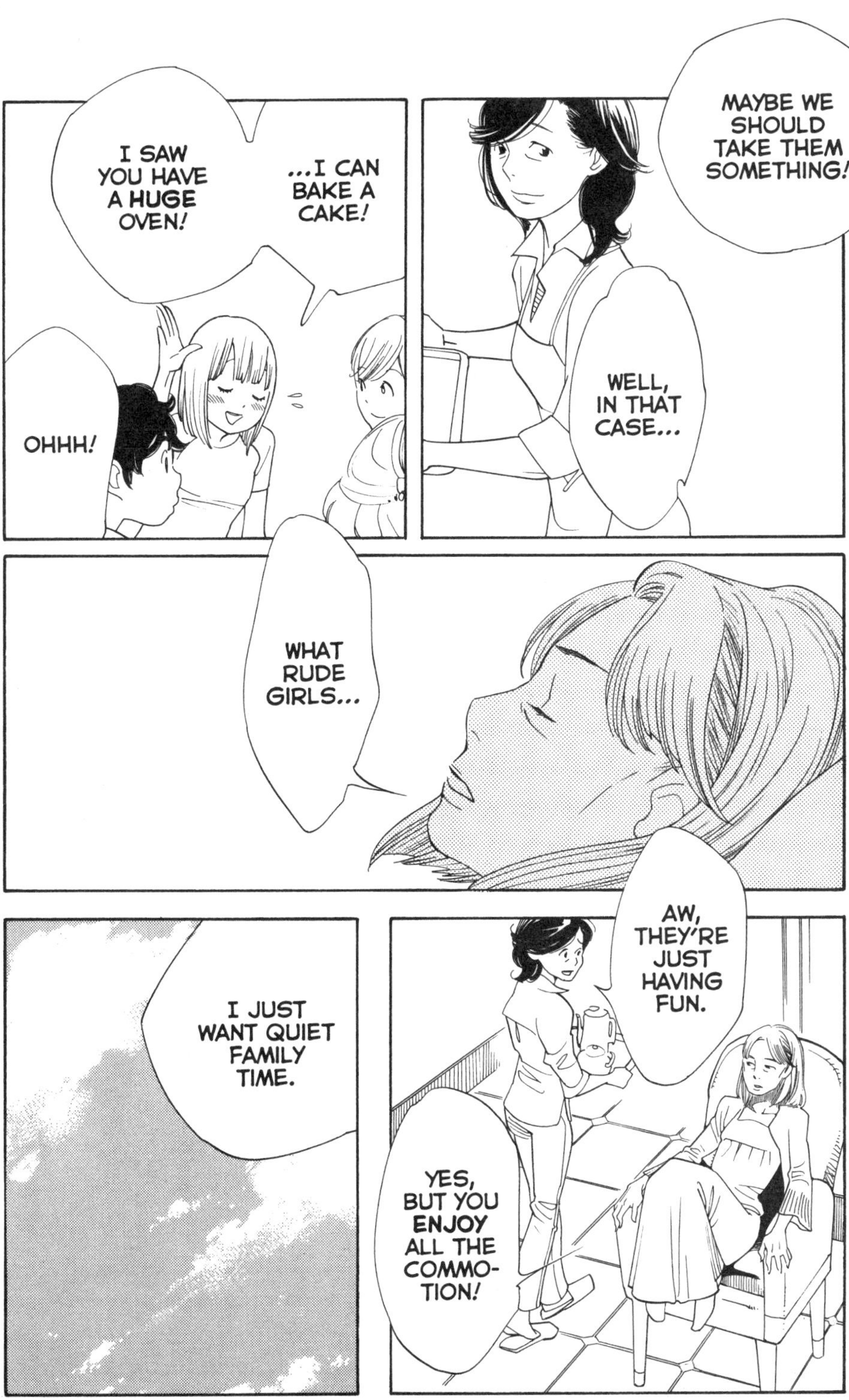
MAYBE WE SHOULD TAKE THEM SOMETHING!
WELL, IN THAT CASE...
I SAW YOU HAVE A HUGE OVEN!
...I CAN BAKE A CAKE!
OHHH!
WHAT RUDE GIRLS...
AW, THEY'RE JUST HAVING FUN.
YES, BUT YOU ENJOY ALL THE COMMOTION!
I JUST WANT QUIET FAMILY TIME.

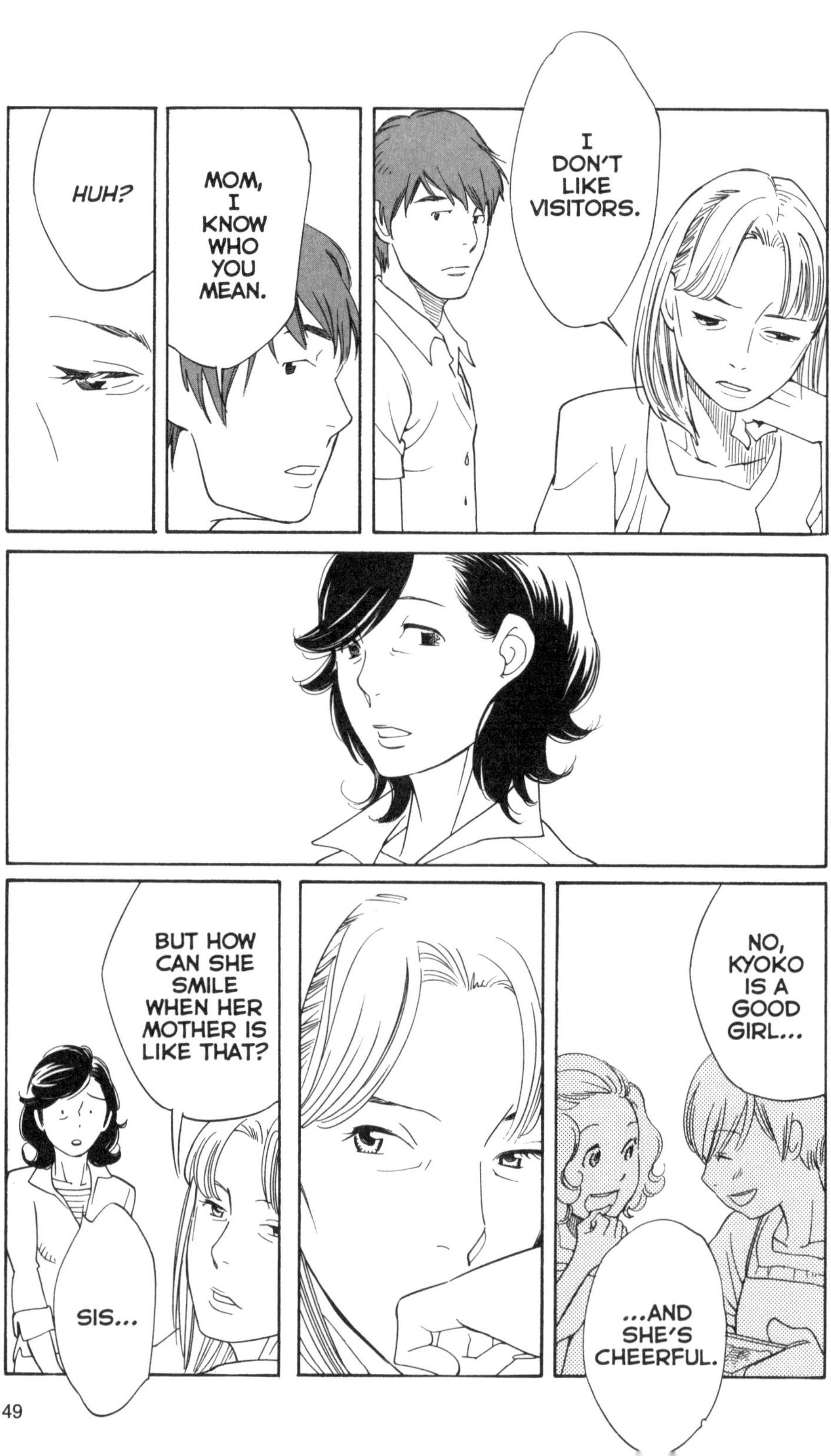
I DON'T LIKE VISITORS.
MOM, I KNOW WHO YOU MEAN.
HUH?
NO, KYOKO IS A GOOD GIRL...
...AND SHE'S CHEERFUL.
BUT HOW CAN SHE SMILE WHEN HER MOTHER IS LIKE THAT?
SIS...

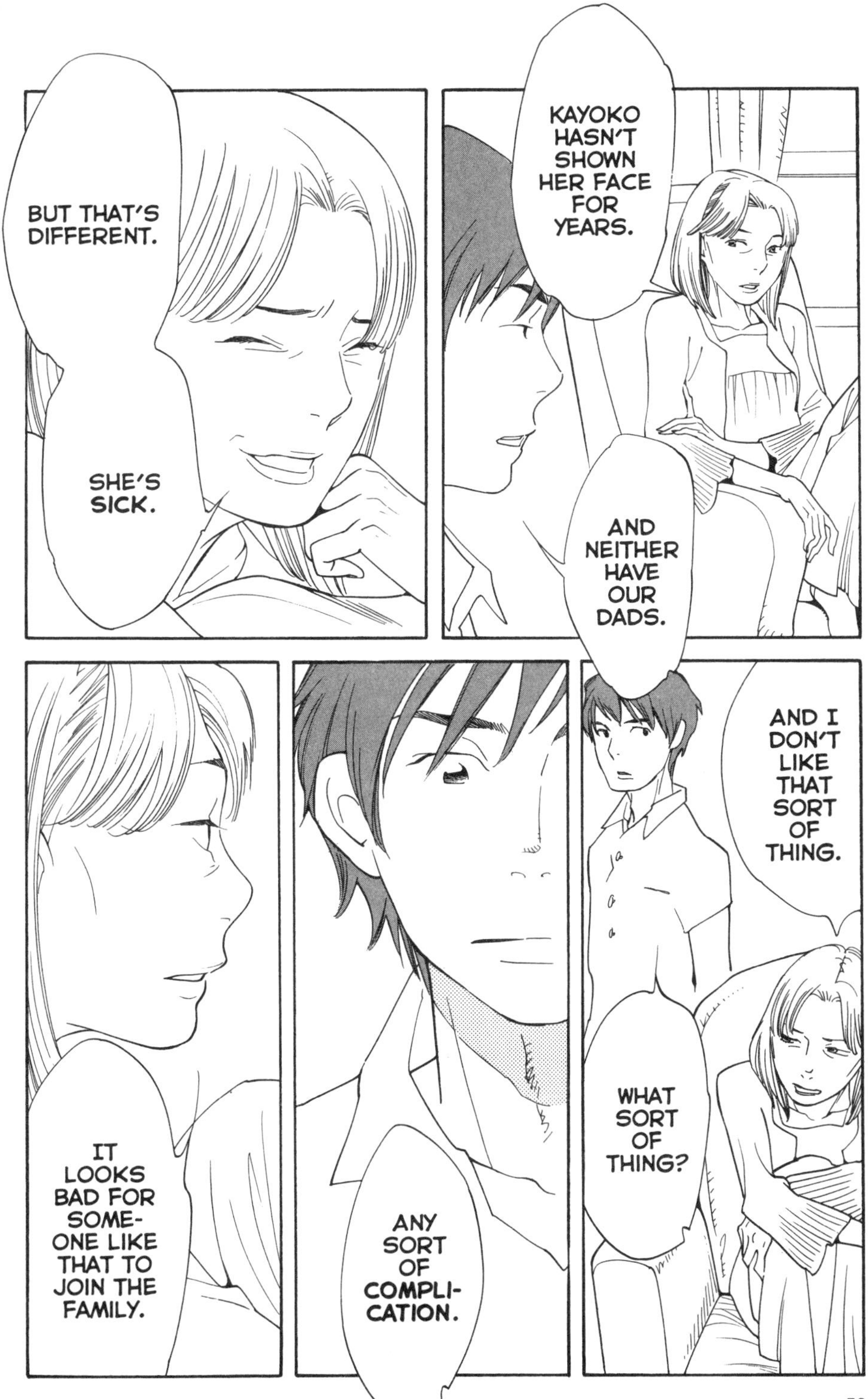
KAYOKO HASN'T SHOWN HER FACE FOR YEARS.
AND NEITHER HAVE OUR DADS.
BUT THAT'S DIFFERENT.
SHE'S SICK.
AND I DON'T LIKE THAT SORT OF THING.
WHAT SORT OF THING?
ANY SORT OF COMPLICATION.
IT LOOKS BAD FOR SOME-ONE LIKE THAT TO JOIN THE FAMILY.

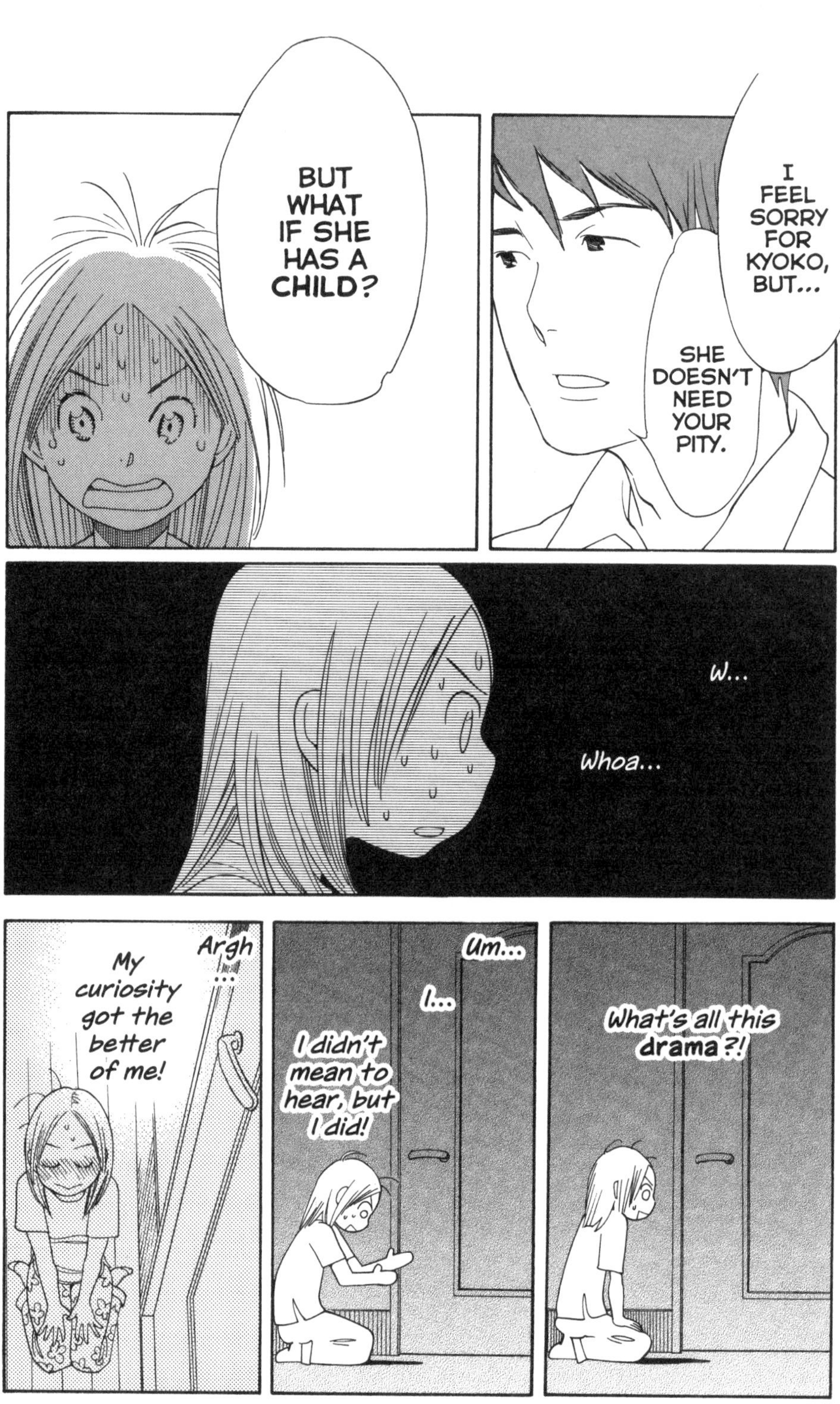
I FEEL SORRY FOR KYOKO, BUT...
SHE DOESN'T NEED YOUR PITY.
BUT WHAT IF SHE HAS A CHILD?
W...
Whoa...
What's all this drama?!
Um...
I...
I didn't mean to hear, but I did!
Argh...
My curiosity got the better of me!

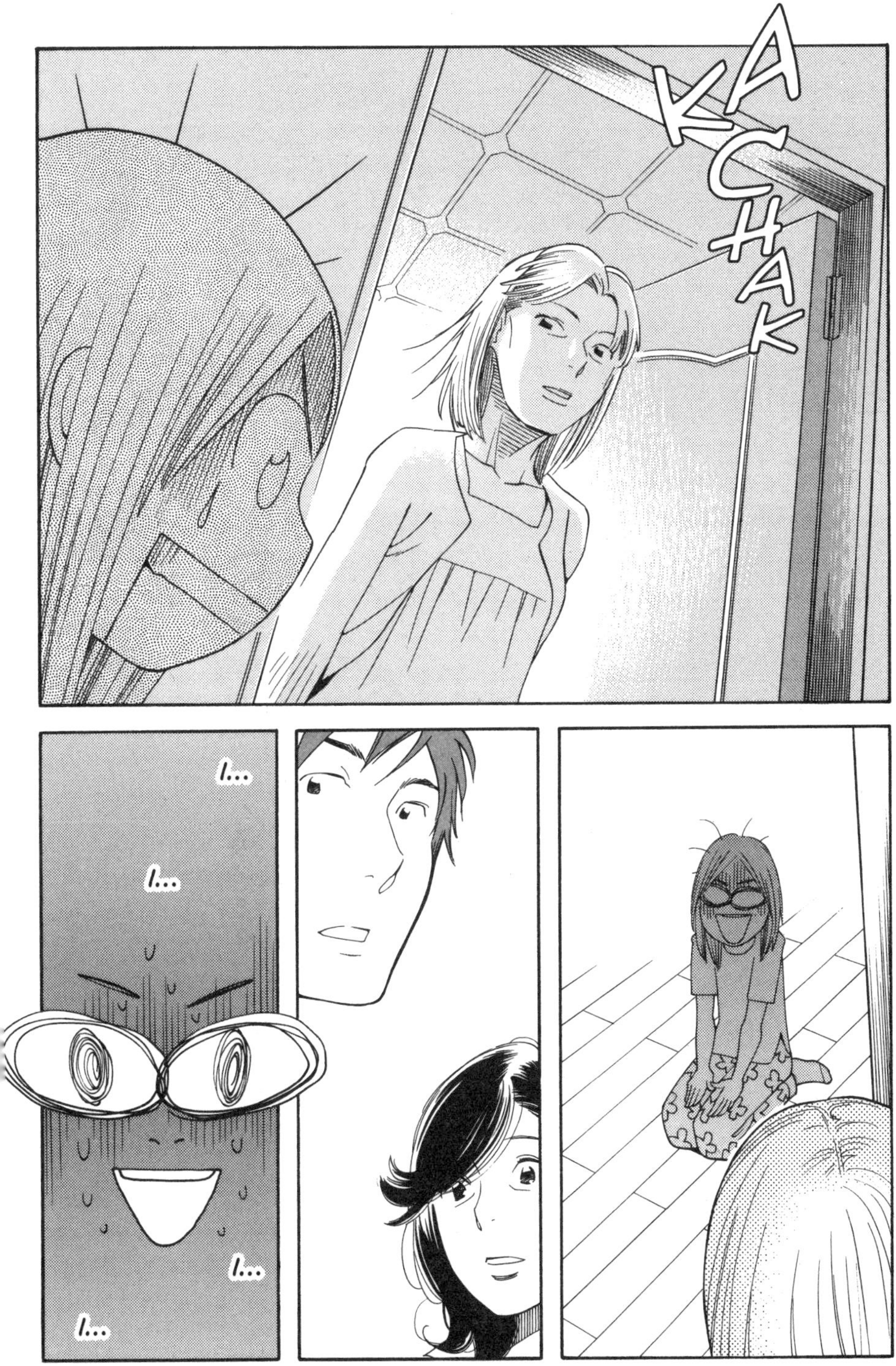
KACHAK
I...
I...
I...
I...

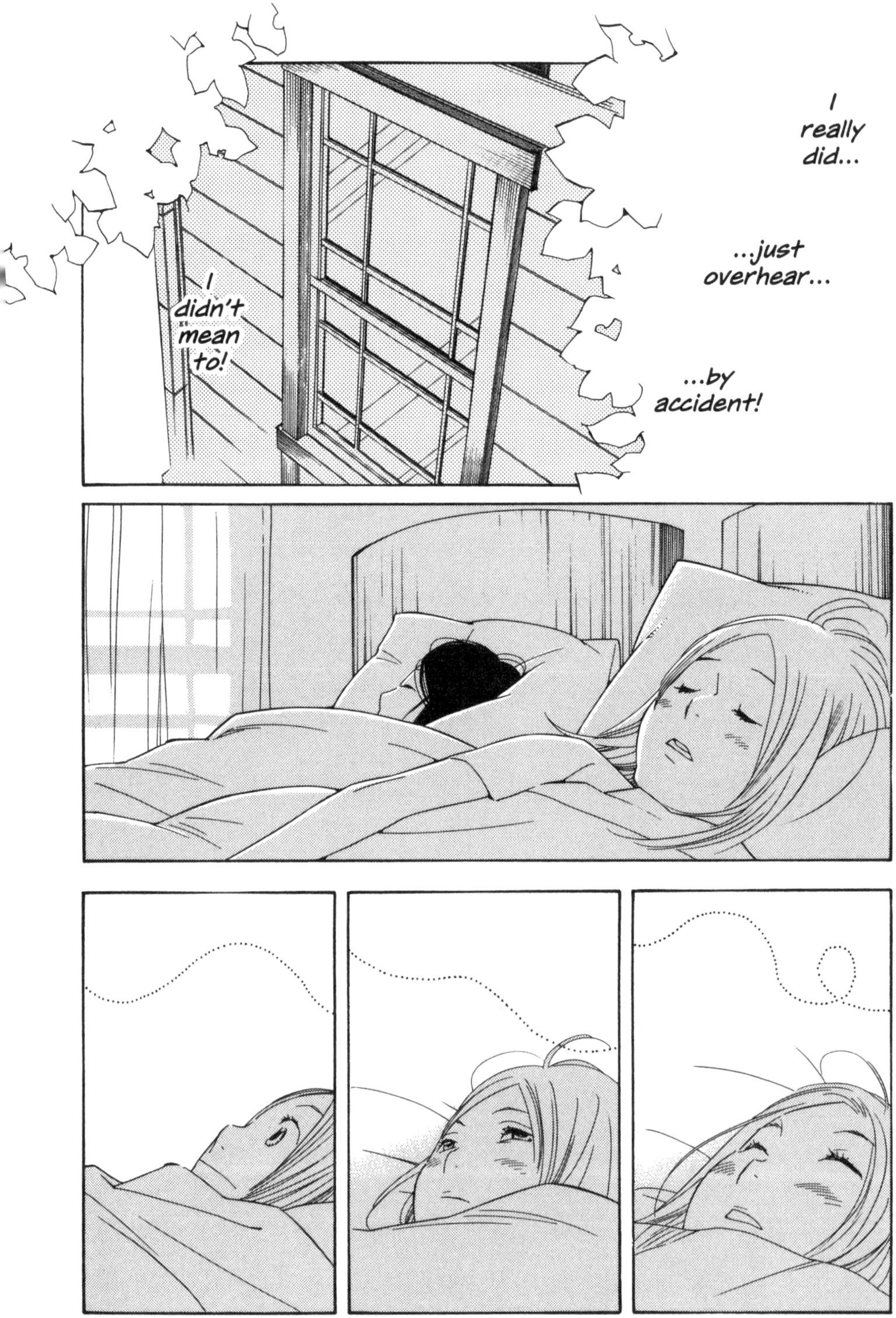
I really did...
...just overhear...
...by accident!
I didn't mean to!

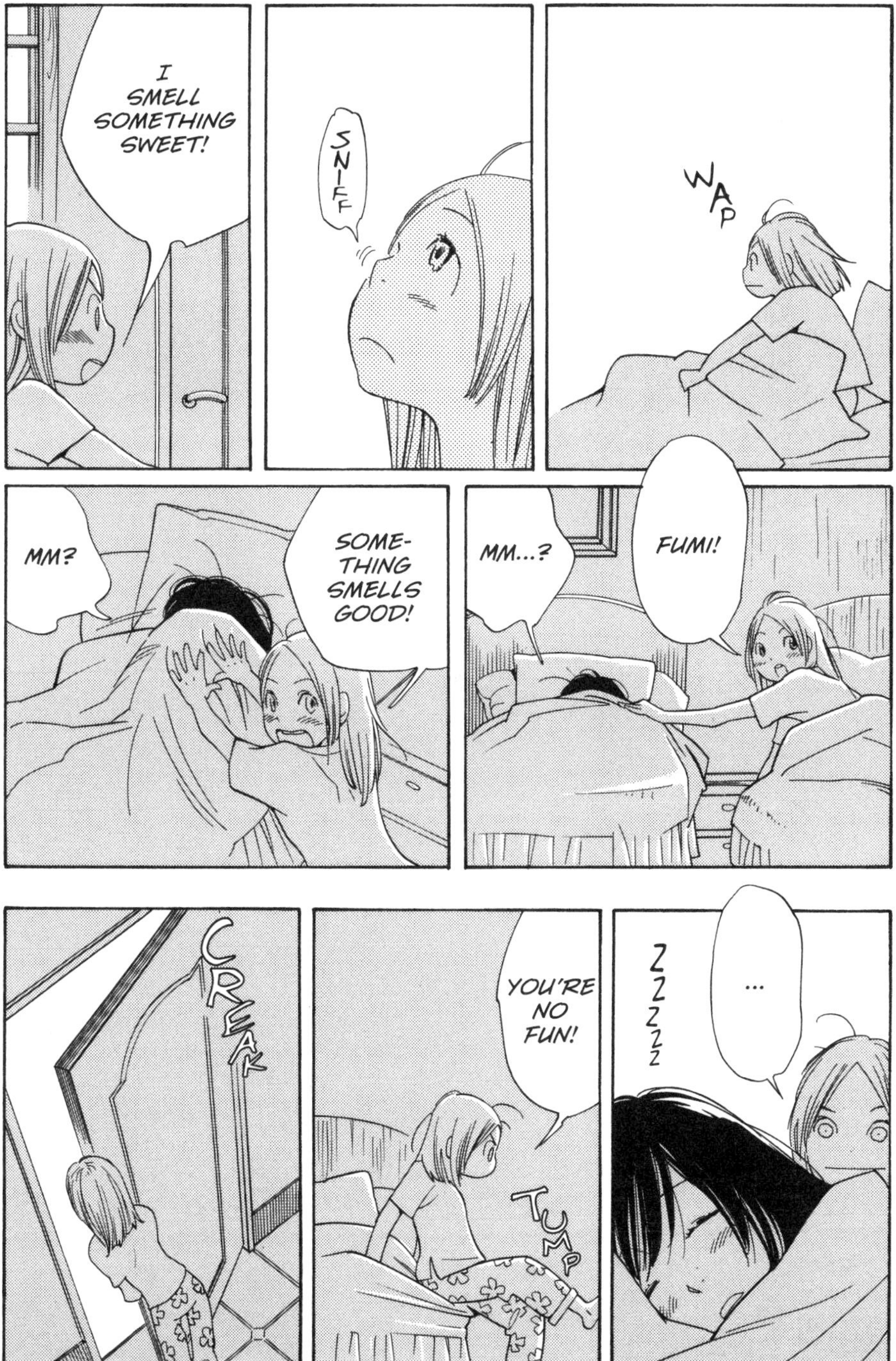
WAP
SNIFF
I SMELL SOMETHING SWEET!
FUMI!
MM...?
SOME-THING SMELLS GOOD!
MM?
...
ZZZZZ
YOU'RE NO FUN!
TUMP
CREAK

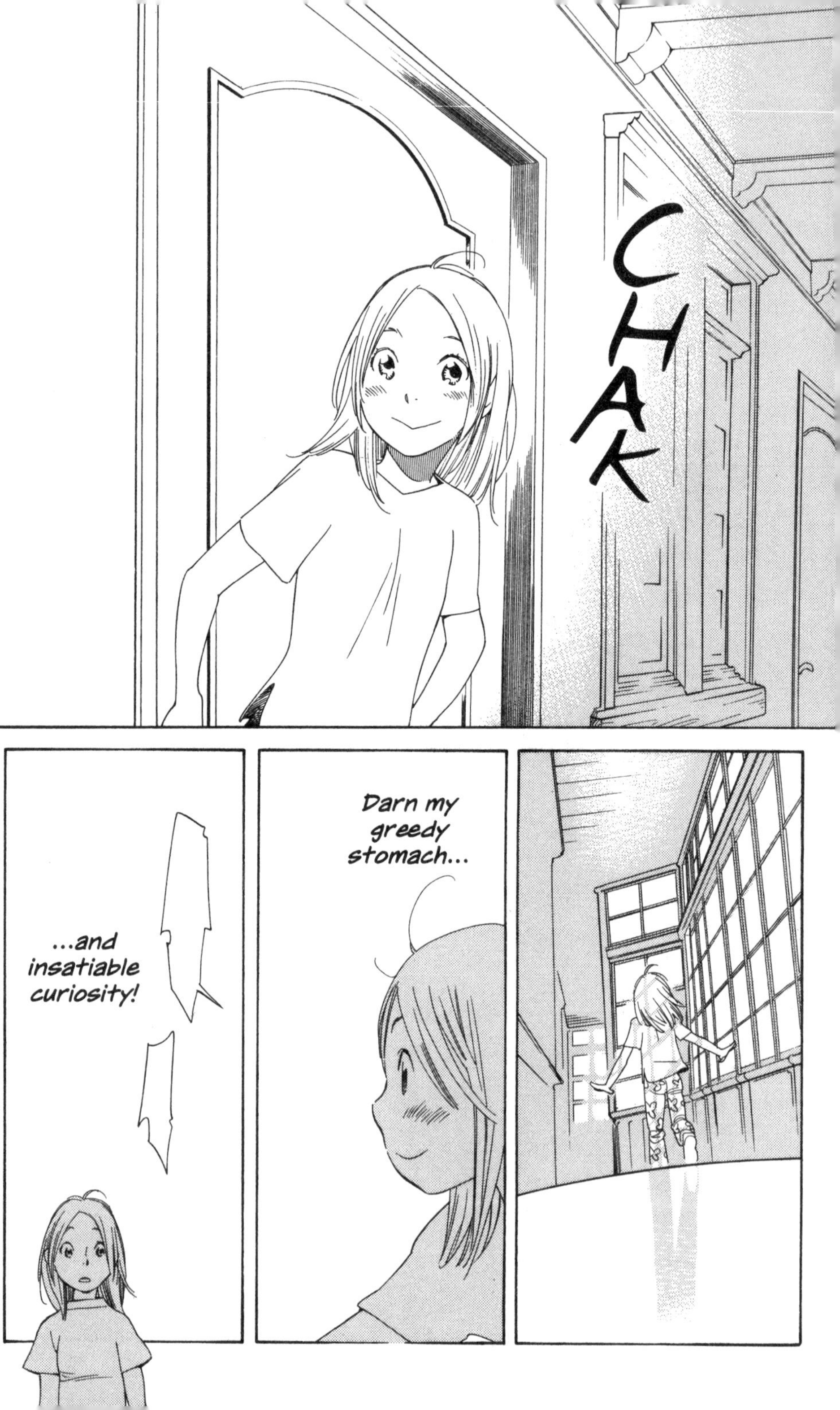
CHAK
Darn my greedy stomach...
...and insatiable curiosity!

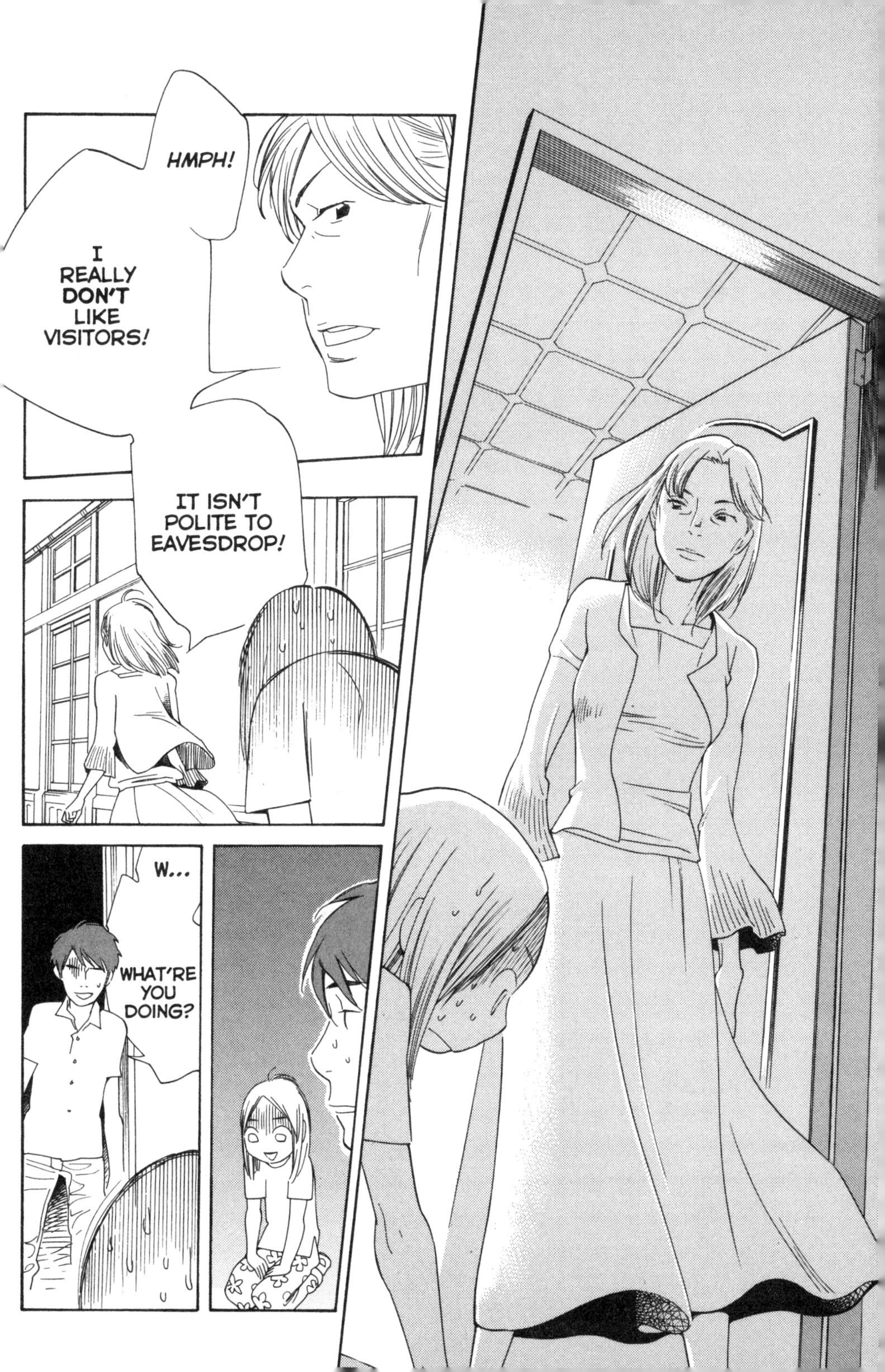
HMPH!
I REALLY DON'T LIKE VISITORS!
IT ISN'T POLITE TO EAVESDROP!
W...
WHAT'RE YOU DOING?

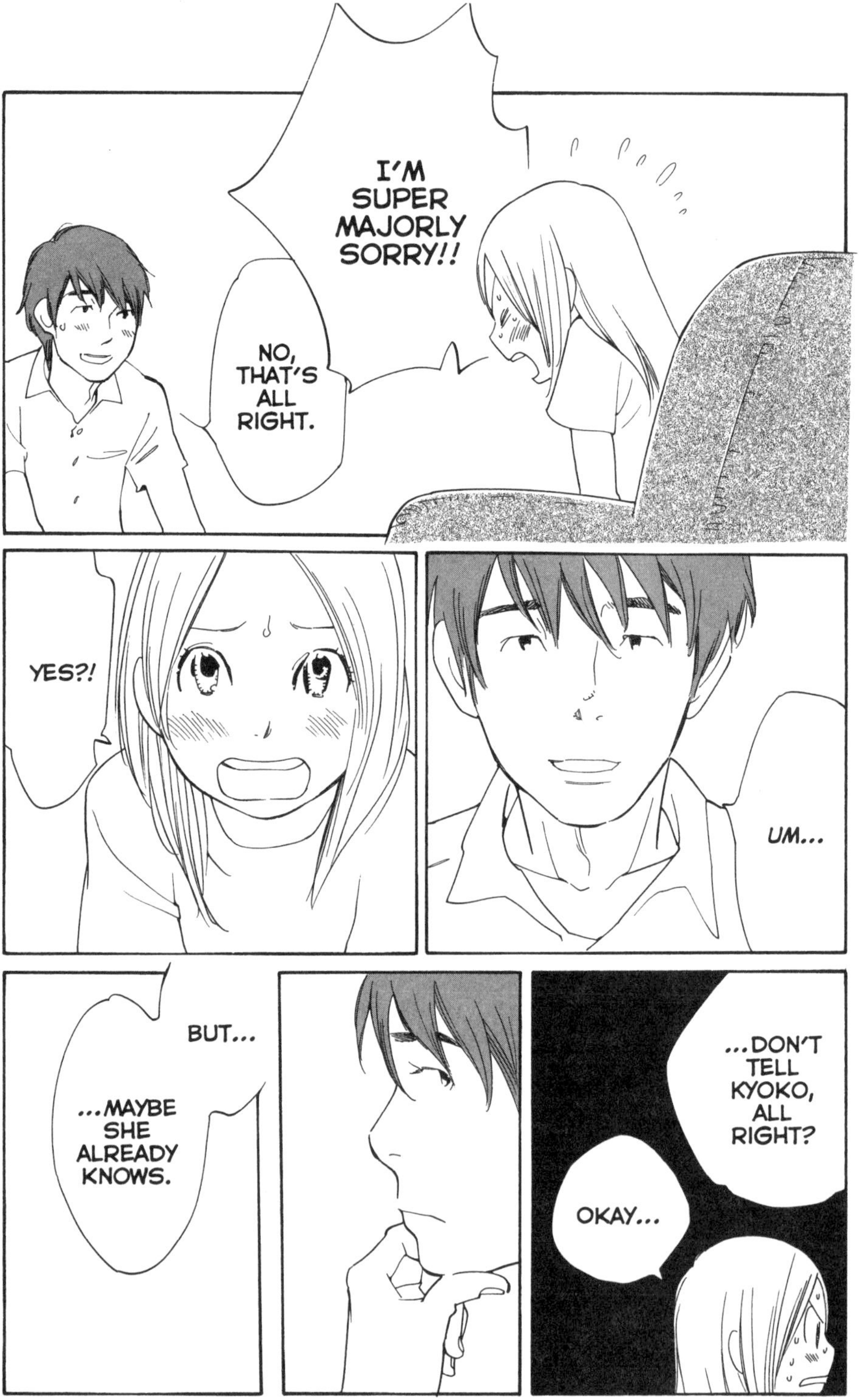
I'M SUPER MAJORLY SORRY!!
NO, THAT'S ALL RIGHT.
UM...
YES?!
...DON'T TELL KYOKO, ALL RIGHT?
OKAY...
BUT...
...MAYBE SHE ALREADY KNOWS.

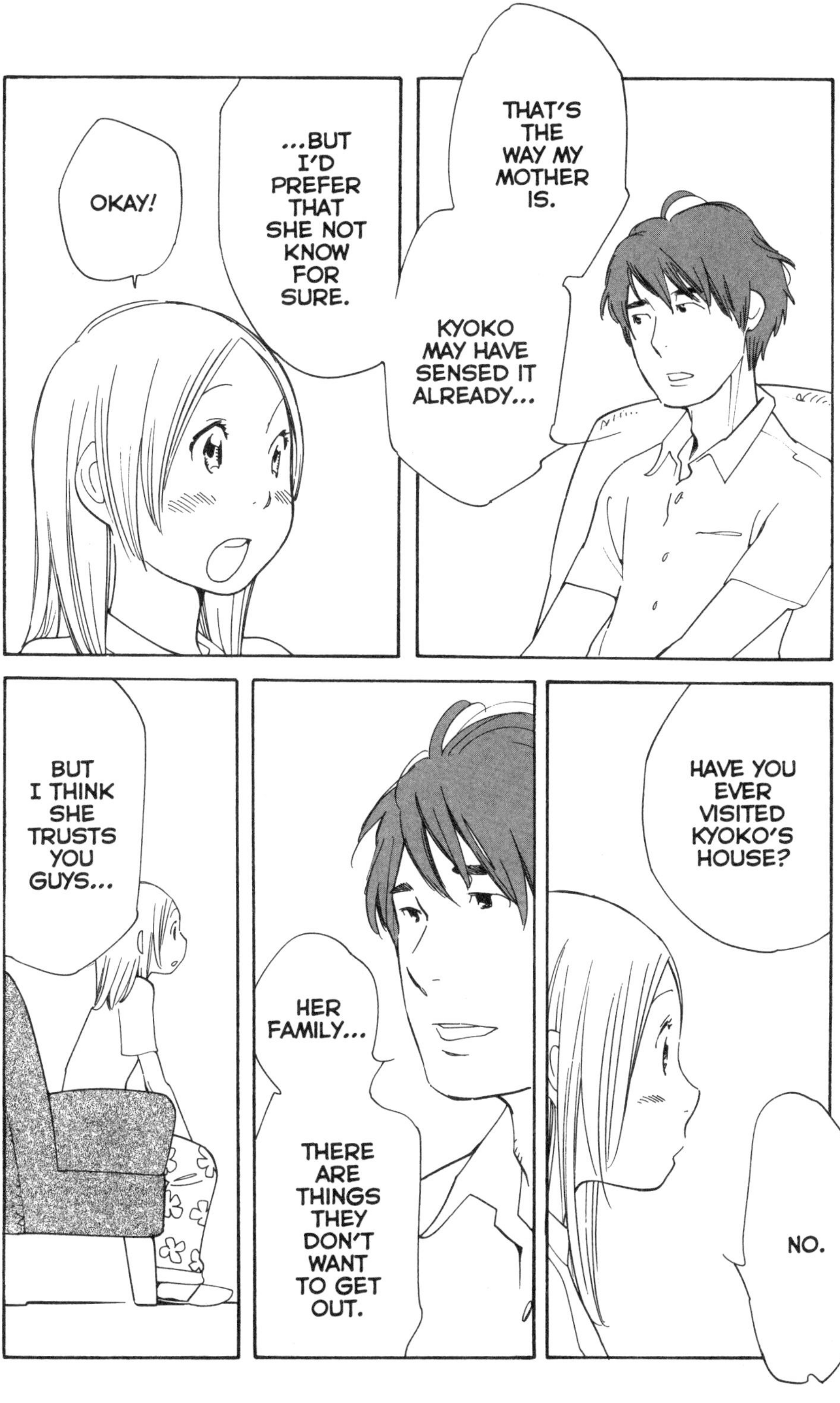
THAT'S THE WAY MY MOTHER IS.
KYOKO MAY HAVE SENSED IT ALREADY...
...BUT I'D PREFER THAT SHE NOT KNOW FOR SURE.
OKAY!
HAVE YOU EVER VISITED KYOKO'S HOUSE?
NO.
HER FAMILY...
THERE ARE THINGS THEY DON'T WANT TO GET OUT.
BUT I THINK SHE TRUSTS YOU GUYS...

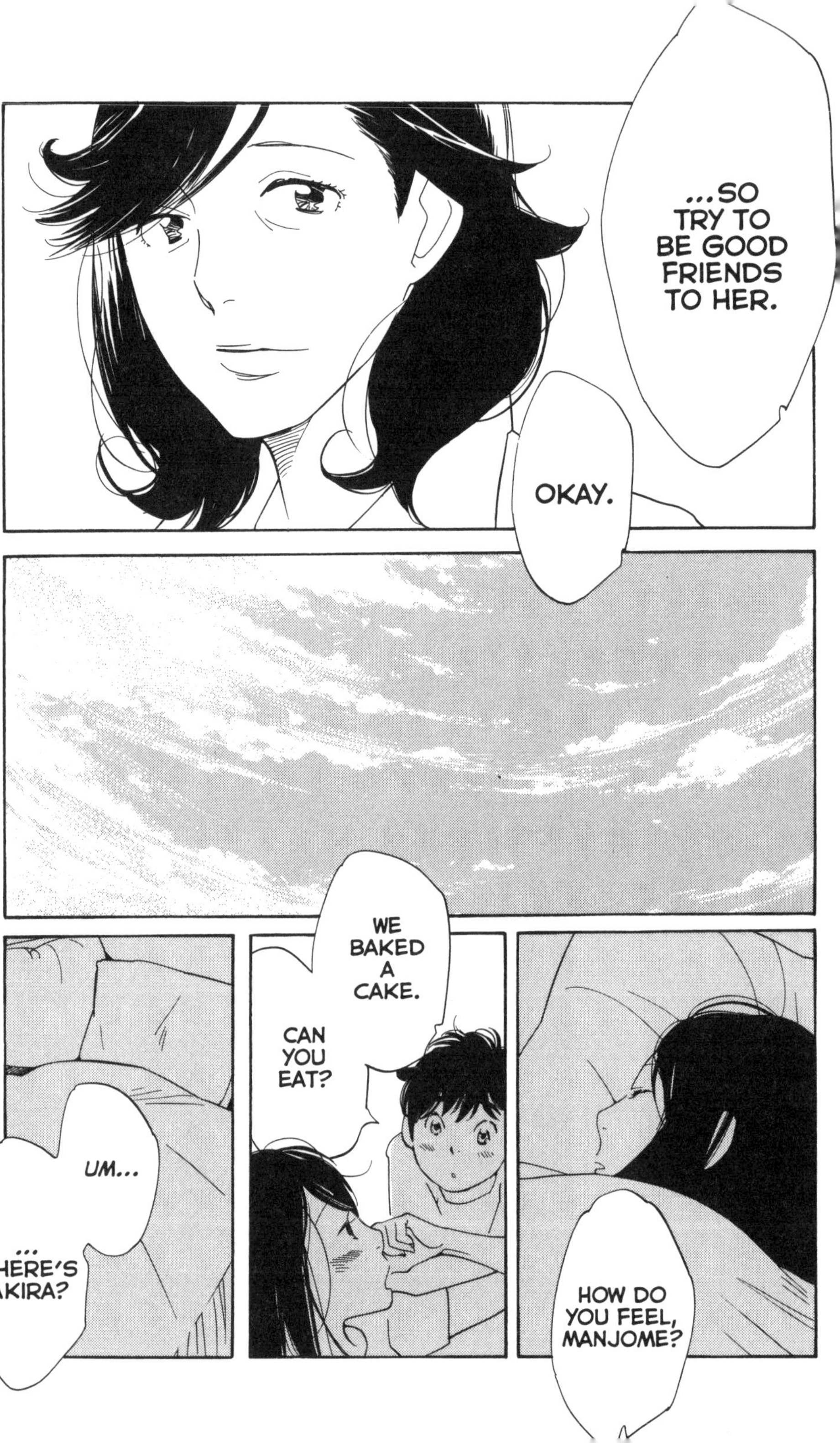
...SO TRY TO BE GOOD FRIENDS TO HER.
OKAY.
HOW DO YOU FEEL, MANJOME?
WE BAKED A CAKE.
CAN YOU EAT?
UM...
...WHERE'S AKIRA?

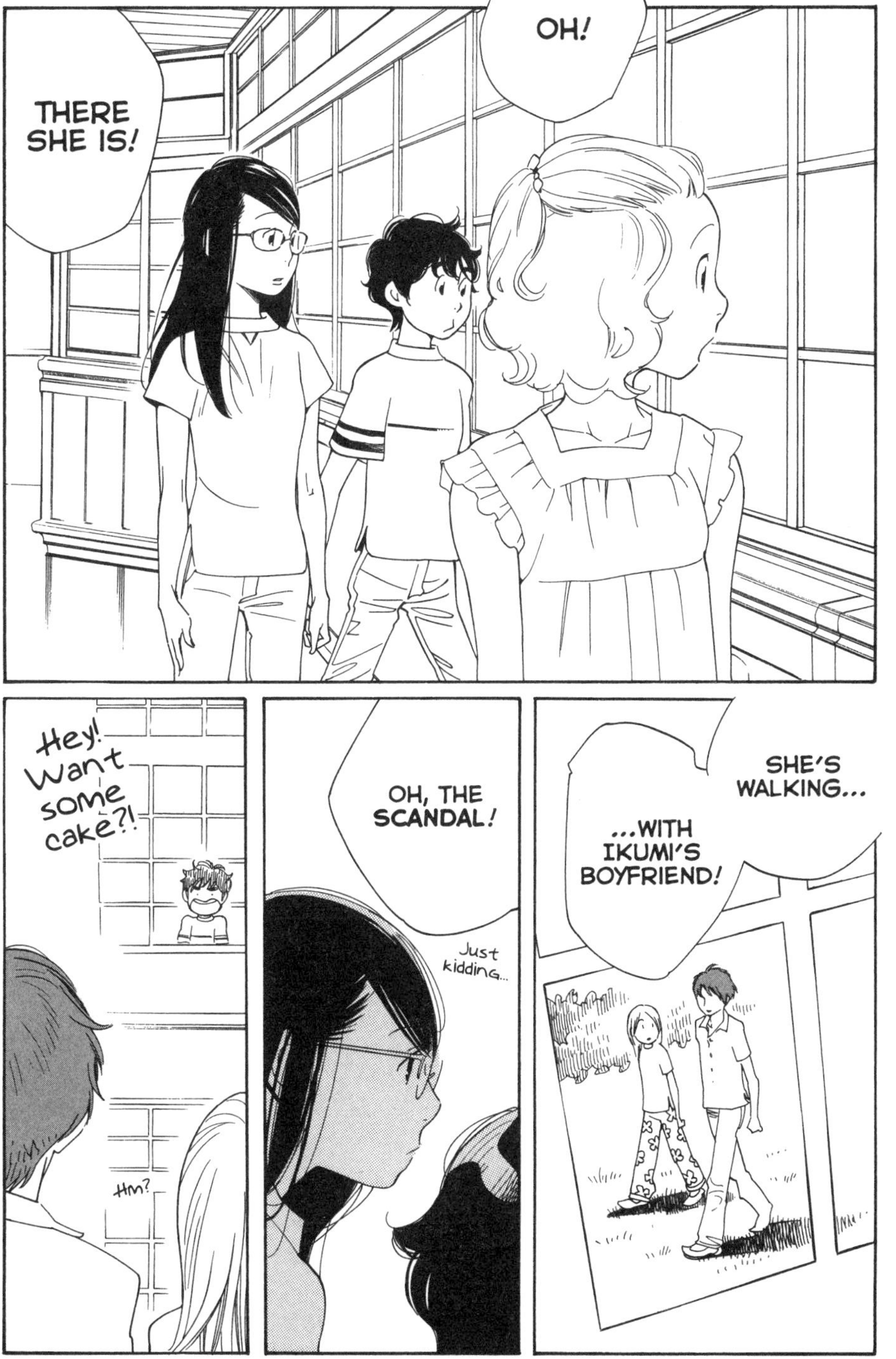
OH!
THERE SHE IS!
SHE'S WALKING...
...WITH IKUMI'S BOYFRIEND!
OH, THE SCANDAL!
Just kidding...
Hey! Want some cake?!
Hm?

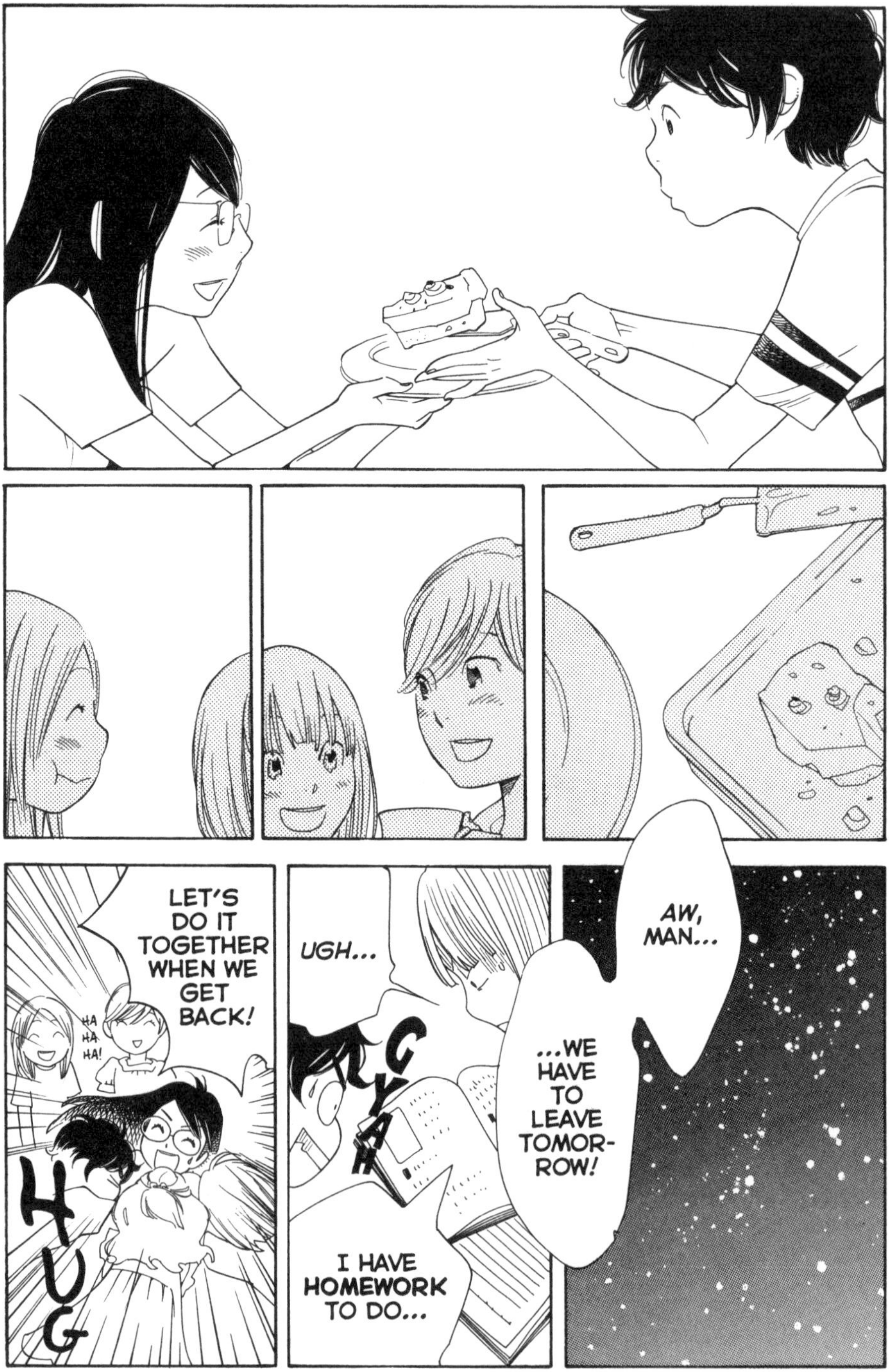
AW, MAN...
...WE HAVE TO LEAVE TOMORROW!
UGH...
GYAH
I HAVE HOMEWORK TO DO...
LET'S DO IT TOGETHER WHEN WE GET BACK!
HA HA HA!
HUG

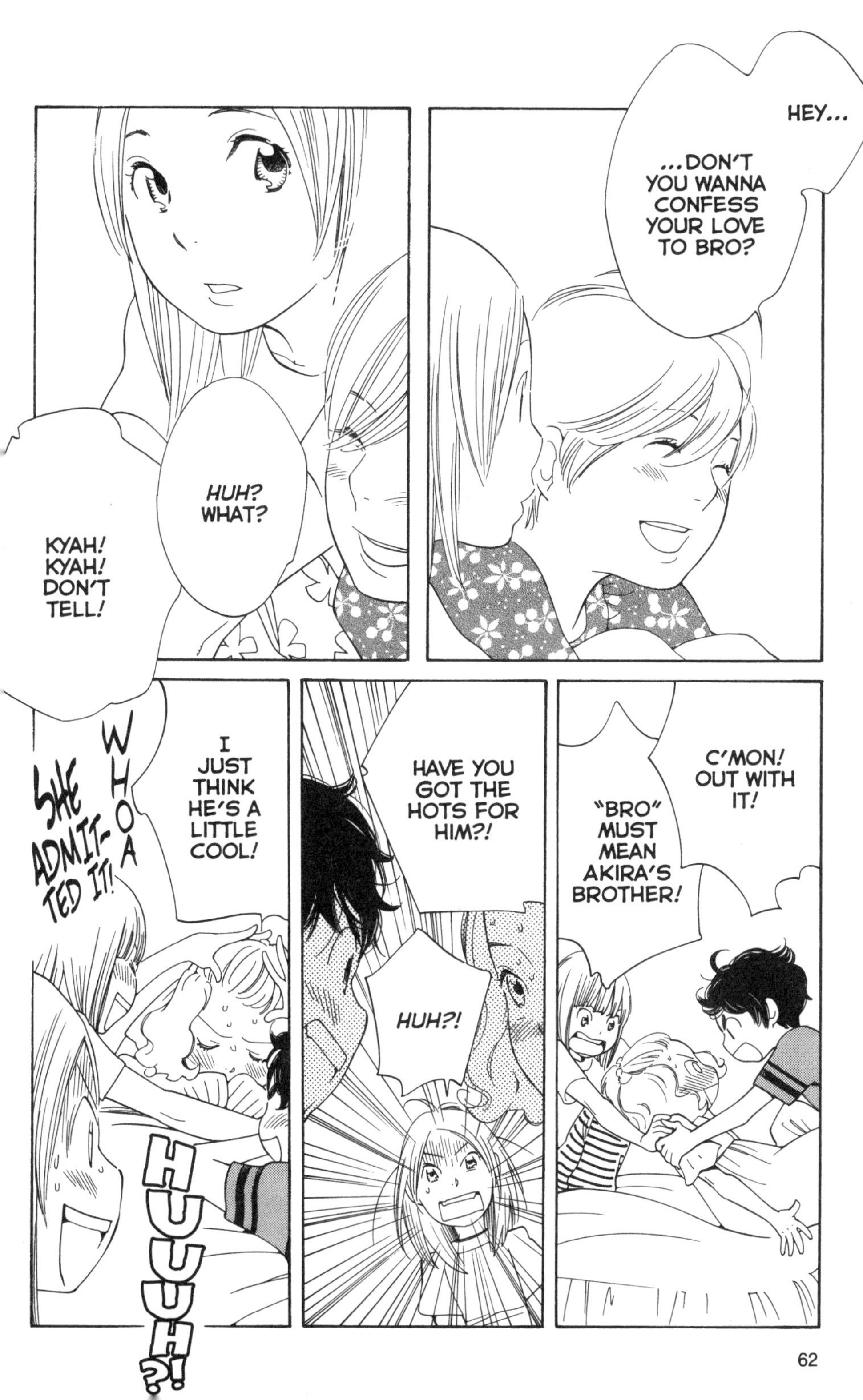
HEY...
...DON'T YOU WANNA CONFESS YOUR LOVE TO BRO?
HUH? WHAT?
KYAH! KYAH! DON'T TELL!
C'MON! OUT WITH IT!
"BRO" MUST MEAN AKIRA'S BROTHER!
HAVE YOU GOT THE HOTS FOR HIM?!
HUH?!
I JUST THINK HE'S A LITTLE COOL!
WHOA
SHE ADMIT-TED IT!
HUUUUH?!

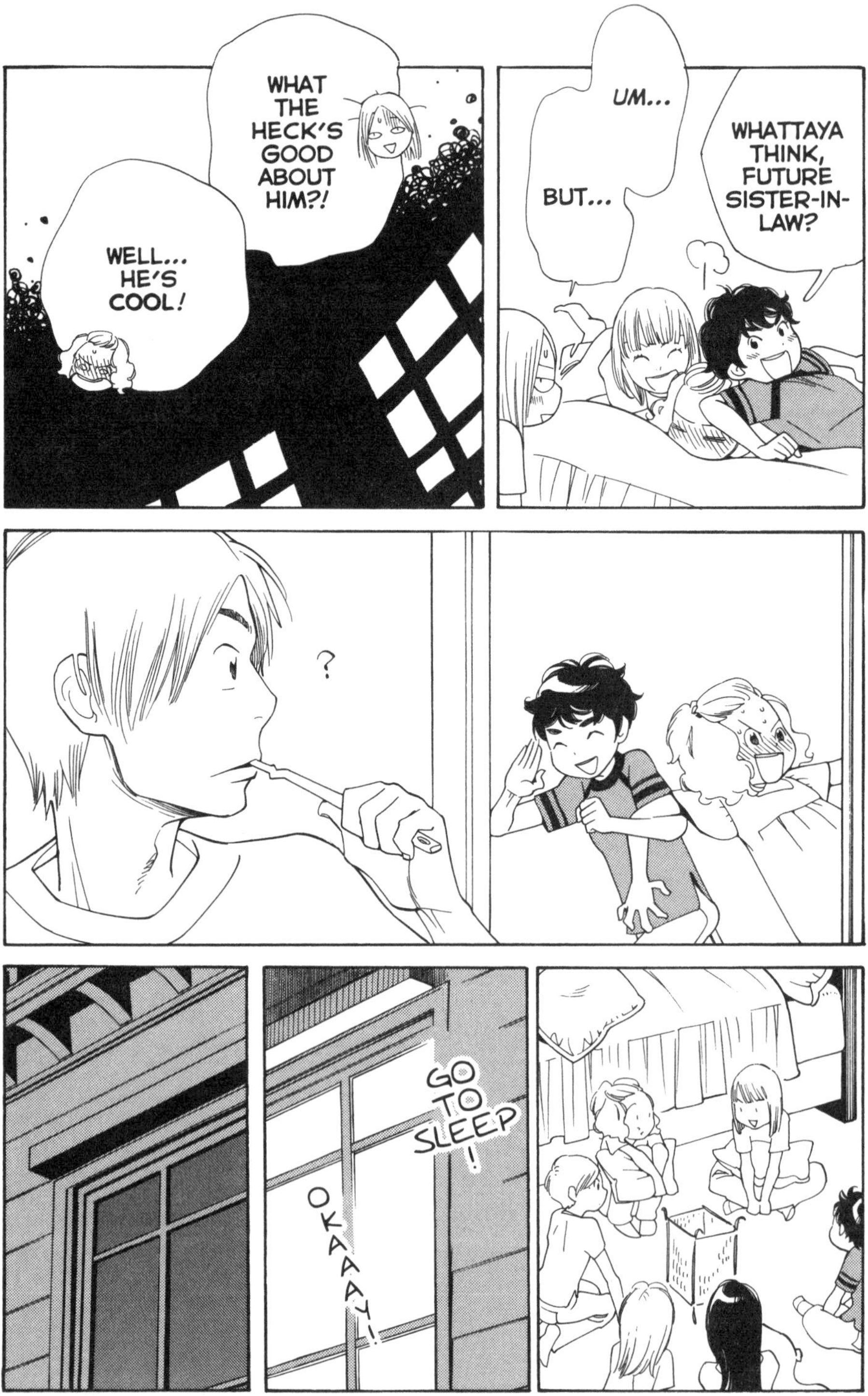
WHATTAYA THINK, FUTURE SISTER-IN-LAW?
UM...
BUT...
WHAT THE HECK'S GOOD ABOUT HIM?!
WELL... HE'S COOL!
?
GO TO SLEEP!
OKAAAAY!

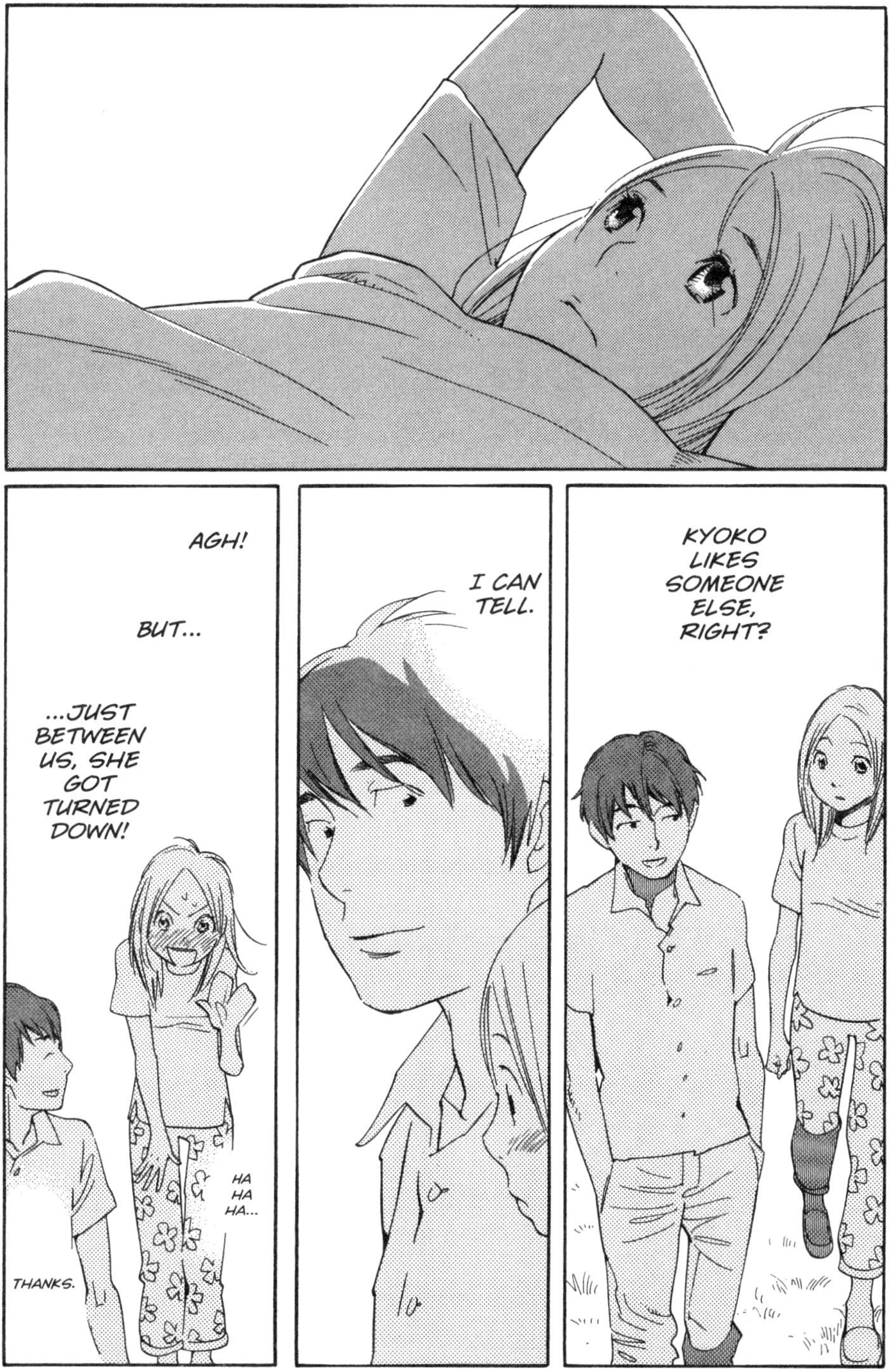
KYOKO LIKES SOMEONE ELSE, RIGHT?
I CAN TELL.
AGH!
BUT...
...JUST BETWEEN US, SHE GOT TURNED DOWN!
HA HA HA...
THANKS.

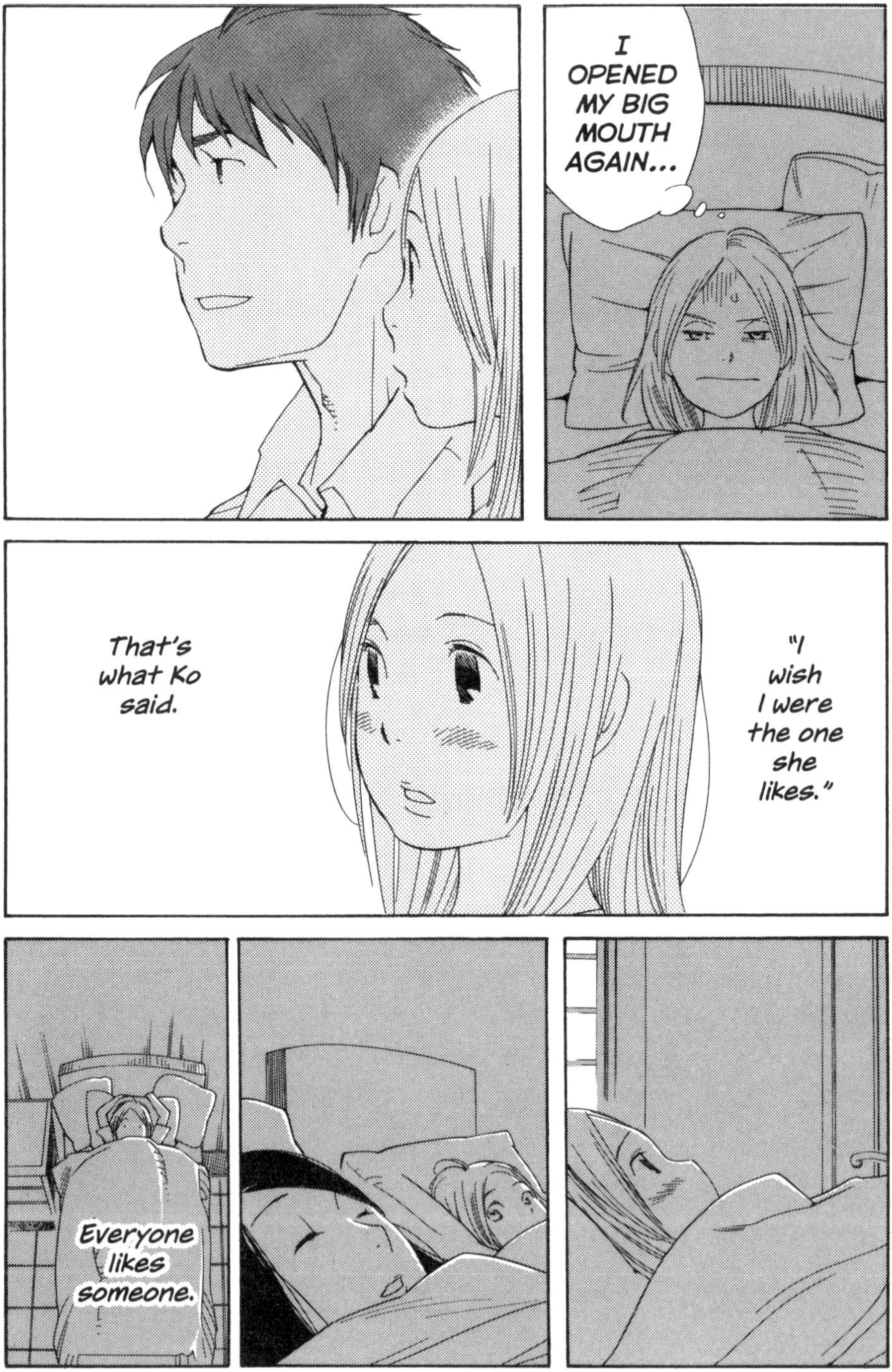
I OPENED MY BIG MOUTH AGAIN...
"I wish I were the one she likes."
That's what Ko said.
Everyone likes someone.

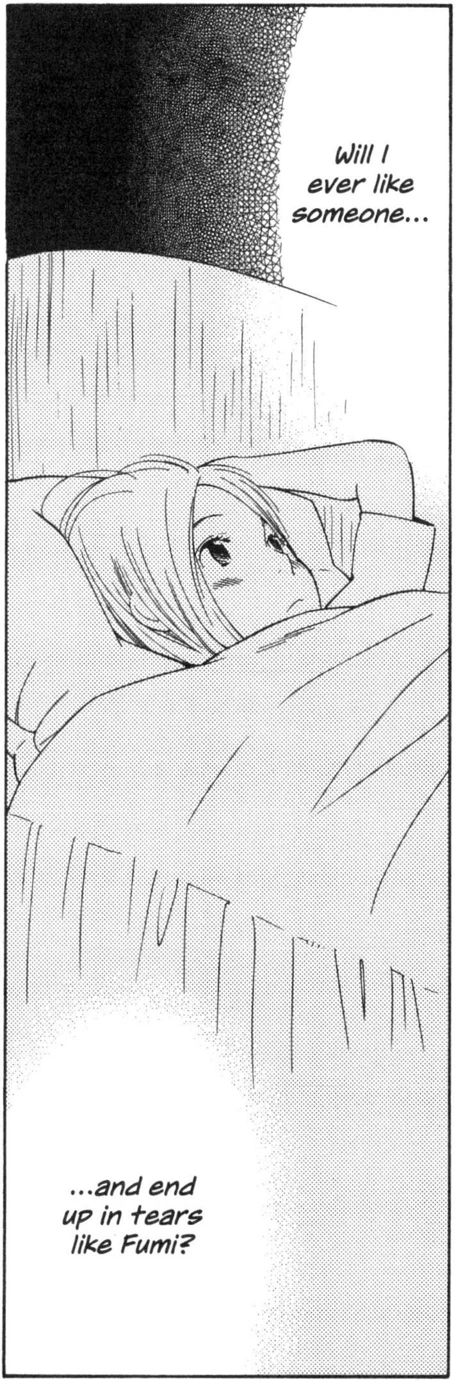
Will I ever like someone...
...and end up in tears like Fumi?

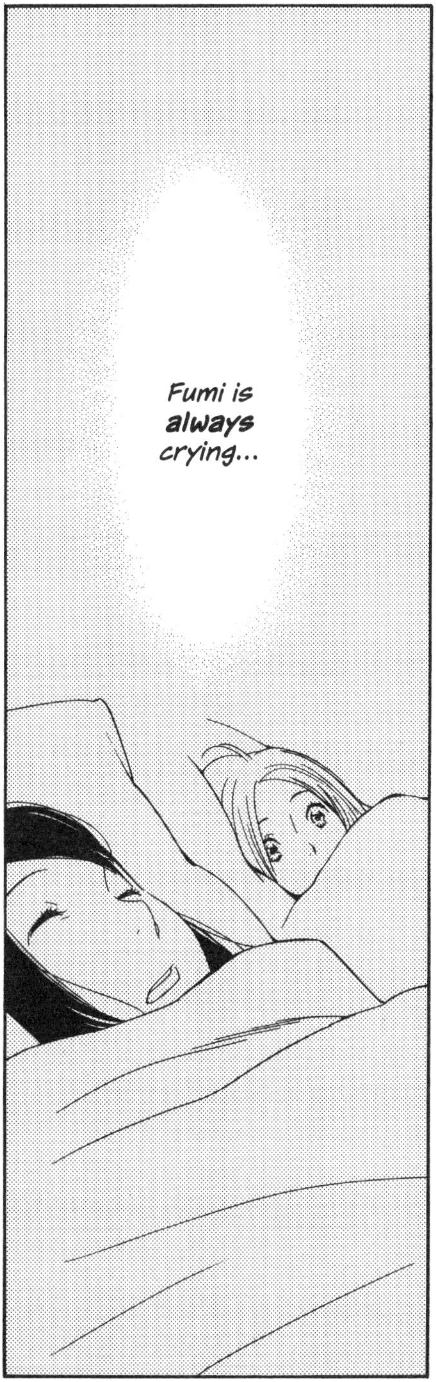
Fumi is **always** crying...

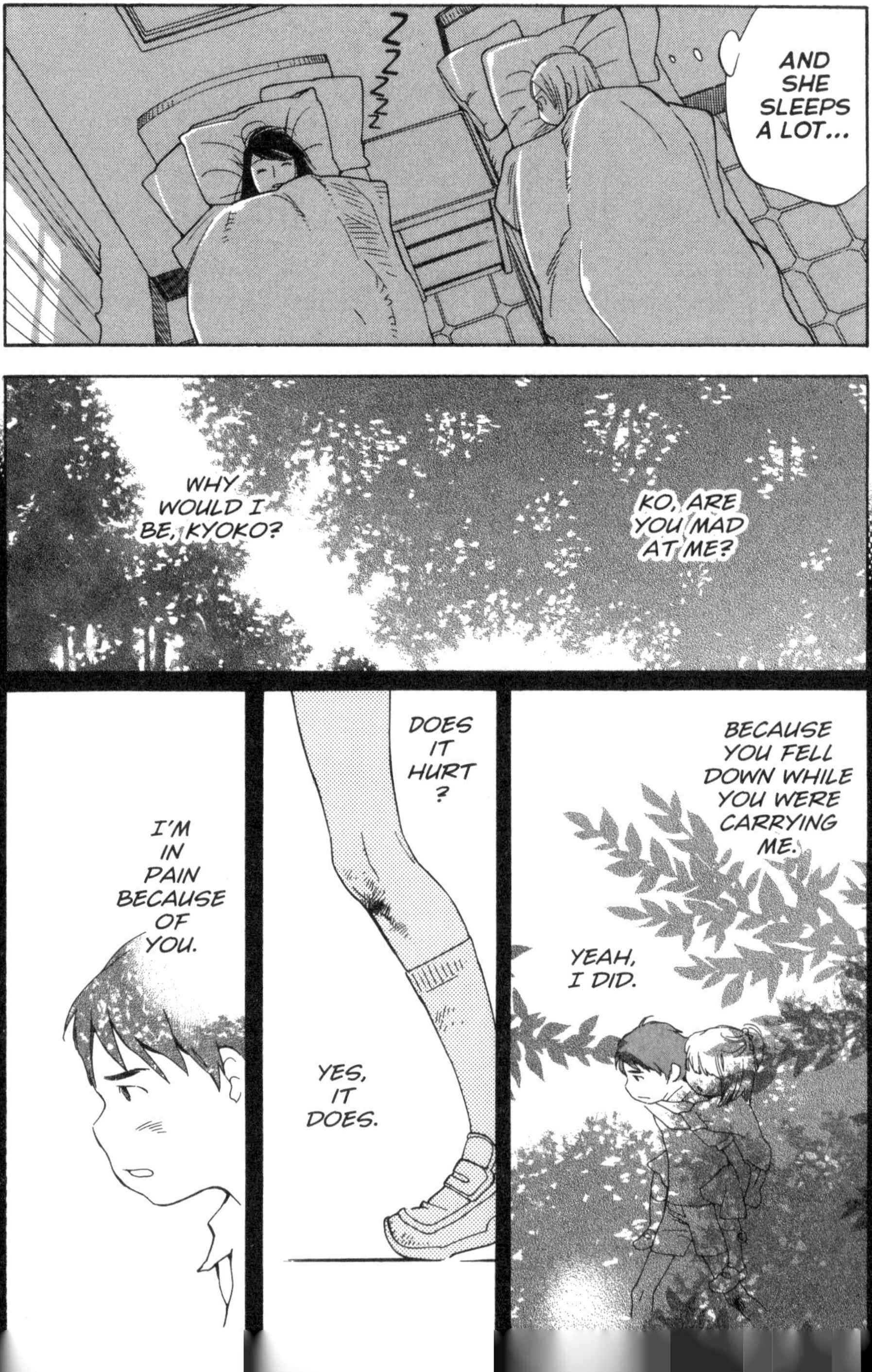
AND SHE SLEEPS A LOT...
KO, ARE YOU MAD AT ME?
WHY WOULD I BE, KYOKO?
BECAUSE YOU FELL DOWN WHILE YOU WERE CARRYING ME.
YEAH, I DID.
DOES IT HURT?
YES, IT DOES.
I'M IN PAIN BECAUSE OF YOU.

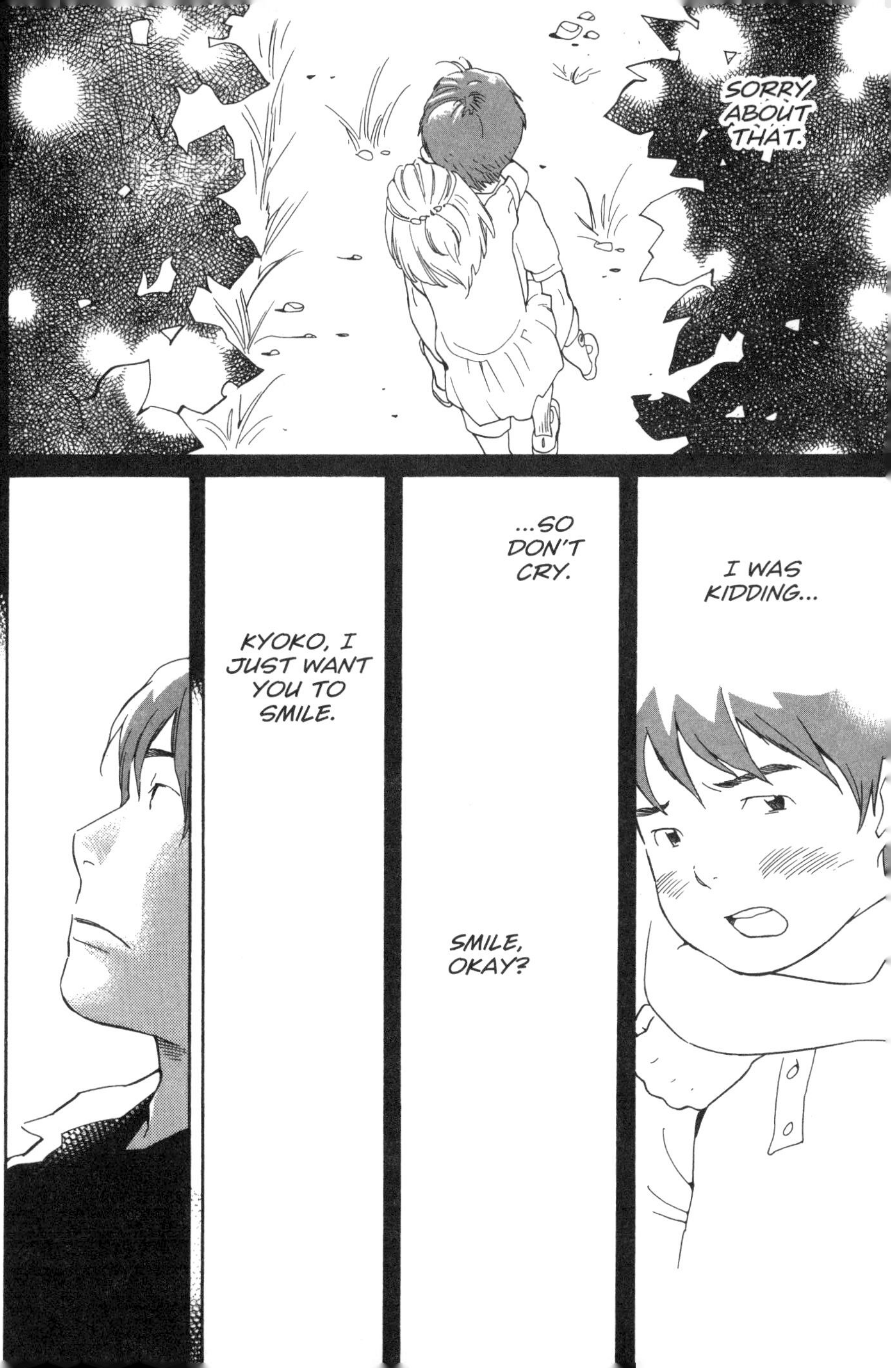
SORRY ABOUT THAT.
I WAS KIDDING...
...SO DON'T CRY.
SMILE, OKAY?
KYOKO, I JUST WANT YOU TO SMILE.

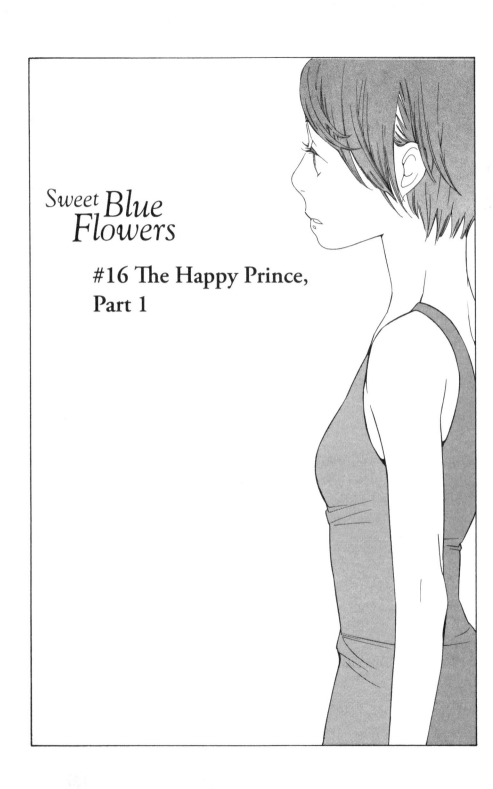

Sweet Blue Flowers

#16 The Happy Prince, Part 1

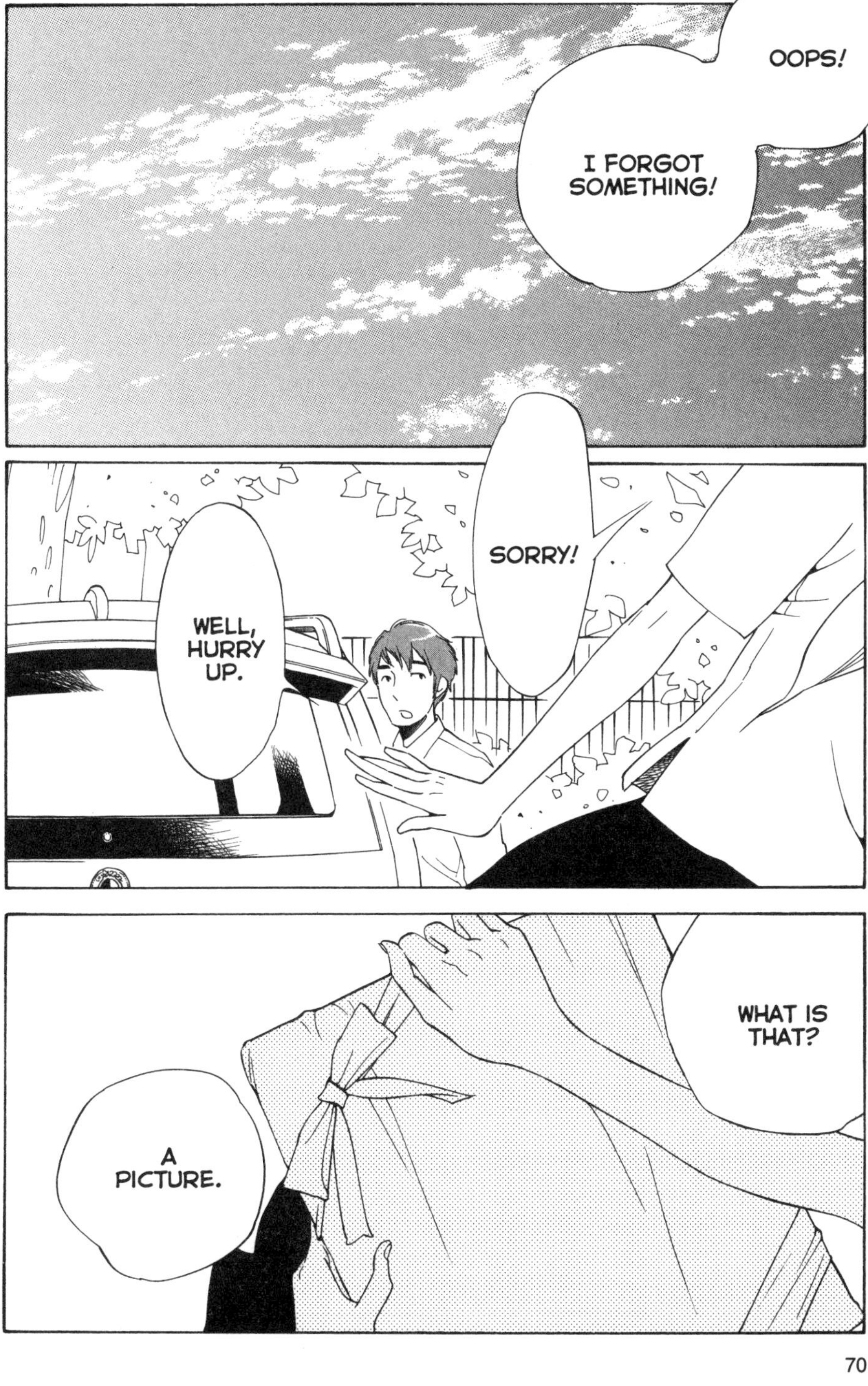
OOPS!
I FORGOT SOMETHING!
SORRY!
WELL, HURRY UP.
WHAT IS THAT?
A PICTURE.

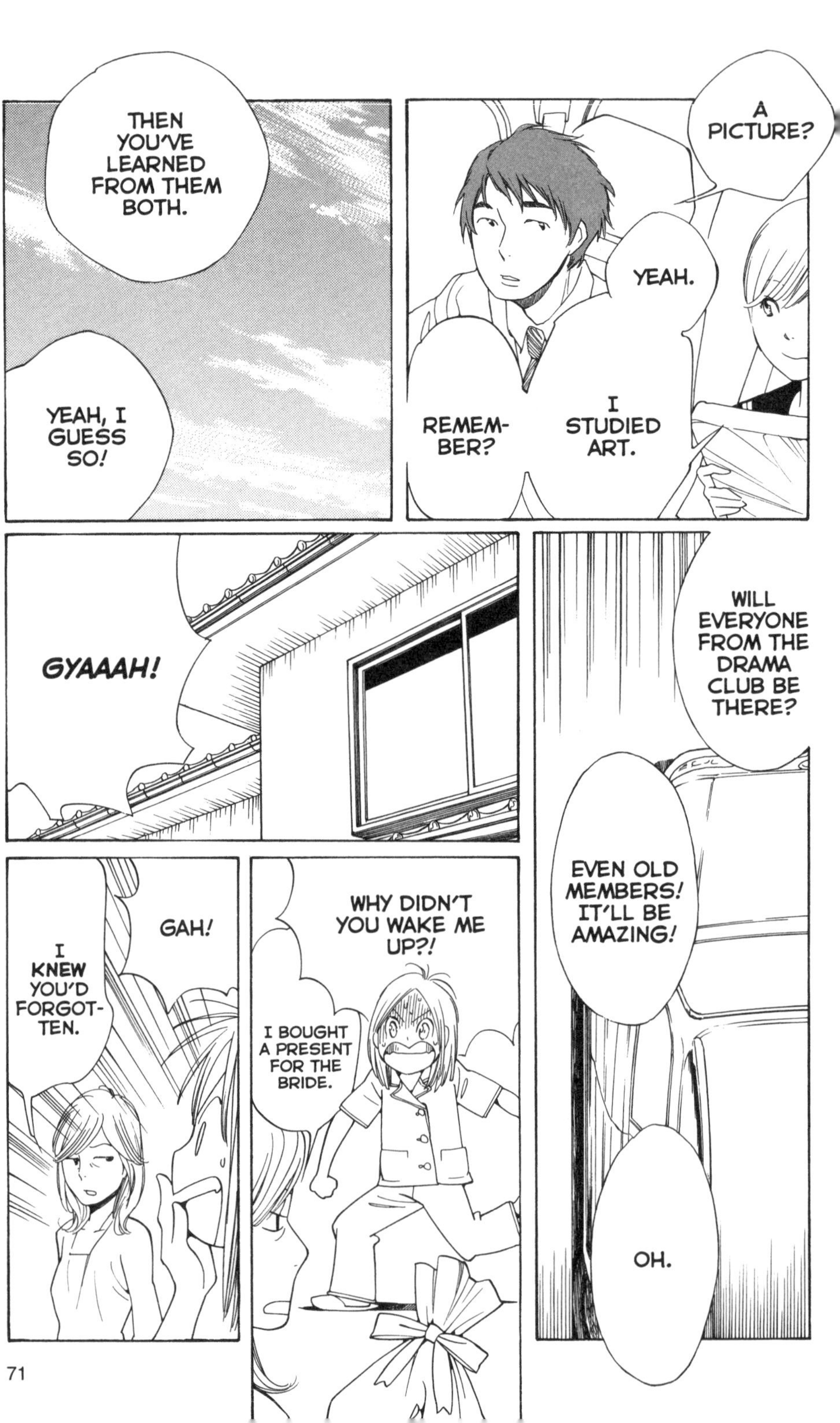
A PICTURE?
YEAH.
I STUDIED ART.
REMEM-BER?
THEN YOU'VE LEARNED FROM THEM BOTH.
YEAH, I GUESS SO!
WILL EVERYONE FROM THE DRAMA CLUB BE THERE?
EVEN OLD MEMBERS! IT'LL BE AMAZING!
OH.
GYAAAH!
WHY DIDN'T YOU WAKE ME UP?!
I BOUGHT A PRESENT FOR THE BRIDE.
GAH!
I KNEW YOU'D FORGOT-TEN.

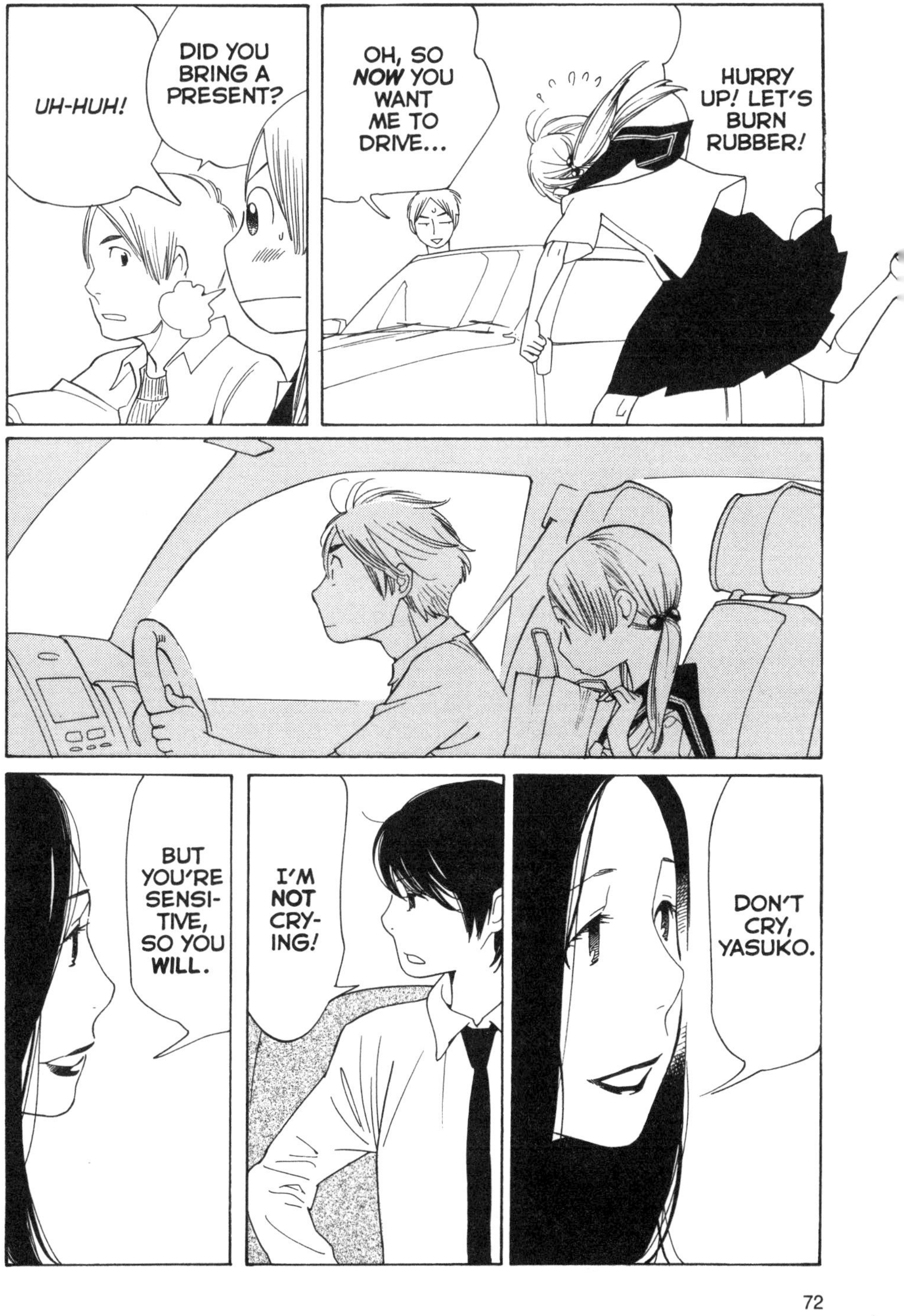
HURRY UP! LET'S BURN RUBBER!
OH, SO *NOW* YOU WANT ME TO DRIVE...
DID YOU BRING A PRESENT?
UH-HUH!
DON'T CRY, YASUKO.
I'M **NOT** CRY-ING!
BUT YOU'RE SENSI-TIVE, SO YOU **WILL**.

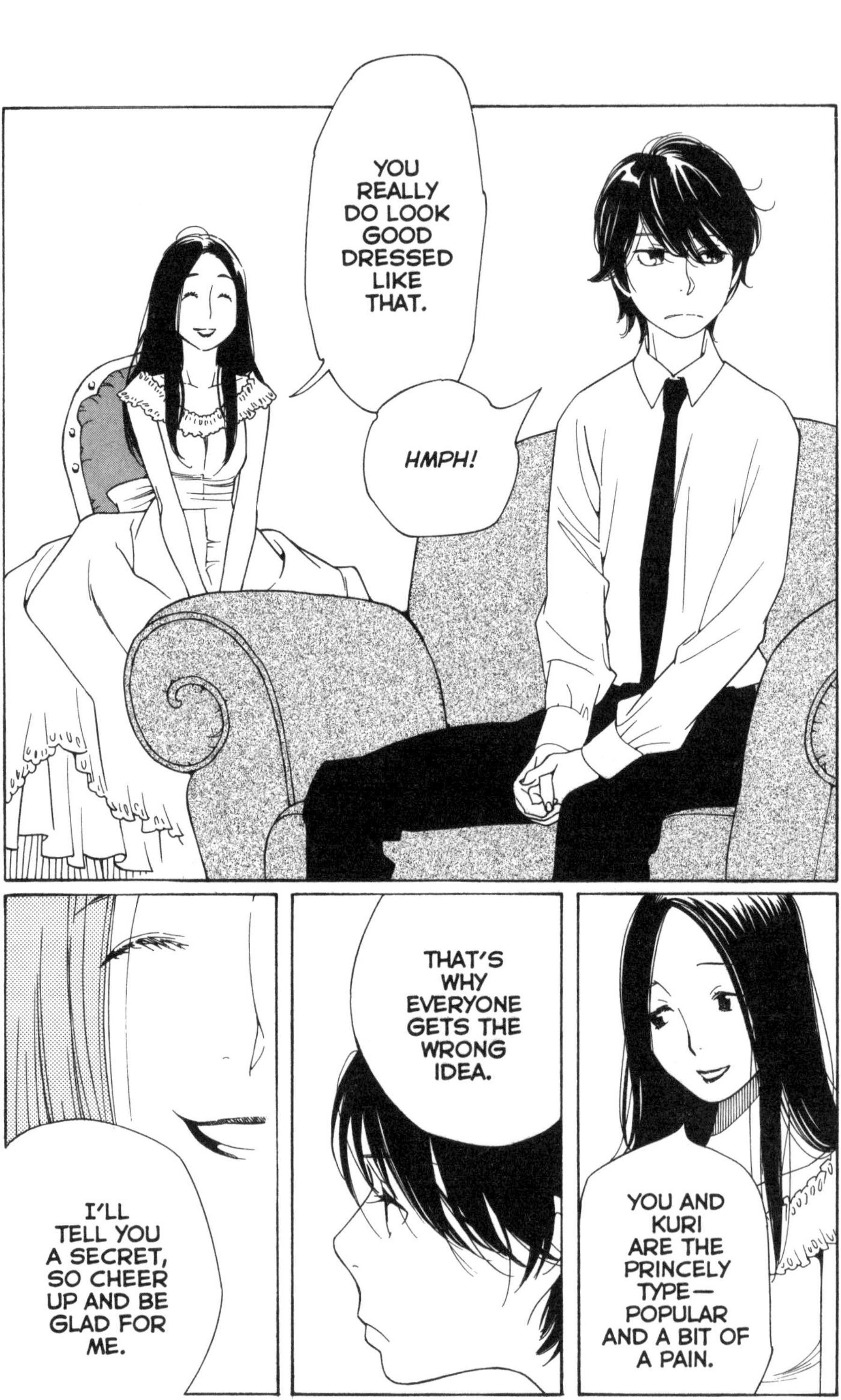
YOU REALLY DO LOOK GOOD DRESSED LIKE THAT.
HMPH!
YOU AND KURI ARE THE PRINCELY TYPE— POPULAR AND A BIT OF A PAIN.
THAT'S WHY EVERYONE GETS THE WRONG IDEA.
I'LL TELL YOU A SECRET, SO CHEER UP AND BE GLAD FOR ME.

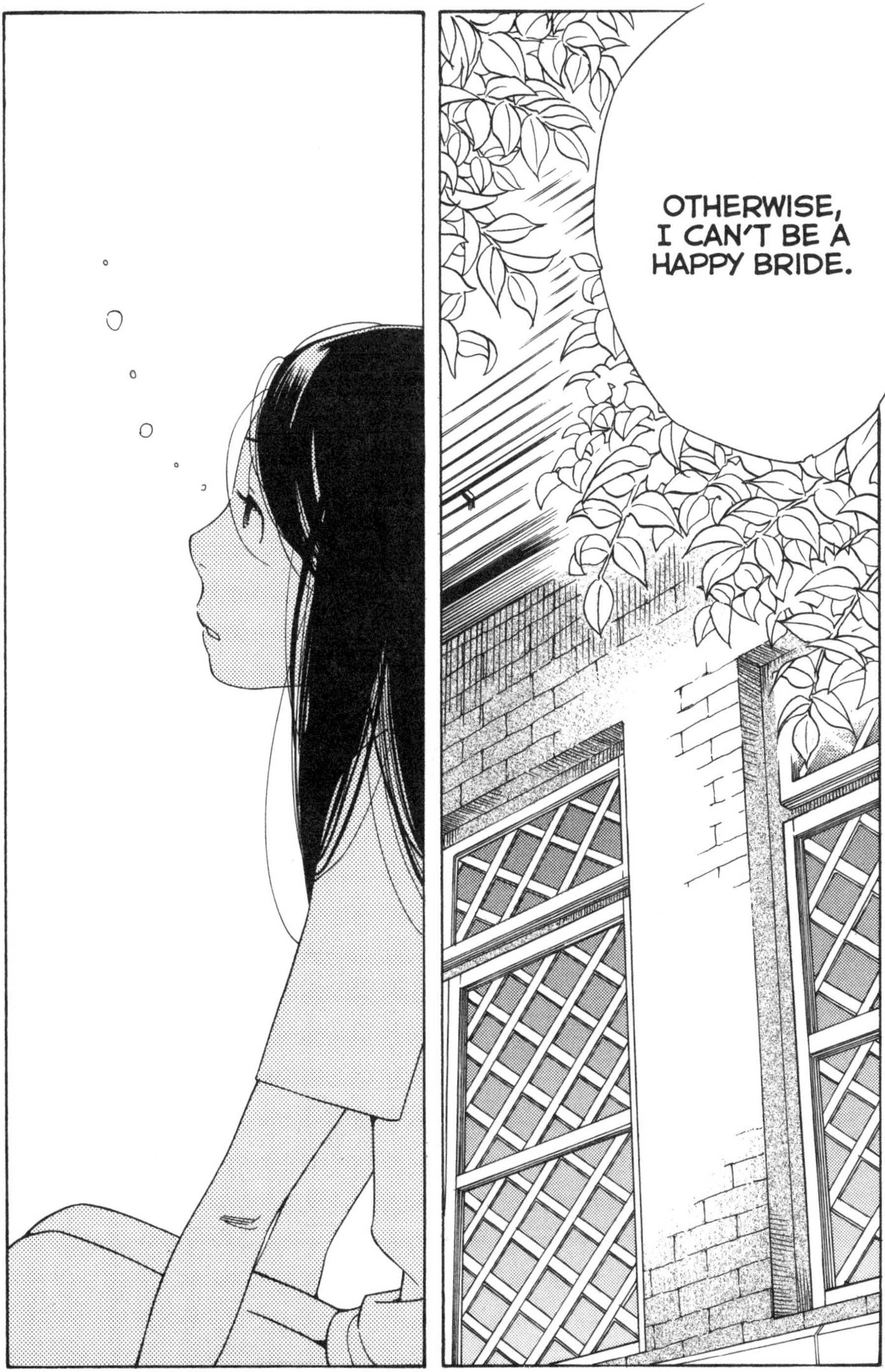
OTHERWISE, I CAN'T BE A HAPPY BRIDE.

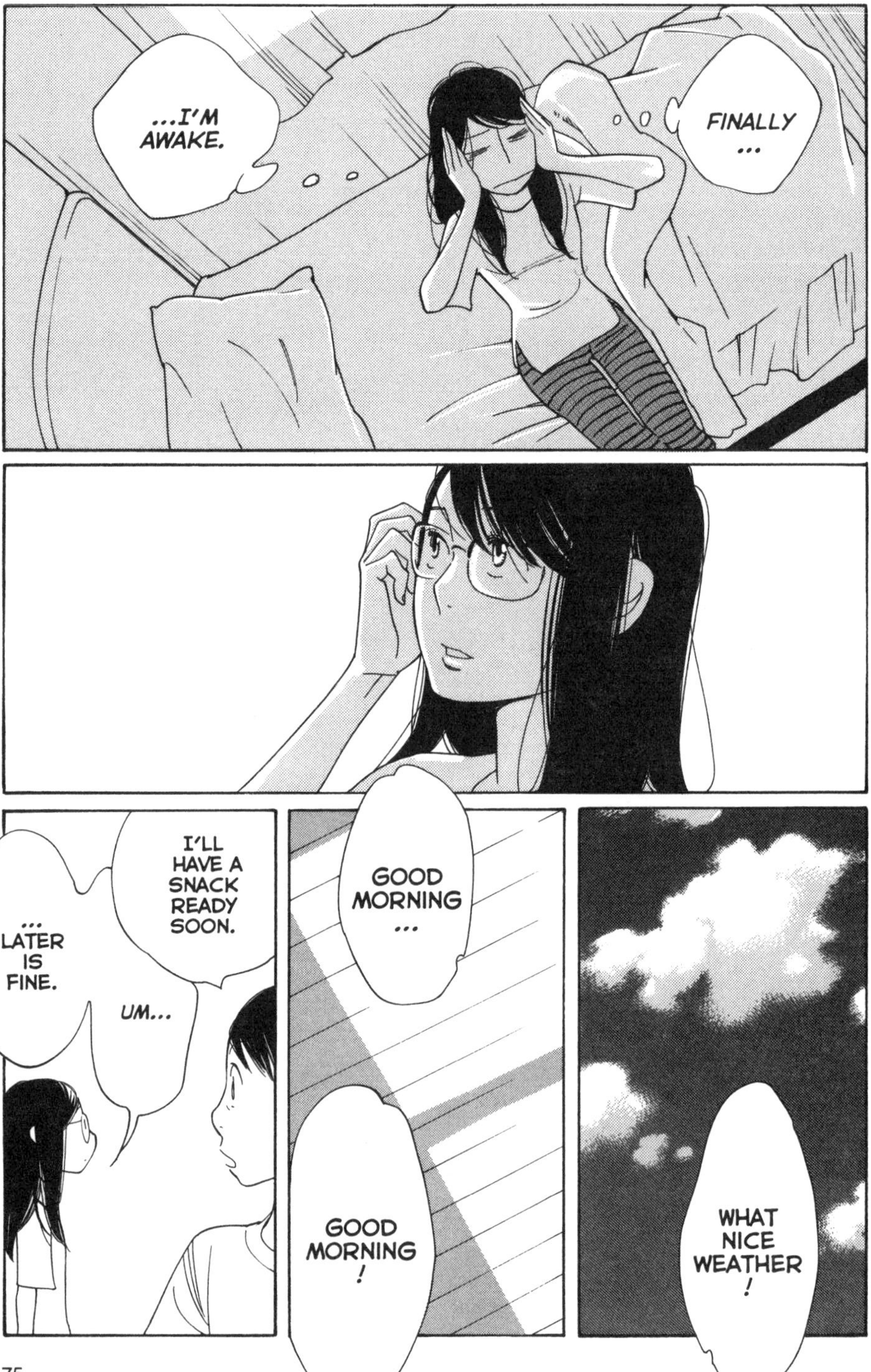
FINALLY...
...I'M AWAKE.
WHAT NICE WEATHER!
GOOD MORNING...
GOOD MORNING!
I'LL HAVE A SNACK READY SOON.
UM...
...LATER IS FINE.

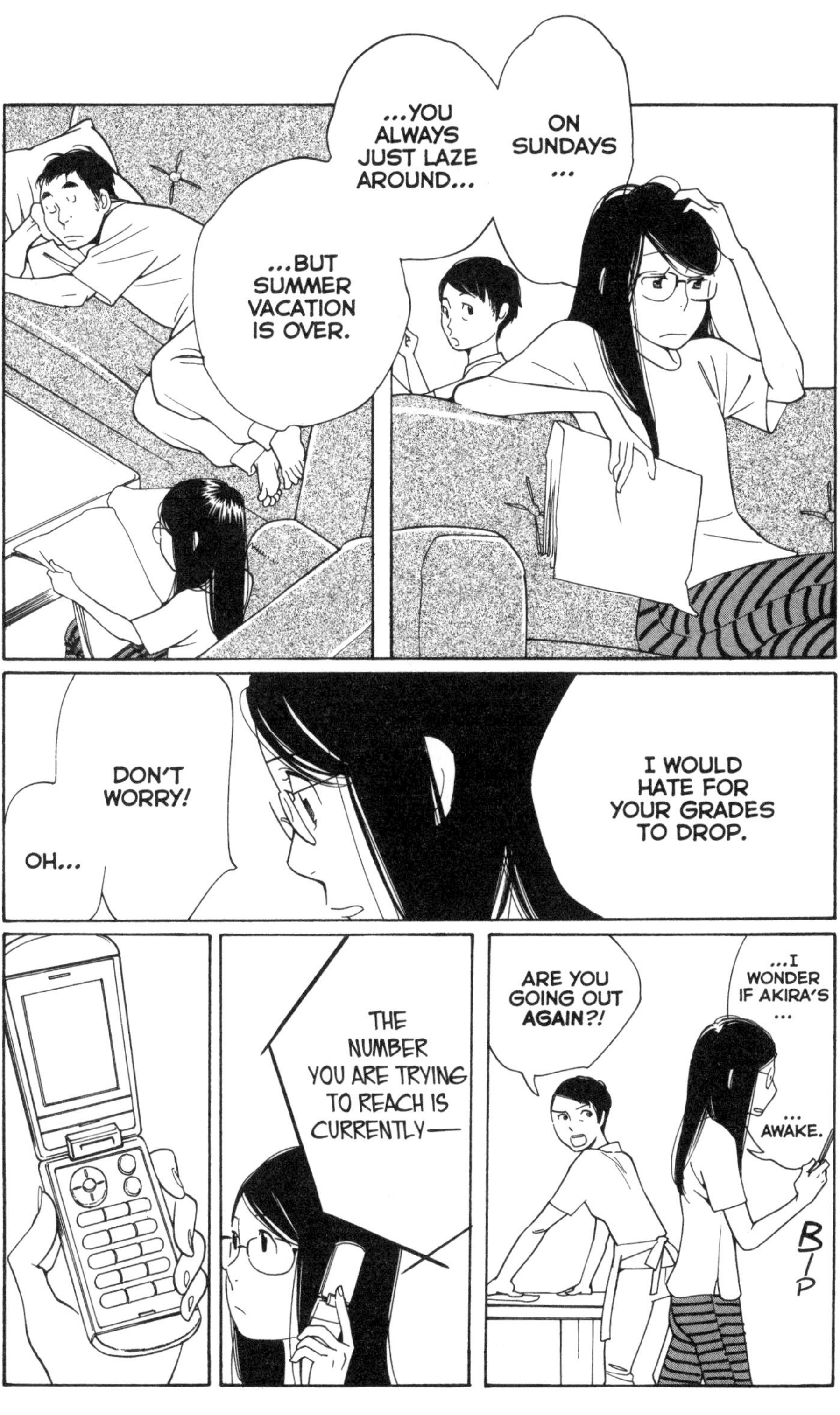
ON SUNDAYS ...
...YOU ALWAYS JUST LAZE AROUND...
...BUT SUMMER VACATION IS OVER.
I WOULD HATE FOR YOUR GRADES TO DROP.
DON'T WORRY!
OH...
...I WONDER IF AKIRA'S ...
ARE YOU GOING OUT AGAIN?!
... AWAKE.
BIP
THE NUMBER YOU ARE TRYING TO REACH IS CURRENTLY—

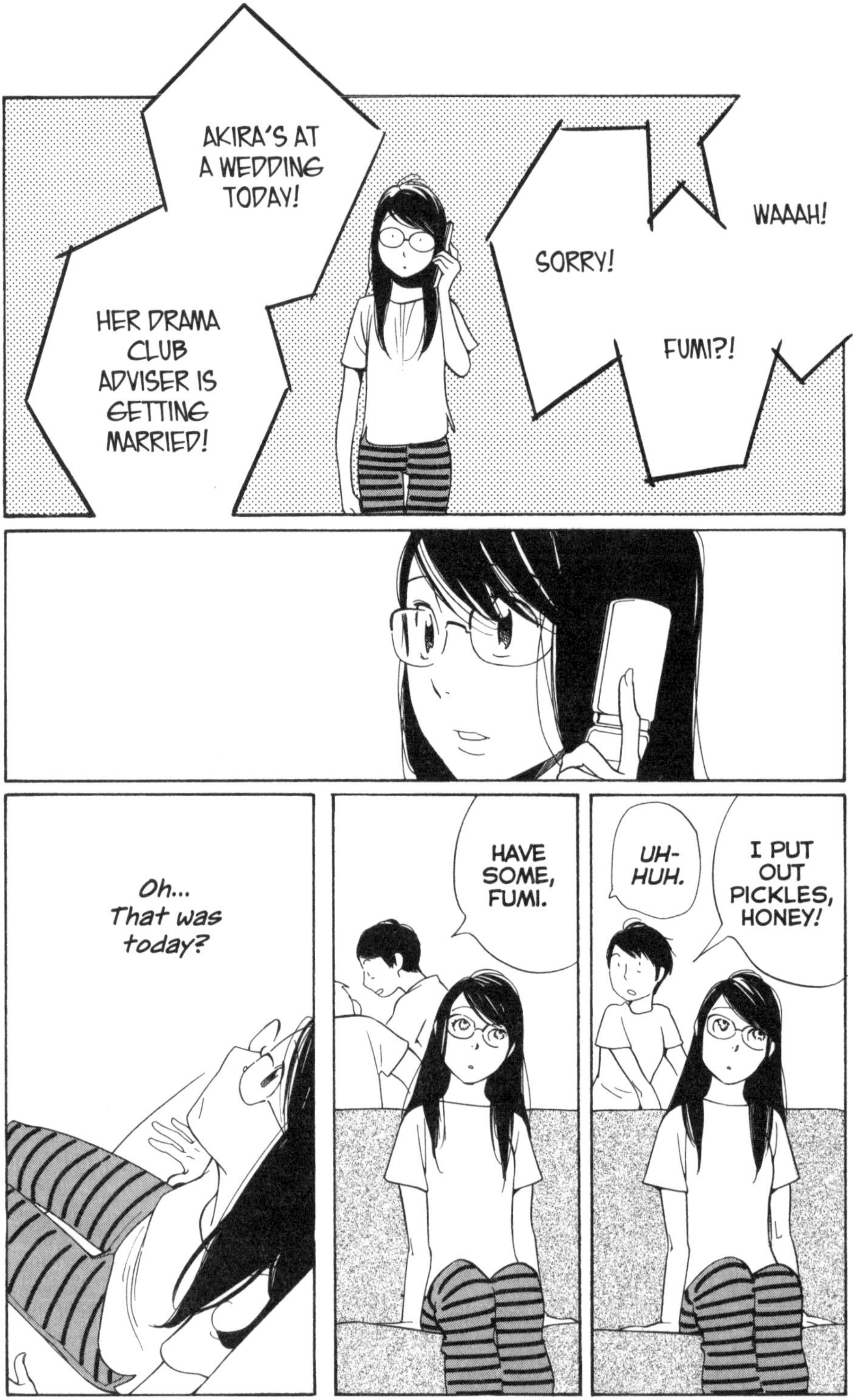
WAAAH!
SORRY!
FUMI?!
AKIRA'S AT A WEDDING TODAY!
HER DRAMA CLUB ADVISER IS GETTING MARRIED!
I PUT OUT PICKLES, HONEY!
UH-HUH.
HAVE SOME, FUMI.
Oh... That was today?

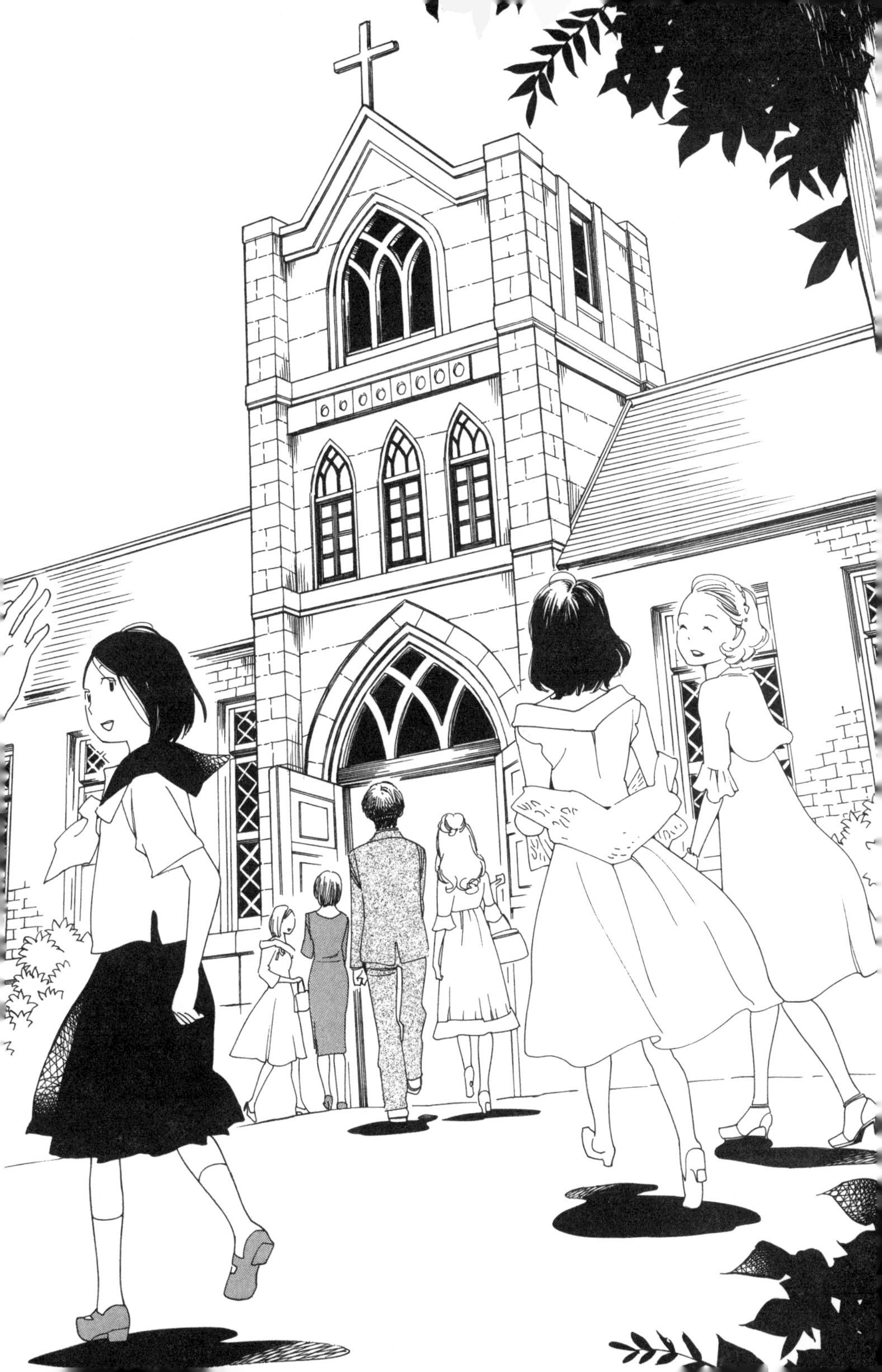

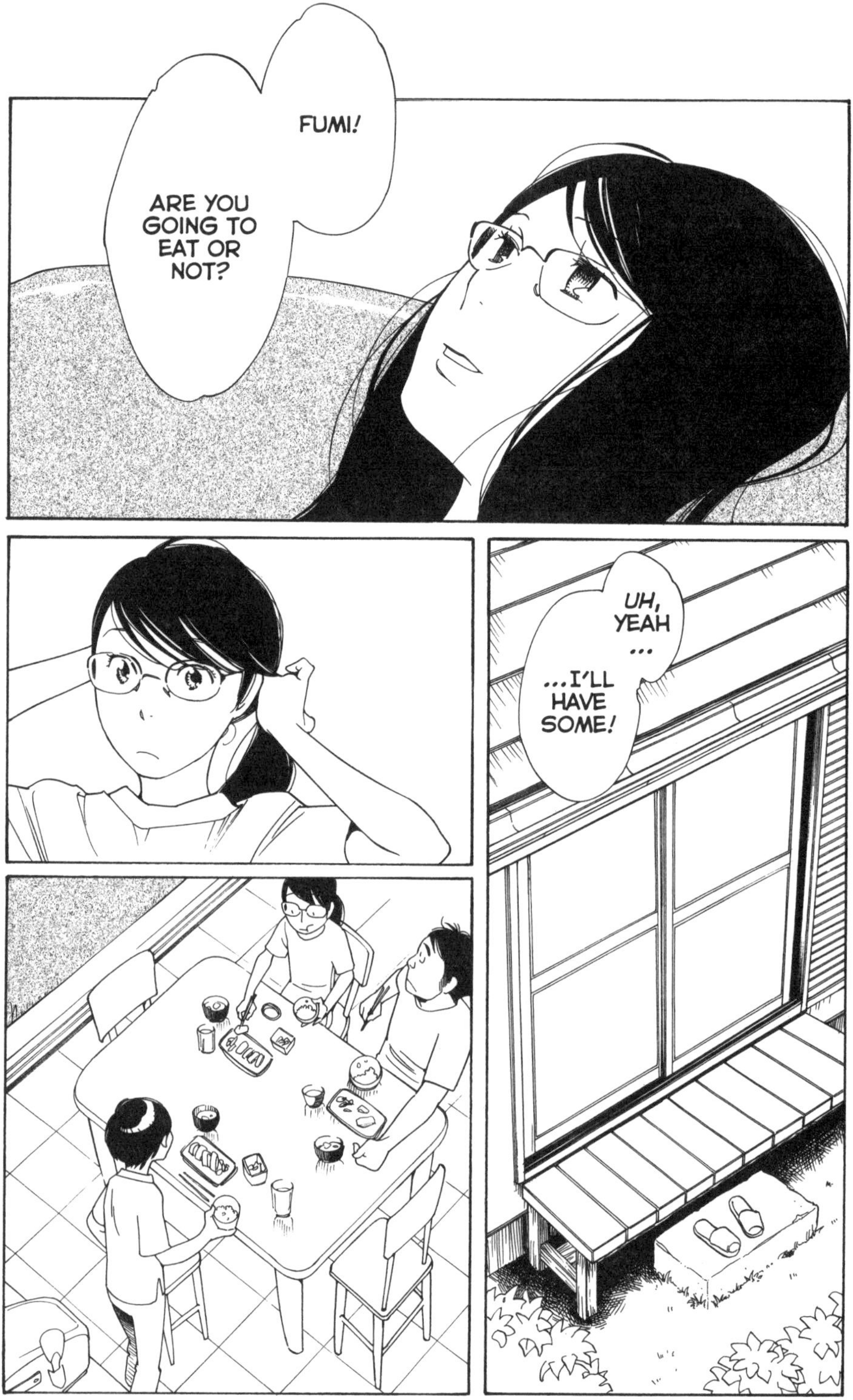
FUMI!
ARE YOU GOING TO EAT OR NOT?
UH, YEAH ...
...I'LL HAVE SOME!

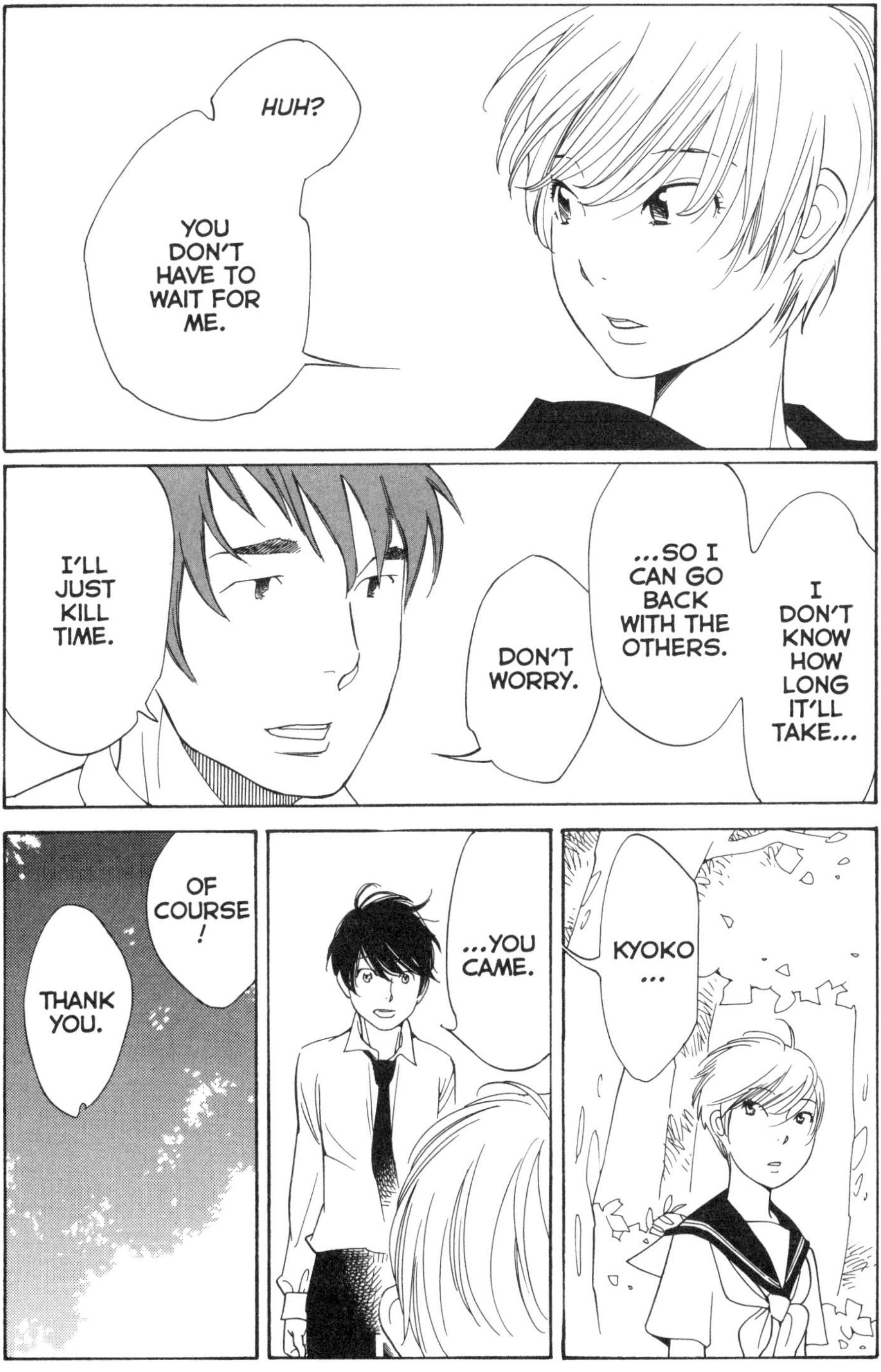
HUH?
YOU DON'T HAVE TO WAIT FOR ME.
I DON'T KNOW HOW LONG IT'LL TAKE...
...SO I CAN GO BACK WITH THE OTHERS.
DON'T WORRY.
I'LL JUST KILL TIME.
KYOKO...
...YOU CAME.
OF COURSE!
THANK YOU.

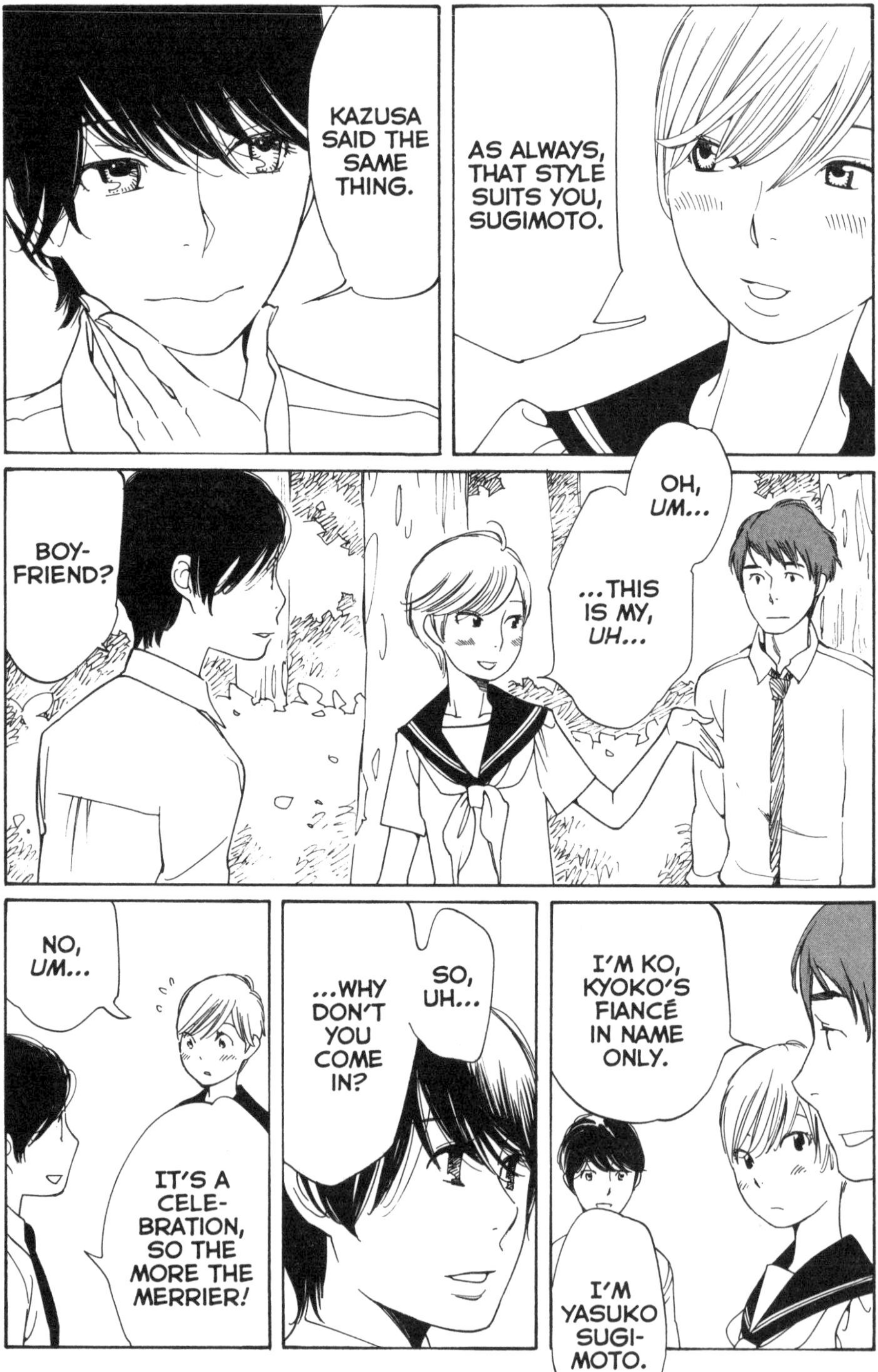
AS ALWAYS, THAT STYLE SUITS YOU, SUGIMOTO.
KAZUSA SAID THE SAME THING.
OH, UM...
...THIS IS MY, UH...
BOY-FRIEND?
I'M KO, KYOKO'S FIANCÉ IN NAME ONLY.
I'M YASUKO SUGI-MOTO.
SO, UH...
...WHY DON'T YOU COME IN?
NO, UM...
IT'S A CELE-BRATION, SO THE MORE THE MERRIER!

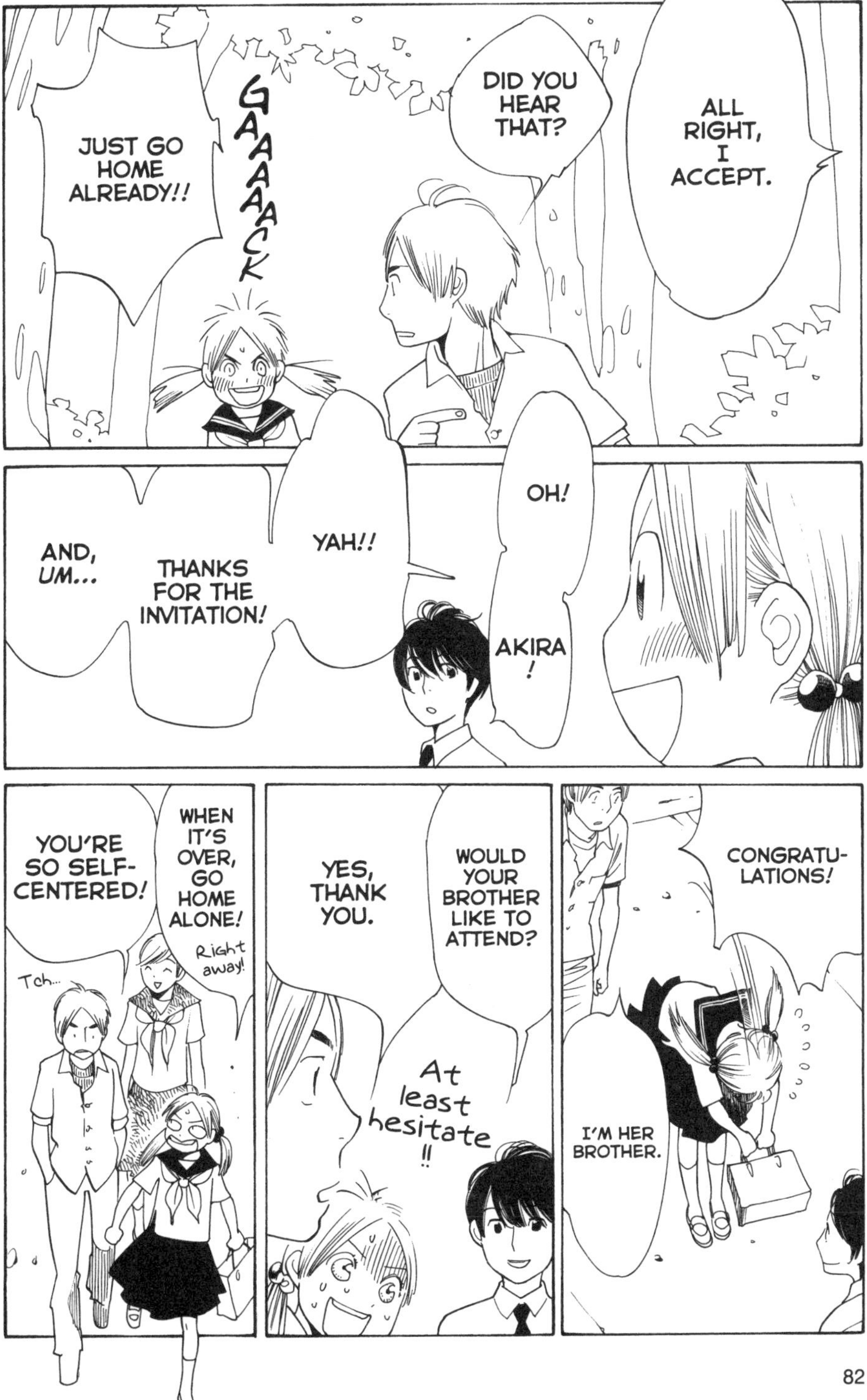
ALL RIGHT, I ACCEPT.
DID YOU HEAR THAT?
GAAAAACK
JUST GO HOME ALREADY!!
OH!
AKIRA!
YAH!!
THANKS FOR THE INVITATION!
AND, UM...
CONGRATULATIONS!
I'M HER BROTHER.
WOULD YOUR BROTHER LIKE TO ATTEND?
YES, THANK YOU.
At least hesitate!!
WHEN IT'S OVER, GO HOME ALONE!
Right away!
YOU'RE SO SELF-CENTERED!
Tch...

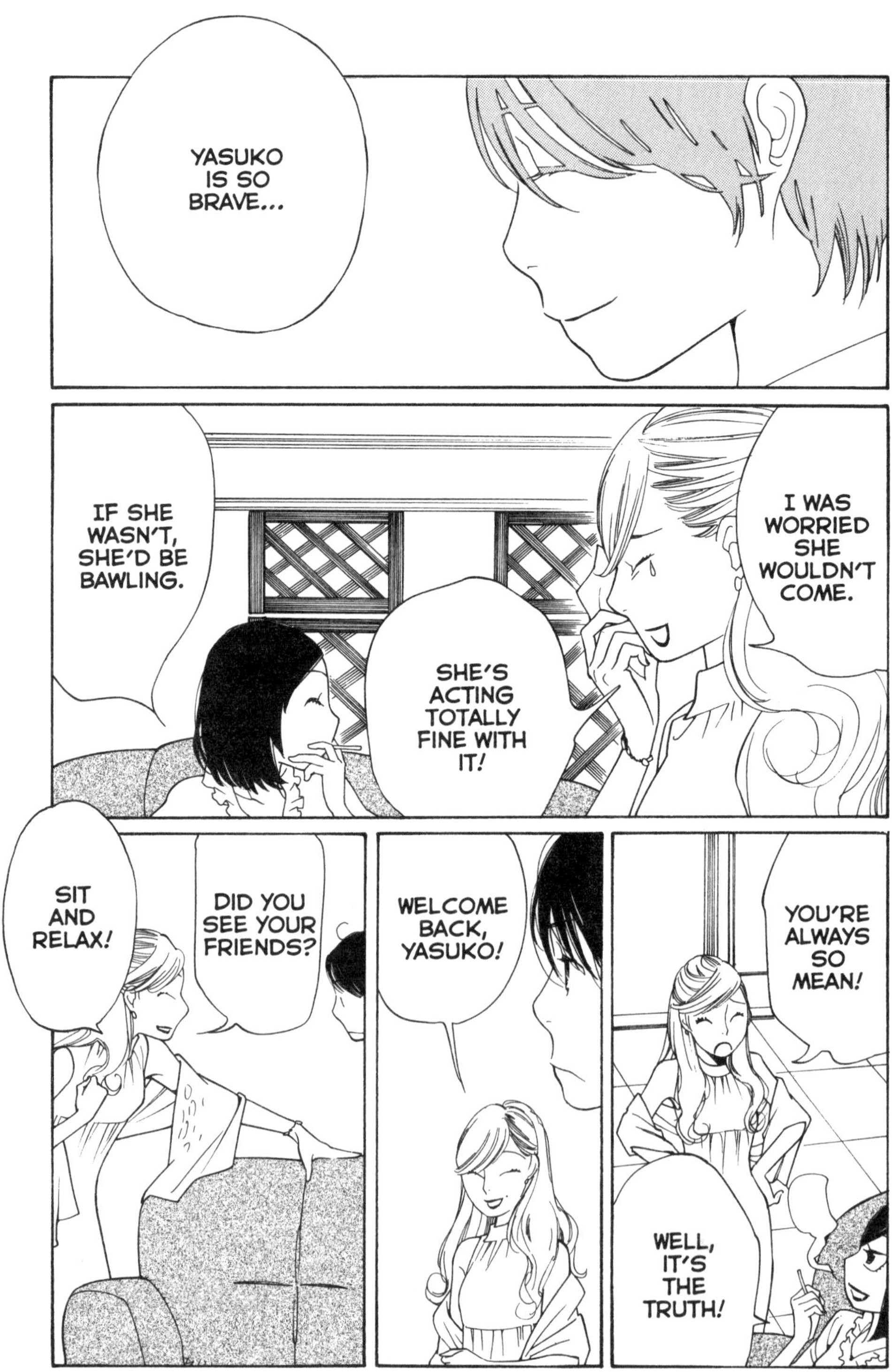
YASUKO IS SO BRAVE...
I WAS WORRIED SHE WOULDN'T COME.
SHE'S ACTING TOTALLY FINE WITH IT!
IF SHE WASN'T, SHE'D BE BAWLING.
YOU'RE ALWAYS SO MEAN!
WELL, IT'S THE TRUTH!
WELCOME BACK, YASUKO!
DID YOU SEE YOUR FRIENDS?
SIT AND RELAX!

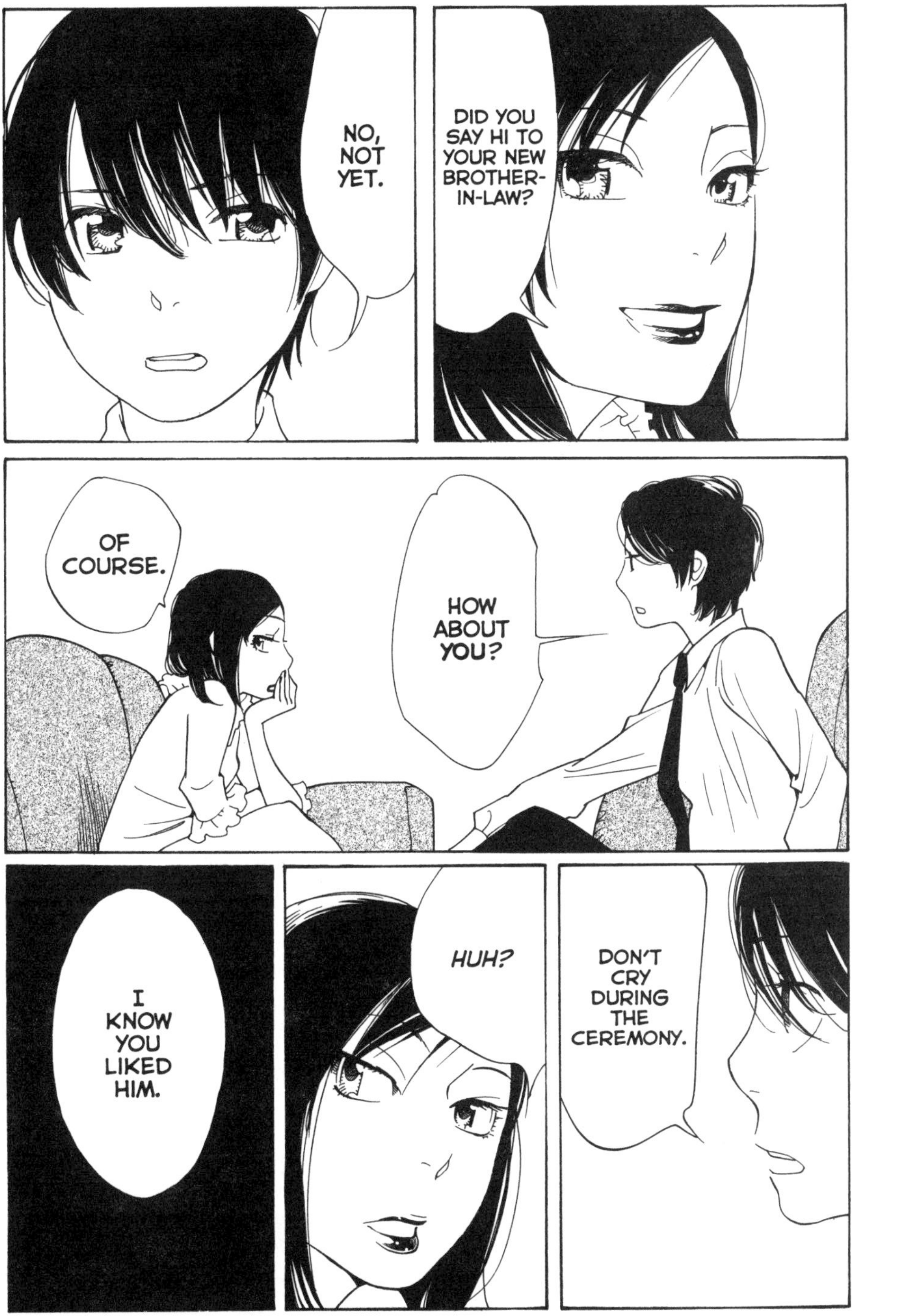
DID YOU SAY HI TO YOUR NEW BROTHER-IN-LAW?
NO, NOT YET.
HOW ABOUT YOU?
OF COURSE.
DON'T CRY DURING THE CEREMONY.
HUH?
I KNOW YOU LIKED HIM.

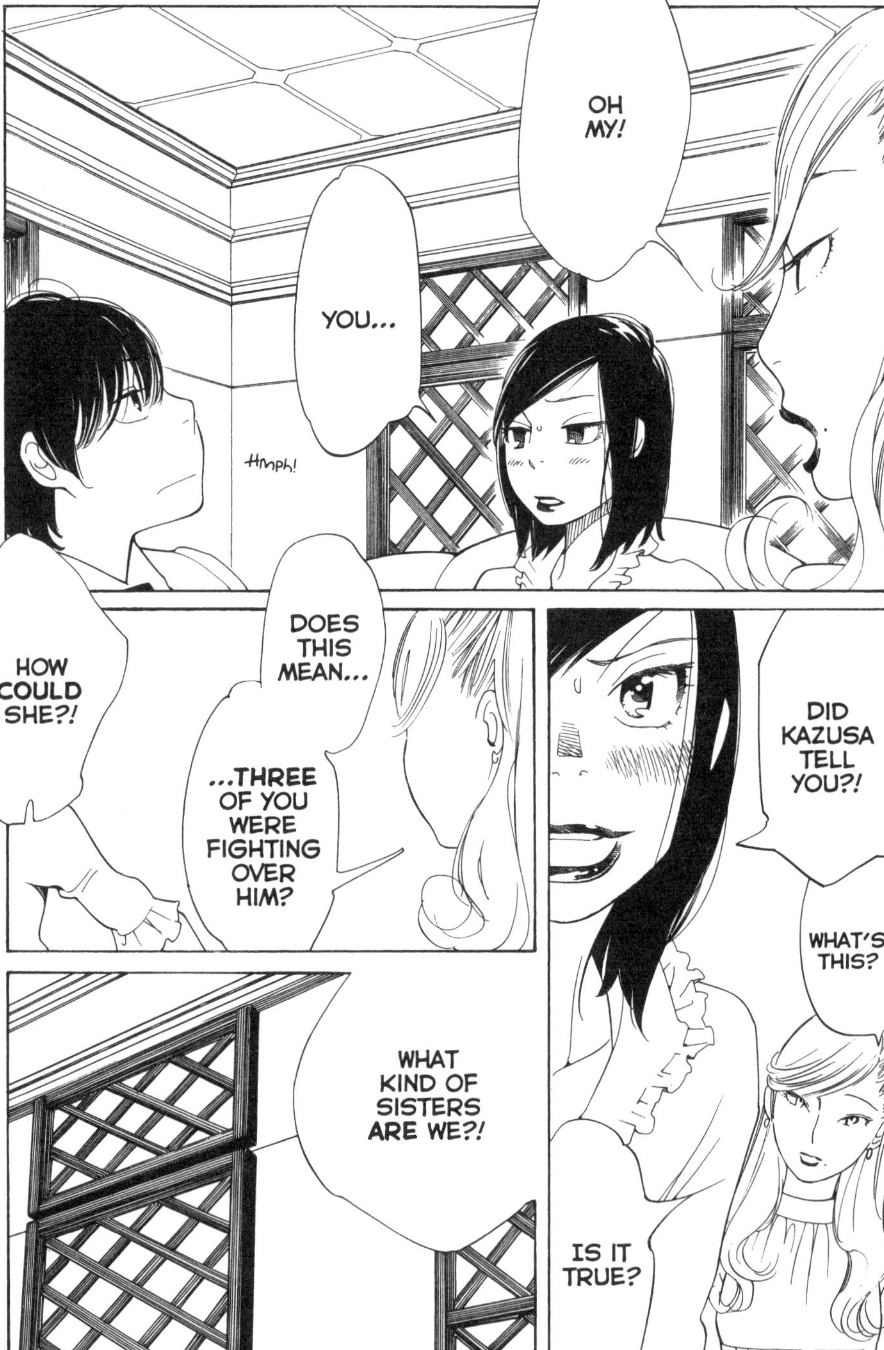
OH MY!
YOU...
Hmph!
DID KAZUSA TELL YOU?!
WHAT'S THIS?
IS IT TRUE?
DOES THIS MEAN...
...THREE OF YOU WERE FIGHTING OVER HIM?
HOW COULD SHE?!
WHAT KIND OF SISTERS ARE WE?!

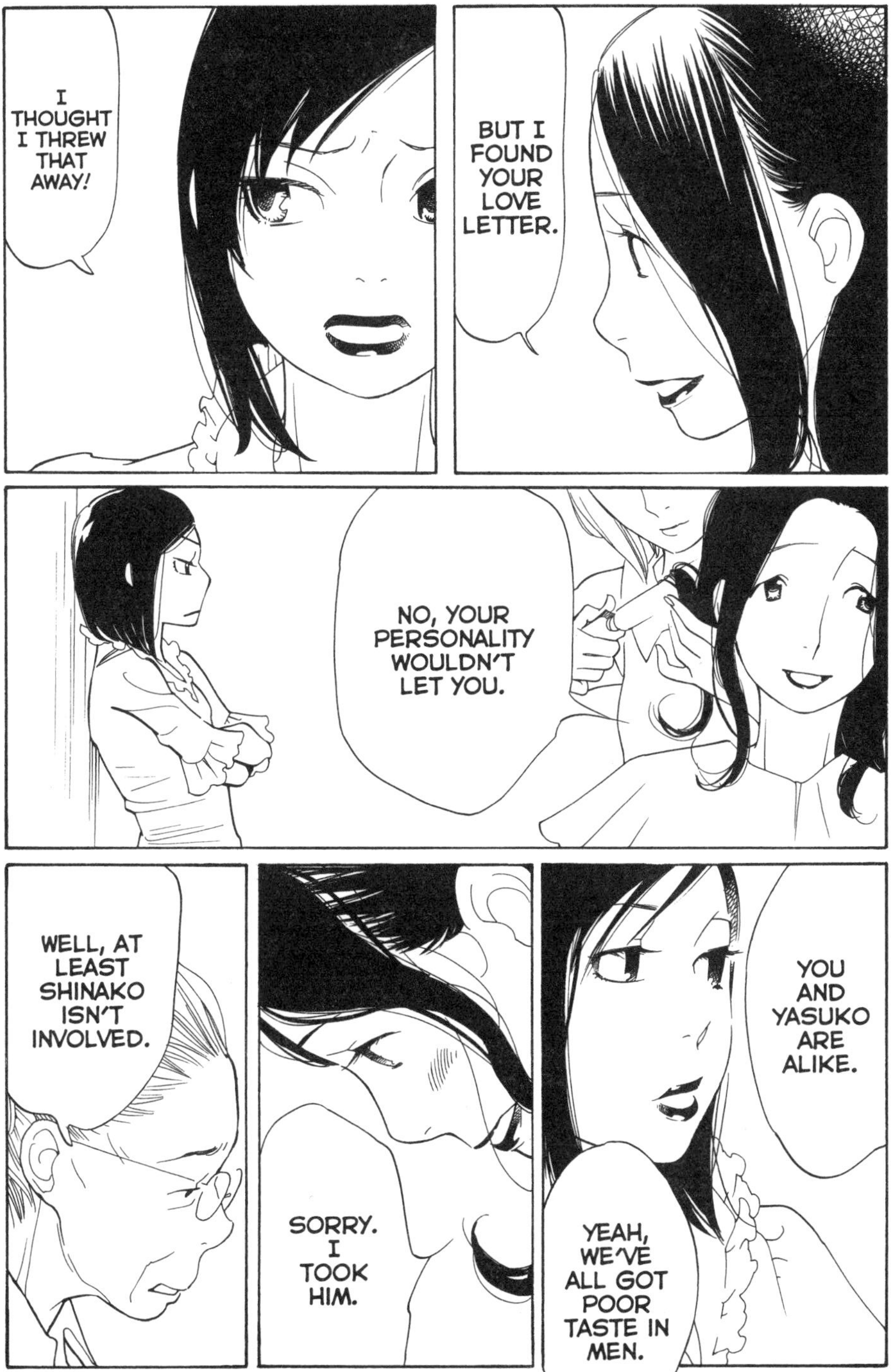
BUT I FOUND YOUR LOVE LETTER.
I THOUGHT I THREW THAT AWAY!
NO, YOUR PERSONALITY WOULDN'T LET YOU.
YOU AND YASUKO ARE ALIKE.
YEAH, WE'VE ALL GOT POOR TASTE IN MEN.
SORRY. I TOOK HIM.
WELL, AT LEAST SHINAKO ISN'T INVOLVED.

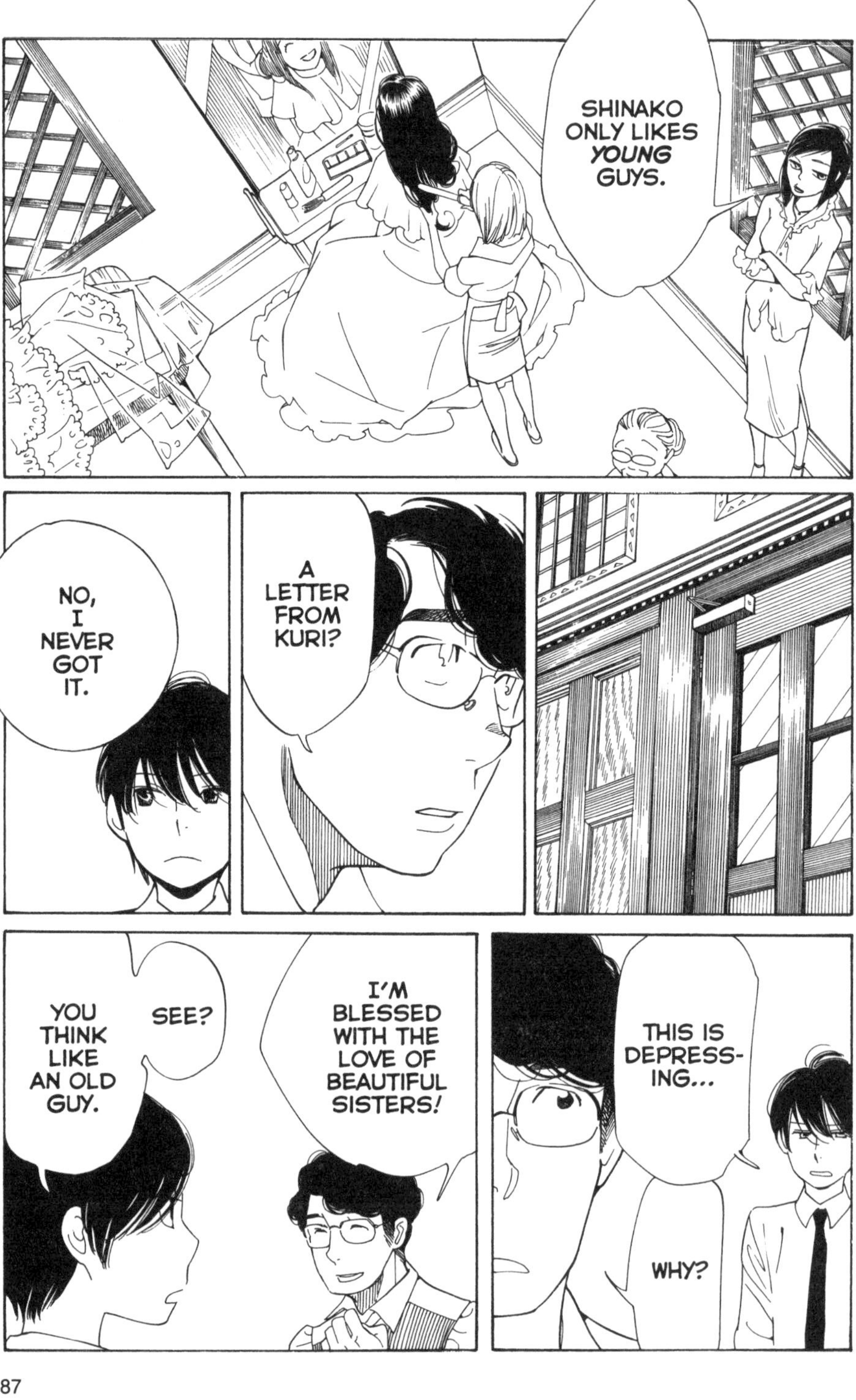
SHINAKO ONLY LIKES *YOUNG* GUYS.
A LETTER FROM KURI?
NO, I NEVER GOT IT.
THIS IS DEPRESS-ING...
WHY?
I'M BLESSED WITH THE LOVE OF BEAUTIFUL SISTERS!
SEE?
YOU THINK LIKE AN OLD GUY.

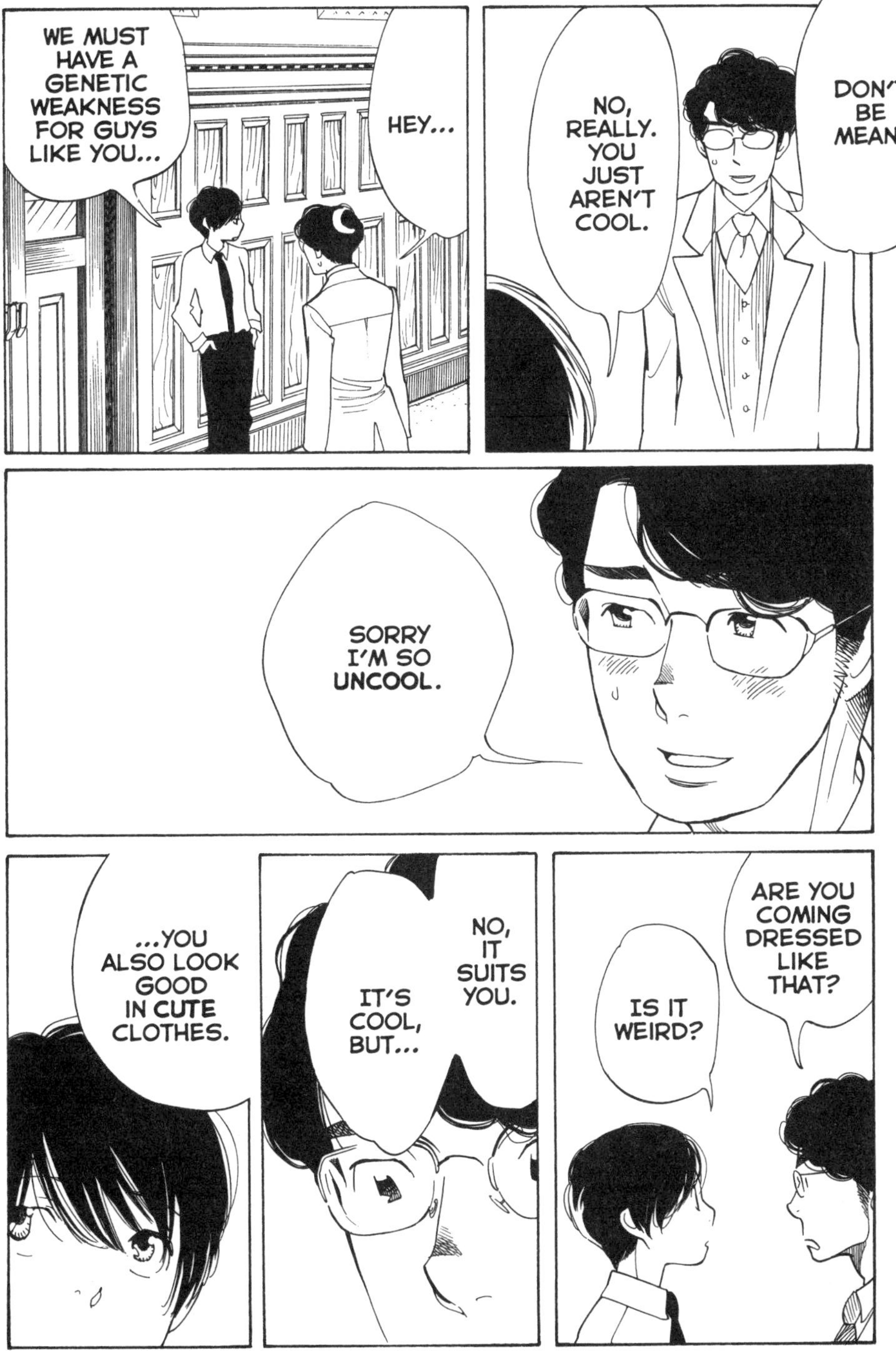
DON'T BE MEAN.
NO, REALLY. YOU JUST AREN'T COOL.
HEY...
WE MUST HAVE A GENETIC WEAKNESS FOR GUYS LIKE YOU...
SORRY I'M SO UNCOOL.
ARE YOU COMING DRESSED LIKE THAT?
IS IT WEIRD?
NO, IT SUITS YOU.
IT'S COOL, BUT...
...YOU ALSO LOOK GOOD IN CUTE CLOTHES.

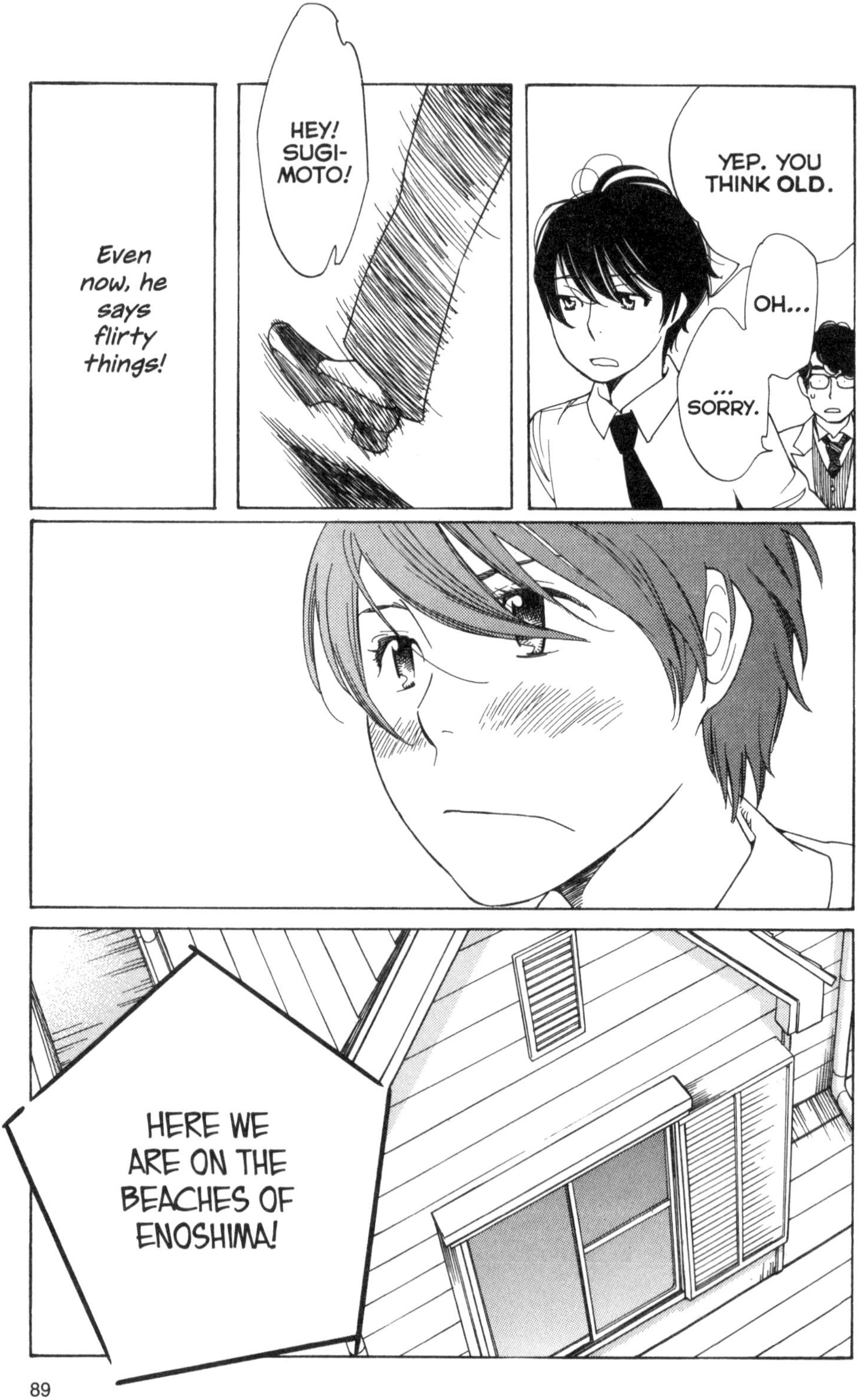
YEP. YOU THINK OLD.
OH...
... SORRY.
HEY! SUGI-MOTO!
Even now, he says flirty things!
HERE WE ARE ON THE BEACHES OF ENOSHIMA!

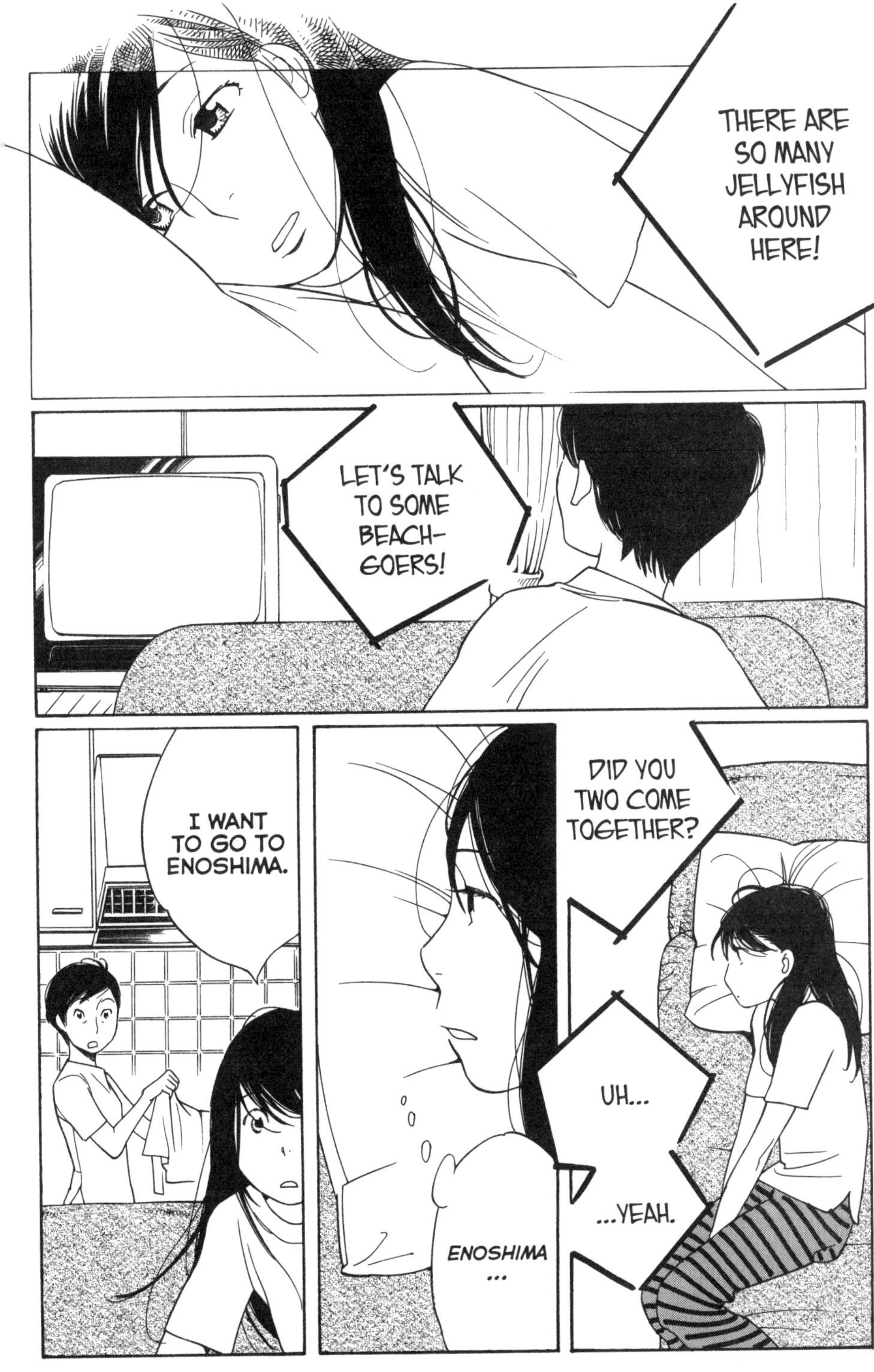
THERE ARE SO MANY JELLYFISH AROUND HERE!
LET'S TALK TO SOME BEACH-GOERS!
DID YOU TWO COME TOGETHER?
UH...
...YEAH.
ENOSHIMA...
I WANT TO GO TO ENOSHIMA.

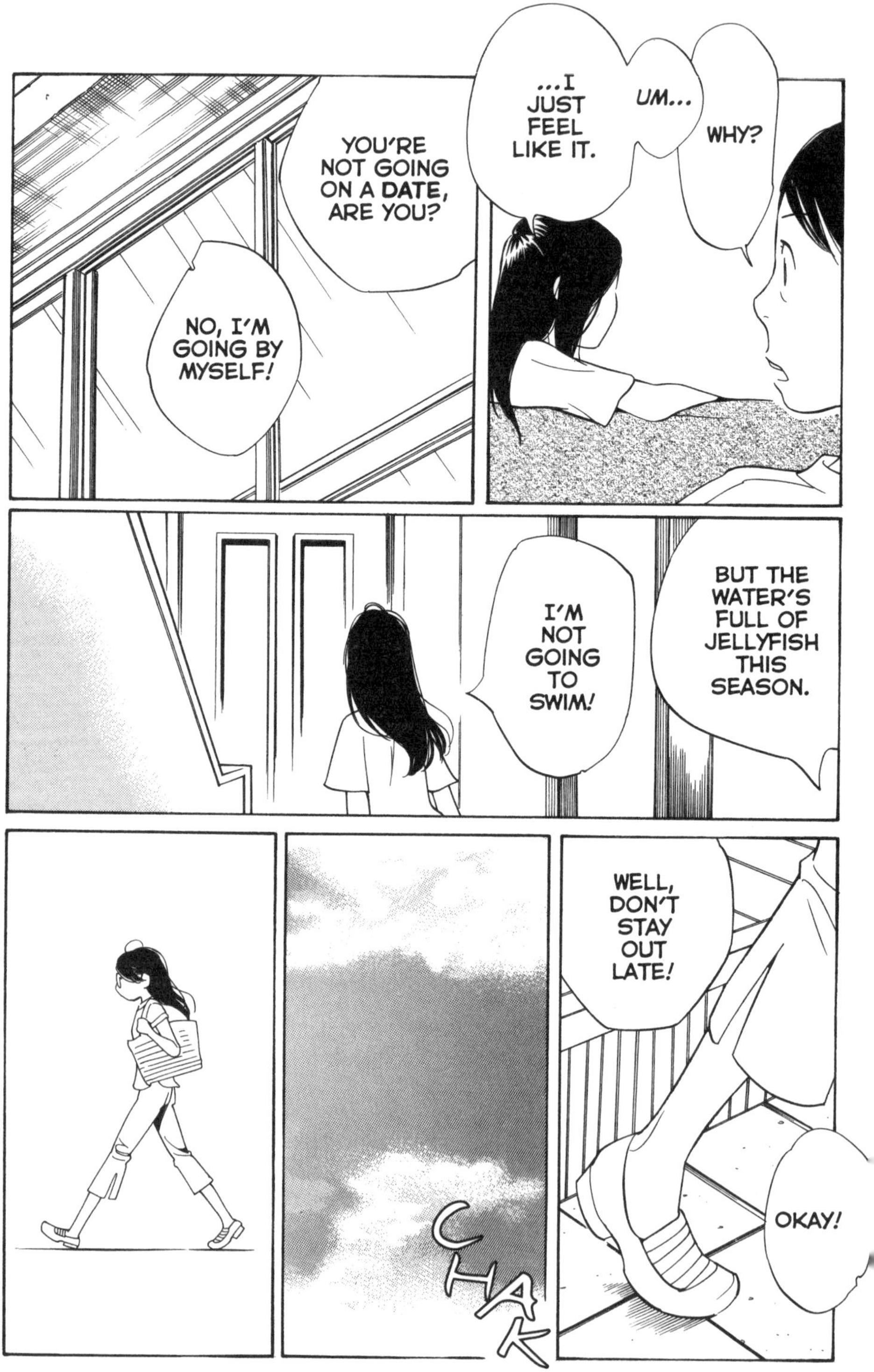
WHY?
UM...
...I JUST FEEL LIKE IT.
YOU'RE NOT GOING ON A DATE, ARE YOU?
NO, I'M GOING BY MYSELF!
BUT THE WATER'S FULL OF JELLYFISH THIS SEASON.
I'M NOT GOING TO SWIM!
WELL, DON'T STAY OUT LATE!
OKAY!
CHAK

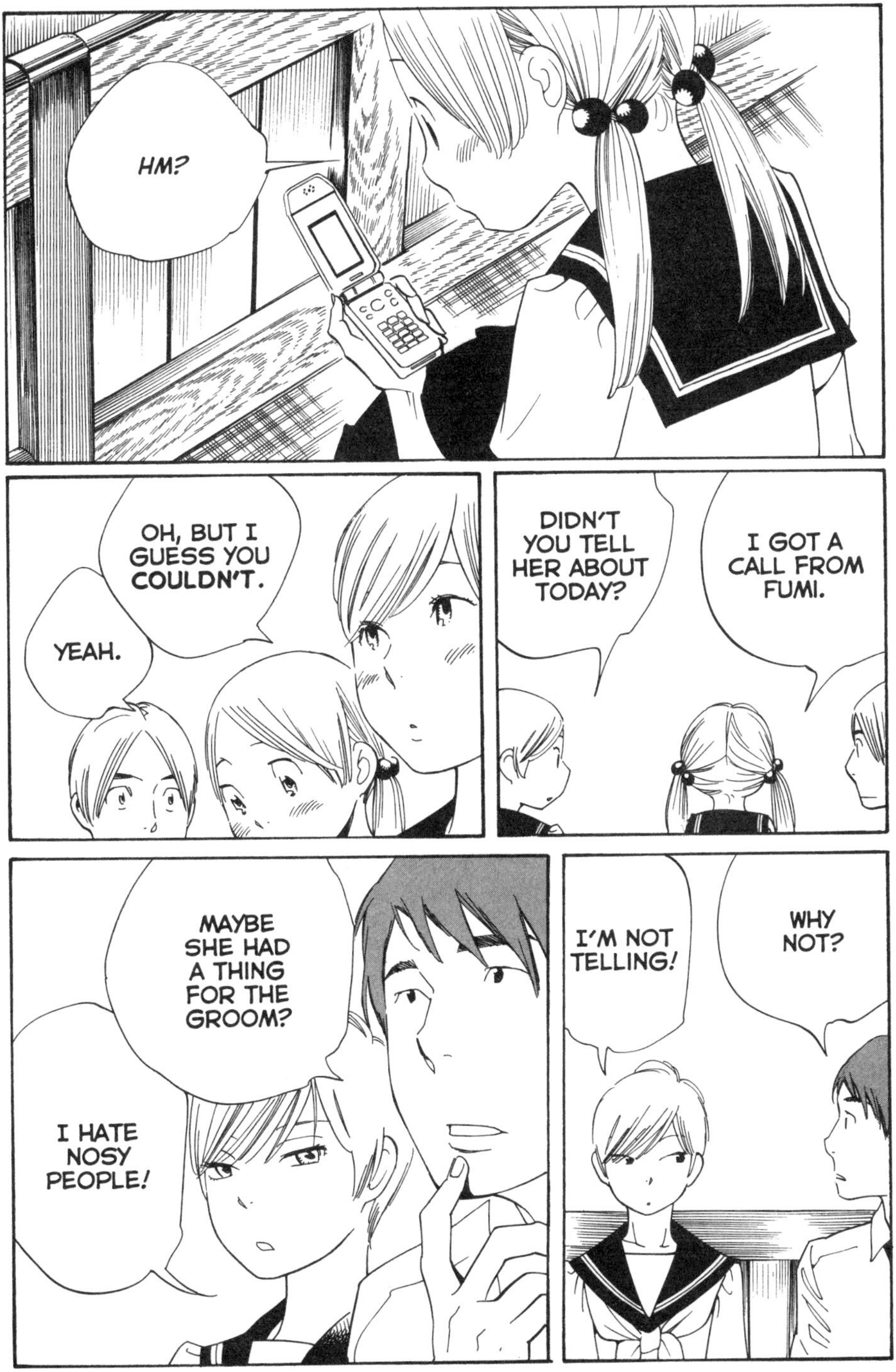
HM?
I GOT A CALL FROM FUMI.
DIDN'T YOU TELL HER ABOUT TODAY?
OH, BUT I GUESS YOU COULDN'T.
YEAH.
WHY NOT?
I'M NOT TELLING!
MAYBE SHE HAD A THING FOR THE GROOM?
I HATE NOSY PEOPLE!

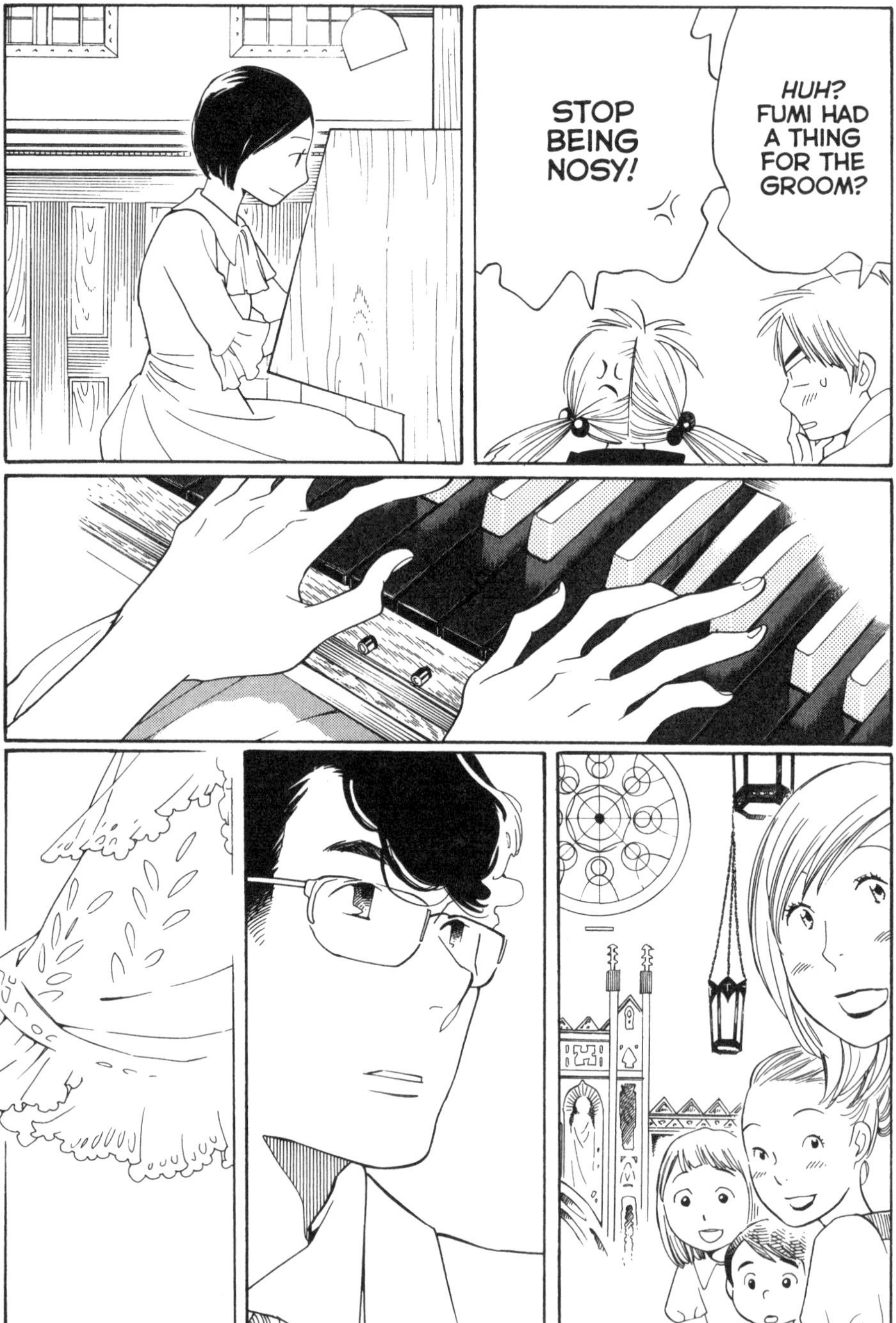
HUH? FUMI HAD A THING FOR THE GROOM?
STOP BEING NOSY!

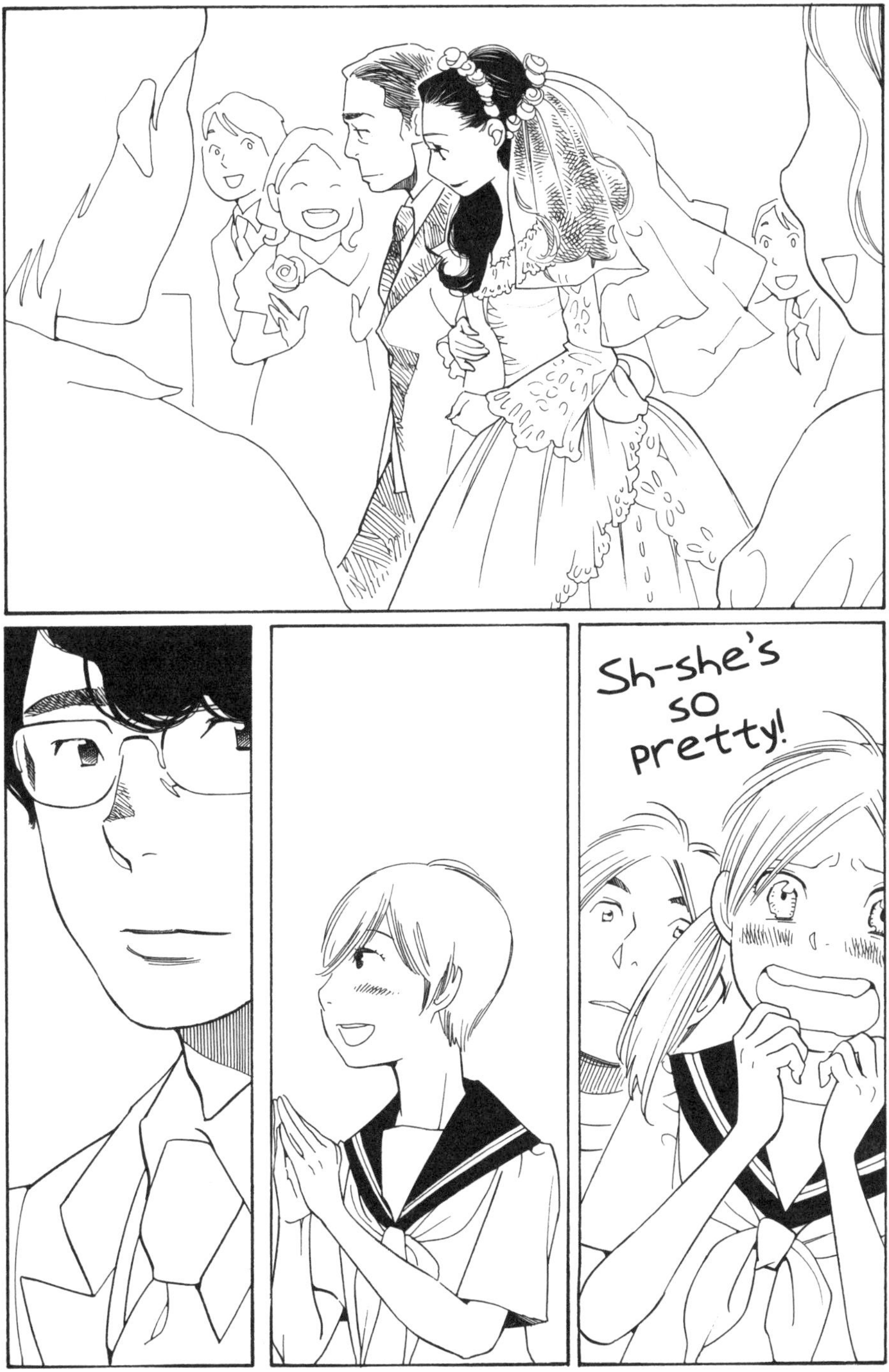
Sh-she's so pretty!

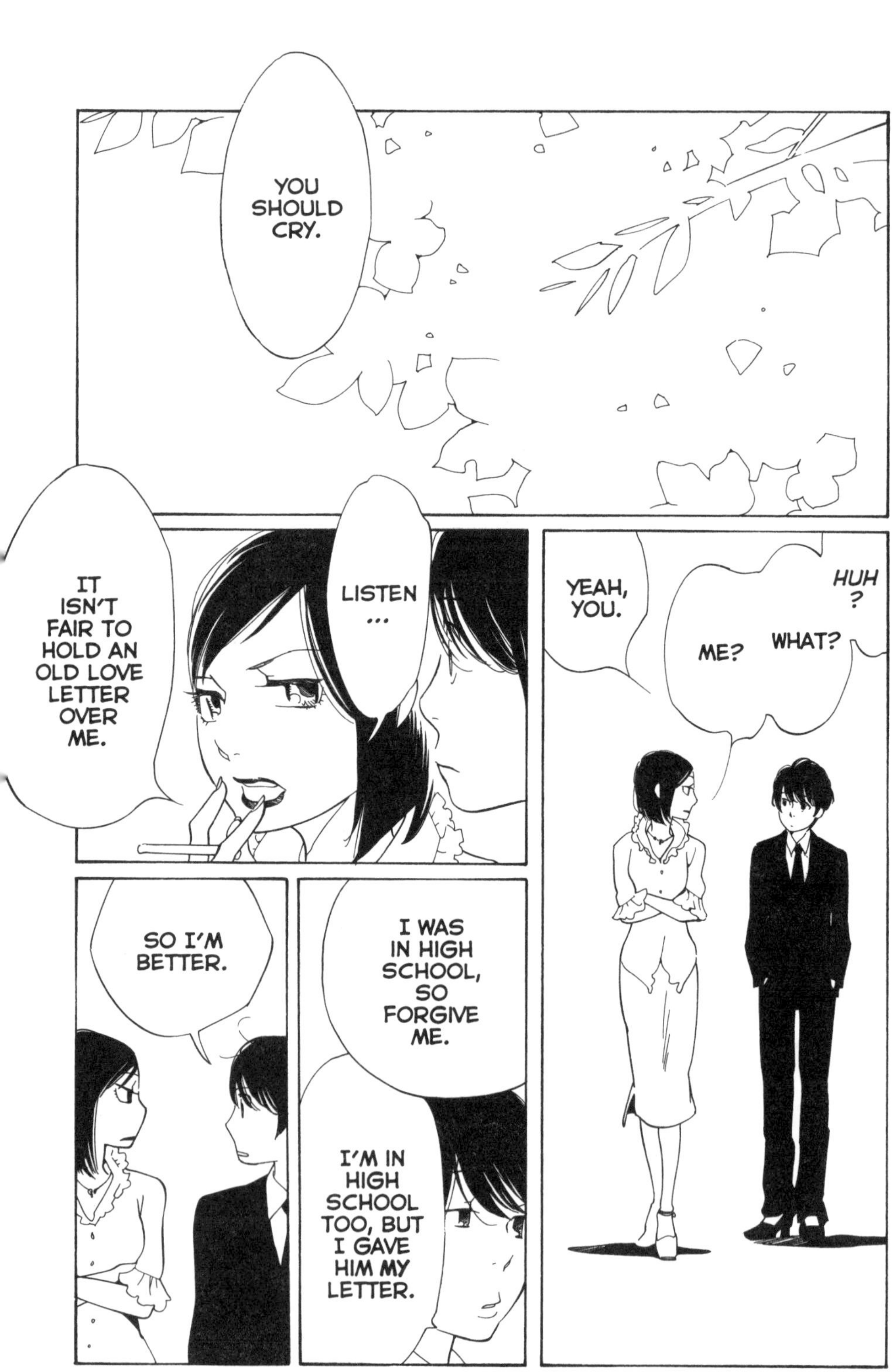
YOU SHOULD CRY.
HUH?
WHAT?
ME?
YEAH, YOU.
LISTEN...
IT ISN'T FAIR TO HOLD AN OLD LOVE LETTER OVER ME.
I WAS IN HIGH SCHOOL, SO FORGIVE ME.
I'M IN HIGH SCHOOL TOO, BUT I GAVE HIM MY LETTER.
SO I'M BETTER.

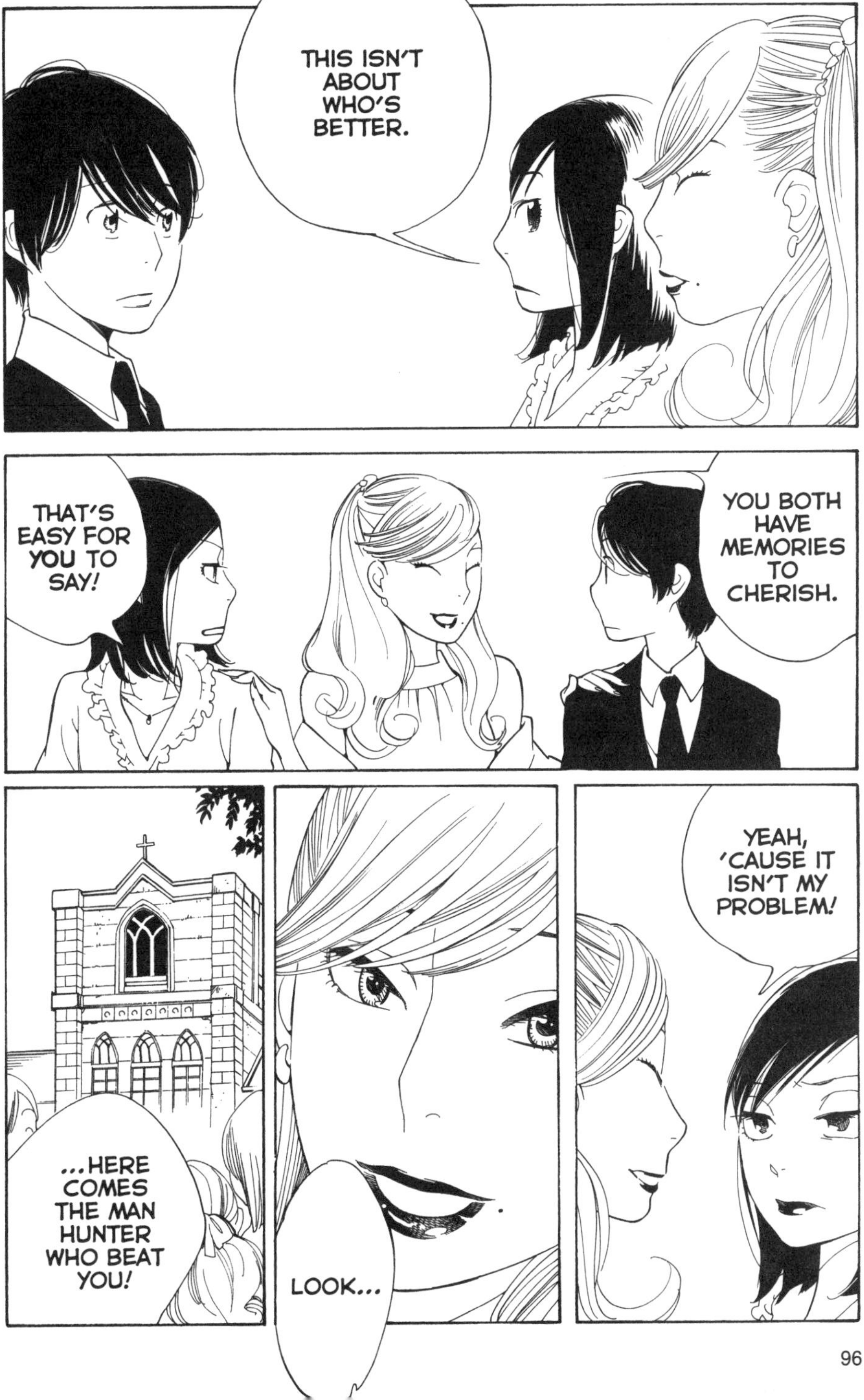
THIS ISN'T ABOUT WHO'S BETTER.
YOU BOTH HAVE MEMORIES TO CHERISH.
THAT'S EASY FOR YOU TO SAY!
YEAH, 'CAUSE IT ISN'T MY PROBLEM!
LOOK...
...HERE COMES THE MAN HUNTER WHO BEAT YOU!

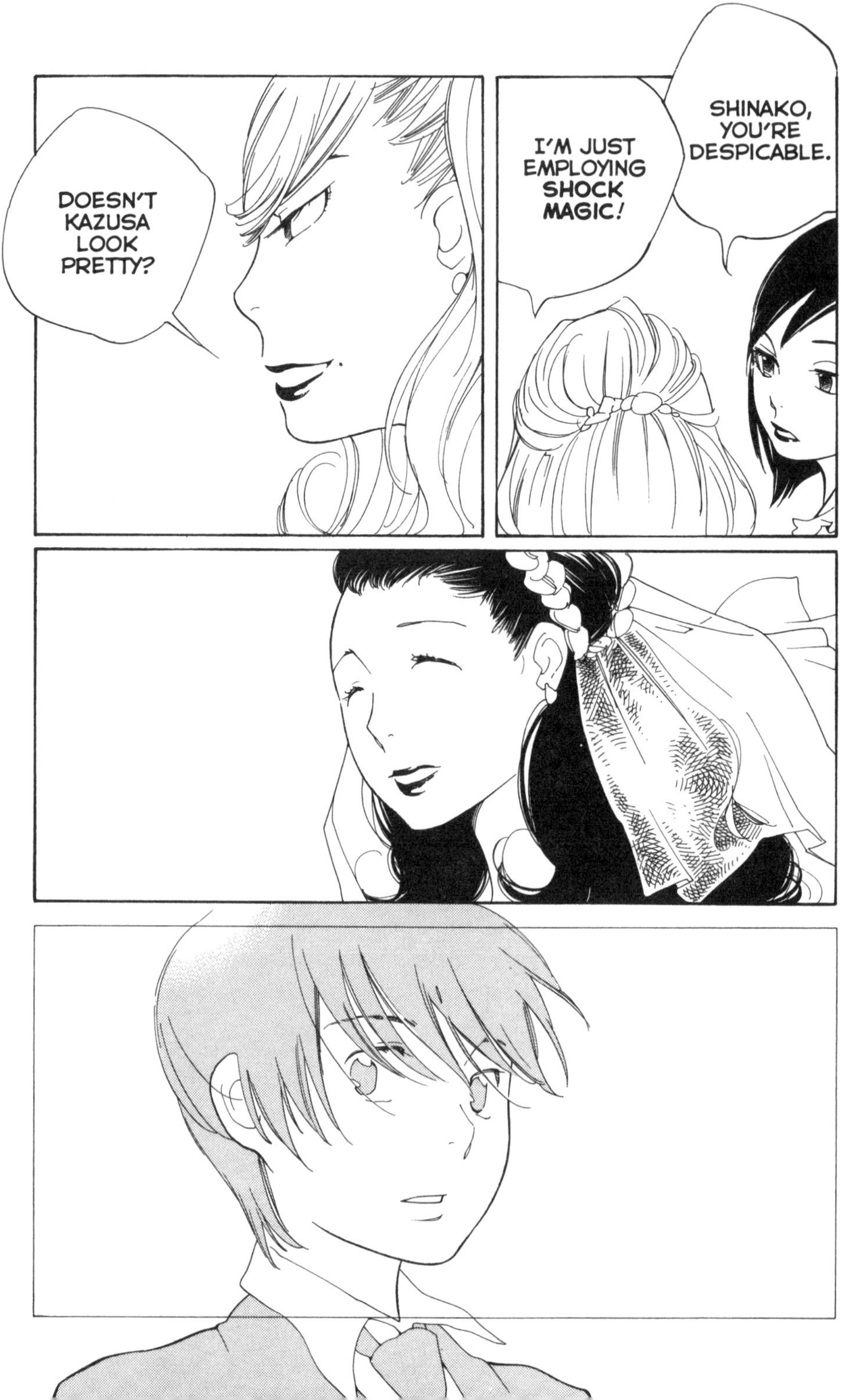
SHINAKO, YOU'RE DESPICABLE.
I'M JUST EMPLOYING SHOCK MAGIC!
DOESN'T KAZUSA LOOK PRETTY?

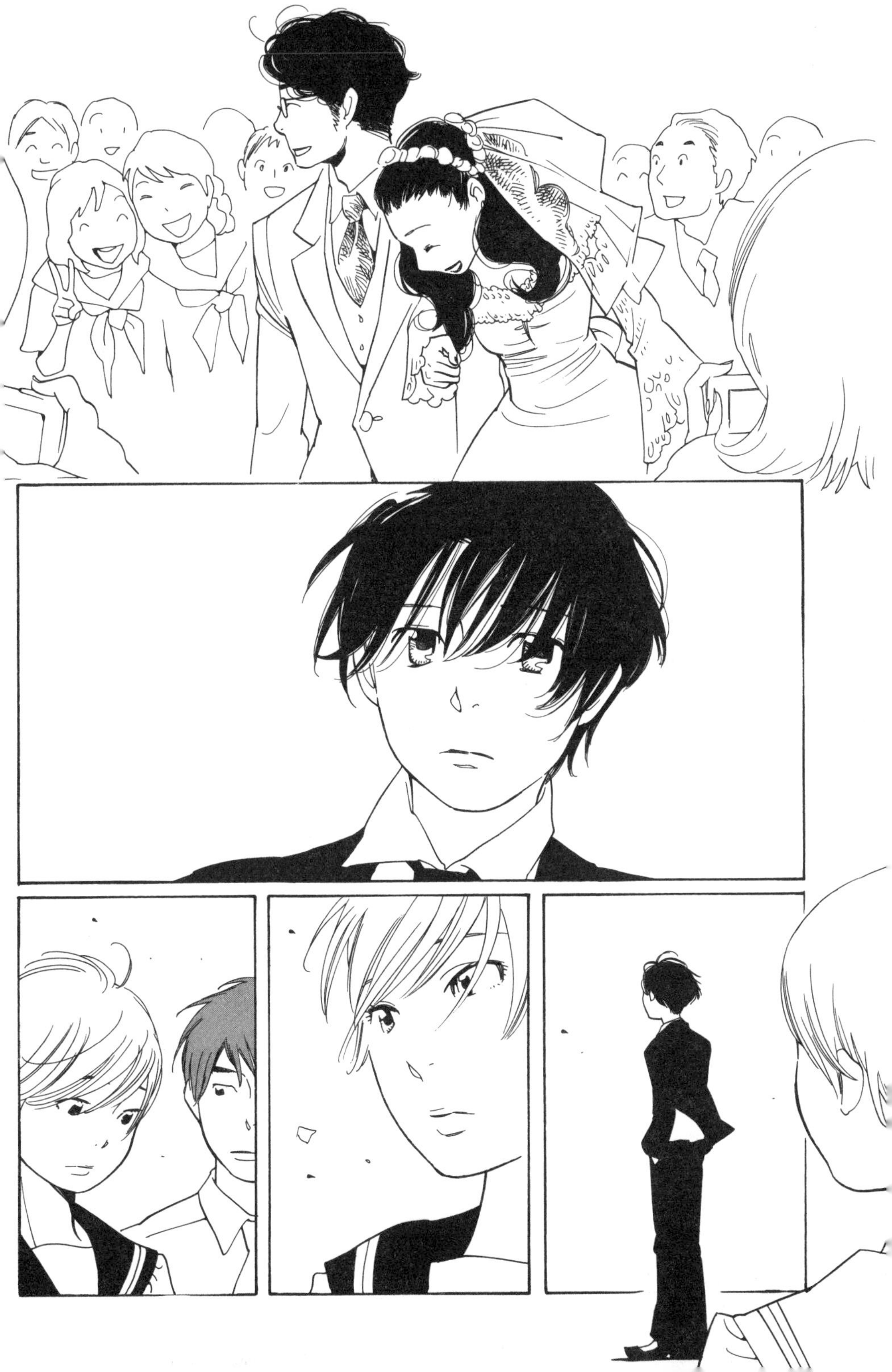

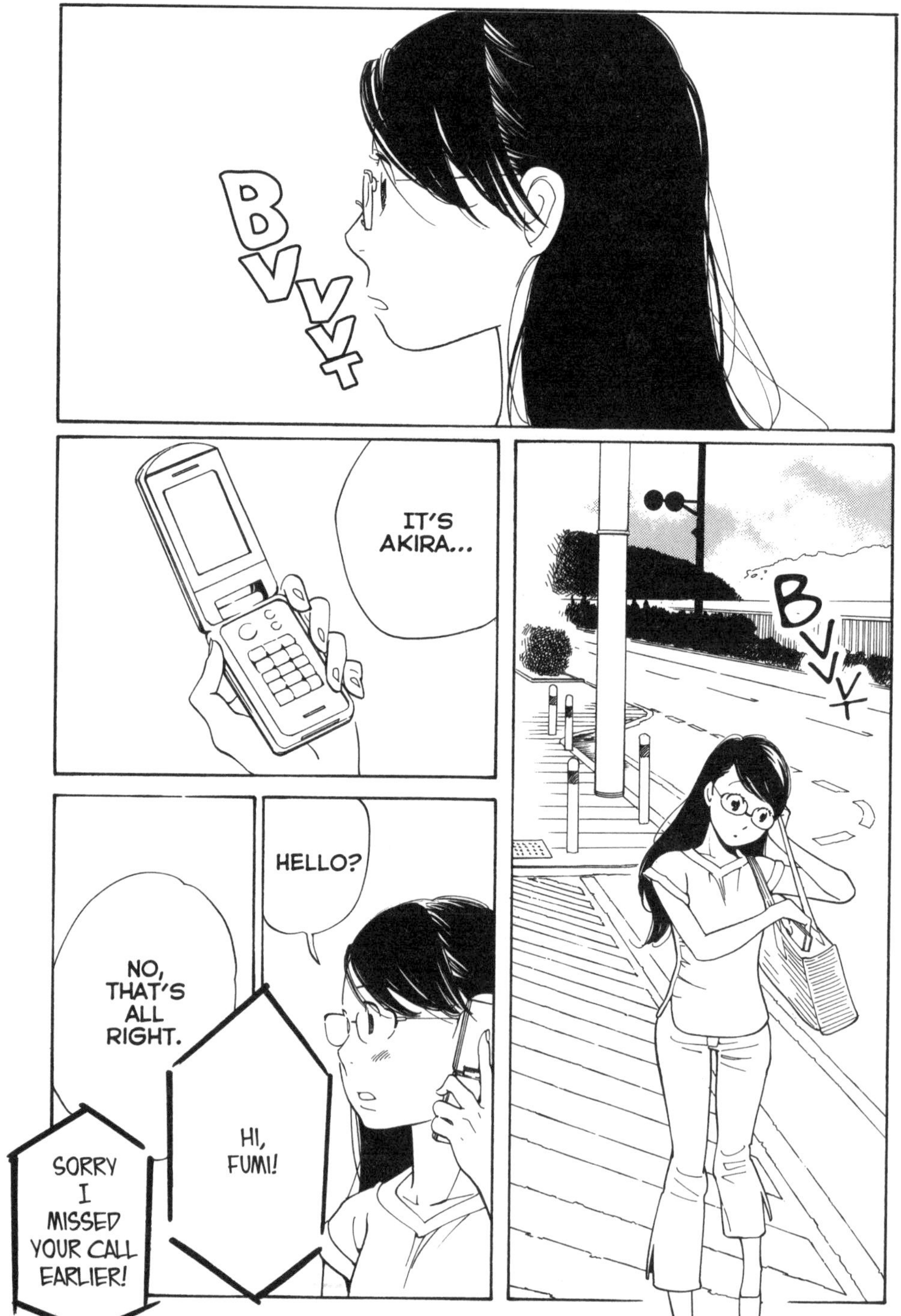
BVVVT
BVVVT
IT'S AKIRA...
HELLO?
HI, FUMI!
SORRY I MISSED YOUR CALL EARLIER!
NO, THAT'S ALL RIGHT.

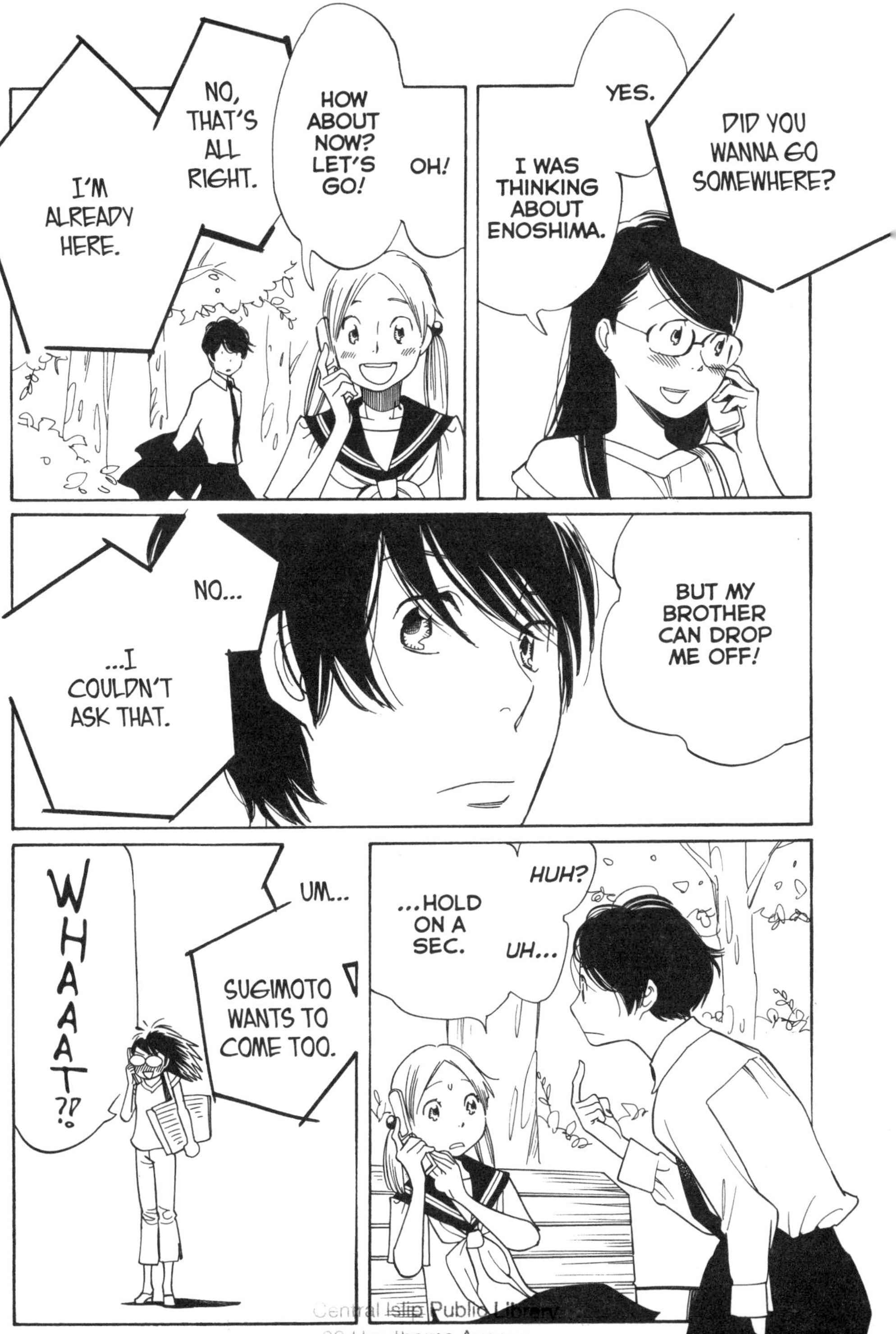
DID YOU WANNA GO SOMEWHERE?
YES.
I WAS THINKING ABOUT ENOSHIMA.
OH!
HOW ABOUT NOW? LET'S GO!
NO, THAT'S ALL RIGHT.
I'M ALREADY HERE.
BUT MY BROTHER CAN DROP ME OFF!
NO...
...I COULDN'T ASK THAT.
HUH?
UH...
...HOLD ON A SEC.
UM...
SUGIMOTO WANTS TO COME TOO.
WHAAAT?!

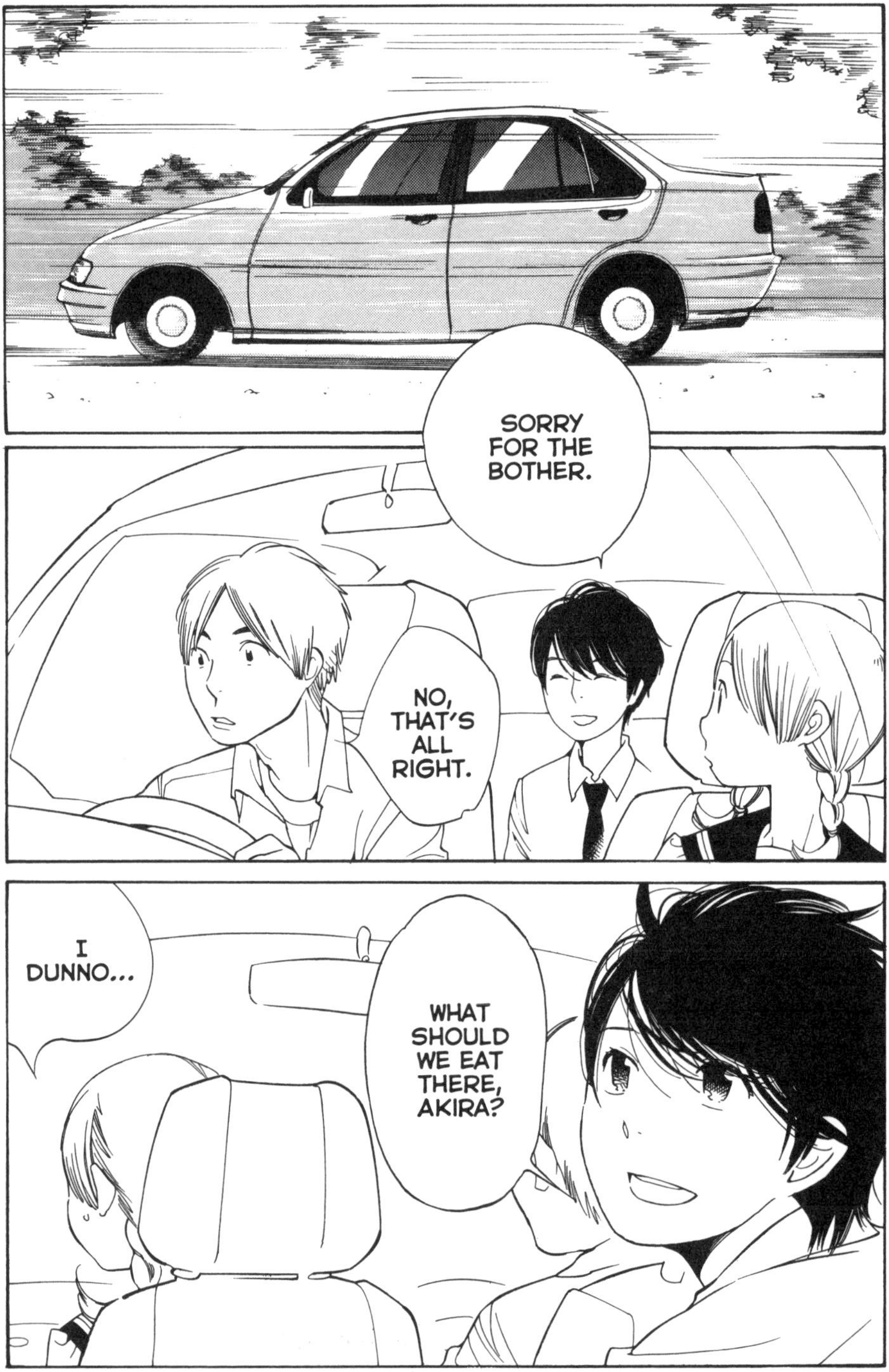
SORRY FOR THE BOTHER.
NO, THAT'S ALL RIGHT.
WHAT SHOULD WE EAT THERE, AKIRA?
I DUNNO...

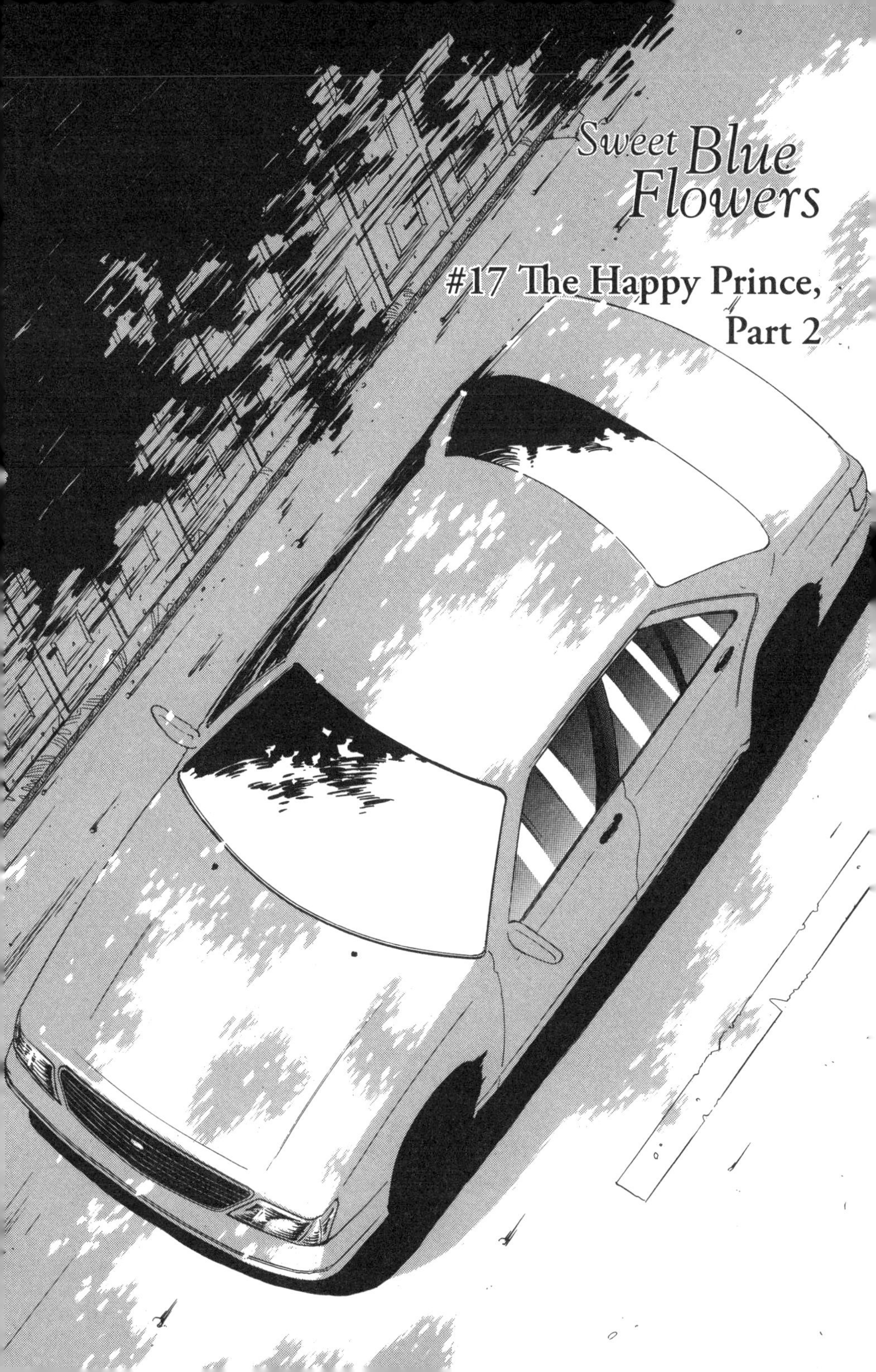
Sweet Blue Flowers
#17 The Happy Prince, Part 2

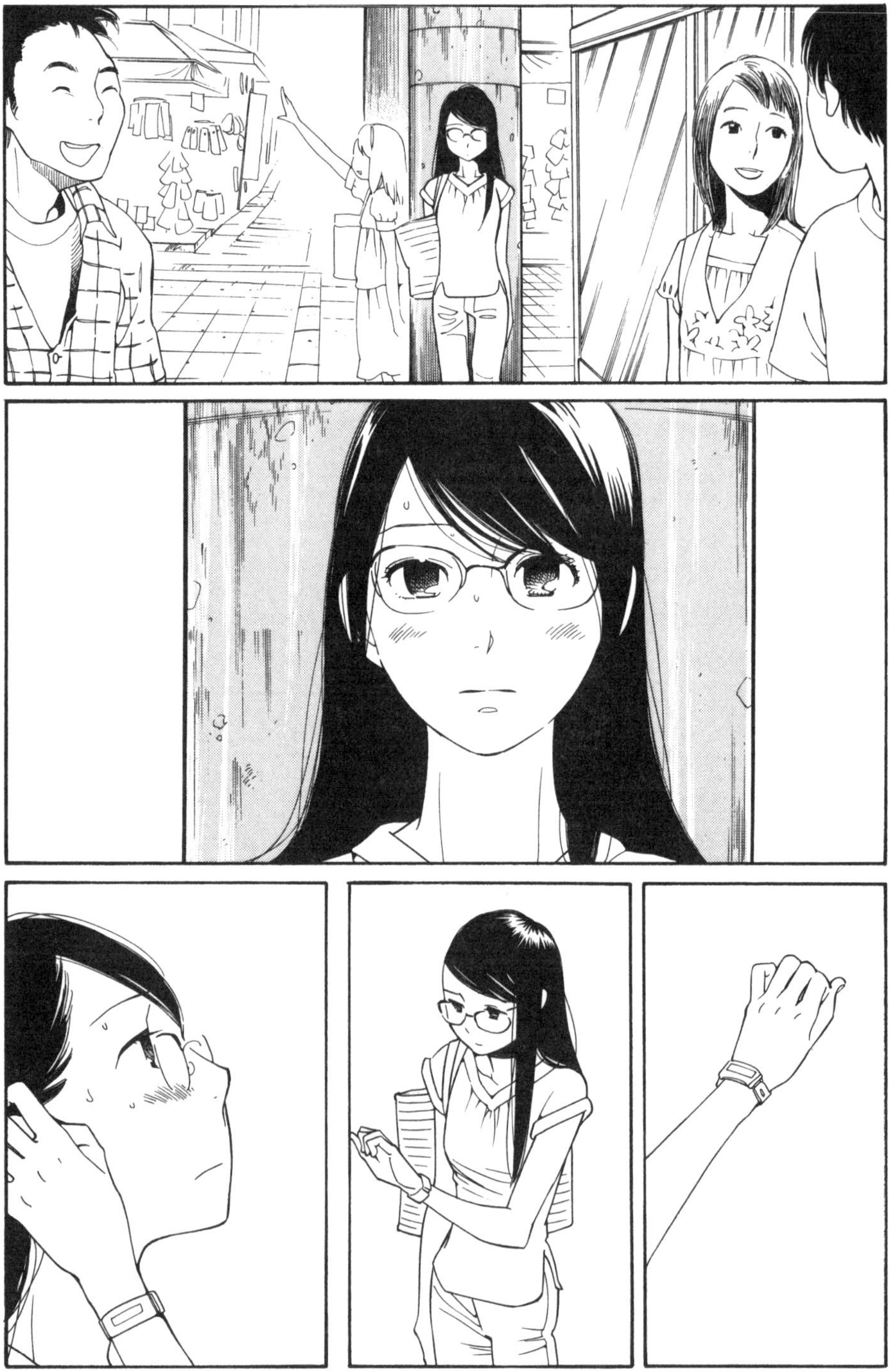

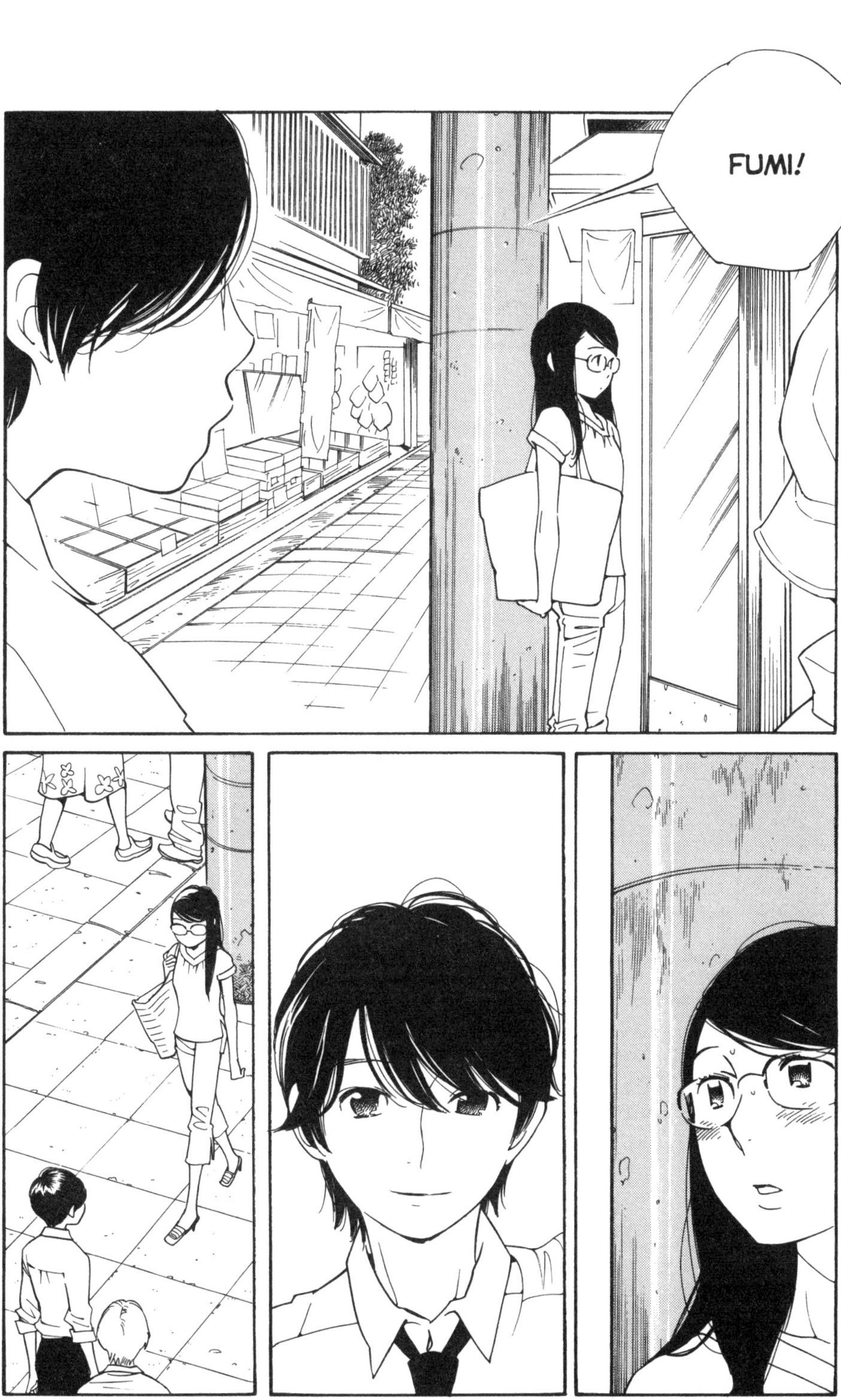
FUMI!

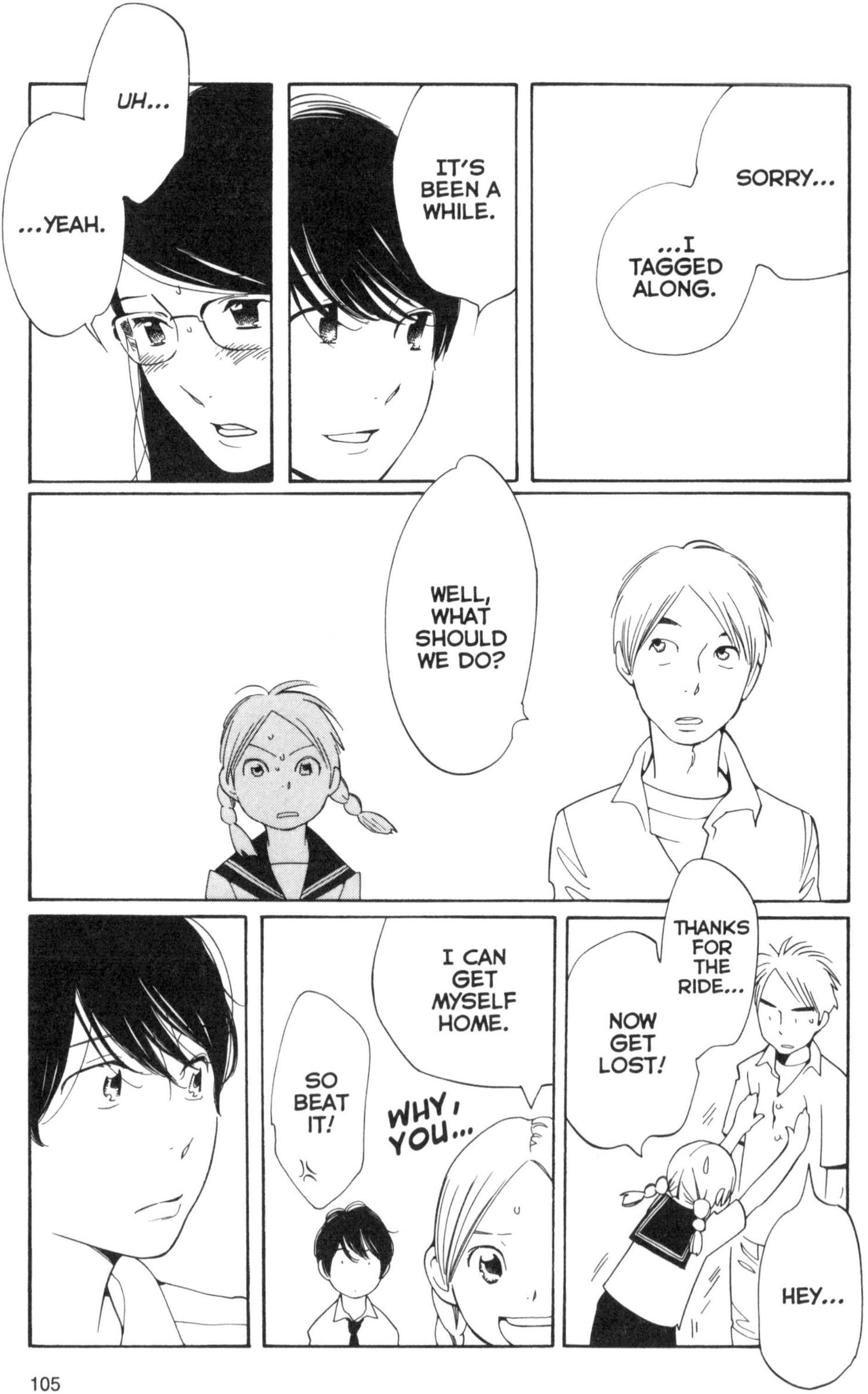
SORRY...
...I TAGGED ALONG.
IT'S BEEN A WHILE.
UH...
...YEAH.
WELL, WHAT SHOULD WE DO?
THANKS FOR THE RIDE...
NOW GET LOST!
HEY...
I CAN GET MYSELF HOME.
SO BEAT IT!
WHY, YOU...

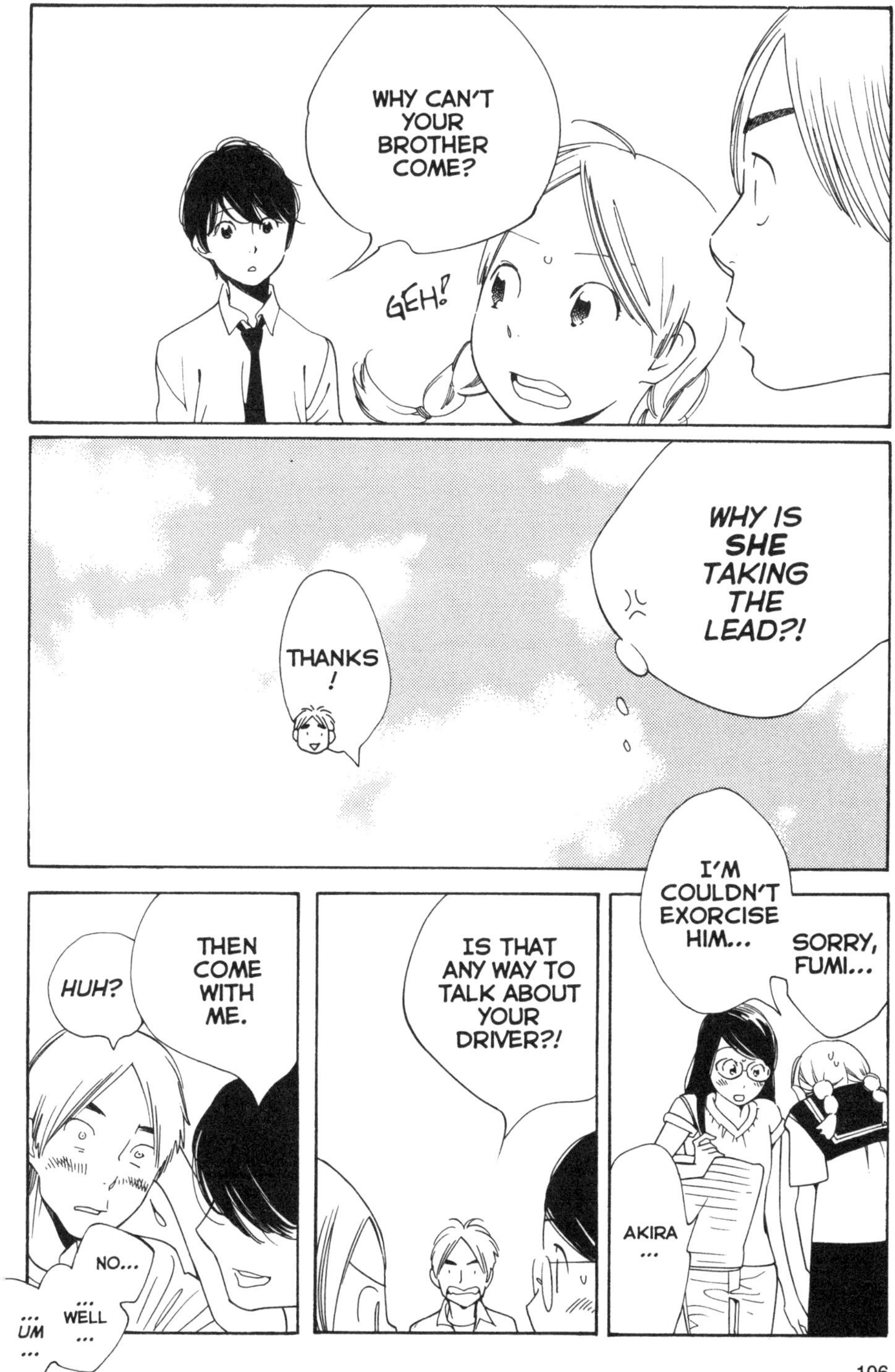
WHY CAN'T YOUR BROTHER COME?
GEH!
WHY IS SHE TAKING THE LEAD?!
THANKS!
SORRY, FUMI...
I'M COULDN'T EXORCISE HIM...
AKIRA ...
IS THAT ANY WAY TO TALK ABOUT YOUR DRIVER?!
THEN COME WITH ME.
HUH?
NO...
... WELL ...
... UM ...

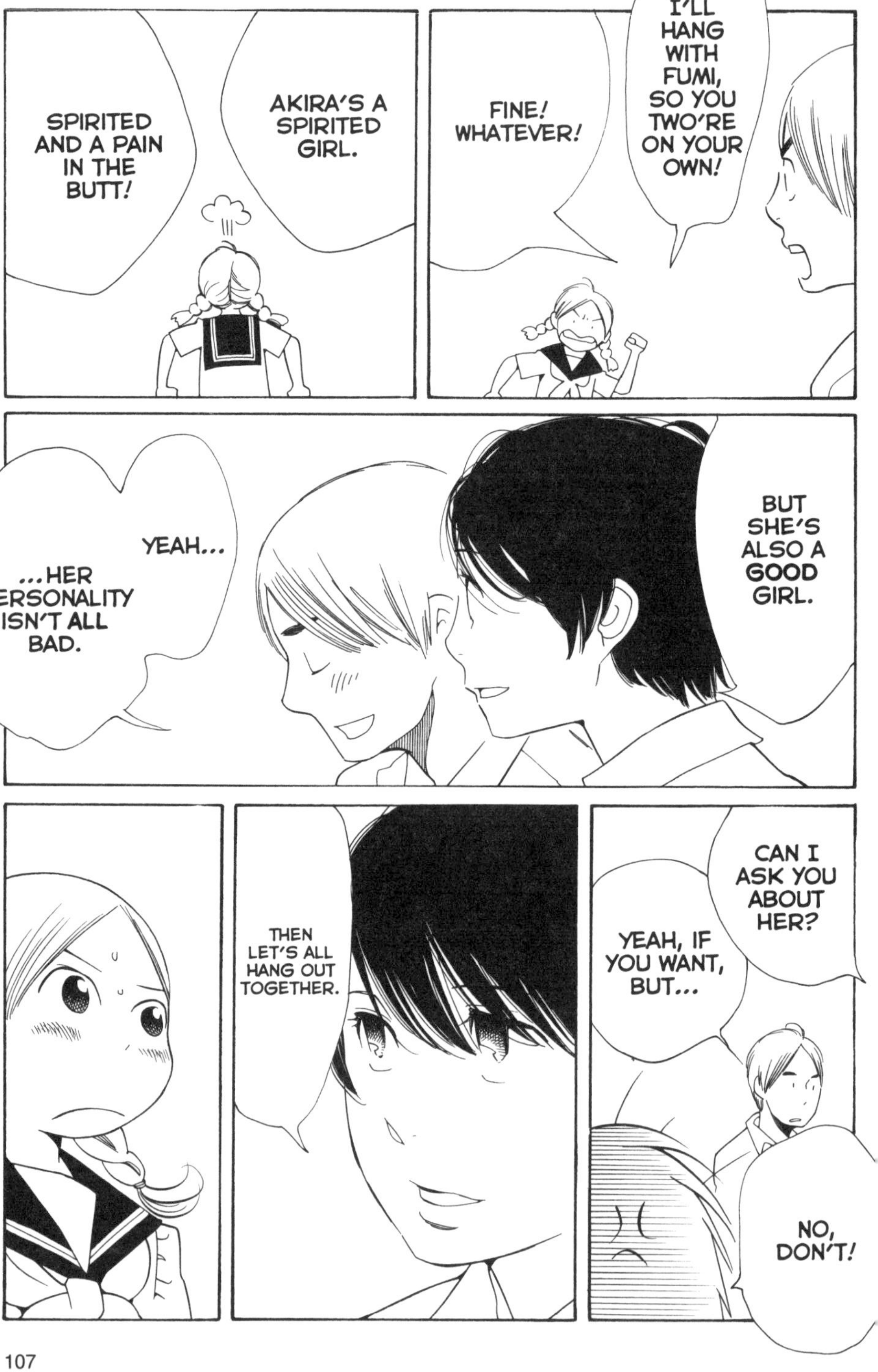
I'LL HANG WITH FUMI, SO YOU TWO'RE ON YOUR OWN!
FINE! WHATEVER!
AKIRA'S A SPIRITED GIRL.
SPIRITED AND A PAIN IN THE BUTT!
BUT SHE'S ALSO A GOOD GIRL.
YEAH...
...HER PERSONALITY ISN'T ALL BAD.
CAN I ASK YOU ABOUT HER?
YEAH, IF YOU WANT, BUT...
NO, DON'T!
THEN LET'S ALL HANG OUT TOGETHER.

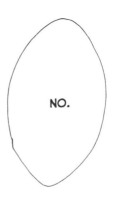

NO.

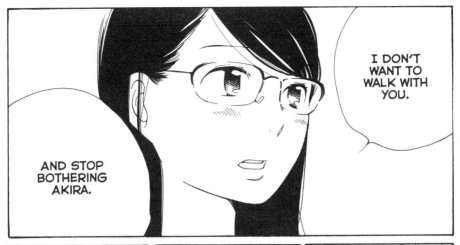

I DON'T WANT TO WALK WITH YOU.

AND STOP BOTHERING AKIRA.

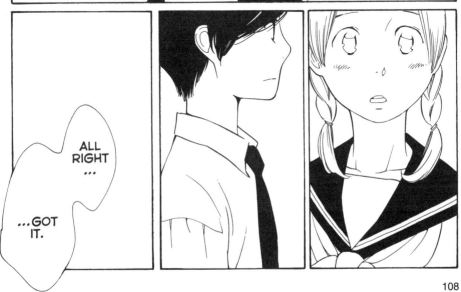

ALL RIGHT ...

...GOT IT.

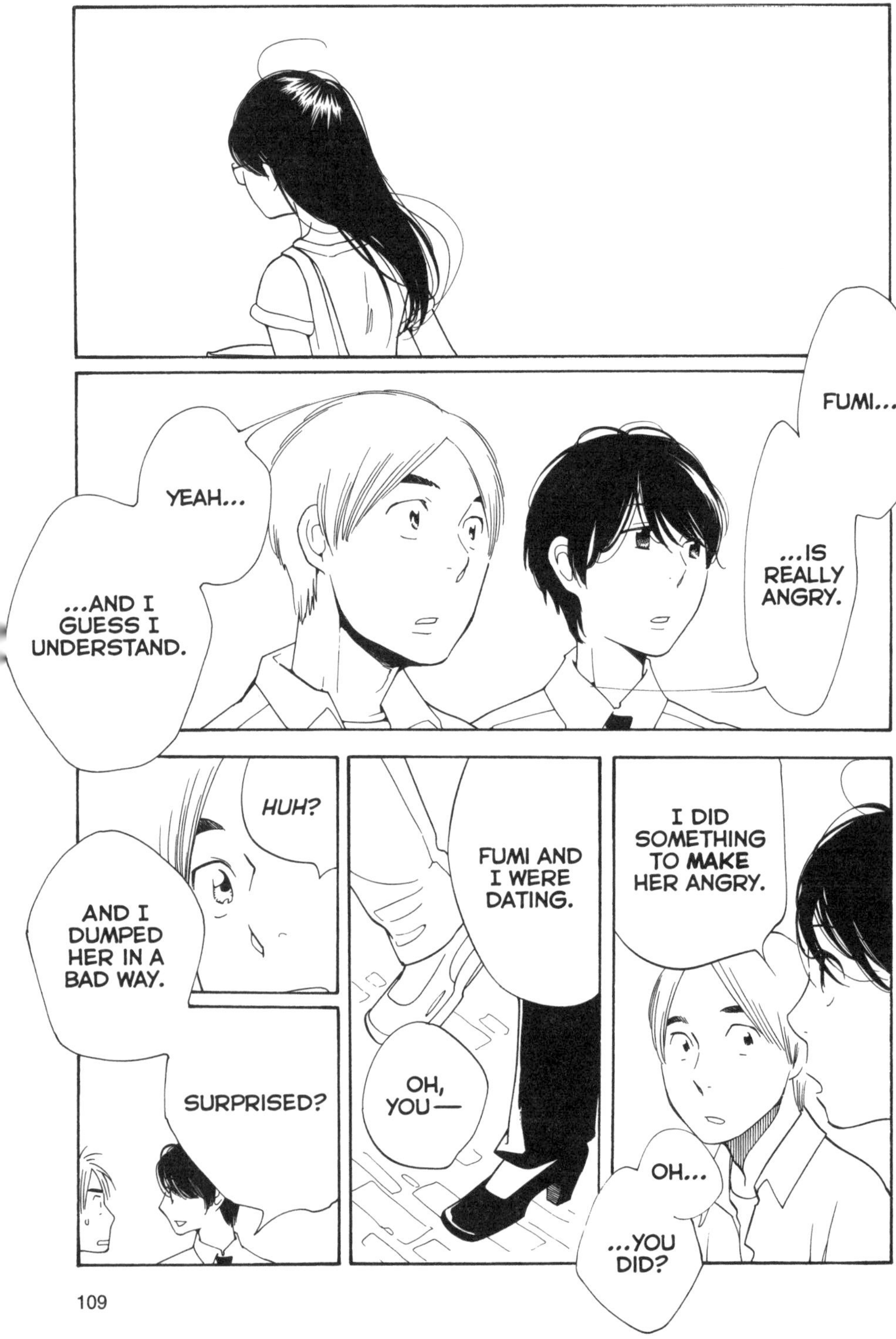
FUMI...
...IS REALLY ANGRY.
YEAH...
...AND I GUESS I UNDERSTAND.
I DID SOMETHING TO MAKE HER ANGRY.
OH...
...YOU DID?
FUMI AND I WERE DATING.
OH, YOU—
HUH?
AND I DUMPED HER IN A BAD WAY.
SURPRISED?

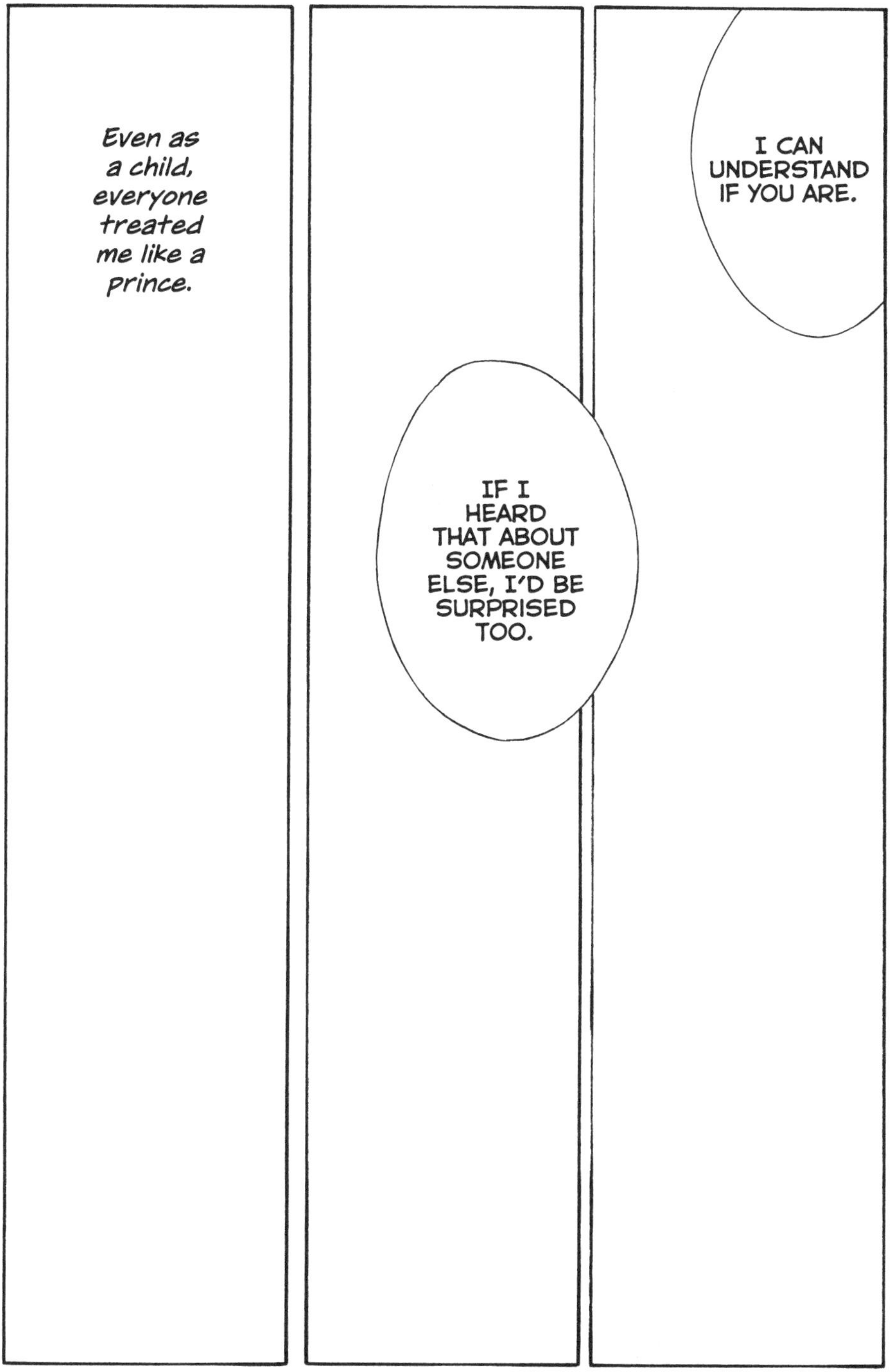
I CAN UNDERSTAND IF YOU ARE.
IF I HEARD THAT ABOUT SOMEONE ELSE, I'D BE SURPRISED TOO.
Even as a child, everyone treated me like a prince.

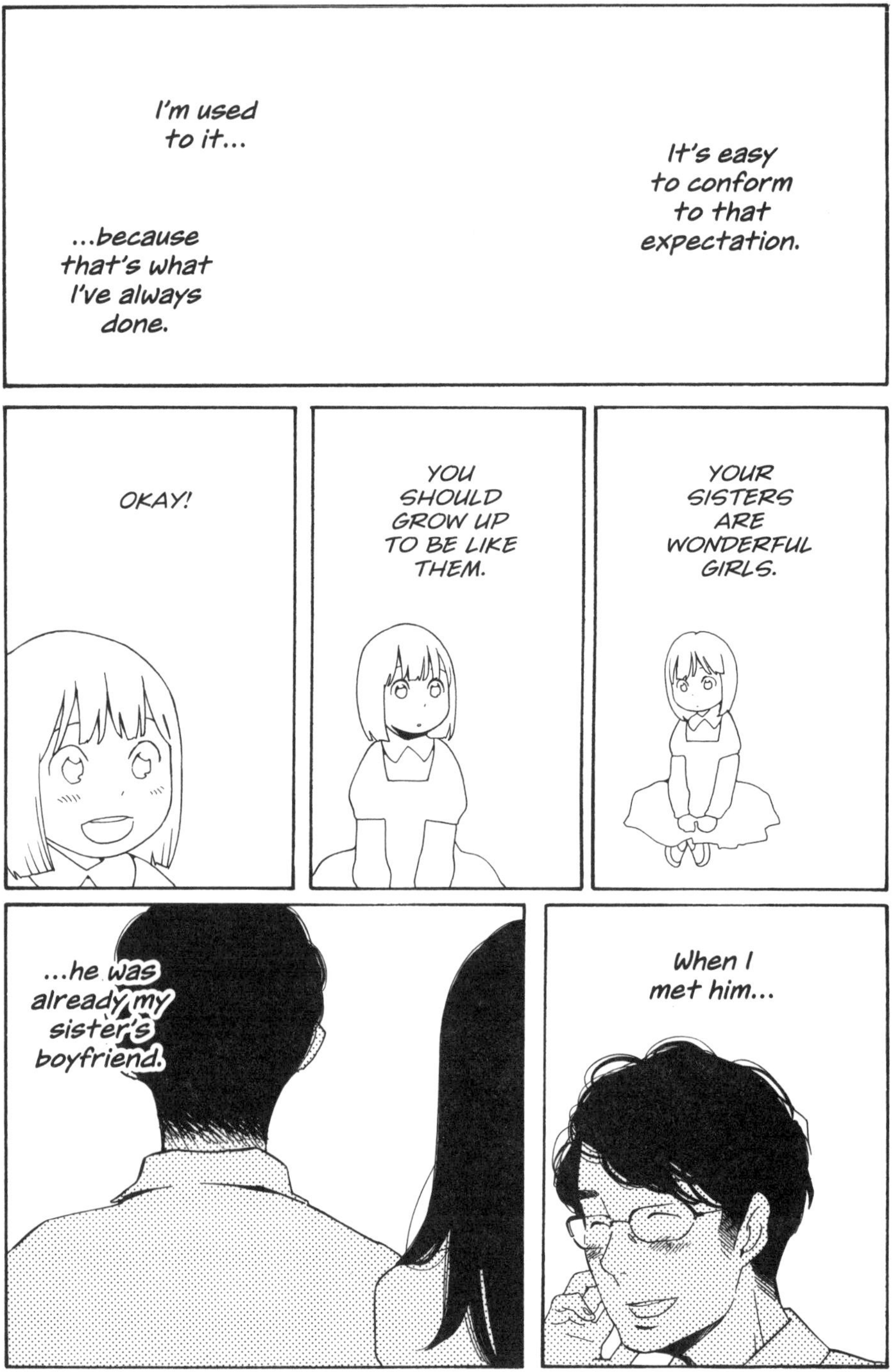
It's easy to conform to that expectation.
I'm used to it...
...because that's what I've always done.
YOUR SISTERS ARE WONDERFUL GIRLS.
YOU SHOULD GROW UP TO BE LIKE THEM.
OKAY!
When I met him...
...he was already my sister's boyfriend.

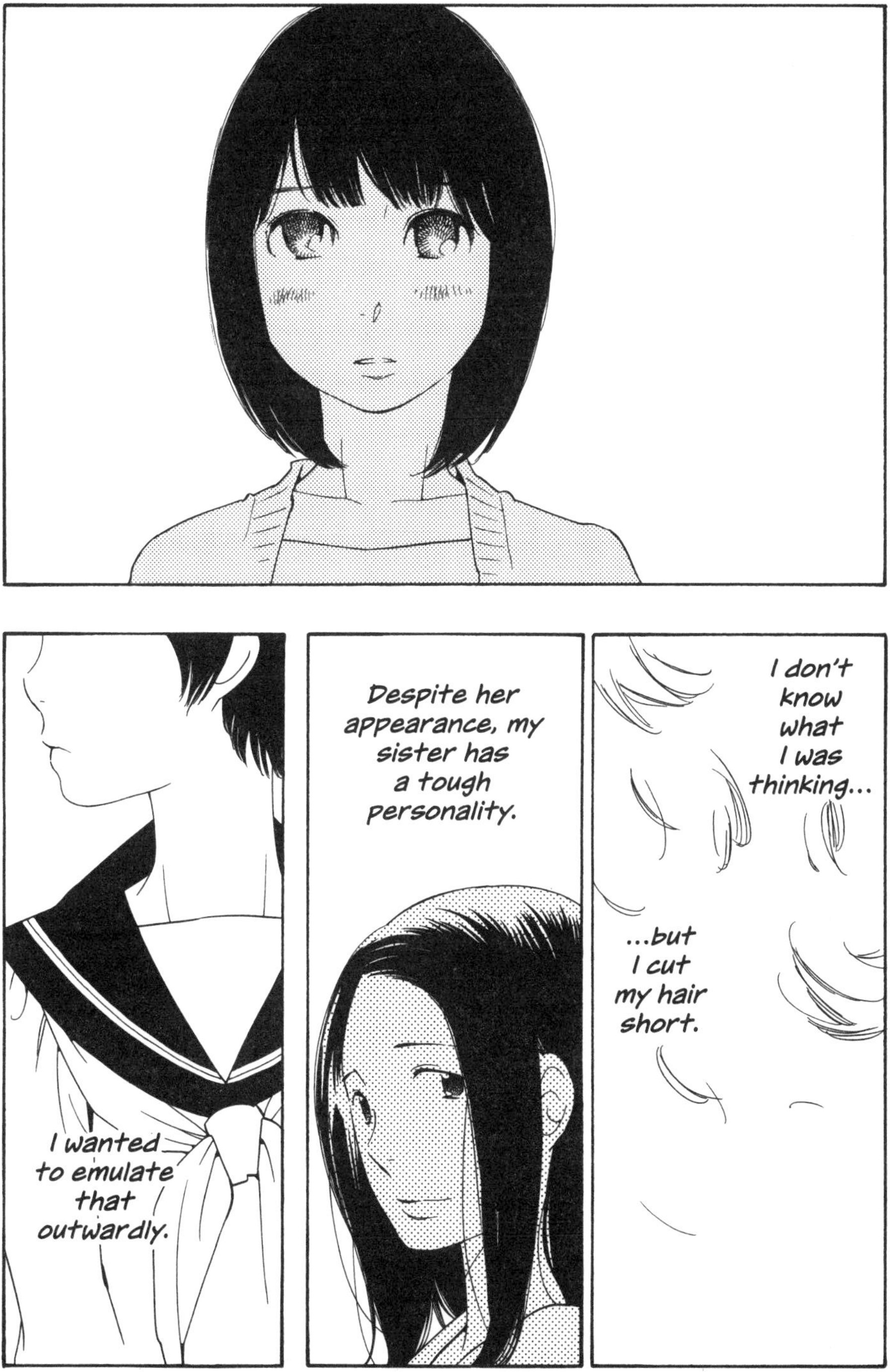
I don't know what I was thinking...
...but I cut my hair short.
Despite her appearance, my sister has a tough personality.
I wanted to emulate that outwardly.

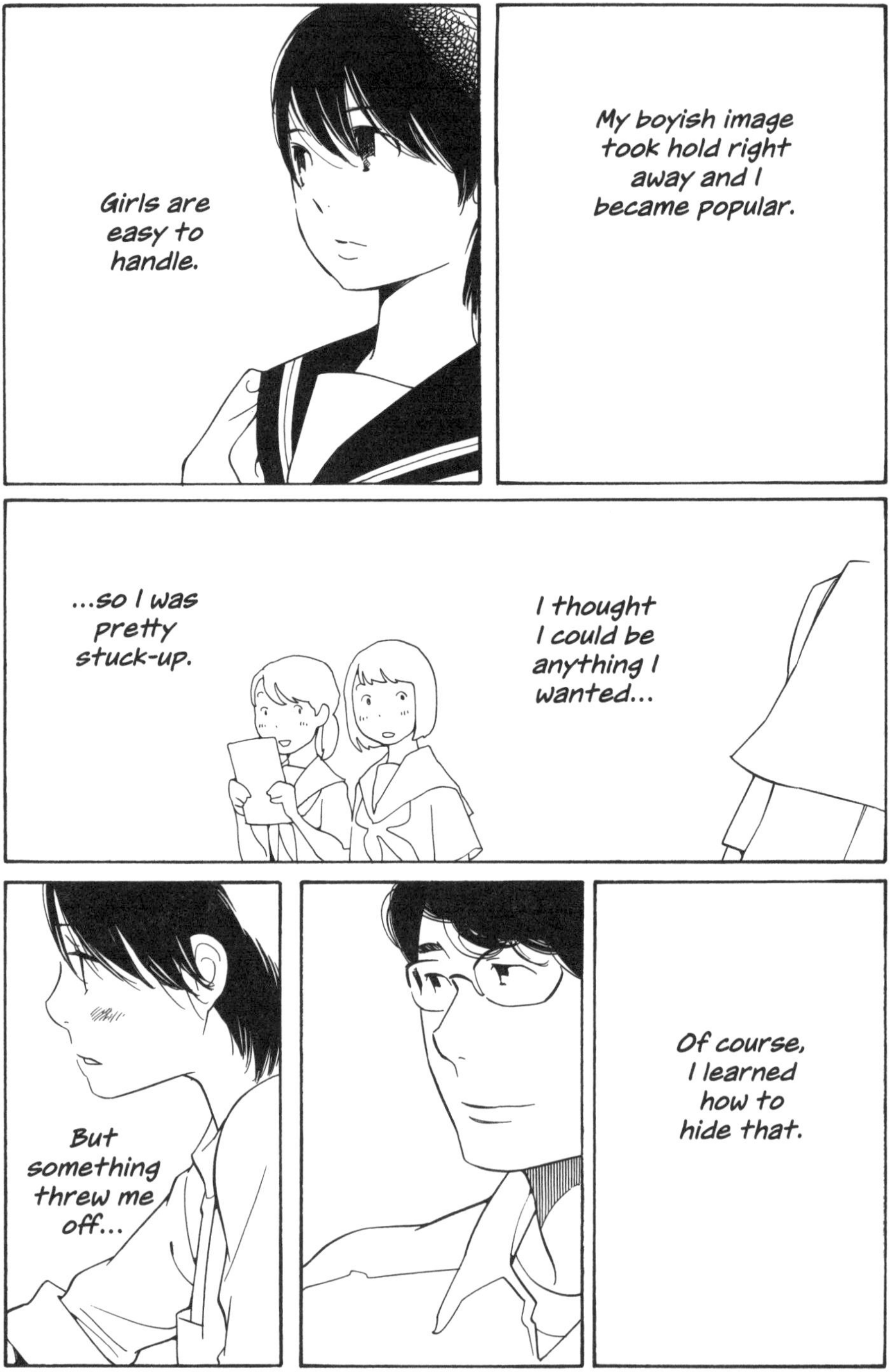
My boyish image took hold right away and I became popular.
Girls are easy to handle.
I thought I could be anything I wanted...
...so I was pretty stuck-up.
Of course, I learned how to hide that.
But something threw me off...

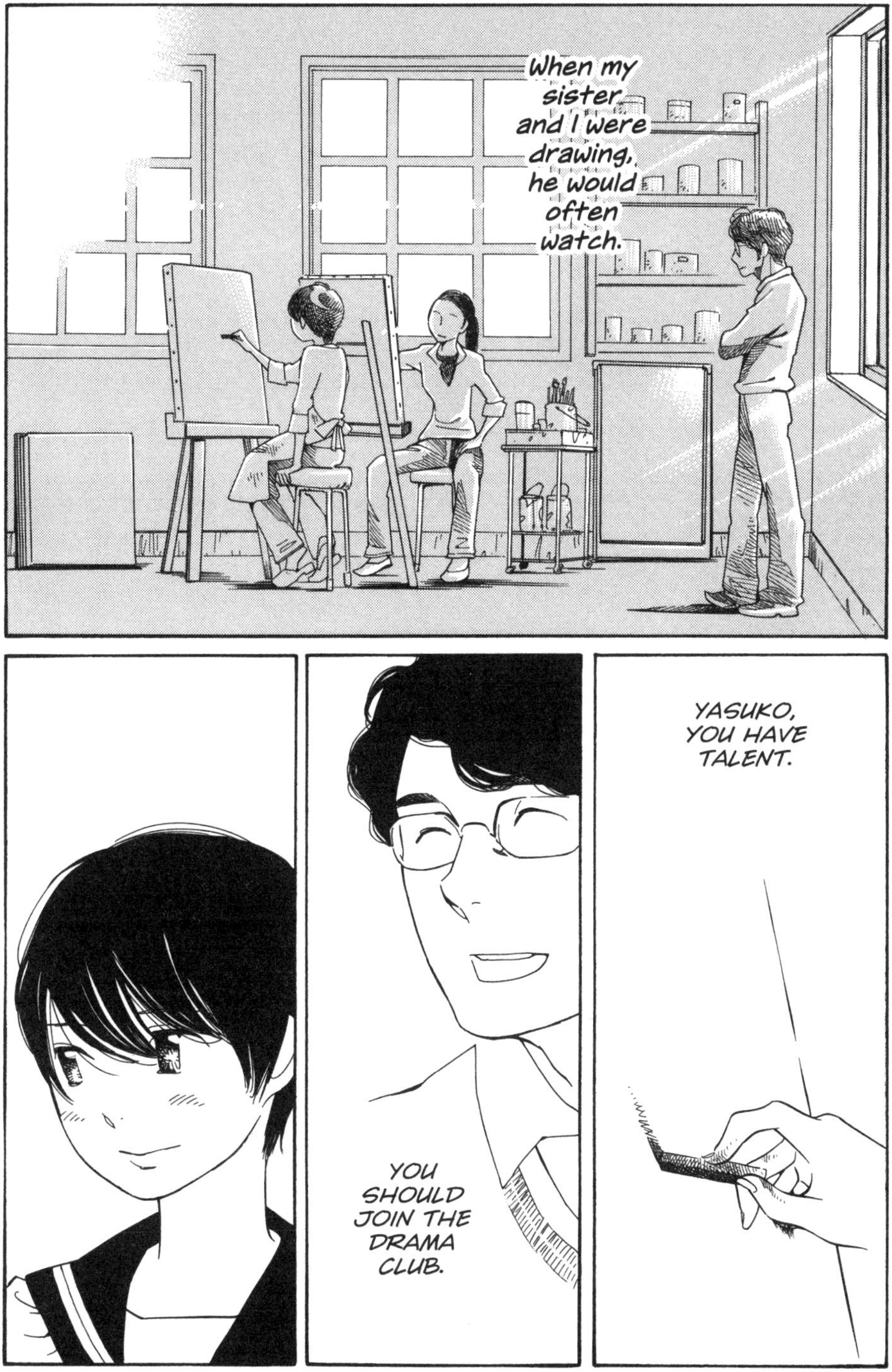
When my sister and I were drawing, he would often watch.
YASUKO, YOU HAVE TALENT.
YOU SHOULD JOIN THE DRAMA CLUB.

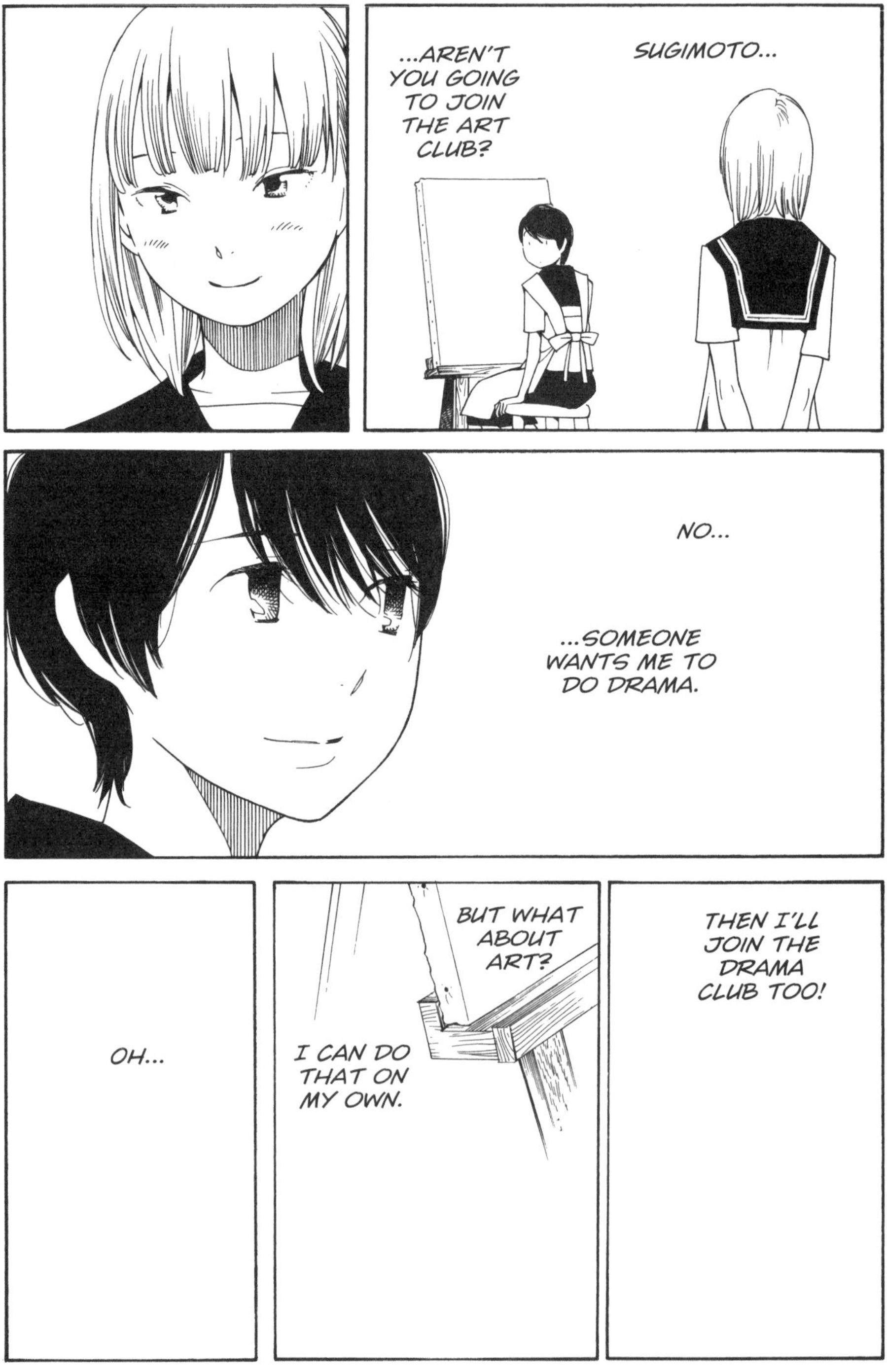
SUGIMOTO...
...AREN'T YOU GOING TO JOIN THE ART CLUB?
NO...
...SOMEONE WANTS ME TO DO DRAMA.
THEN I'LL JOIN THE DRAMA CLUB TOO!
BUT WHAT ABOUT ART?
I CAN DO THAT ON MY OWN.
OH...

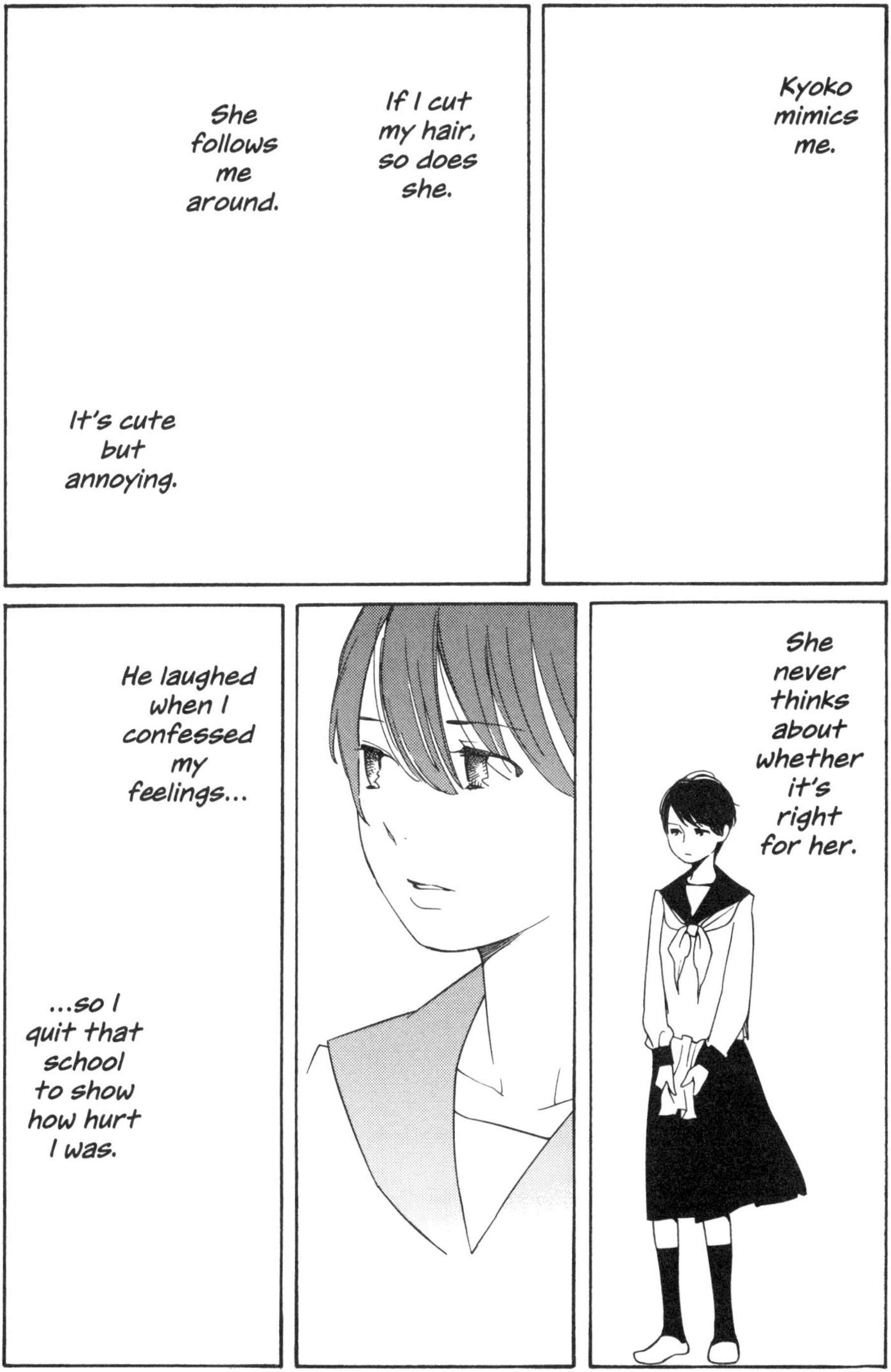
Kyoko mimics me.
If I cut my hair, so does she.
She follows me around.
It's cute but annoying.
She never thinks about whether it's right for her.
He laughed when I confessed my feelings...
...so I quit that school to show how hurt I was.

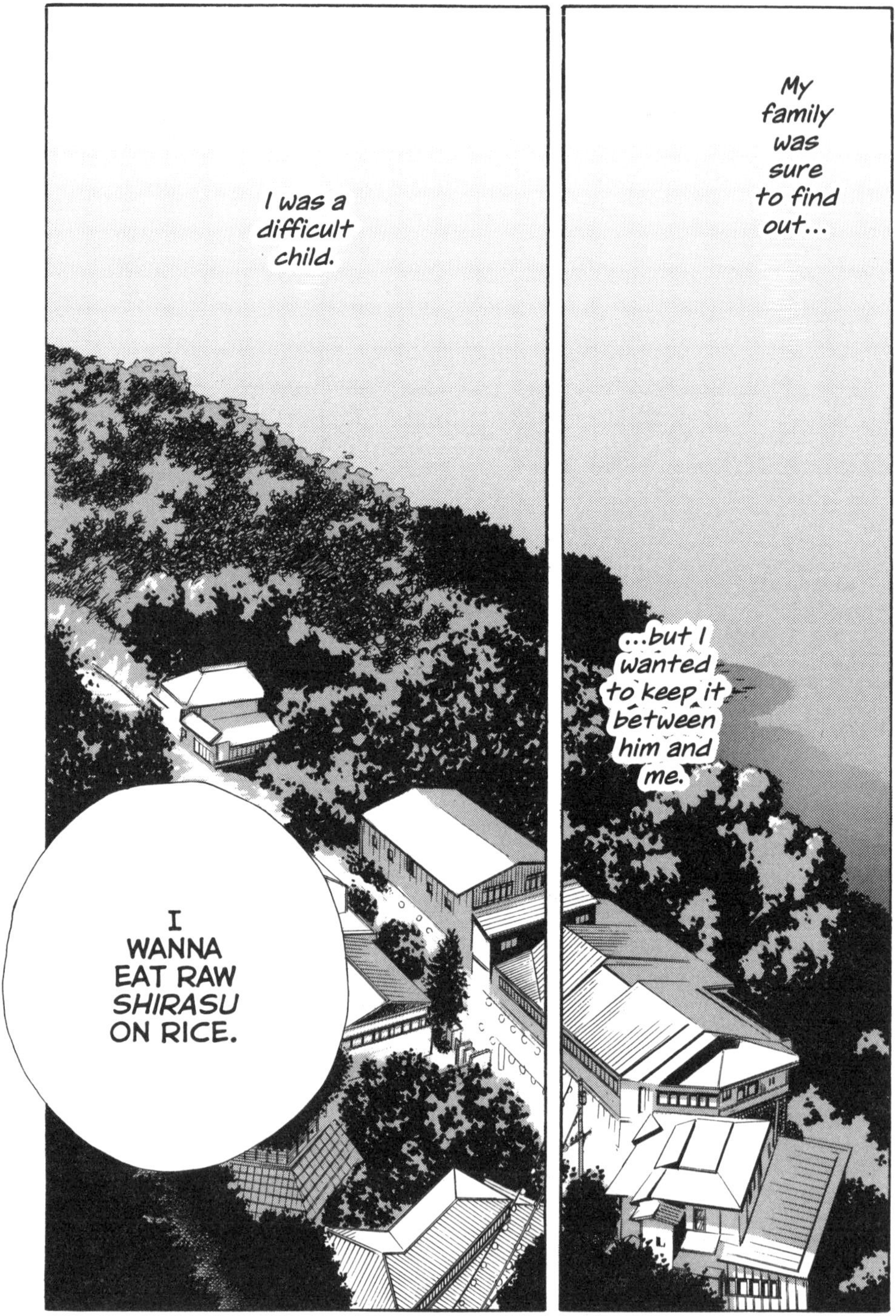
My family was sure to find out...
...but I wanted to keep it between him and me.
I was a difficult child.
I WANNA EAT RAW SHIRASU ON RICE.

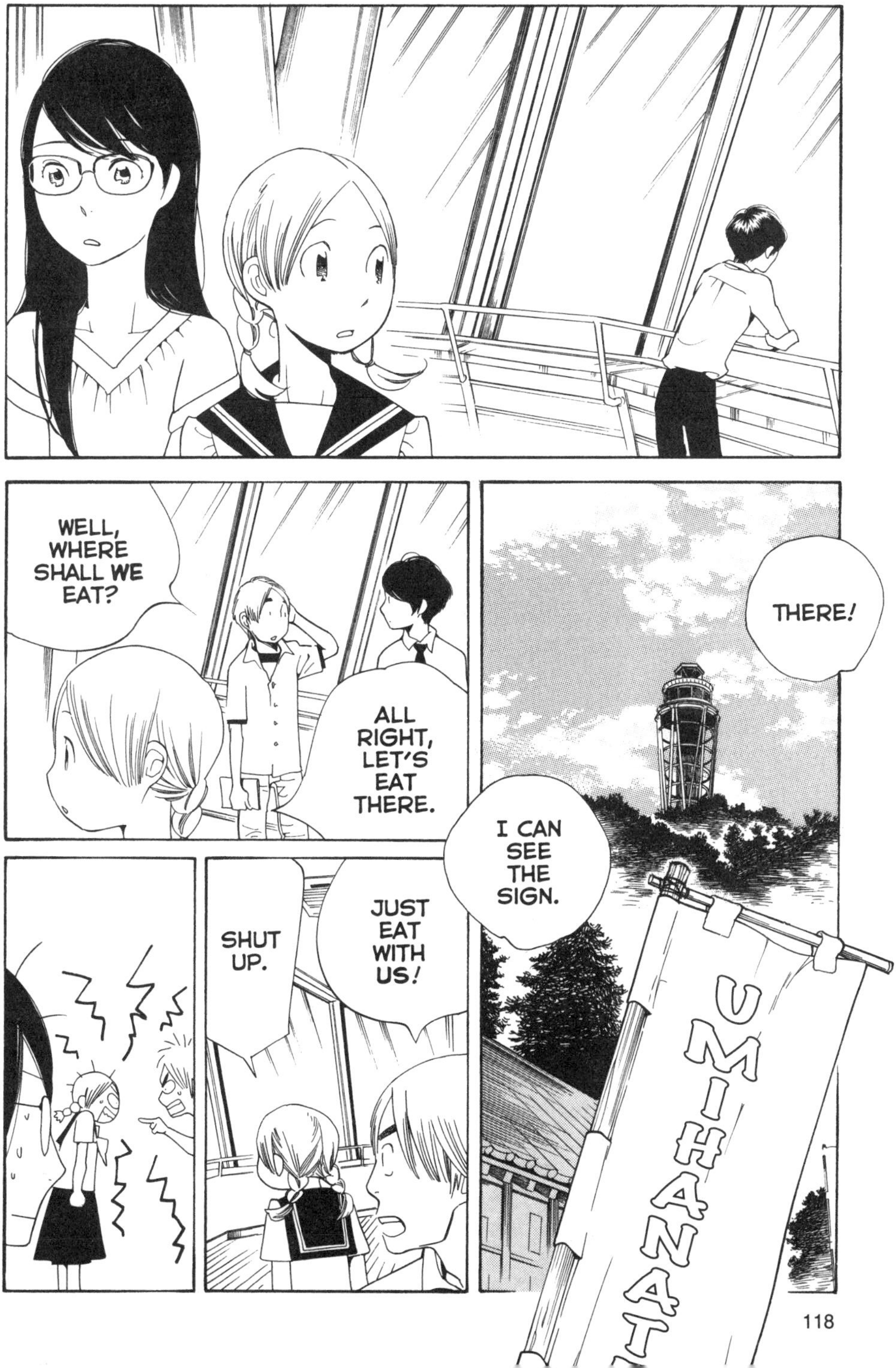
THERE!
I CAN SEE THE SIGN.
UMIHANAT
WELL, WHERE SHALL WE EAT?
ALL RIGHT, LET'S EAT THERE.
JUST EAT WITH US!
SHUT UP.

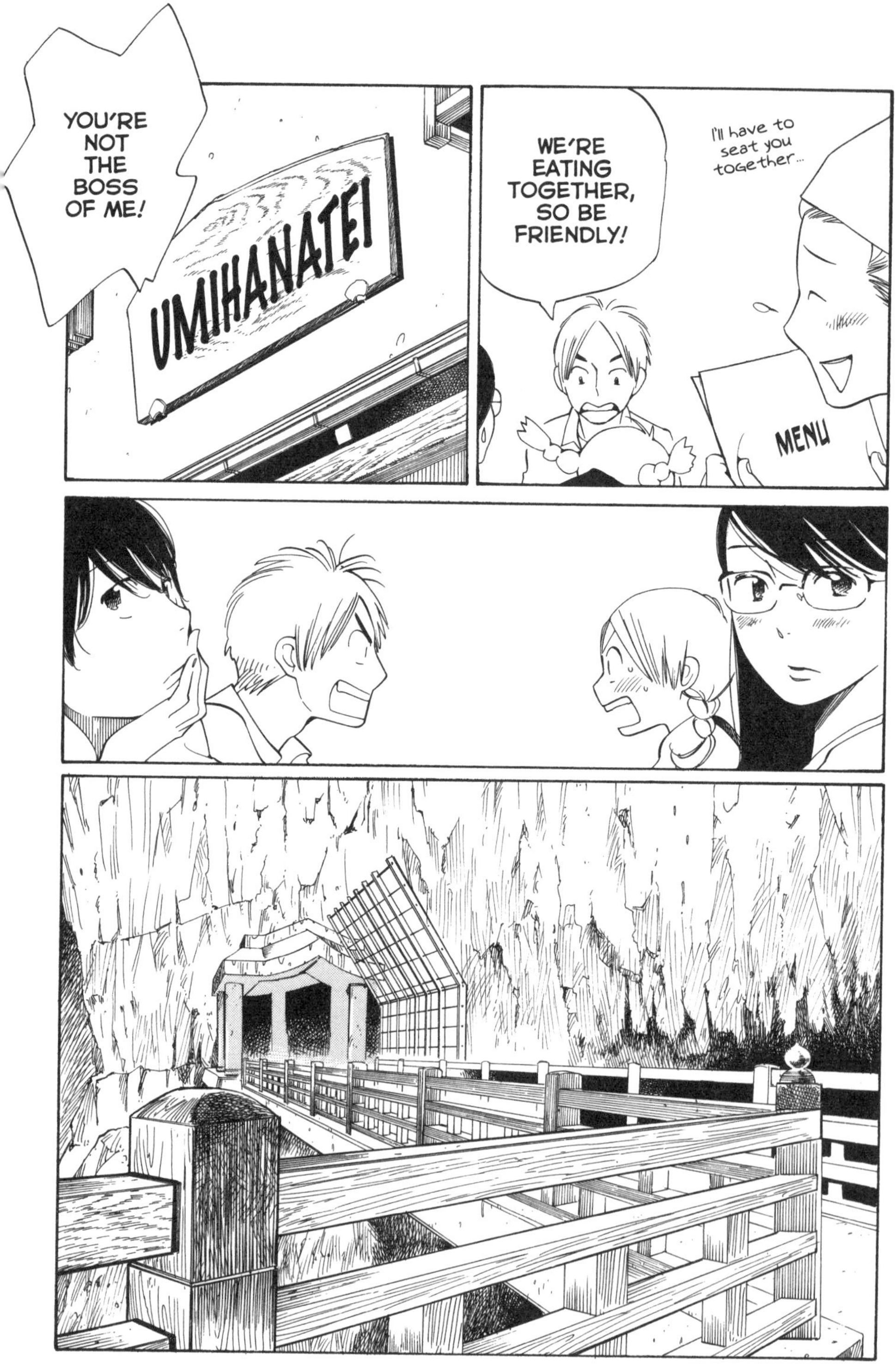
I'll have to seat you together...
WE'RE EATING TOGETHER, SO BE FRIENDLY!
MENU
YOU'RE NOT THE BOSS OF ME!
UMIHANATEI

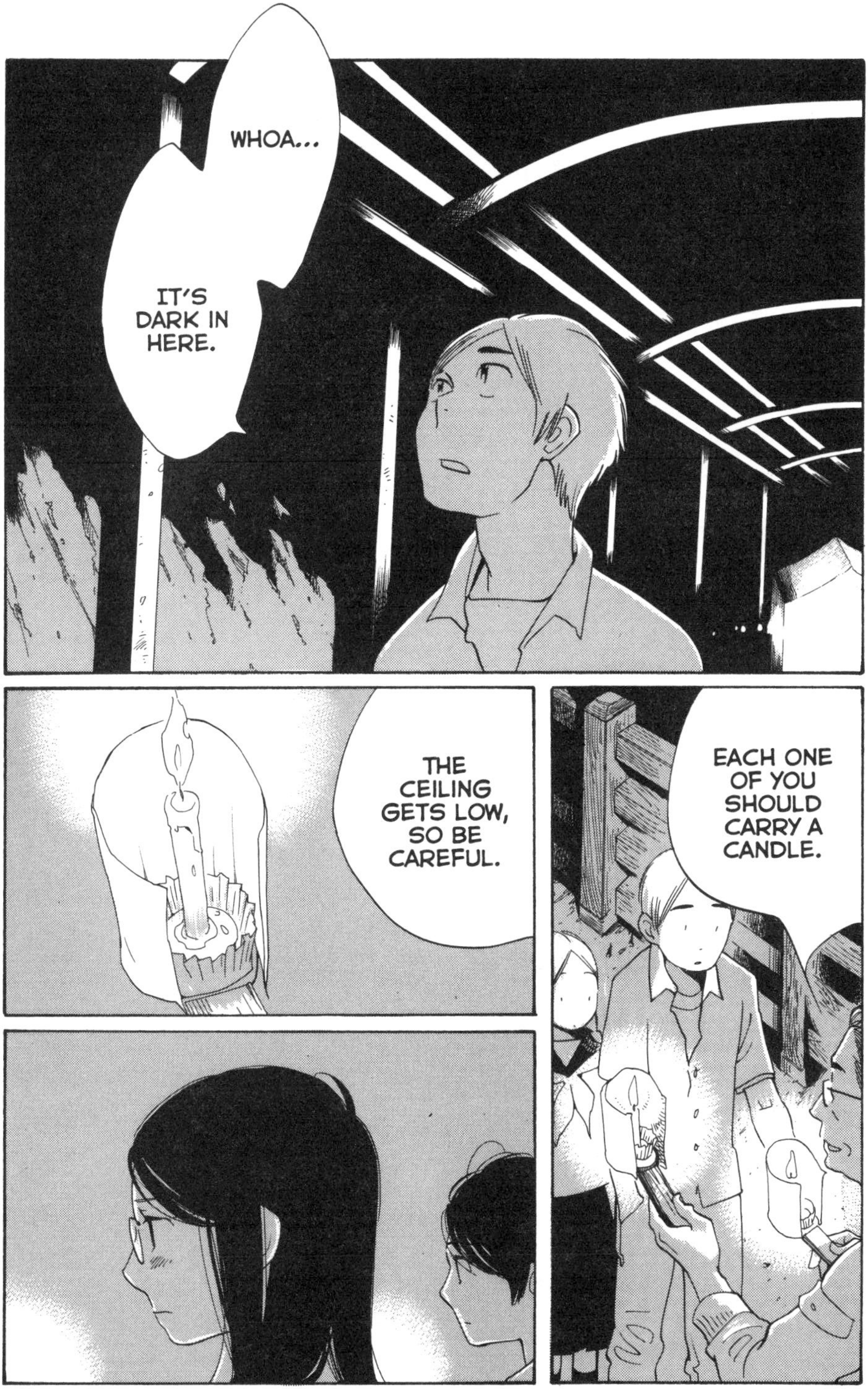
WHOA...
IT'S DARK IN HERE.
EACH ONE OF YOU SHOULD CARRY A CANDLE.
THE CEILING GETS LOW, SO BE CAREFUL.

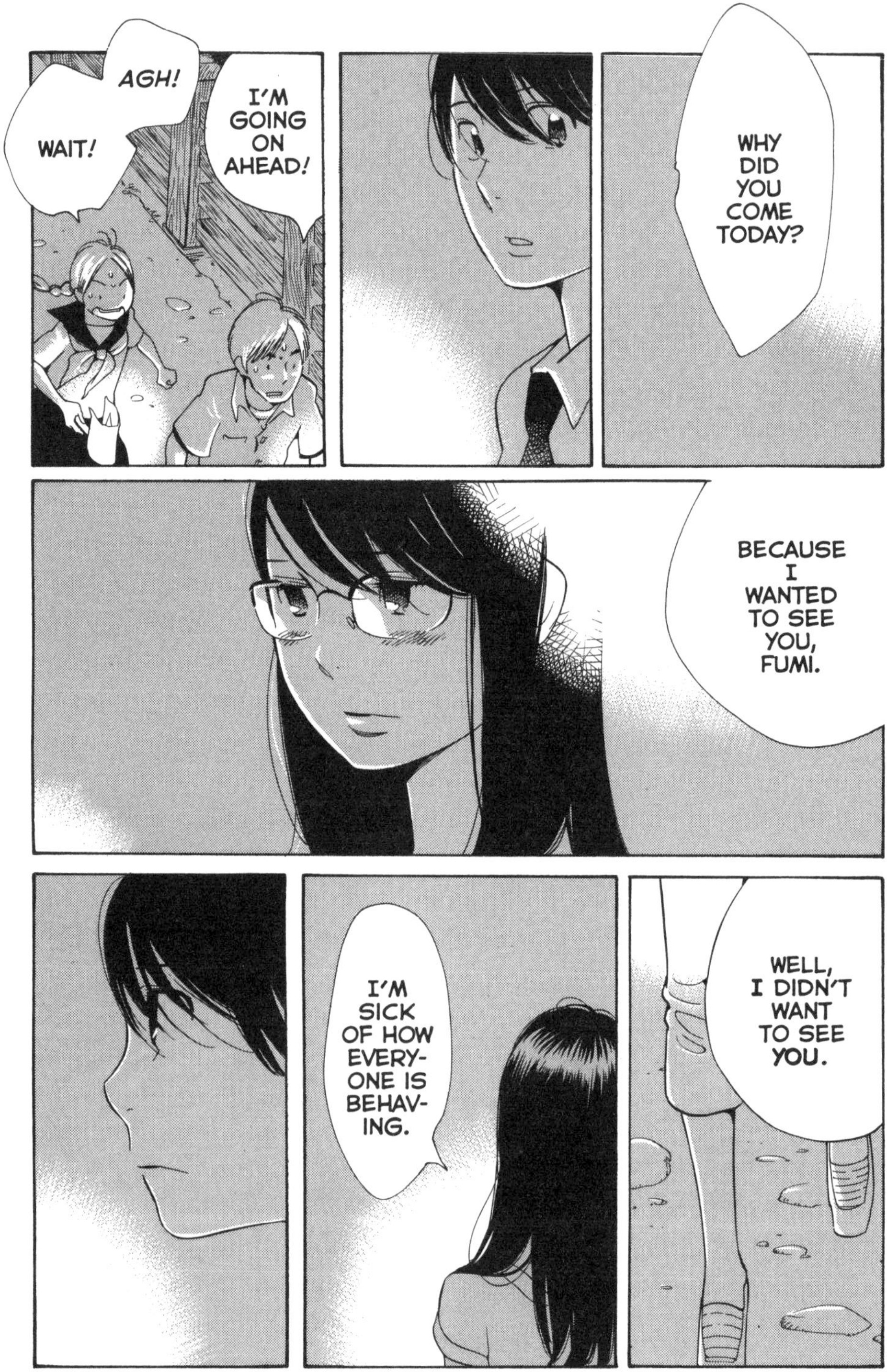
WHY DID YOU COME TODAY?
I'M GOING ON AHEAD!
AGH! WAIT!
BECAUSE I WANTED TO SEE YOU, FUMI.
WELL, I DIDN'T WANT TO SEE YOU.
I'M SICK OF HOW EVERY-ONE IS BEHAV-ING.

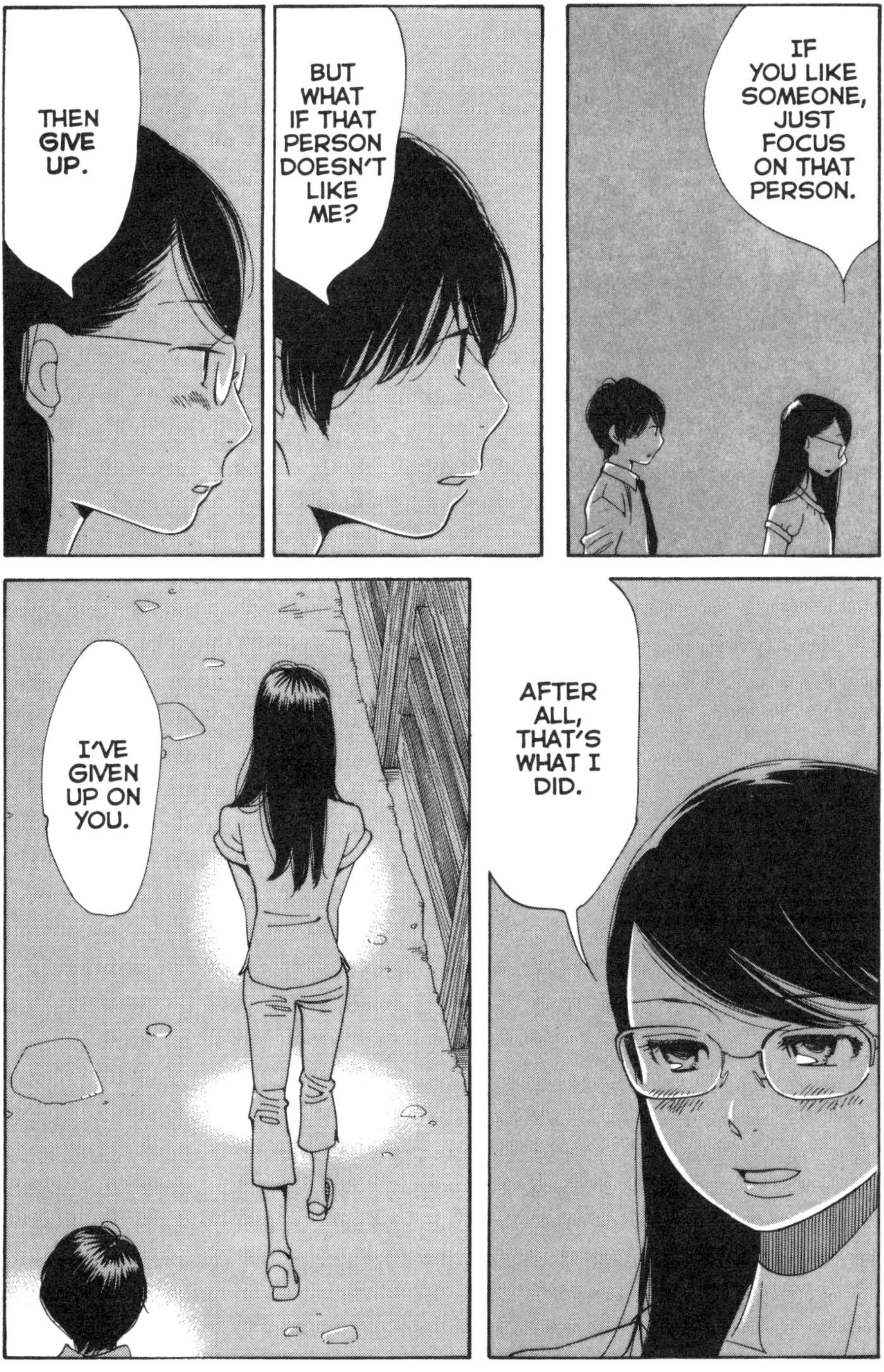
IF YOU LIKE SOMEONE, JUST FOCUS ON THAT PERSON.
BUT WHAT IF THAT PERSON DOESN'T LIKE ME?
THEN GIVE UP.
AFTER ALL, THAT'S WHAT I DID.
I'VE GIVEN UP ON YOU.

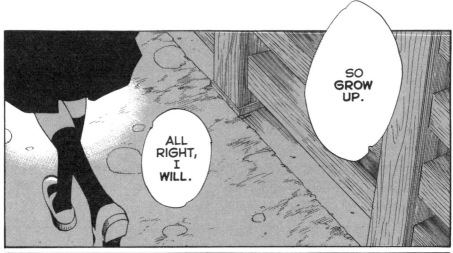

SO GROW UP.

ALL RIGHT, I WILL.

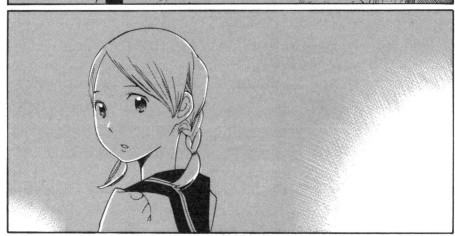

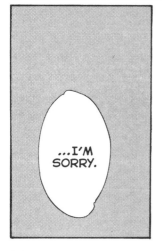

...I'M SORRY.

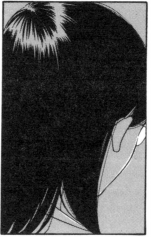

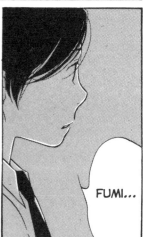

FUMI...

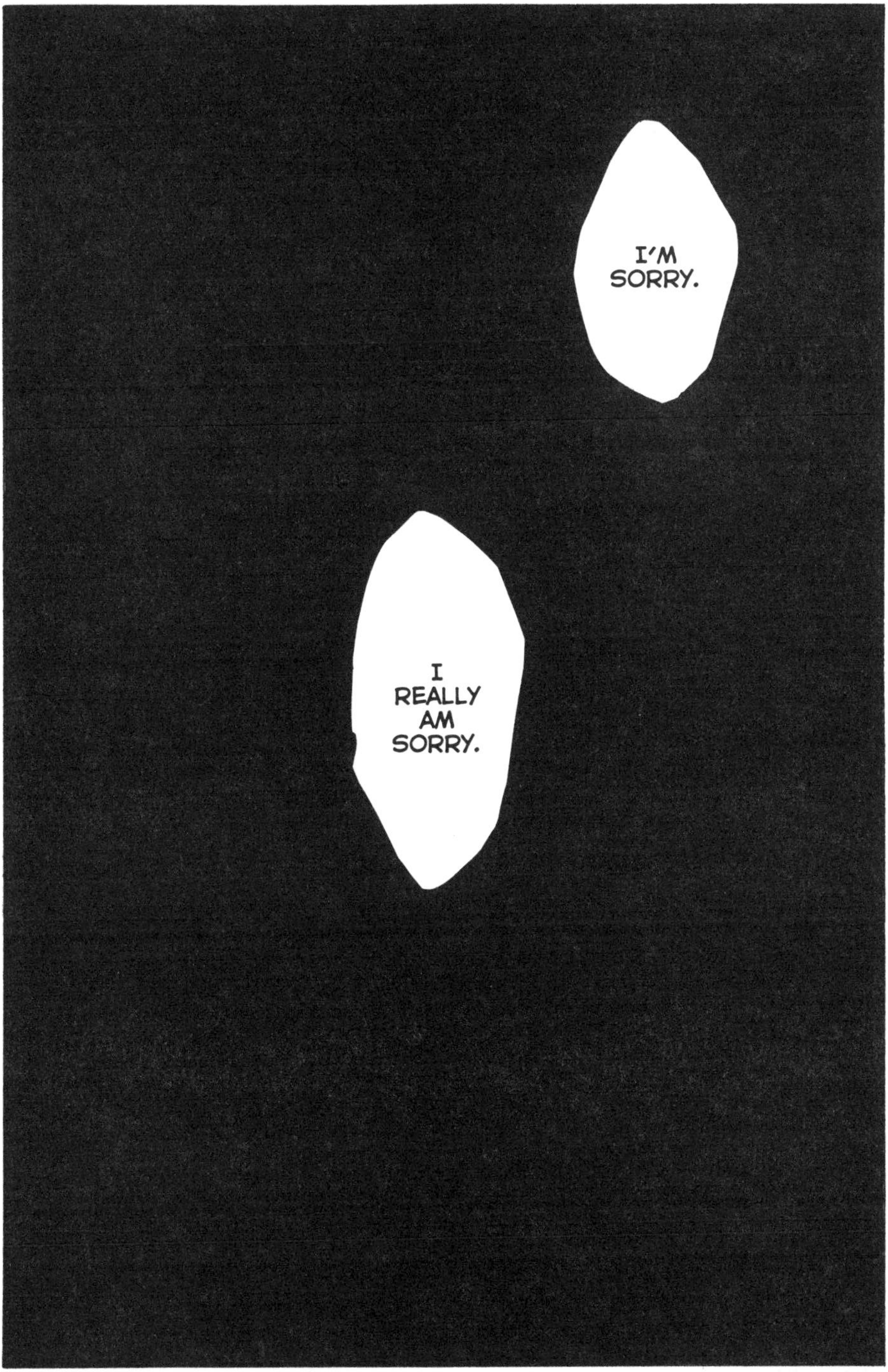
I'M SORRY.
I REALLY AM SORRY.

Sweet Blue Flowers

#18 Winter Fireworks

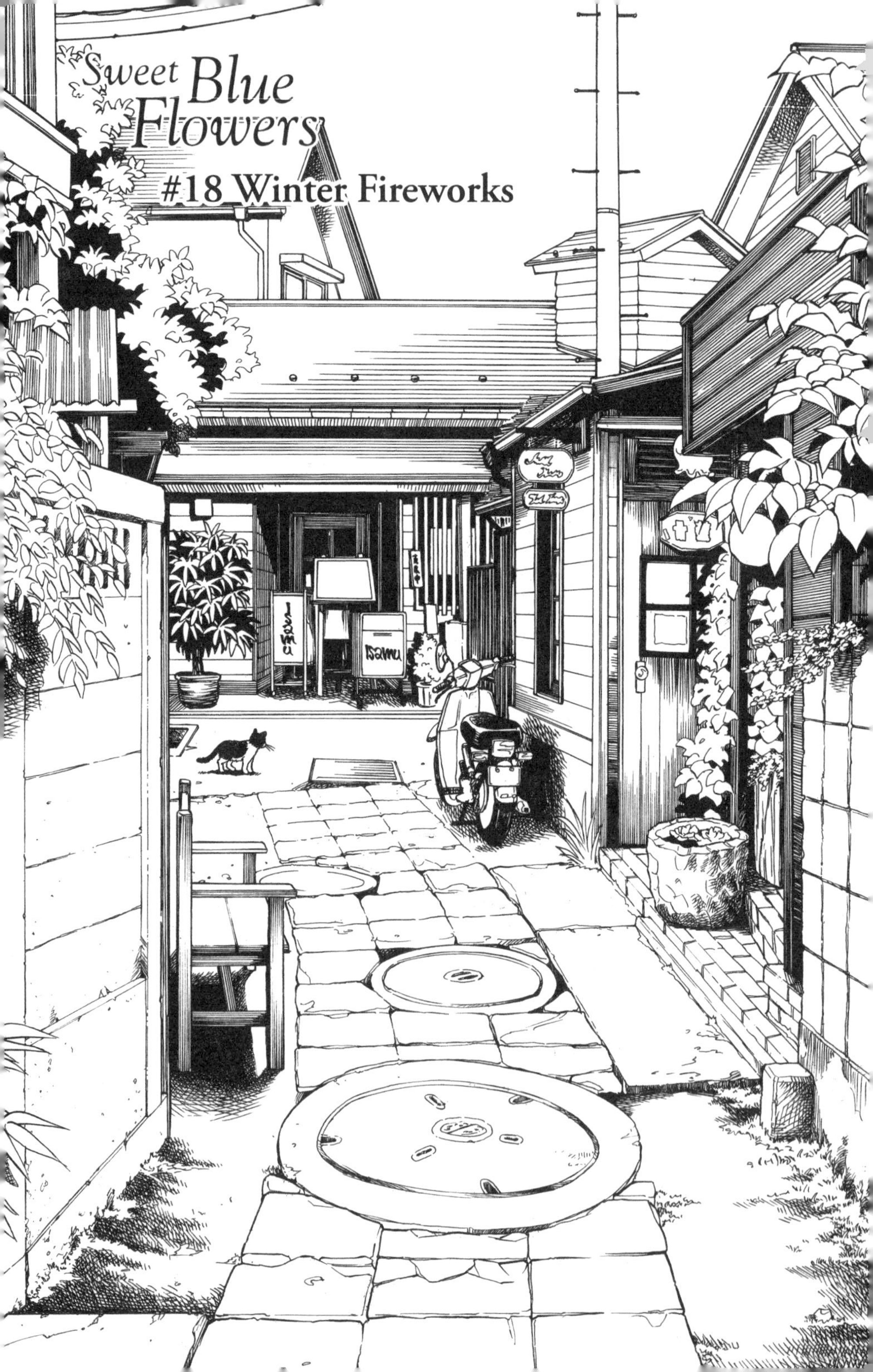
isamu
Isamu

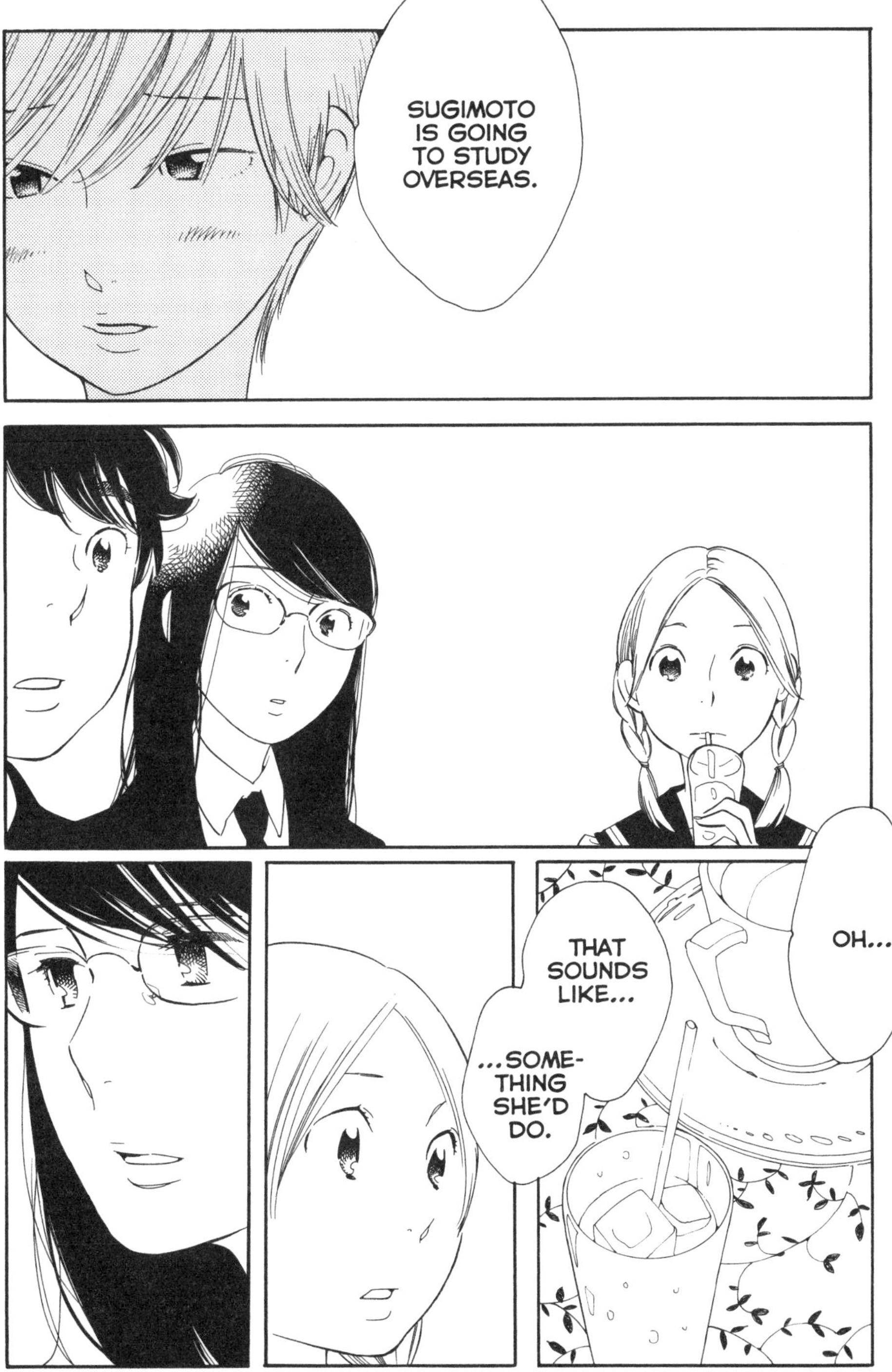
SUGIMOTO IS GOING TO STUDY OVERSEAS.
OH...
THAT SOUNDS LIKE...
...SOME-THING SHE'D DO.

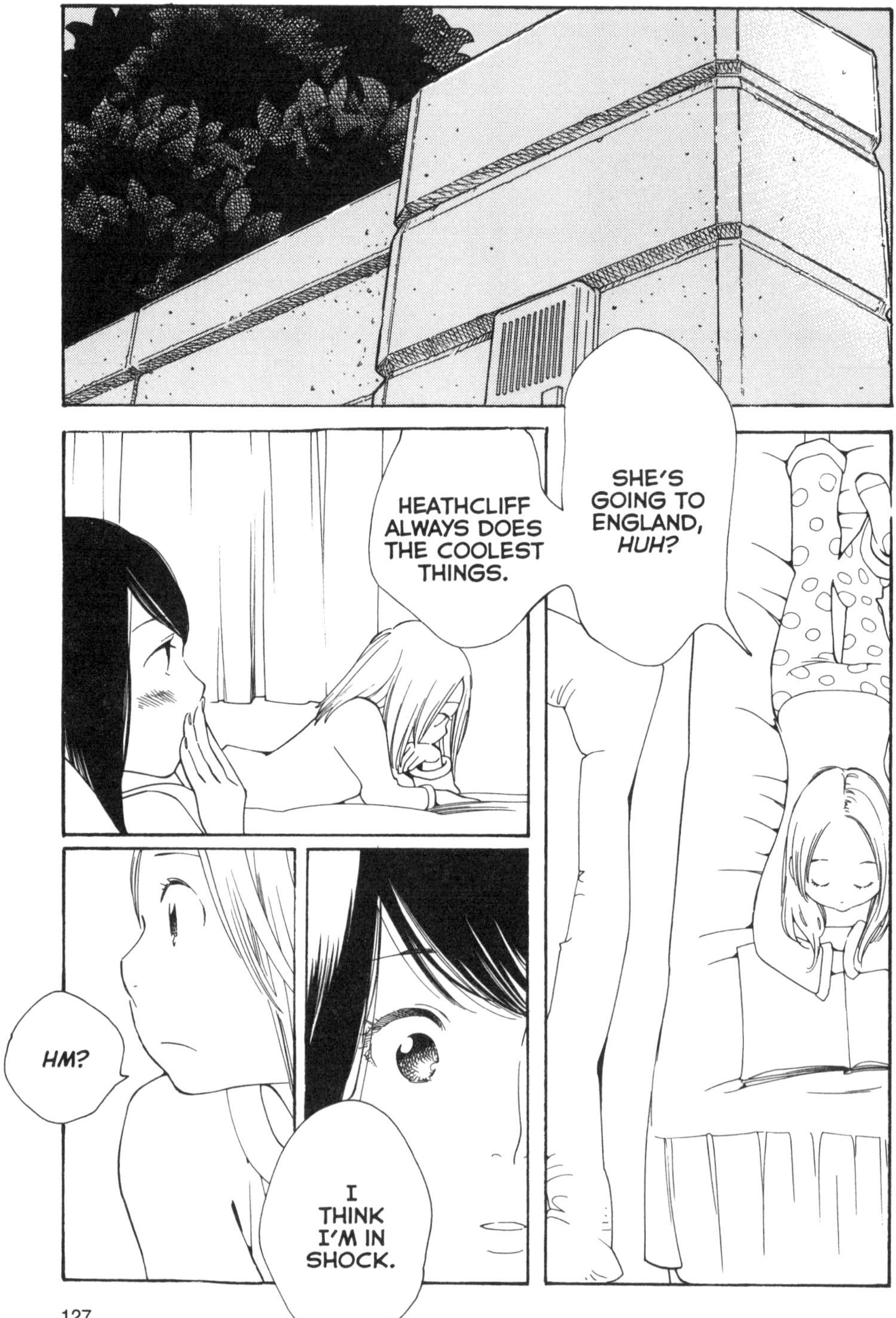
SHE'S GOING TO ENGLAND, *HUH?*
HEATHCLIFF ALWAYS DOES THE COOLEST THINGS.
I THINK I'M IN SHOCK.
HM?

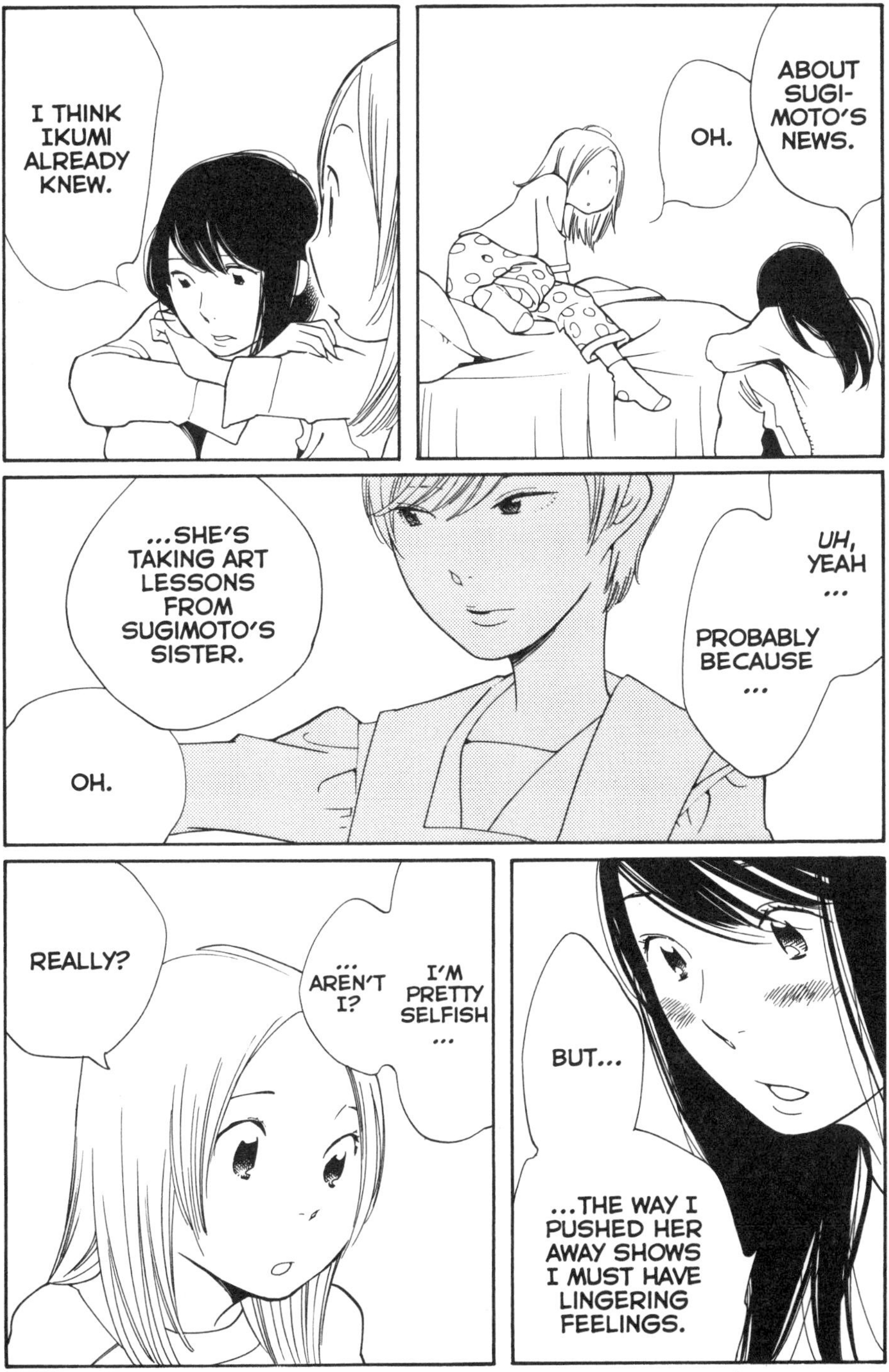
ABOUT SUGI-MOTO'S NEWS.
OH.
I THINK IKUMI ALREADY KNEW.
UH, YEAH ...
PROBABLY BECAUSE ...
...SHE'S TAKING ART LESSONS FROM SUGIMOTO'S SISTER.
OH.
BUT...
...THE WAY I PUSHED HER AWAY SHOWS I MUST HAVE LINGERING FEELINGS.
I'M PRETTY SELFISH ...
... AREN'T I?
REALLY?

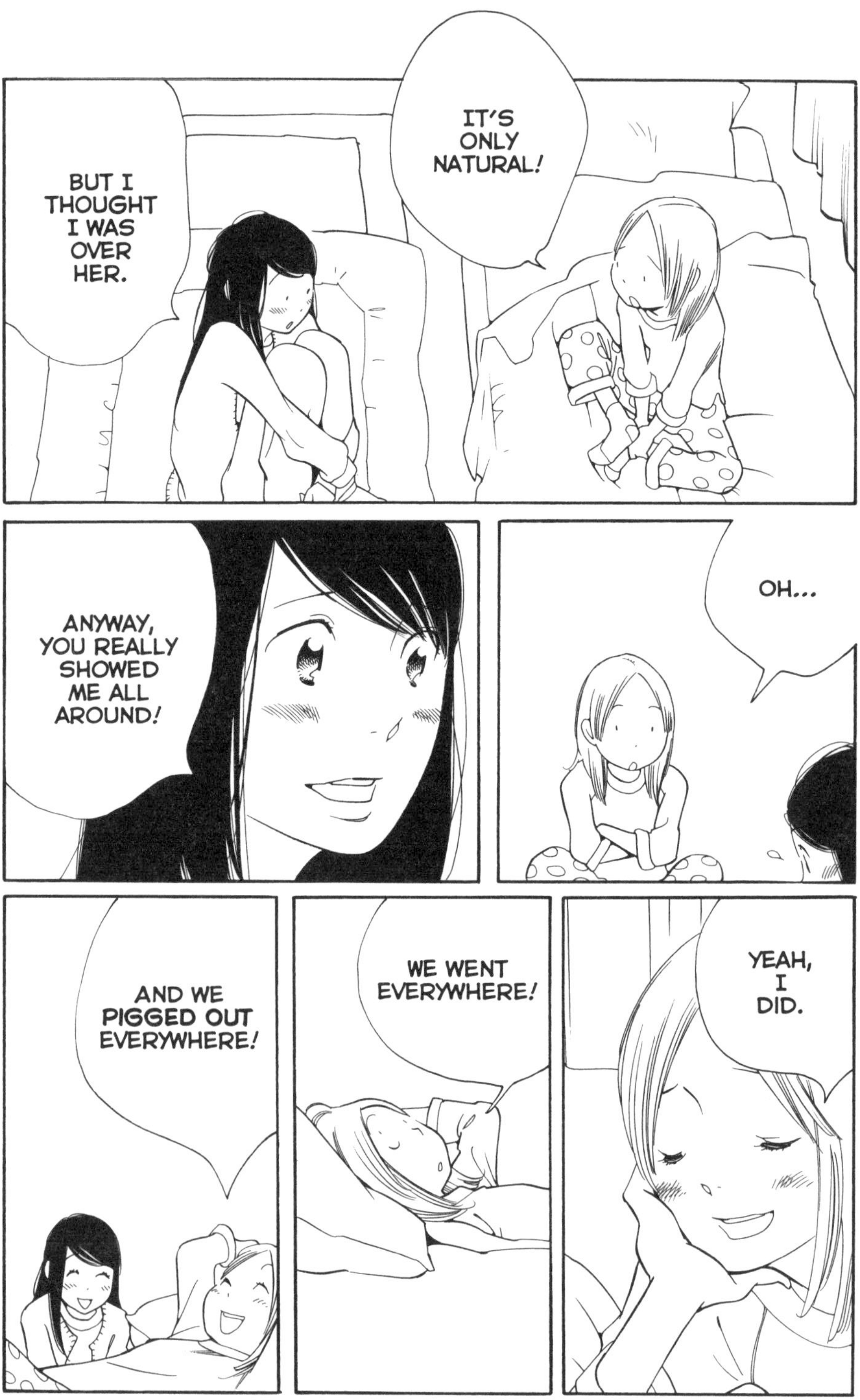
IT'S ONLY NATURAL!
BUT I THOUGHT I WAS OVER HER.
OH...
ANYWAY, YOU REALLY SHOWED ME ALL AROUND!
YEAH, I DID.
WE WENT EVERYWHERE!
AND WE PIGGED OUT EVERYWHERE!

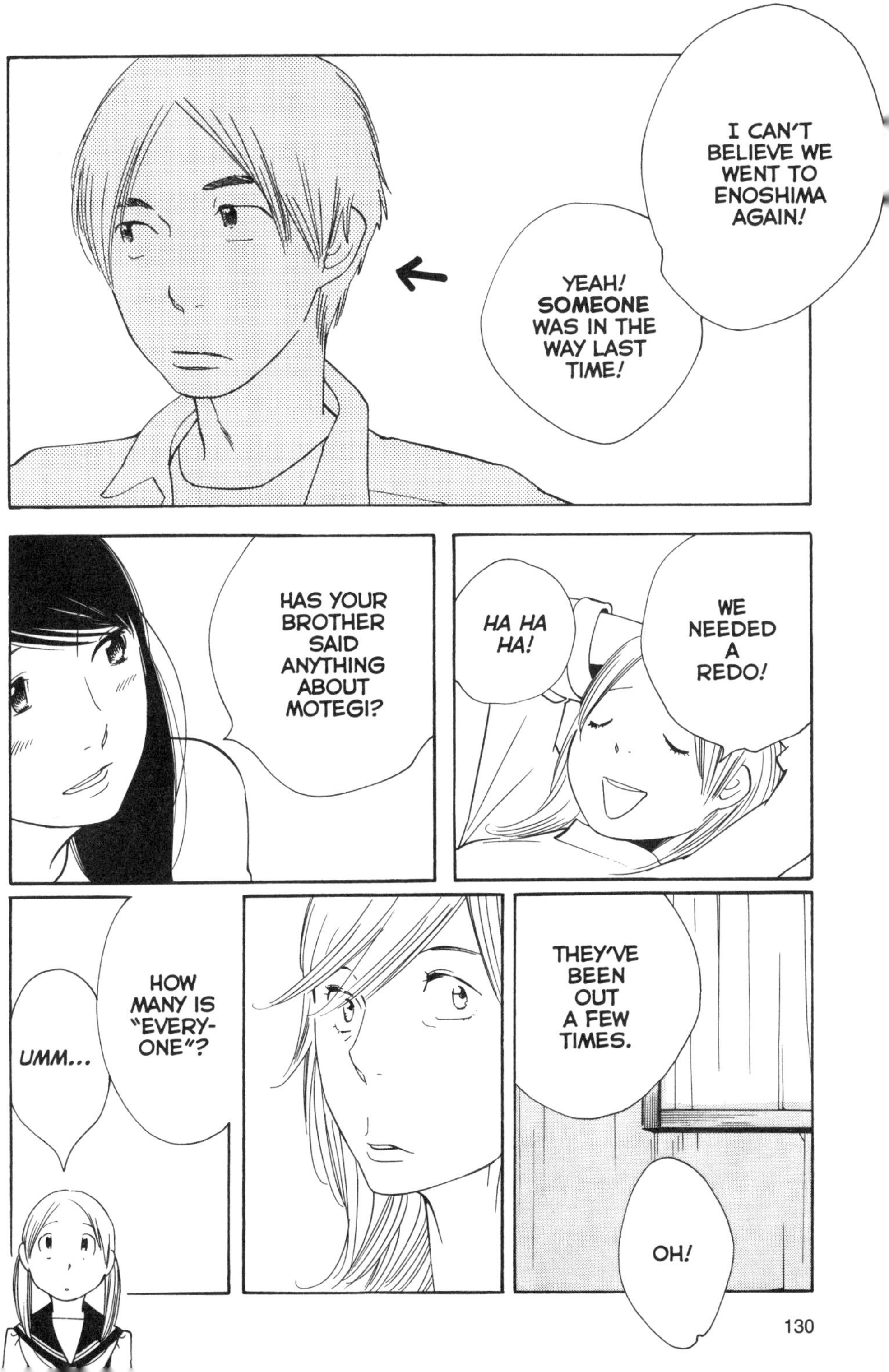
I CAN'T BELIEVE WE WENT TO ENOSHIMA AGAIN!
YEAH! SOMEONE WAS IN THE WAY LAST TIME!
WE NEEDED A REDO!
HA HA HA!
HAS YOUR BROTHER SAID ANYTHING ABOUT MOTEGI?
THEY'VE BEEN OUT A FEW TIMES.
OH!
HOW MANY IS "EVERY-ONE"?
UMM...

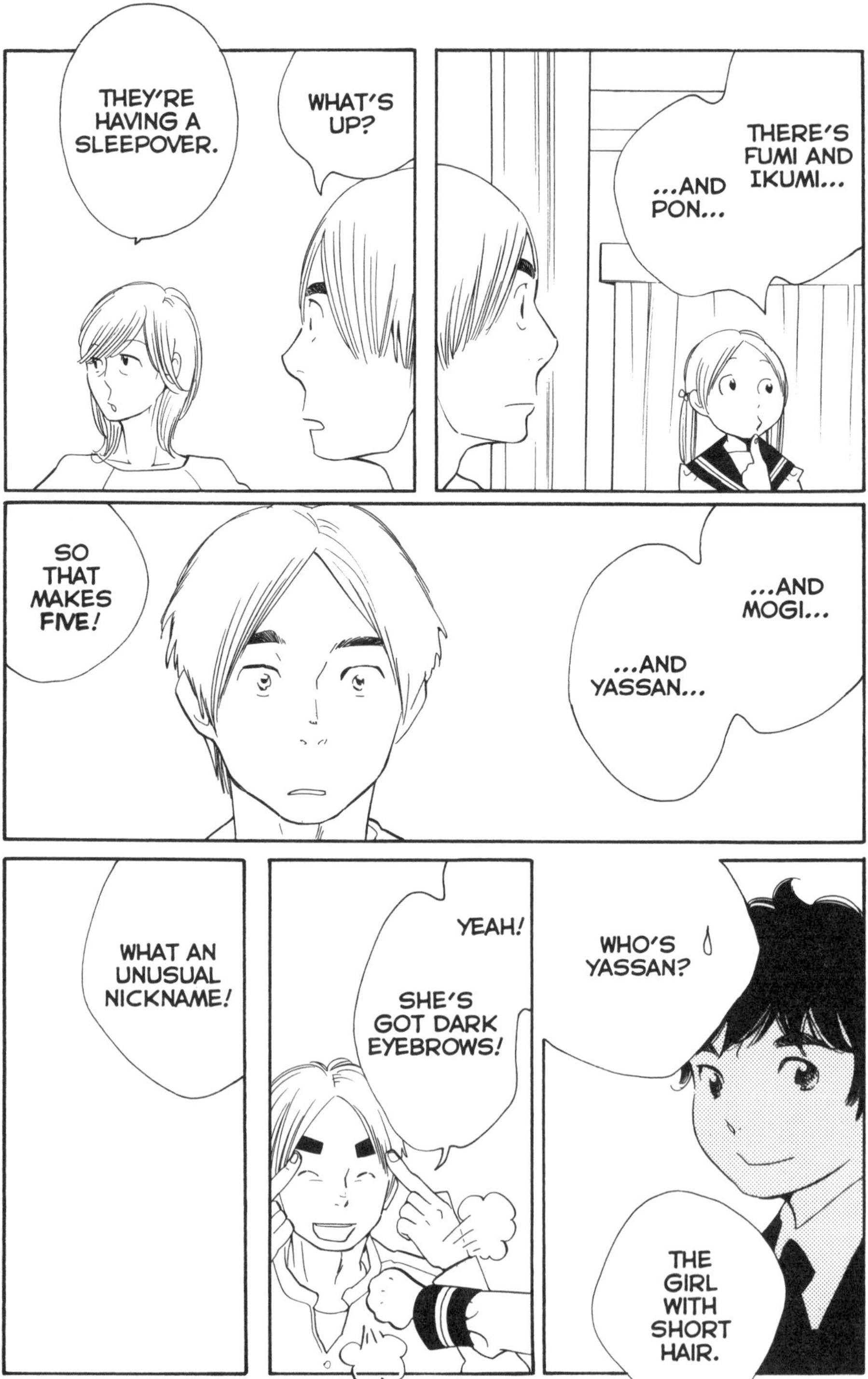
THERE'S FUMI AND IKUMI...
...AND PON...
WHAT'S UP?
THEY'RE HAVING A SLEEPOVER.
...AND MOGI...
...AND YASSAN...
SO THAT MAKES FIVE!
WHO'S YASSAN?
THE GIRL WITH SHORT HAIR.
YEAH!
SHE'S GOT DARK EYEBROWS!
WHAT AN UNUSUAL NICKNAME!

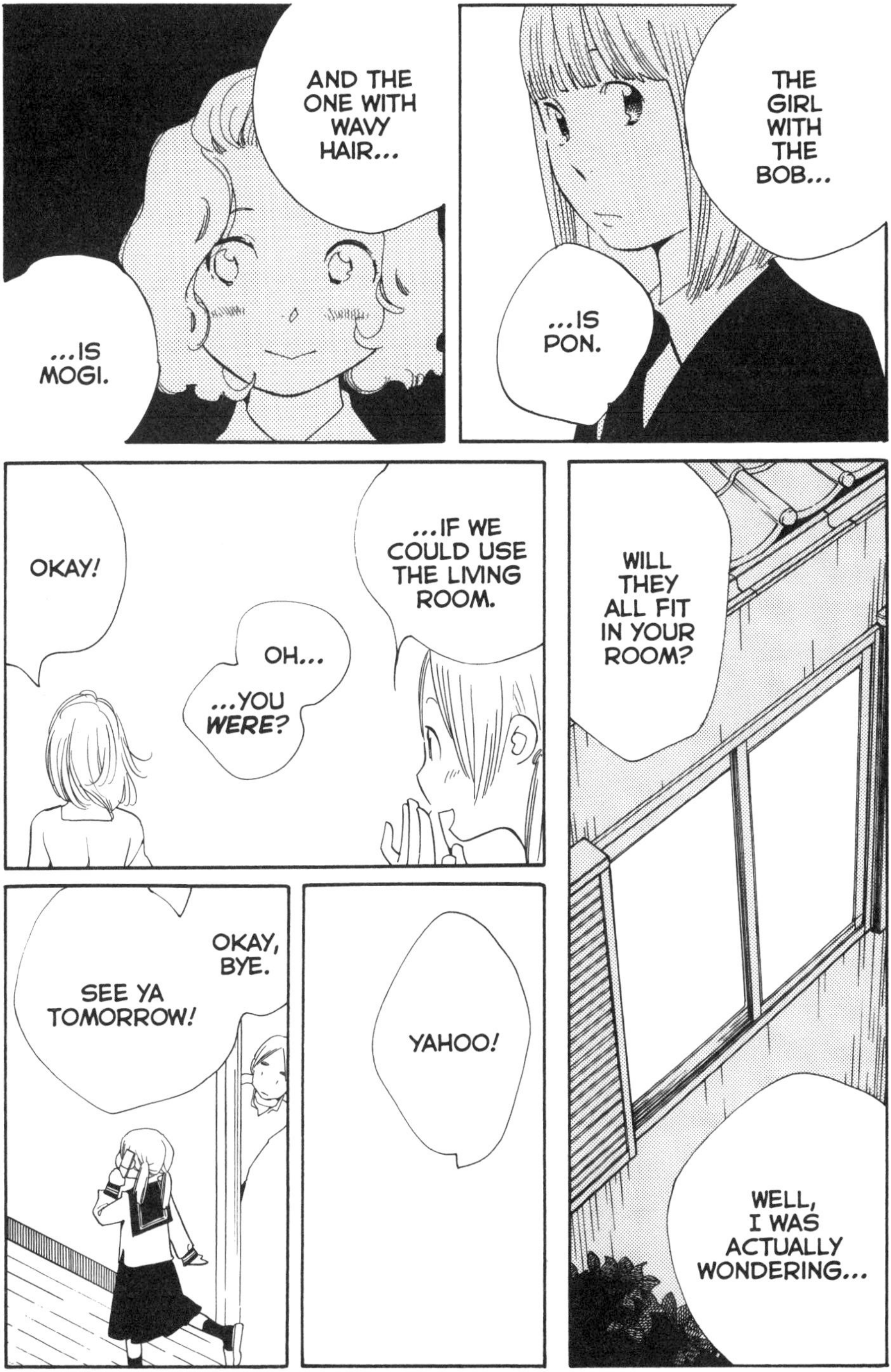
THE GIRL WITH THE BOB...
...IS PON.
AND THE ONE WITH WAVY HAIR...
...IS MOGI.
WILL THEY ALL FIT IN YOUR ROOM?
WELL, I WAS ACTUALLY WONDERING...
...IF WE COULD USE THE LIVING ROOM.
OH...
...YOU *WERE*?
OKAY!
YAHOO!
OKAY, BYE.
SEE YA TOMORROW!

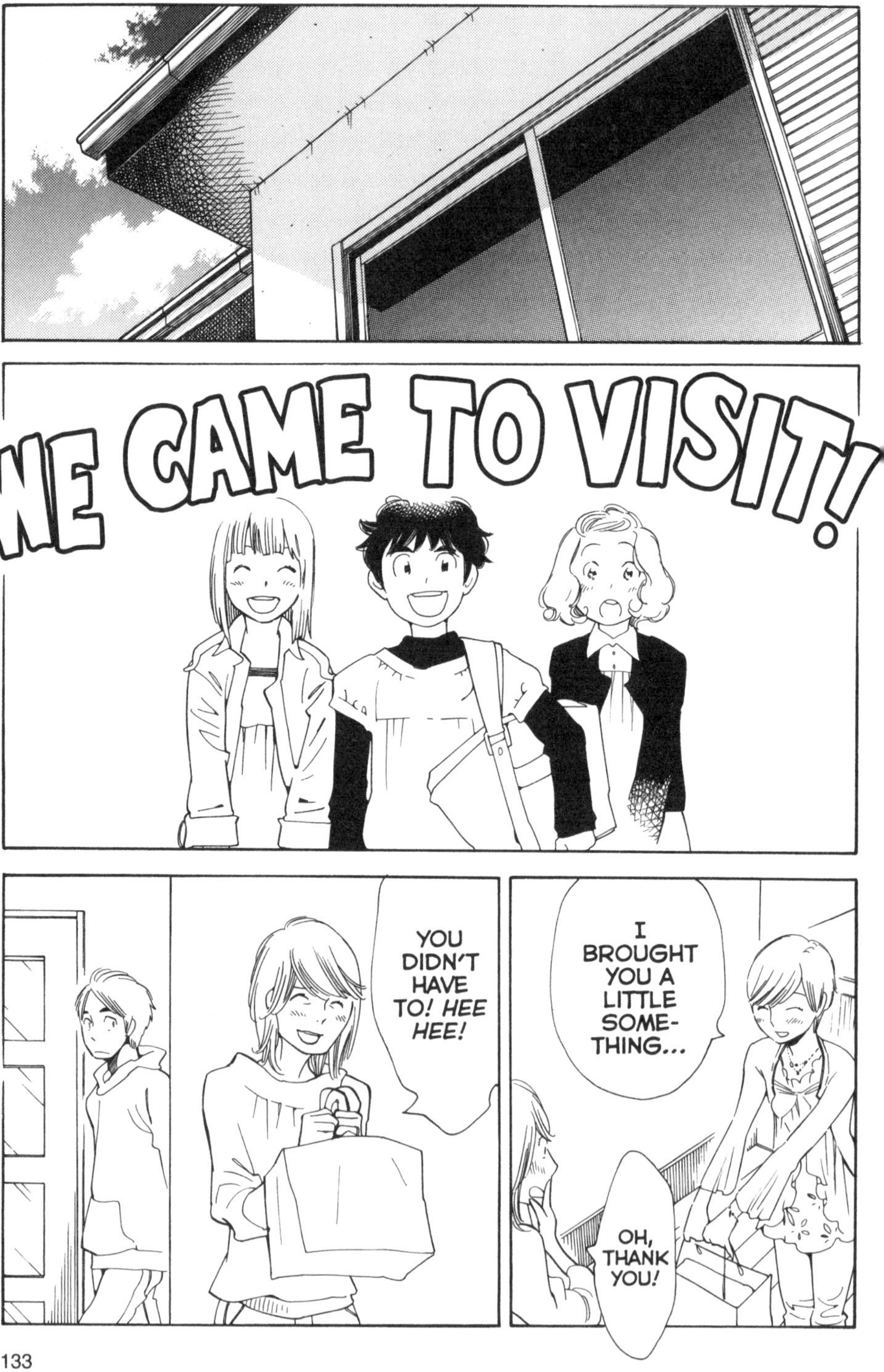
WE CAME TO VISIT!
I BROUGHT YOU A LITTLE SOME-THING...
OH, THANK YOU!
YOU DIDN'T HAVE TO! *HEE HEE!*

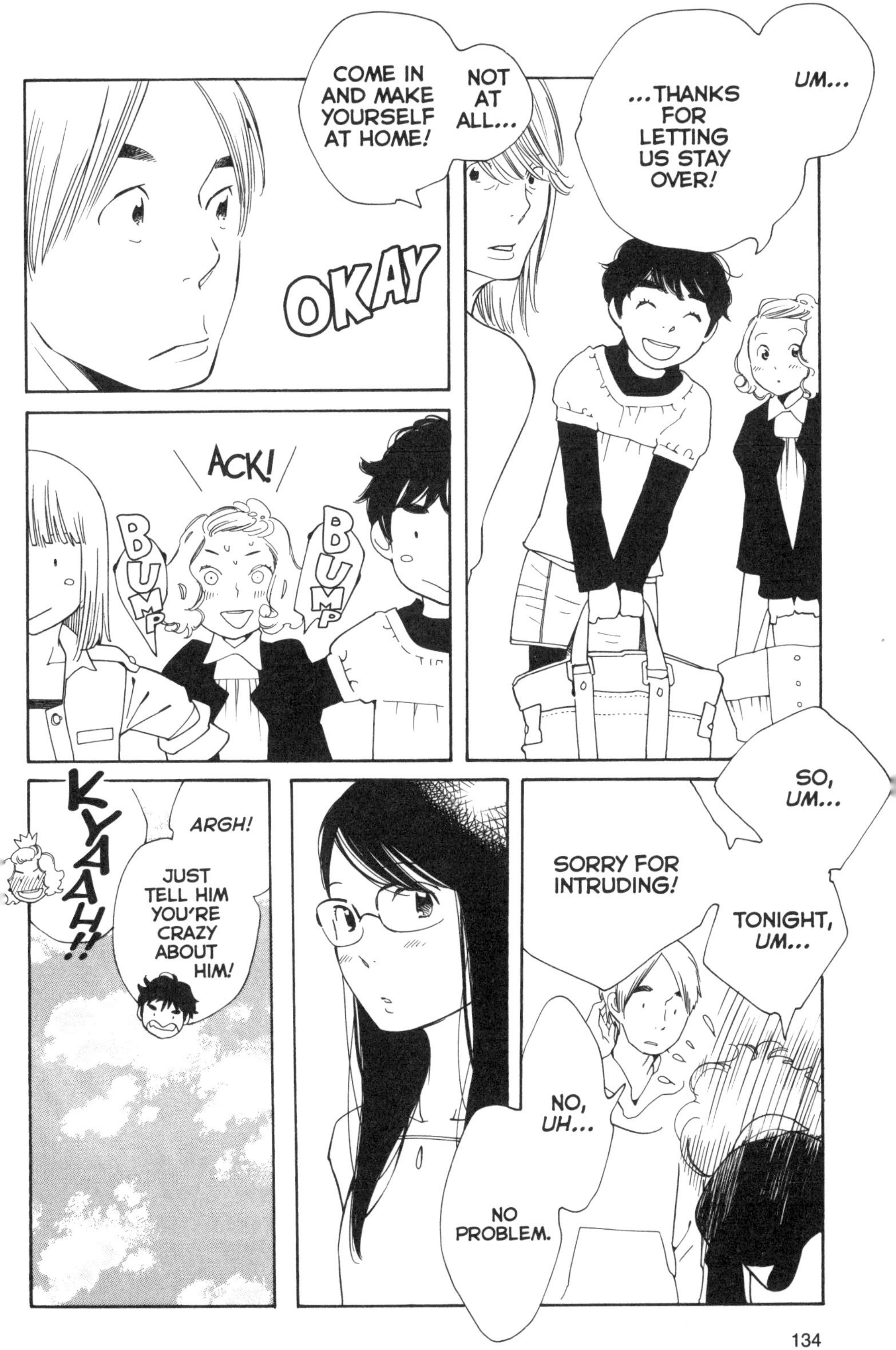
UM...
...THANKS FOR LETTING US STAY OVER!
NOT AT ALL...
COME IN AND MAKE YOURSELF AT HOME!
OKAY
ACK!
BUMP
BUMP
SO, UM...
SORRY FOR INTRUDING!
TONIGHT, UM...
NO, UH...
NO PROBLEM.
KYAAH!!
ARGH!
JUST TELL HIM YOU'RE CRAZY ABOUT HIM!

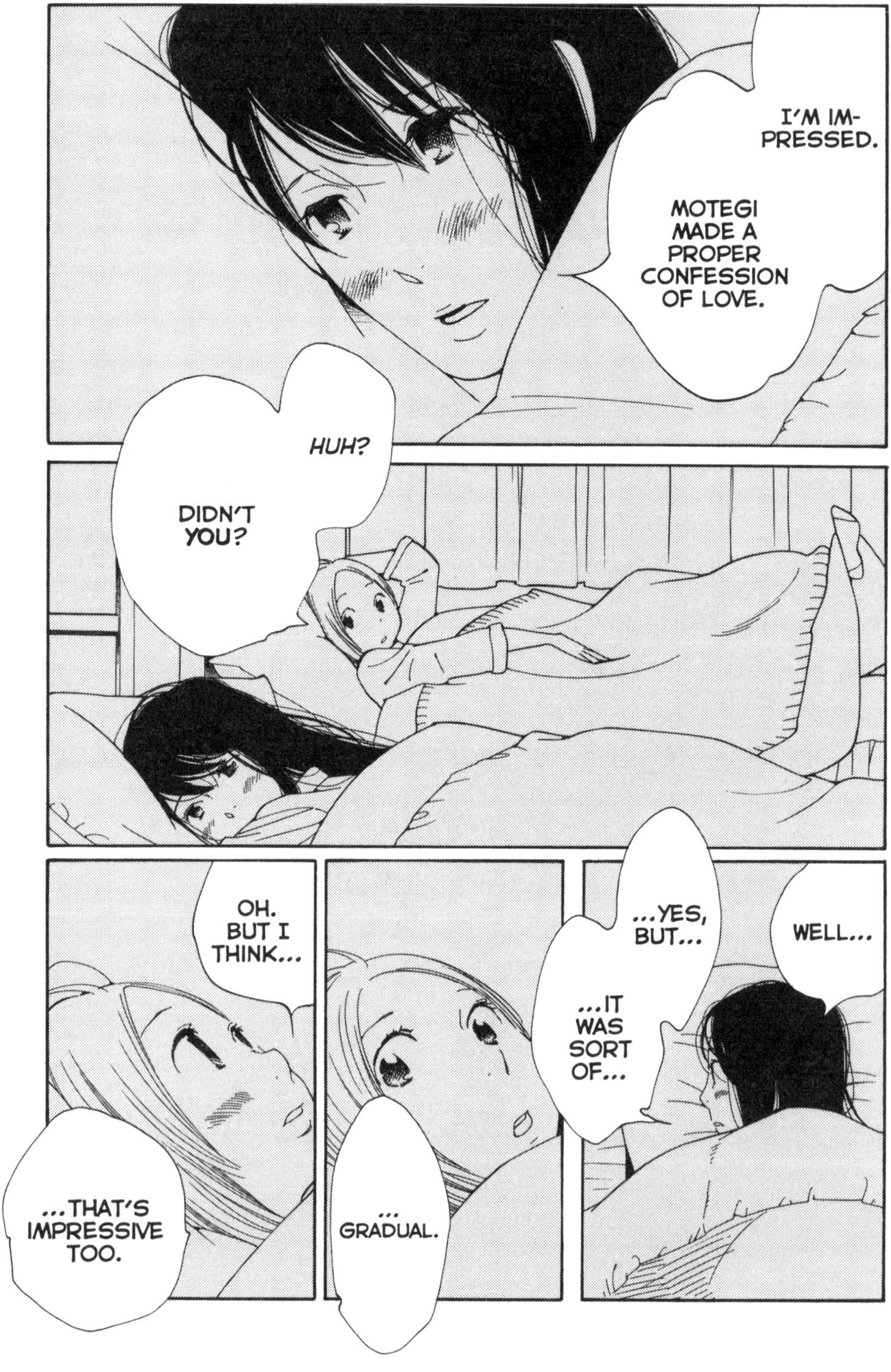
I'M IM-PRESSED.
MOTEGI MADE A PROPER CONFESSION OF LOVE.
HUH?
DIDN'T YOU?
WELL...
...YES, BUT...
...IT WAS SORT OF...
...GRADUAL.
OH. BUT I THINK...
...THAT'S IMPRESSIVE TOO.

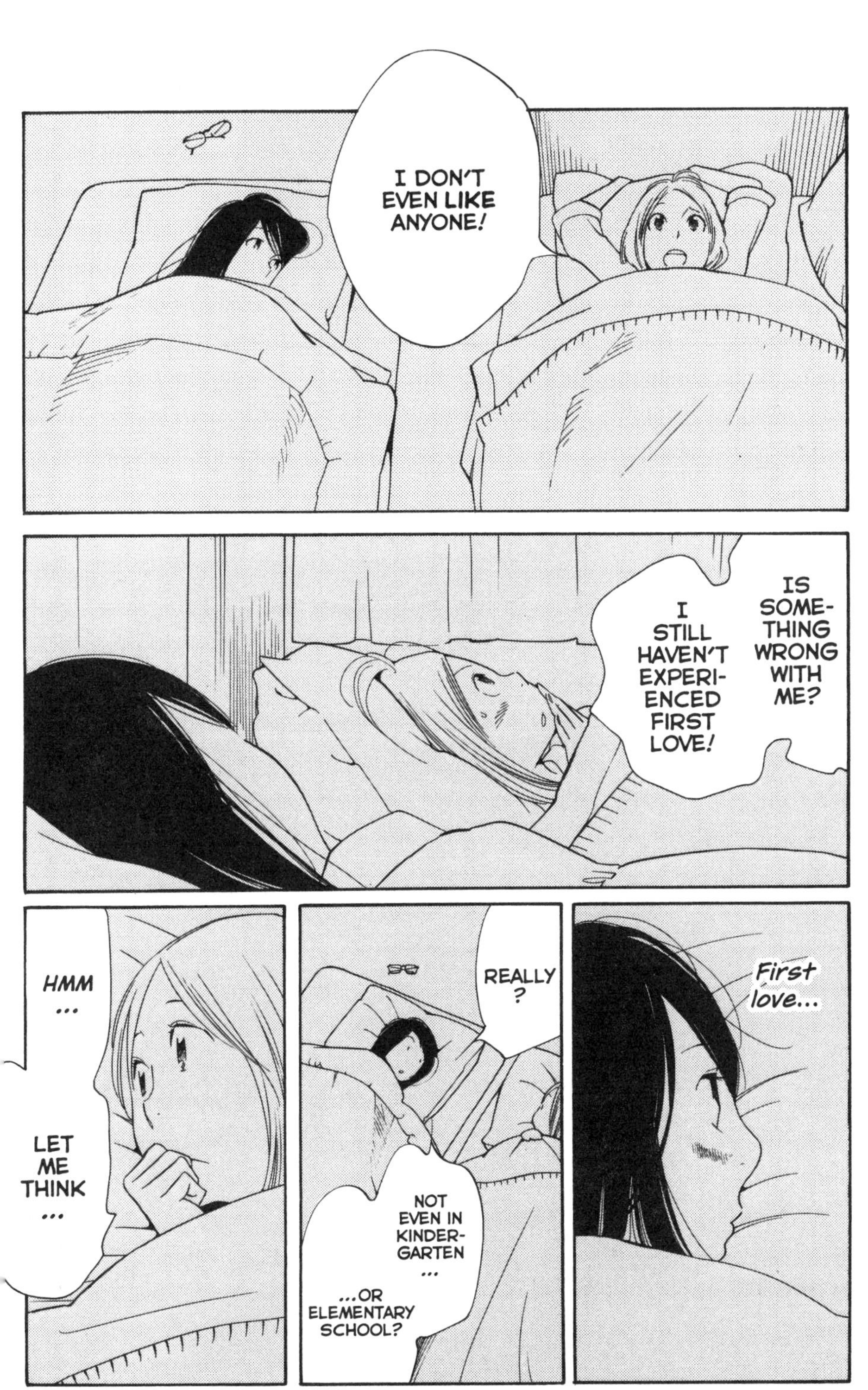
I DON'T EVEN LIKE ANYONE!
I STILL HAVEN'T EXPERIENCED FIRST LOVE!
IS SOMETHING WRONG WITH ME?
First love...
REALLY?
NOT EVEN IN KINDERGARTEN...
...OR ELEMENTARY SCHOOL?
HMM...
LET ME THINK...

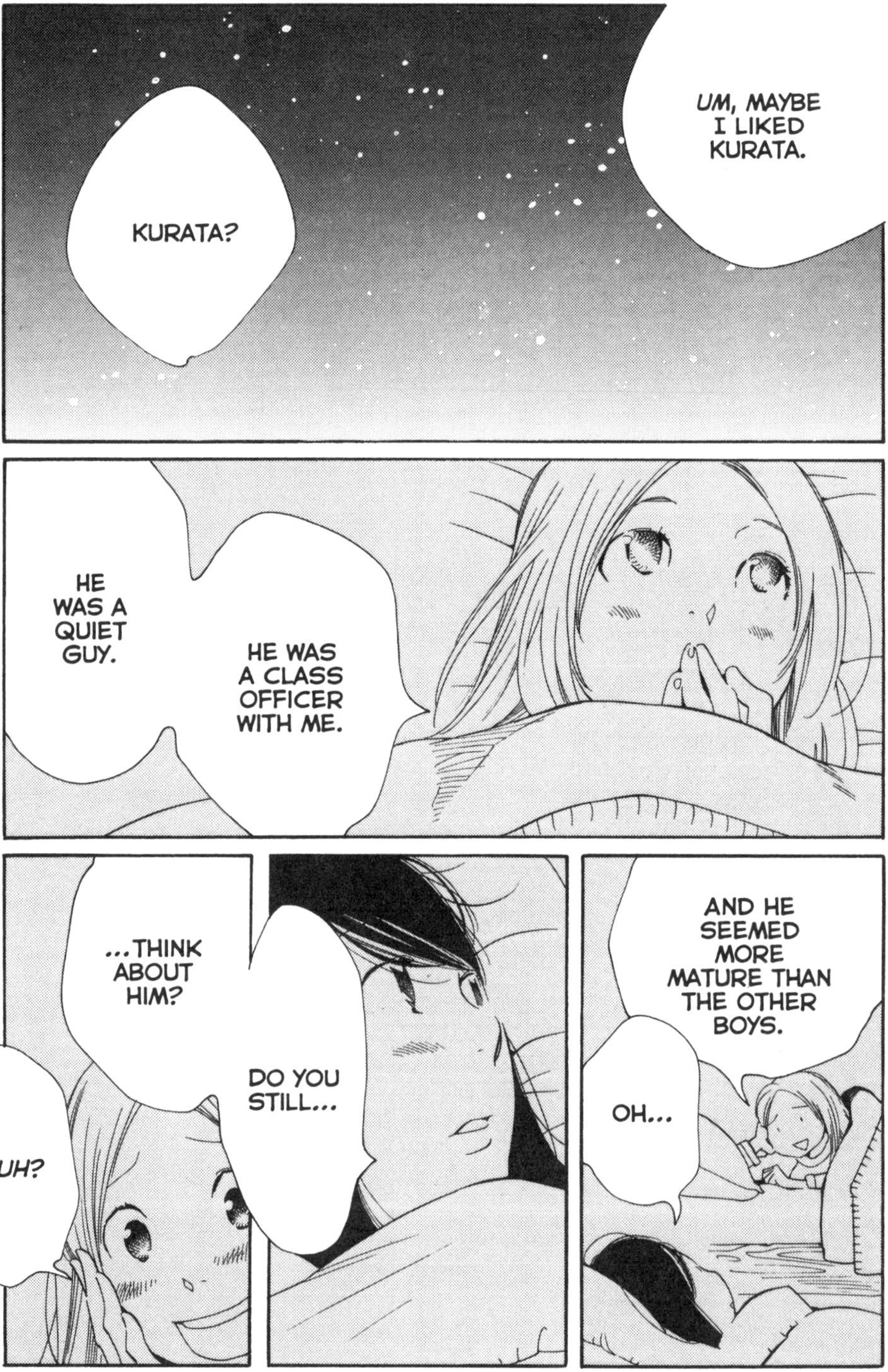
UM, MAYBE I LIKED KURATA.
KURATA?
HE WAS A CLASS OFFICER WITH ME.
HE WAS A QUIET GUY.
AND HE SEEMED MORE MATURE THAN THE OTHER BOYS.
OH...
DO YOU STILL...
...THINK ABOUT HIM?
HUH?

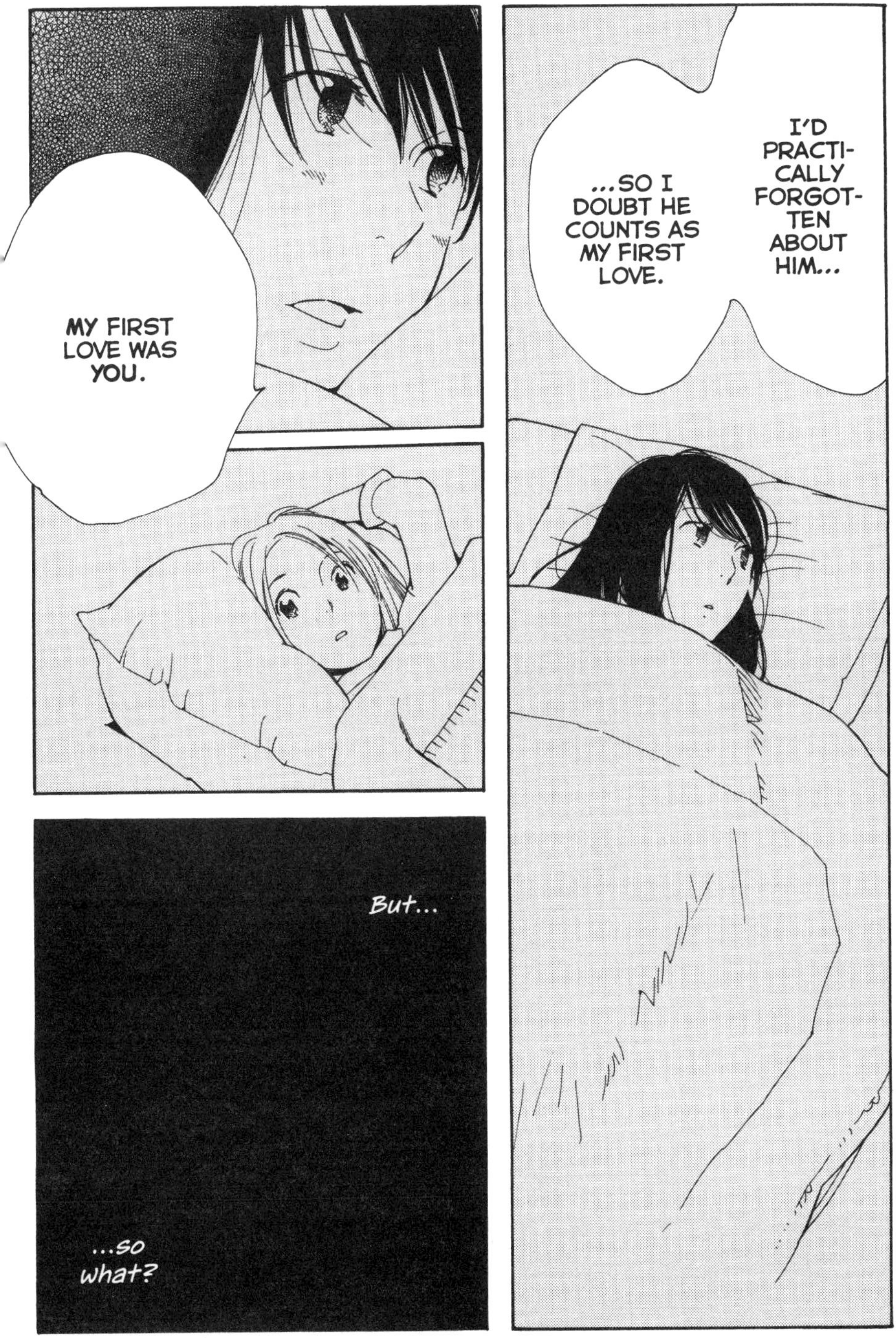
I'D PRACTI-CALLY FORGOT-TEN ABOUT HIM...
...SO I DOUBT HE COUNTS AS MY FIRST LOVE.
MY FIRST LOVE WAS YOU.
But...
...so what?

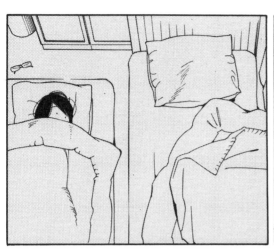
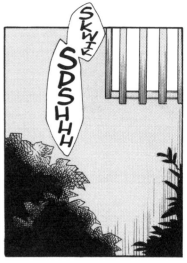

SKWIK
SDSHH

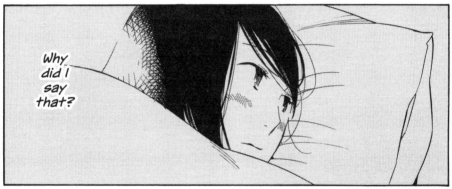

Why did I say that?

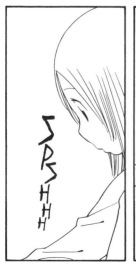

SDSHH

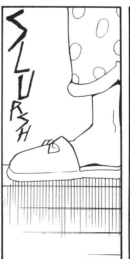

SLURSH

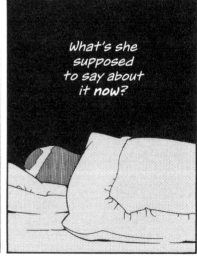

What's she supposed to say about it *now*?

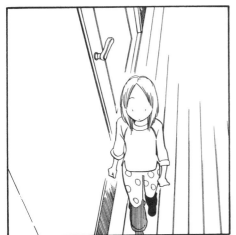

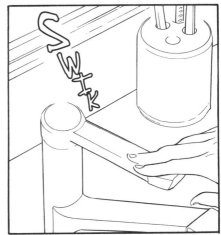

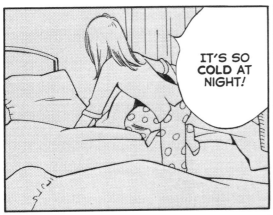

IT'S SO COLD AT NIGHT!

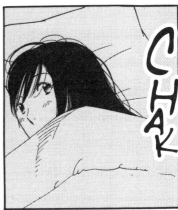

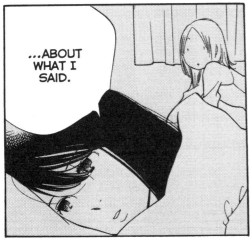

...ABOUT WHAT I SAID.

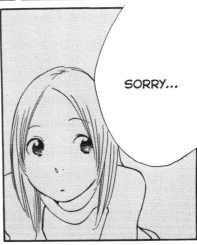

SORRY...

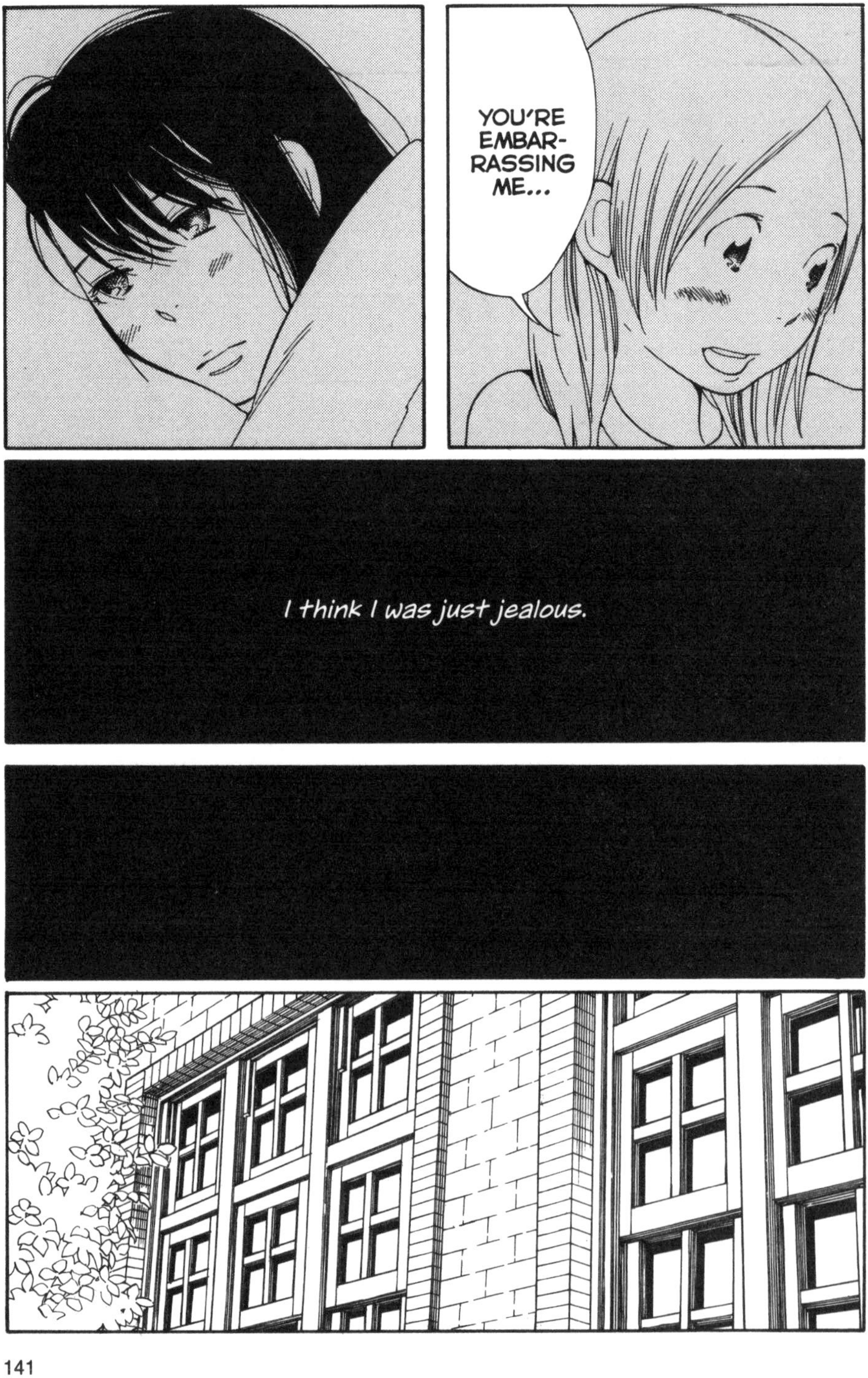
YOU'RE EMBARRASSING ME...
I think I was just jealous.

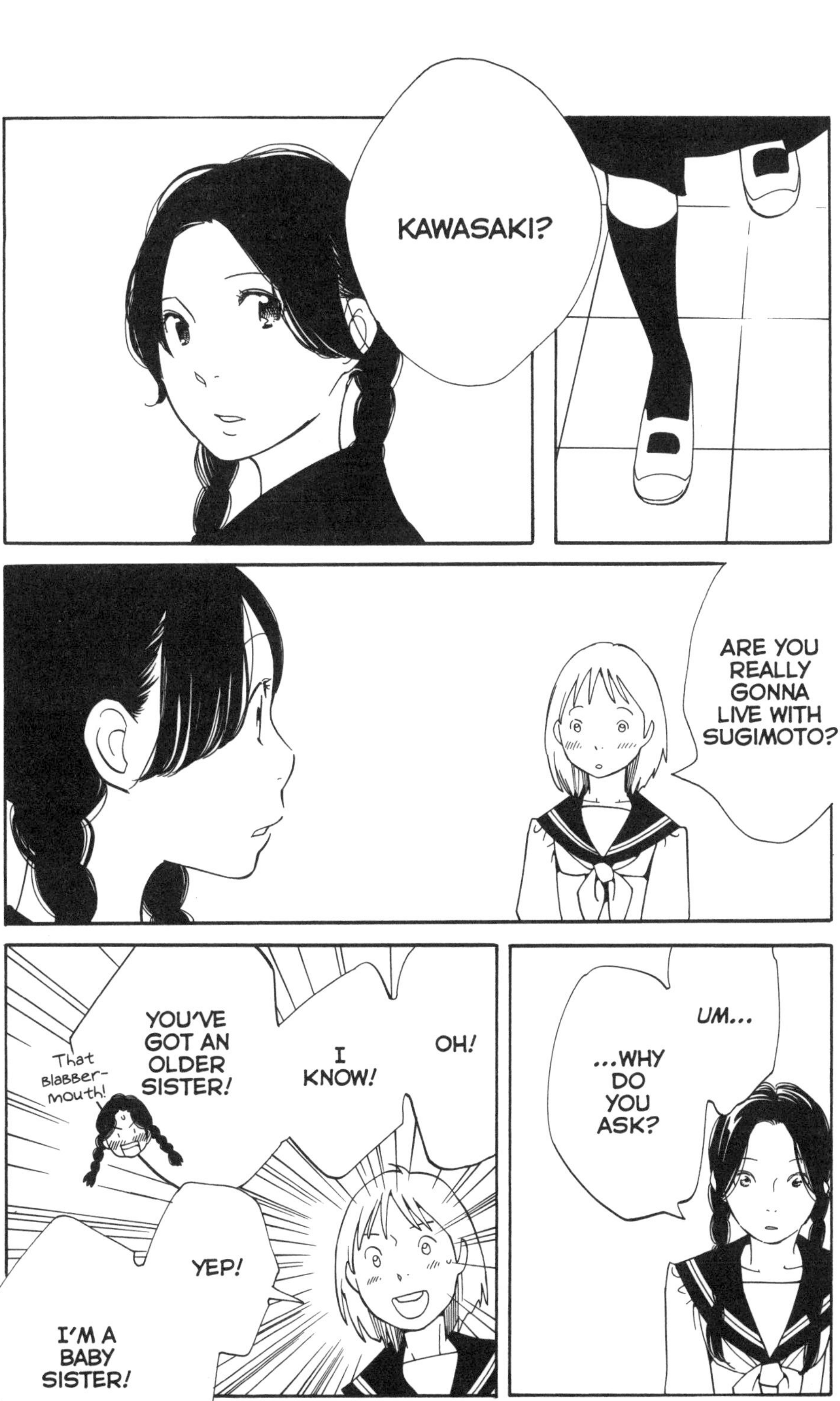
KAWASAKI?
ARE YOU REALLY GONNA LIVE WITH SUGIMOTO?
UM...
...WHY DO YOU ASK?
OH!
I KNOW!
YOU'VE GOT AN OLDER SISTER!
That blabber-mouth!
YEP!
I'M A BABY SISTER!

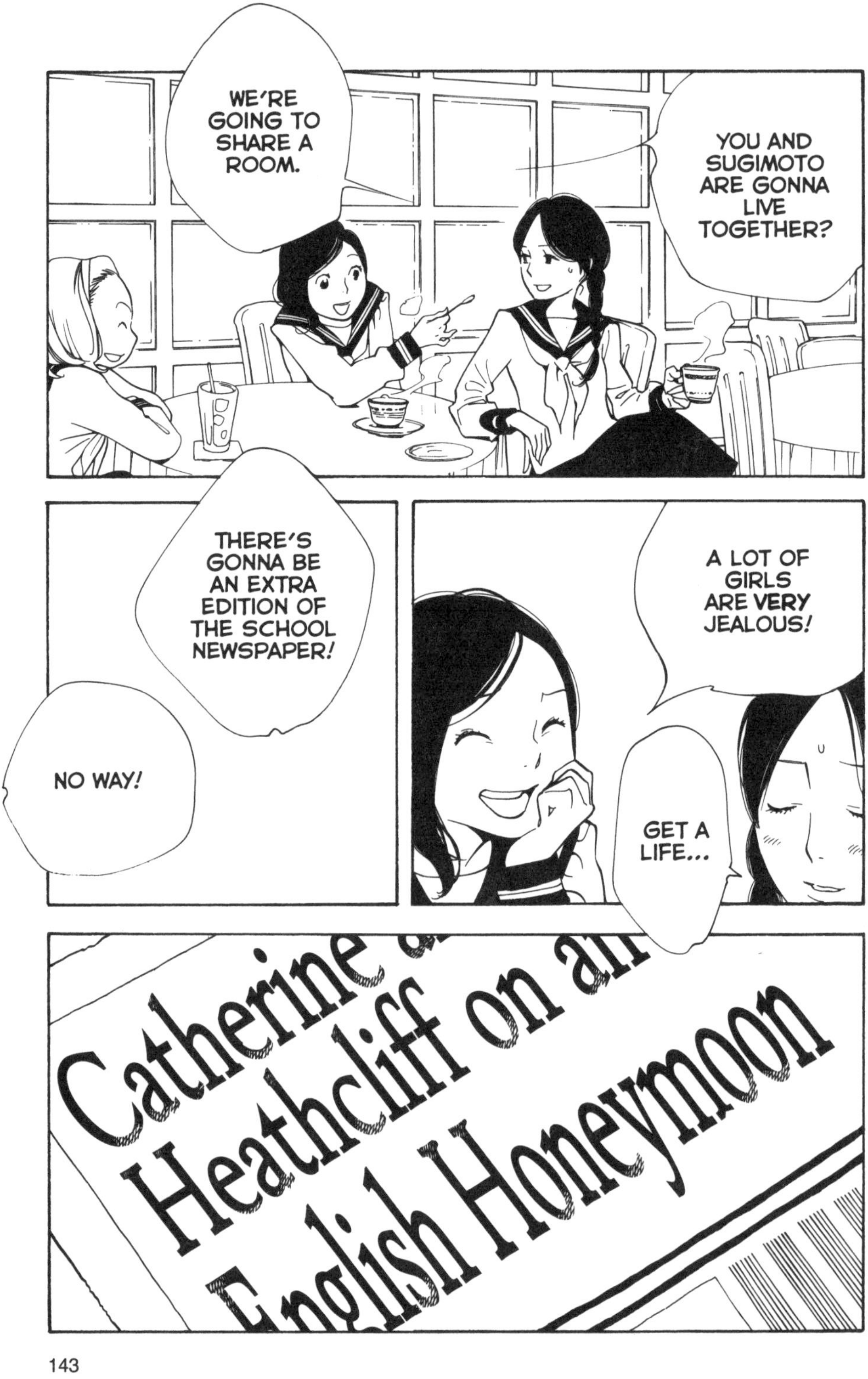
YOU AND SUGIMOTO ARE GONNA LIVE TOGETHER?
WE'RE GOING TO SHARE A ROOM.
A LOT OF GIRLS ARE VERY JEALOUS!
GET A LIFE...
THERE'S GONNA BE AN EXTRA EDITION OF THE SCHOOL NEWSPAPER!
NO WAY!
Catherine a
Heathcliff on an
English Honeymoon

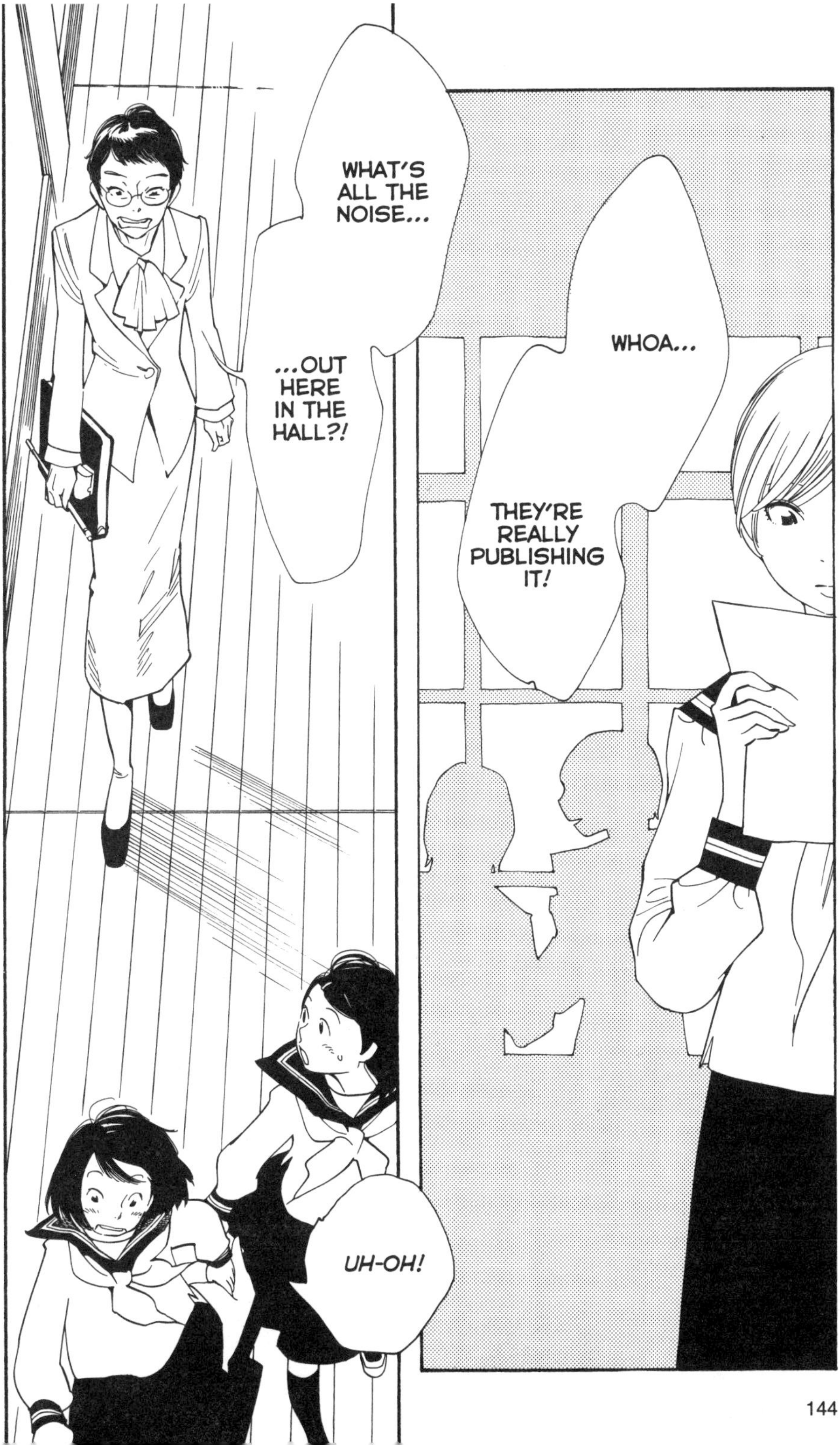
WHOA...
THEY'RE REALLY PUBLISHING IT!
WHAT'S ALL THE NOISE...
...OUT HERE IN THE HALL?!
UH-OH!

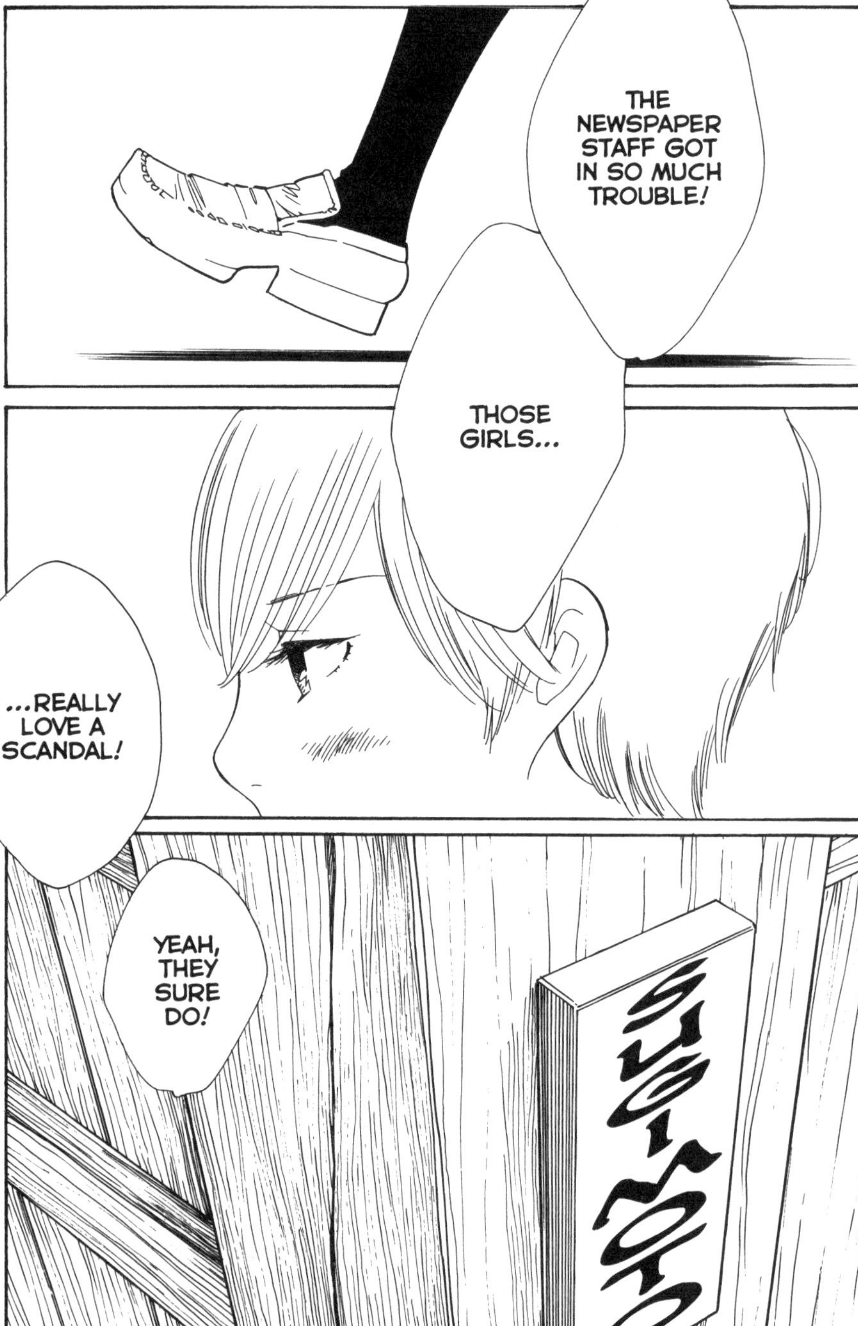
THE NEWSPAPER STAFF GOT IN SO MUCH TROUBLE!
THOSE GIRLS...
...REALLY LOVE A SCANDAL!
YEAH, THEY SURE DO!
SUGIMOTO

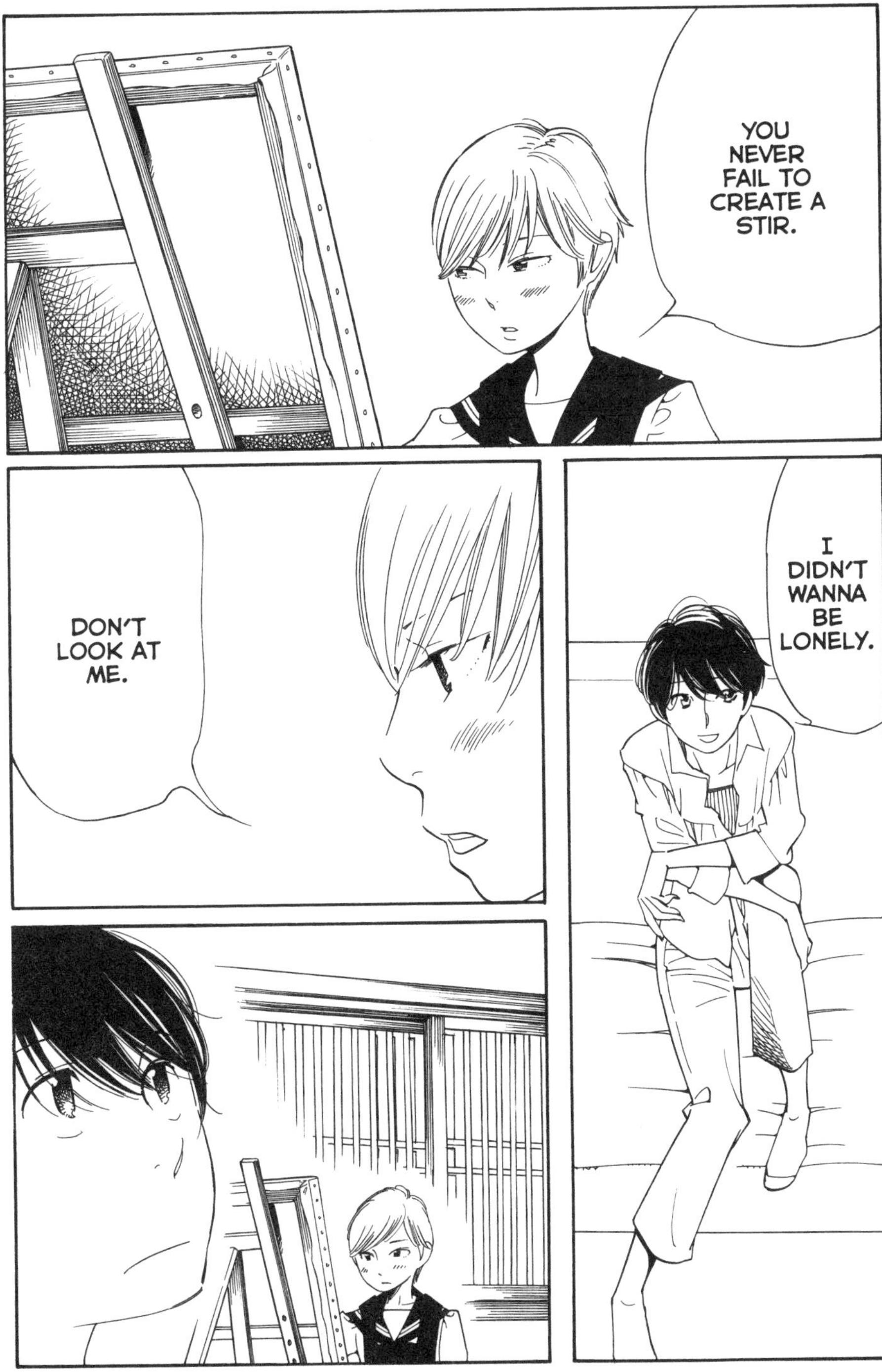
YOU NEVER FAIL TO CREATE A STIR.
I DIDN'T WANNA BE LONELY.
DON'T LOOK AT ME.

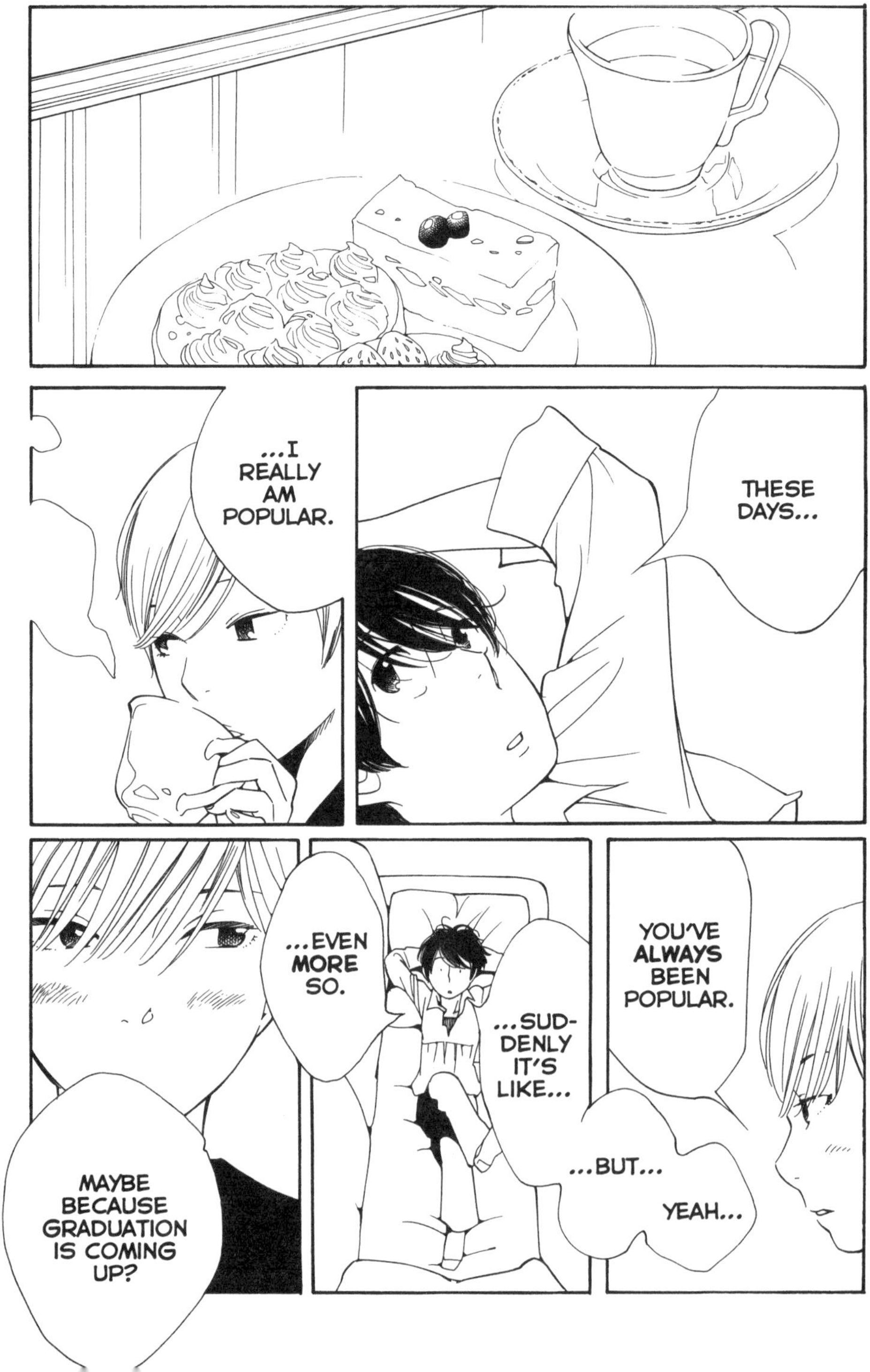
THESE DAYS...
...I REALLY AM POPULAR.
YOU'VE ALWAYS BEEN POPULAR.
...BUT... YEAH...
...SUD-DENLY IT'S LIKE...
...EVEN MORE SO.
MAYBE BECAUSE GRADUATION IS COMING UP?

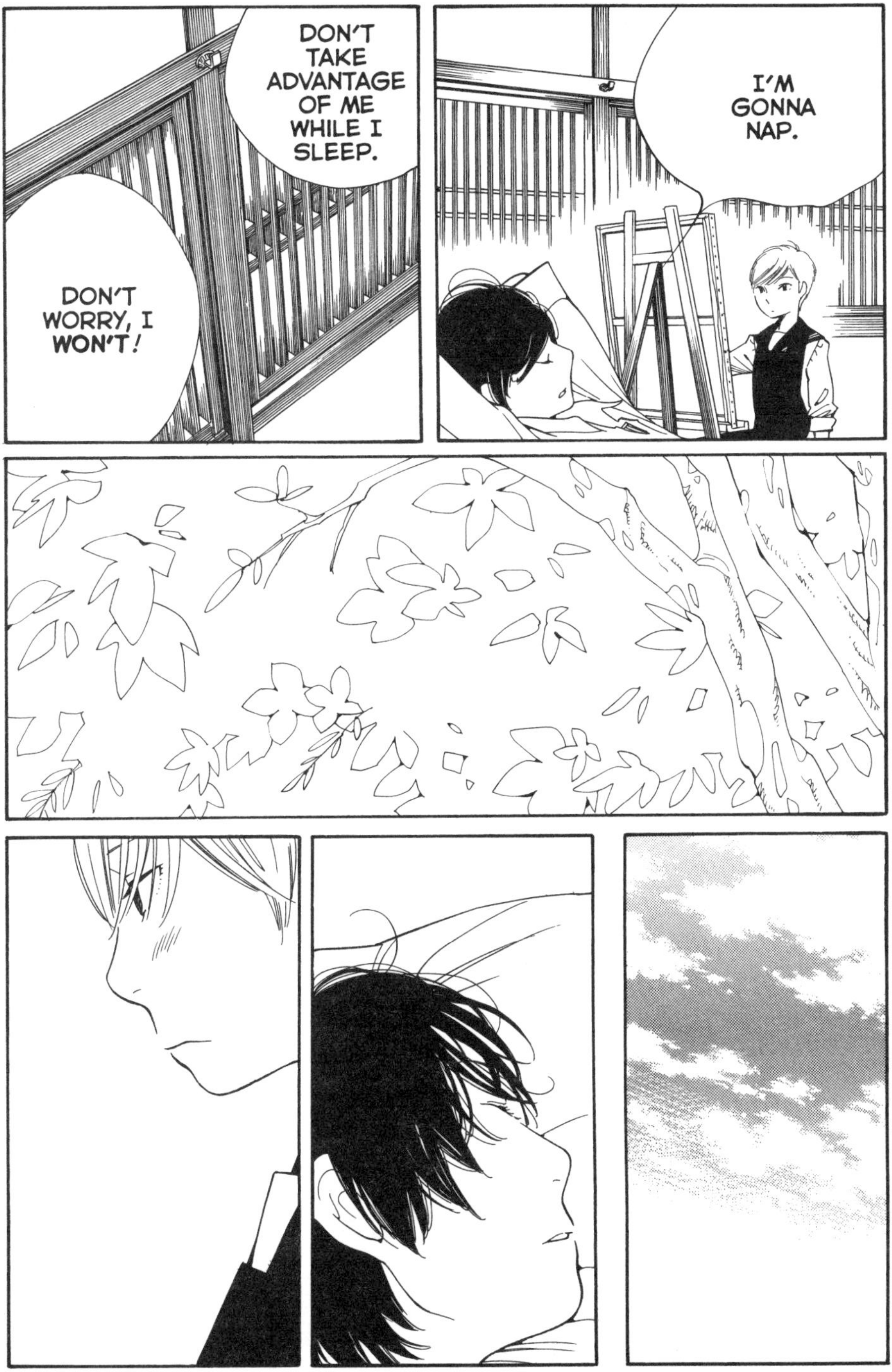
I'M GONNA NAP.
DON'T TAKE ADVANTAGE OF ME WHILE I SLEEP.
DON'T WORRY, I WON'T!

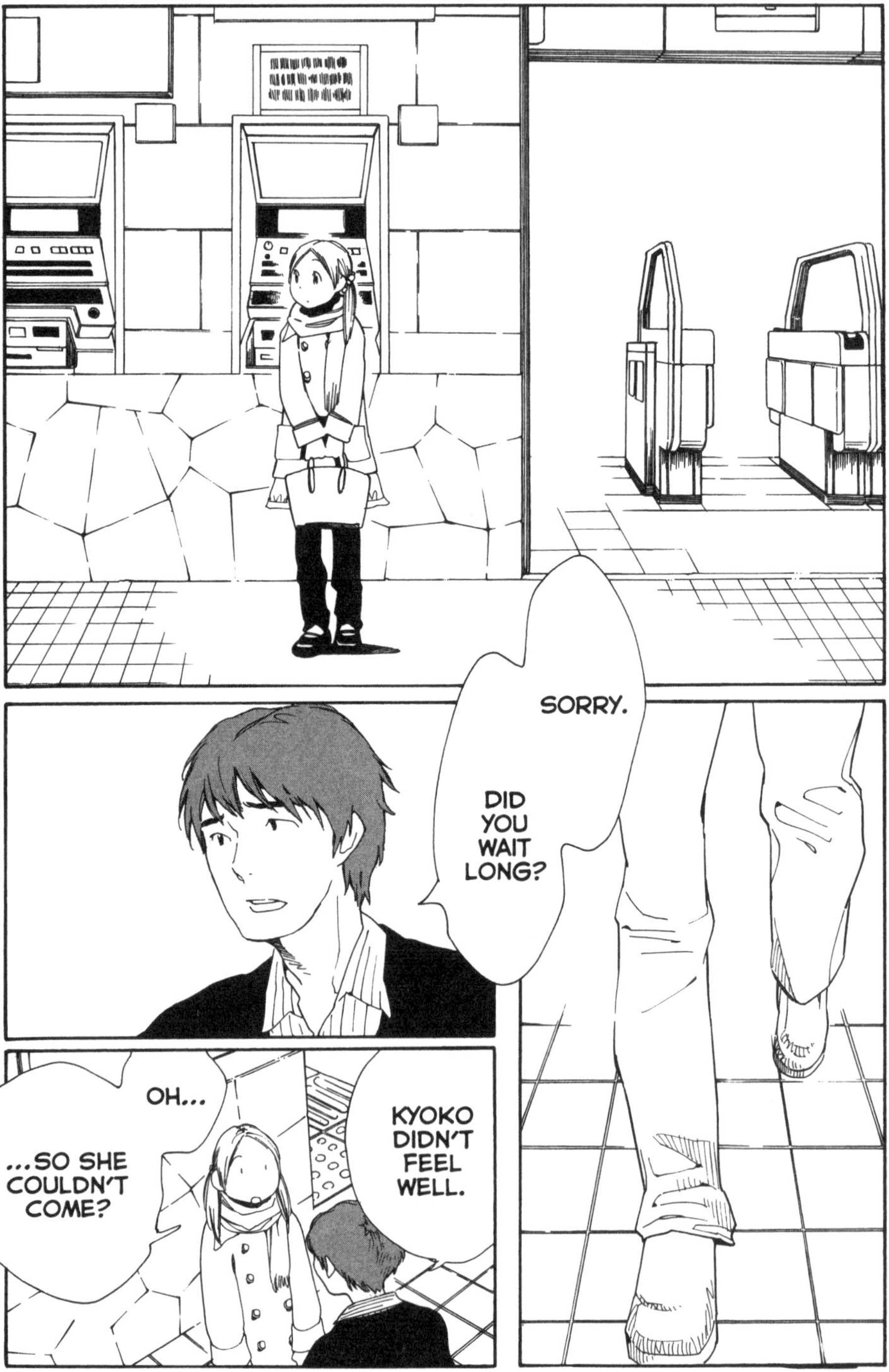
SORRY.
DID YOU WAIT LONG?
KYOKO DIDN'T FEEL WELL.
OH...
...SO SHE COULDN'T COME?

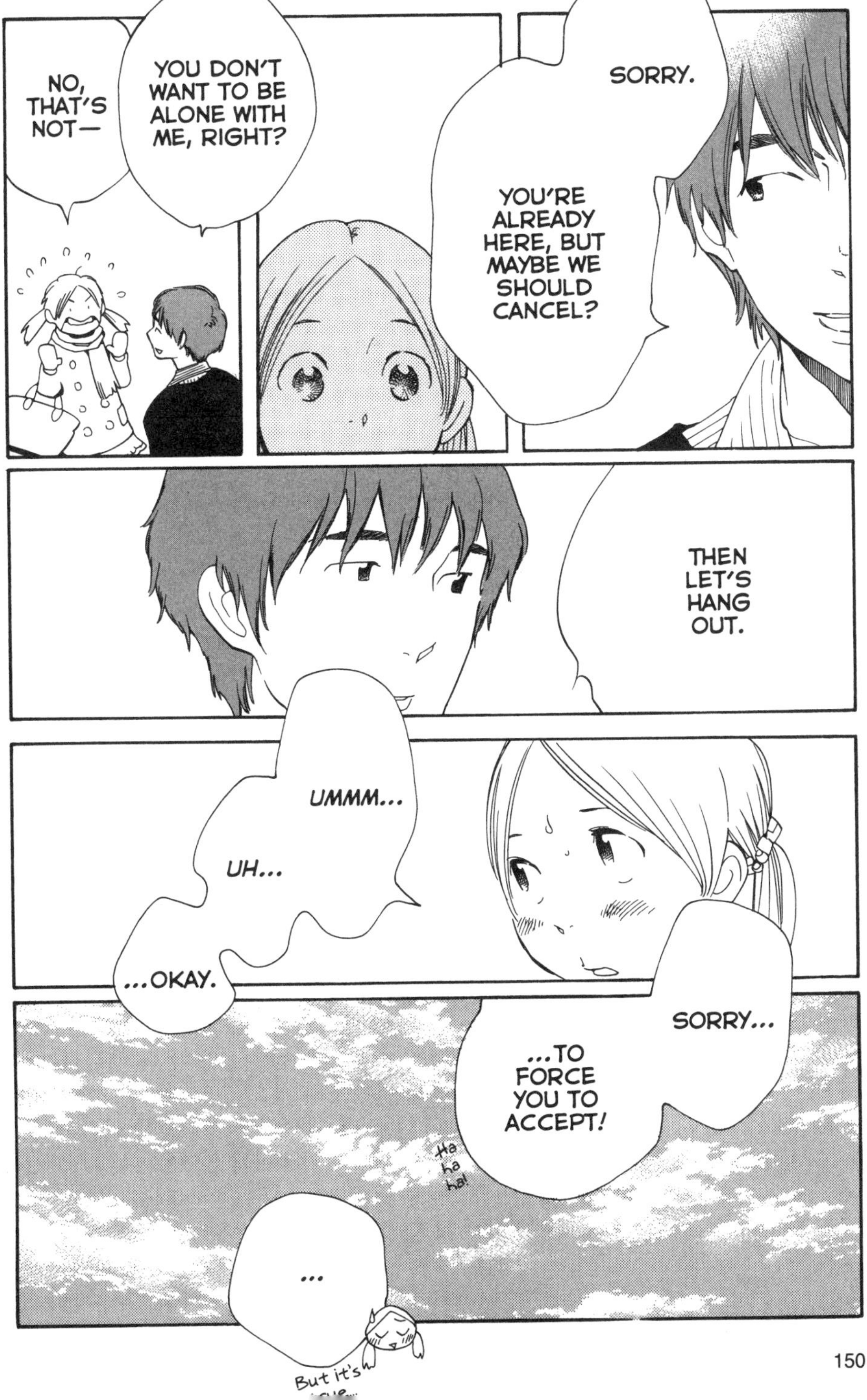
SORRY.
YOU'RE ALREADY HERE, BUT MAYBE WE SHOULD CANCEL?
YOU DON'T WANT TO BE ALONE WITH ME, RIGHT?
NO, THAT'S NOT—
THEN LET'S HANG OUT.
UMMM...
UH...
...OKAY.
SORRY...
...TO FORCE YOU TO ACCEPT!
Ha ha ha!
...
But it's

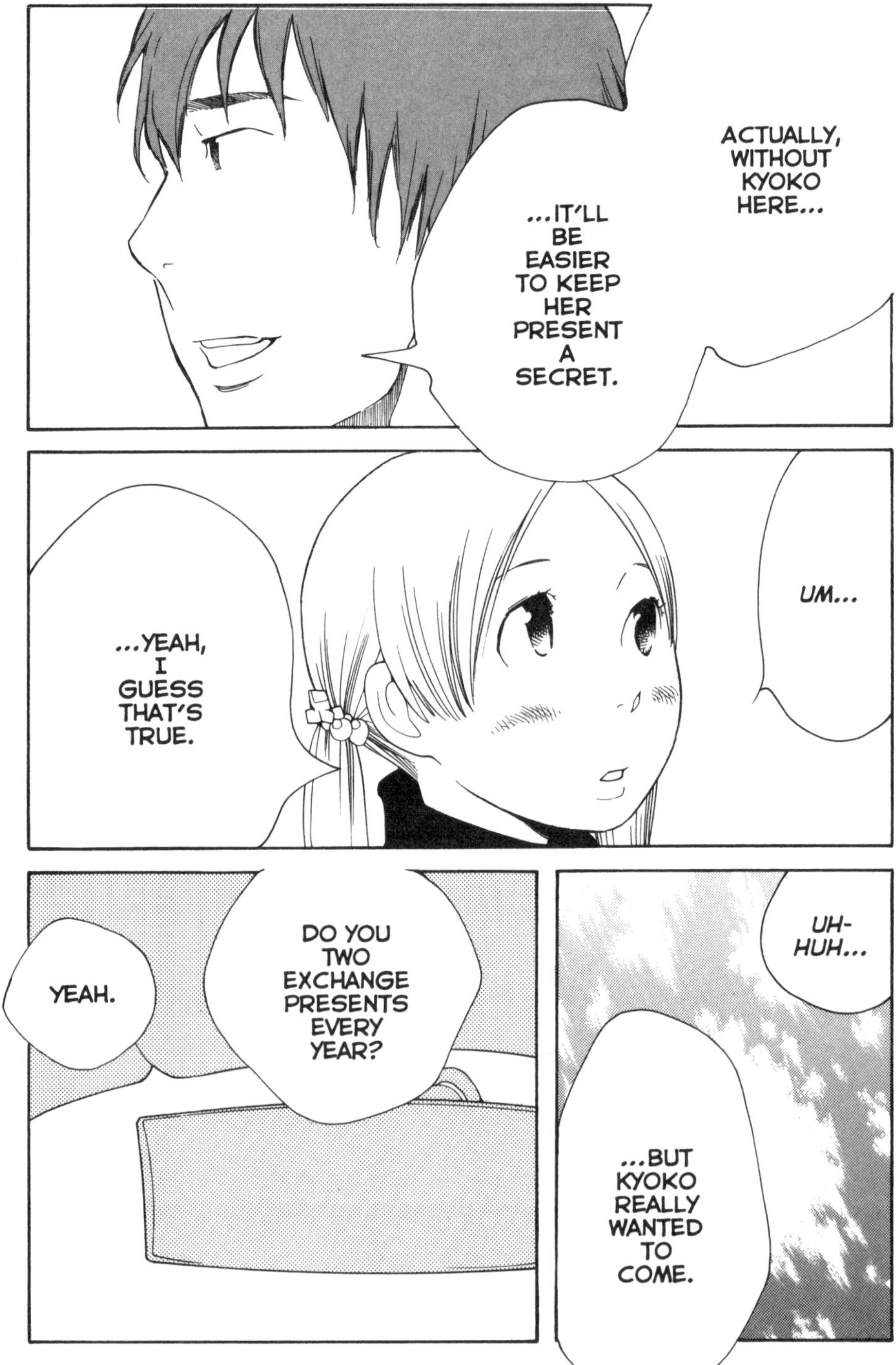
ACTUALLY, WITHOUT KYOKO HERE...
...IT'LL BE EASIER TO KEEP HER PRESENT A SECRET.
UM...
...YEAH, I GUESS THAT'S TRUE.
UH-HUH...
...BUT KYOKO REALLY WANTED TO COME.
DO YOU TWO EXCHANGE PRESENTS EVERY YEAR?
YEAH.

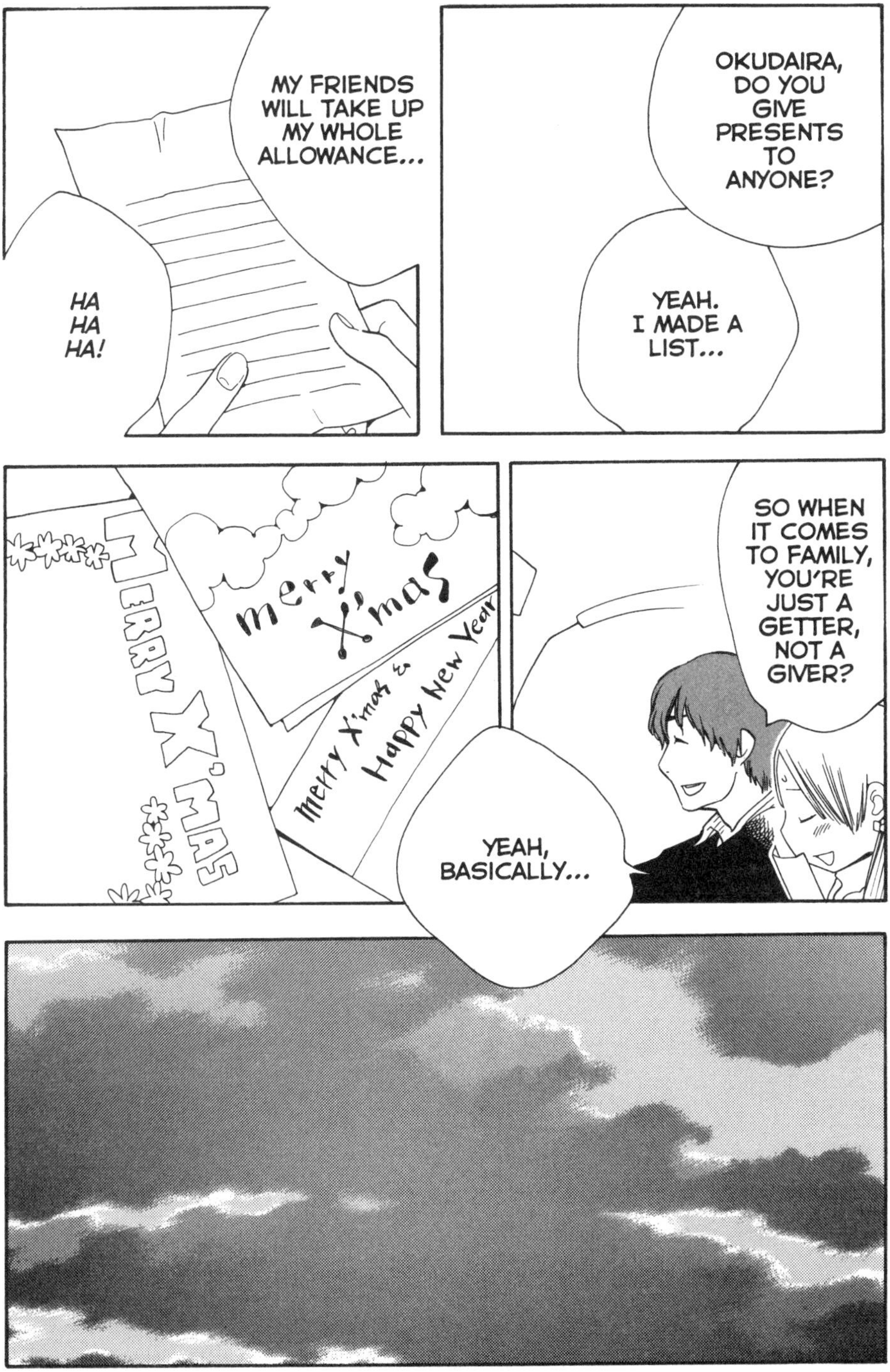
OKUDAIRA, DO YOU GIVE PRESENTS TO ANYONE?
YEAH. I MADE A LIST...
MY FRIENDS WILL TAKE UP MY WHOLE ALLOWANCE...
HA HA HA!
SO WHEN IT COMES TO FAMILY, YOU'RE JUST A GETTER, NOT A GIVER?
YEAH, BASICALLY...
merry X'mas
MERRY X'MAS
merry X'mas & Happy New Year

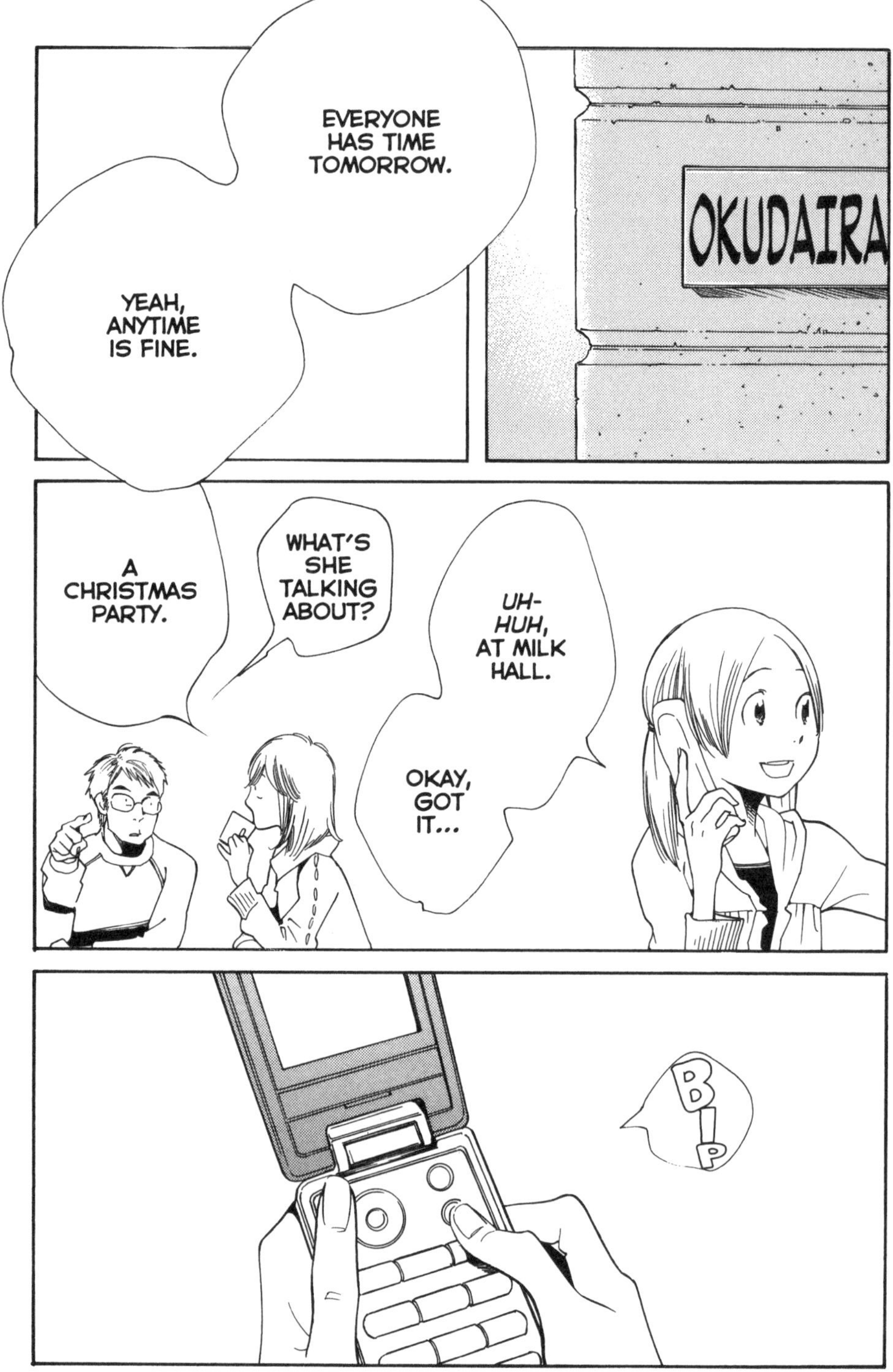
OKUDAIRA
EVERYONE HAS TIME TOMORROW.
YEAH, ANYTIME IS FINE.
UH-HUH, AT MILK HALL.
OKAY, GOT IT...
WHAT'S SHE TALKING ABOUT?
A CHRISTMAS PARTY.
BIP

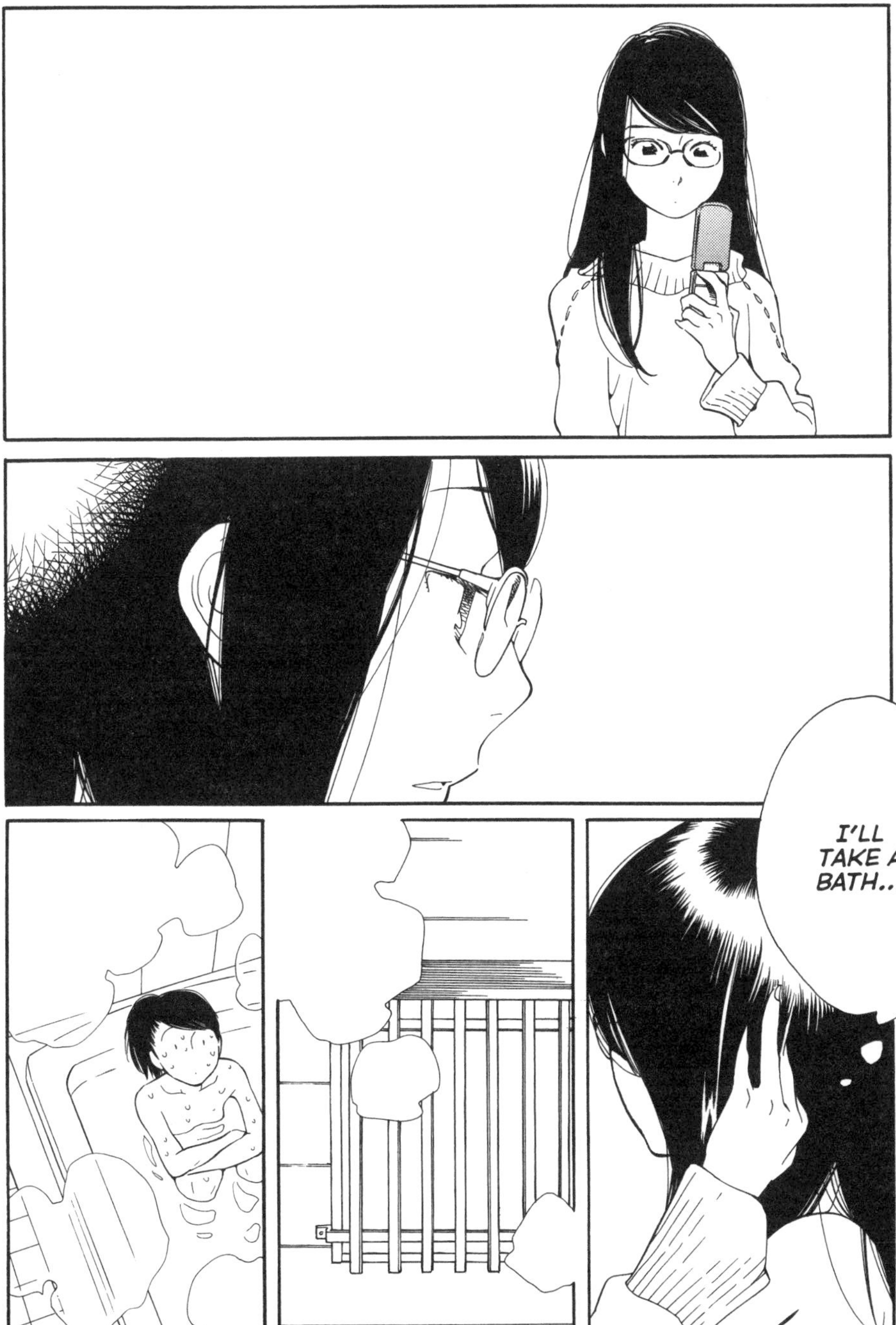
I'LL TAKE A BATH...

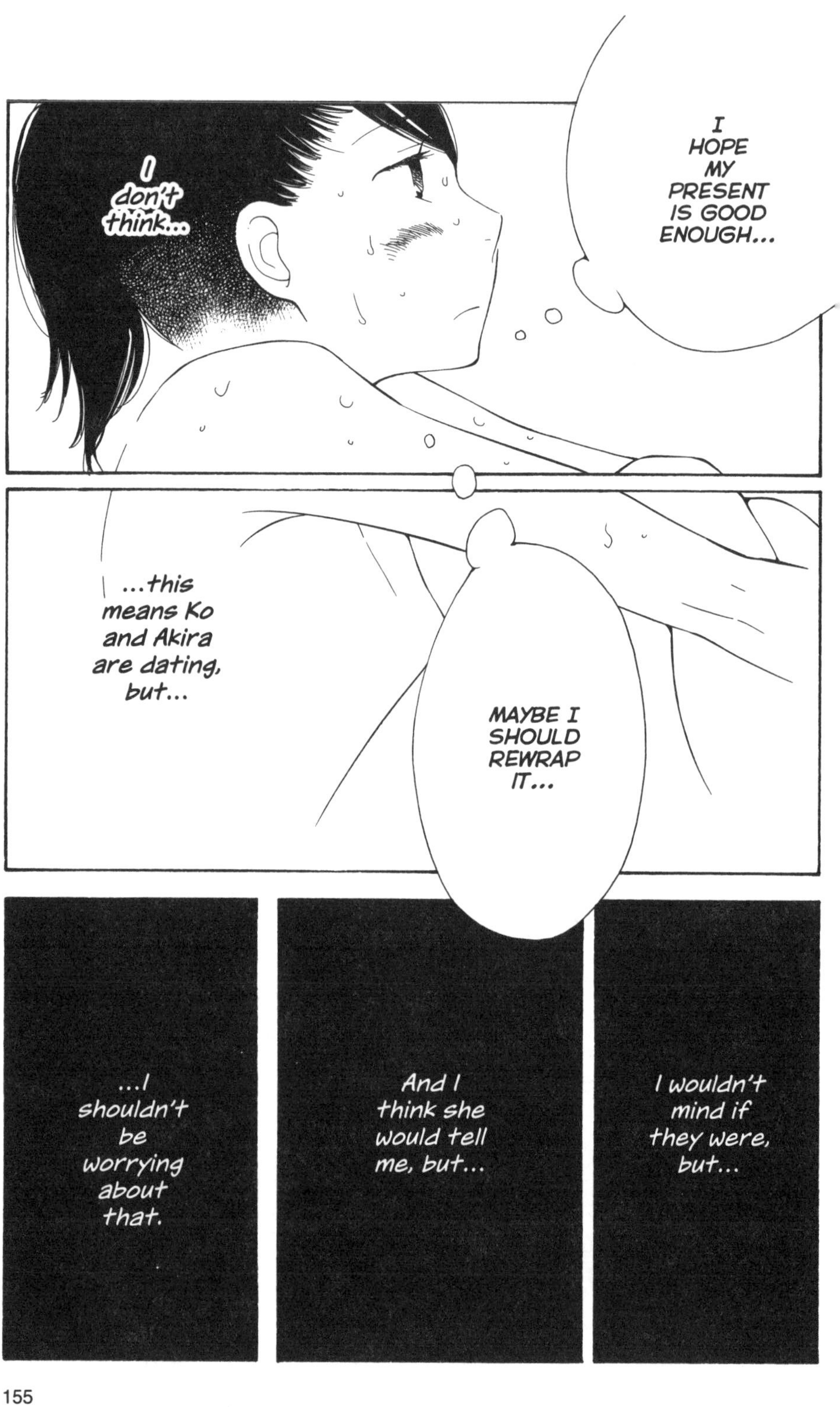
I HOPE MY PRESENT IS GOOD ENOUGH...
I don't think...
MAYBE I SHOULD REWRAP IT...
...this means Ko and Akira are dating, but...
I wouldn't mind if they were, but...
And I think she would tell me, but...
...I shouldn't be worrying about that.

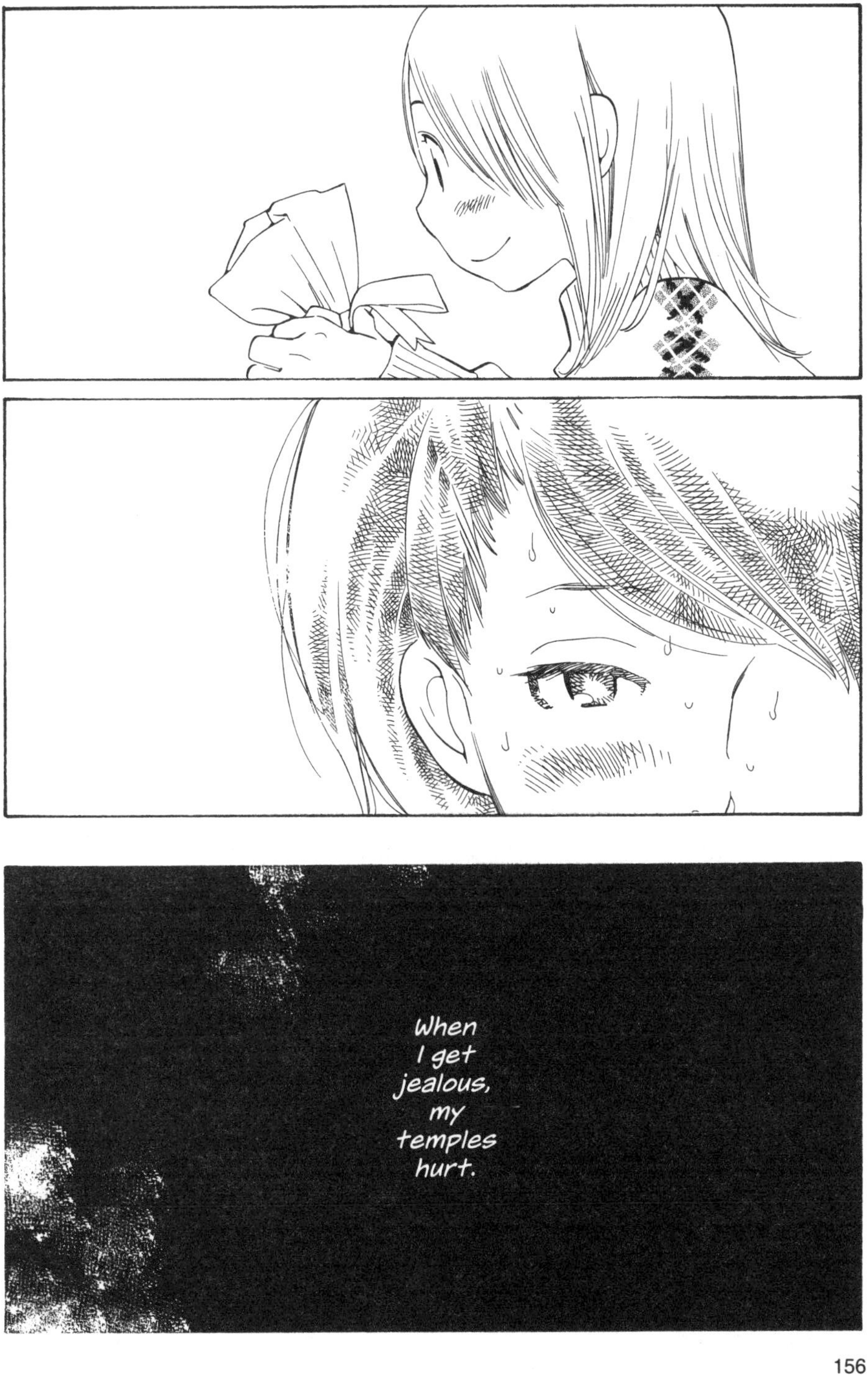
When I get jealous, my temples hurt.

Sweet **Blue**
Flowers

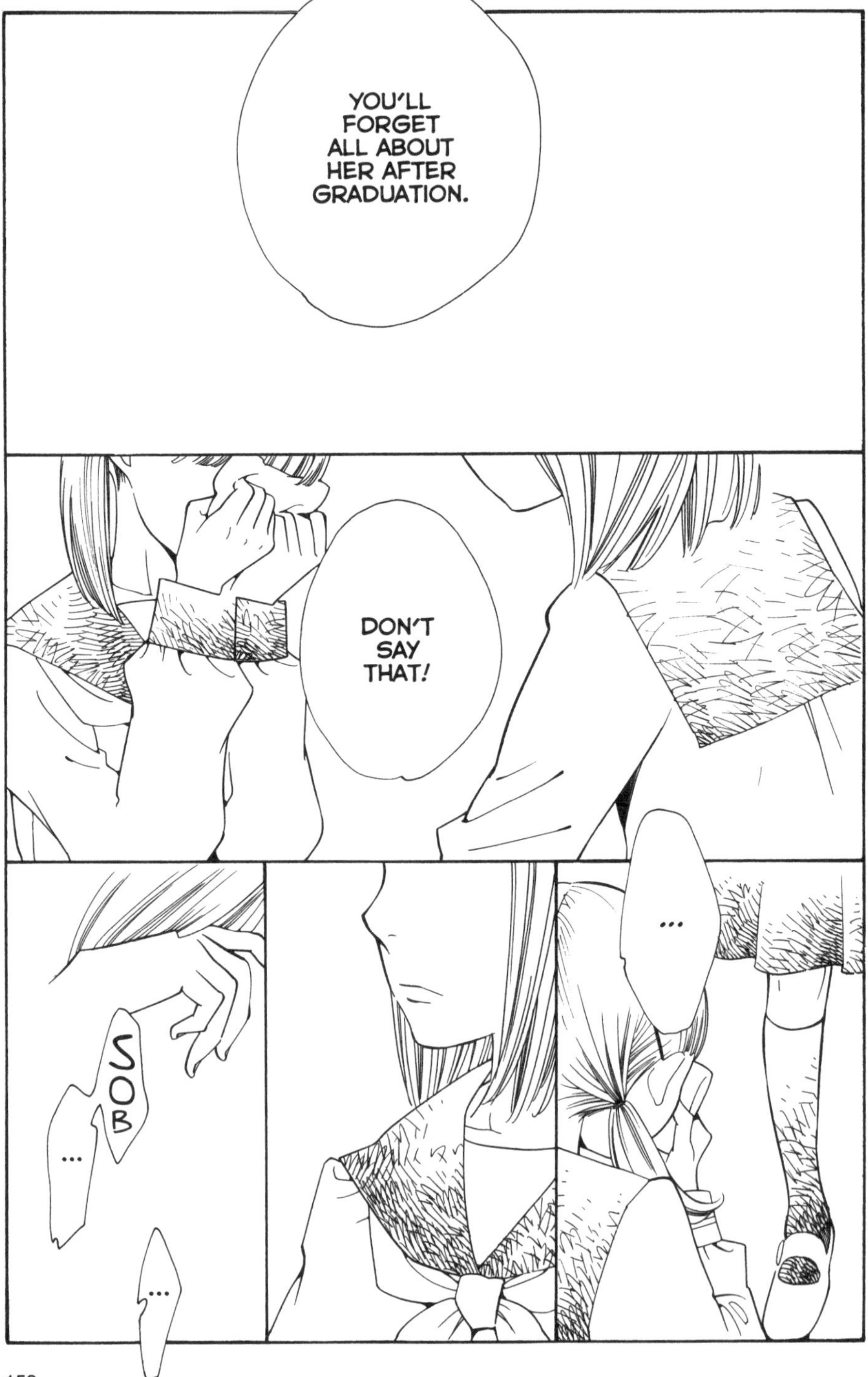
YOU'LL FORGET ALL ABOUT HER AFTER GRADUATION.
DON'T SAY THAT!
...
SOB
...
...

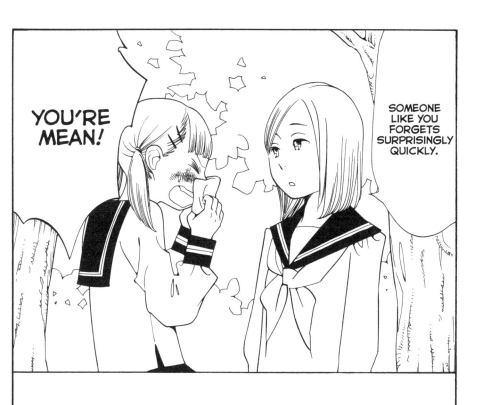

YOU'RE MEAN!

SOMEONE LIKE YOU FORGETS SURPRISINGLY QUICKLY.

And then Orie and Hinako graduated.

LITTLE WOMEN

Orie and Hinako

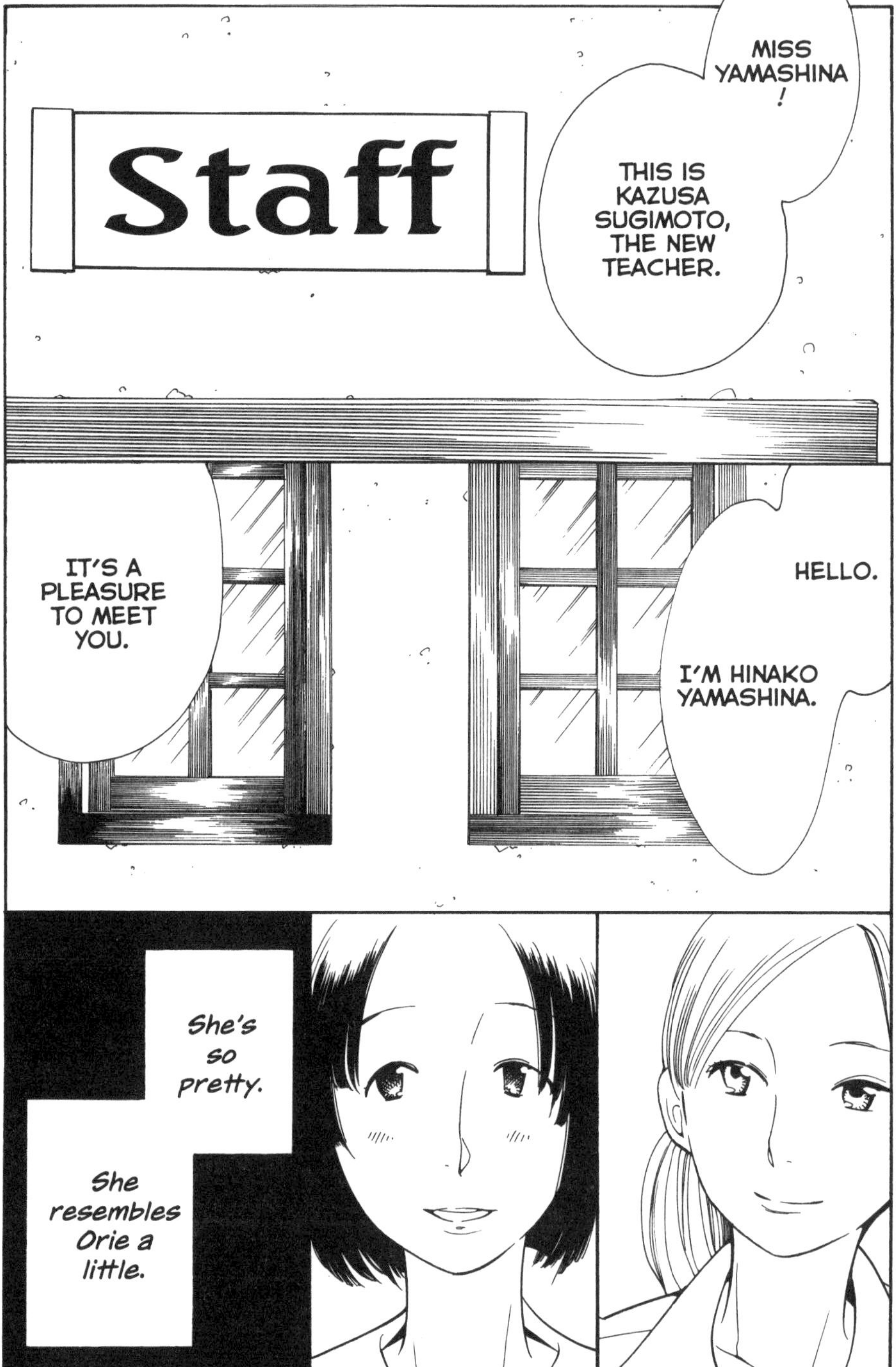
Staff
MISS YAMASHINA!
THIS IS KAZUSA SUGIMOTO, THE NEW TEACHER.
HELLO.
I'M HINAKO YAMASHINA.
IT'S A PLEASURE TO MEET YOU.
She's so pretty.
She resembles Orie a little.

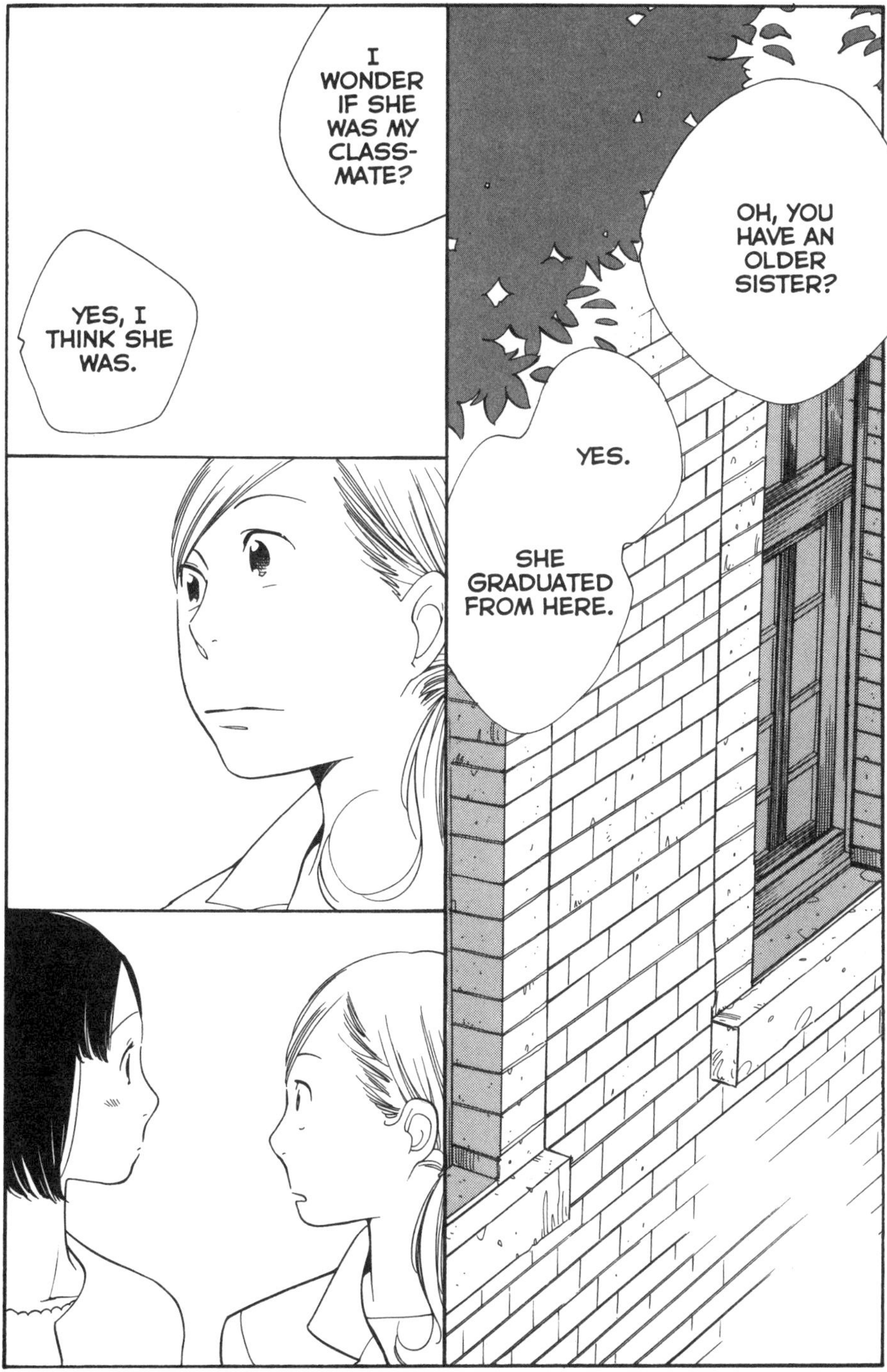
OH, YOU HAVE AN OLDER SISTER?
YES.
SHE GRADUATED FROM HERE.
I WONDER IF SHE WAS MY CLASS-MATE?
YES, I THINK SHE WAS.

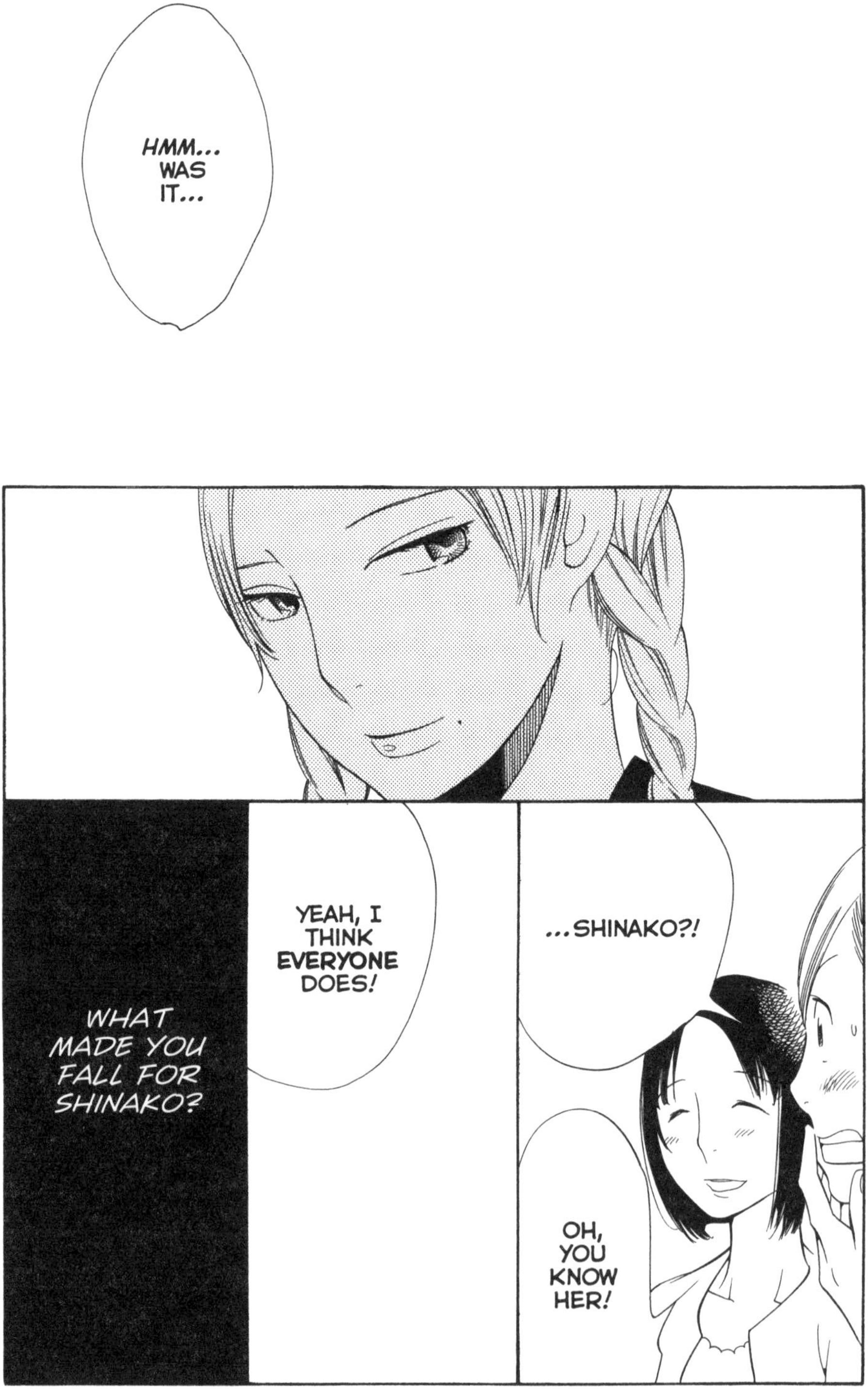
HMM... WAS IT...
...SHINAKO?!
OH, YOU KNOW HER!
YEAH, I THINK EVERYONE DOES!
WHAT MADE YOU FALL FOR SHINAKO?

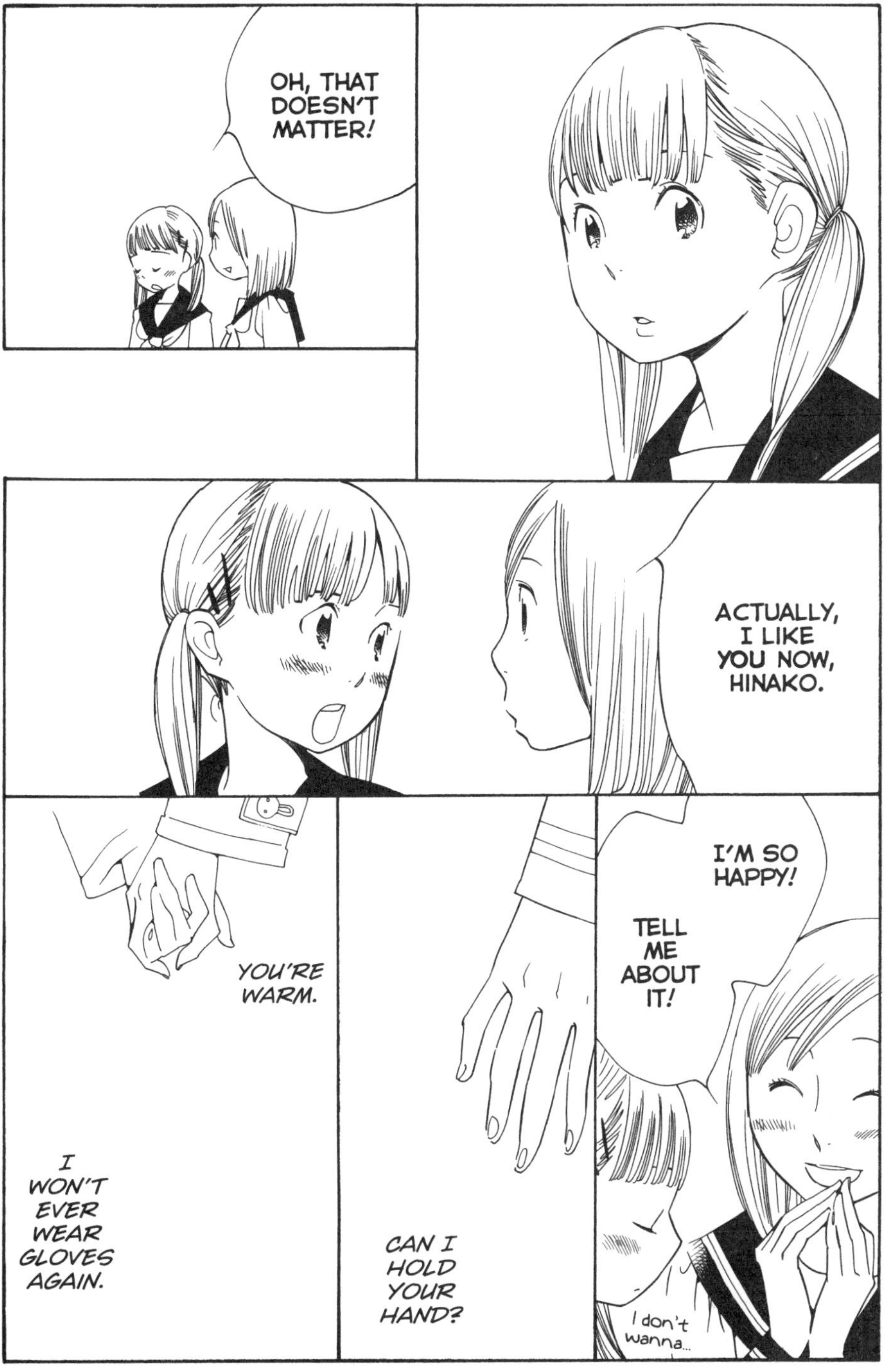
OH, THAT DOESN'T MATTER!
ACTUALLY, I LIKE YOU NOW, HINAKO.
I'M SO HAPPY!
TELL ME ABOUT IT!
I don't wanna...
CAN I HOLD YOUR HAND?
YOU'RE WARM.
I WON'T EVER WEAR GLOVES AGAIN.

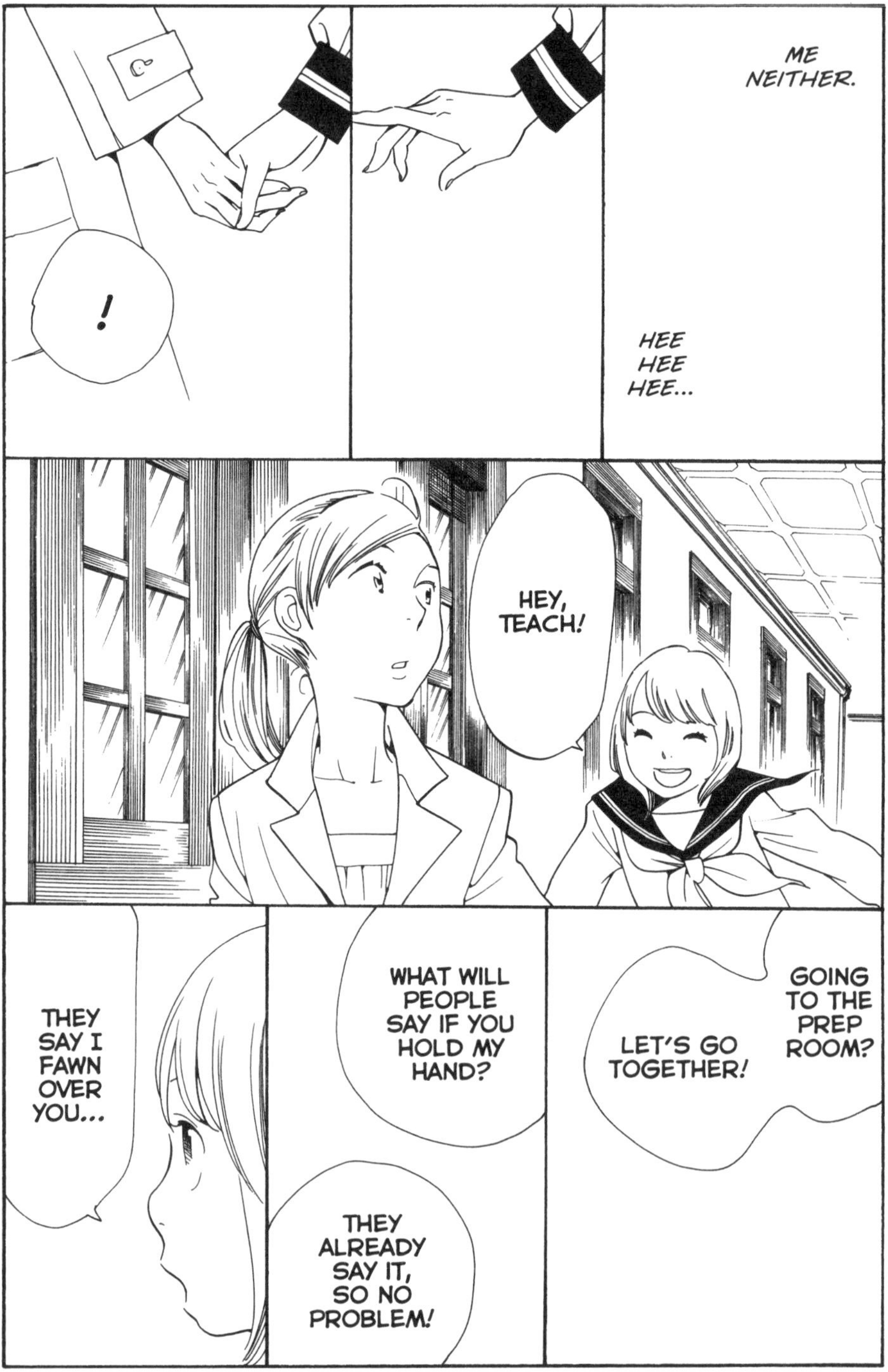
ME NEITHER.
HEE HEE HEE...
!
HEY, TEACH!
GOING TO THE PREP ROOM?
LET'S GO TOGETHER!
WHAT WILL PEOPLE SAY IF YOU HOLD MY HAND?
THEY ALREADY SAY IT, SO NO PROBLEM!
THEY SAY I FAWN OVER YOU...

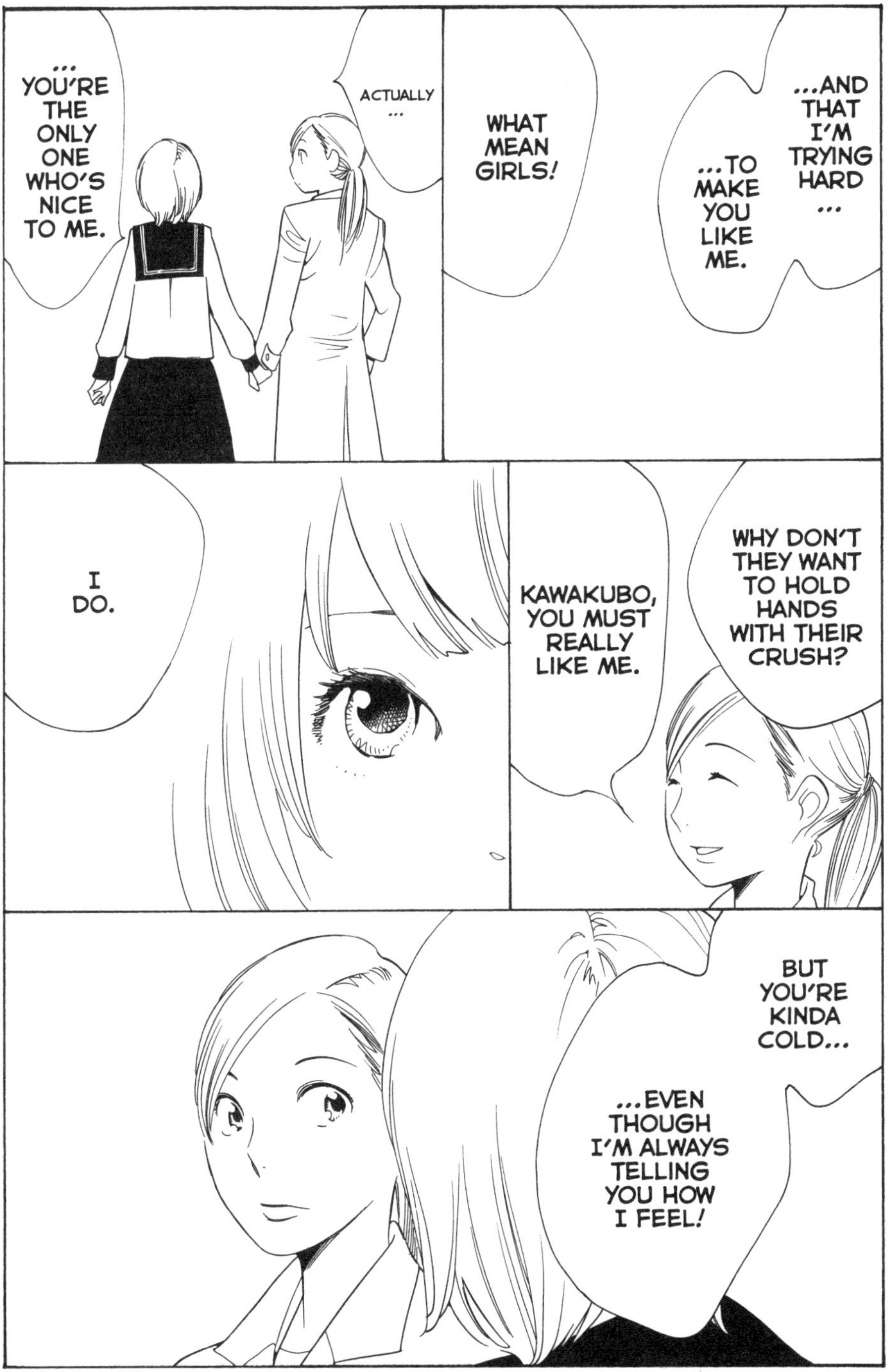
...AND THAT I'M TRYING HARD...
...TO MAKE YOU LIKE ME.
WHAT MEAN GIRLS!
ACTUALLY...
...YOU'RE THE ONLY ONE WHO'S NICE TO ME.
WHY DON'T THEY WANT TO HOLD HANDS WITH THEIR CRUSH?
KAWAKUBO, YOU MUST REALLY LIKE ME.
I DO.
BUT YOU'RE KINDA COLD...
...EVEN THOUGH I'M ALWAYS TELLING YOU HOW I FEEL!

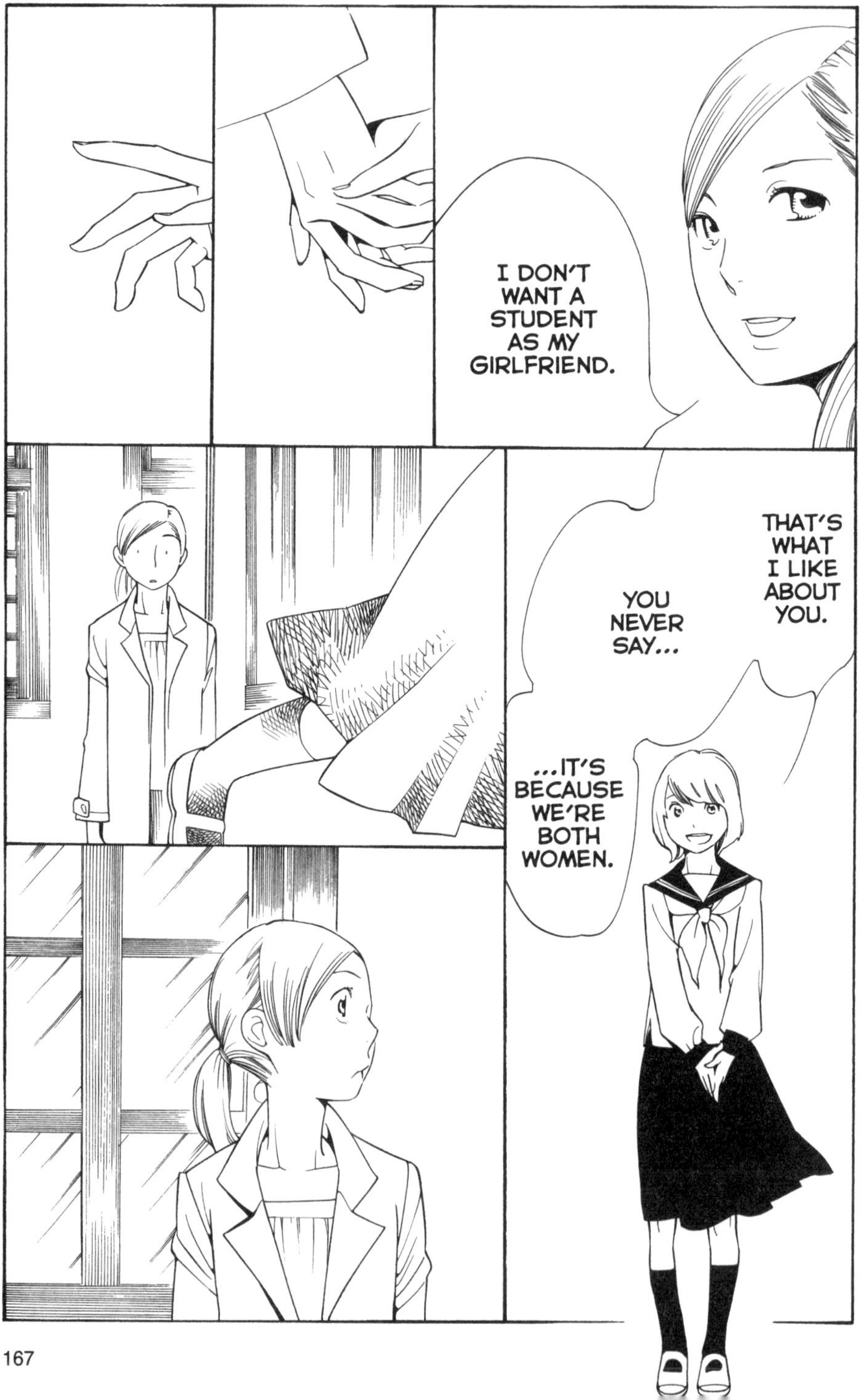
I DON'T WANT A STUDENT AS MY GIRLFRIEND.
THAT'S WHAT I LIKE ABOUT YOU.
YOU NEVER SAY...
...IT'S BECAUSE WE'RE BOTH WOMEN.

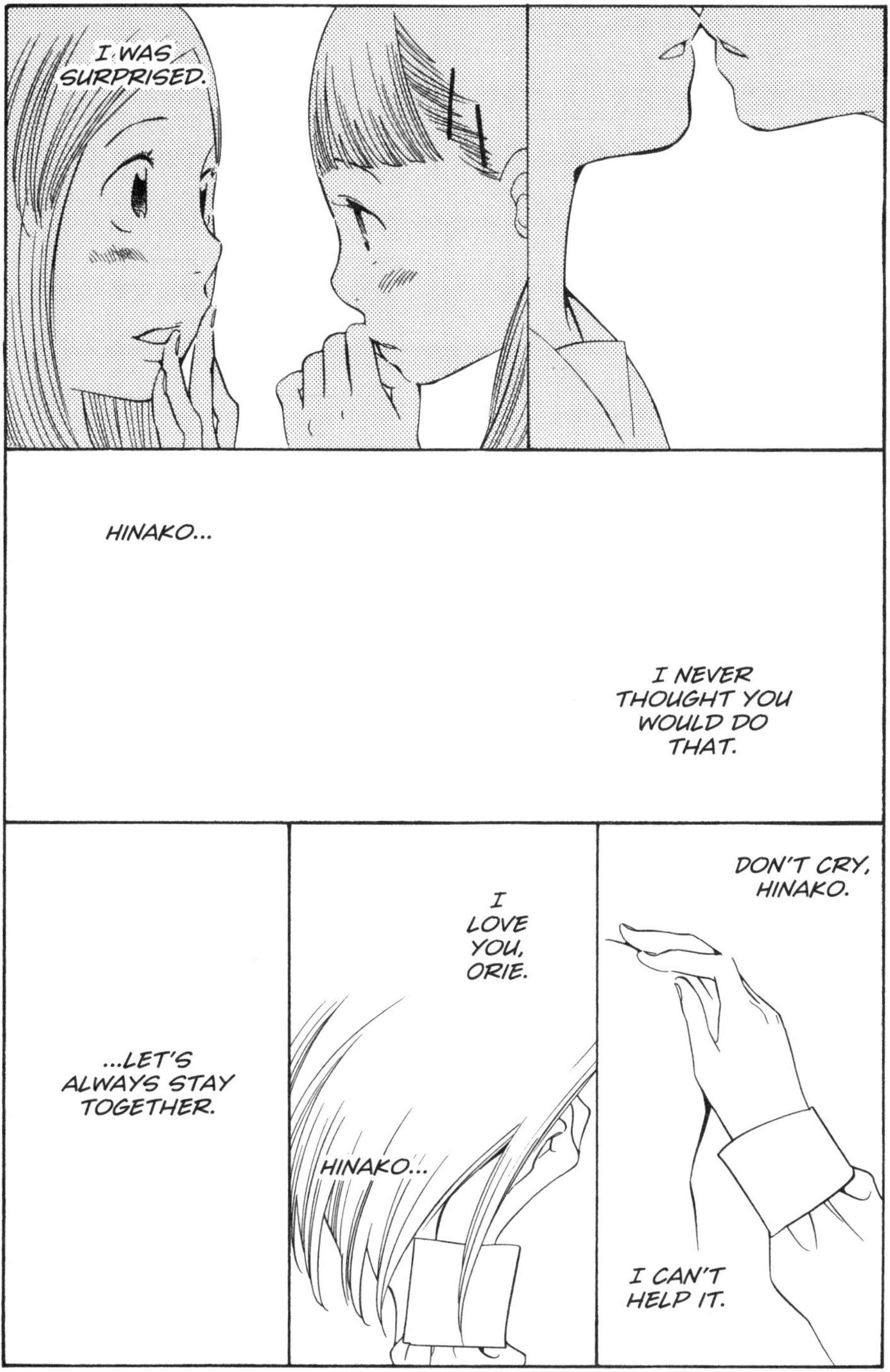
I WAS SURPRISED.
HINAKO...
I NEVER THOUGHT YOU WOULD DO THAT.
DON'T CRY, HINAKO.
I CAN'T HELP IT.
I LOVE YOU, ORIE.
HINAKO...
...LET'S ALWAYS STAY TOGETHER.

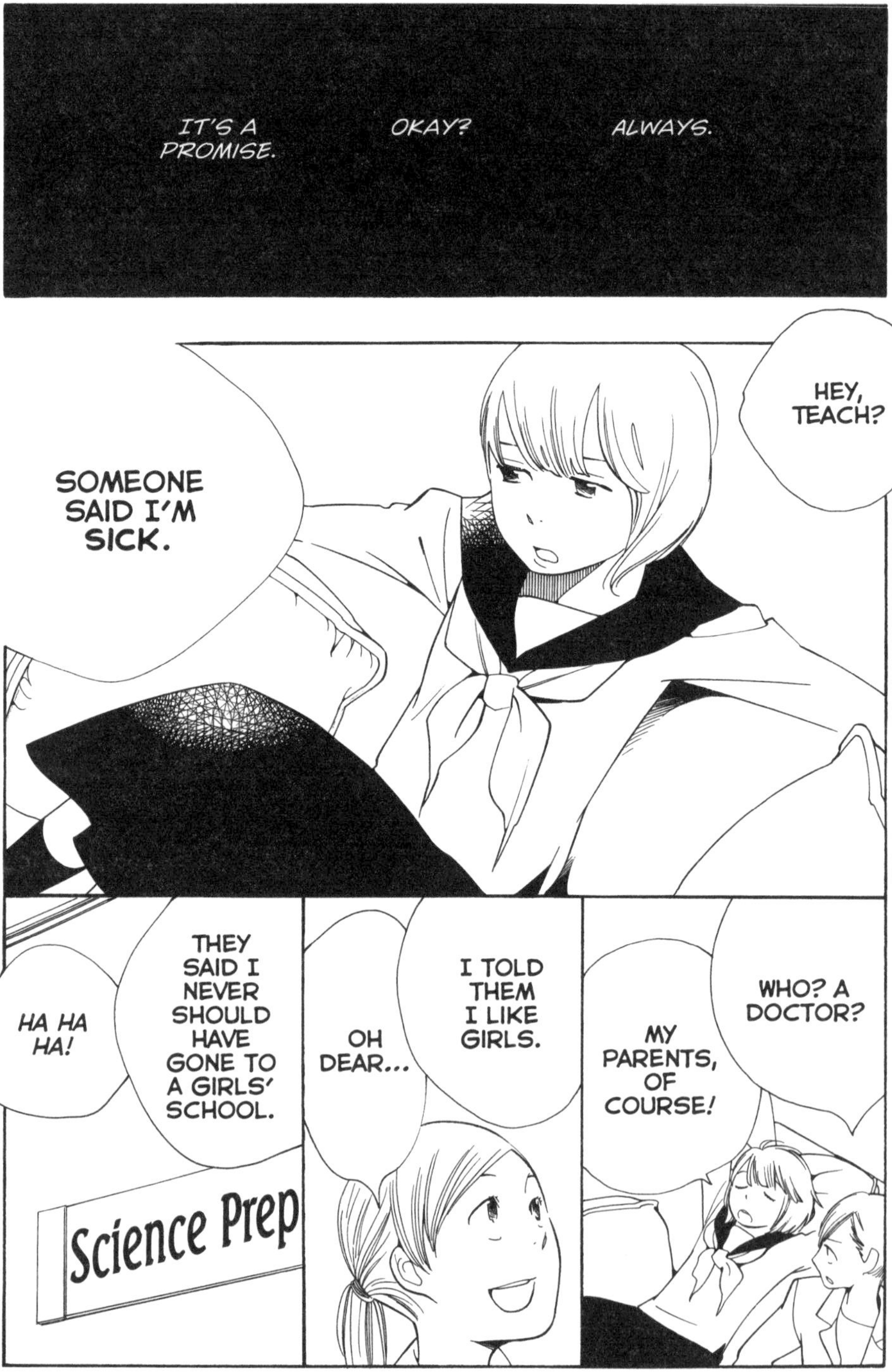
ALWAYS.
OKAY?
IT'S A PROMISE.
HEY, TEACH?
SOMEONE SAID I'M SICK.
WHO? A DOCTOR?
MY PARENTS, OF COURSE!
I TOLD THEM I LIKE GIRLS.
OH DEAR...
THEY SAID I NEVER SHOULD HAVE GONE TO A GIRLS' SCHOOL.
HA HA HA!
Science Prep

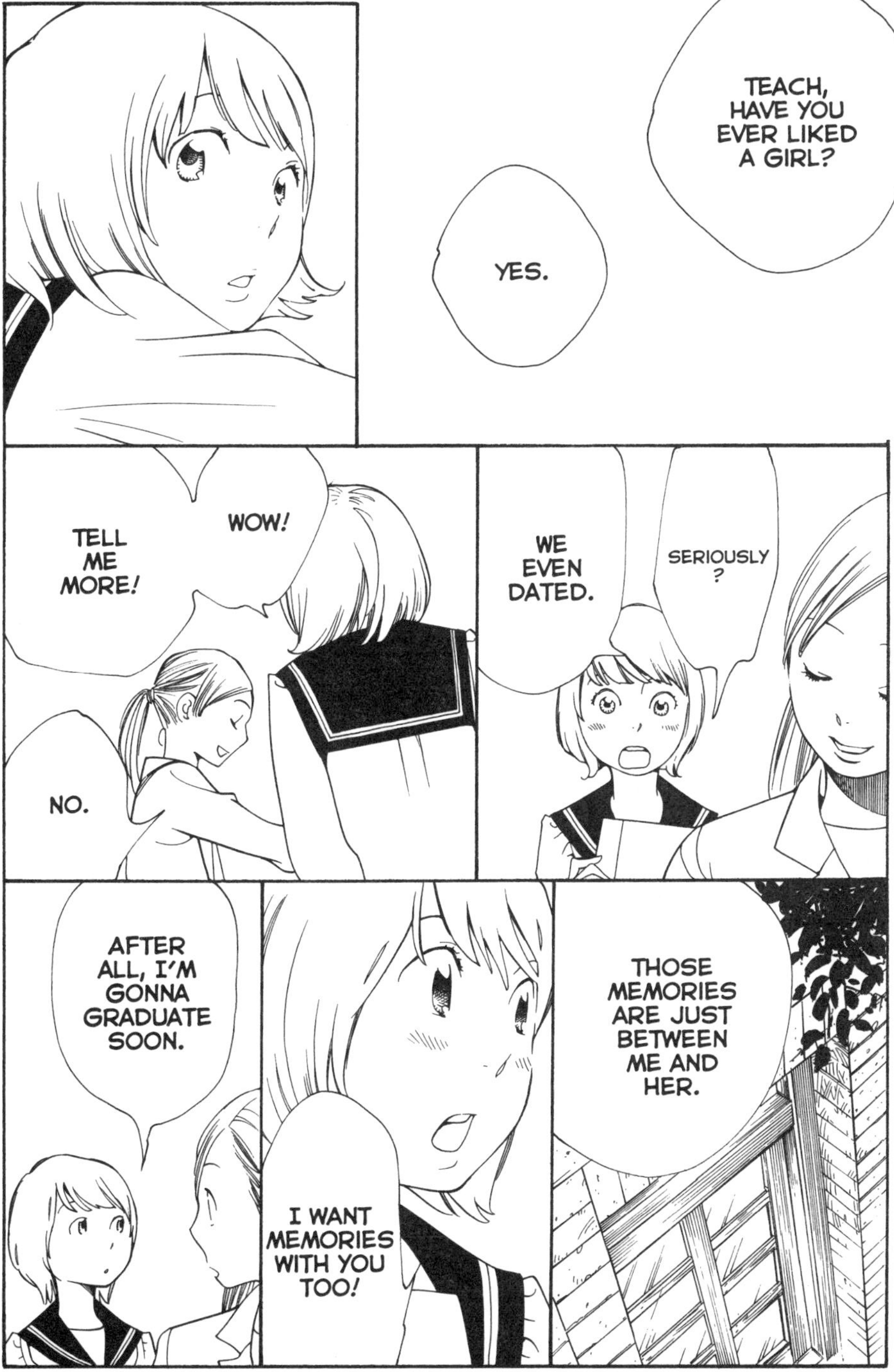
TEACH, HAVE YOU EVER LIKED A GIRL?
YES.
SERIOUSLY?
WE EVEN DATED.
WOW!
TELL ME MORE!
NO.
THOSE MEMORIES ARE JUST BETWEEN ME AND HER.
I WANT MEMORIES WITH YOU TOO!
AFTER ALL, I'M GONNA GRADUATE SOON.

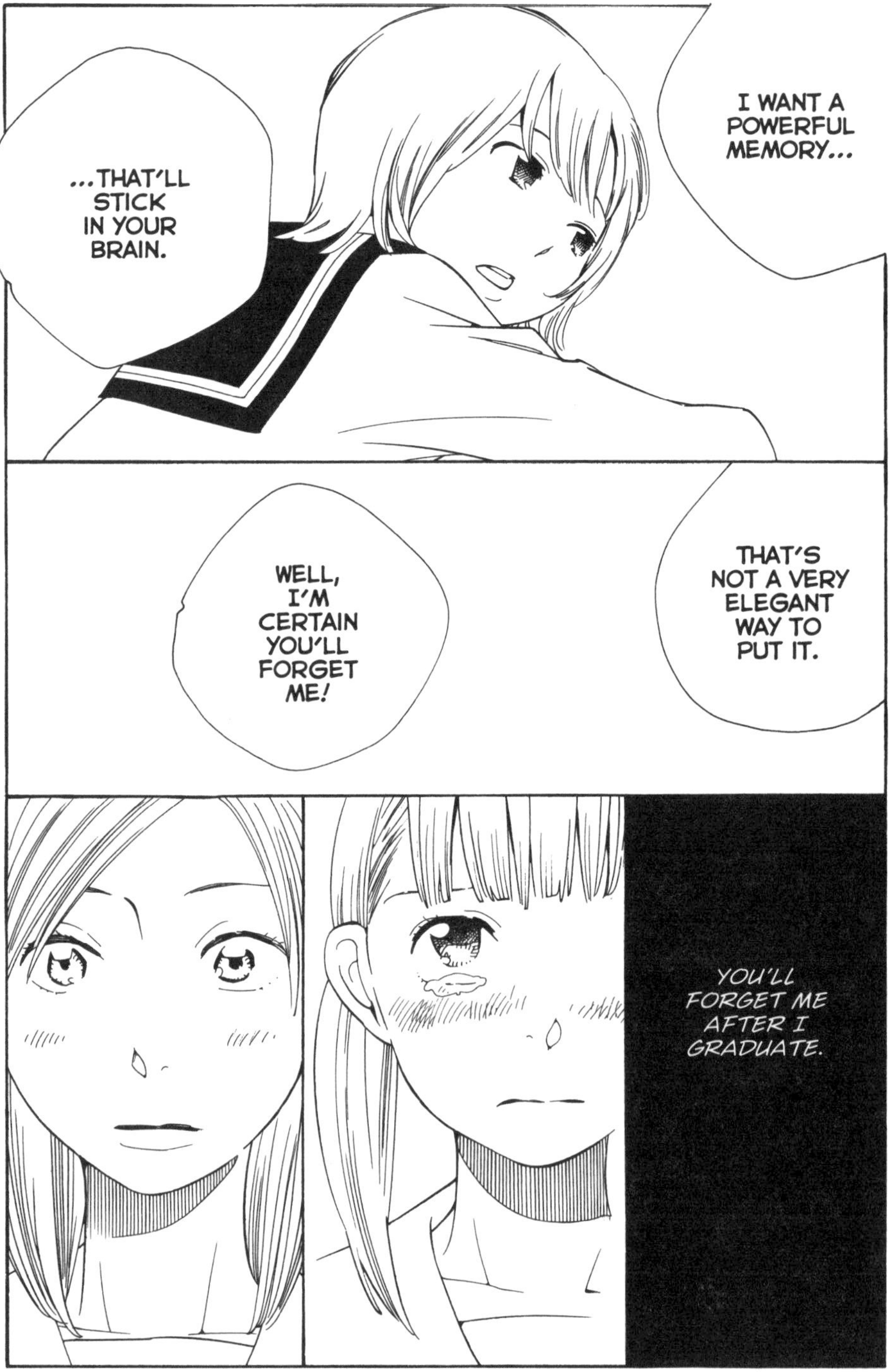
I WANT A POWERFUL MEMORY...
...THAT'LL STICK IN YOUR BRAIN.
THAT'S NOT A VERY ELEGANT WAY TO PUT IT.
WELL, I'M CERTAIN YOU'LL FORGET ME!
YOU'LL FORGET ME AFTER I GRADUATE.

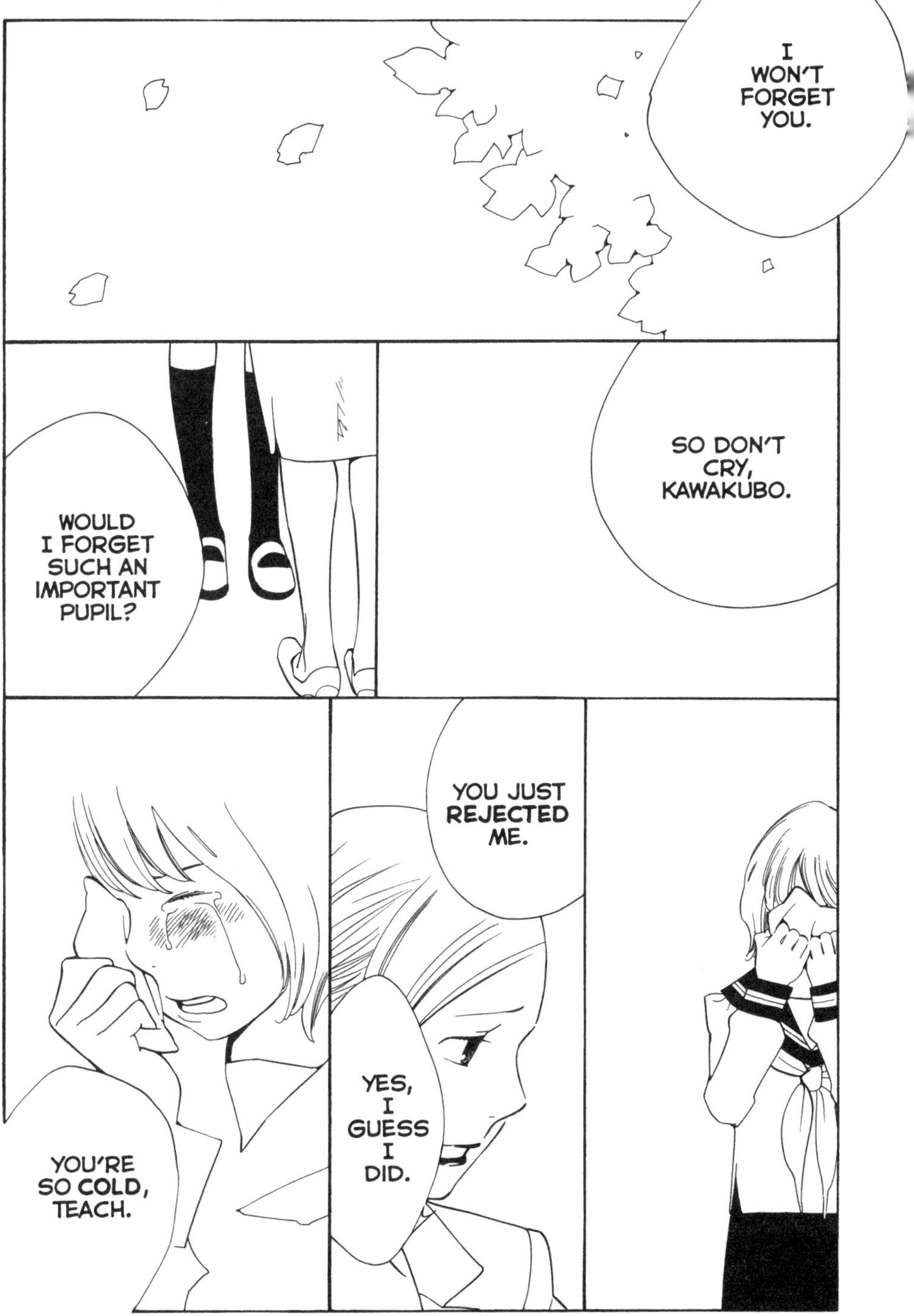
I WON'T FORGET YOU.
SO DON'T CRY, KAWAKUBO.
WOULD I FORGET SUCH AN IMPORTANT PUPIL?
YOU JUST REJECTED ME.
YES, I GUESS I DID.
YOU'RE SO COLD, TEACH.

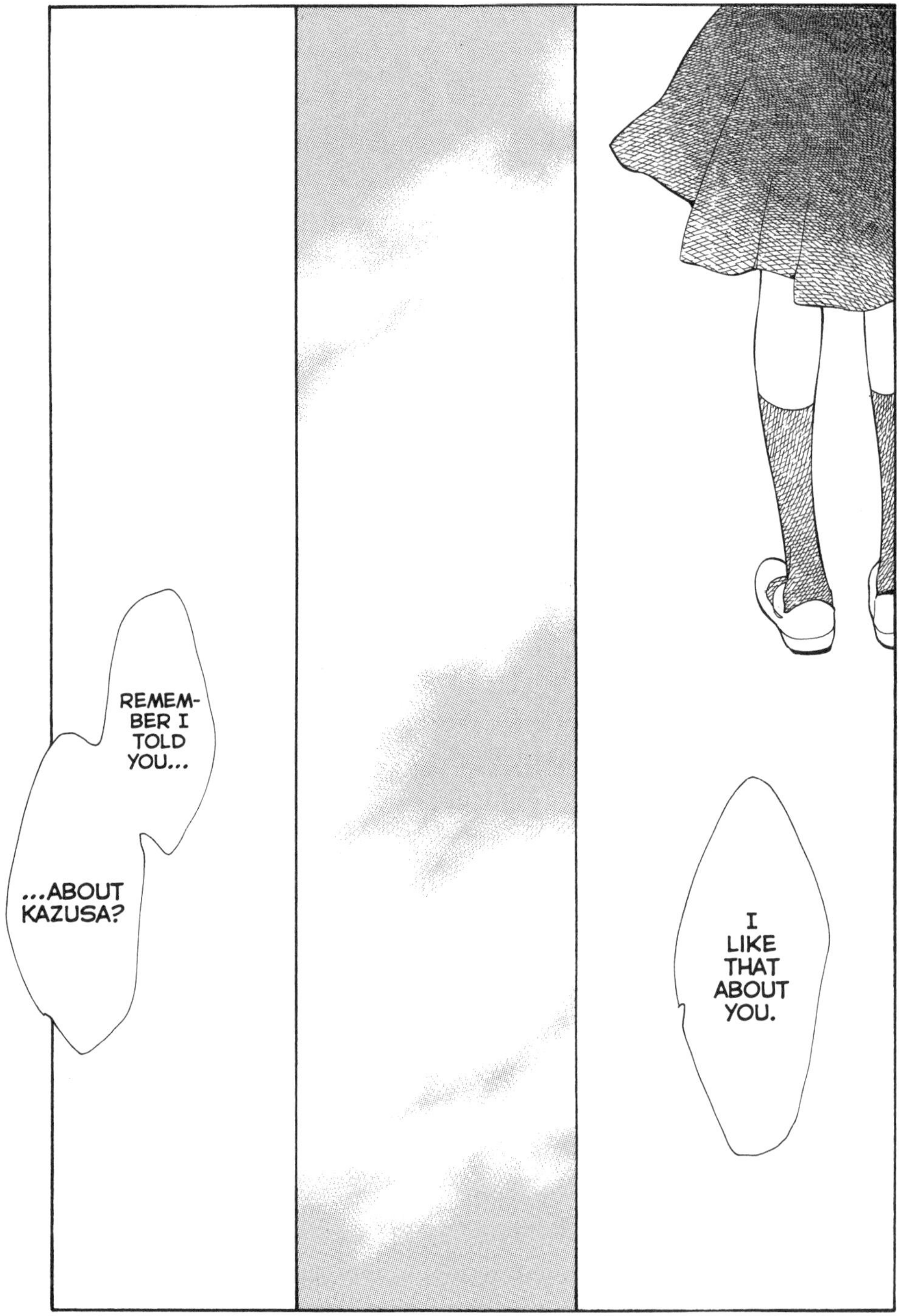
I LIKE THAT ABOUT YOU.
REMEMBER I TOLD YOU...
...ABOUT KAZUSA?

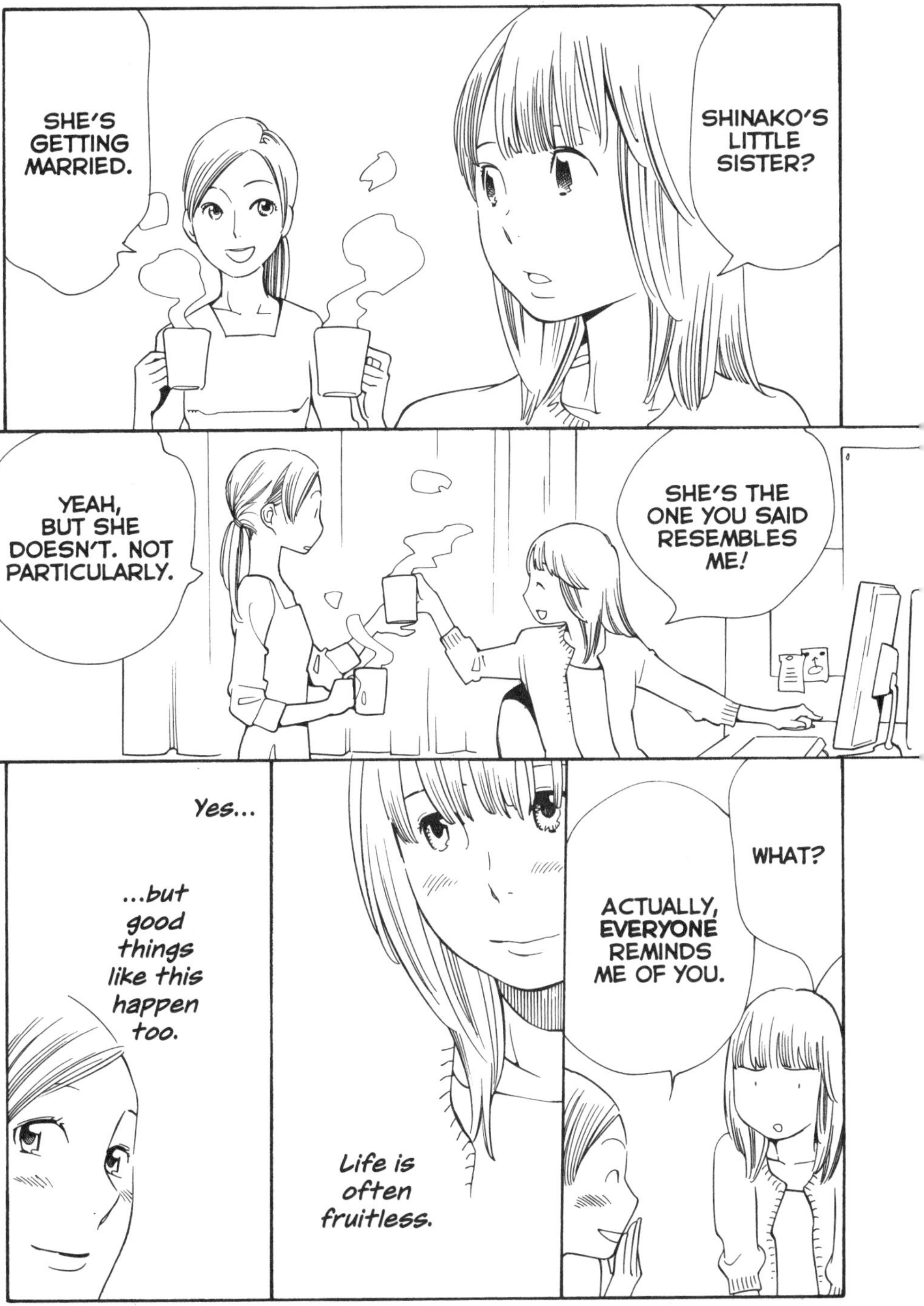
SHINAKO'S LITTLE SISTER?
SHE'S GETTING MARRIED.
SHE'S THE ONE YOU SAID RESEMBLES ME!
YEAH, BUT SHE DOESN'T. NOT PARTICULARLY.
WHAT?
ACTUALLY, **EVERYONE** REMINDS ME OF YOU.
Life is often fruitless.
Yes...
...but good things like this happen too.

Sweet Blue
Flowers

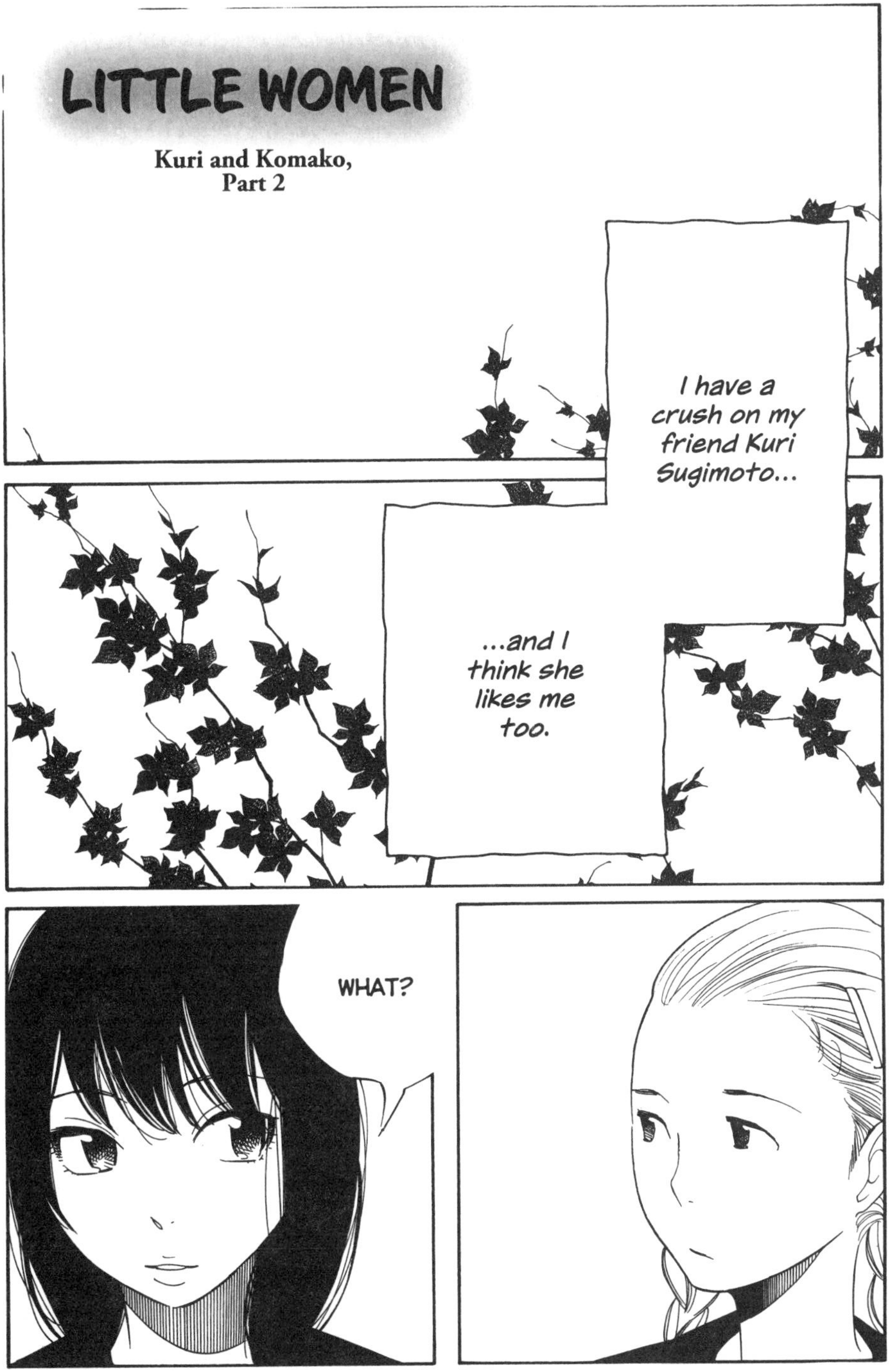
LITTLE WOMEN
Kuri and Komako, Part 2
I have a crush on my friend Kuri Sugimoto...
...and I think she likes me too.
WHAT?

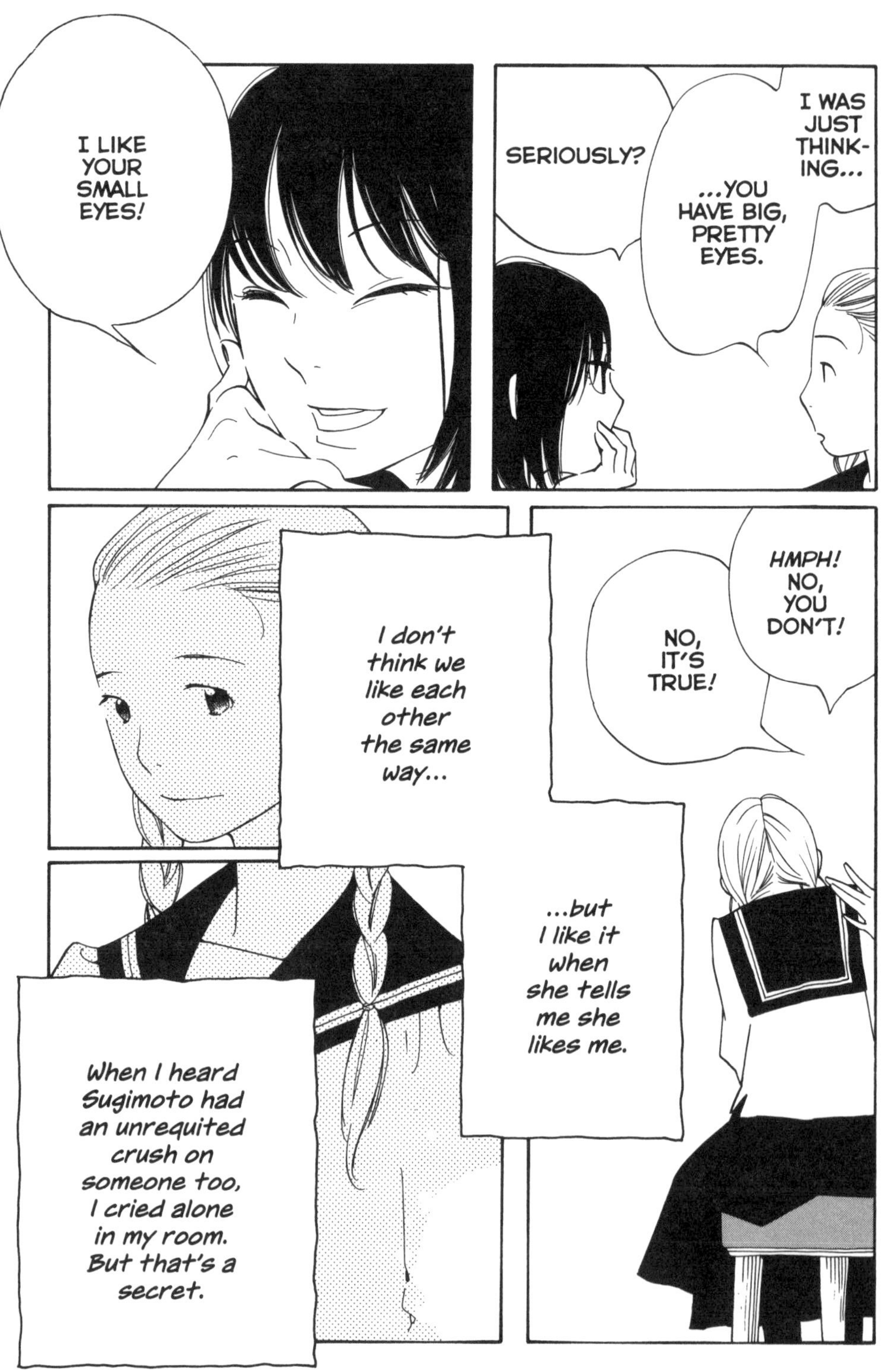
I WAS JUST THINKING...
...YOU HAVE BIG, PRETTY EYES.
SERIOUSLY?
I LIKE YOUR SMALL EYES!
HMPH! NO, YOU DON'T!
NO, IT'S TRUE!
I don't think we like each other the same way...
...but I like it when she tells me she likes me.
When I heard Sugimoto had an unrequited crush on someone too, I cried alone in my room. But that's a secret.

The End

Sweet **Blue**
Flowers

Sweet *Blue* *Flowers*

Part Four

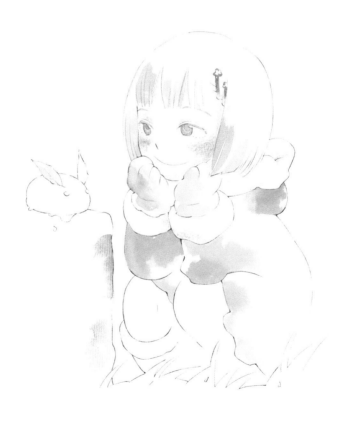

Story and Art by
Takako Shimura

By Haruka Ono

Sweet Blue Flowers Characters

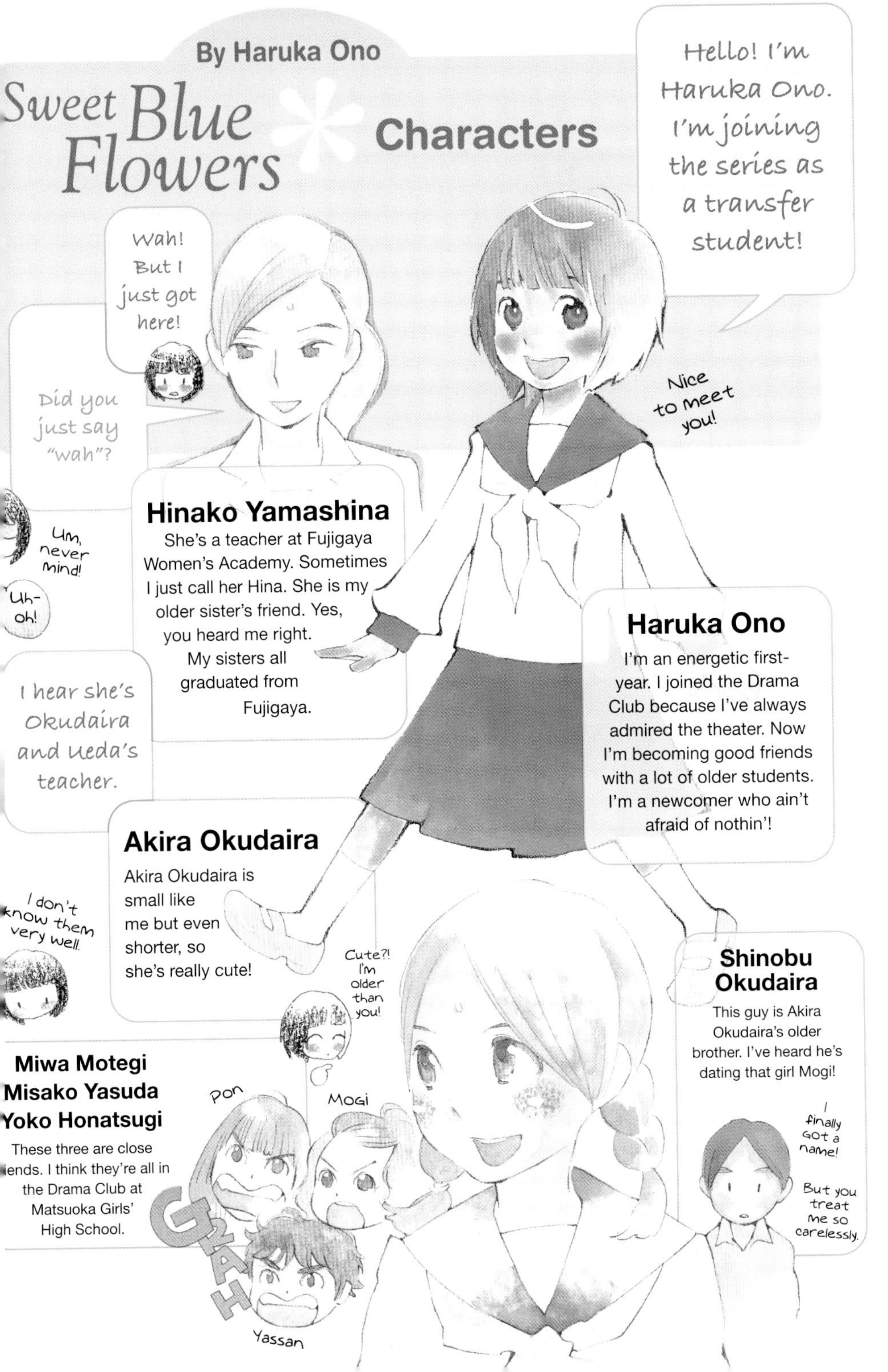
Hello! I'm Haruka Ono. I'm joining the series as a transfer student!
Nice to meet you!
Wah! But I just got here!
Did you just say "wah"?
Um, never mind!
Uh-oh!
I hear she's Okudaira and Ueda's teacher.
I don't know them very well.
Cute?! I'm older than you!
Pon
Mogi
GWAH
Yassan
I finally got a name!
But you treat me so carelessly.

Hinako Yamashina

She's a teacher at Fujigaya Women's Academy. Sometimes I just call her Hina. She is my older sister's friend. Yes, you heard me right. My sisters all graduated from Fujigaya.

Haruka Ono

I'm an energetic first-year. I joined the Drama Club because I've always admired the theater. Now I'm becoming good friends with a lot of older students. I'm a newcomer who ain't afraid of nothin'!

Akira Okudaira

Akira Okudaira is small like me but even shorter, so she's really cute!

Shinobu Okudaira

This guy is Akira Okudaira's older brother. I've heard he's dating that girl Mogi!

Miwa Motegi
Misako Yasuda
Yoko Honatsugi

These three are close iends. I think they're all in the Drama Club at Matsuoka Girls' High School.

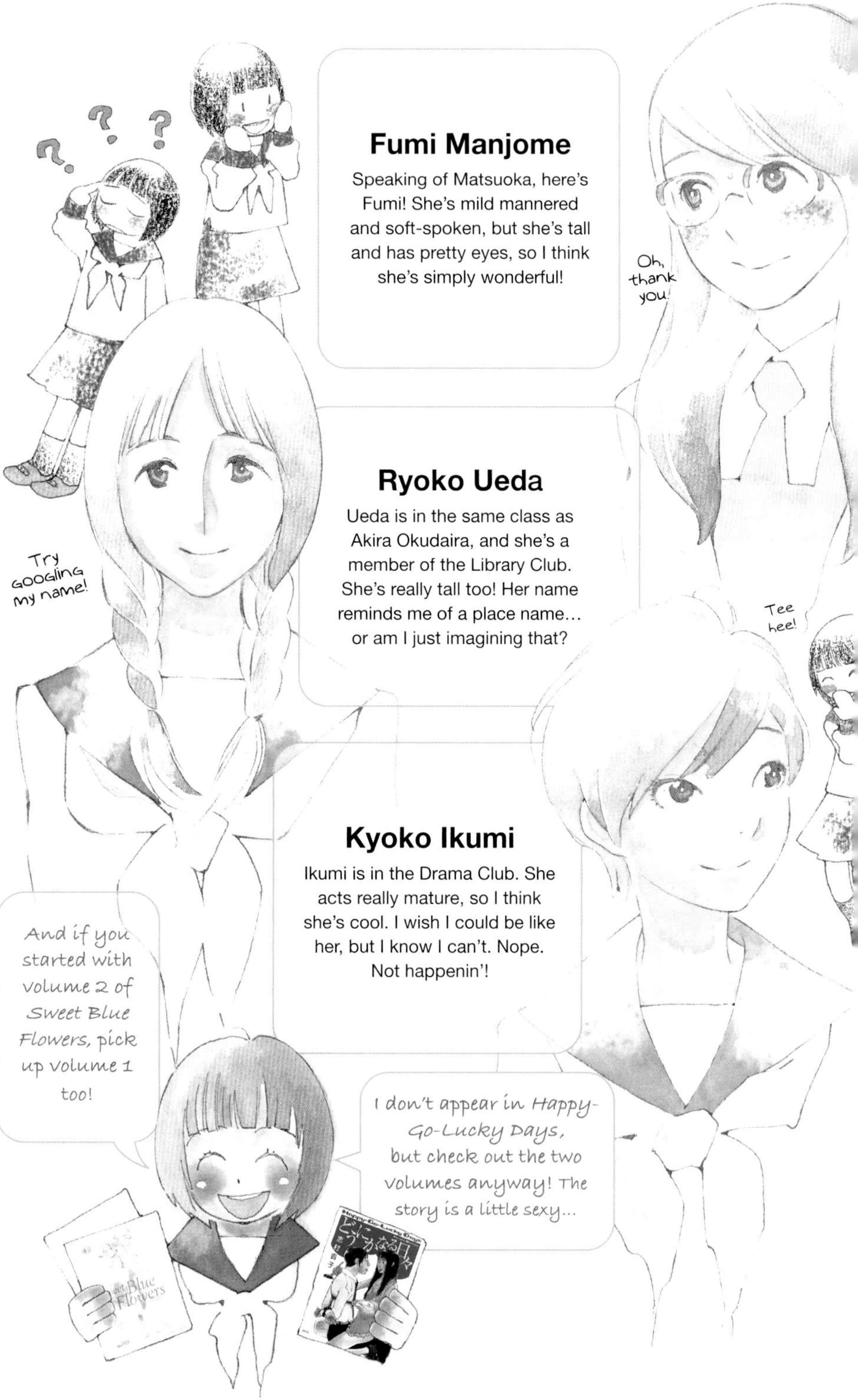
Fumi Manjome
Speaking of Matsuoka, here's Fumi! She's mild mannered and soft-spoken, but she's tall and has pretty eyes, so I think she's simply wonderful!
Oh, thank you!
Ryoko Ueda
Ueda is in the same class as Akira Okudaira, and she's a member of the Library Club. She's really tall too! Her name reminds me of a place name… or am I just imagining that?
Try GOOGLING my name!
Tee hee!
Kyoko Ikumi
Ikumi is in the Drama Club. She acts really mature, so I think she's cool. I wish I could be like her, but I know I can't. Nope. Not happenin'!
I don't appear in Happy-Go-Lucky Days, but check out the two volumes anyway! The story is a little sexy…
And if you started with volume 2 of Sweet Blue Flowers, pick up volume 1 too!

Sweet Blue Flowers

Part Four

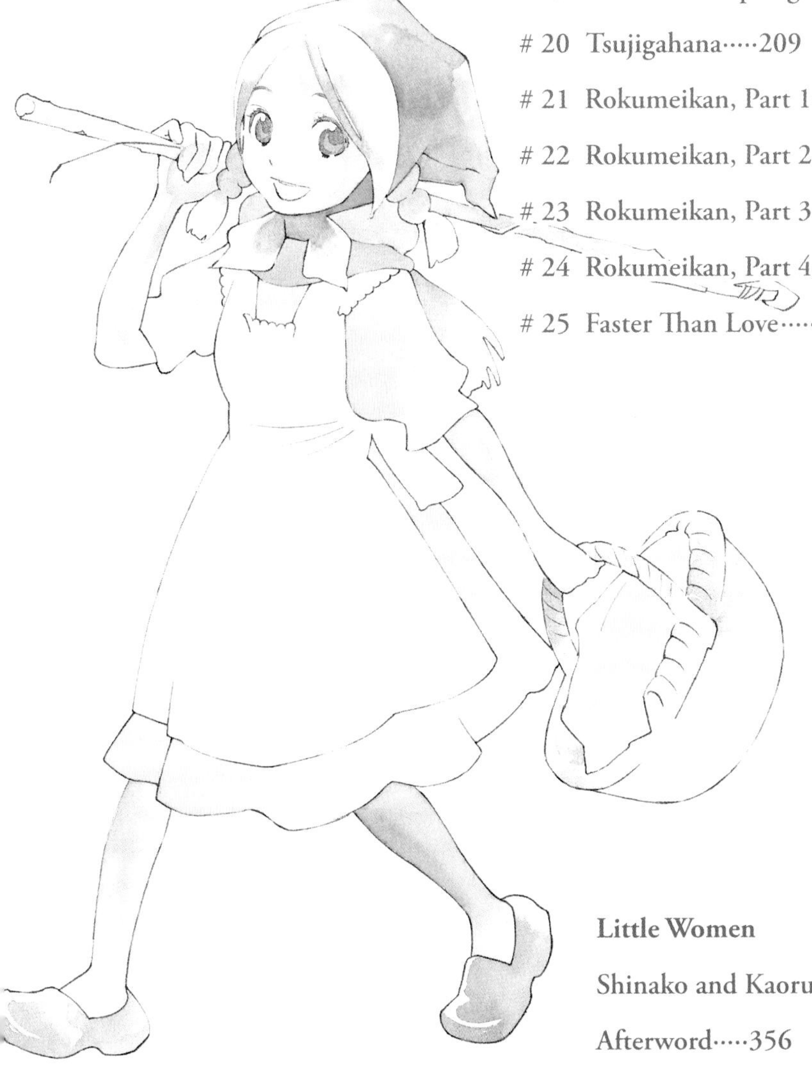

Little Women

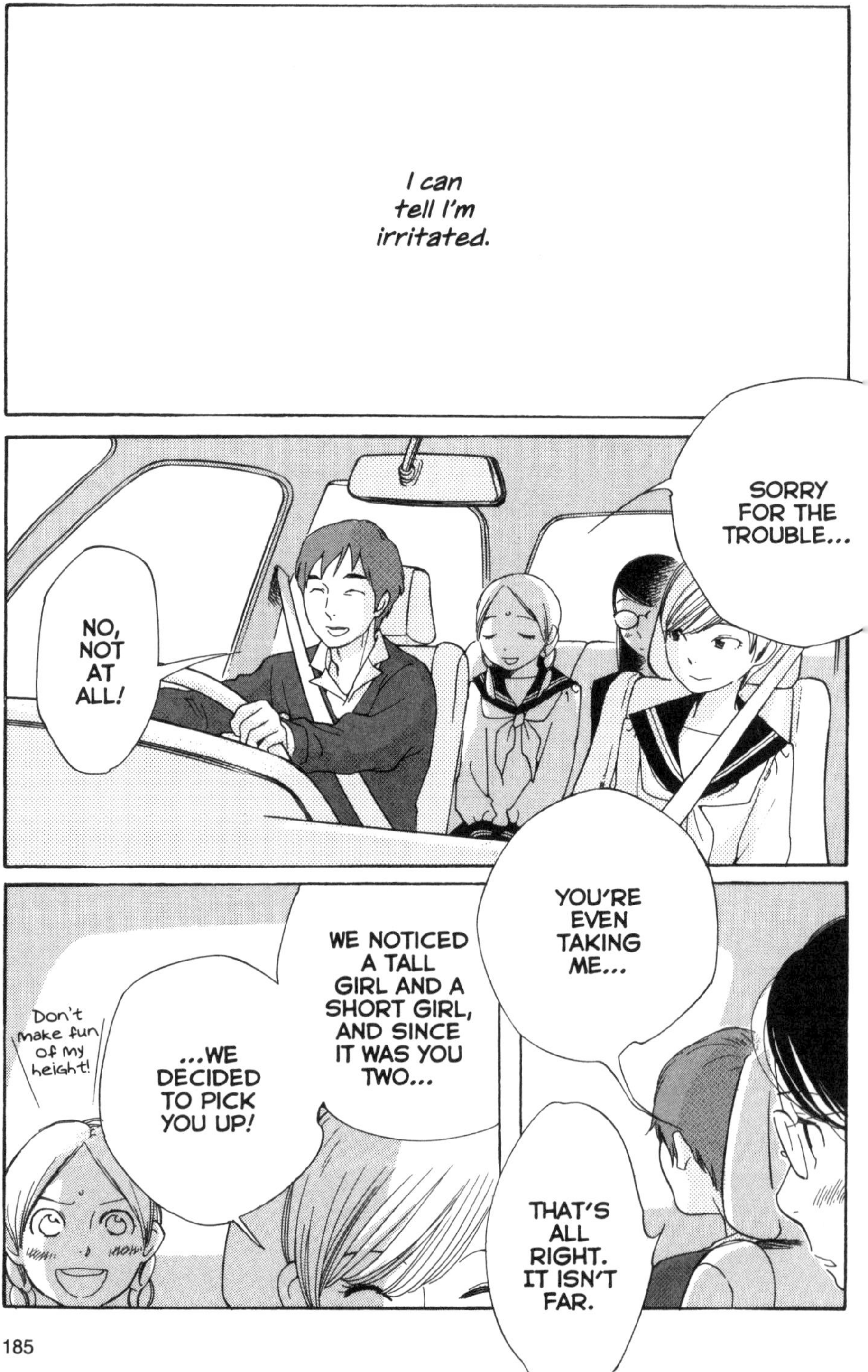
I can tell I'm irritated.
SORRY FOR THE TROUBLE...
NO, NOT AT ALL!
YOU'RE EVEN TAKING ME...
THAT'S ALL RIGHT. IT ISN'T FAR.
WE NOTICED A TALL GIRL AND A SHORT GIRL, AND SINCE IT WAS YOU TWO...
...WE DECIDED TO PICK YOU UP!
Don't make fun of my height!

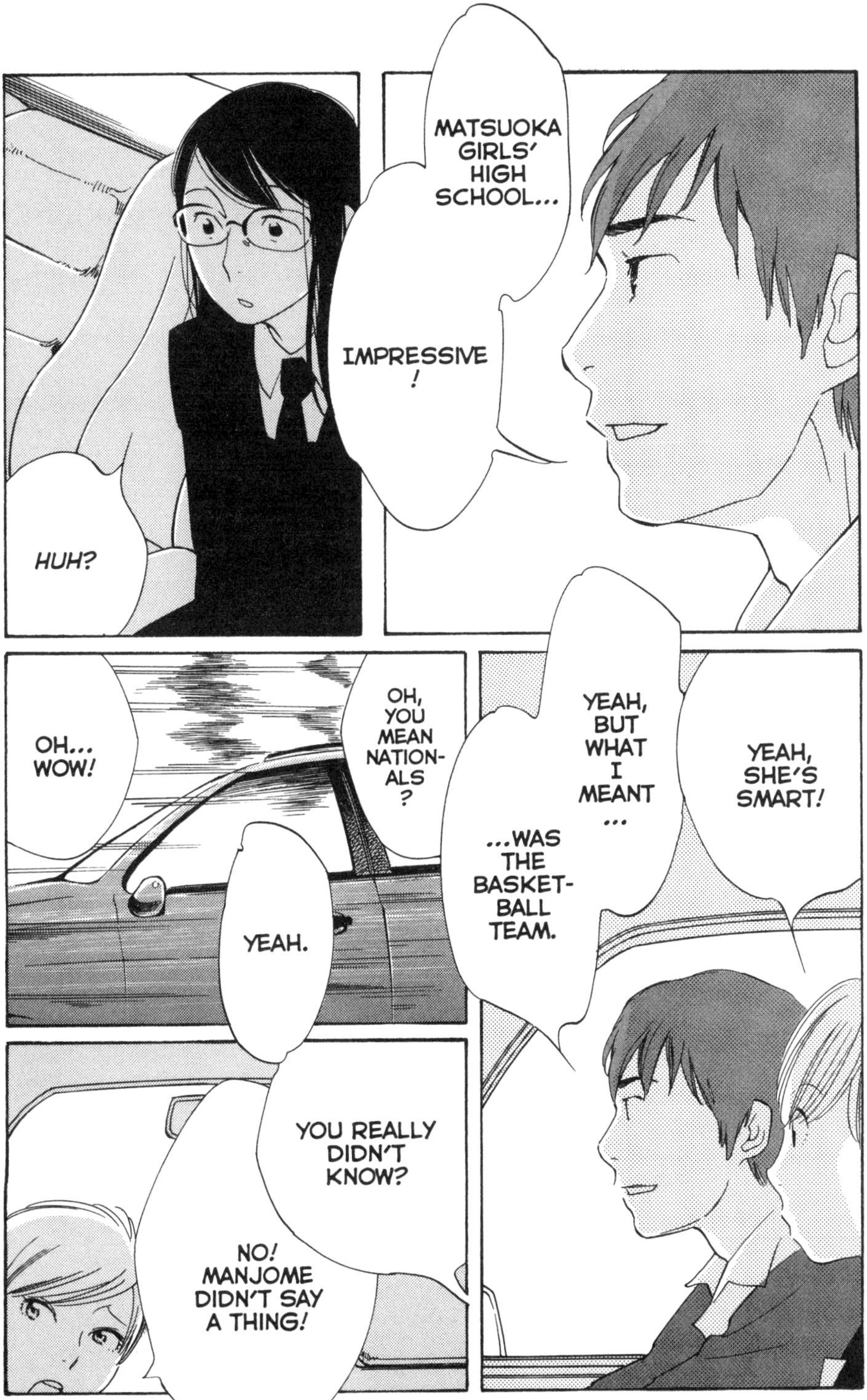
MATSUOKA GIRLS' HIGH SCHOOL...
IMPRESSIVE!
HUH?
YEAH, SHE'S SMART!
YEAH, BUT WHAT I MEANT...
...WAS THE BASKETBALL TEAM.
OH, YOU MEAN NATIONALS?
YEAH.
OH... WOW!
YOU REALLY DIDN'T KNOW?
NO! MANJOME DIDN'T SAY A THING!

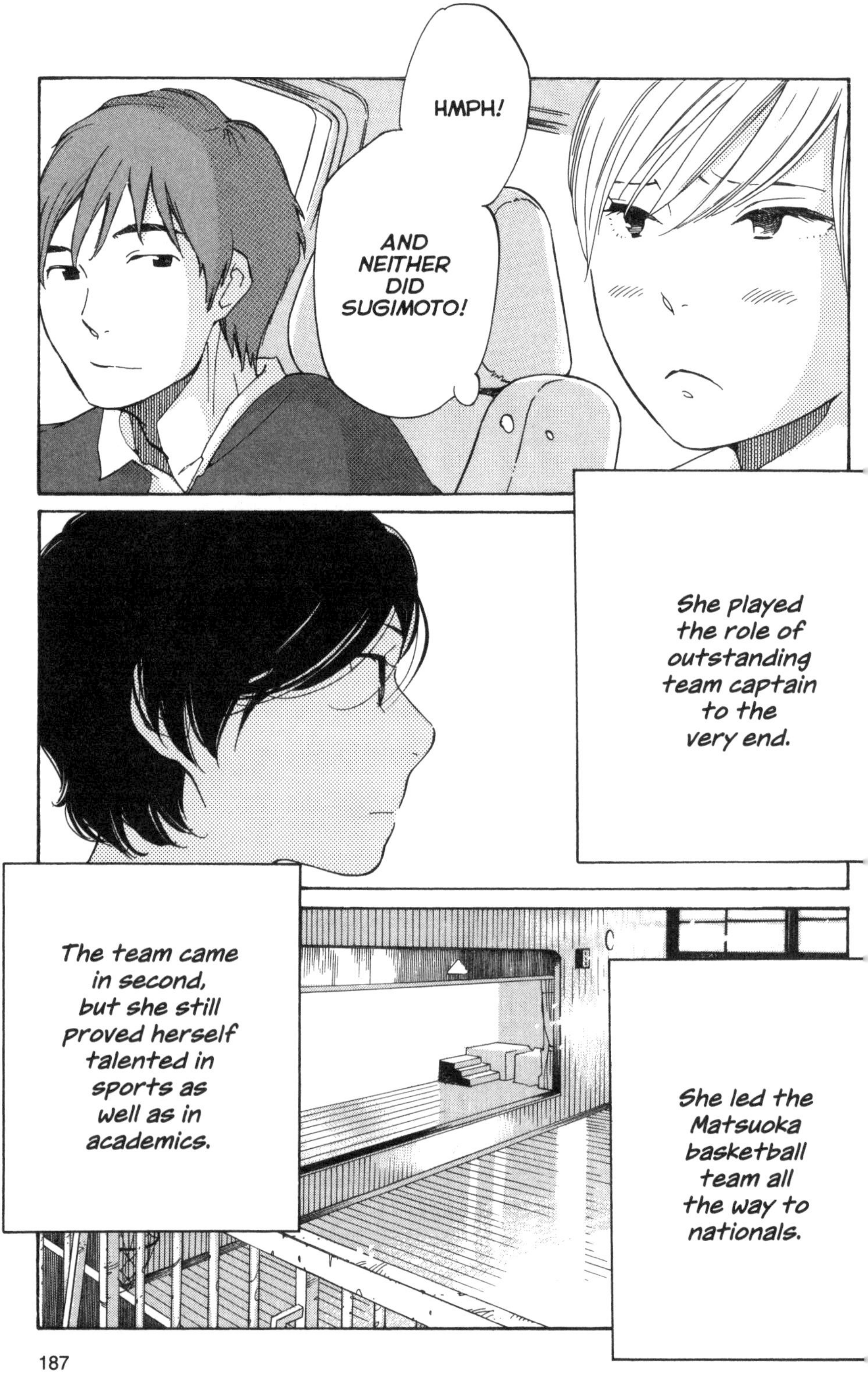
HMPH!
AND NEITHER DID SUGIMOTO!
She played the role of outstanding team captain to the very end.
She led the Matsuoka basketball team all the way to nationals.
The team came in second, but she still proved herself talented in sports as well as in academics.

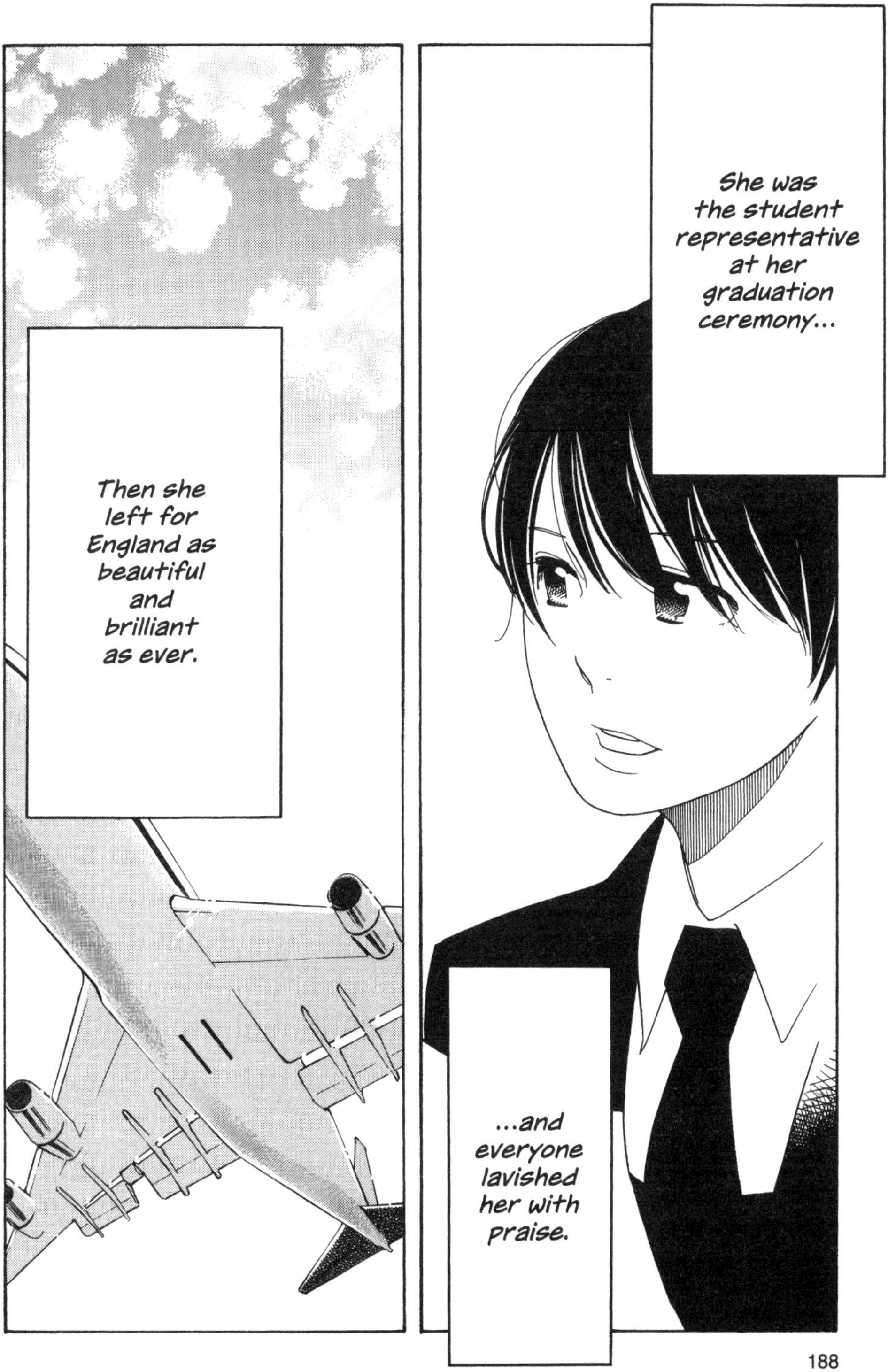
She was the student representative at her graduation ceremony...
...and everyone lavished her with praise.
Then she left for England as beautiful and brilliant as ever.

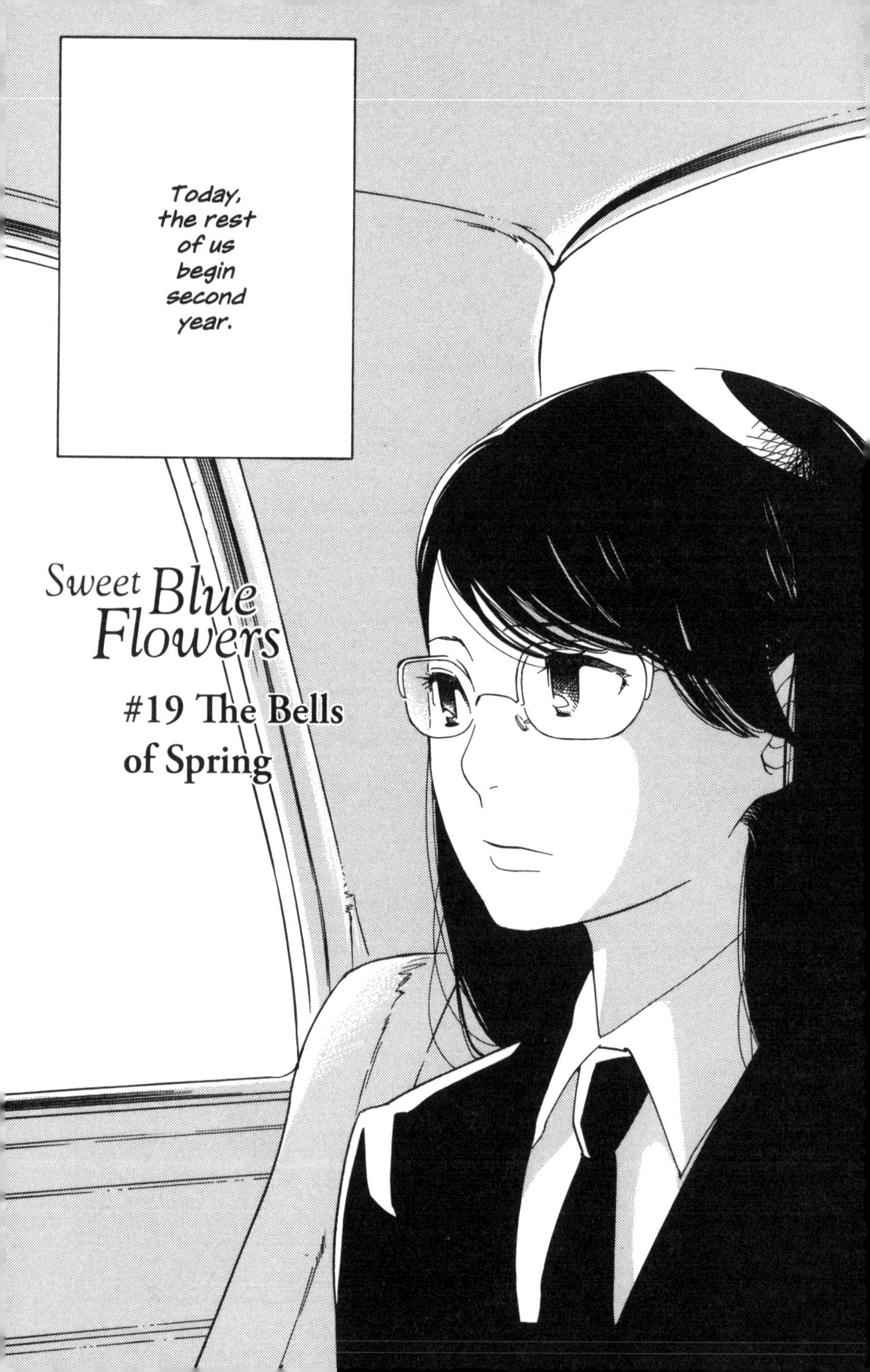
Today, the rest of us begin second year.
Sweet Blue Flowers
#19 The Bells of Spring

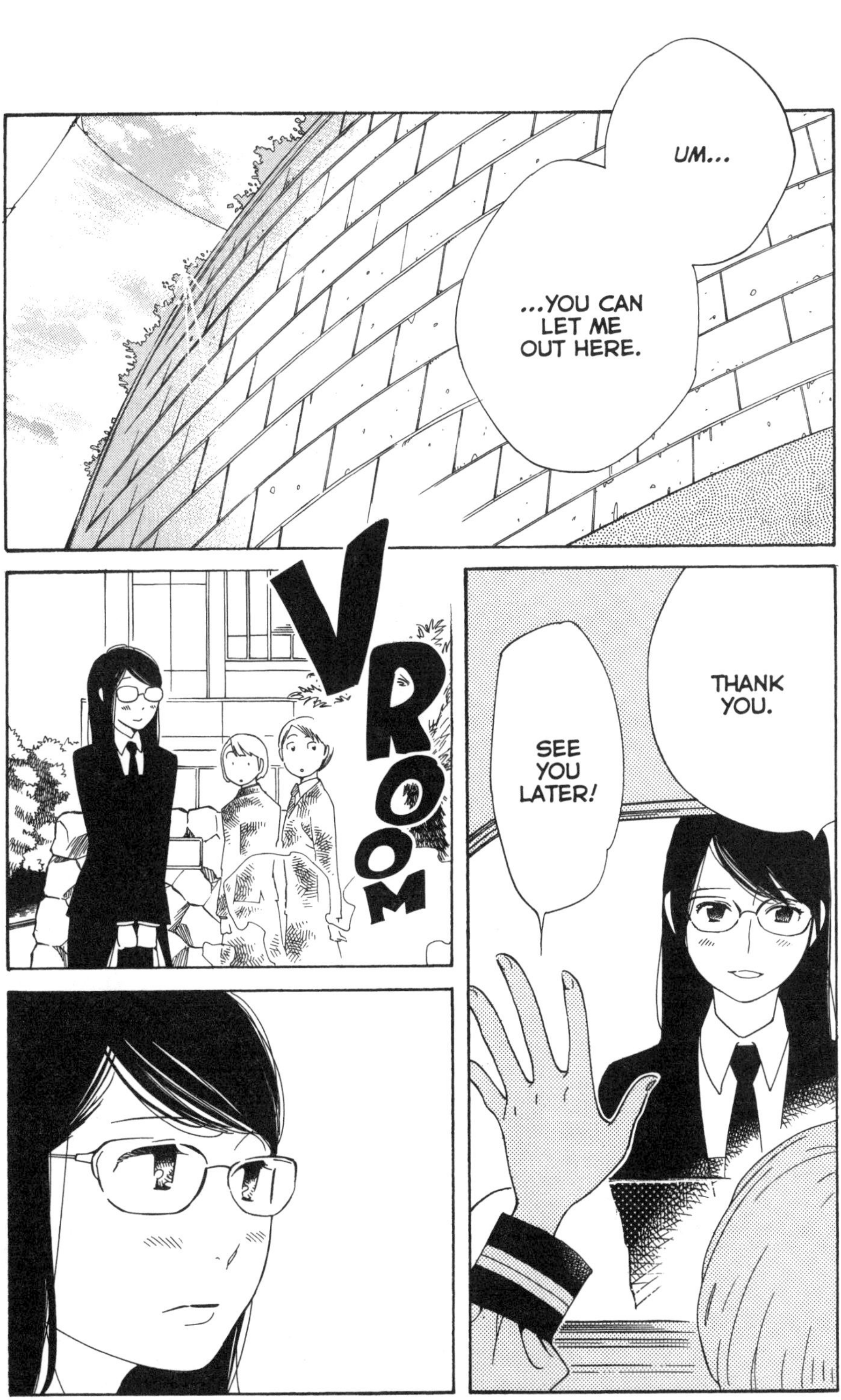
UM...
...YOU CAN LET ME OUT HERE.
THANK YOU.
SEE YOU LATER!
VROOM

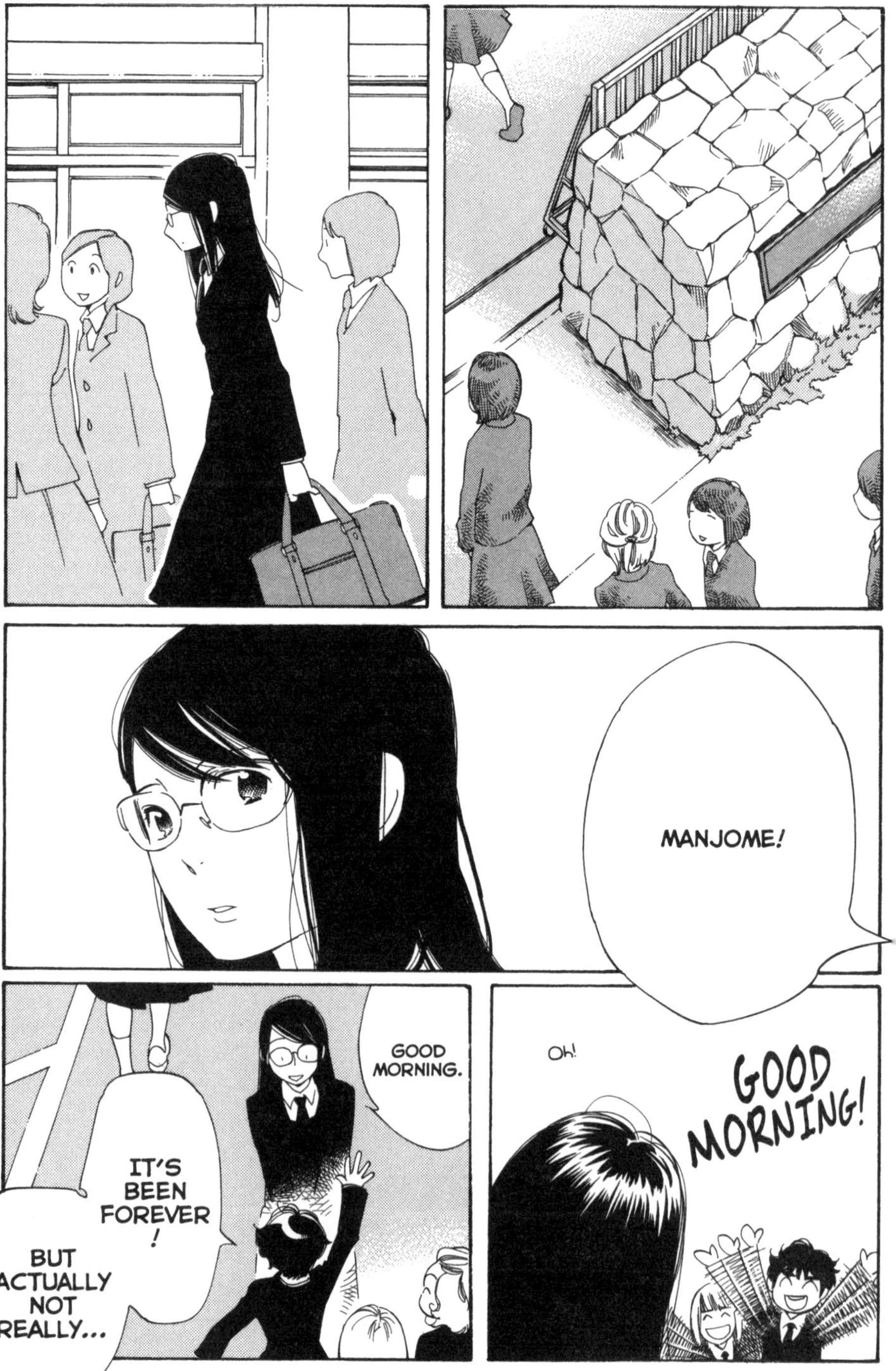
MANJOME!
Oh!
GOOD MORNING!
GOOD MORNING.
IT'S BEEN FOREVER!
BUT ACTUALLY NOT REALLY...

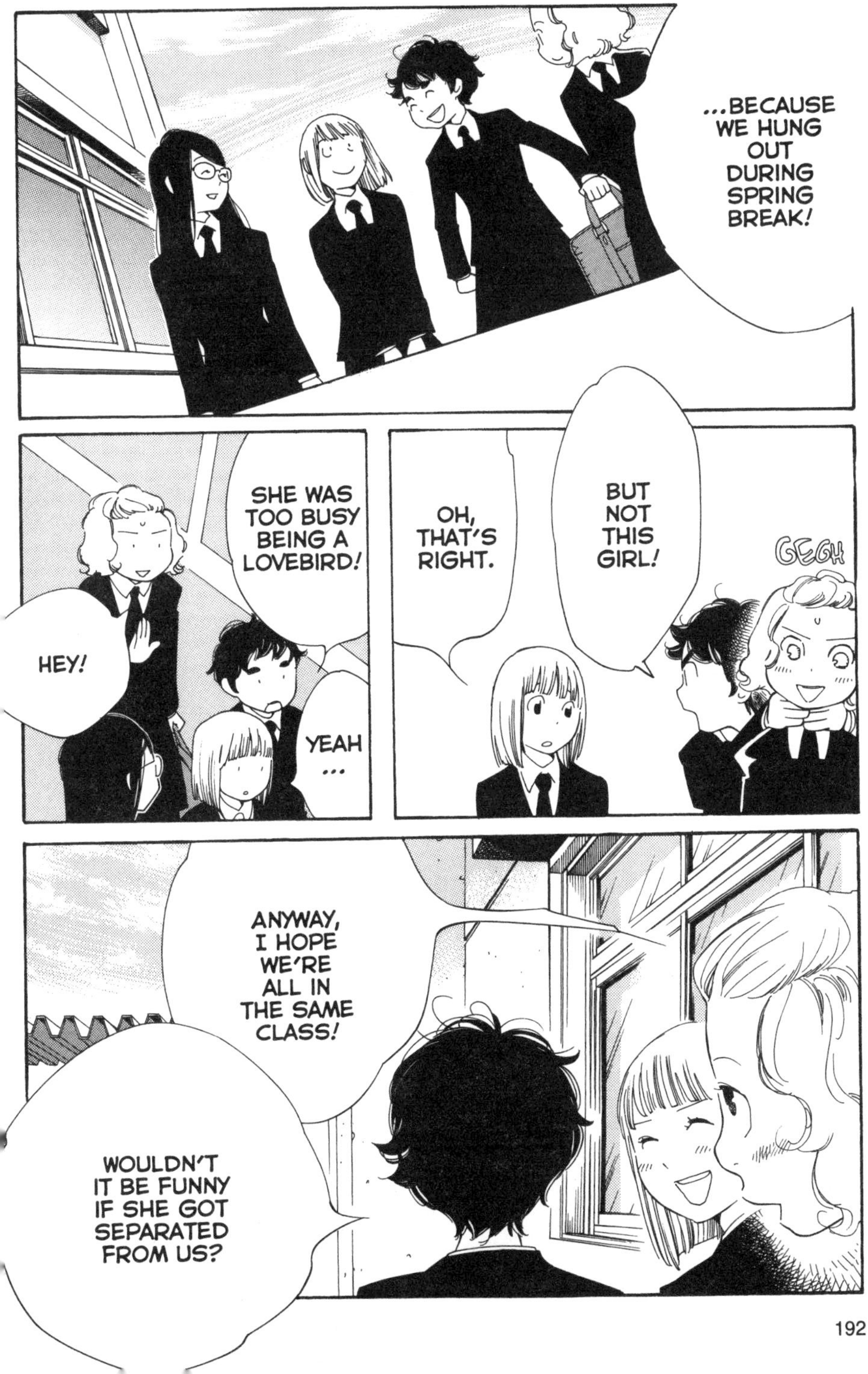
...BECAUSE WE HUNG OUT DURING SPRING BREAK!
GEGH
BUT NOT THIS GIRL!
OH, THAT'S RIGHT.
SHE WAS TOO BUSY BEING A LOVEBIRD!
HEY!
YEAH...
ANYWAY, I HOPE WE'RE ALL IN THE SAME CLASS!
WOULDN'T IT BE FUNNY IF SHE GOT SEPARATED FROM US?

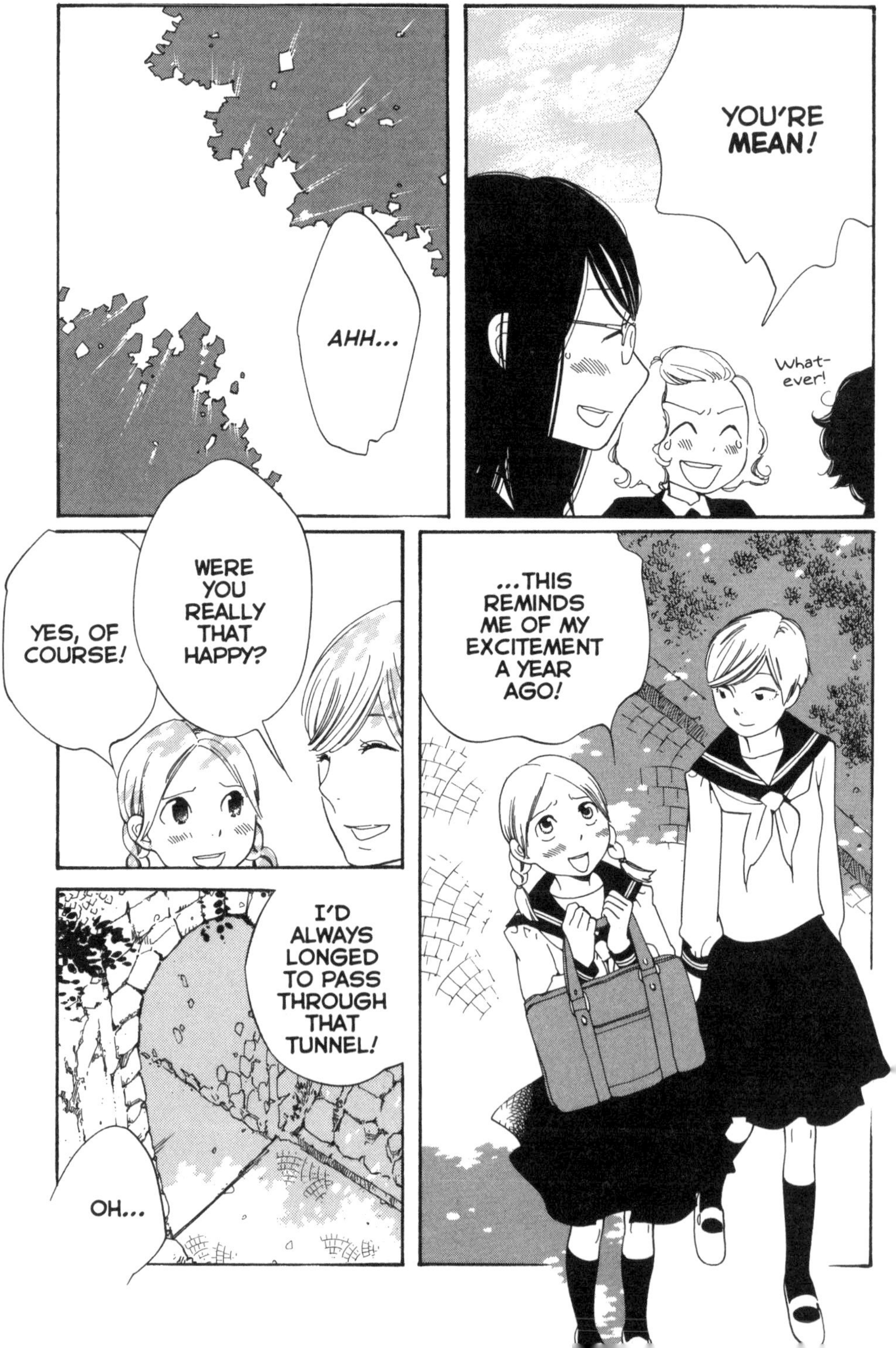
YOU'RE MEAN!
What-ever!
AHH...
...THIS REMINDS ME OF MY EXCITEMENT A YEAR AGO!
WERE YOU REALLY THAT HAPPY?
YES, OF COURSE!
I'D ALWAYS LONGED TO PASS THROUGH THAT TUNNEL!
OH...

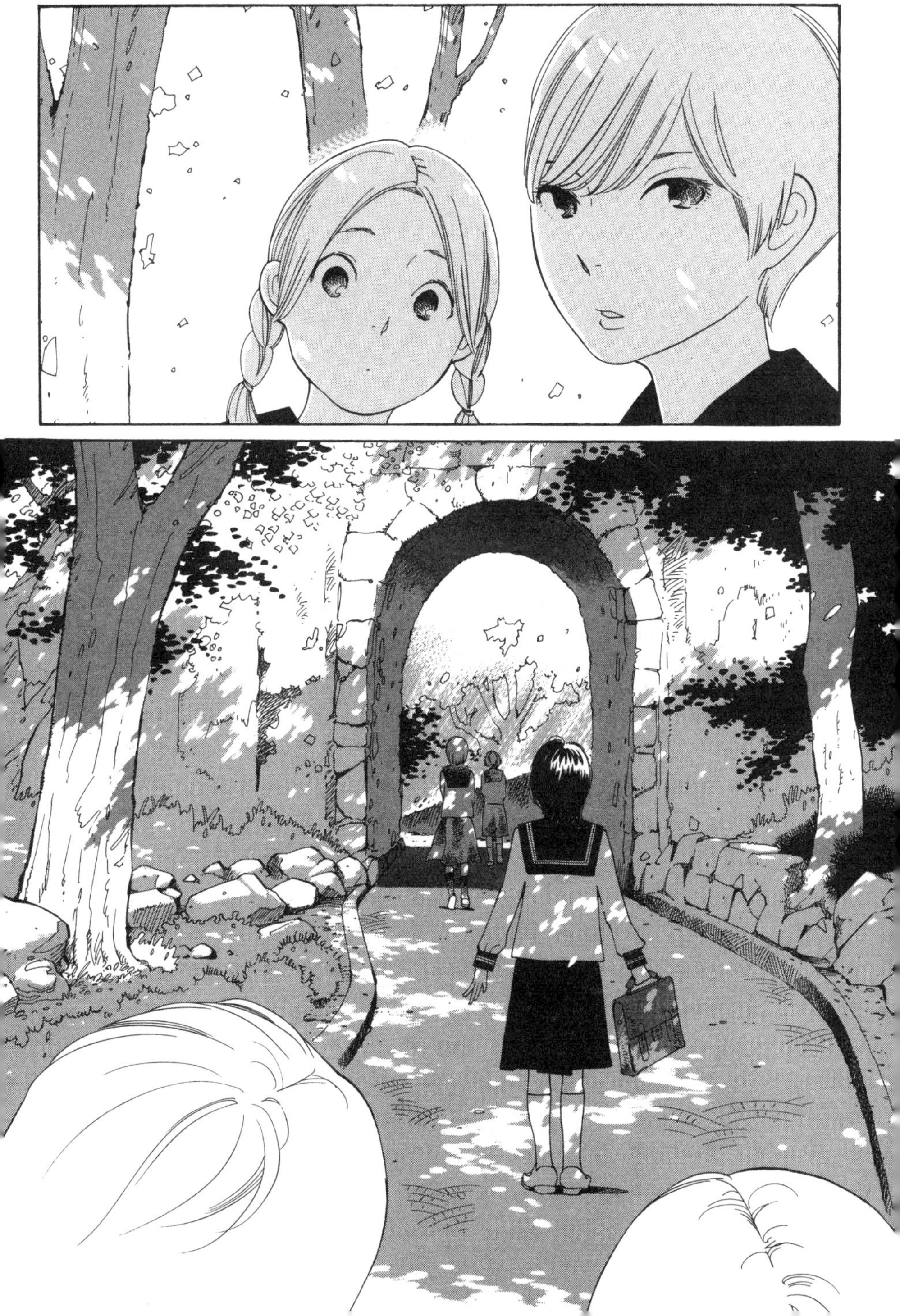

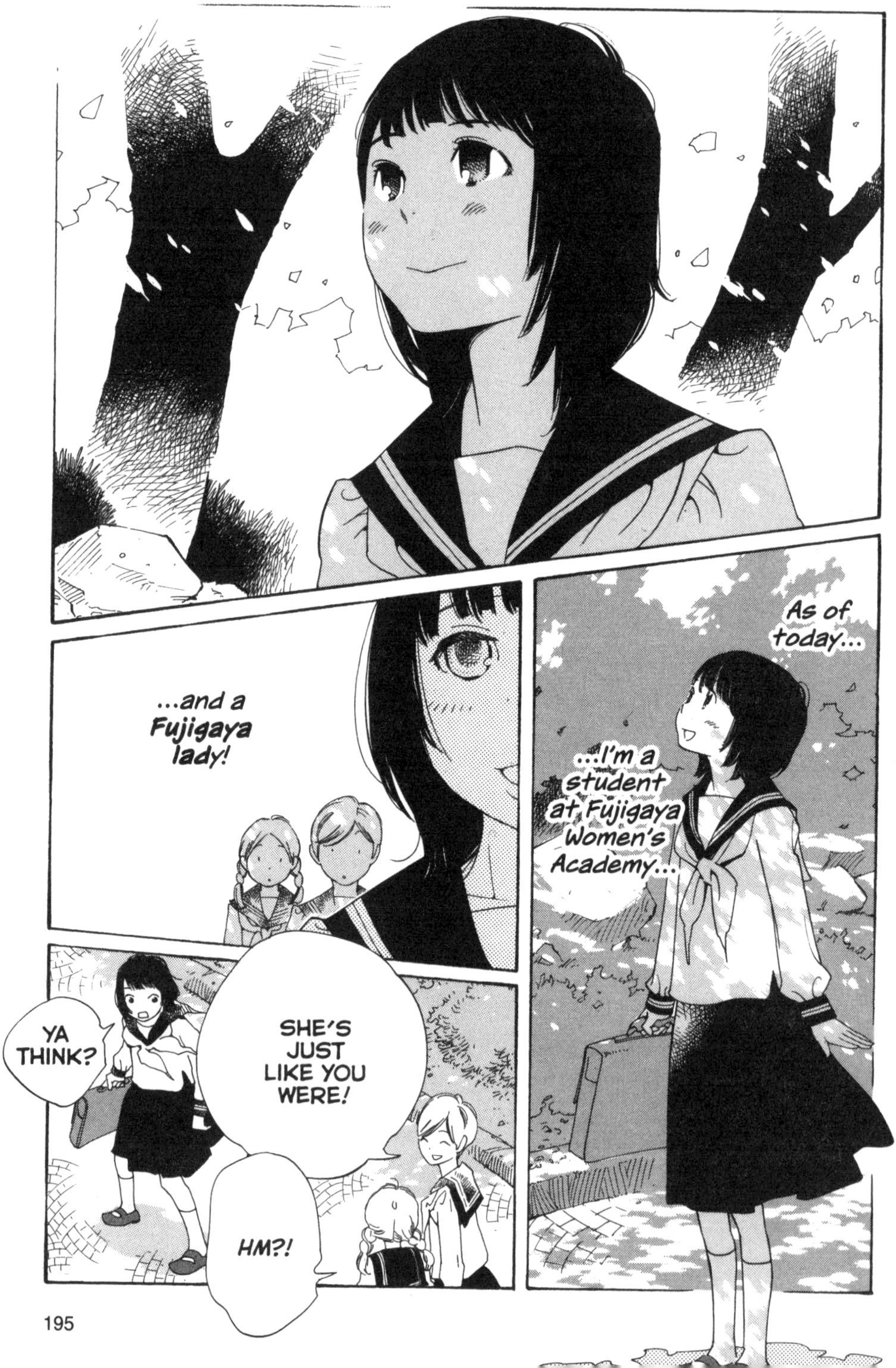
As of today...
...I'm a student at Fujigaya Women's Academy...
...and a Fujigaya lady!
SHE'S JUST LIKE YOU WERE!
HM?!
YA THINK?

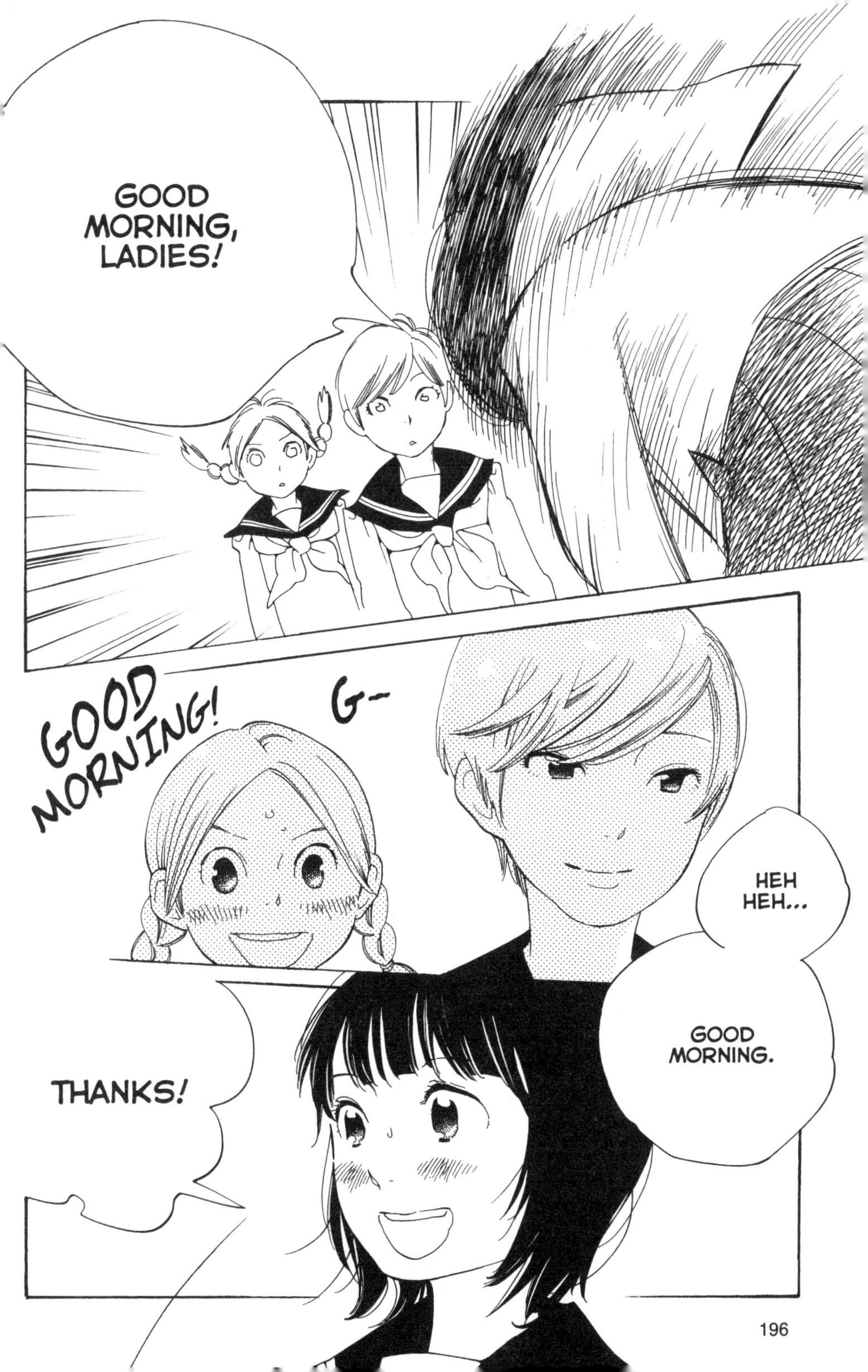
GOOD MORNING, LADIES!
HEH HEH...
GOOD MORNING.
G--
GOOD MORNING!
THANKS!

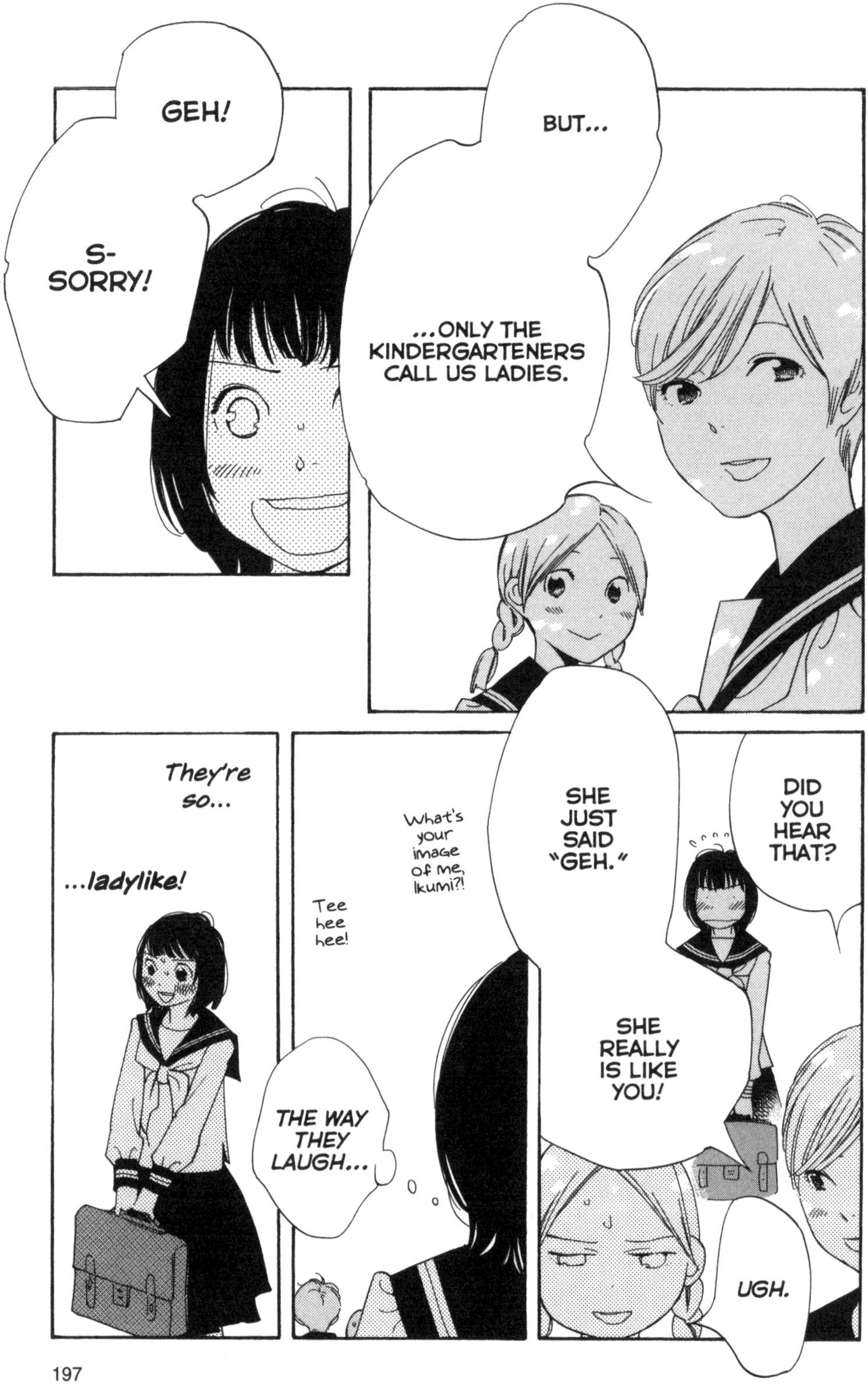
BUT...
...ONLY THE KINDERGARTENERS CALL US LADIES.
GEH!
S-SORRY!
DID YOU HEAR THAT?
SHE JUST SAID "GEH."
SHE REALLY IS LIKE YOU!
UGH.
What's your image of me, Ikumi?!
Tee hee hee!
THE WAY THEY LAUGH...
They're so...
...ladylike!

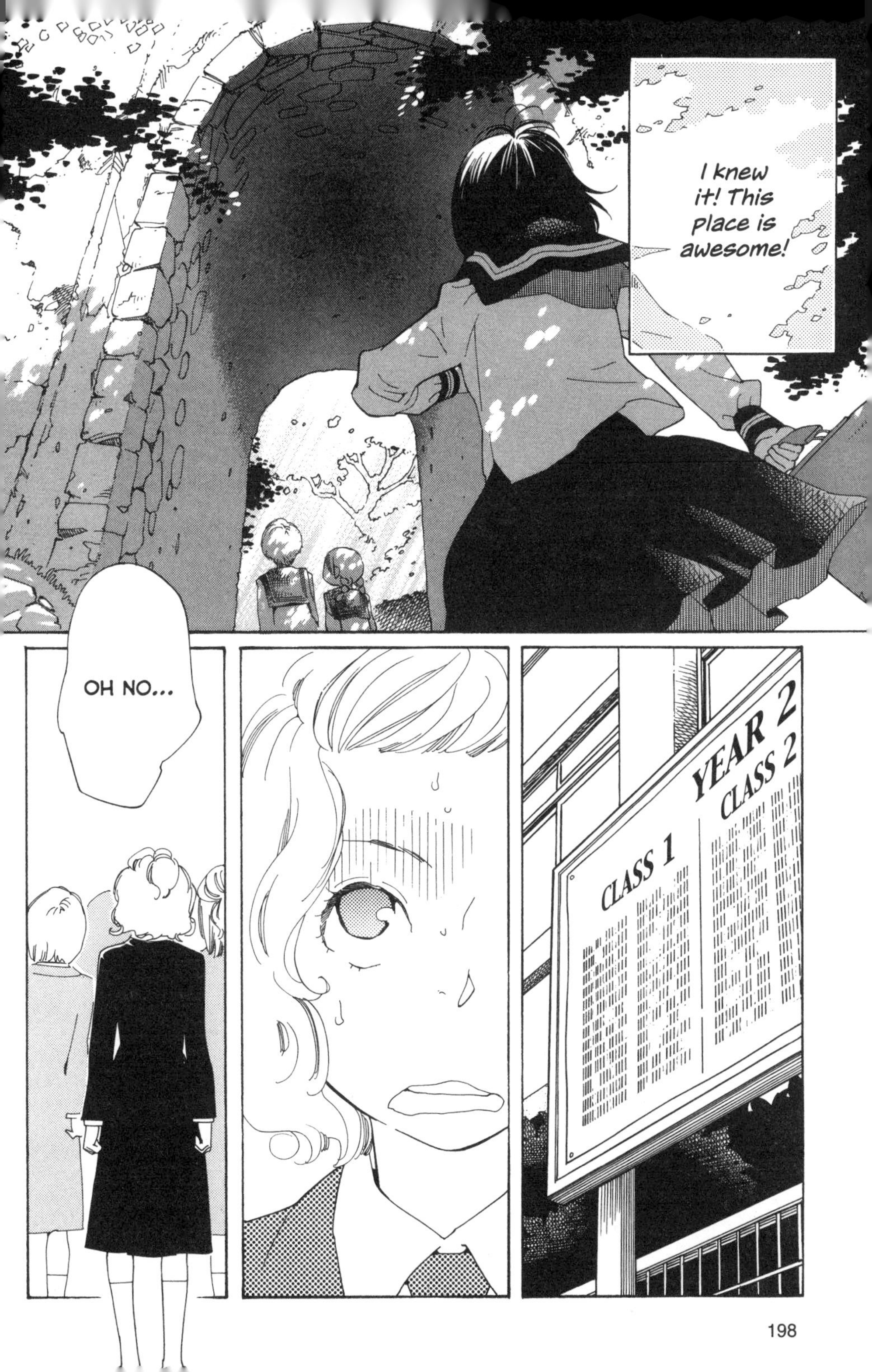

I knew it! This place is awesome!
YEAR 2
CLASS 2
CLASS 1
OH NO...

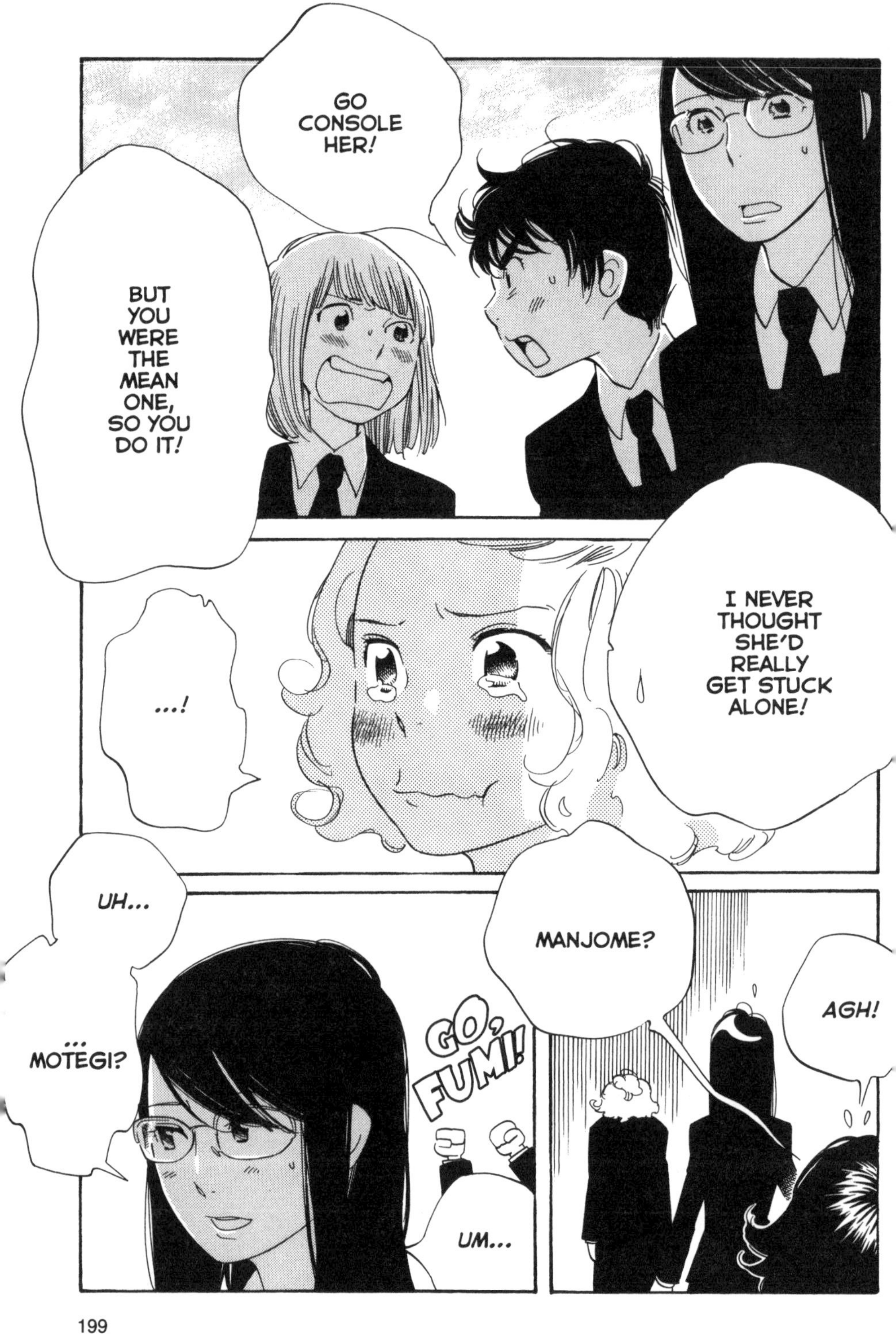
GO CONSOLE HER!
BUT YOU WERE THE MEAN ONE, SO YOU DO IT!
I NEVER THOUGHT SHE'D REALLY GET STUCK ALONE!
...!
MANJOME?
AGH!
GO, FUMI!
UH...
... MOTEGI?
UM...

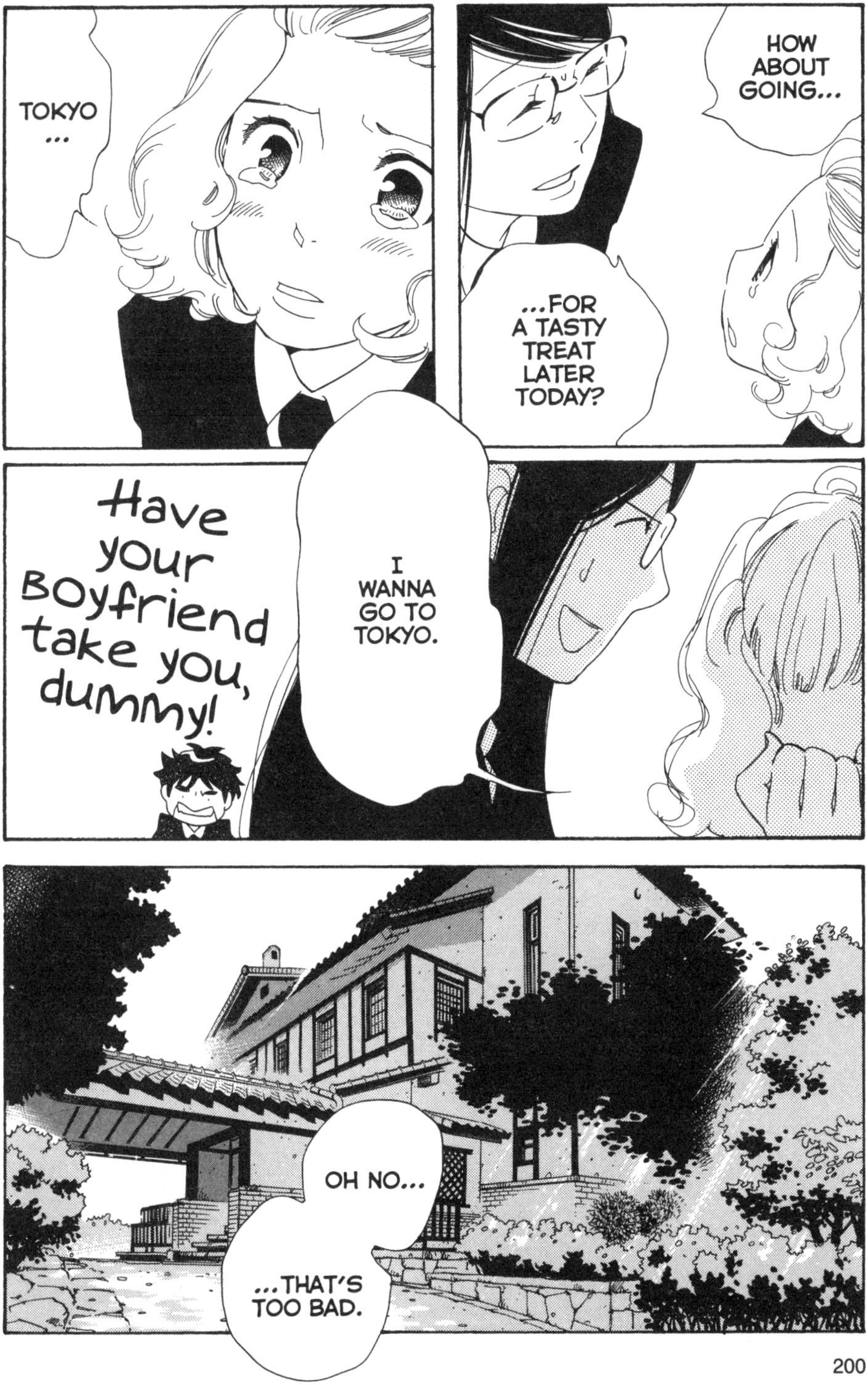
HOW ABOUT GOING...
...FOR A TASTY TREAT LATER TODAY?
TOKYO ...
I WANNA GO TO TOKYO.
Have your Boyfriend take you, dummy!
OH NO...
...THAT'S TOO BAD.

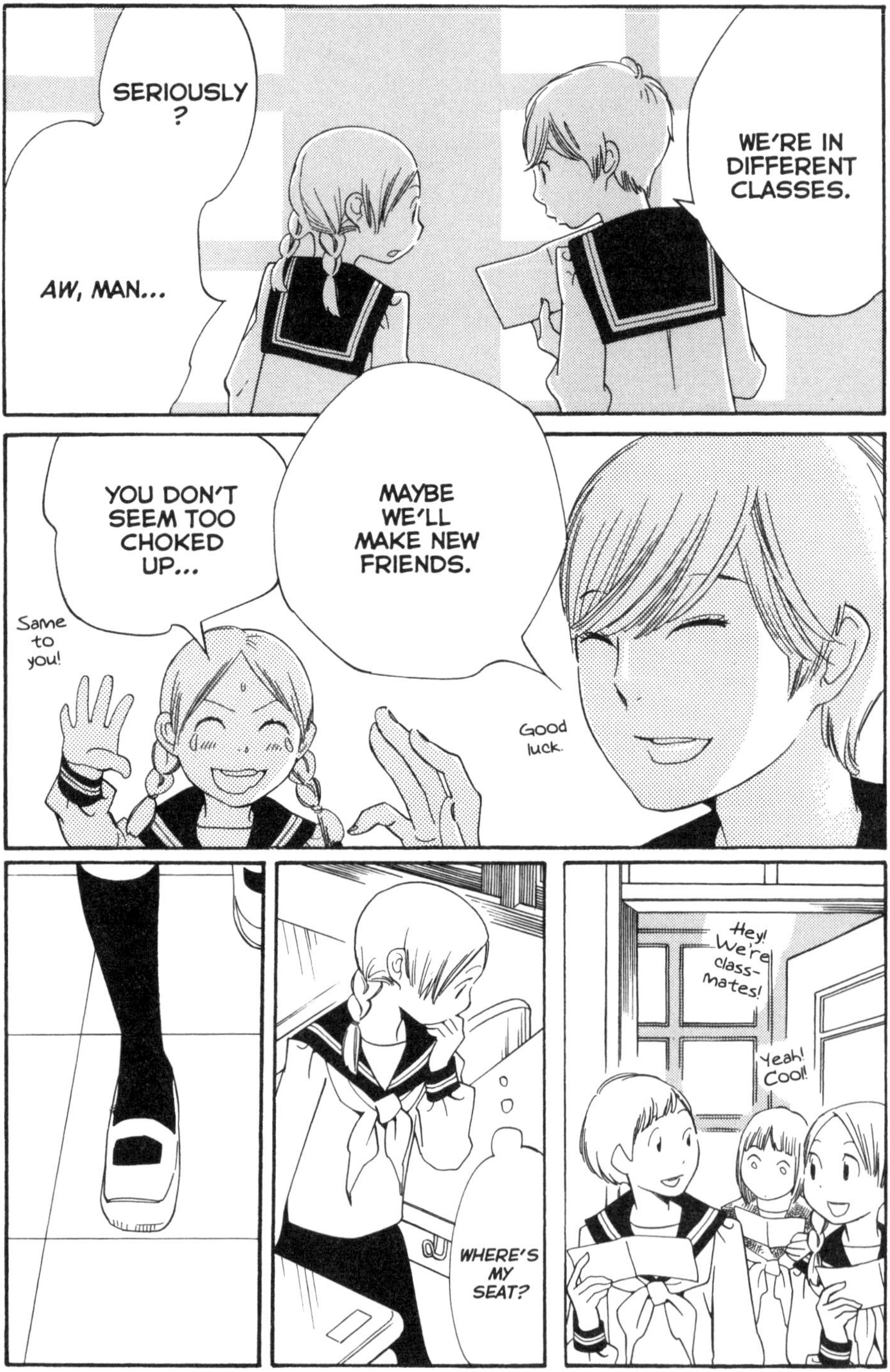
WE'RE IN DIFFERENT CLASSES.
SERIOUSLY?
AW, MAN...
Good luck.
MAYBE WE'LL MAKE NEW FRIENDS.
YOU DON'T SEEM TOO CHOKED UP...
Same to you!
Hey! We're class-mates!
Yeah! Cool!
WHERE'S MY SEAT?

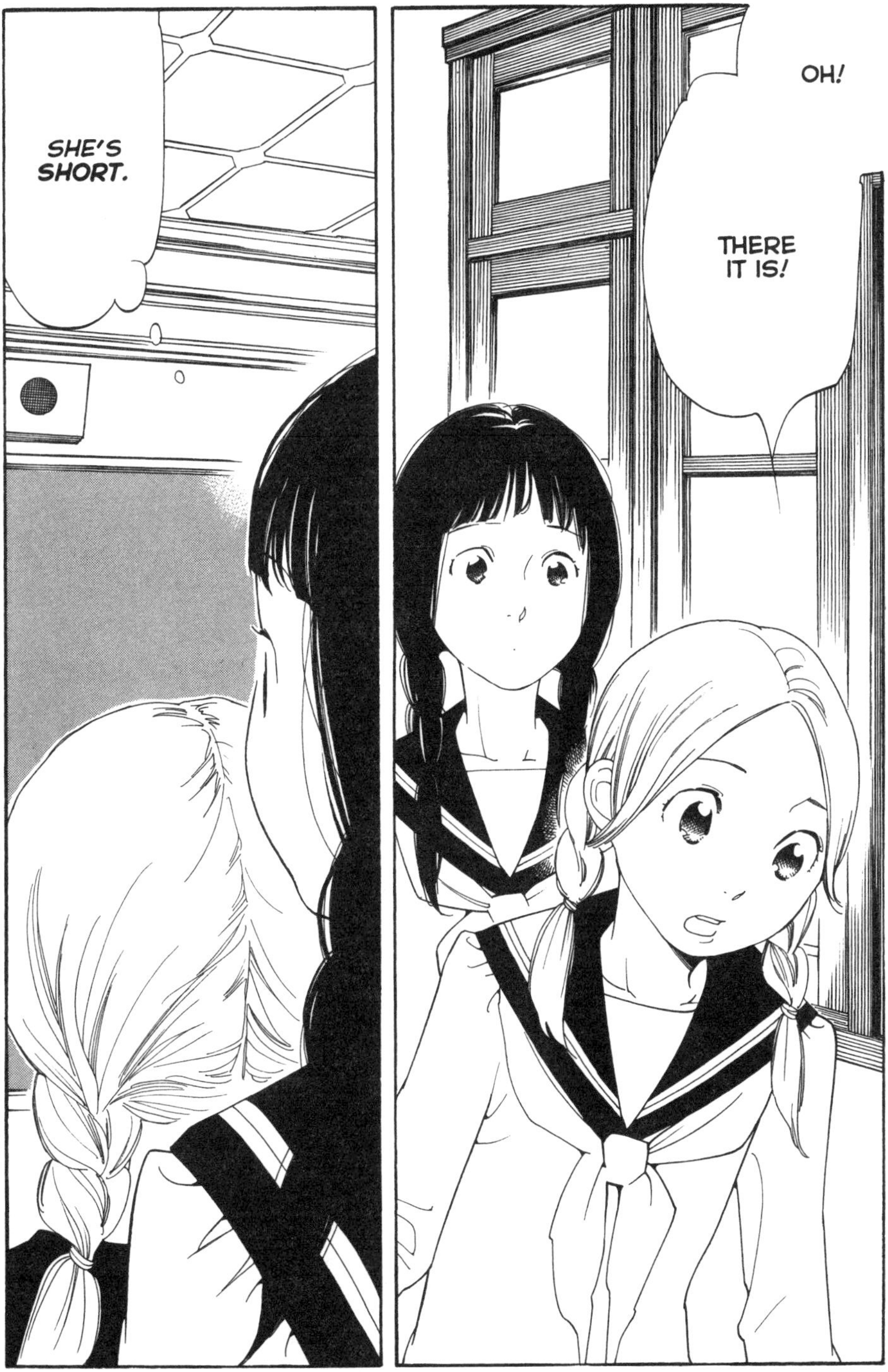
OH!
THERE IT IS!
SHE'S SHORT.

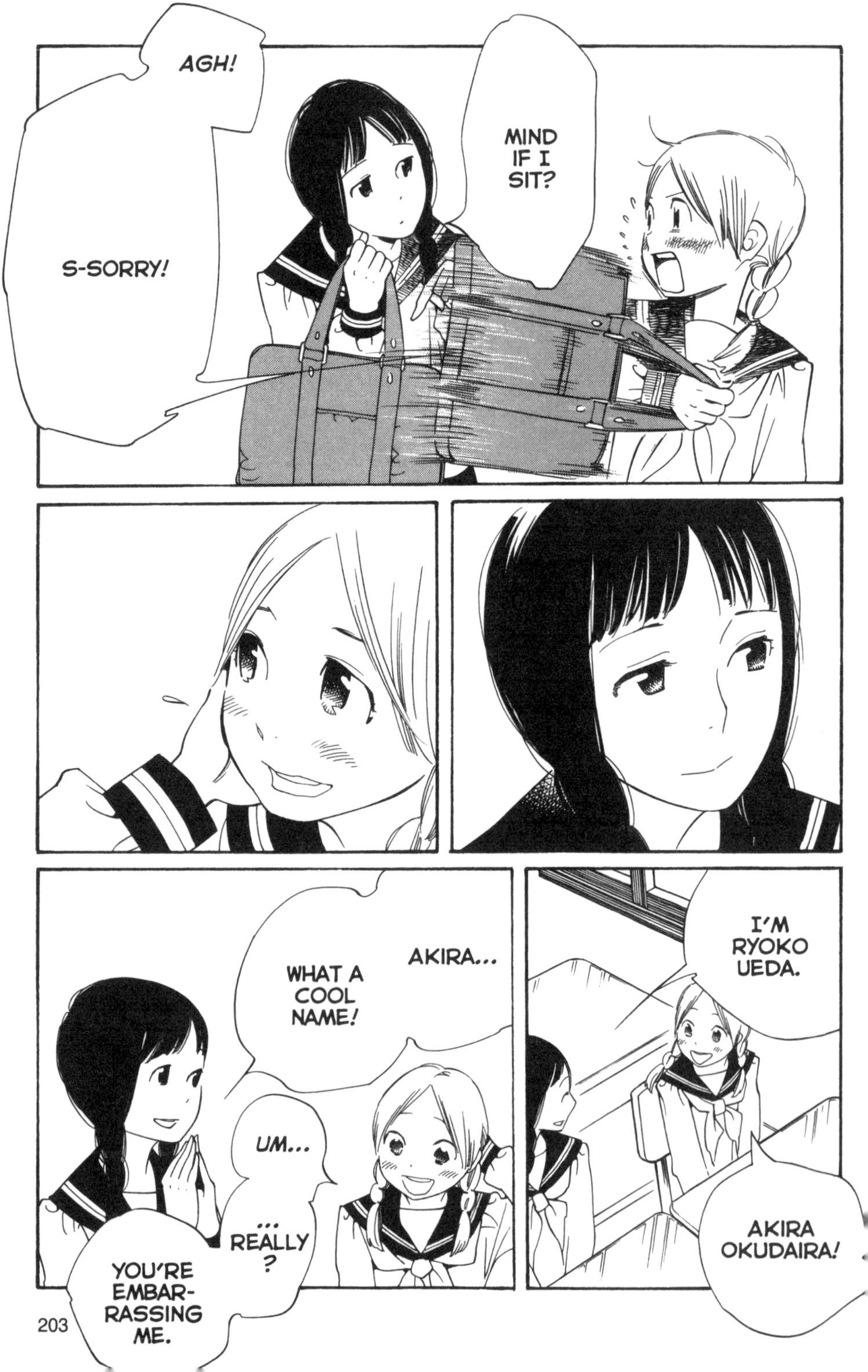
MIND IF I SIT?
AGH!
S-SORRY!
I'M RYOKO UEDA.
AKIRA OKUDAIRA!
AKIRA...
WHAT A COOL NAME!
UM...
...REALLY?
YOU'RE EMBAR-RASSING ME.

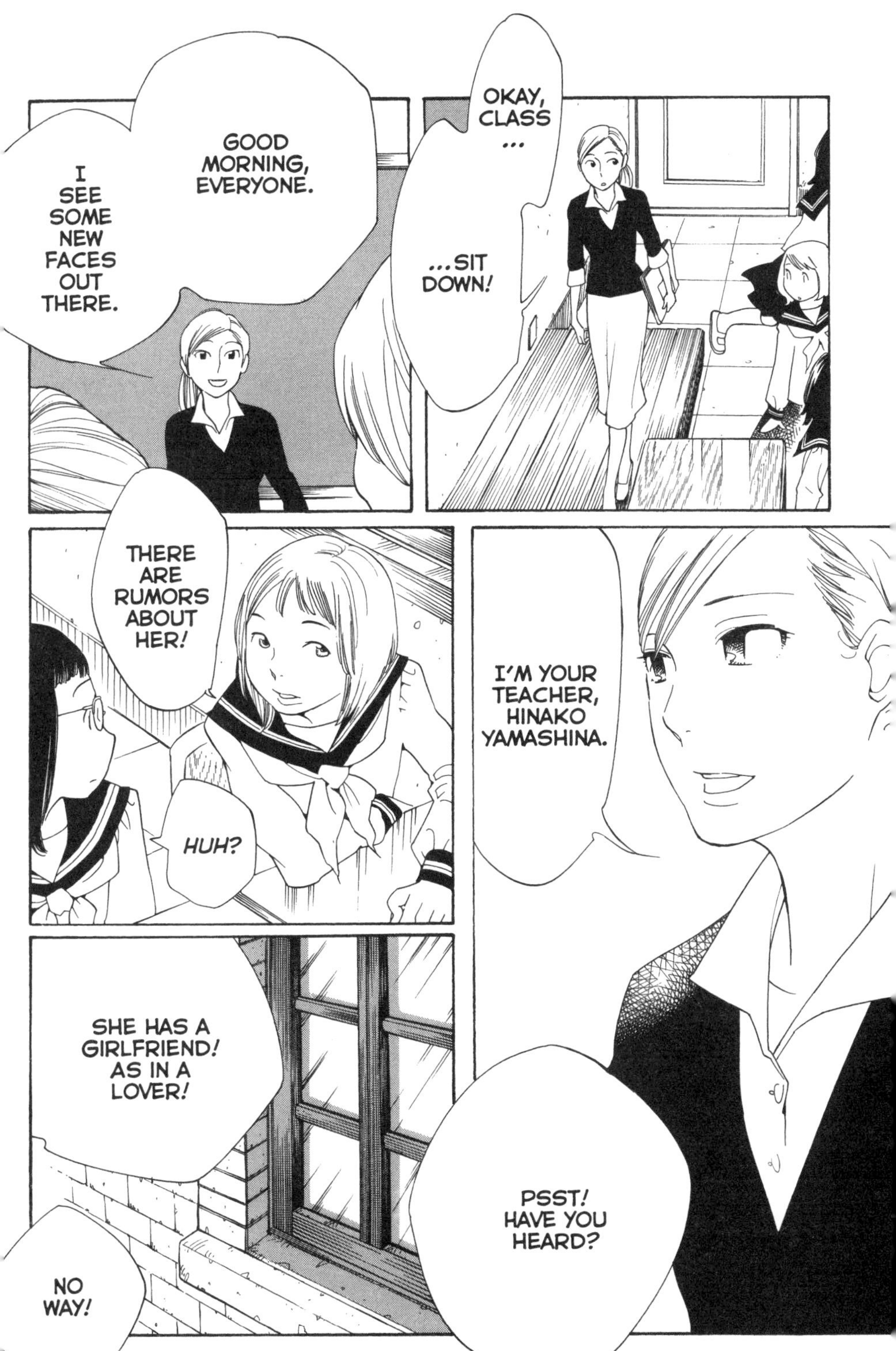
OKAY, CLASS...
...SIT DOWN!
GOOD MORNING, EVERYONE.
I SEE SOME NEW FACES OUT THERE.
I'M YOUR TEACHER, HINAKO YAMASHINA.
PSST! HAVE YOU HEARD?
THERE ARE RUMORS ABOUT HER!
HUH?
SHE HAS A GIRLFRIEND! AS IN A LOVER!
NO WAY!

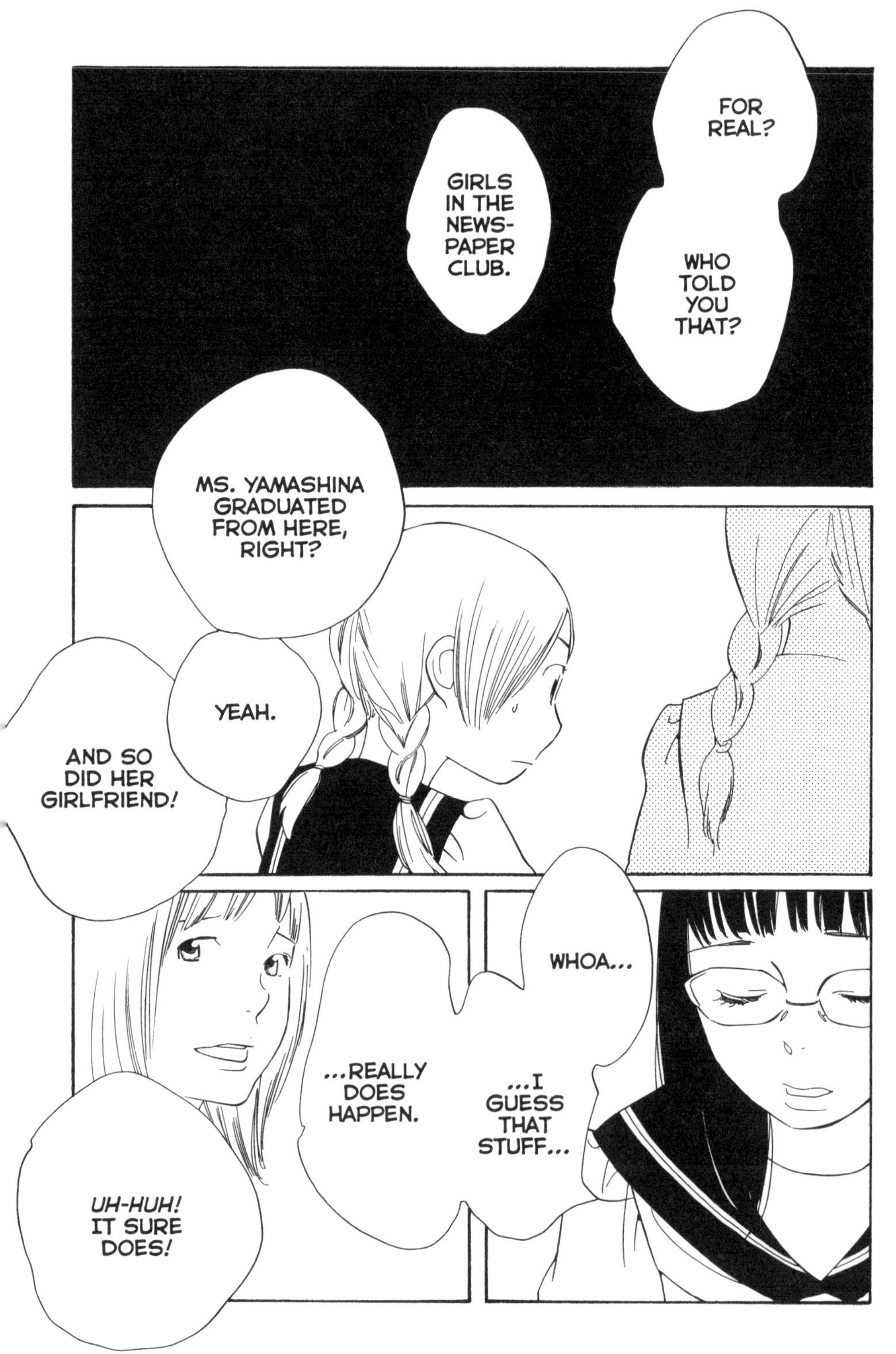
FOR REAL?
WHO TOLD YOU THAT?
GIRLS IN THE NEWS-PAPER CLUB.
MS. YAMASHINA GRADUATED FROM HERE, RIGHT?
YEAH.
AND SO DID HER GIRLFRIEND!
WHOA...
...I GUESS THAT STUFF...
...REALLY DOES HAPPEN.
UH-HUH! IT SURE DOES!

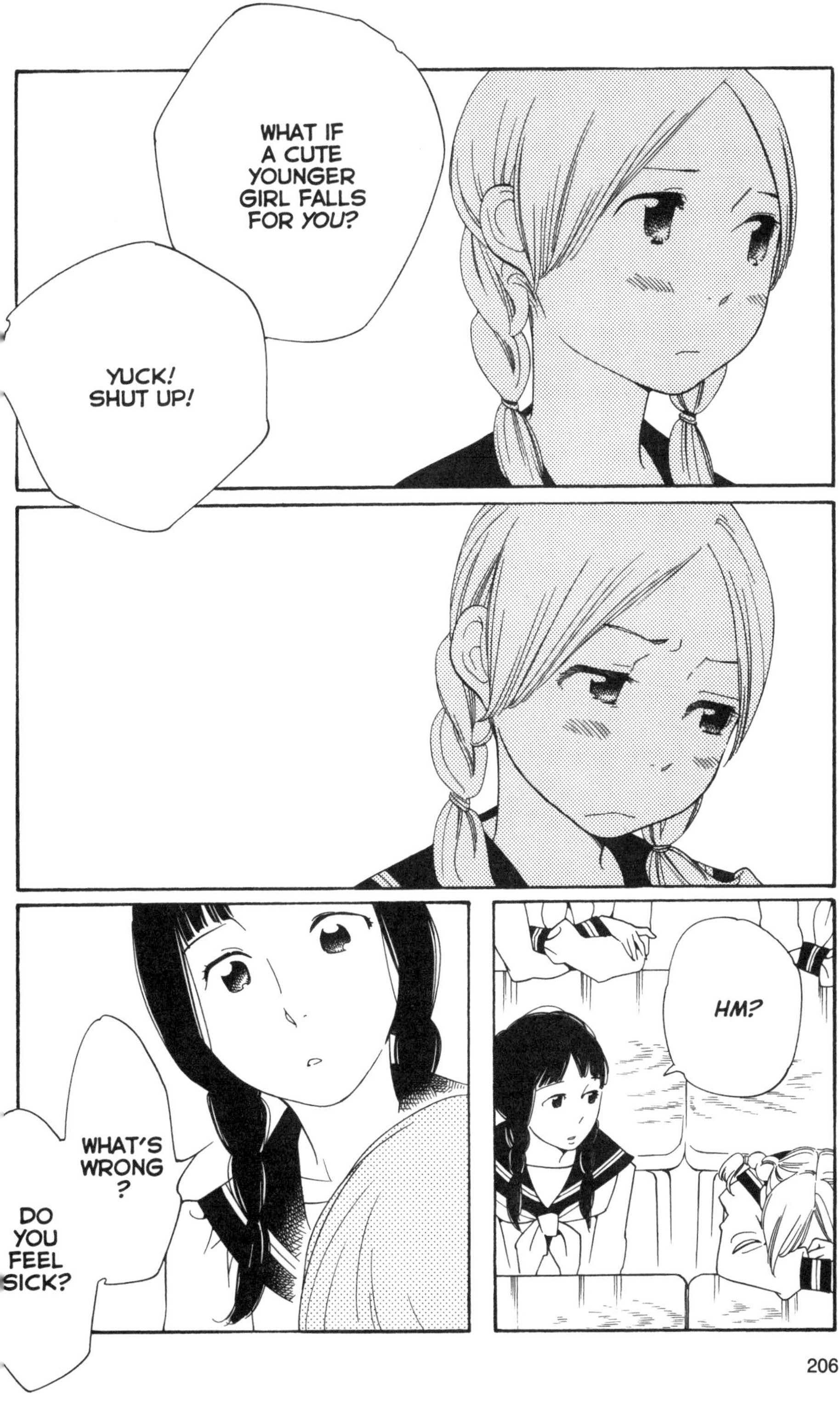
WHAT IF A CUTE YOUNGER GIRL FALLS FOR *YOU*?
YUCK! SHUT UP!
HM?
WHAT'S WRONG?
DO YOU FEEL SICK?

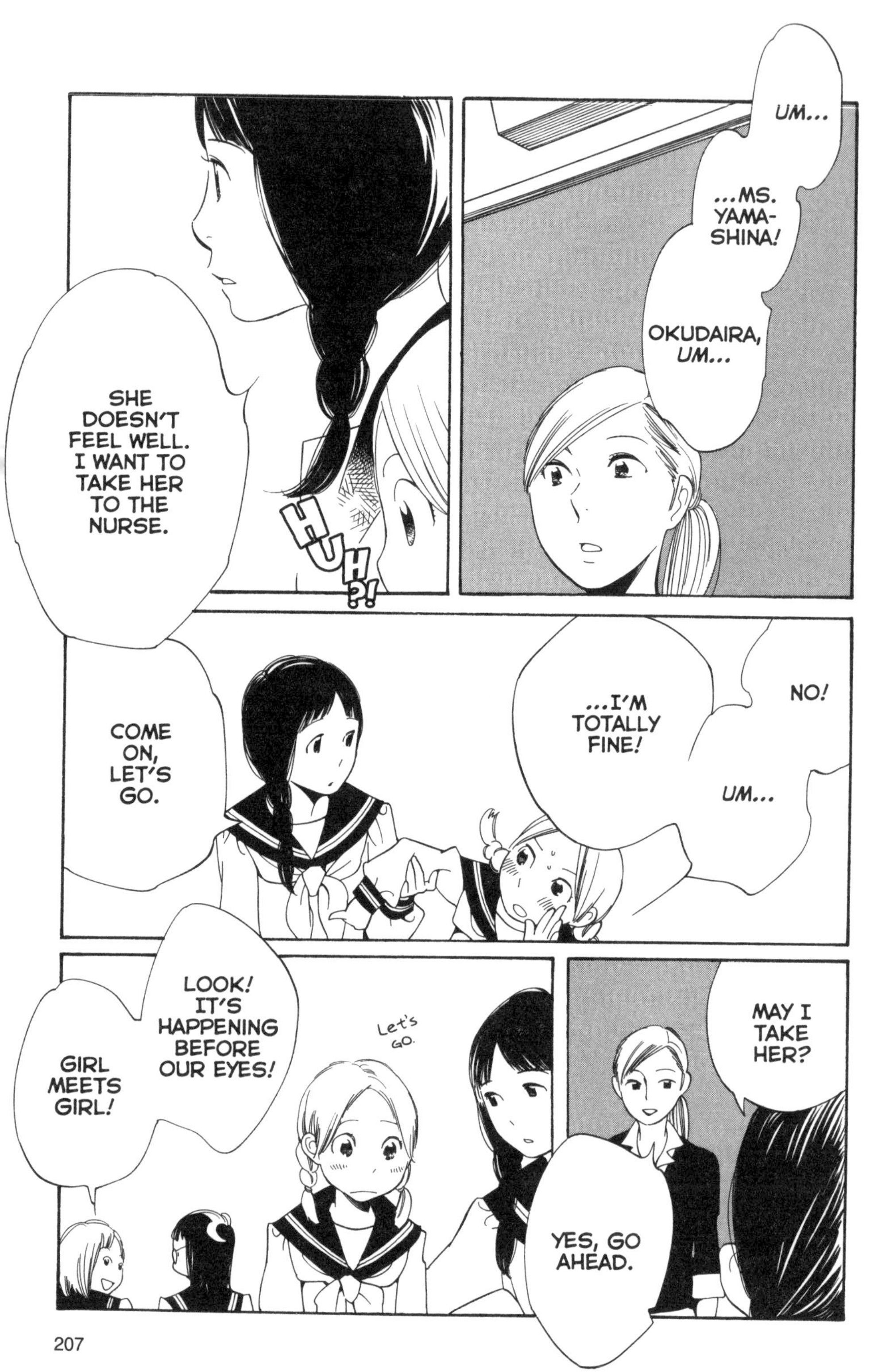
UM...
...MS. YAMA-SHINA!
OKUDAIRA, UM...
SHE DOESN'T FEEL WELL. I WANT TO TAKE HER TO THE NURSE.
HUH?!
NO!
UM...
...I'M TOTALLY FINE!
COME ON, LET'S GO.
MAY I TAKE HER?
YES, GO AHEAD.
Let's GO.
LOOK! IT'S HAPPENING BEFORE OUR EYES!
GIRL MEETS GIRL!

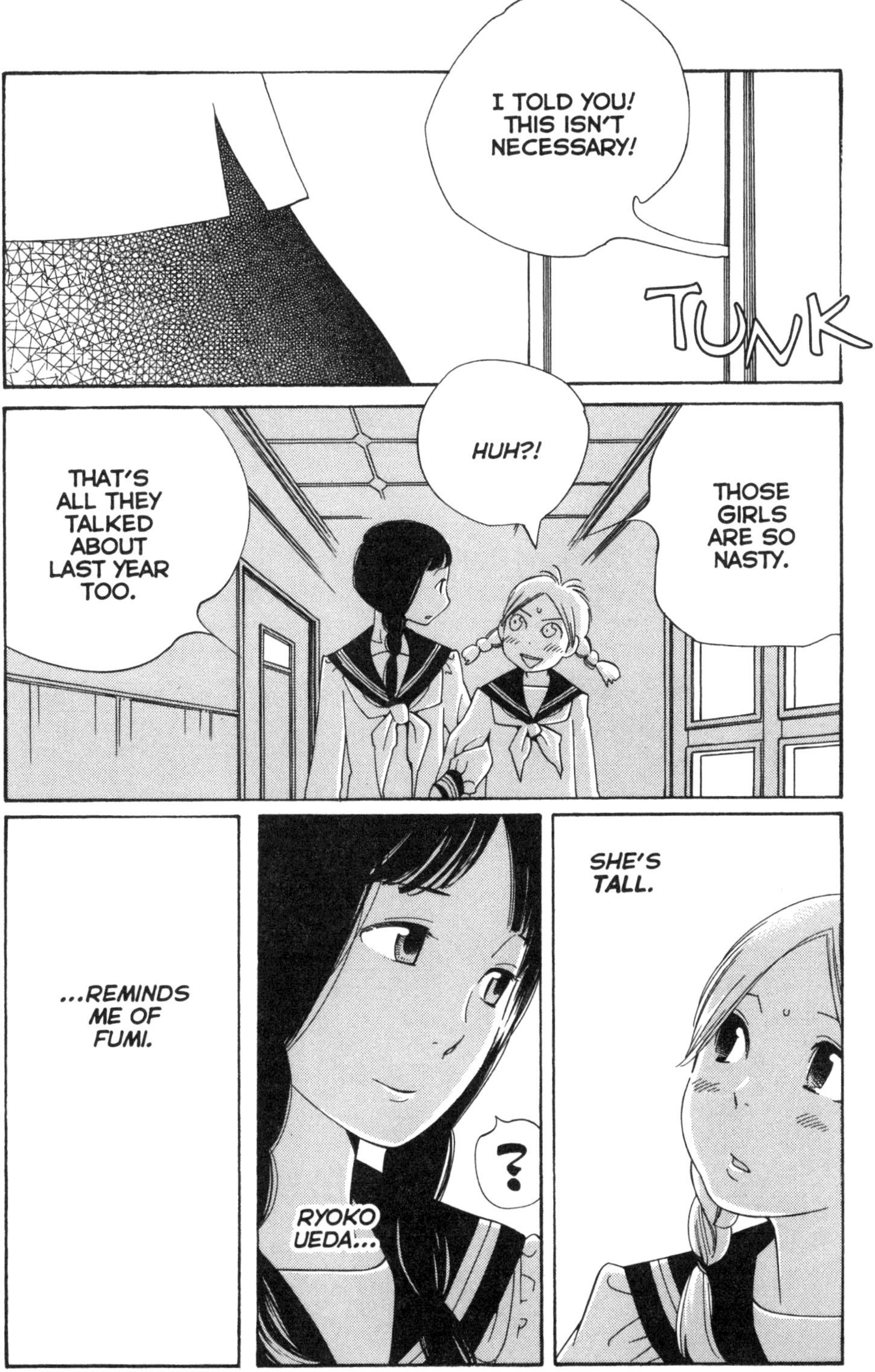
I TOLD YOU! THIS ISN'T NECESSARY!
TUNK
THOSE GIRLS ARE SO NASTY.
HUH?!
THAT'S ALL THEY TALKED ABOUT LAST YEAR TOO.
SHE'S TALL.
?
RYOKO UEDA...
...REMINDS ME OF FUMI.

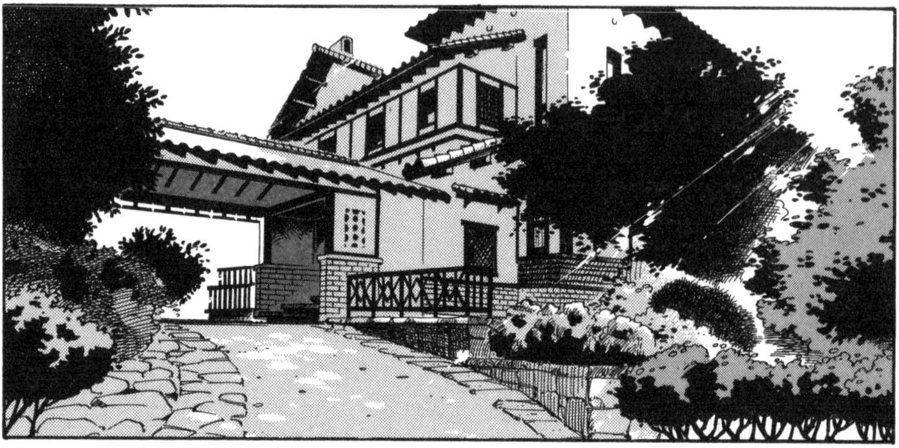
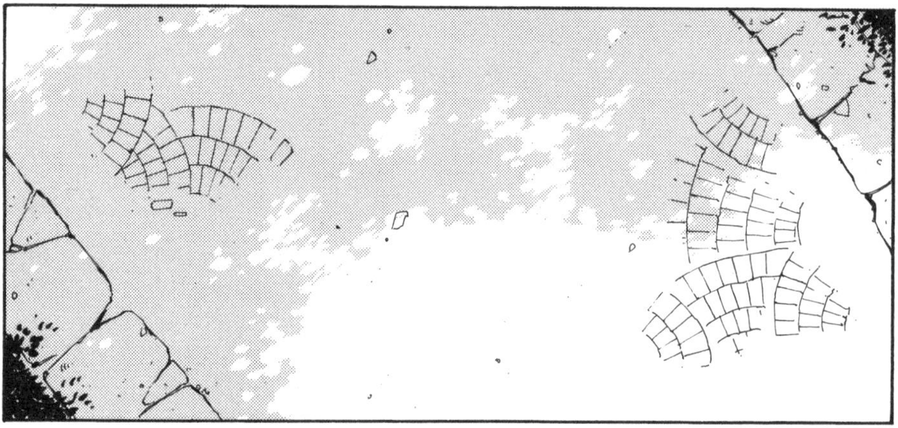
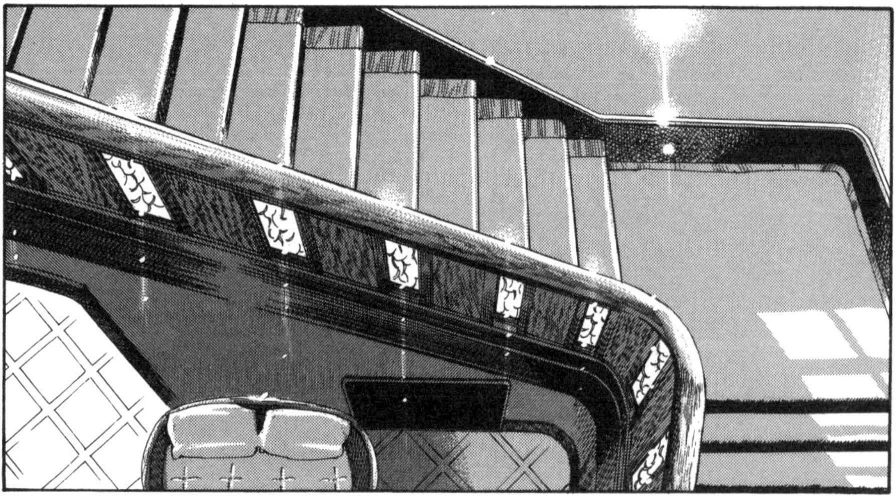

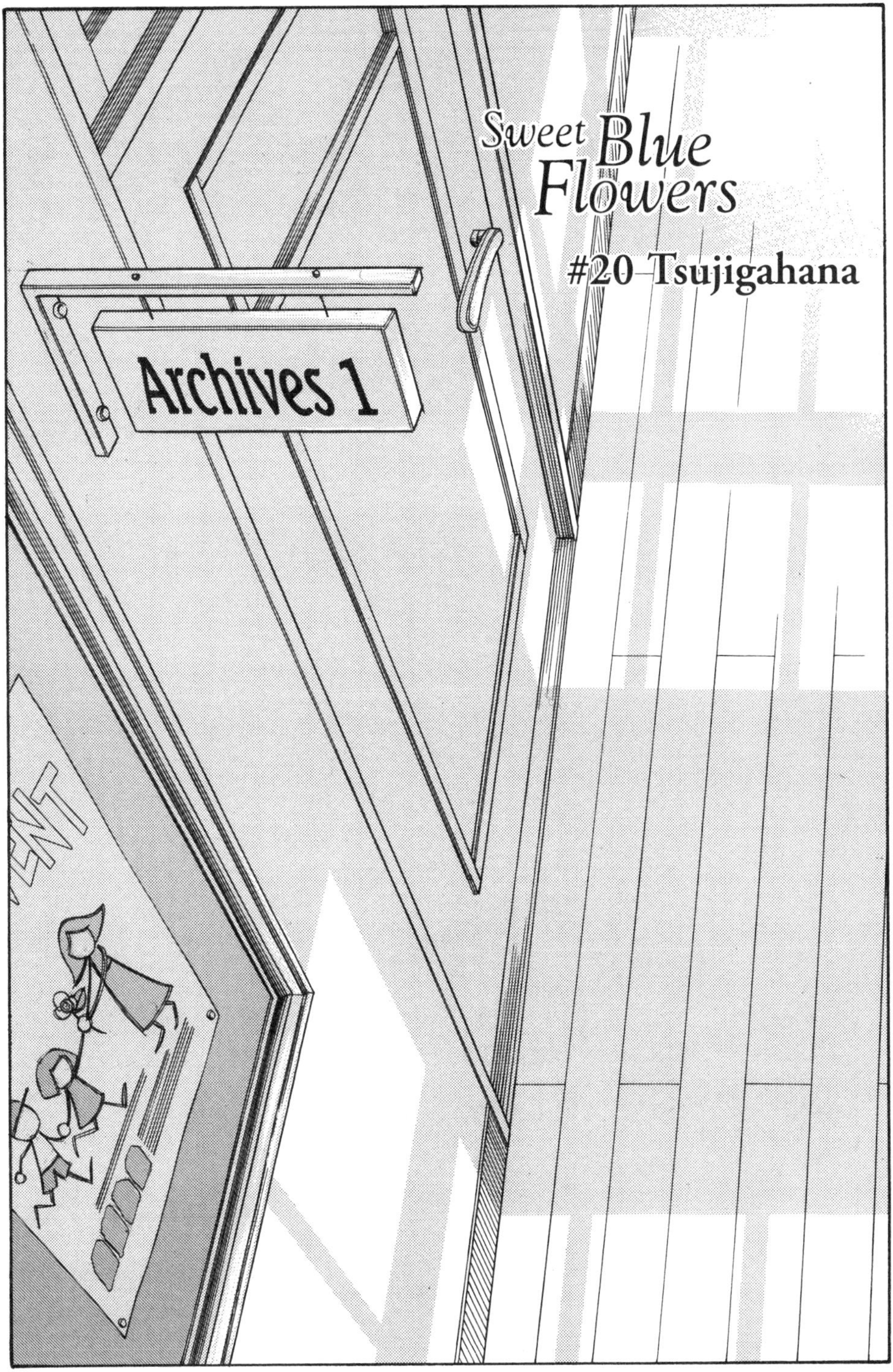
Sweet Blue Flowers
#20 Tsujigahana
Archives 1

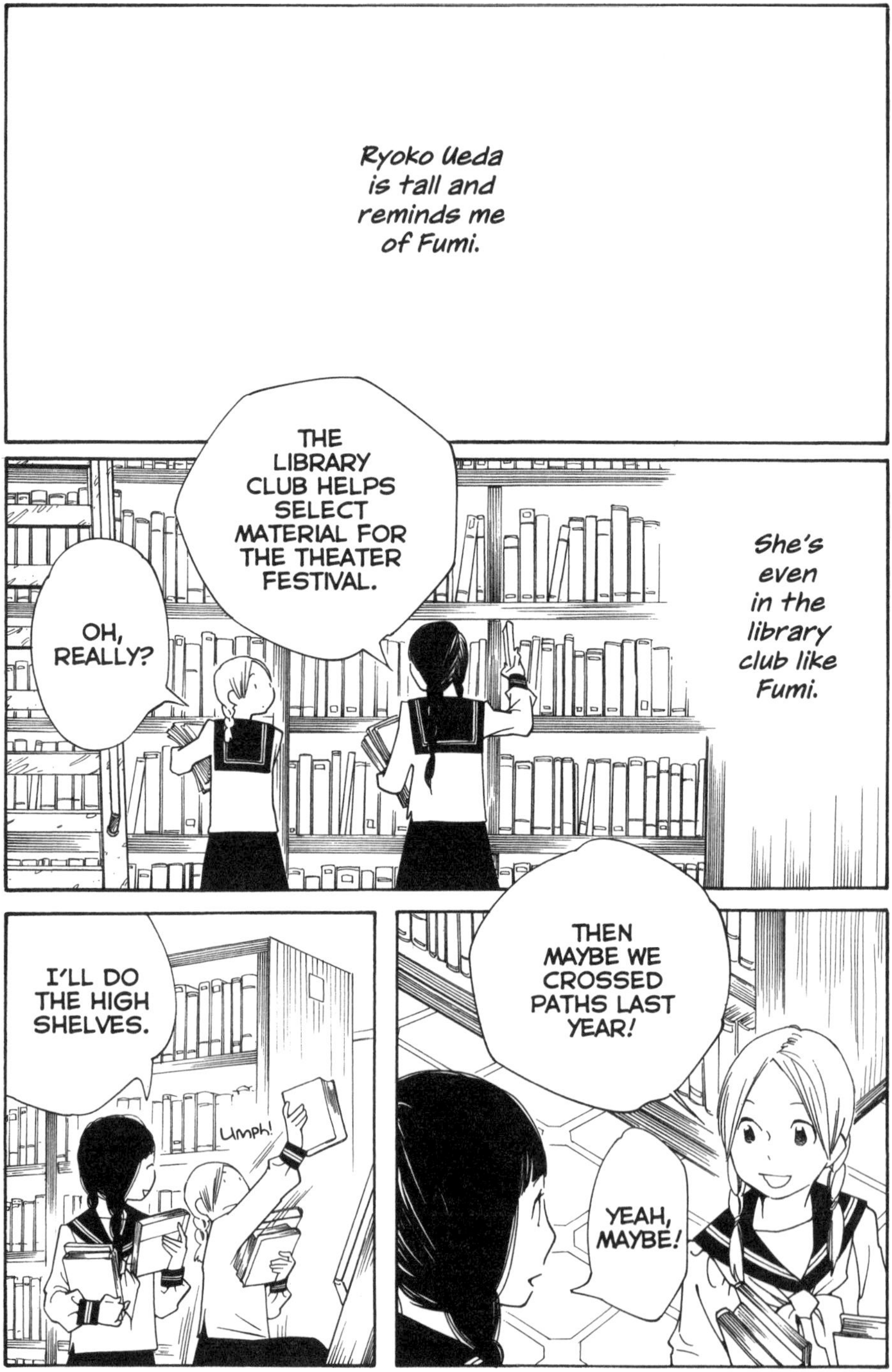
Ryoko Ueda is tall and reminds me of Fumi.
She's even in the library club like Fumi.
THE LIBRARY CLUB HELPS SELECT MATERIAL FOR THE THEATER FESTIVAL.
OH, REALLY?
THEN MAYBE WE CROSSED PATHS LAST YEAR!
YEAH, MAYBE!
I'LL DO THE HIGH SHELVES.
Umph!

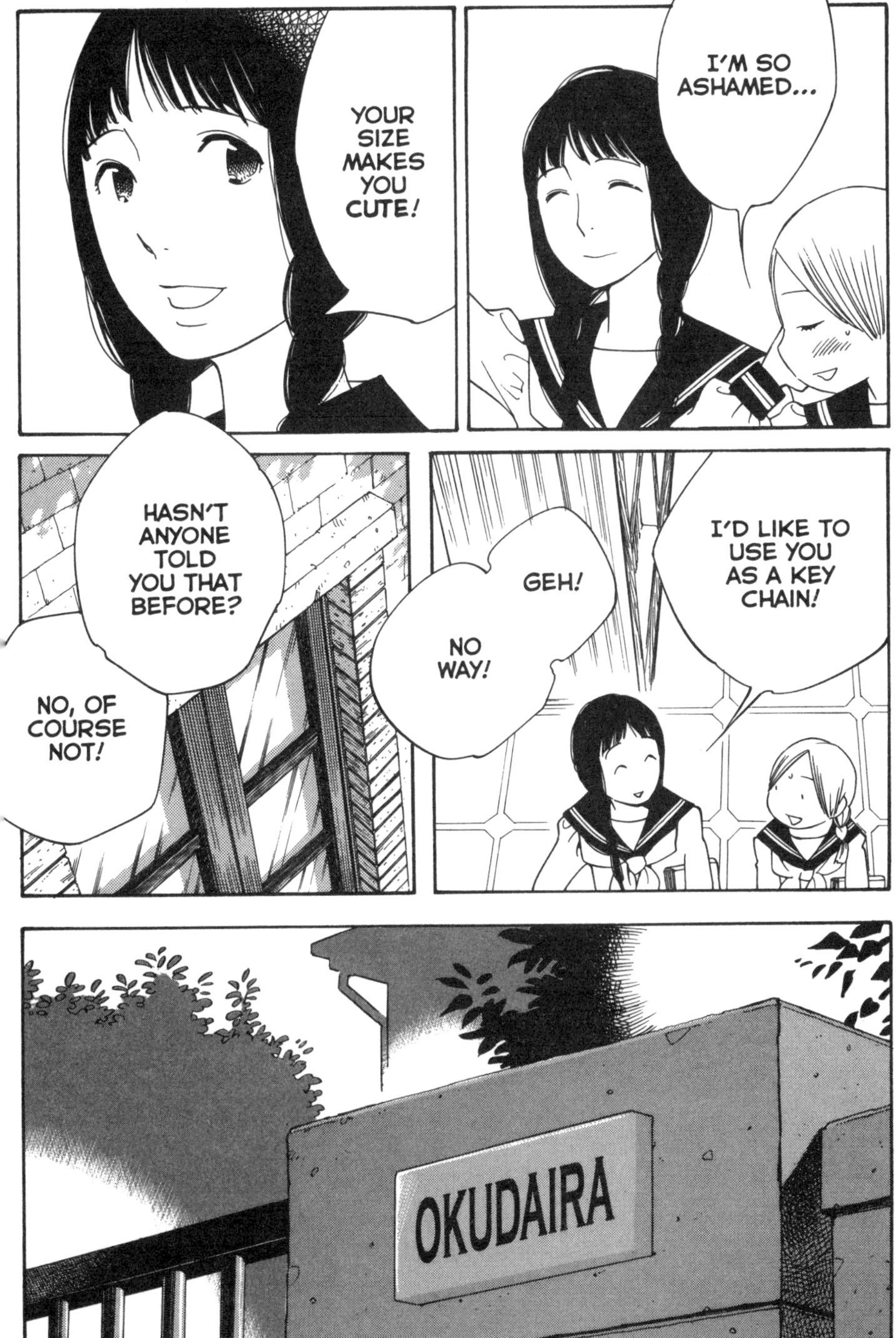
I'M SO ASHAMED...
YOUR SIZE MAKES YOU CUTE!
I'D LIKE TO USE YOU AS A KEY CHAIN!
GEH!
NO WAY!
HASN'T ANYONE TOLD YOU THAT BEFORE?
NO, OF COURSE NOT!
OKUDAIRA

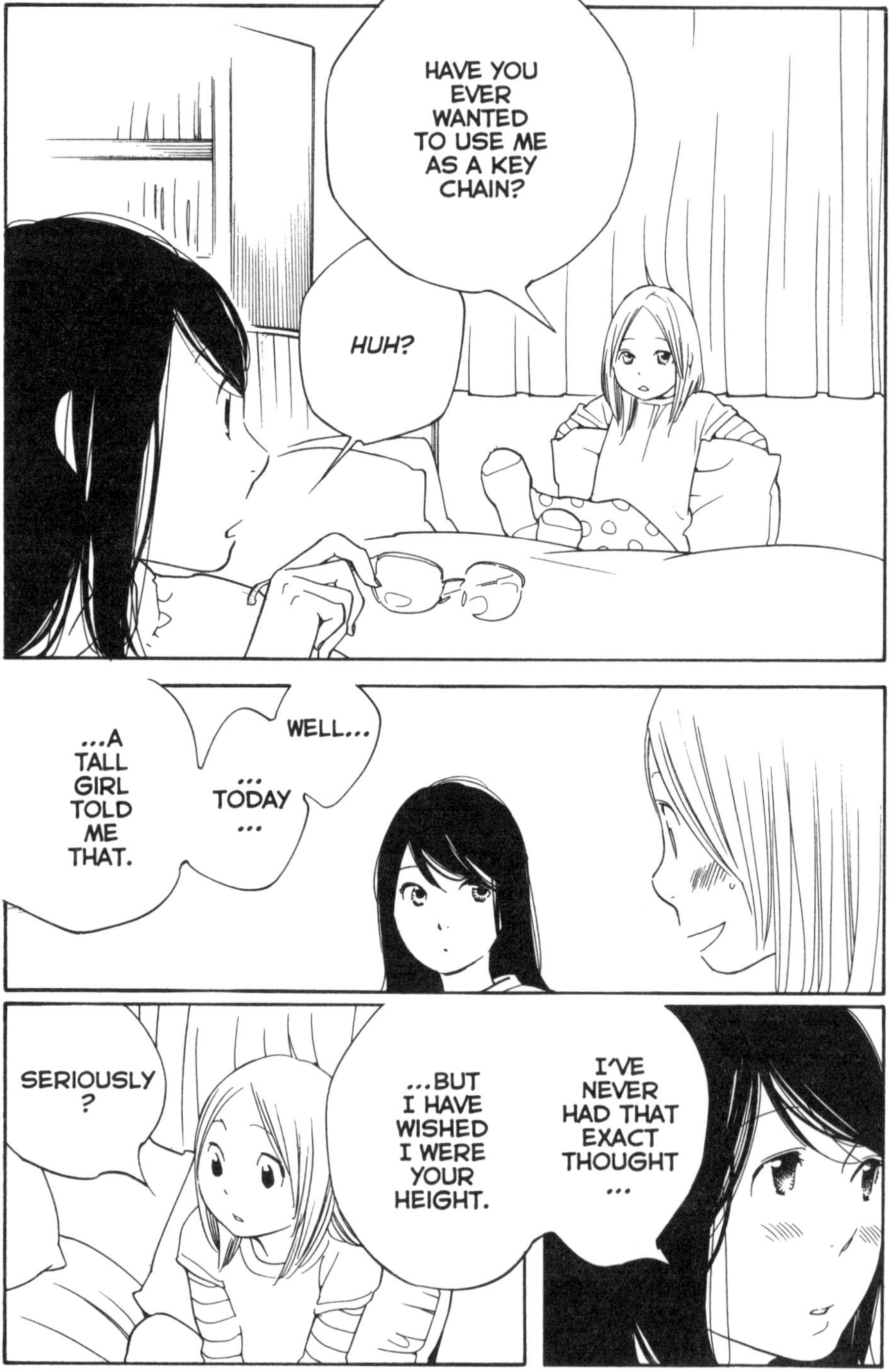
HAVE YOU EVER WANTED TO USE ME AS A KEY CHAIN?
HUH?
WELL...
...TODAY...
...A TALL GIRL TOLD ME THAT.
I'VE NEVER HAD THAT EXACT THOUGHT...
...BUT I HAVE WISHED I WERE YOUR HEIGHT.
SERIOUSLY?

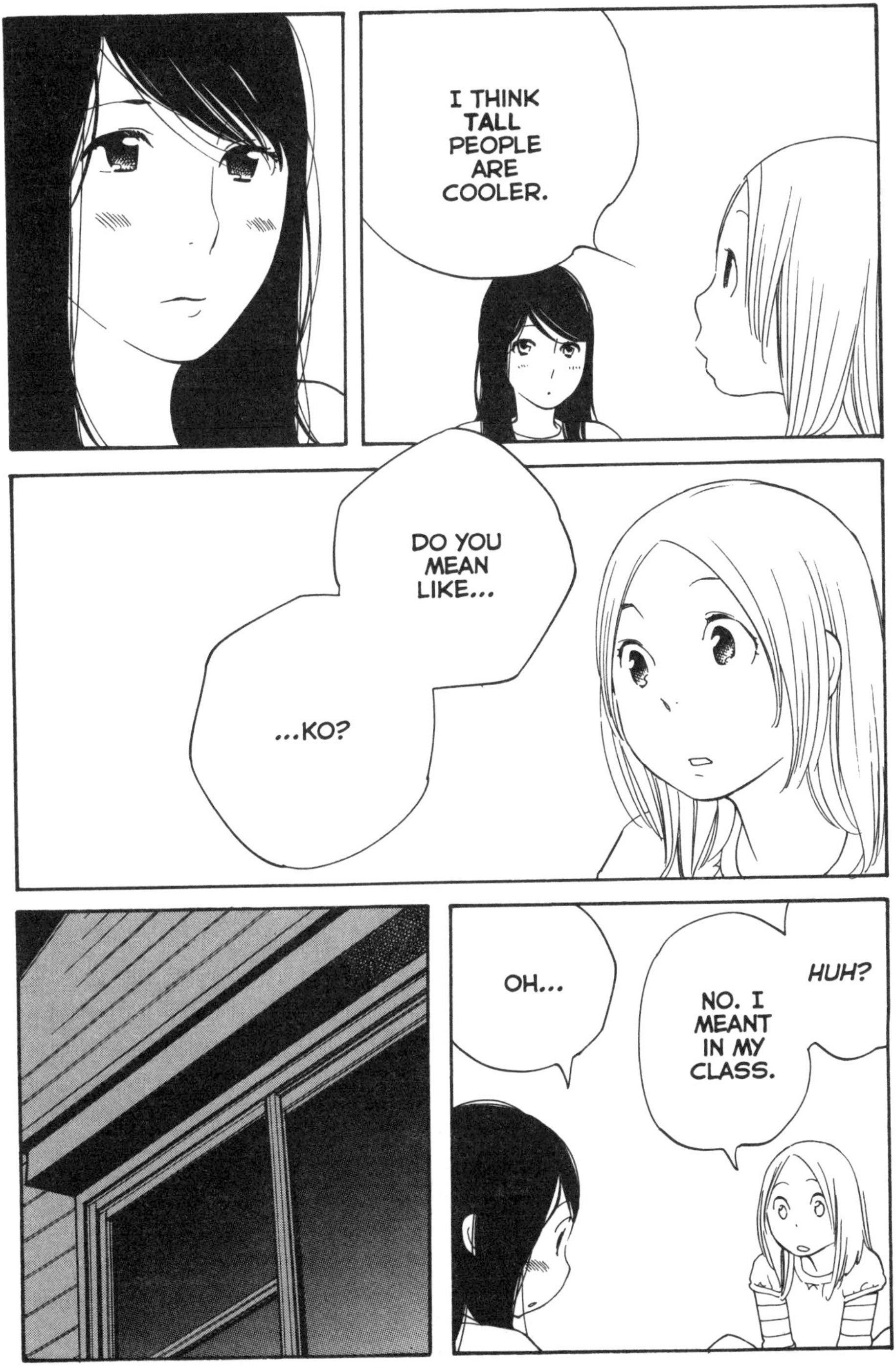
I THINK TALL PEOPLE ARE COOLER.
DO YOU MEAN LIKE...
...KO?
HUH?
NO. I MEANT IN MY CLASS.
OH...

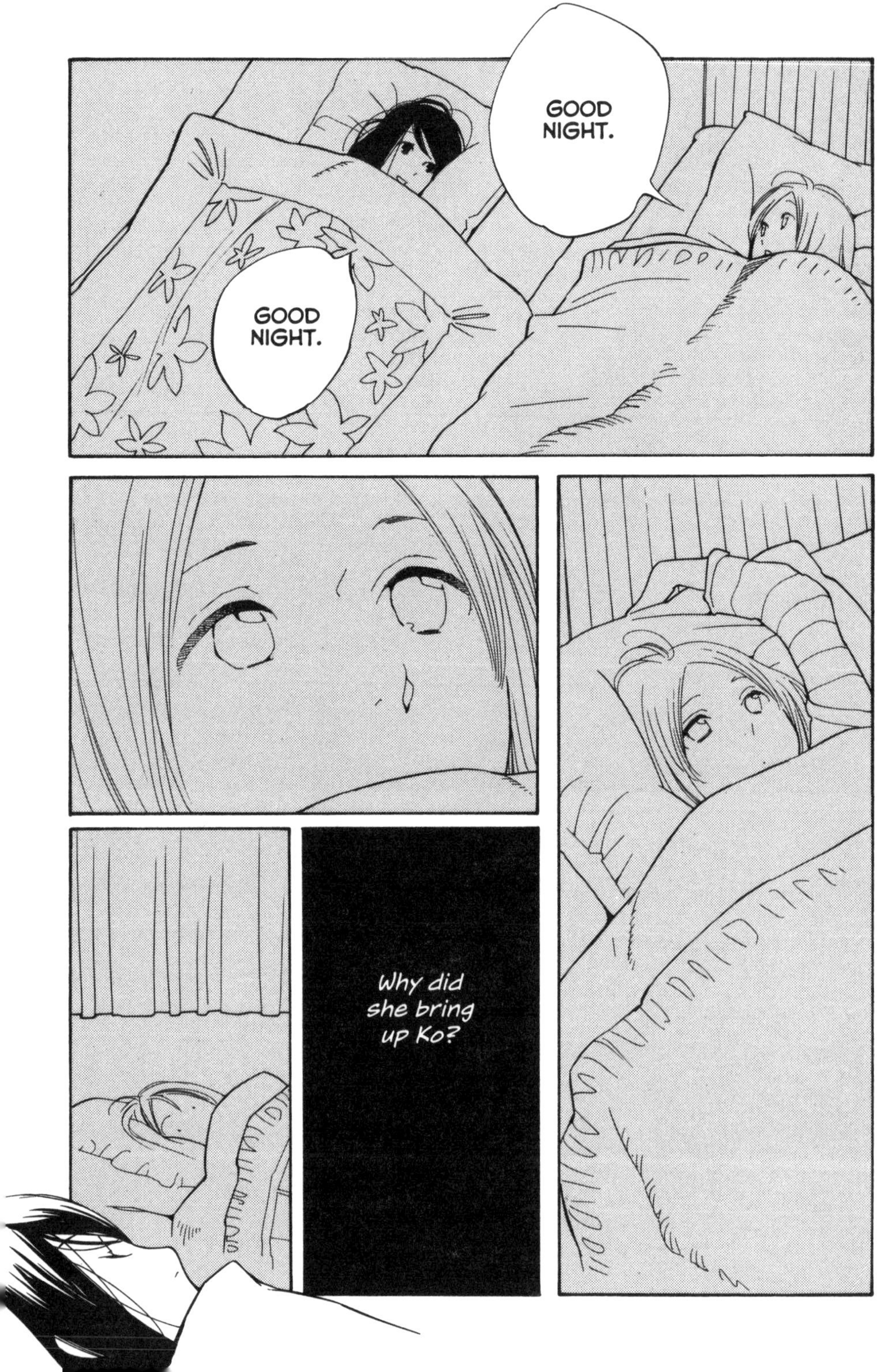
GOOD NIGHT.
GOOD NIGHT.
Why did she bring up Ko?

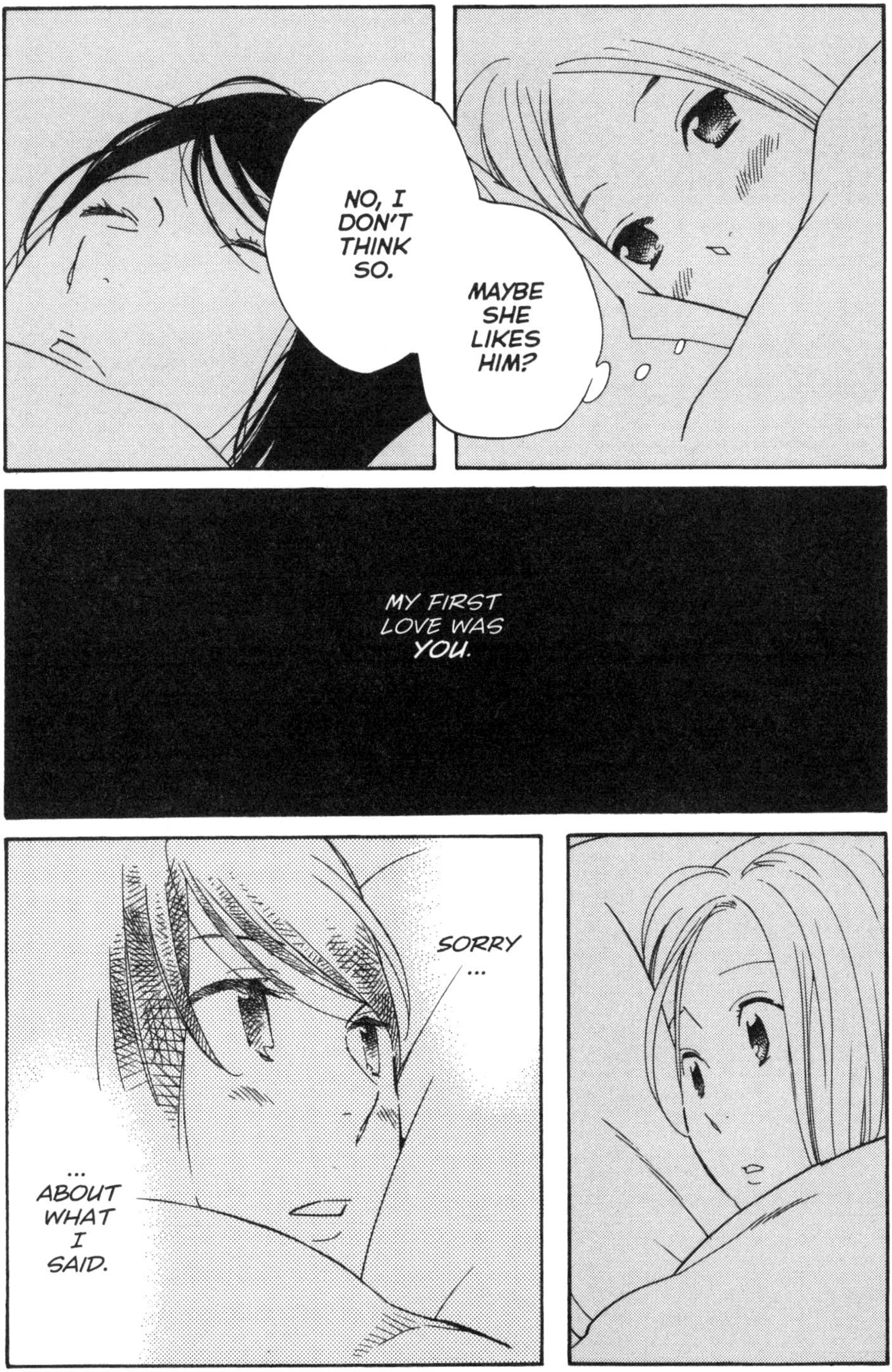
MAYBE SHE LIKES HIM?
NO, I DON'T THINK SO.
MY FIRST LOVE WAS YOU.
SORRY ...
... ABOUT WHAT I SAID.

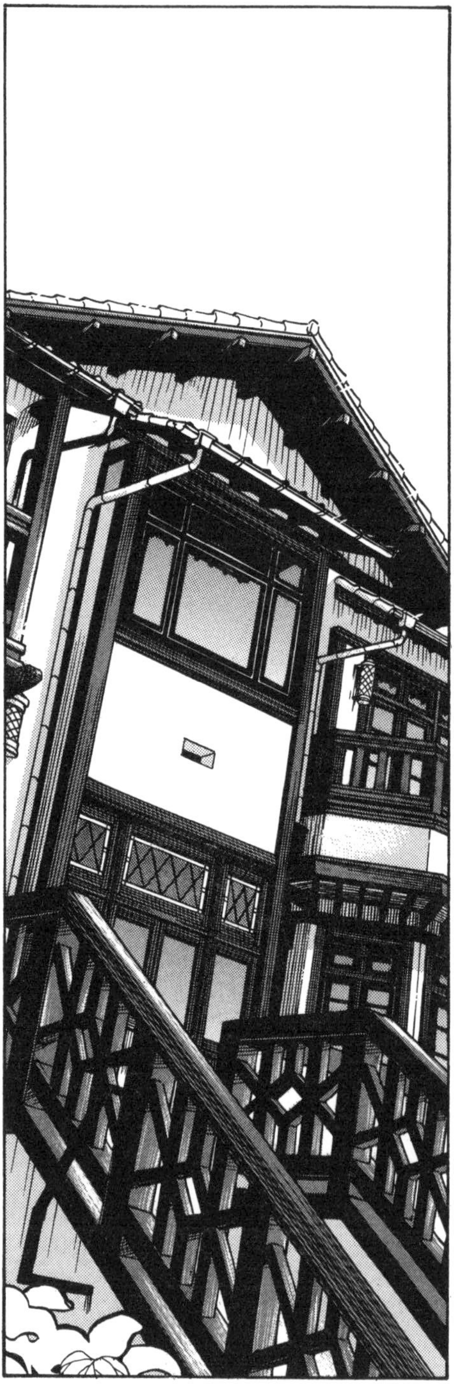
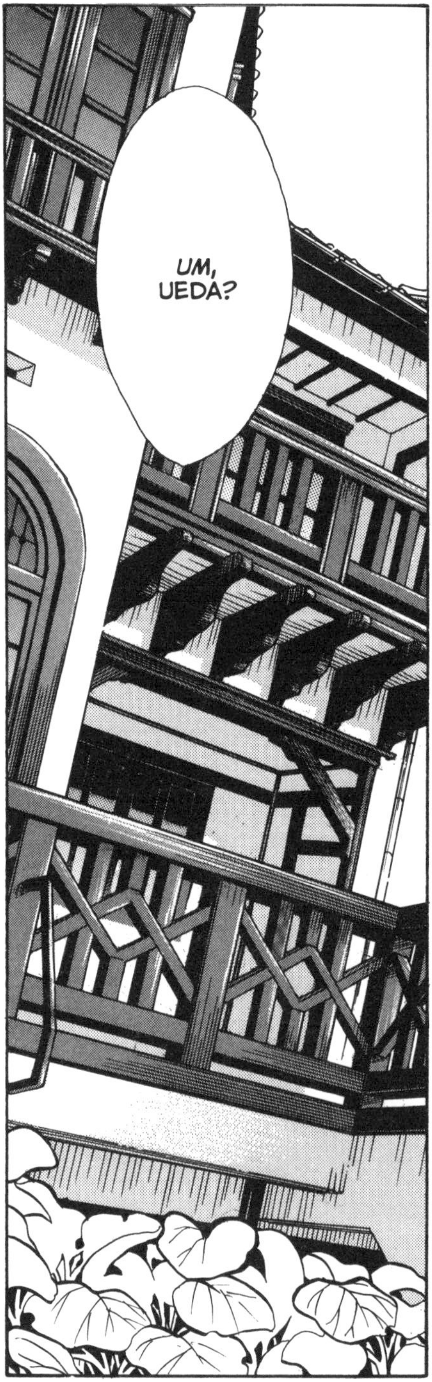
UM, UEDA?

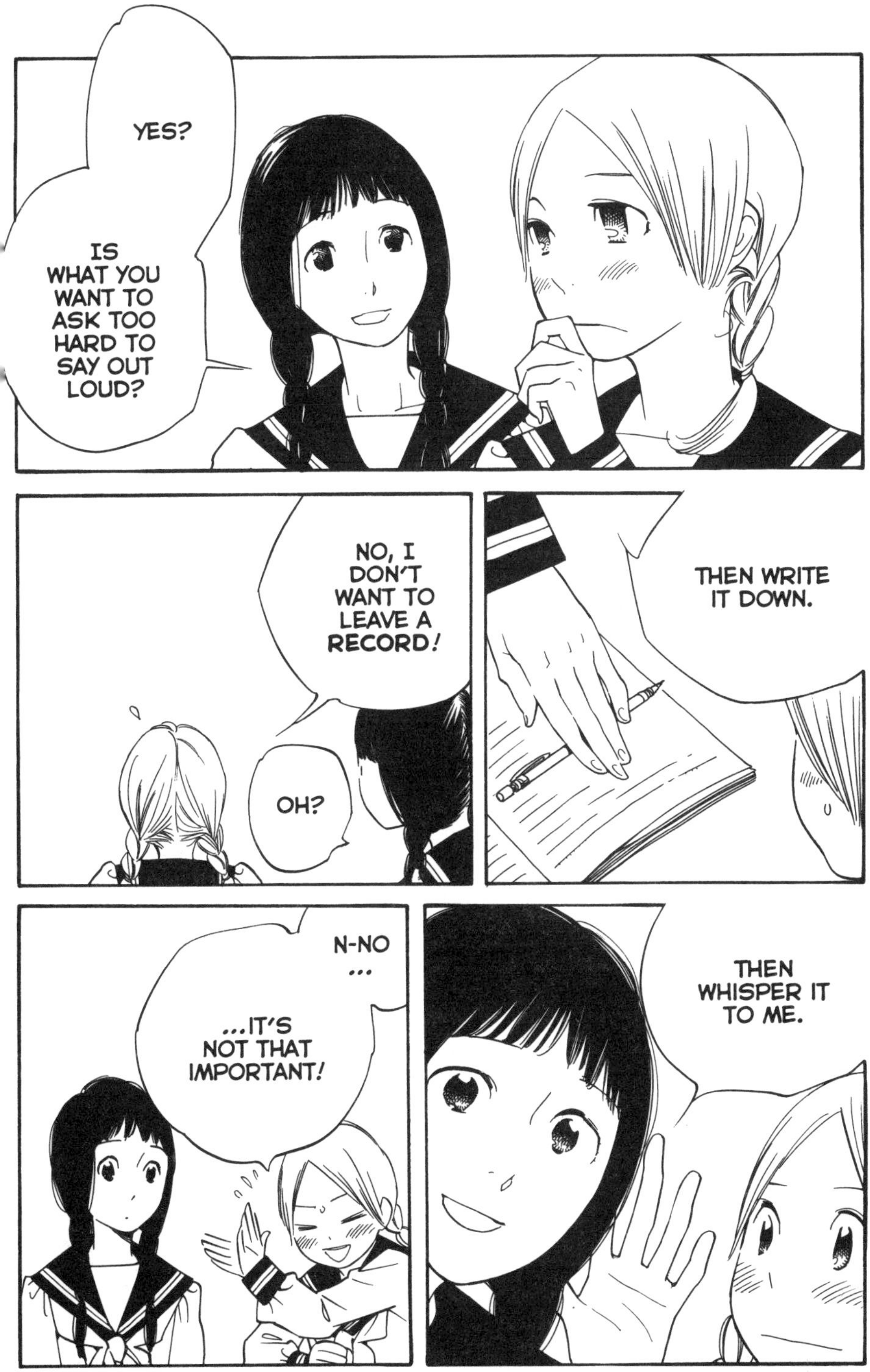
YES?
IS WHAT YOU WANT TO ASK TOO HARD TO SAY OUT LOUD?
THEN WRITE IT DOWN.
NO, I DON'T WANT TO LEAVE A RECORD!
OH?
THEN WHISPER IT TO ME.
N-NO ...
...IT'S NOT THAT IMPORTANT!

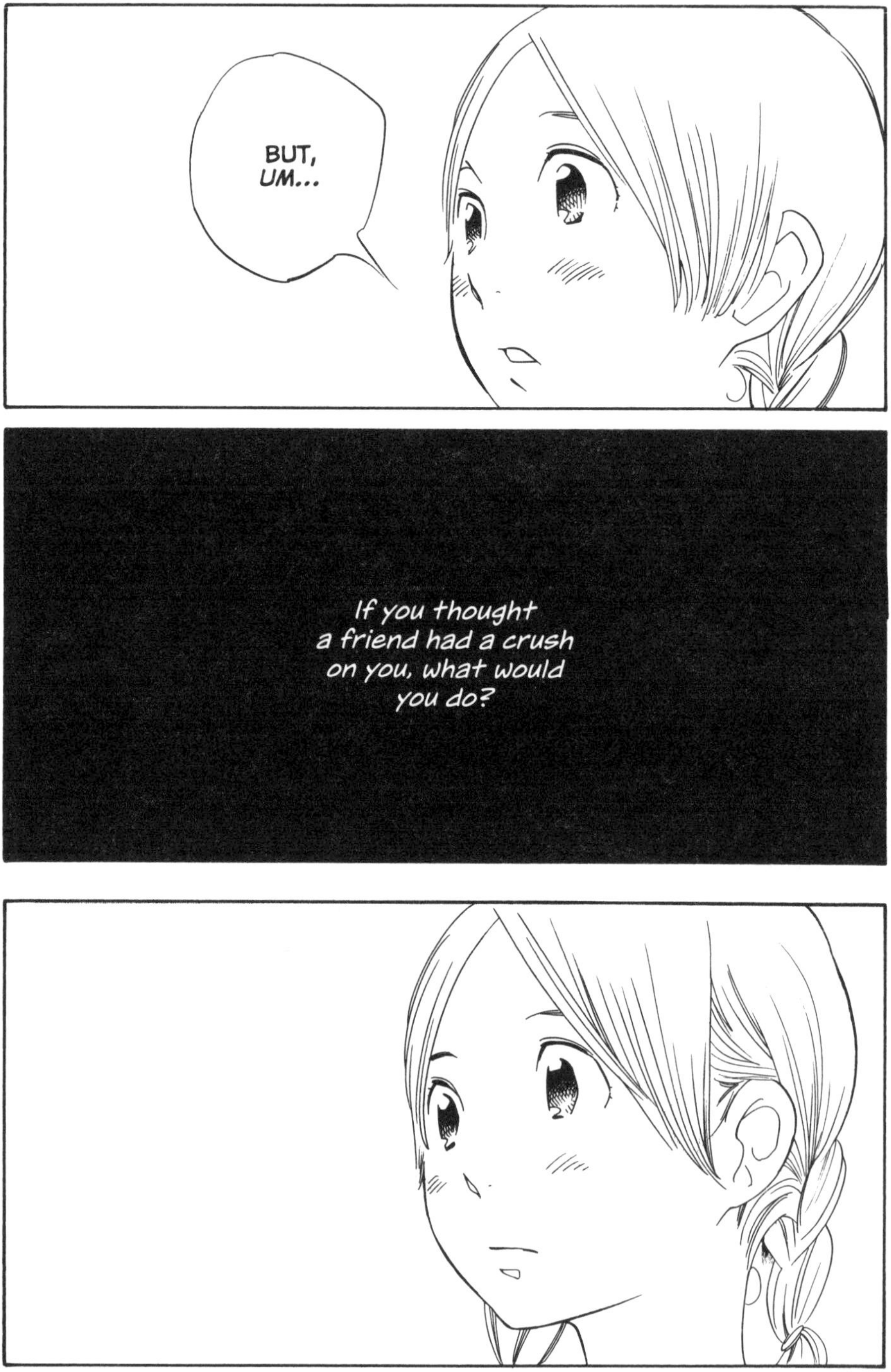
BUT, UM...
If you thought a friend had a crush on you, what would you do?

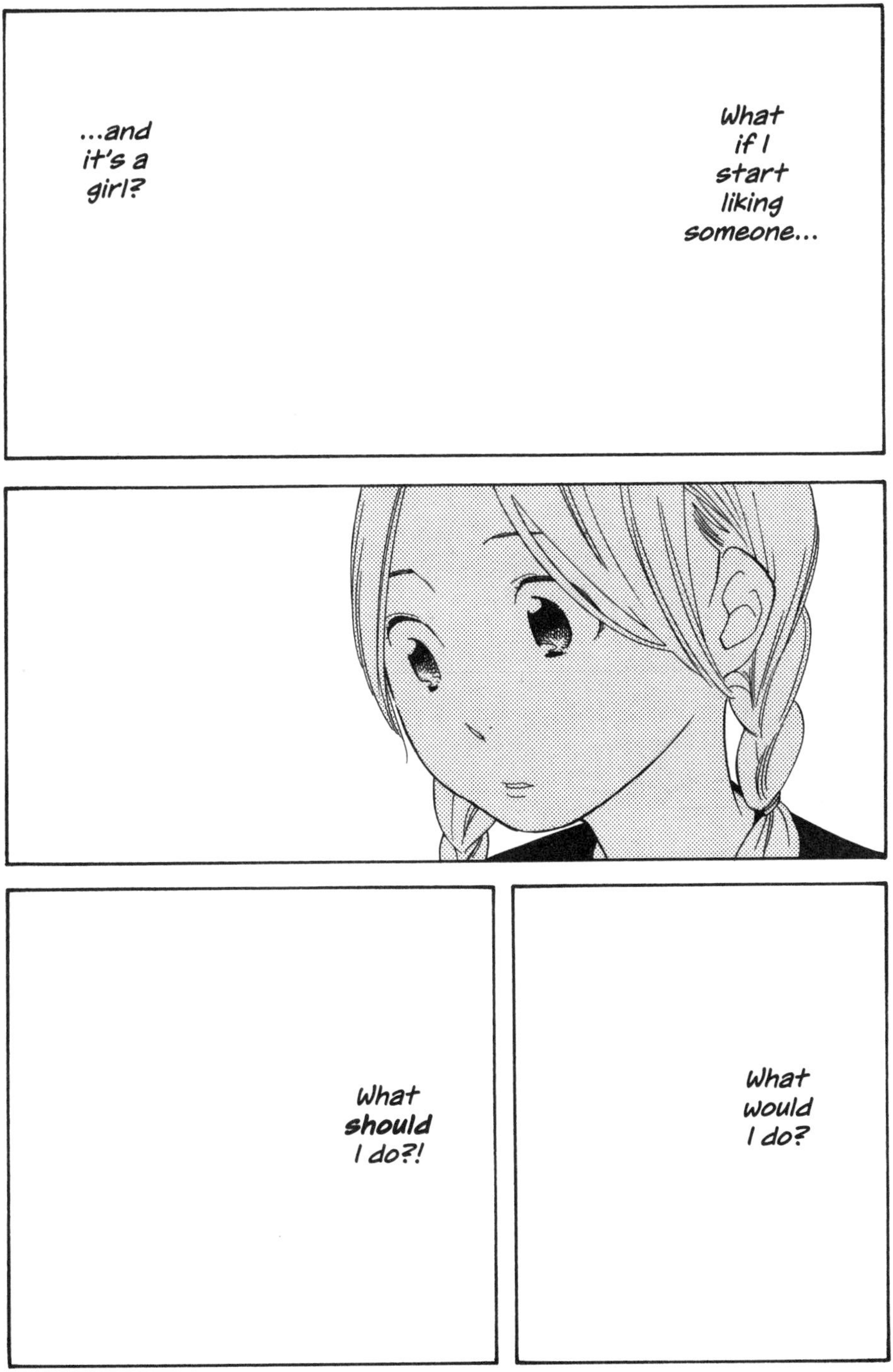
What if I start liking someone...
...and it's a girl?
What would I do?
What should I do?!

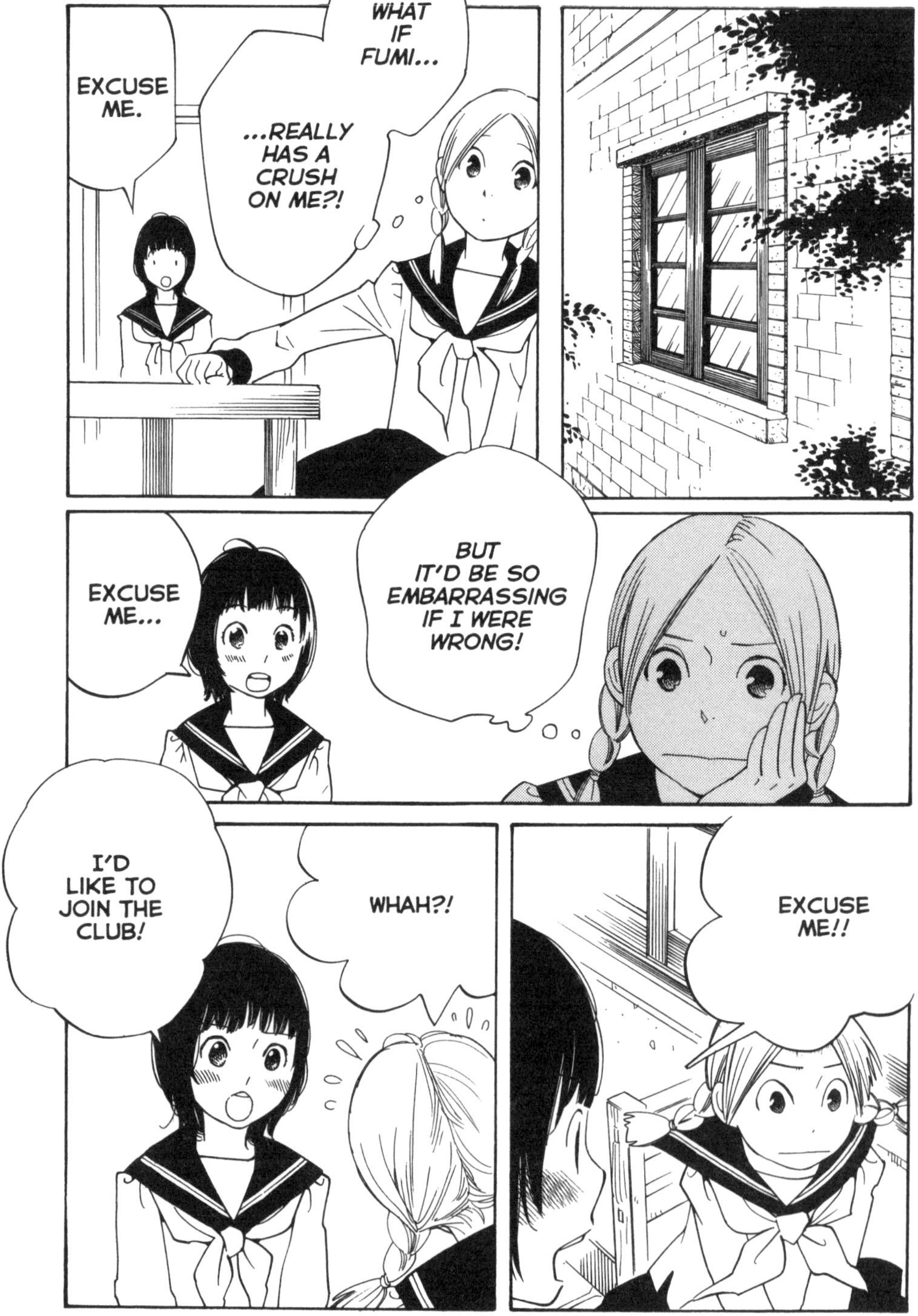
WHAT IF FUMI...
...REALLY HAS A CRUSH ON ME?!
EXCUSE ME.
BUT IT'D BE SO EMBARRASSING IF I WERE WRONG!
EXCUSE ME...
EXCUSE ME!!
I'D LIKE TO JOIN THE CLUB!
WHAH?!

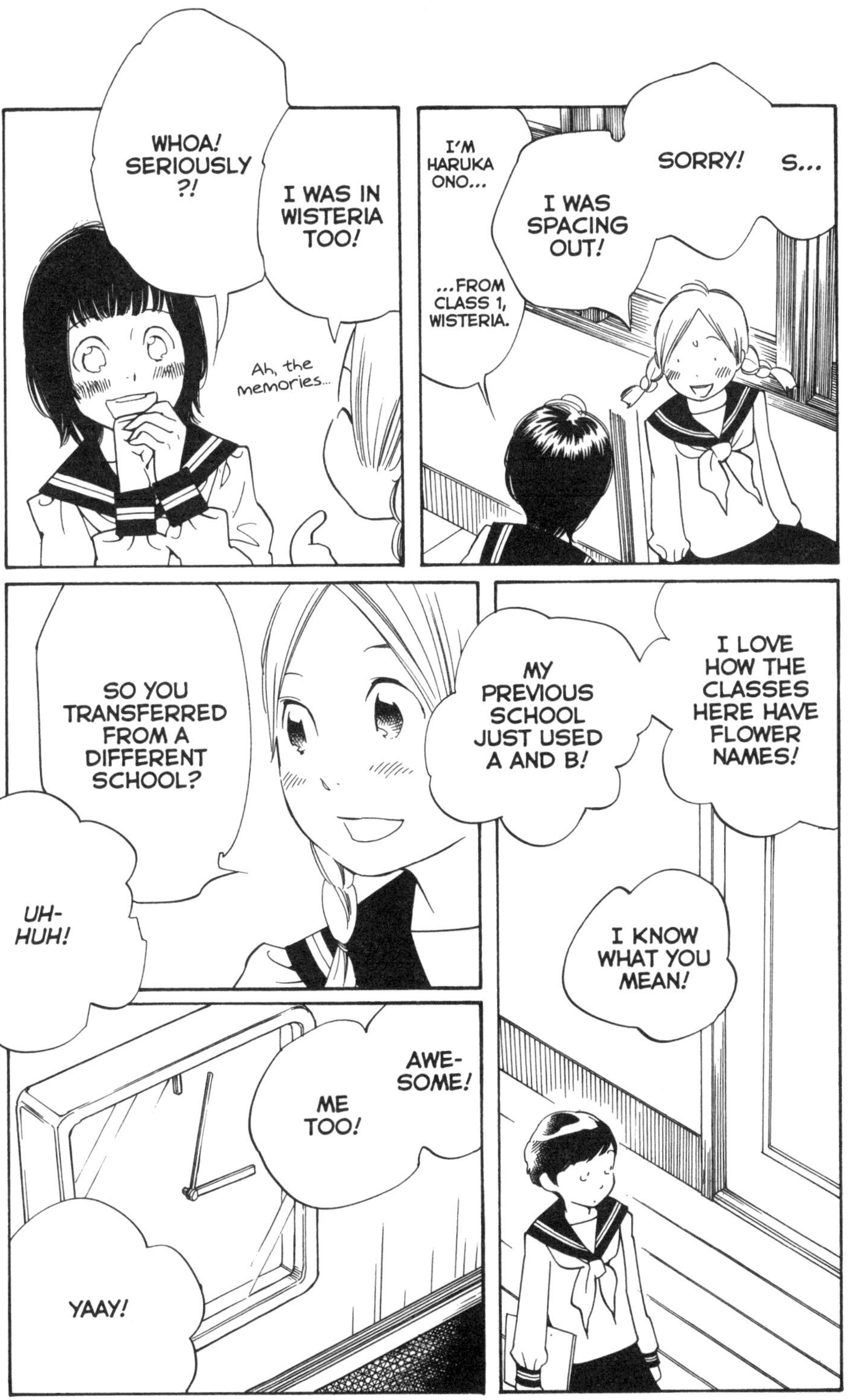
S...
SORRY!
I WAS SPACING OUT!
I'M HARUKA ONO...
...FROM CLASS 1, WISTERIA.
I WAS IN WISTERIA TOO!
WHOA! SERIOUSLY?!
Ah, the memories...
SO YOU TRANSFERRED FROM A DIFFERENT SCHOOL?
UH-HUH!
I LOVE HOW THE CLASSES HERE HAVE FLOWER NAMES!
MY PREVIOUS SCHOOL JUST USED A AND B!
I KNOW WHAT YOU MEAN!
AWE-SOME!
ME TOO!
YAAY!

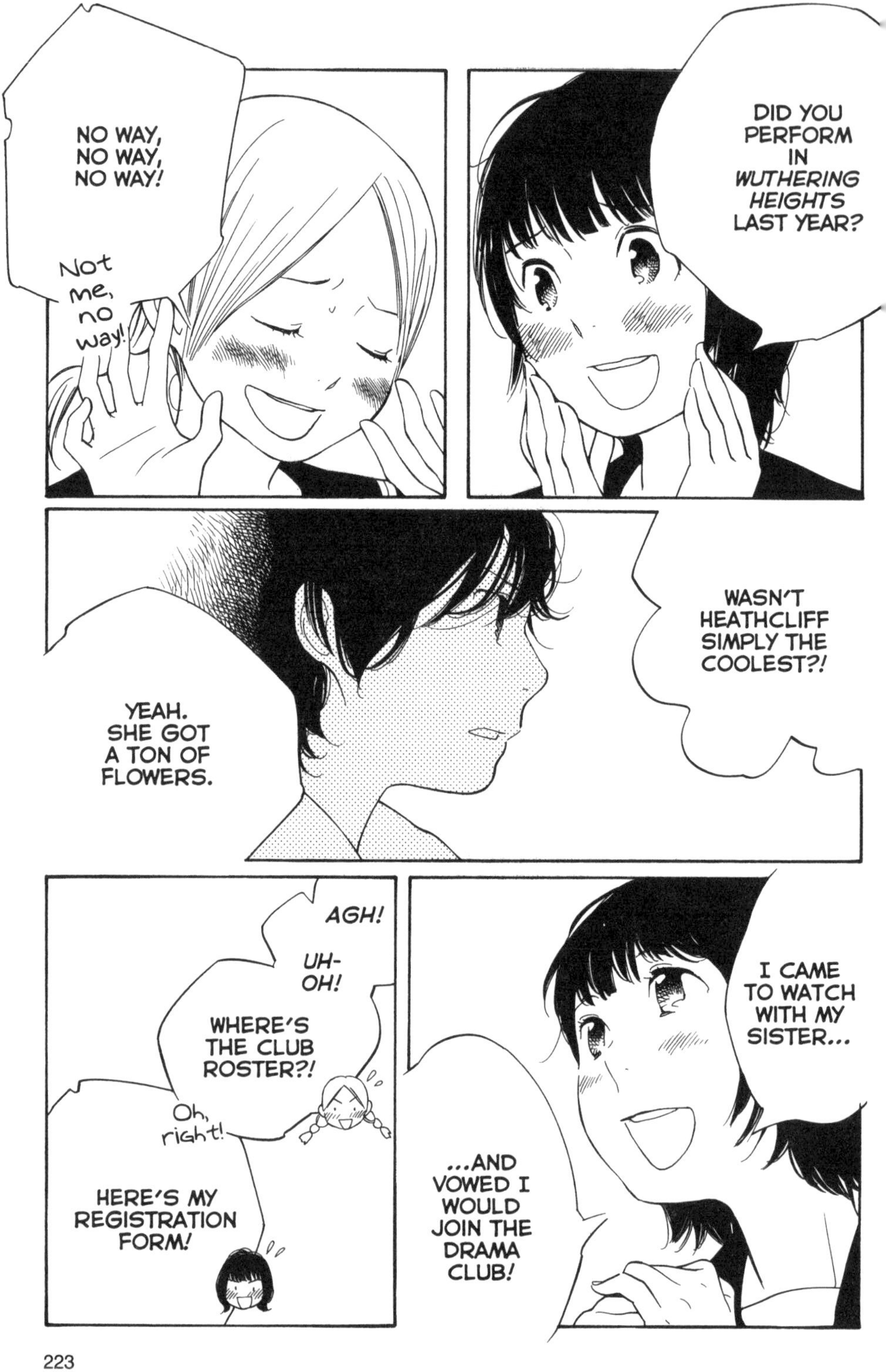
DID YOU PERFORM IN *WUTHERING HEIGHTS* LAST YEAR?
NO WAY, NO WAY, NO WAY!
Not me, no way!
WASN'T HEATHCLIFF SIMPLY THE COOLEST?!
YEAH. SHE GOT A TON OF FLOWERS.
I CAME TO WATCH WITH MY SISTER...
...AND VOWED I WOULD JOIN THE DRAMA CLUB!
AGH!
UH-OH!
WHERE'S THE CLUB ROSTER?!
Oh, right!
HERE'S MY REGISTRATION FORM!

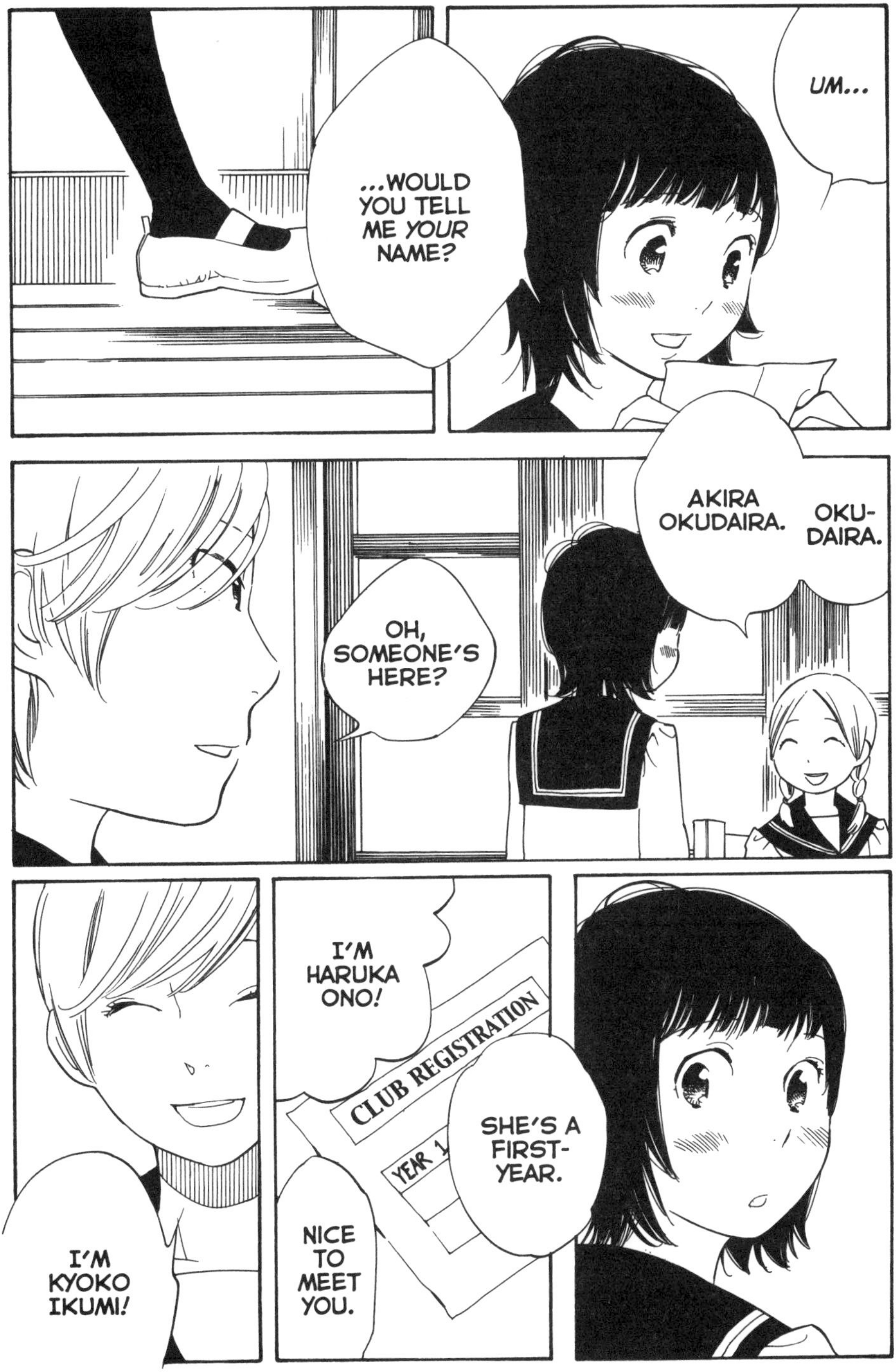
UM...
...WOULD YOU TELL ME *YOUR* NAME?
AKIRA OKUDAIRA. OKU-DAIRA.
OH, SOMEONE'S HERE?
SHE'S A FIRST-YEAR.
I'M HARUKA ONO!
CLUB REGISTRATION
YEAR 1
NICE TO MEET YOU.
I'M KYOKO IKUMI!

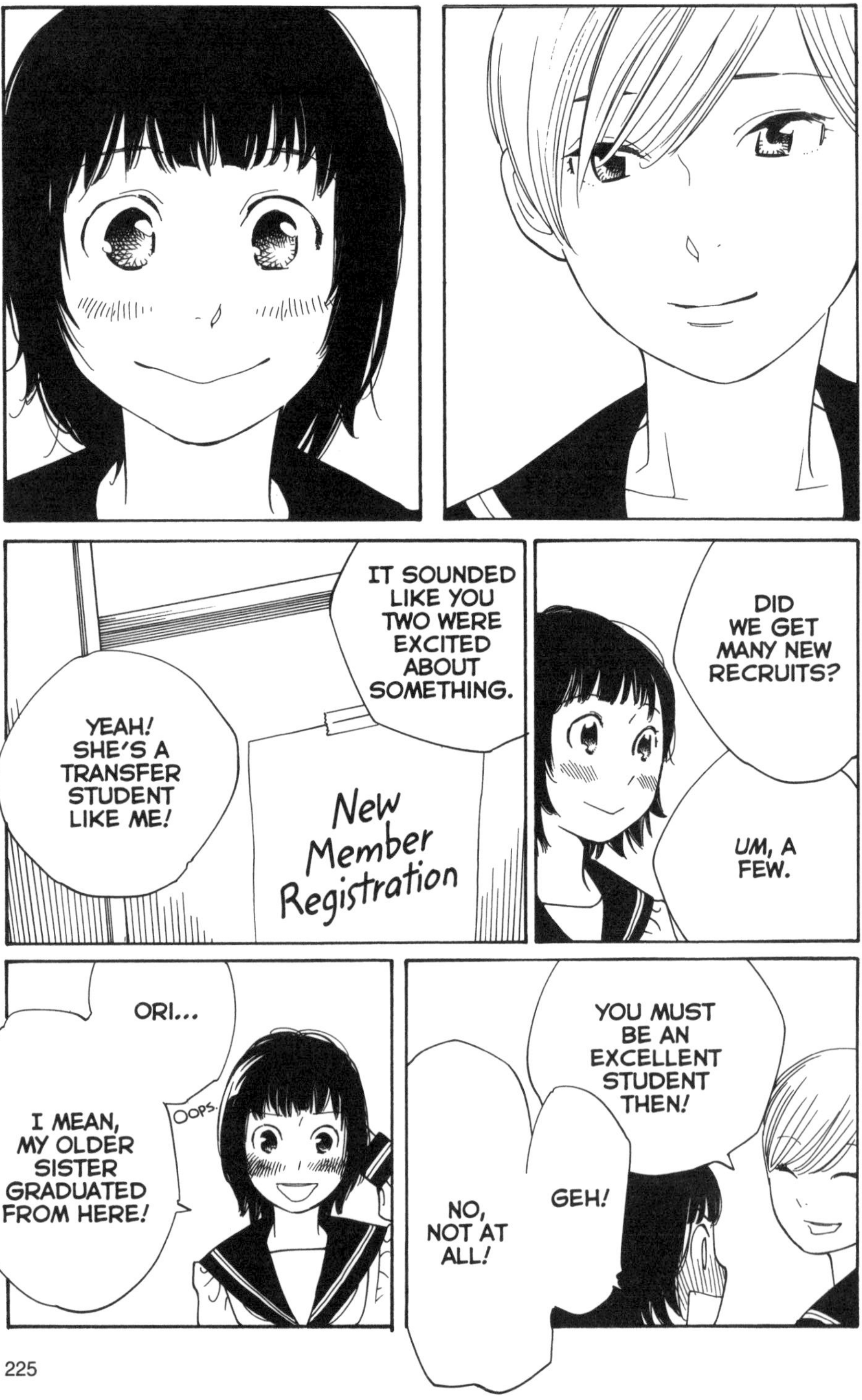
DID WE GET MANY NEW RECRUITS?
UM, A FEW.
IT SOUNDED LIKE YOU TWO WERE EXCITED ABOUT SOMETHING.
YEAH! SHE'S A TRANSFER STUDENT LIKE ME!
New Member Registration
YOU MUST BE AN EXCELLENT STUDENT THEN!
GEH!
NO, NOT AT ALL!
ORI...
OOPS.
I MEAN, MY OLDER SISTER GRADUATED FROM HERE!

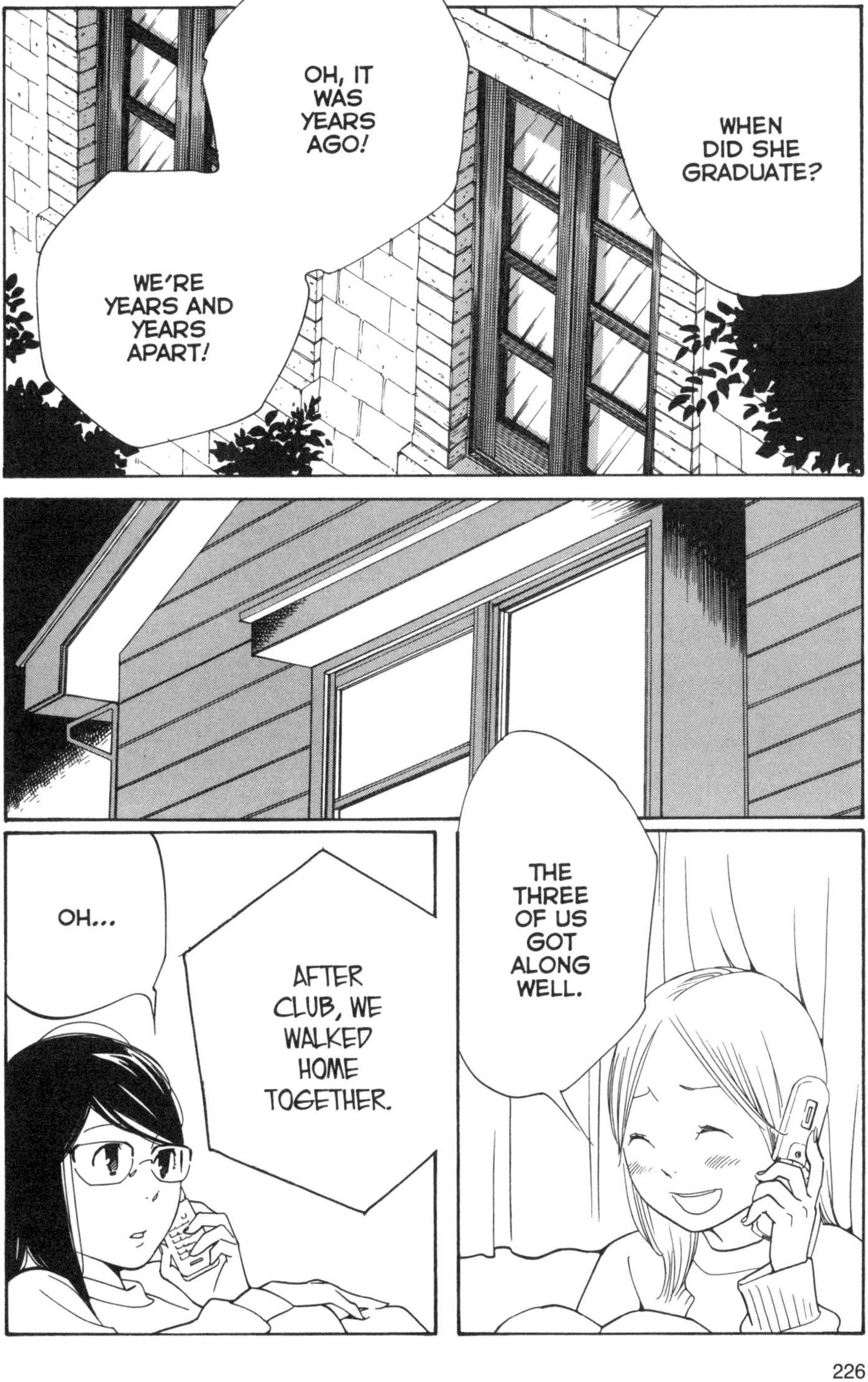
WHEN DID SHE GRADUATE?
OH, IT WAS YEARS AGO!
WE'RE YEARS AND YEARS APART!
THE THREE OF US GOT ALONG WELL.
AFTER CLUB, WE WALKED HOME TOGETHER.
OH...

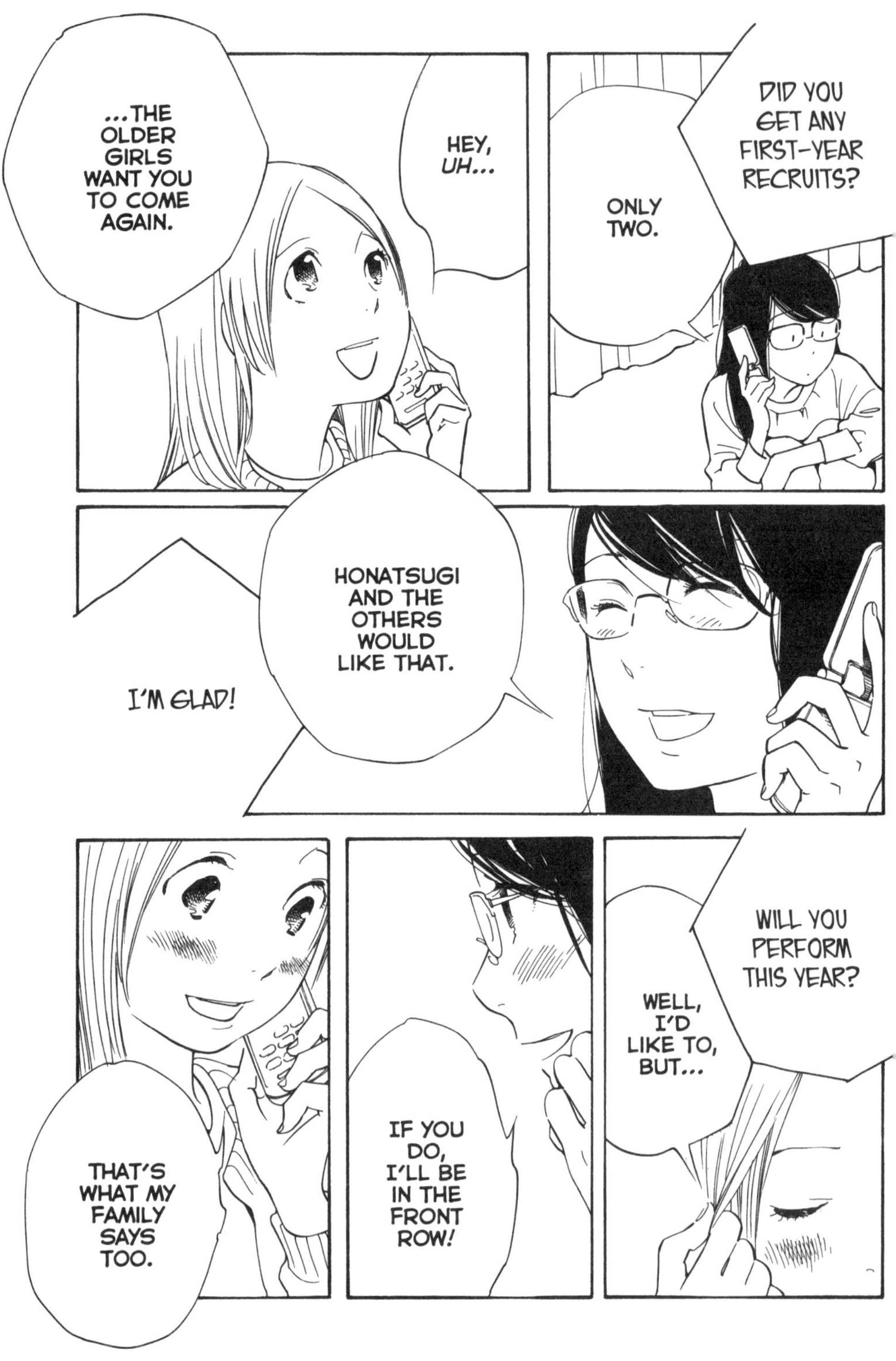
DID YOU GET ANY FIRST-YEAR RECRUITS?
ONLY TWO.
HEY, UH...
...THE OLDER GIRLS WANT YOU TO COME AGAIN.
HONATSUGI AND THE OTHERS WOULD LIKE THAT.
I'M GLAD!
WILL YOU PERFORM THIS YEAR?
WELL, I'D LIKE TO, BUT...
IF YOU DO, I'LL BE IN THE FRONT ROW!
THAT'S WHAT MY FAMILY SAYS TOO.

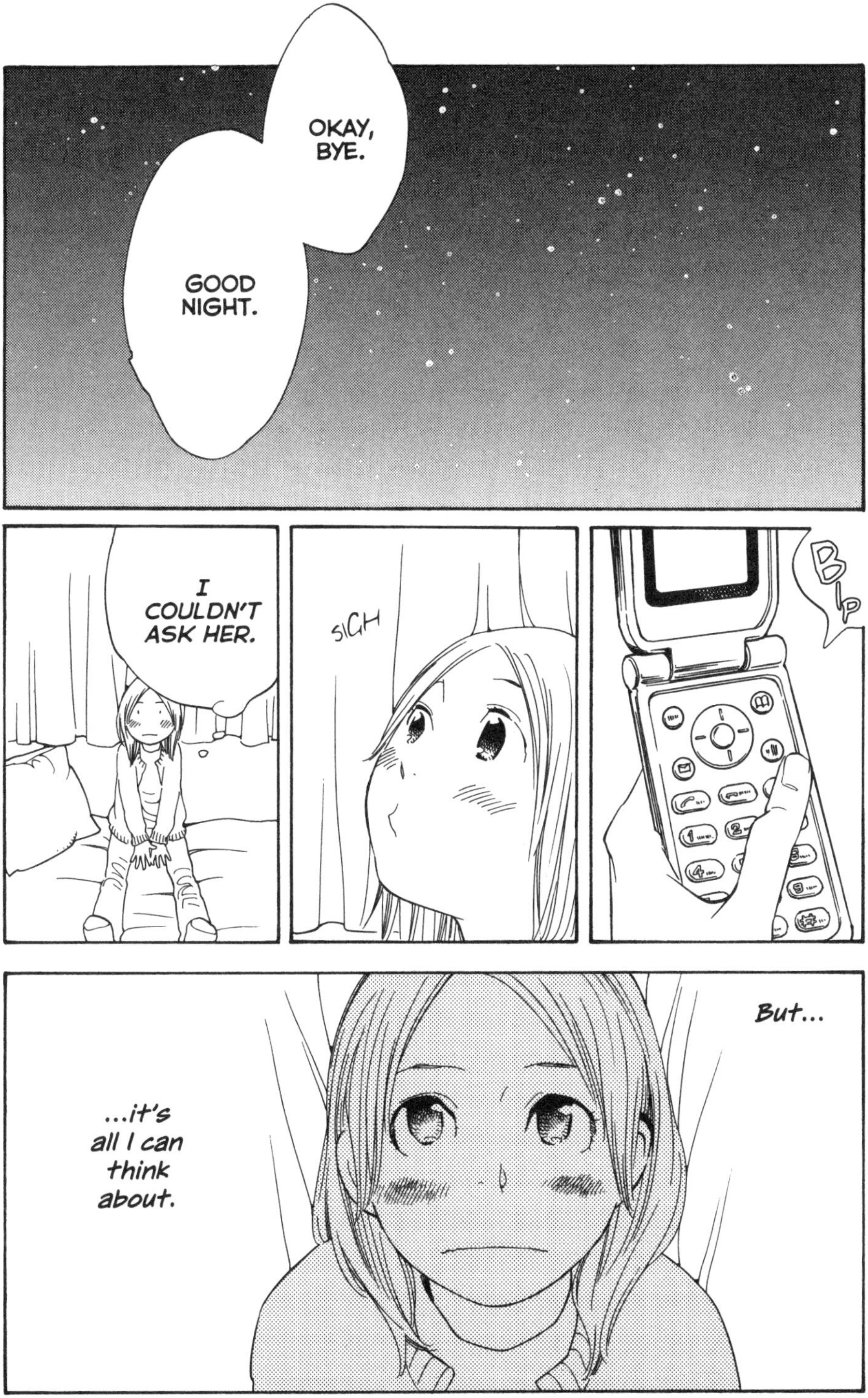
OKAY, BYE.
GOOD NIGHT.
Blp
SIGH
I COULDN'T ASK HER.
But...
...it's all I can think about.

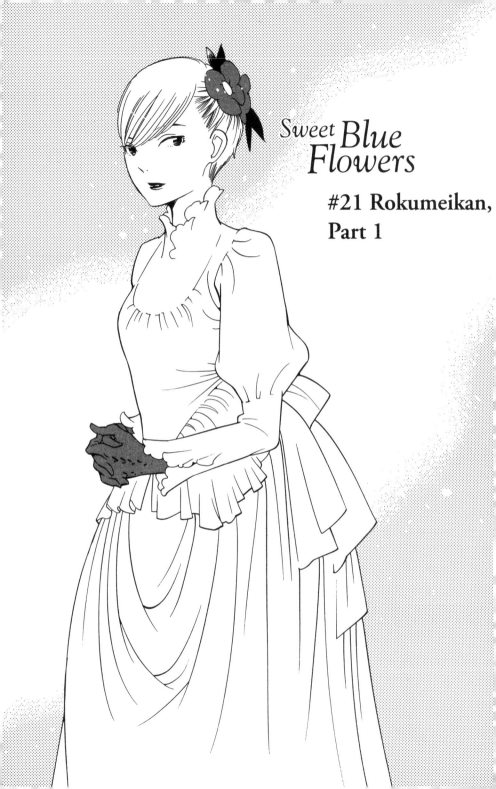

Sweet Blue Flowers

#21 Rokumeikan, Part 1

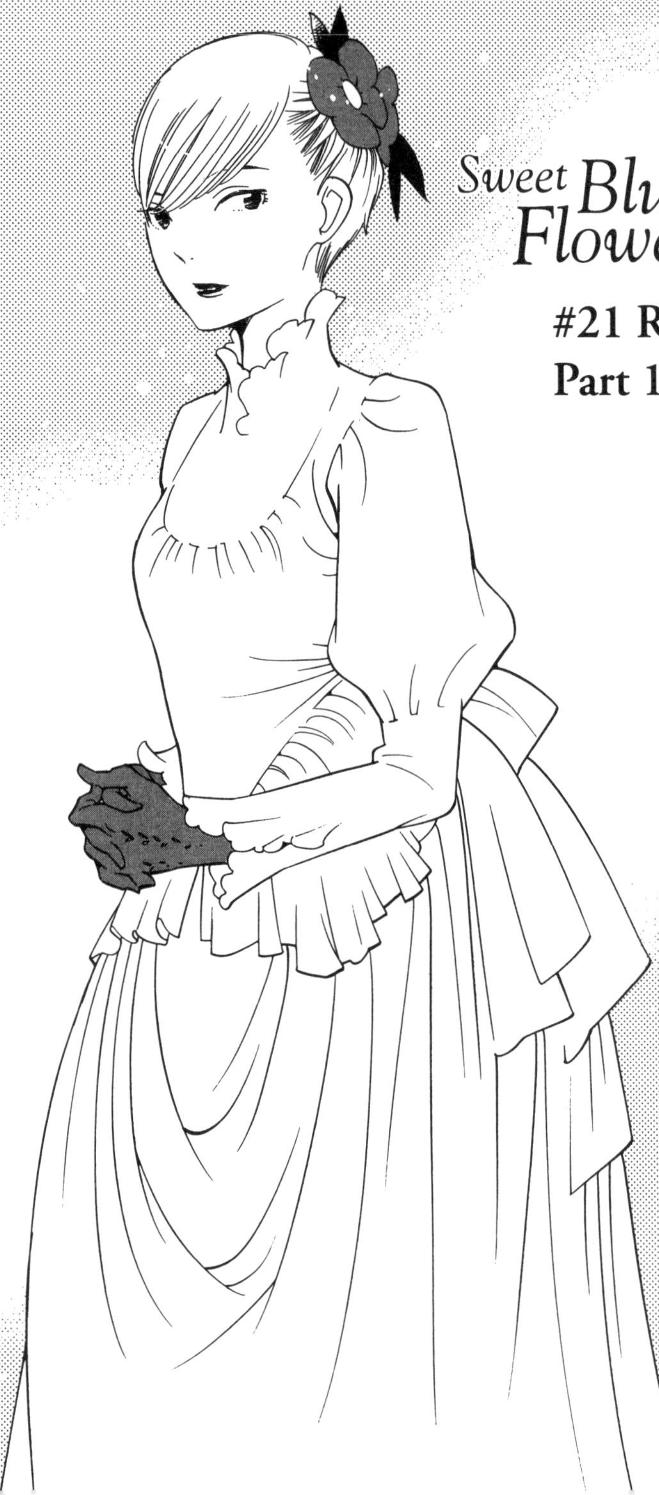

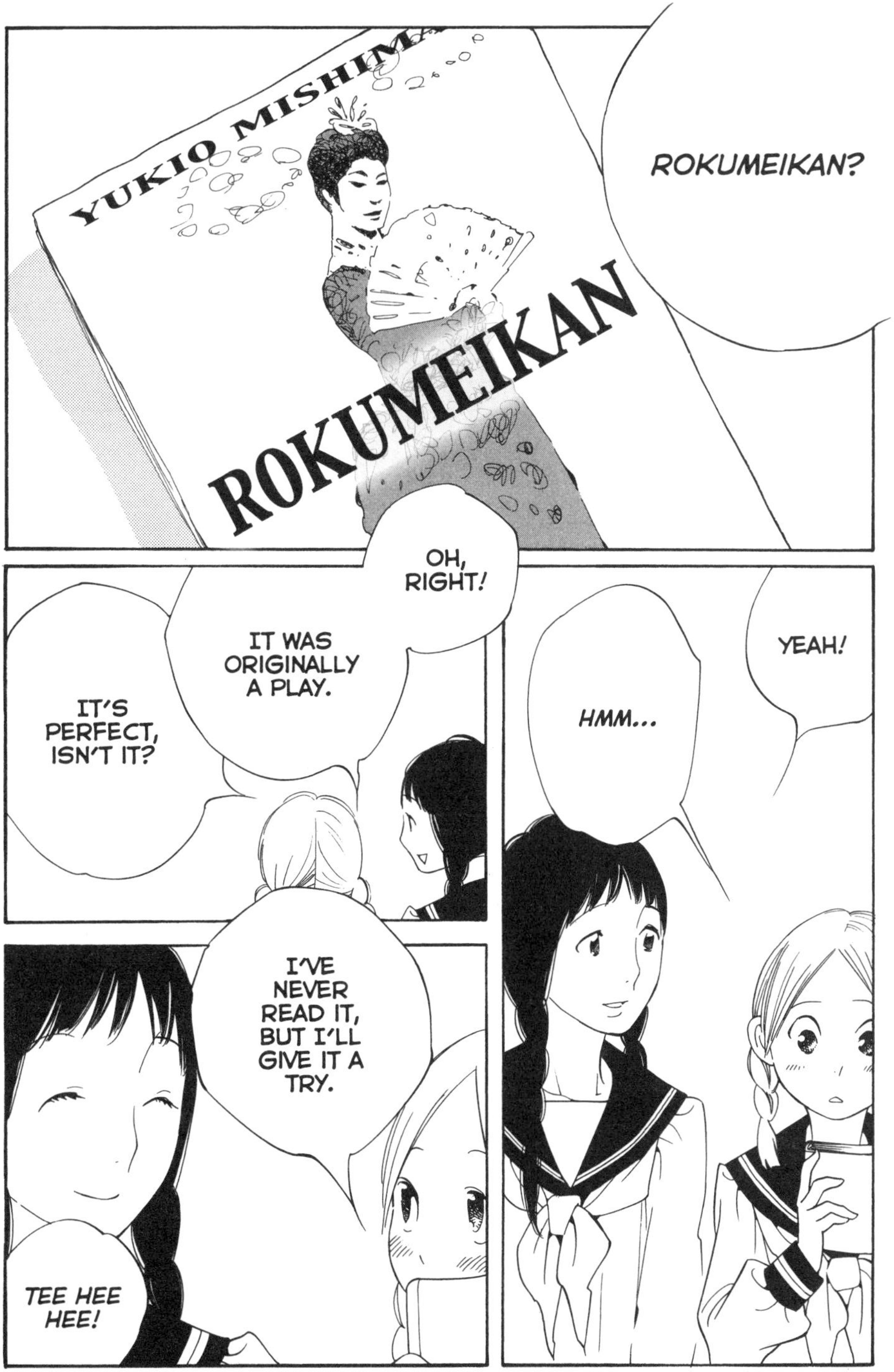
ROKUMEIKAN?
YUKIO MISHIMA
ROKUMEIKAN
YEAH!
HMM...
OH, RIGHT!
IT WAS ORIGINALLY A PLAY.
IT'S PERFECT, ISN'T IT?
I'VE NEVER READ IT, BUT I'LL GIVE IT A TRY.
TEE HEE HEE!

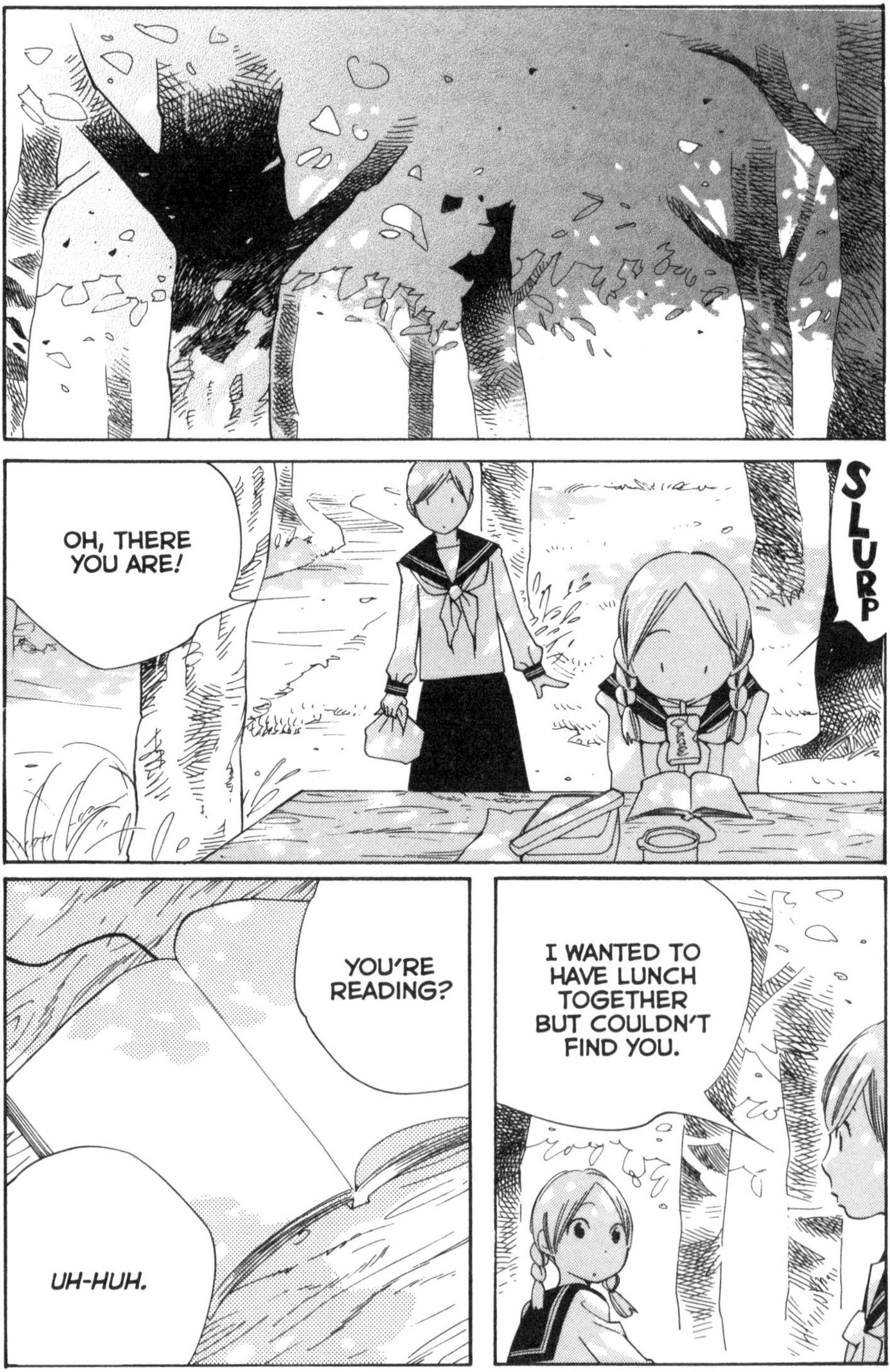
SLURP
OH, THERE YOU ARE!
I WANTED TO HAVE LUNCH TOGETHER BUT COULDN'T FIND YOU.
YOU'RE READING?
UH-HUH.

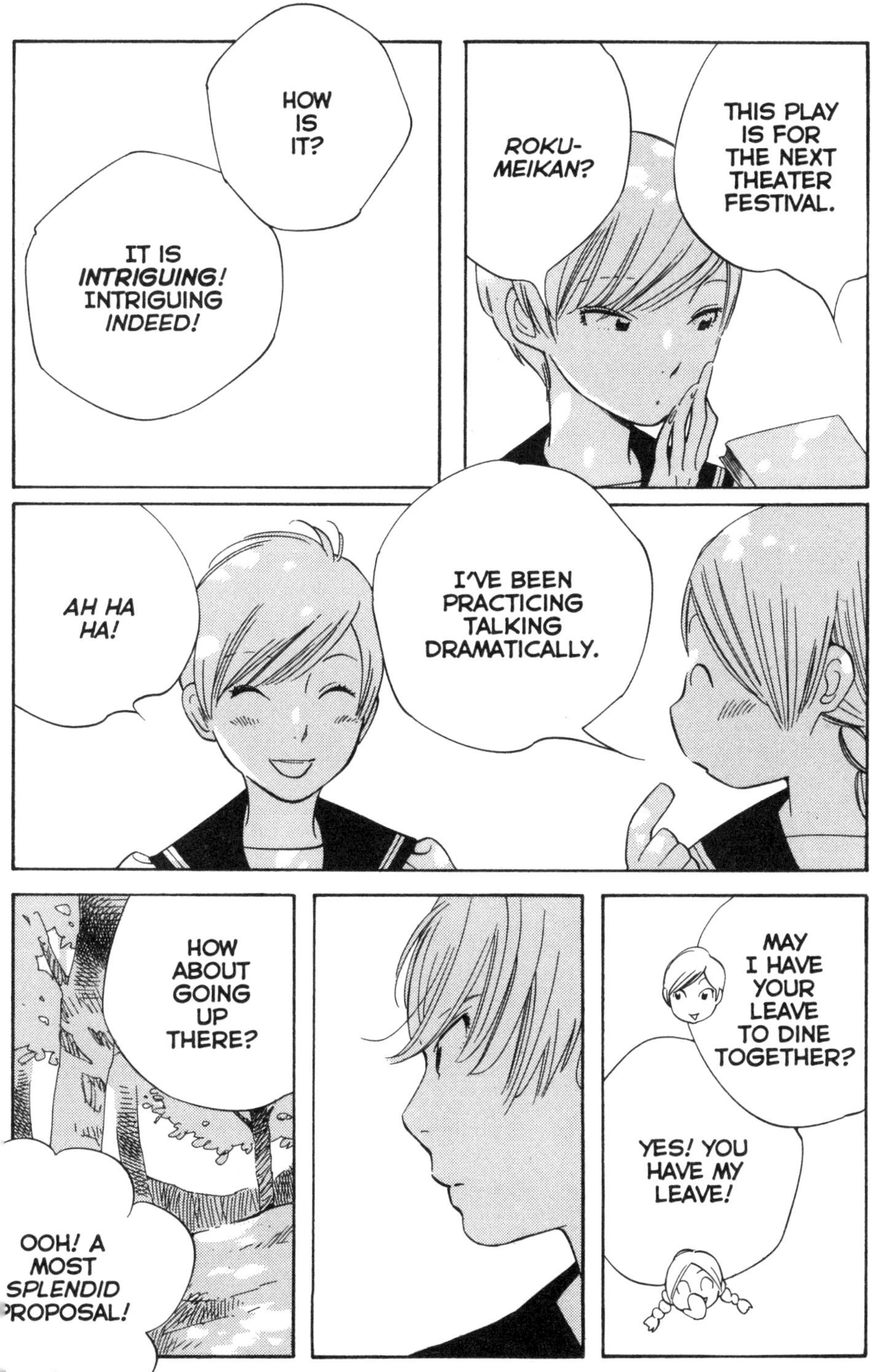
THIS PLAY IS FOR THE NEXT THEATER FESTIVAL.
ROKU-MEIKAN?
HOW IS IT?
IT IS INTRIGUING! INTRIGUING INDEED!
I'VE BEEN PRACTICING TALKING DRAMATICALLY.
AH HA HA!
MAY I HAVE YOUR LEAVE TO DINE TOGETHER?
YES! YOU HAVE MY LEAVE!
HOW ABOUT GOING UP THERE?
OOH! A MOST SPLENDID PROPOSAL!

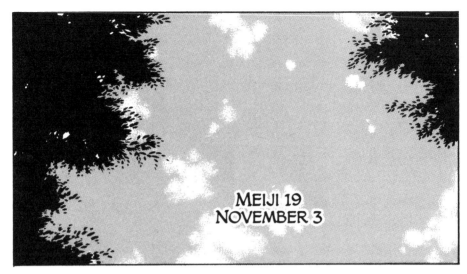

MEIJI 19
NOVEMBER 3

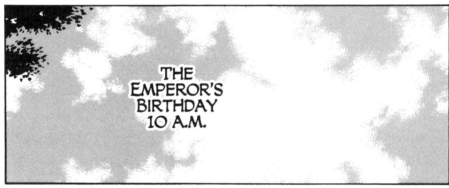

THE
EMPEROR'S
BIRTHDAY
10 A.M.

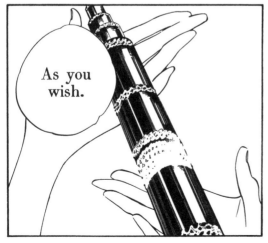

As you wish.

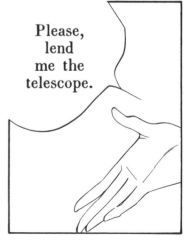

Please, lend me the telescope.

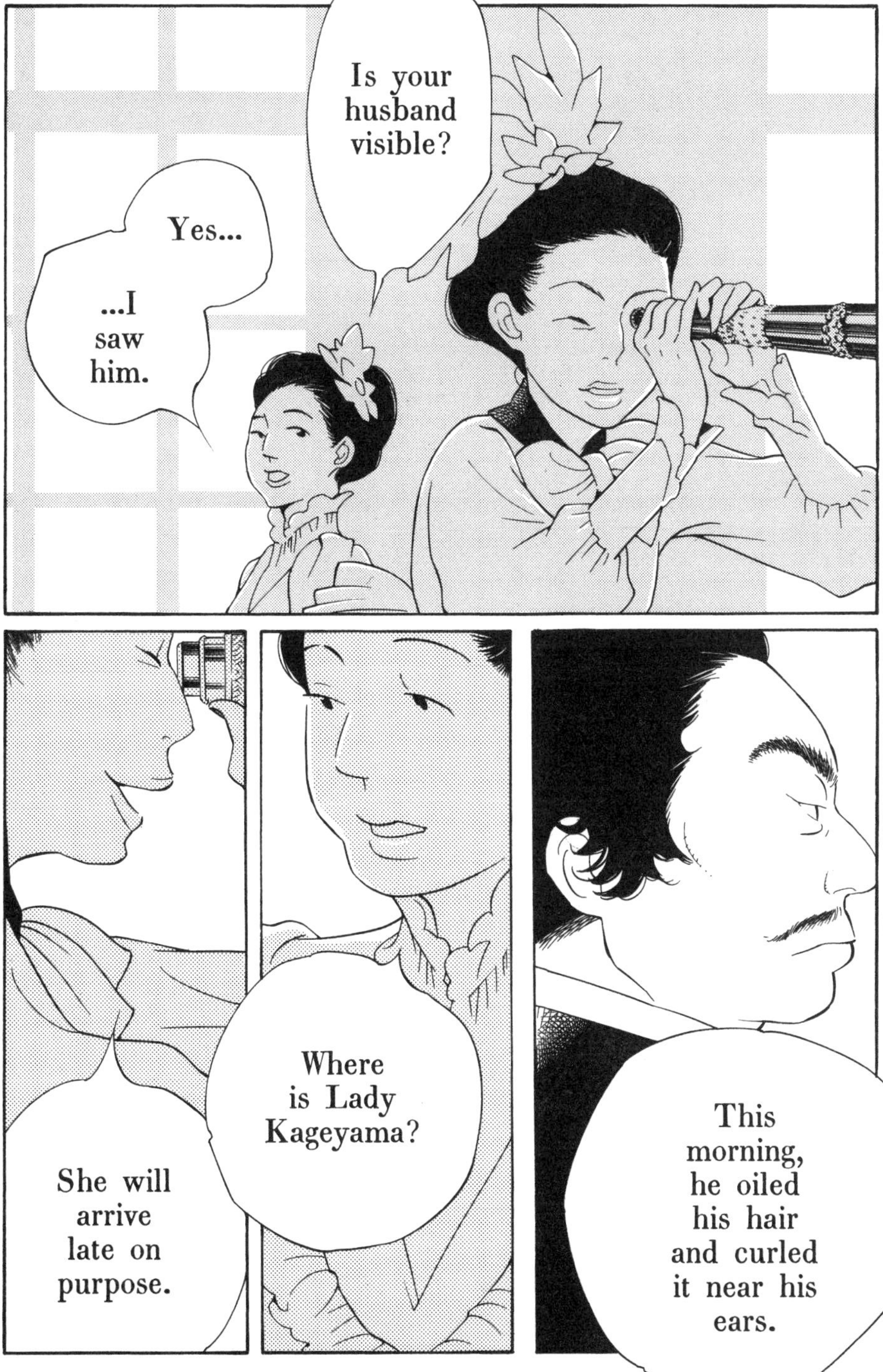
Is your husband visible?
Yes... ...I saw him.
This morning, he oiled his hair and curled it near his ears.
Where is Lady Kageyama?
She will arrive late on purpose.

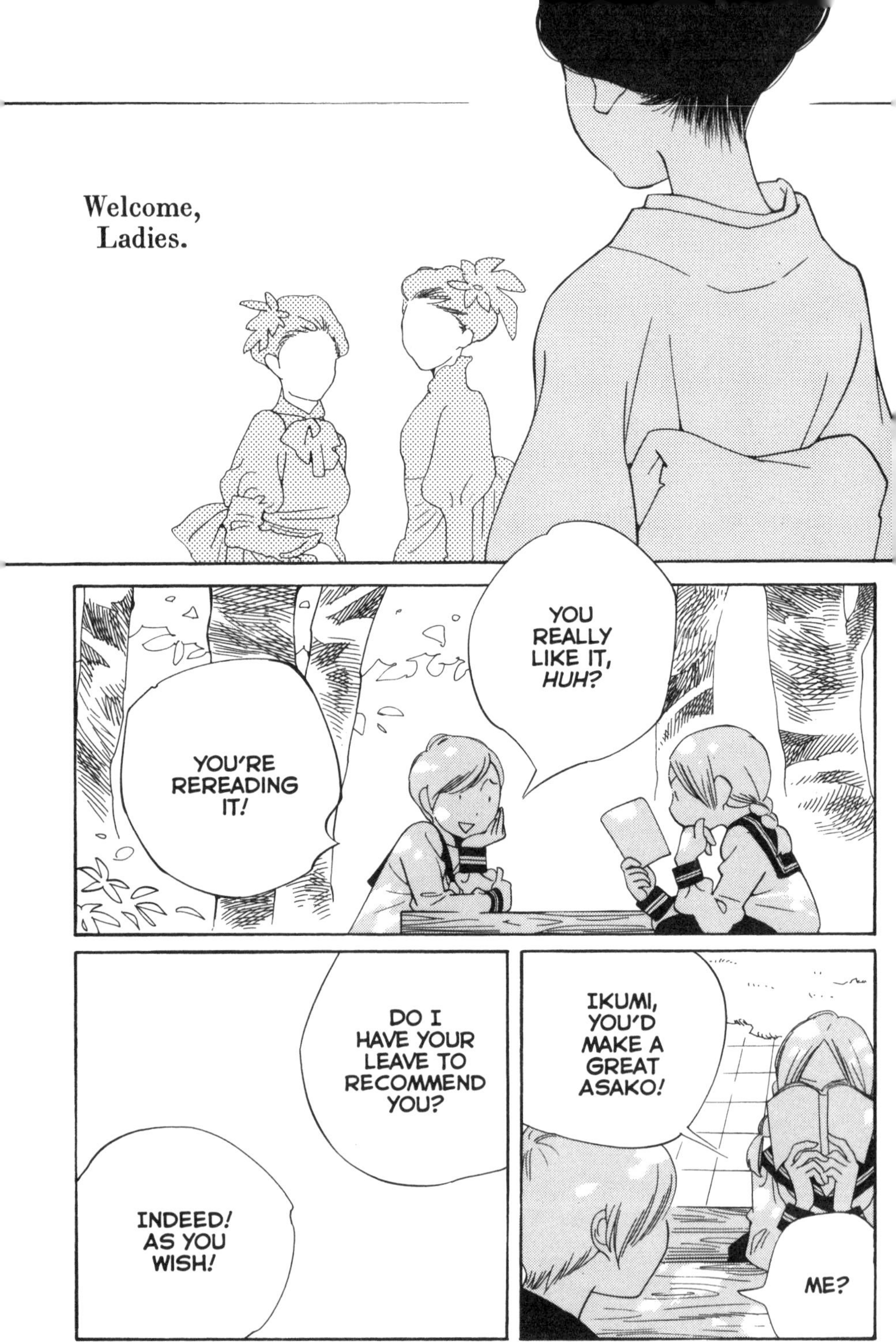
Welcome, Ladies.
YOU REALLY LIKE IT, HUH?
YOU'RE REREADING IT!
IKUMI, YOU'D MAKE A GREAT ASAKO!
ME?
DO I HAVE YOUR LEAVE TO RECOMMEND YOU?
INDEED! AS YOU WISH!

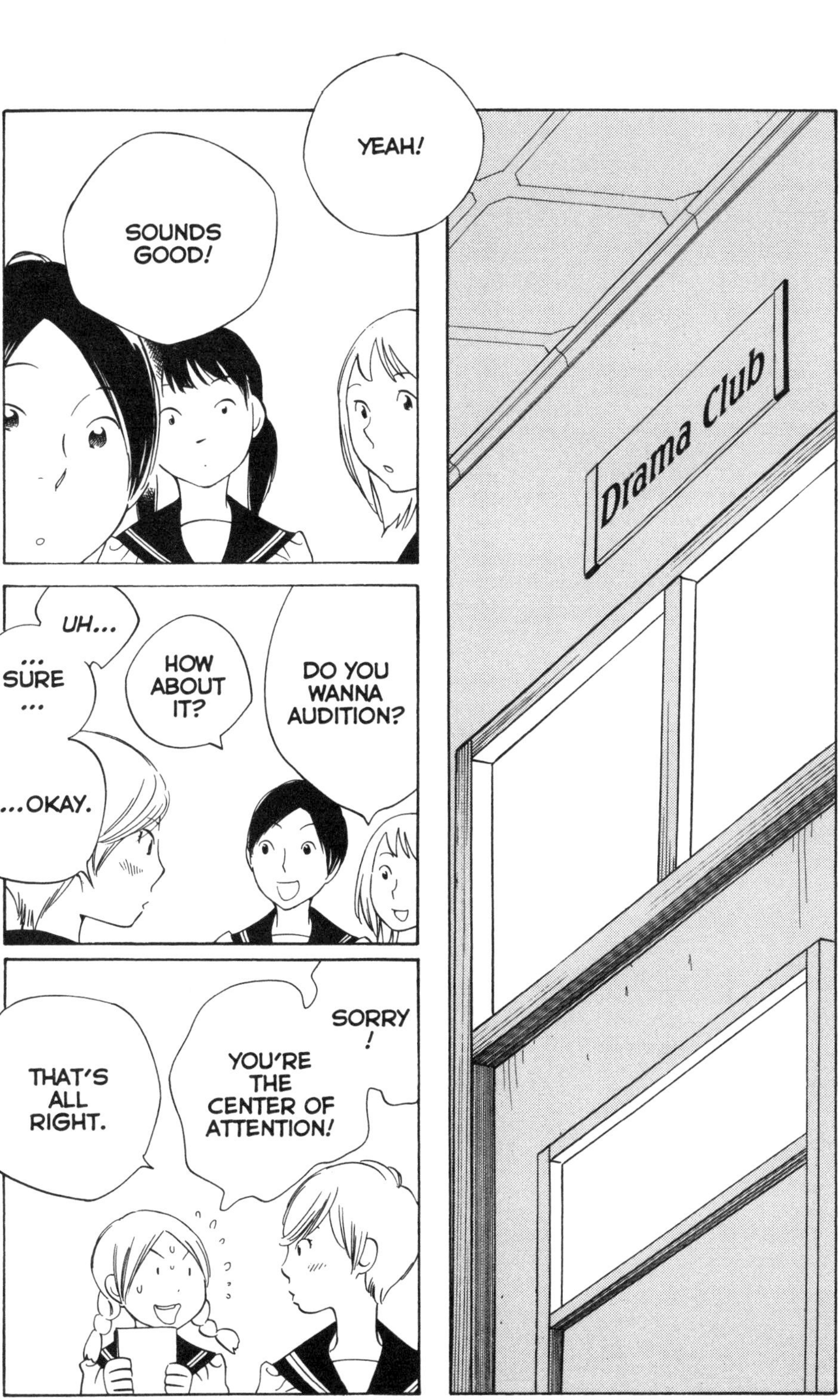
Drama Club
YEAH!
SOUNDS GOOD!
DO YOU WANNA AUDITION?
HOW ABOUT IT?
UH...
...SURE...
...OKAY.
SORRY!
YOU'RE THE CENTER OF ATTENTION!
THAT'S ALL RIGHT.

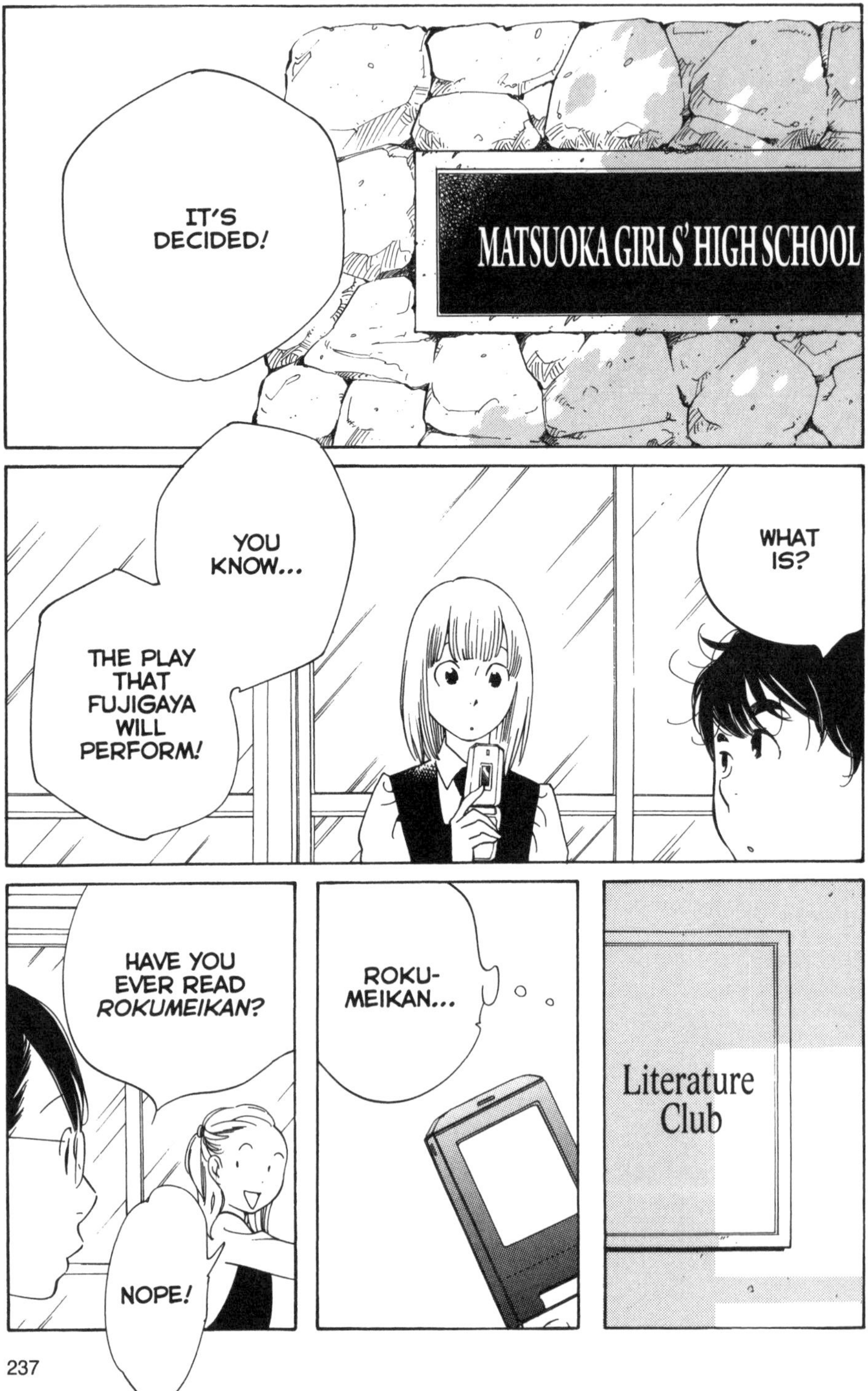
MATSUOKA GIRLS' HIGH SCHOOL
IT'S DECIDED!
WHAT IS?
YOU KNOW...
THE PLAY THAT FUJIGAYA WILL PERFORM!
Literature Club
ROKU-MEIKAN...
HAVE YOU EVER READ *ROKUMEIKAN*?
NOPE!

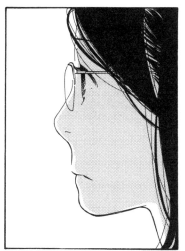

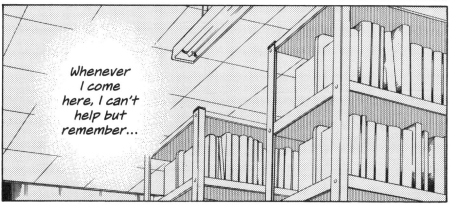

Whenever I come here, I can't help but remember...

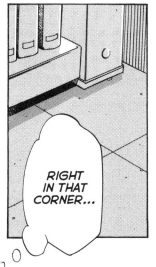

RIGHT IN THAT CORNER...

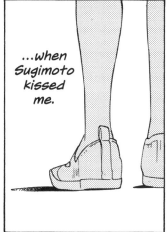

...when Sugimoto kissed me.

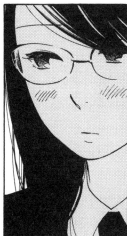

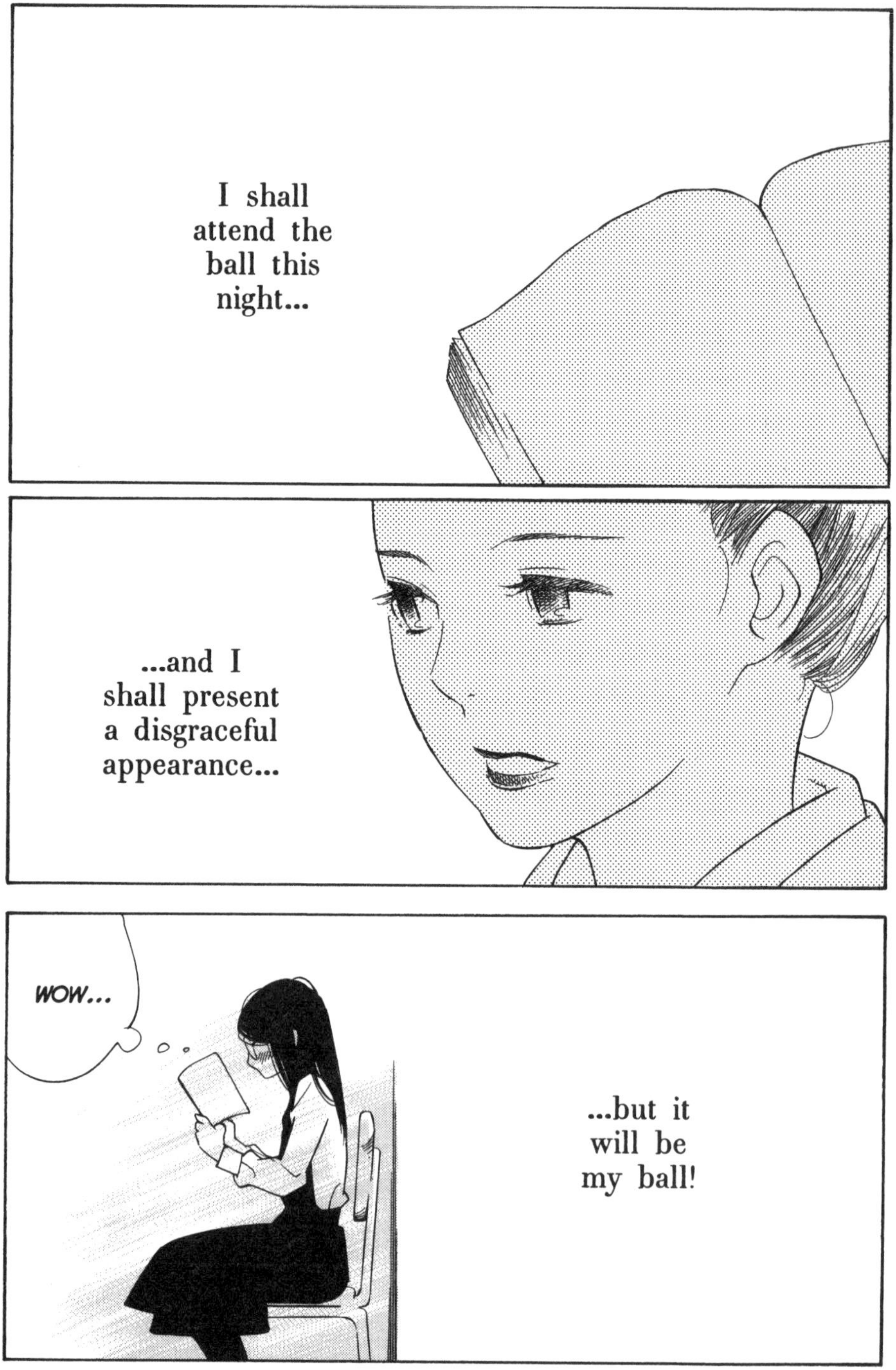
I shall attend the ball this night...
...and I shall present a disgraceful appearance...
...but it will be my ball!
WOW...

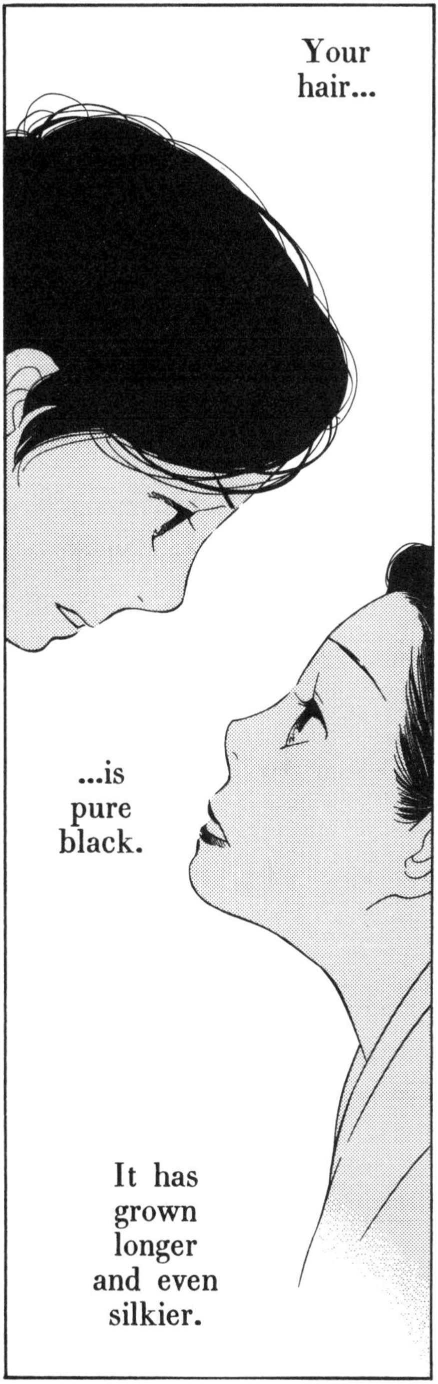
Your hair...
...is pure black.
It has grown longer and even silkier.
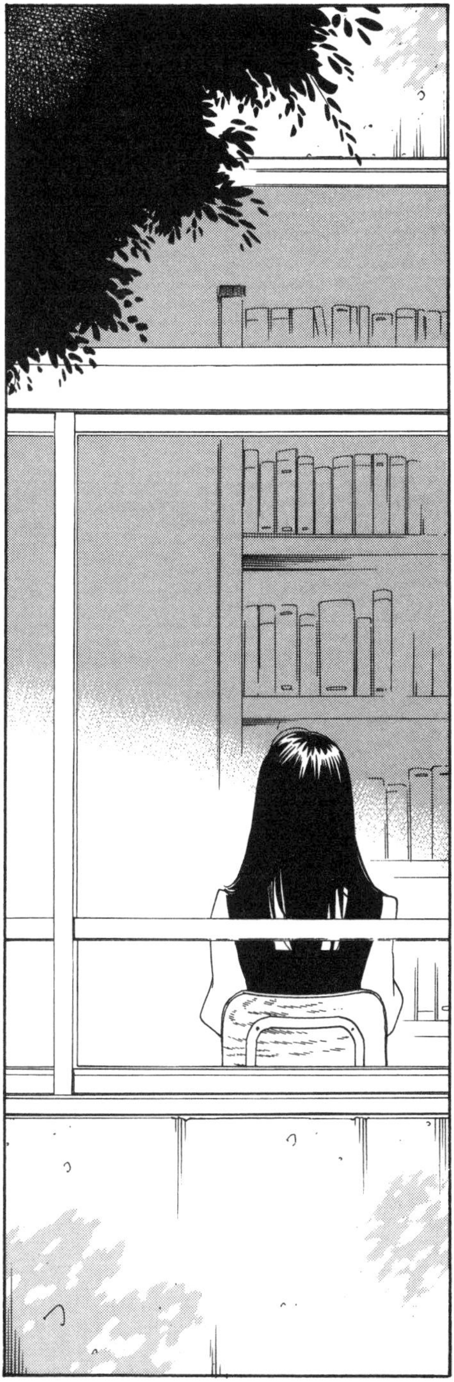

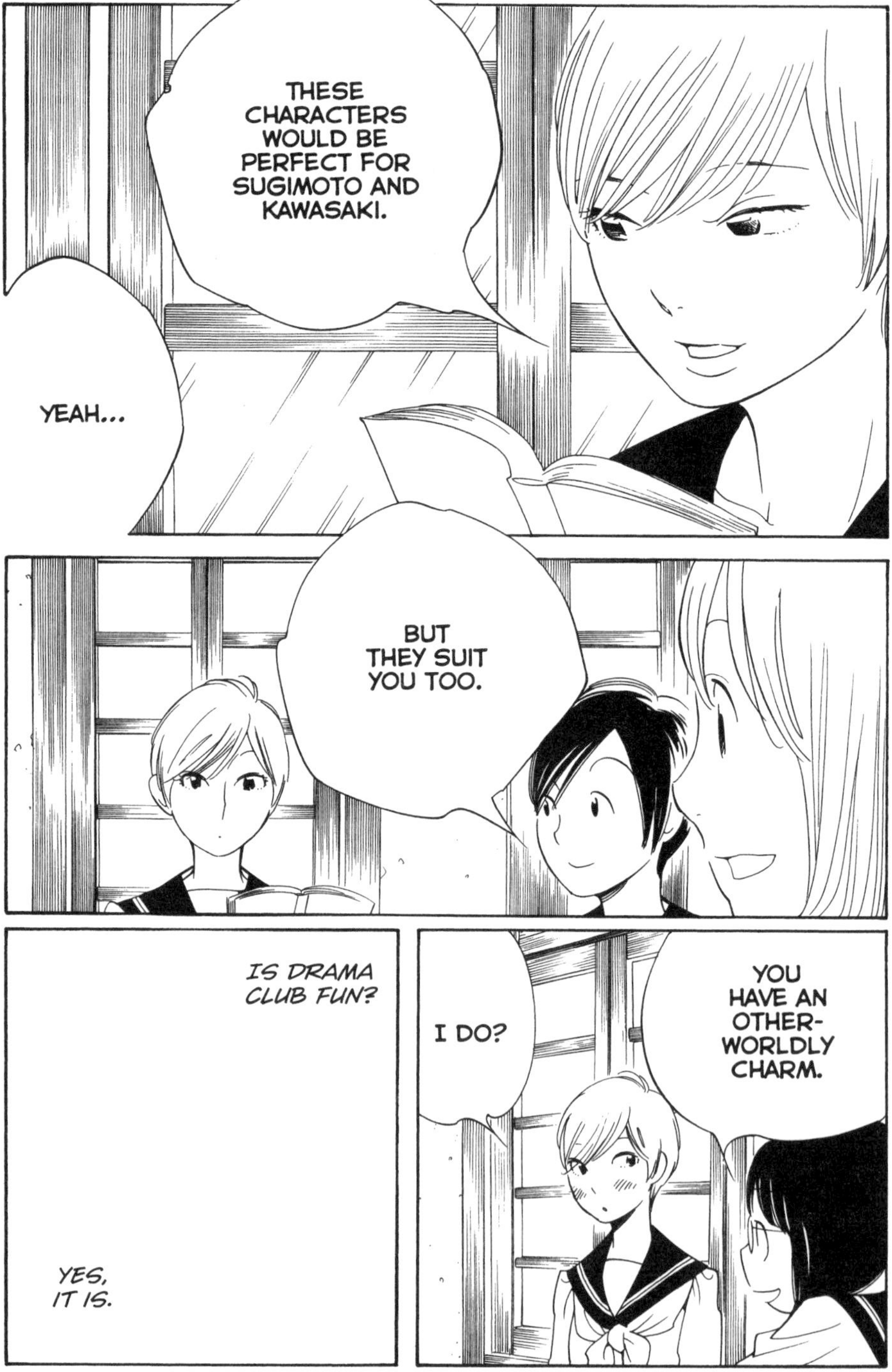
THESE CHARACTERS WOULD BE PERFECT FOR SUGIMOTO AND KAWASAKI.
YEAH...
BUT THEY SUIT YOU TOO.
YOU HAVE AN OTHER-WORLDLY CHARM.
I DO?
IS DRAMA CLUB FUN?
YES, IT IS.

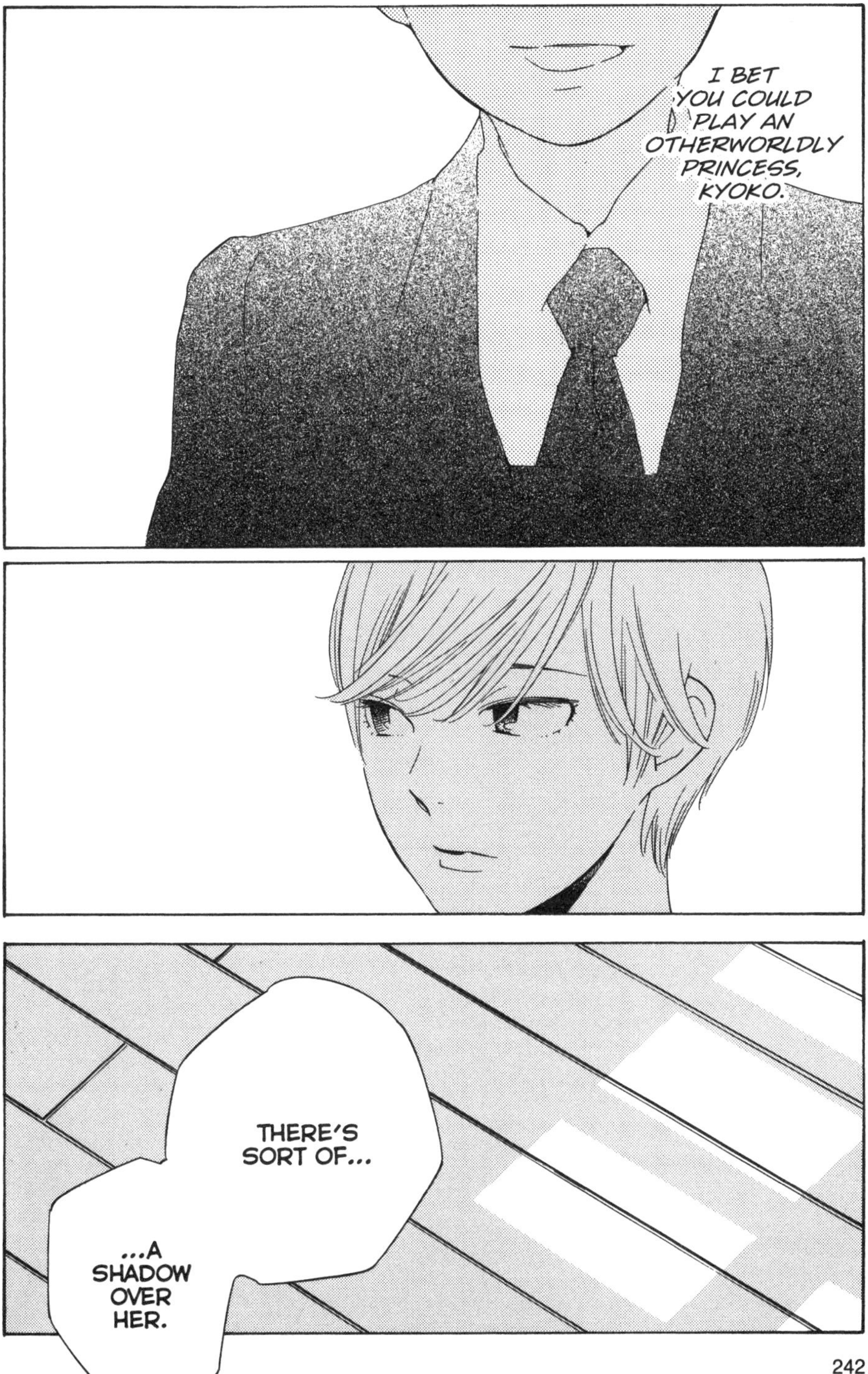
I BET YOU COULD PLAY AN OTHERWORLDLY PRINCESS, KYOKO.
THERE'S SORT OF...
...A SHADOW OVER HER.

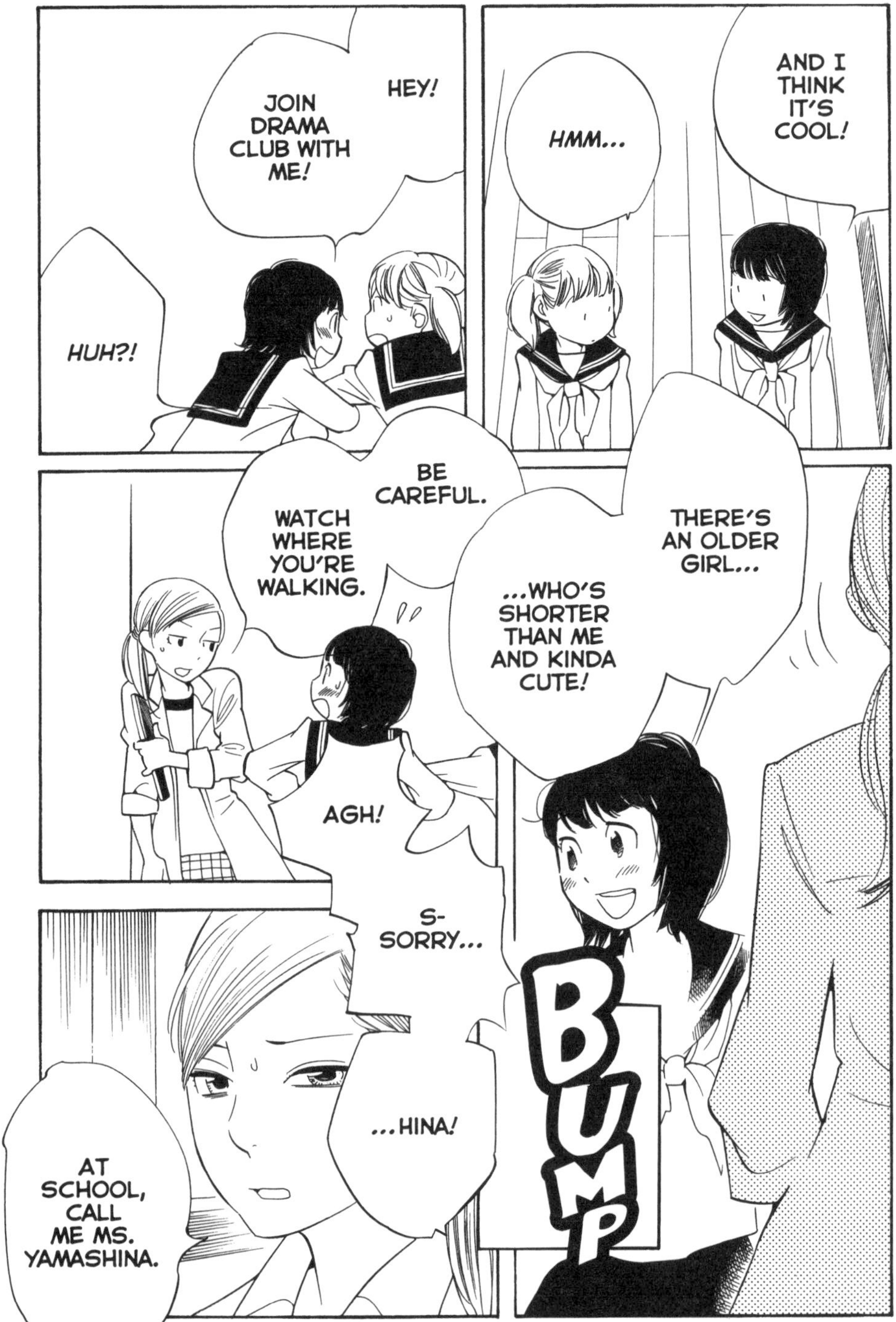
AND I THINK IT'S COOL!
HMM...
HEY!
JOIN DRAMA CLUB WITH ME!
HUH?!
THERE'S AN OLDER GIRL...
...WHO'S SHORTER THAN ME AND KINDA CUTE!
BUMP
BE CAREFUL.
WATCH WHERE YOU'RE WALKING.
AGH!
S-SORRY...
...HINA!
AT SCHOOL, CALL ME MS. YAMASHINA.

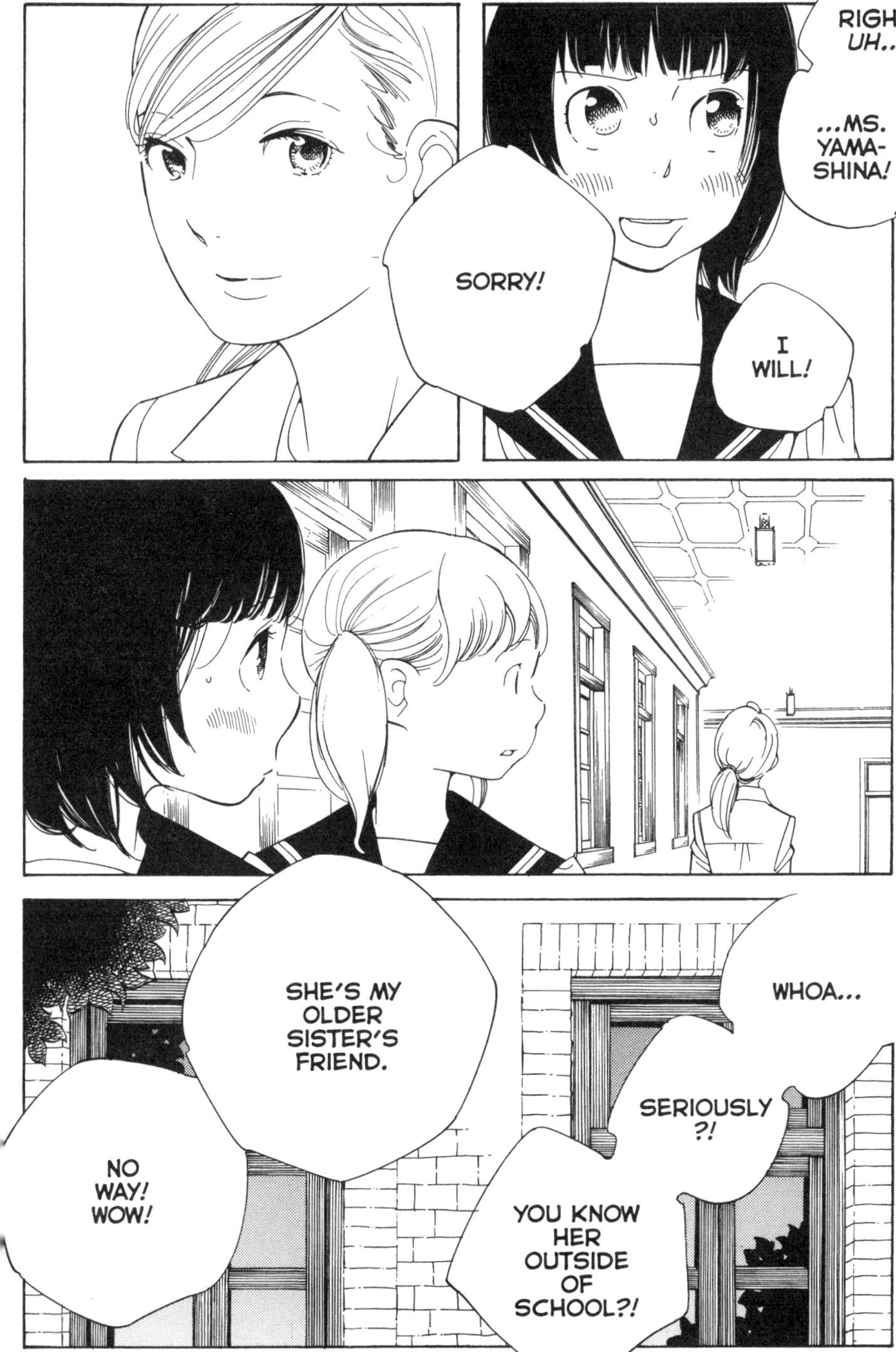
RIGHT, UH...
...MS. YAMA-SHINA!
SORRY!
I WILL!
WHOA...
SERIOUSLY?!
YOU KNOW HER OUTSIDE OF SCHOOL?!
SHE'S MY OLDER SISTER'S FRIEND.
NO WAY! WOW!

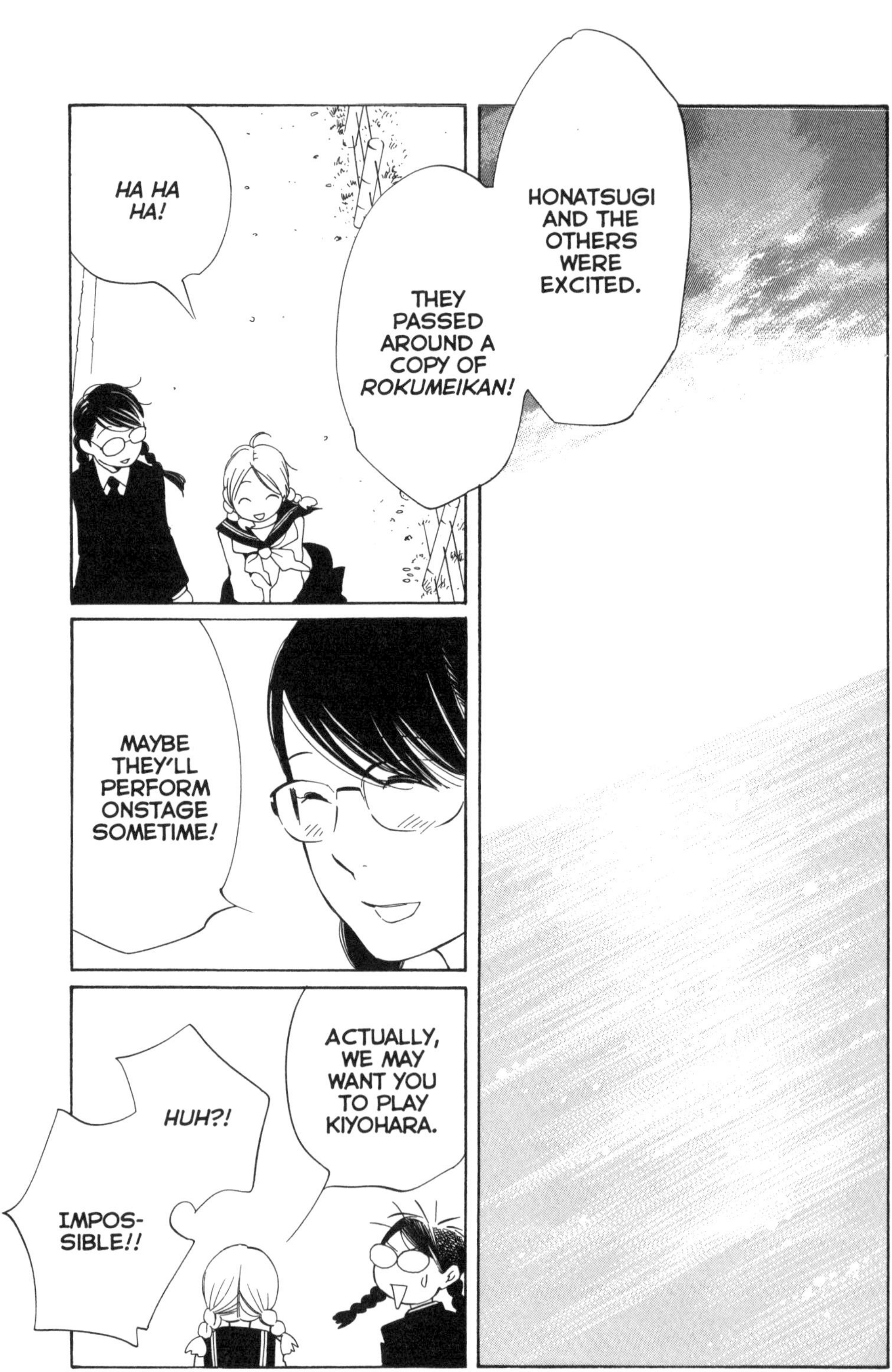
HONATSUGI AND THE OTHERS WERE EXCITED.
THEY PASSED AROUND A COPY OF *ROKUMEIKAN!*
HA HA HA!
MAYBE THEY'LL PERFORM ONSTAGE SOMETIME!
ACTUALLY, WE MAY WANT YOU TO PLAY KIYOHARA.
HUH?!
IMPOSSIBLE!!

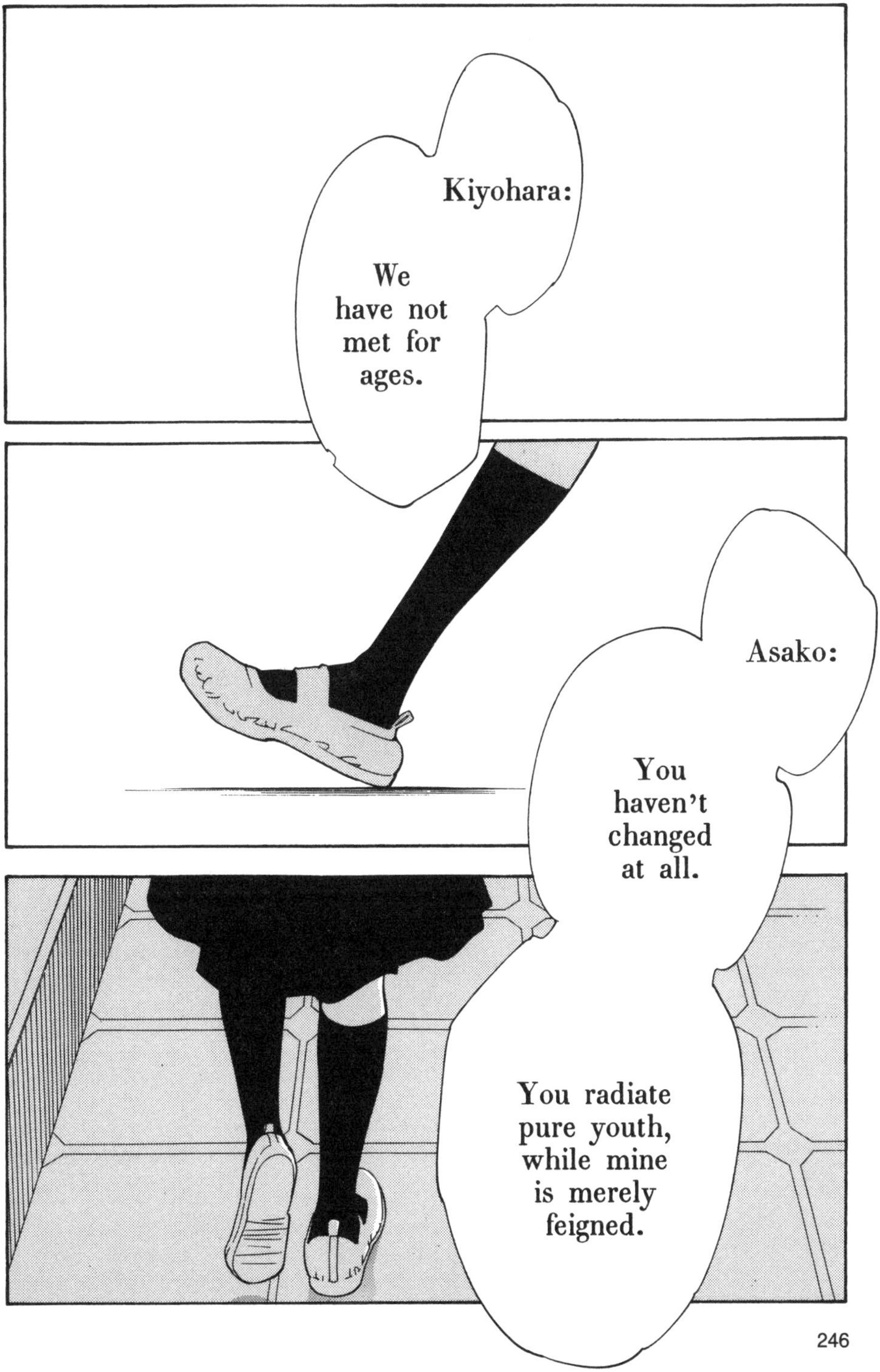
Kiyohara:
We have not met for ages.
Asako:
You haven't changed at all.
You radiate pure youth, while mine is merely feigned.

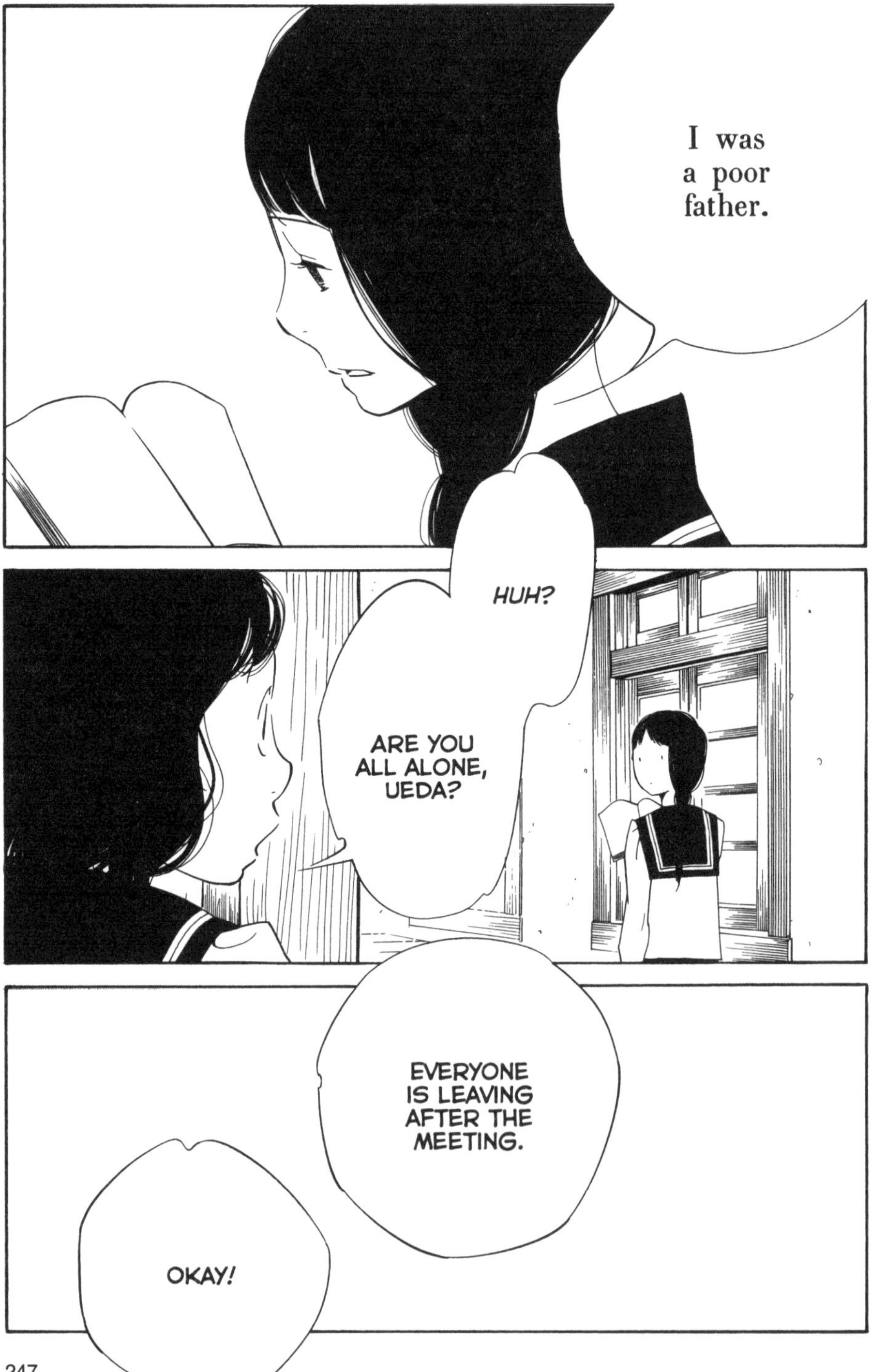
I was a poor father.
HUH?
ARE YOU ALL ALONE, UEDA?
EVERYONE IS LEAVING AFTER THE MEETING.
OKAY!

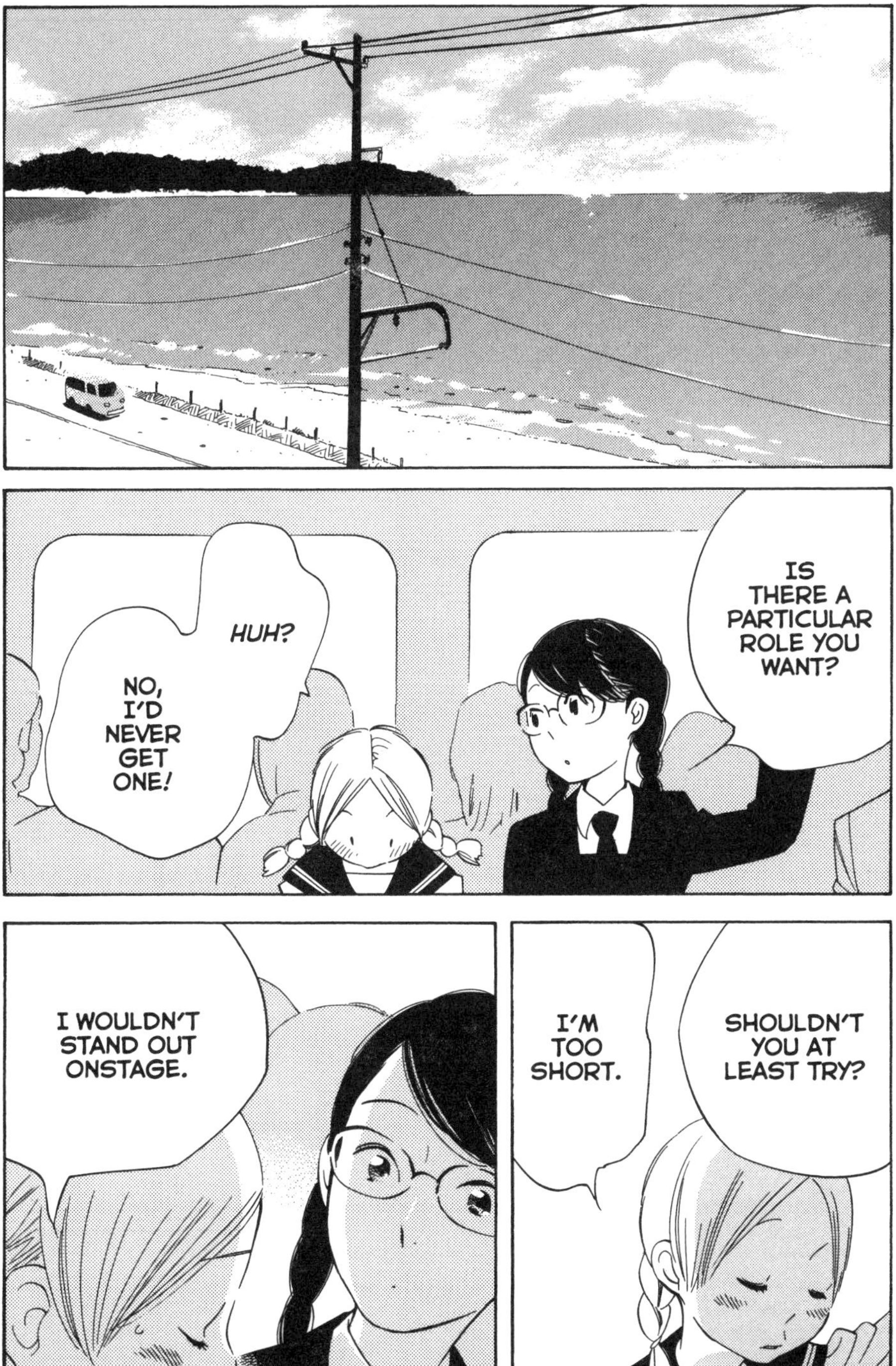
IS THERE A PARTICULAR ROLE YOU WANT?
HUH?
NO, I'D NEVER GET ONE!
SHOULDN'T YOU AT LEAST TRY?
I'M TOO SHORT.
I WOULDN'T STAND OUT ONSTAGE.

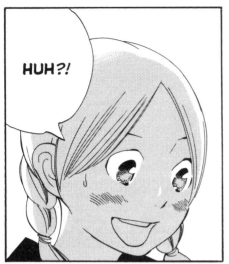

HUH?!

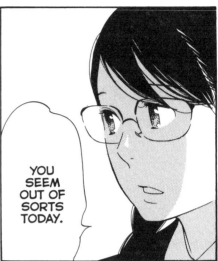

YOU SEEM OUT OF SORTS TODAY.

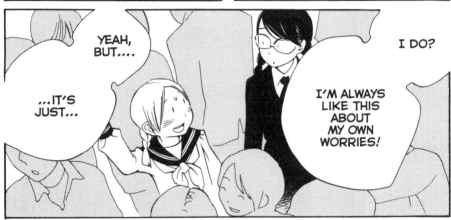

YEAH, BUT....

...IT'S JUST...

I DO?

I'M ALWAYS LIKE THIS ABOUT MY OWN WORRIES!

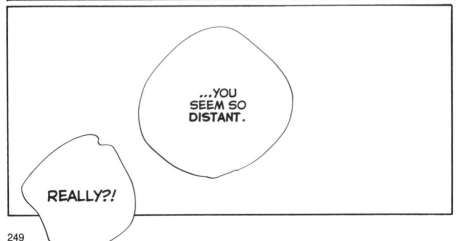

...YOU SEEM SO **DISTANT**.

REALLY?!

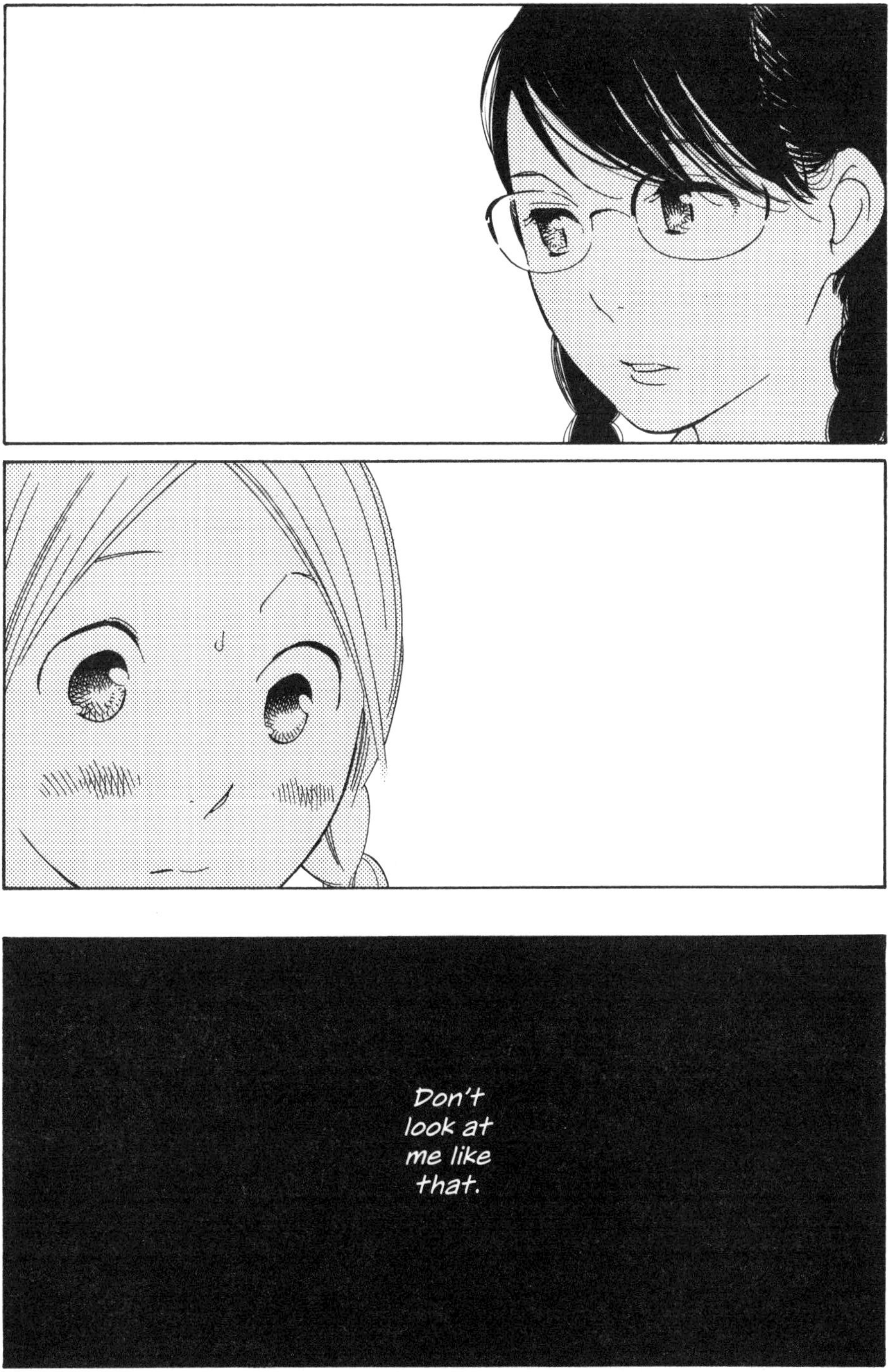
Don't look at me like that.

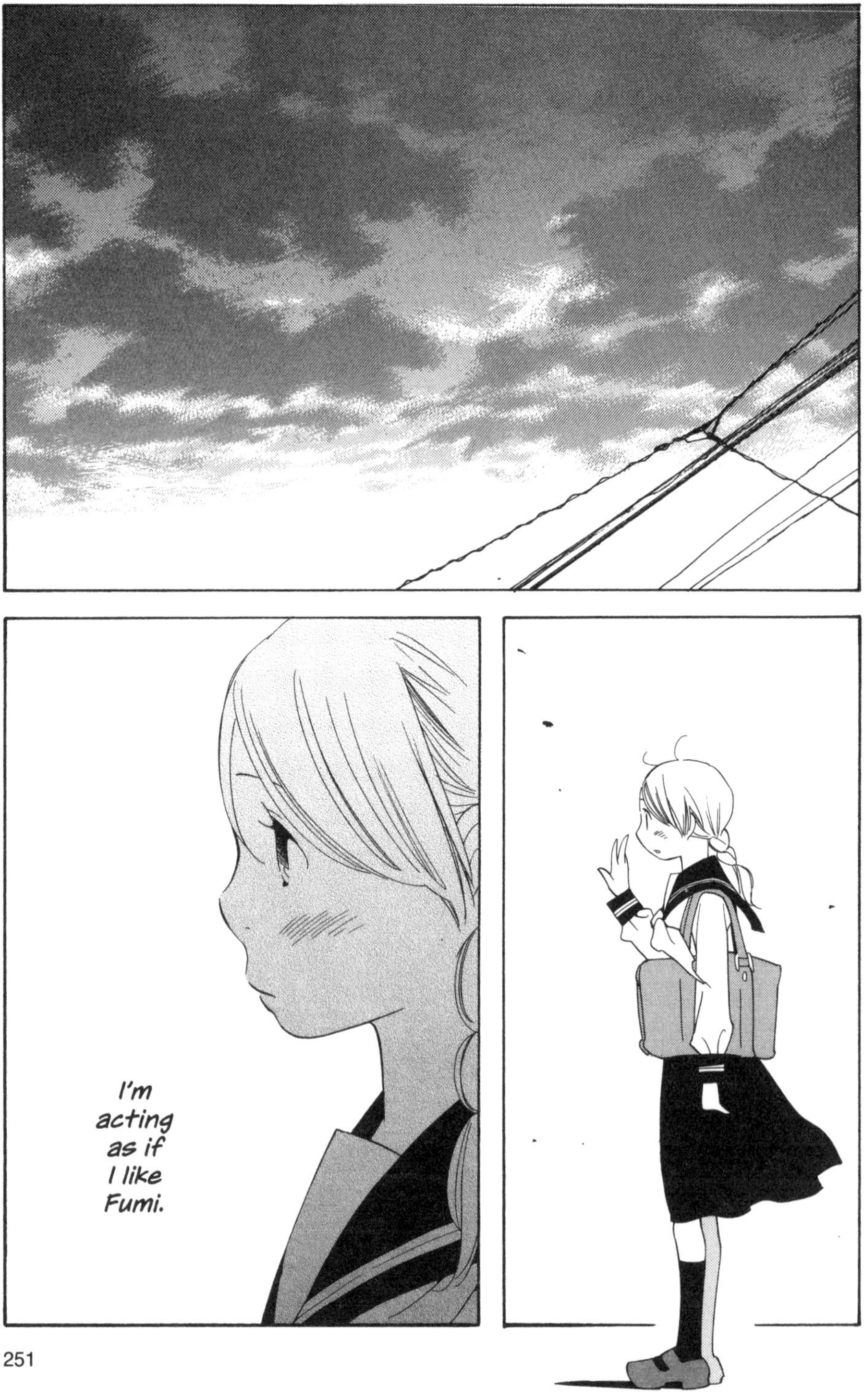
I'm acting as if I like Fumi.

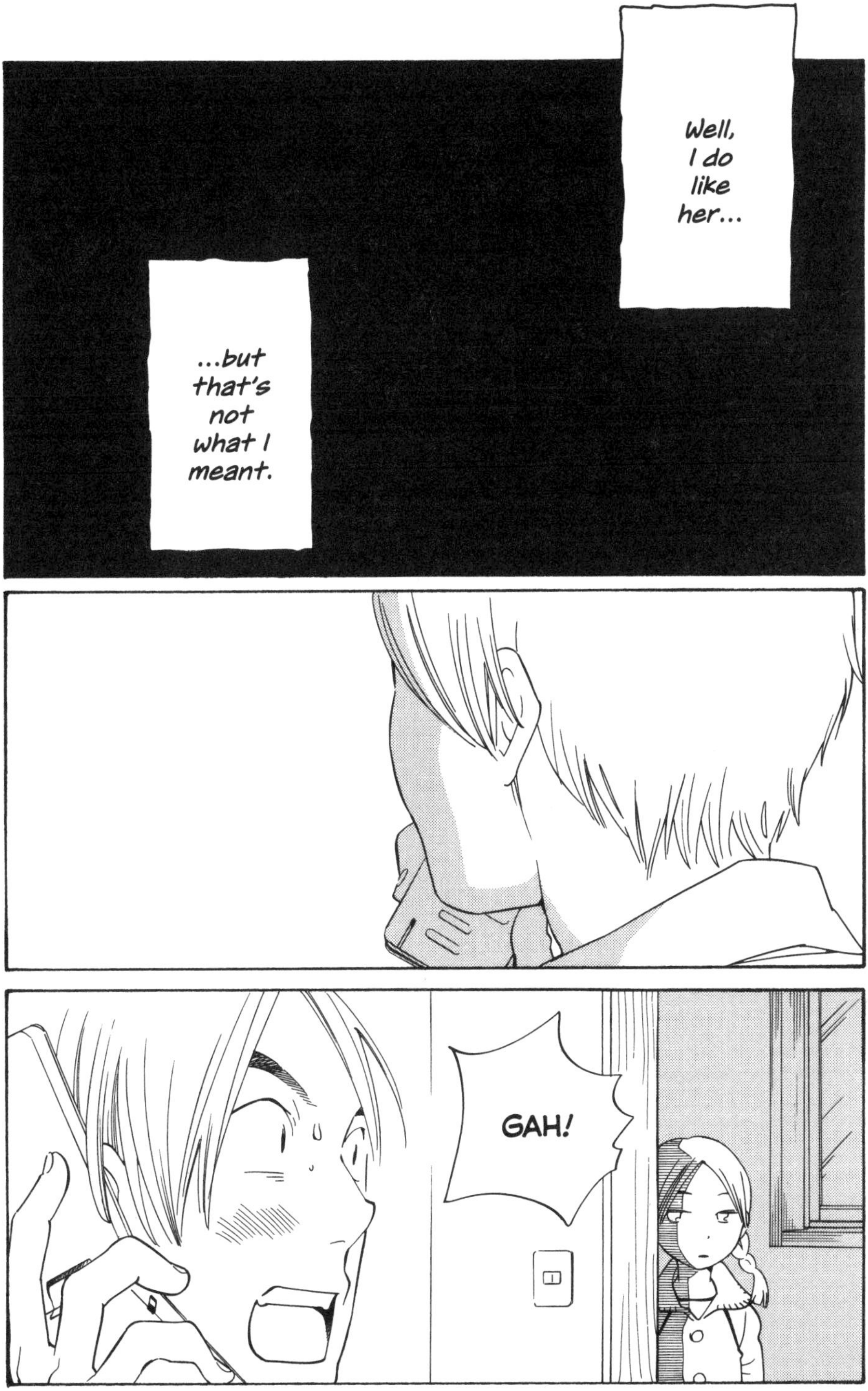
Well, I do like her...
...but that's not what I meant.
GAH!

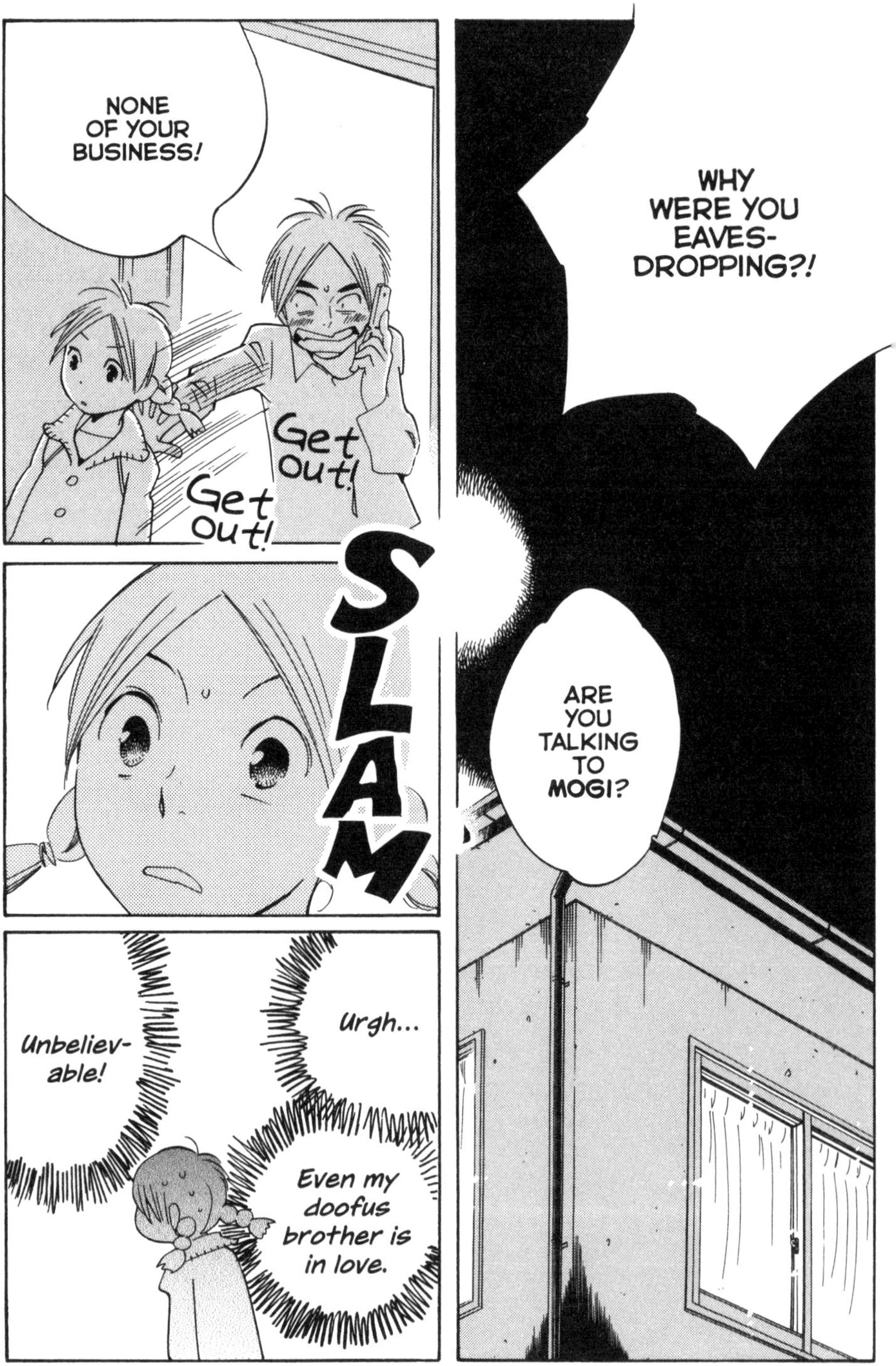
WHY WERE YOU EAVES-DROPPING?!
ARE YOU TALKING TO MOGI?
NONE OF YOUR BUSINESS!
Get out!
Get out!
SLAM
Urgh...
Unbeliev-able!
Even my doofus brother is in love.

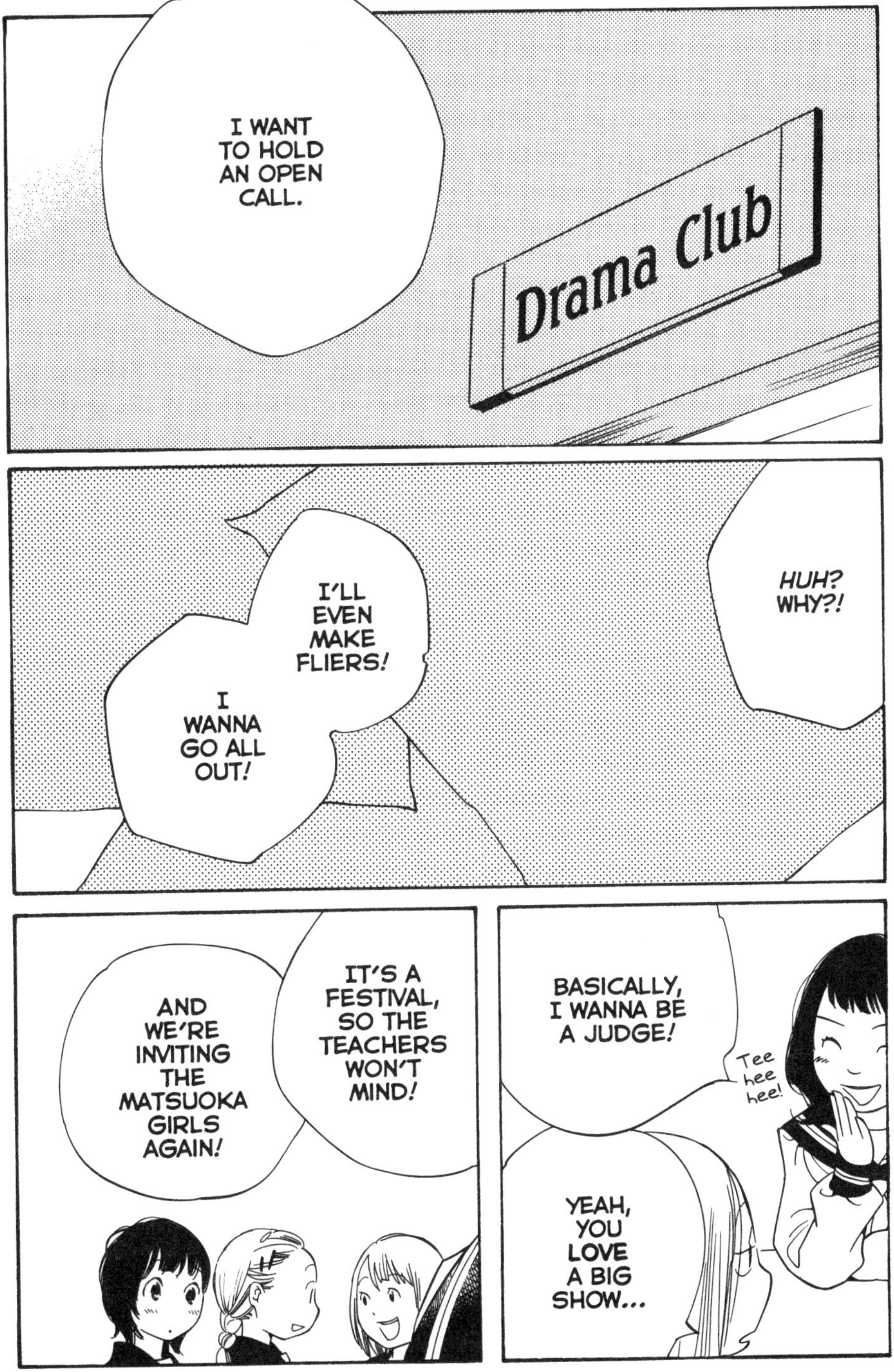
I WANT TO HOLD AN OPEN CALL.
Drama Club
HUH? WHY?!
I'LL EVEN MAKE FLIERS!
I WANNA GO ALL OUT!
BASICALLY, I WANNA BE A JUDGE!
Tee hee hee!
YEAH, YOU LOVE A BIG SHOW...
IT'S A FESTIVAL, SO THE TEACHERS WON'T MIND!
AND WE'RE INVITING THE MATSUOKA GIRLS AGAIN!

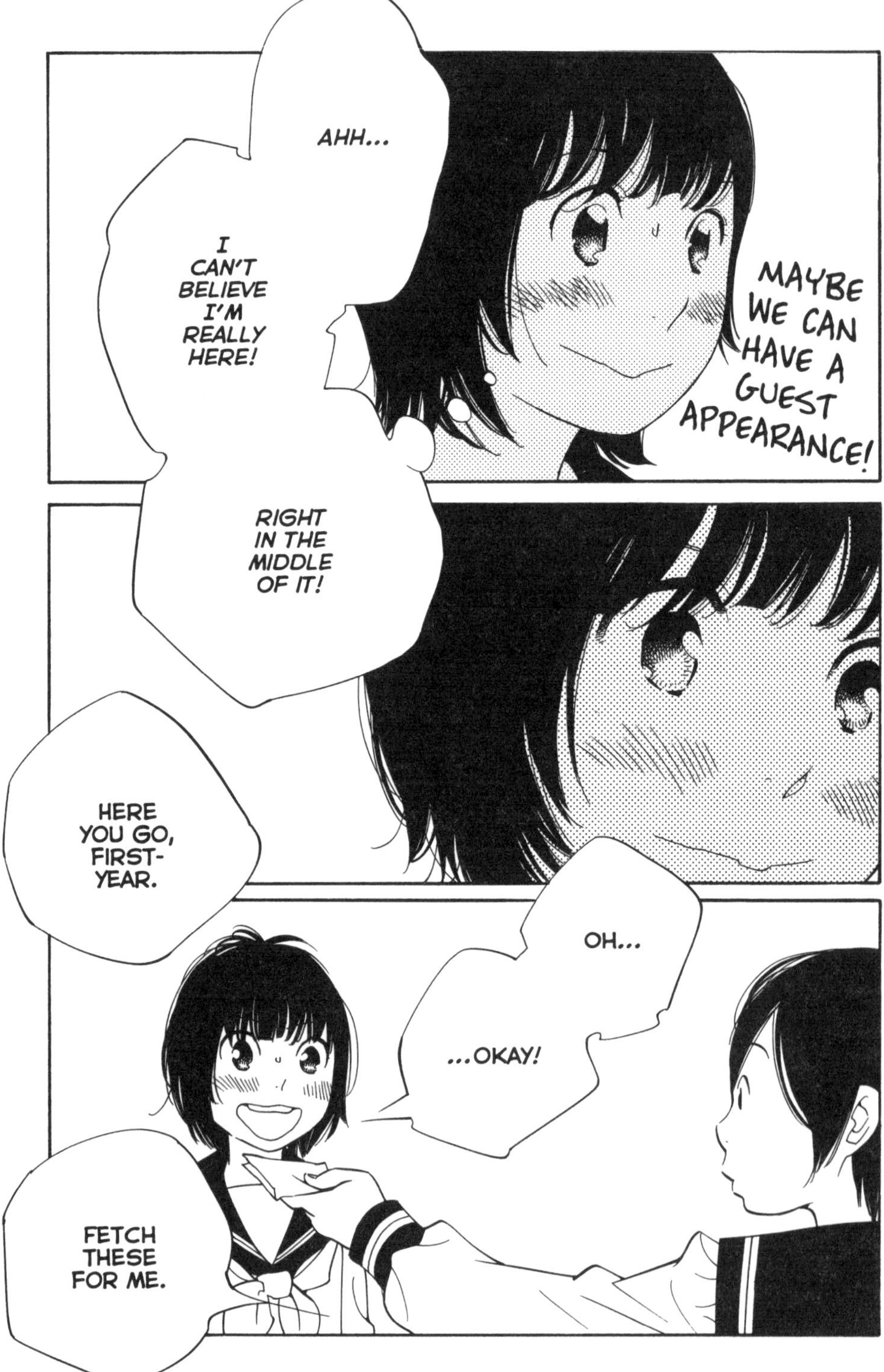
MAYBE WE CAN HAVE A GUEST APPEARANCE!
AHH...
I CAN'T BELIEVE I'M REALLY HERE!
RIGHT IN THE MIDDLE OF IT!
HERE YOU GO, FIRST-YEAR.
OH...
...OKAY!
FETCH THESE FOR ME.

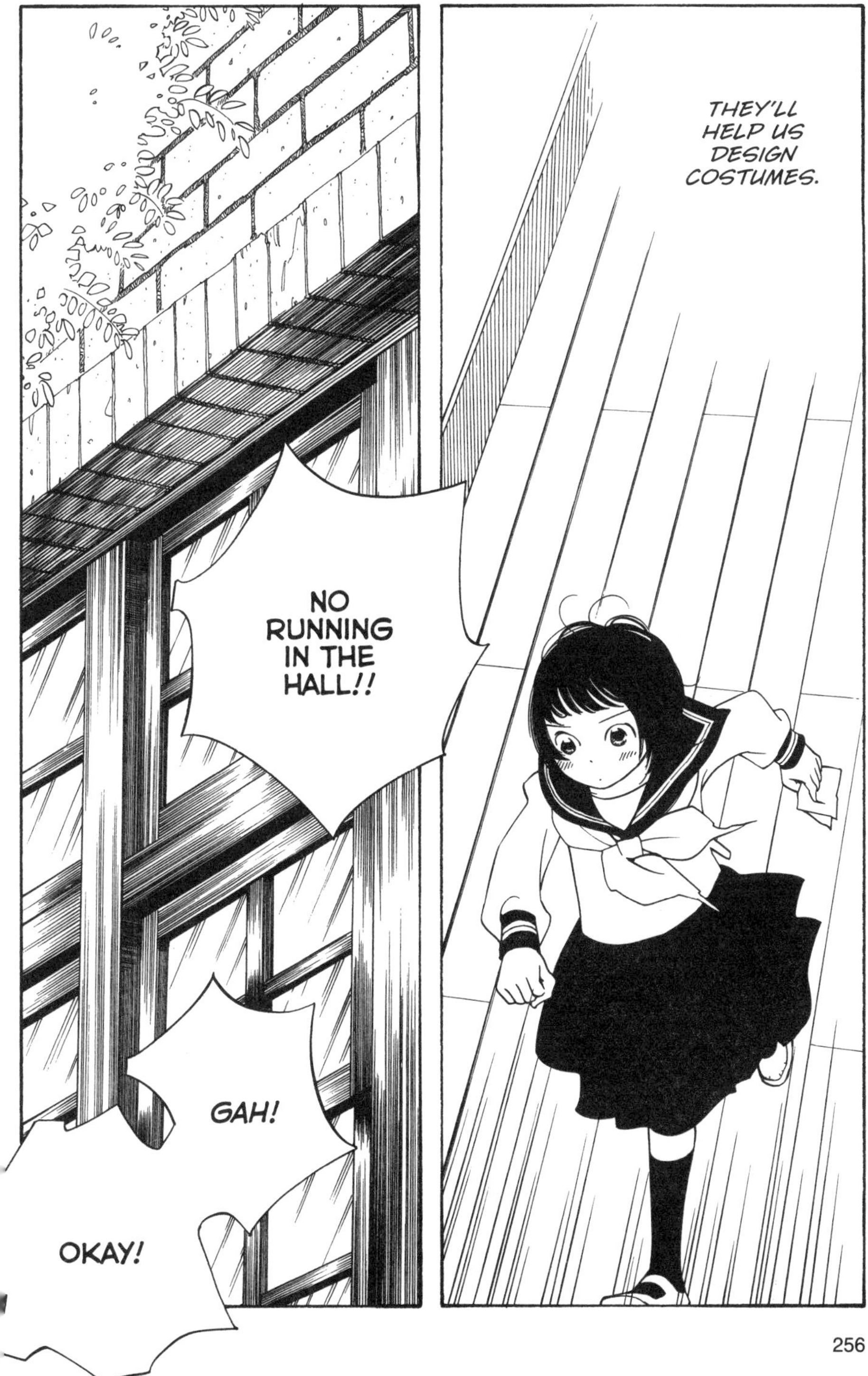
THEY'LL HELP US DESIGN COSTUMES.
NO RUNNING IN THE HALL!!
GAH!
OKAY!

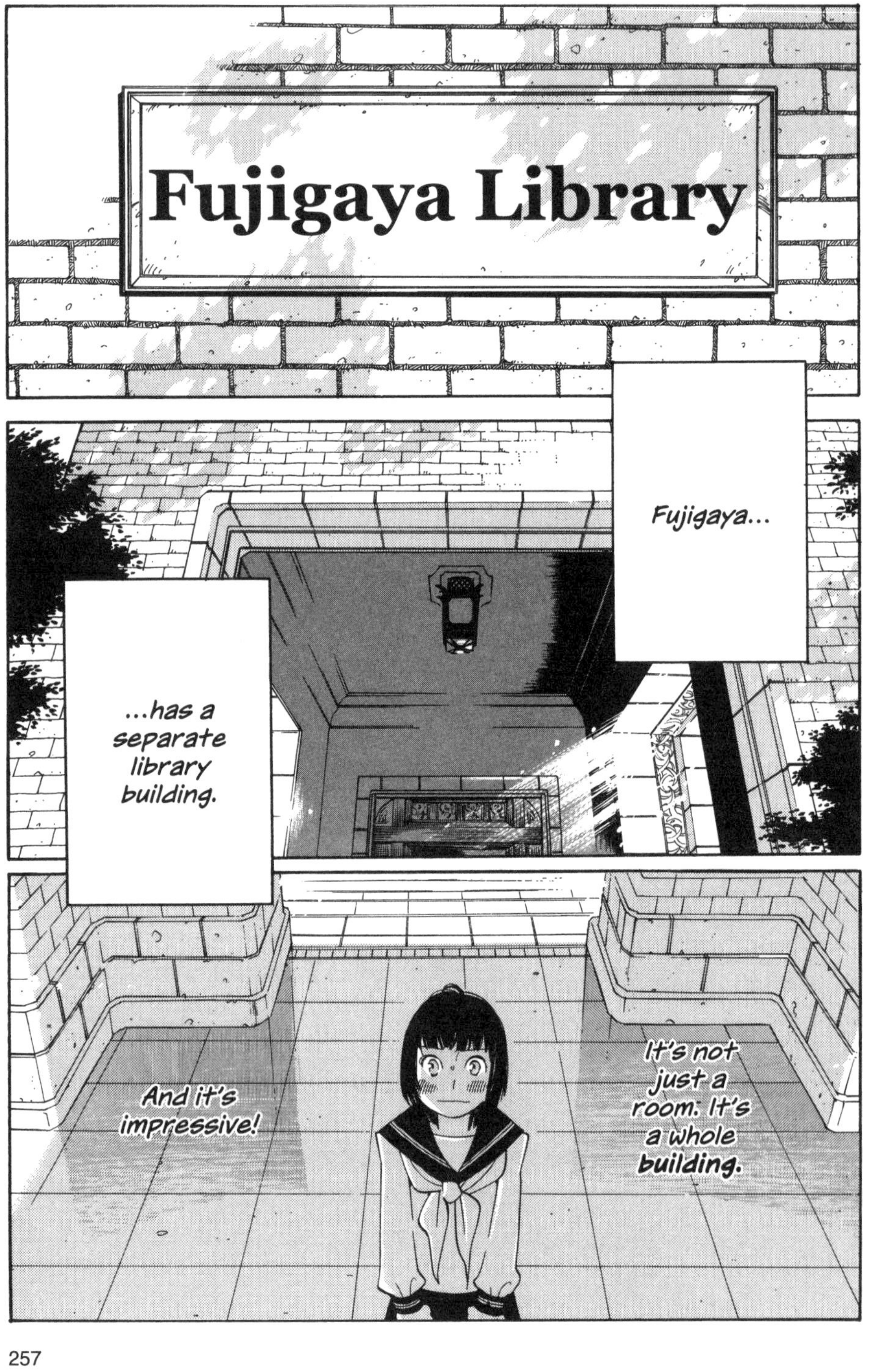
Fujigaya Library
Fujigaya...
...has a separate library building.
It's not just a room. It's a whole building.
And it's impressive!

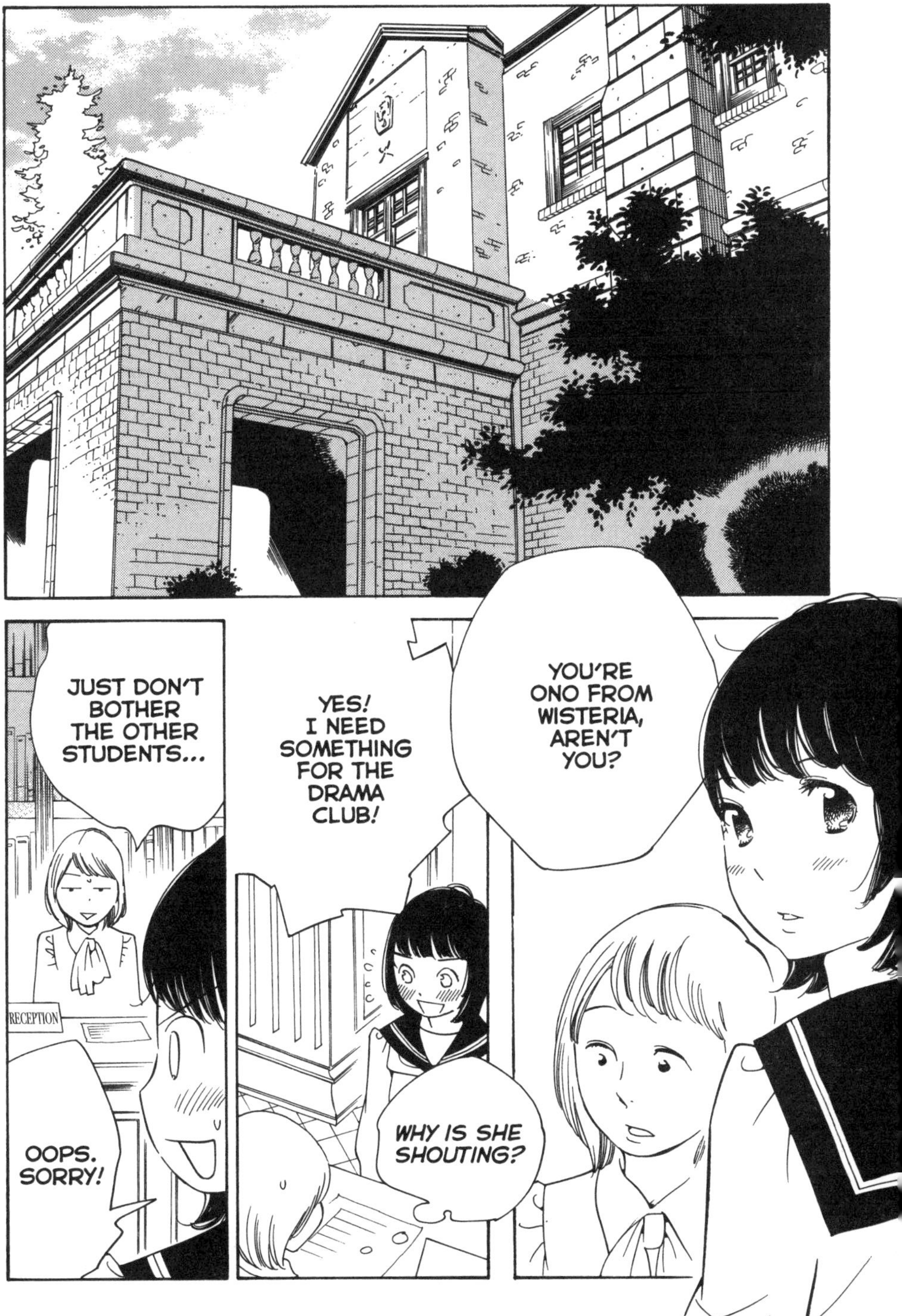
YOU'RE ONO FROM WISTERIA, AREN'T YOU?
YES! I NEED SOMETHING FOR THE DRAMA CLUB!
WHY IS SHE SHOUTING?
JUST DON'T BOTHER THE OTHER STUDENTS...
RECEPTION
OOPS. SORRY!

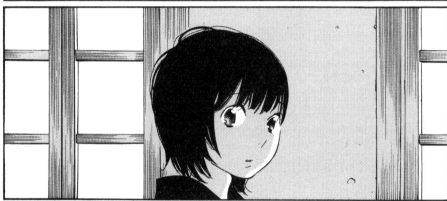

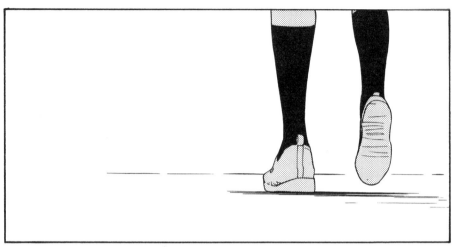

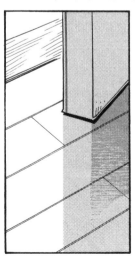

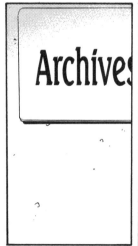

Archives

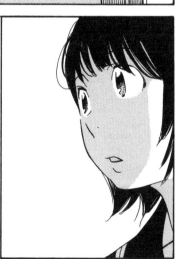

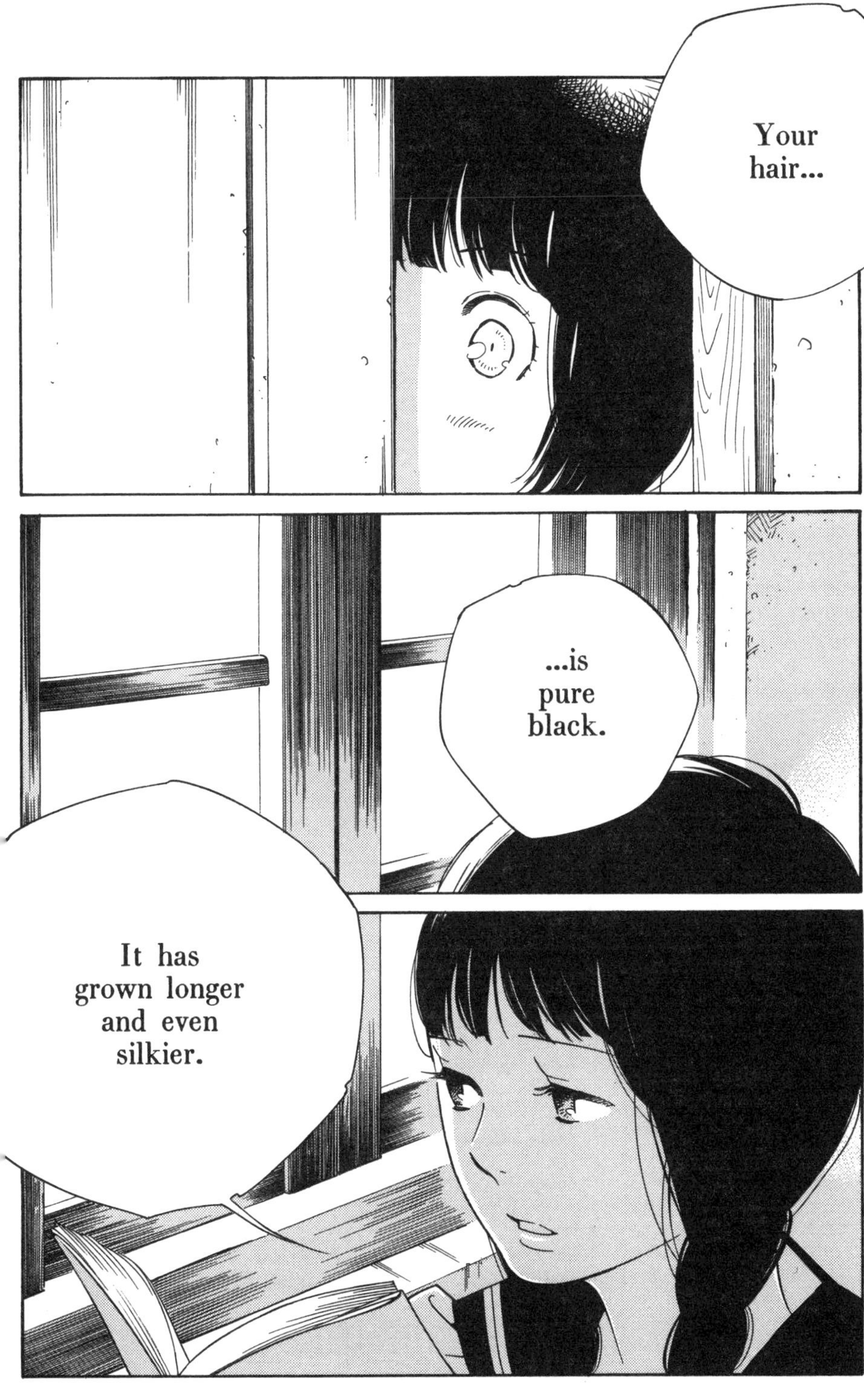
Your hair...
...is pure black.
It has grown longer and even silkier.

Sweet *Blue Flowers*

#22 Rokumeikan, Part 2

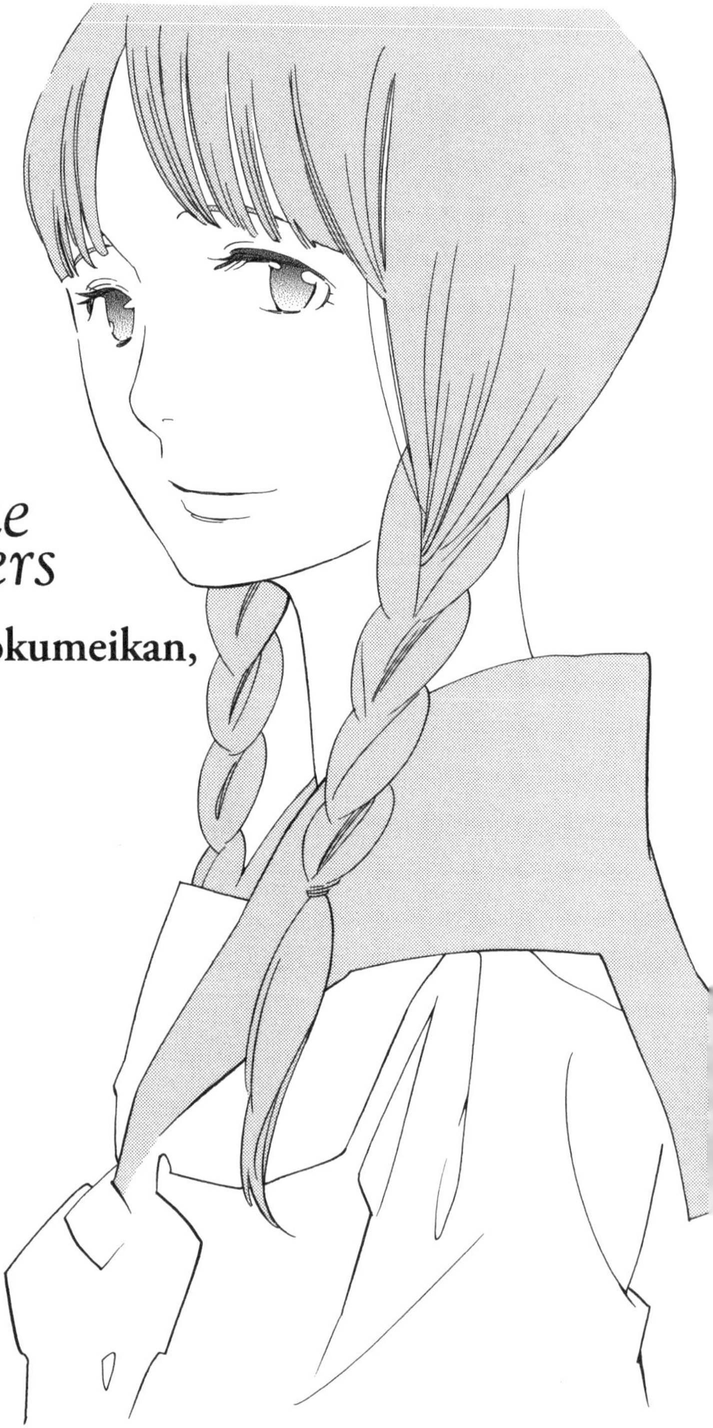

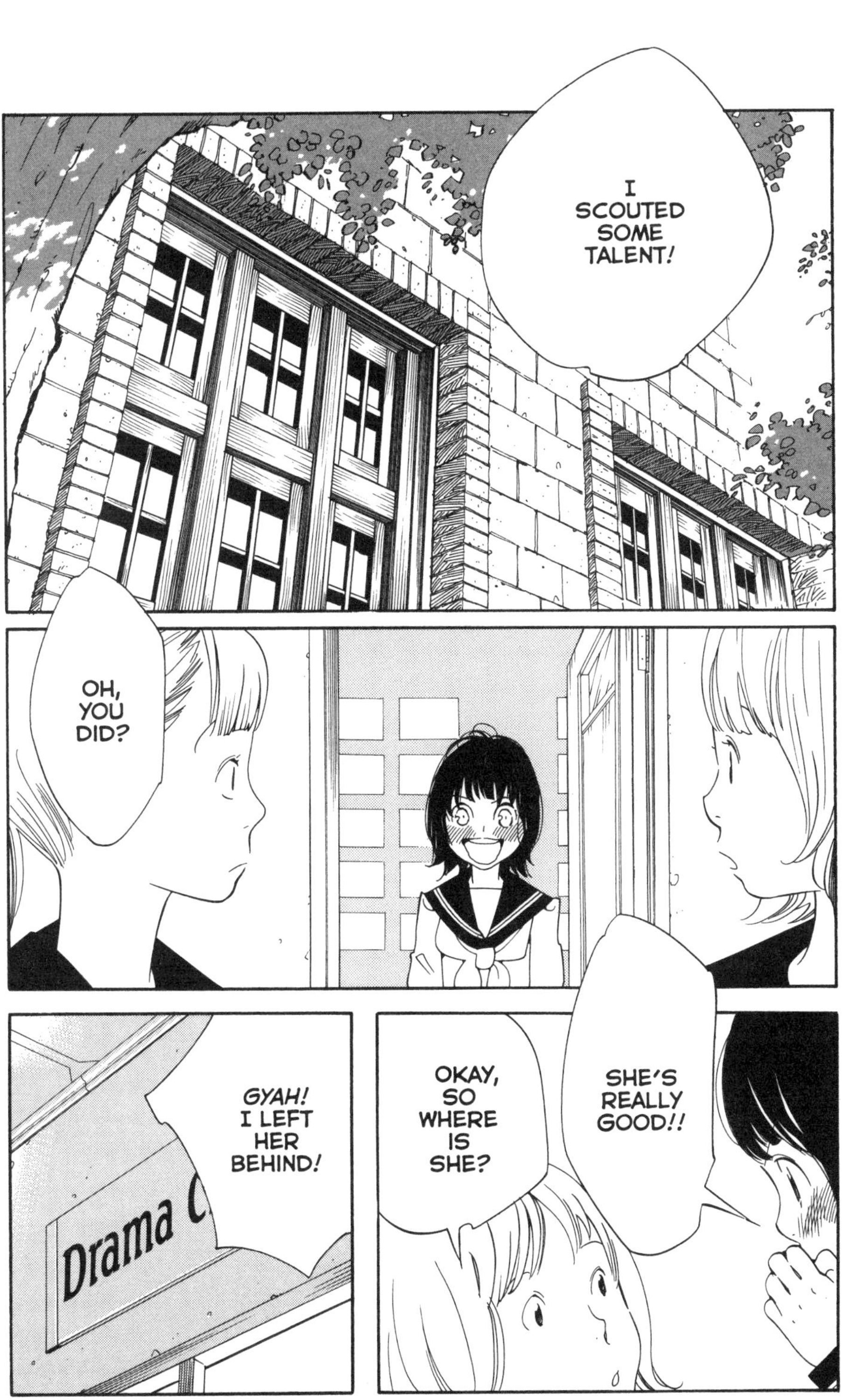
I SCOUTED SOME TALENT!
OH, YOU DID?
SHE'S REALLY GOOD!!
OKAY, SO WHERE IS SHE?
GYAH! I LEFT HER BEHIND!
Drama

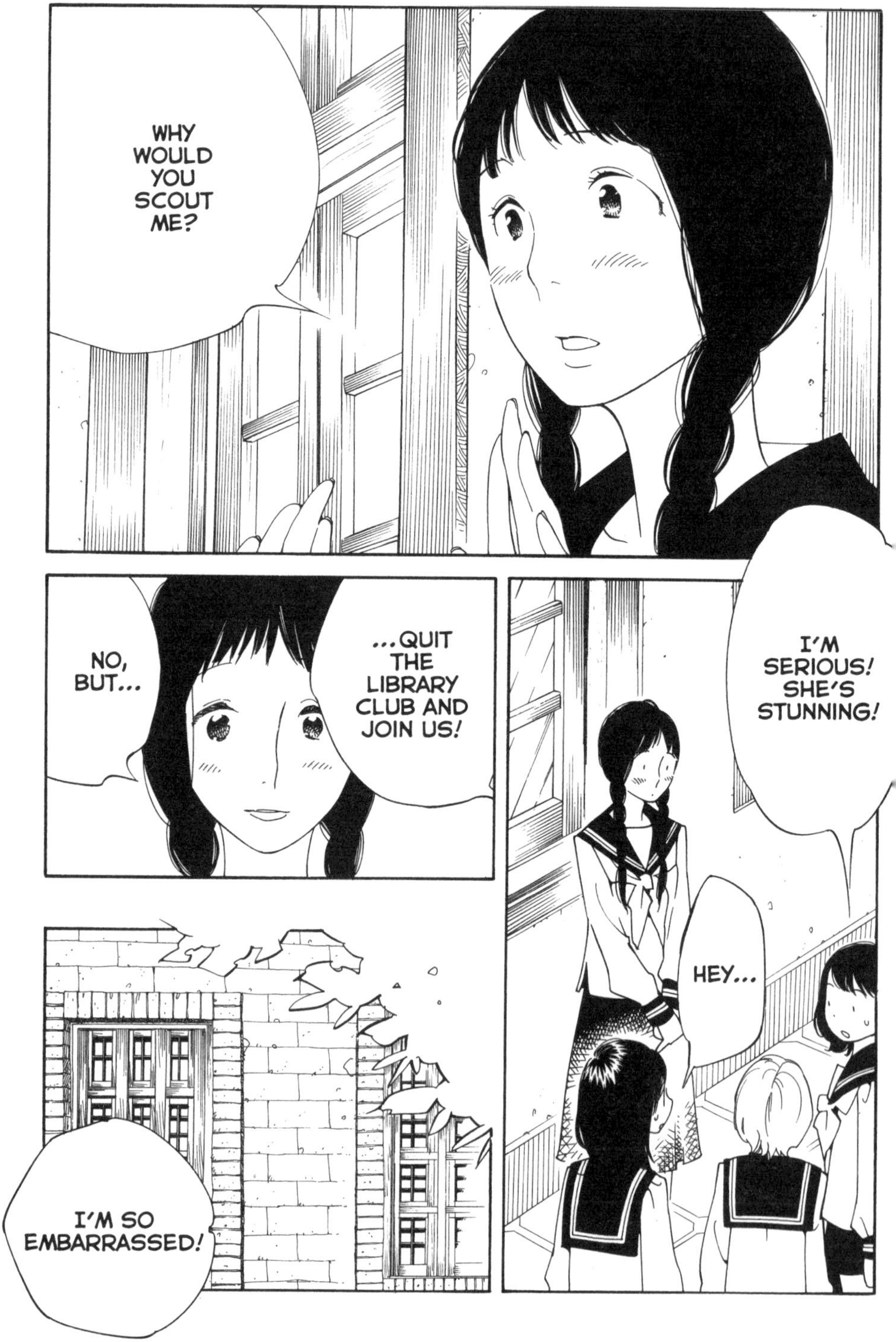
WHY WOULD YOU SCOUT ME?
I'M SERIOUS! SHE'S STUNNING!
HEY...
...QUIT THE LIBRARY CLUB AND JOIN US!
NO, BUT...
I'M SO EMBARRASSED!

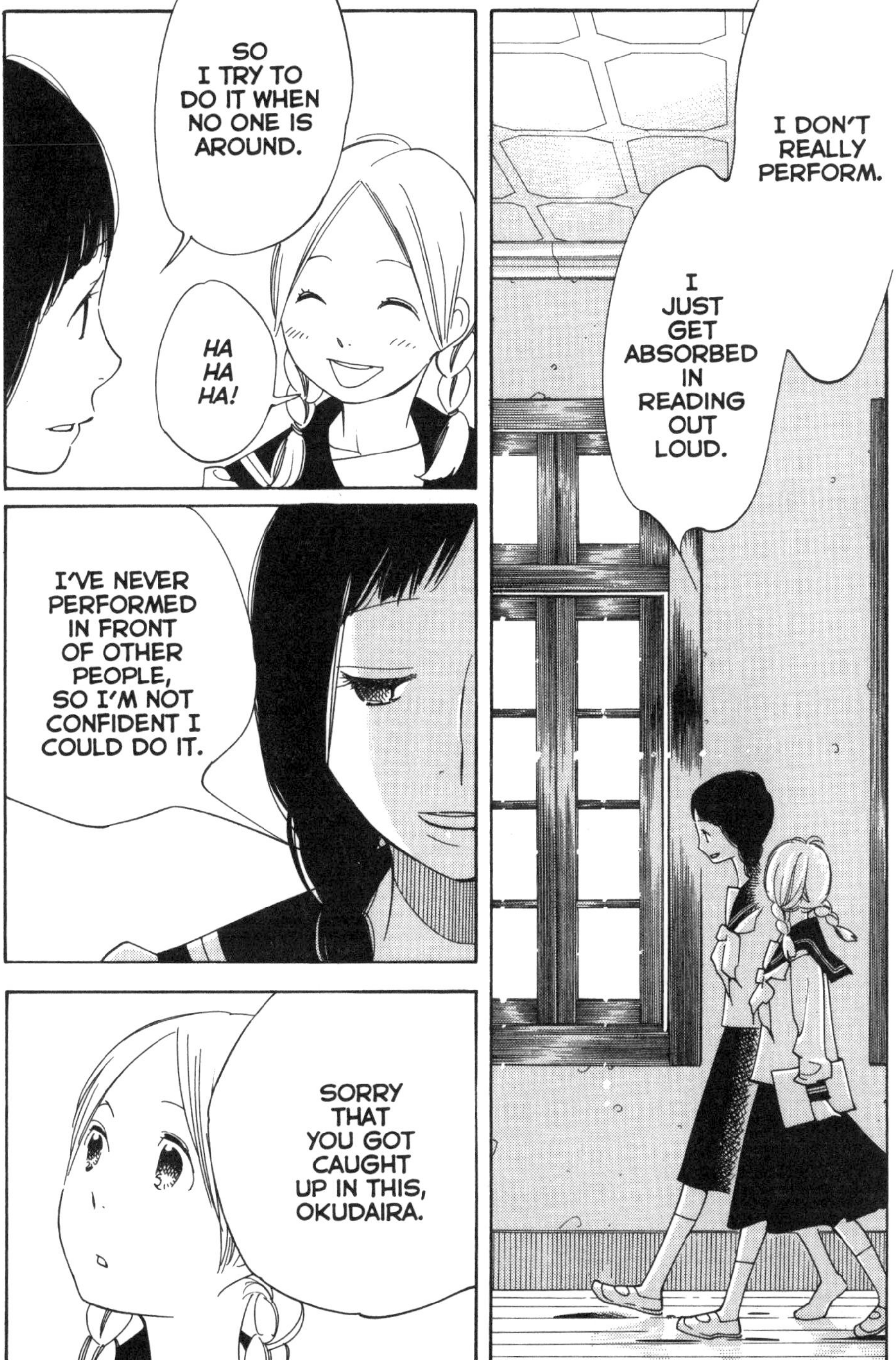
I DON'T REALLY PERFORM.
I JUST GET ABSORBED IN READING OUT LOUD.
SO I TRY TO DO IT WHEN NO ONE IS AROUND.
HA HA HA!
I'VE NEVER PERFORMED IN FRONT OF OTHER PEOPLE, SO I'M NOT CONFIDENT I COULD DO IT.
SORRY THAT YOU GOT CAUGHT UP IN THIS, OKUDAIRA.

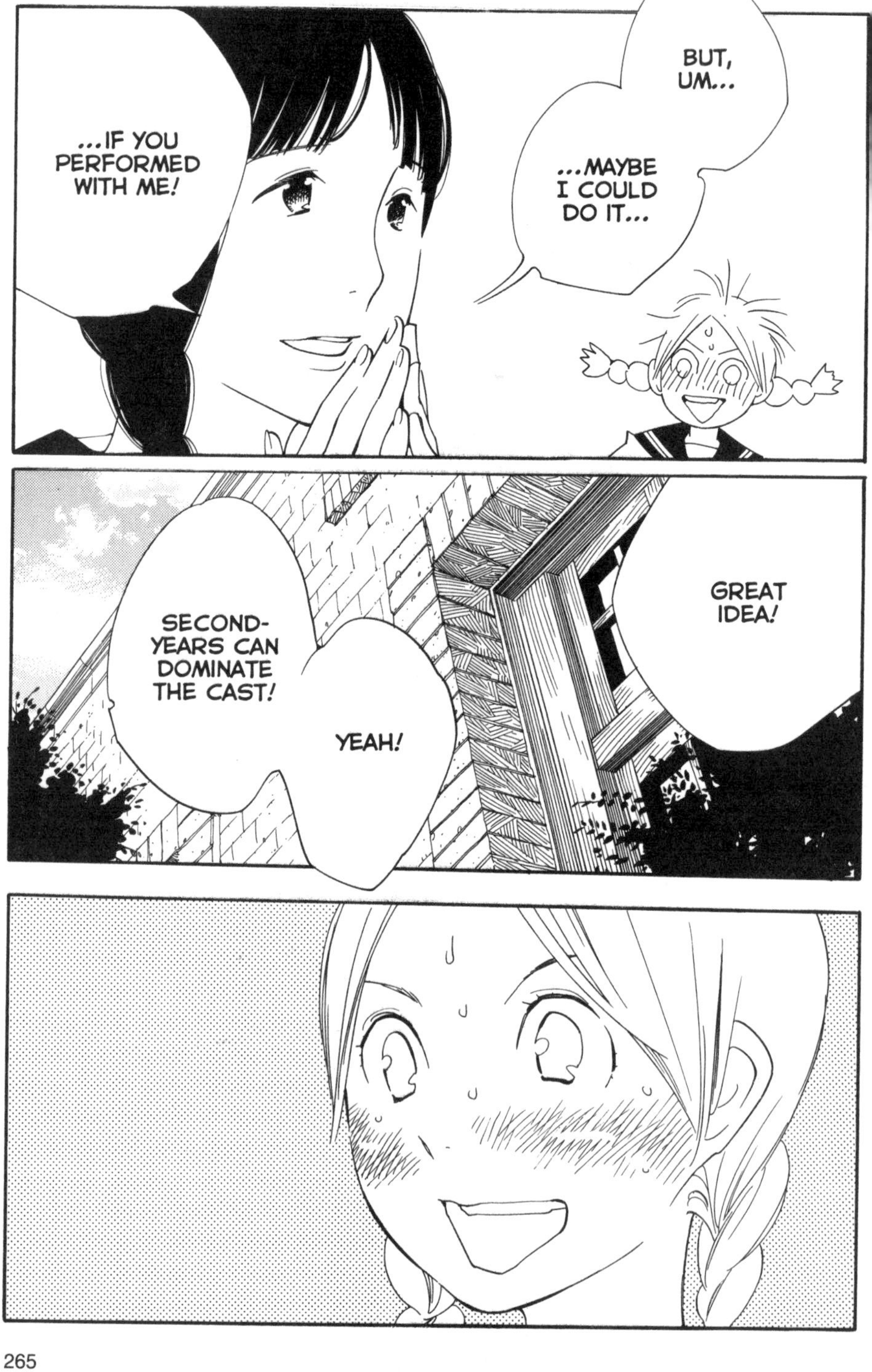
BUT, UM...
...MAYBE I COULD DO IT...
...IF YOU PERFORMED WITH ME!
GREAT IDEA!
SECOND-YEARS CAN DOMINATE THE CAST!
YEAH!

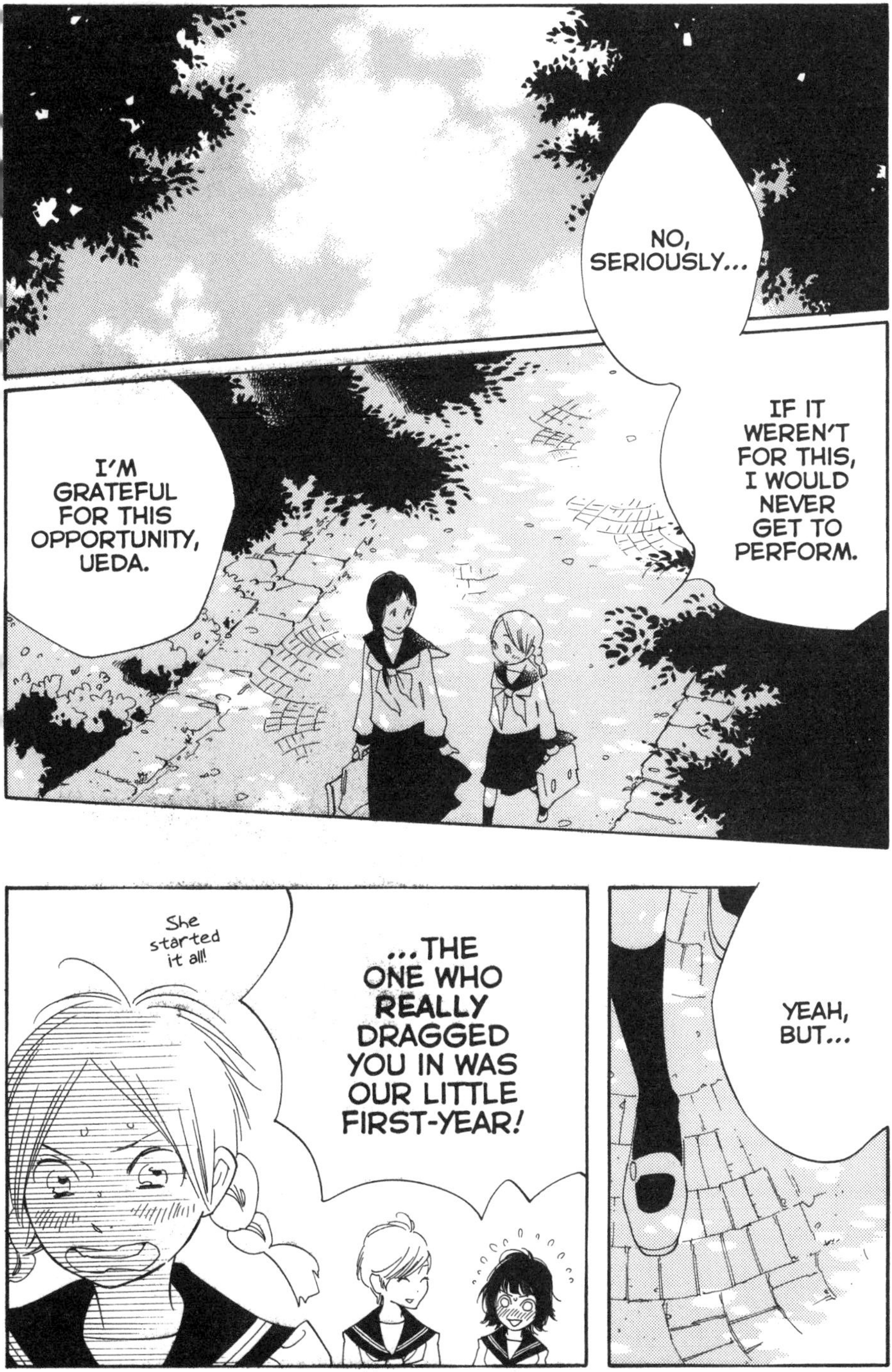
NO, SERIOUSLY...
IF IT WEREN'T FOR THIS, I WOULD NEVER GET TO PERFORM.
I'M GRATEFUL FOR THIS OPPORTUNITY, UEDA.
YEAH, BUT...
...THE ONE WHO REALLY DRAGGED YOU IN WAS OUR LITTLE FIRST-YEAR!
She started it all!

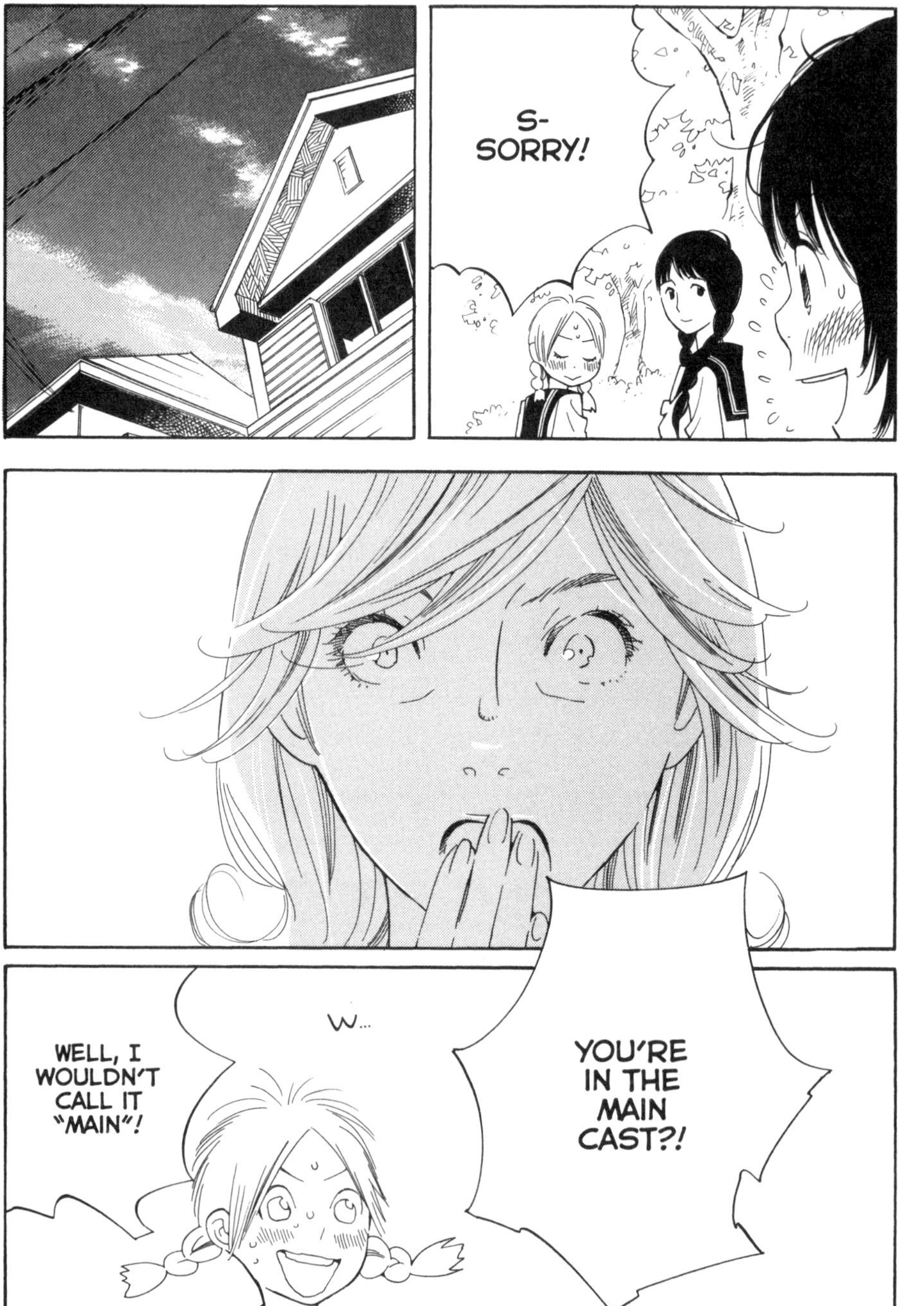
S-
SORRY!
YOU'RE IN THE MAIN CAST?!
W...
WELL, I WOULDN'T CALL IT "MAIN"!

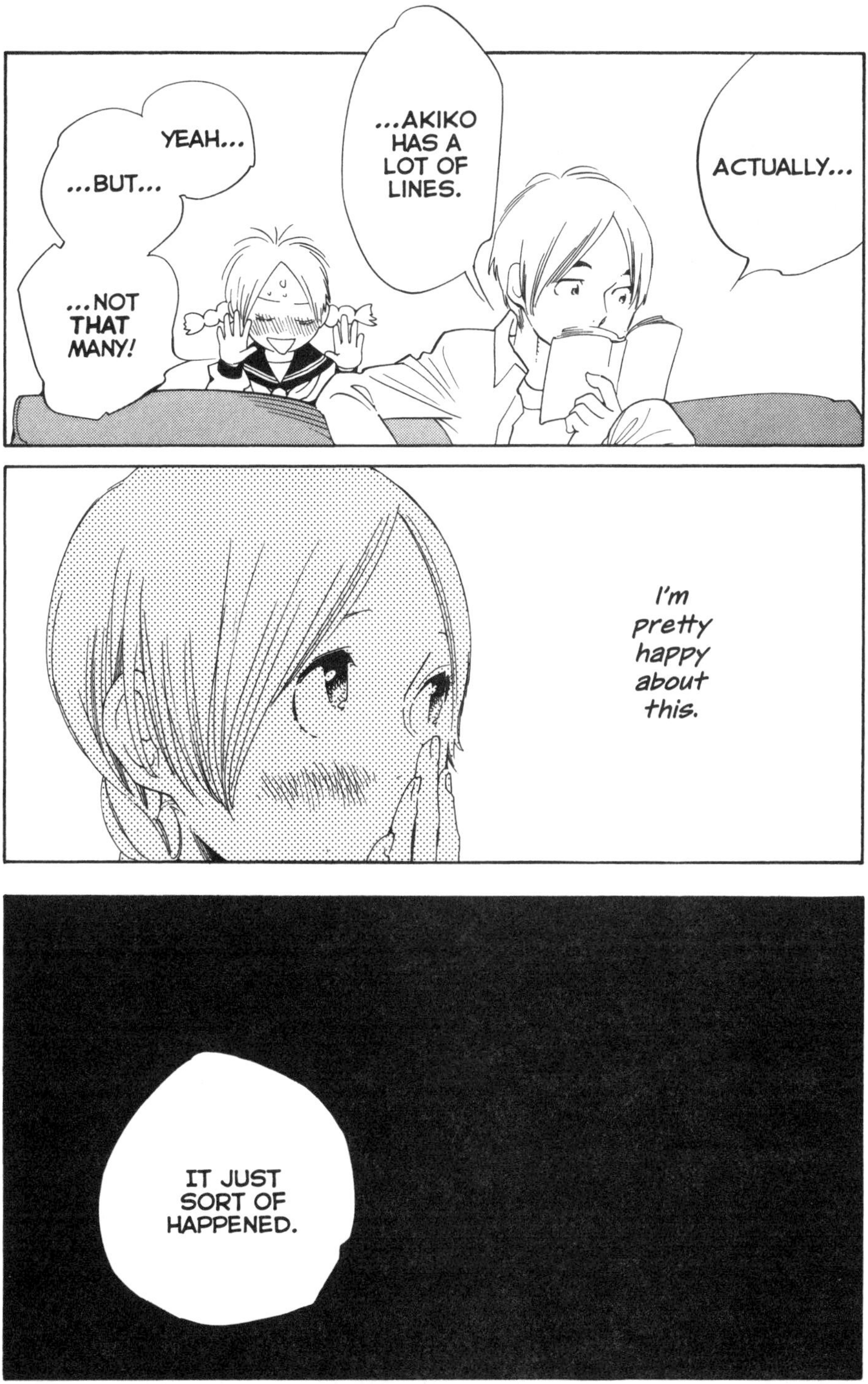
ACTUALLY...
...AKIKO HAS A LOT OF LINES.
YEAH...
...BUT...
...NOT THAT MANY!
I'm pretty happy about this.
IT JUST SORT OF HAPPENED.

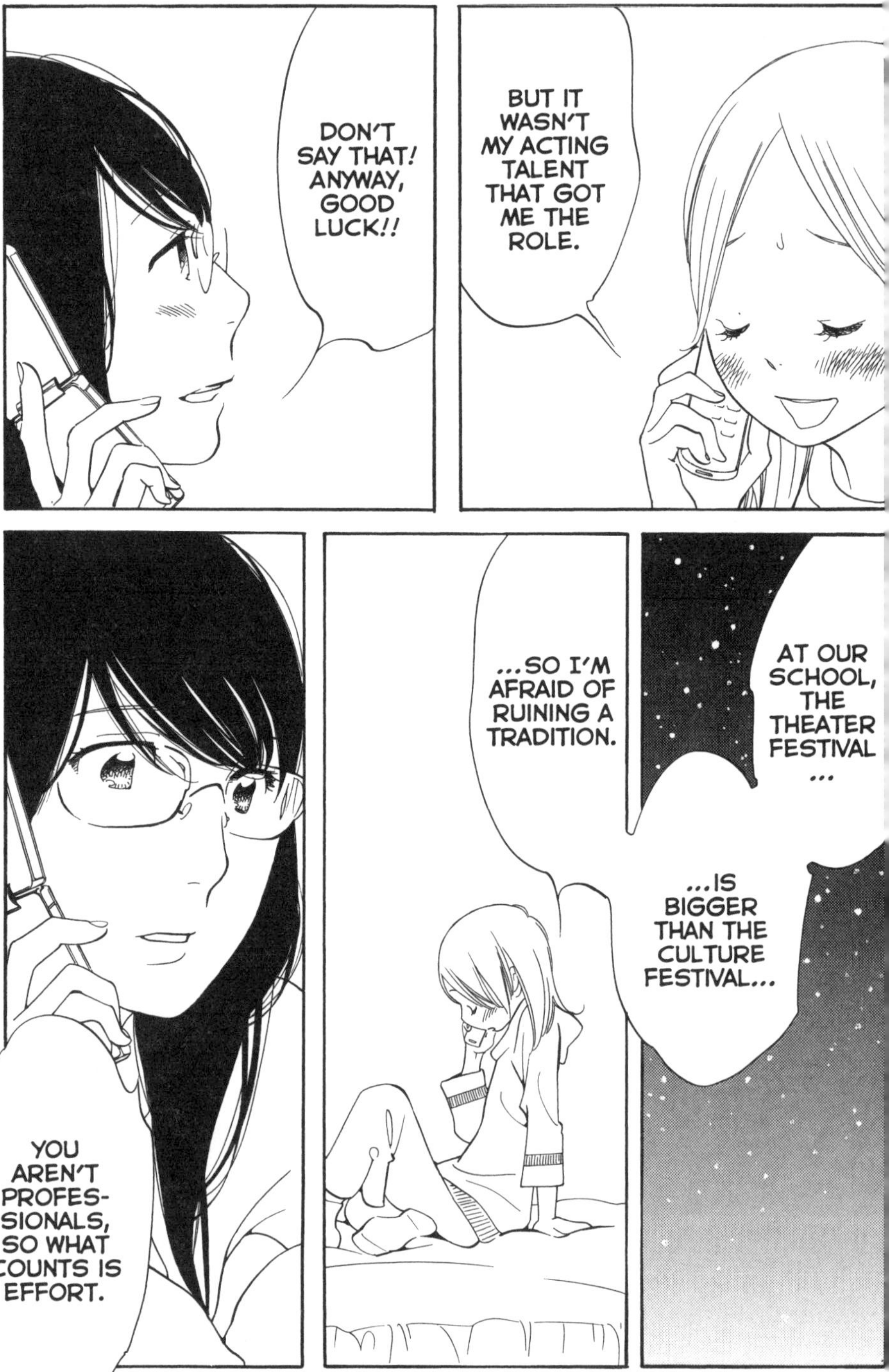
BUT IT WASN'T MY ACTING TALENT THAT GOT ME THE ROLE.
DON'T SAY THAT! ANYWAY, GOOD LUCK!!
AT OUR SCHOOL, THE THEATER FESTIVAL ...
...IS BIGGER THAN THE CULTURE FESTIVAL...
...SO I'M AFRAID OF RUINING A TRADITION.
YOU AREN'T PROFES-SIONALS, SO WHAT COUNTS IS EFFORT.

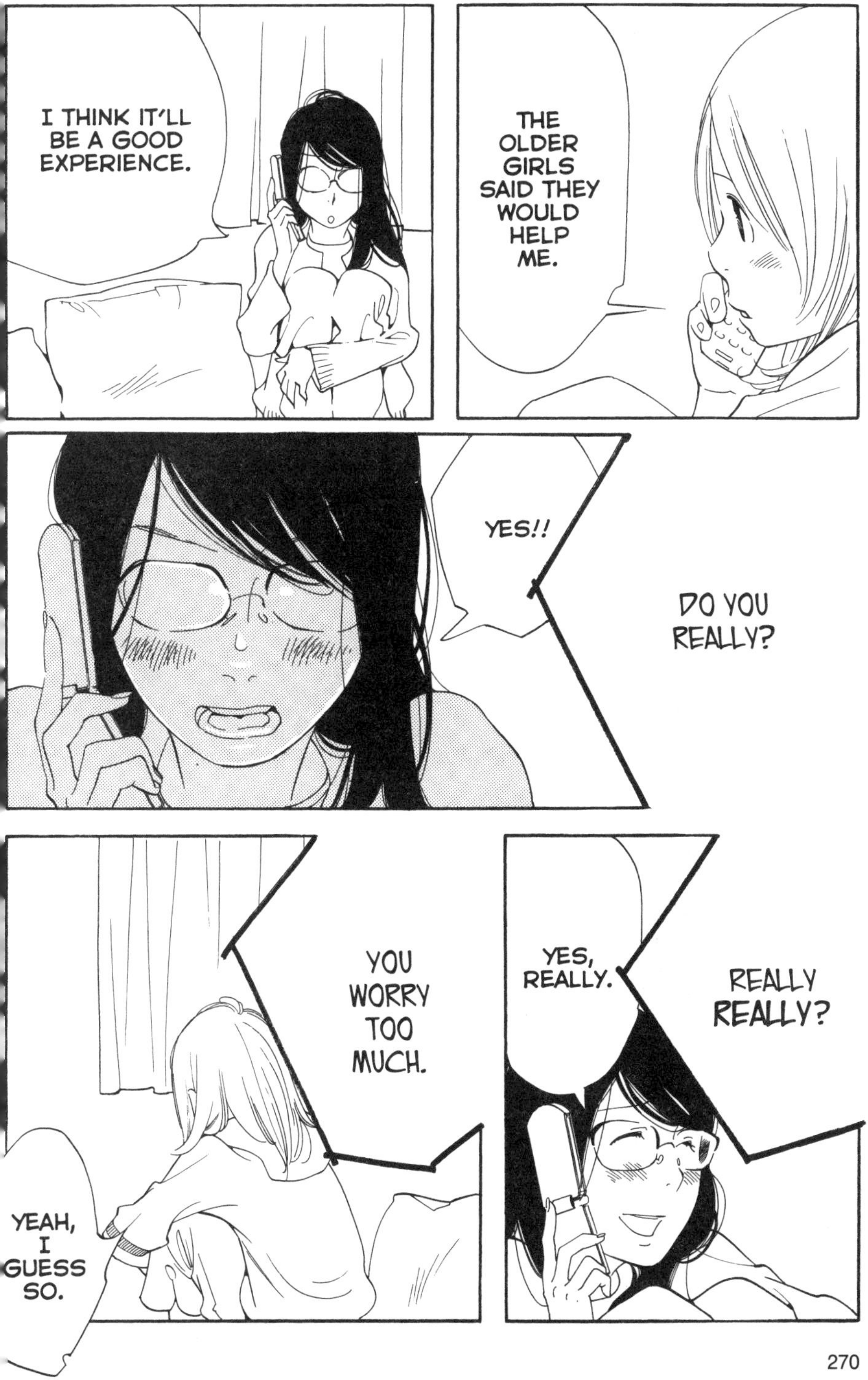
THE OLDER GIRLS SAID THEY WOULD HELP ME.
I THINK IT'LL BE A GOOD EXPERIENCE.
DO YOU REALLY?
YES!!
REALLY REALLY?
YES, REALLY.
YOU WORRY TOO MUCH.
YEAH, I GUESS SO.

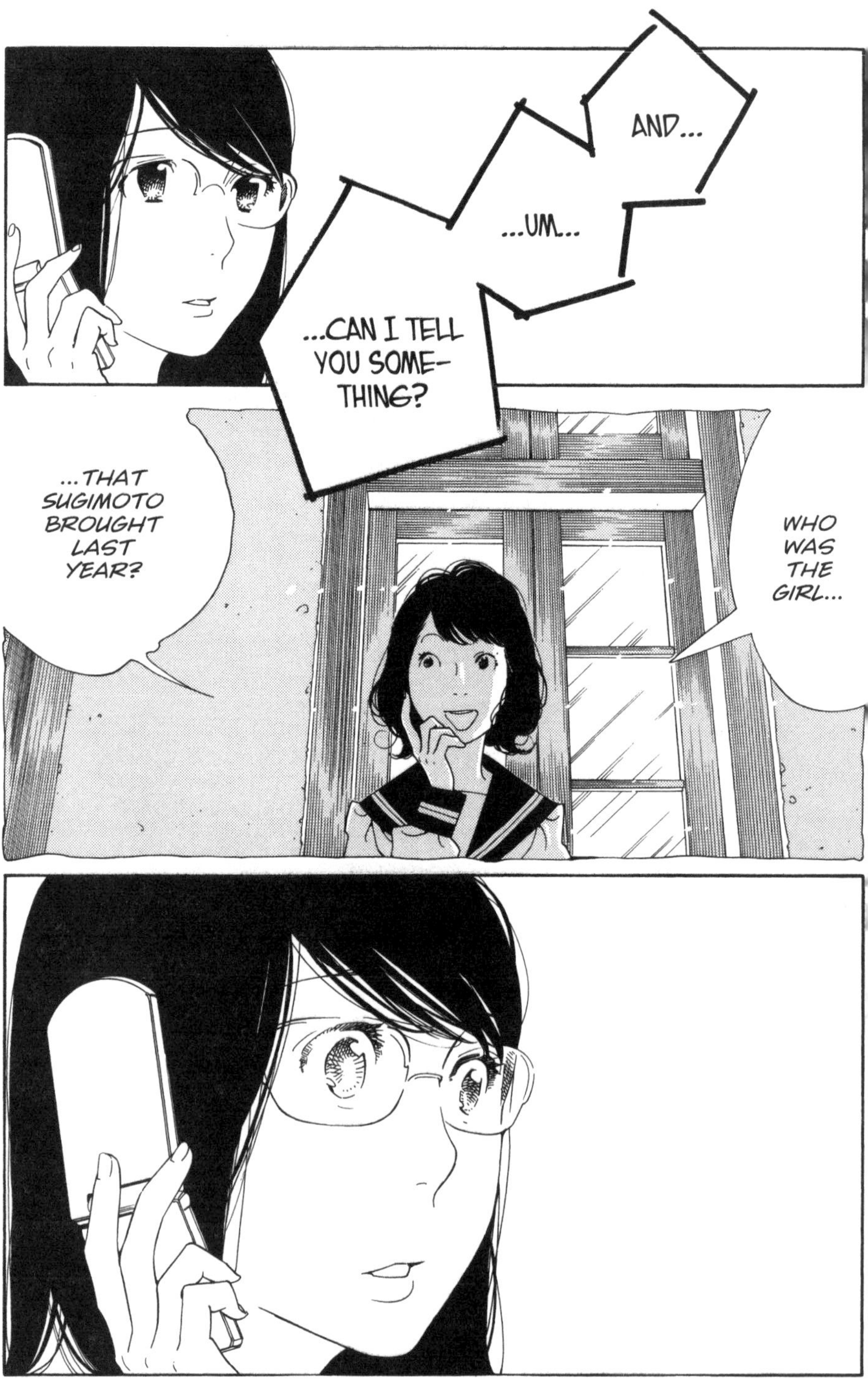
AND...
...UM...
...CAN I TELL YOU SOME-THING?
WHO WAS THE GIRL...
...THAT SUGIMOTO BROUGHT LAST YEAR?

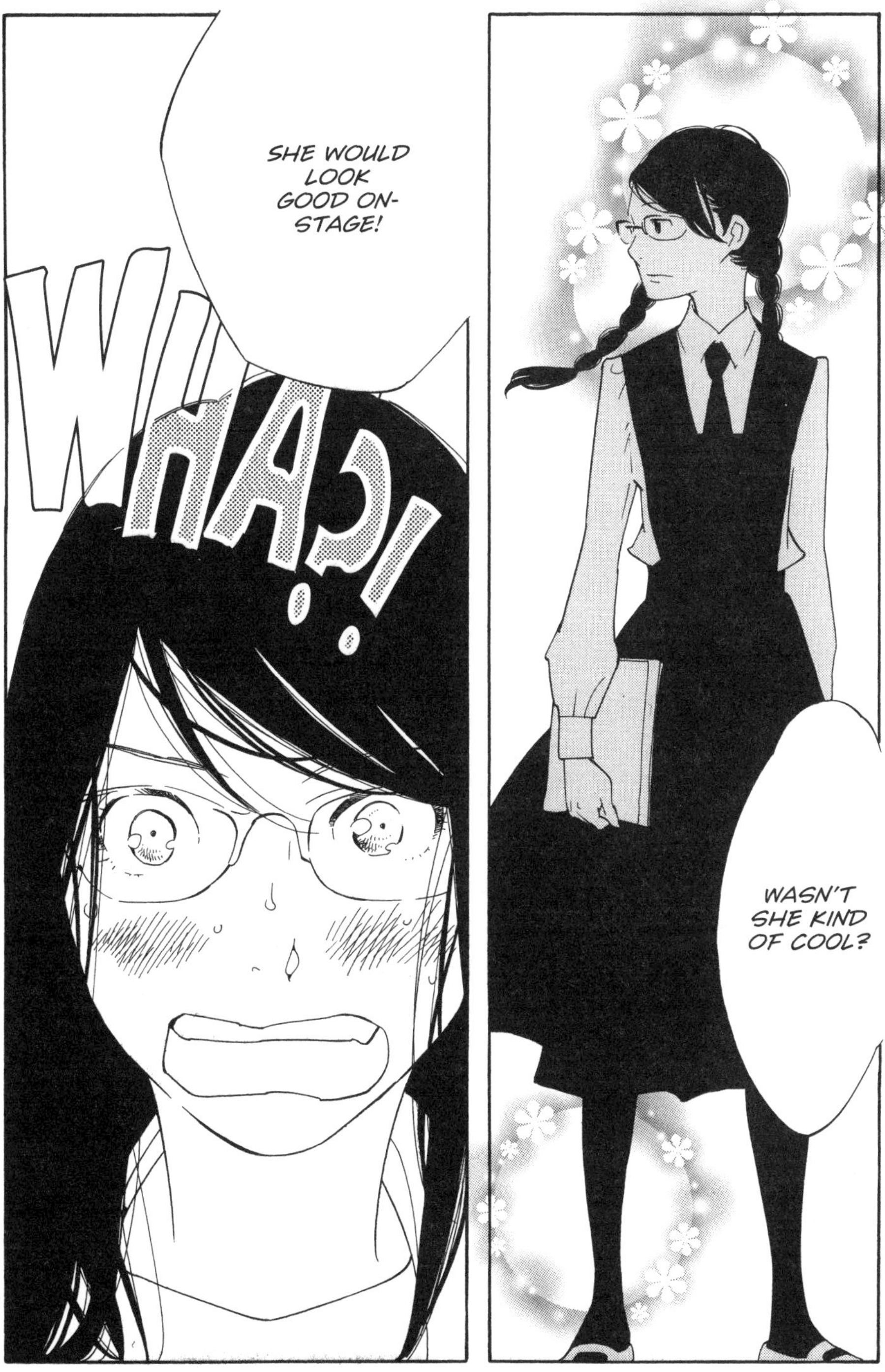
WASN'T SHE KIND OF COOL?
SHE WOULD LOOK GOOD ON-STAGE!
WHA?!

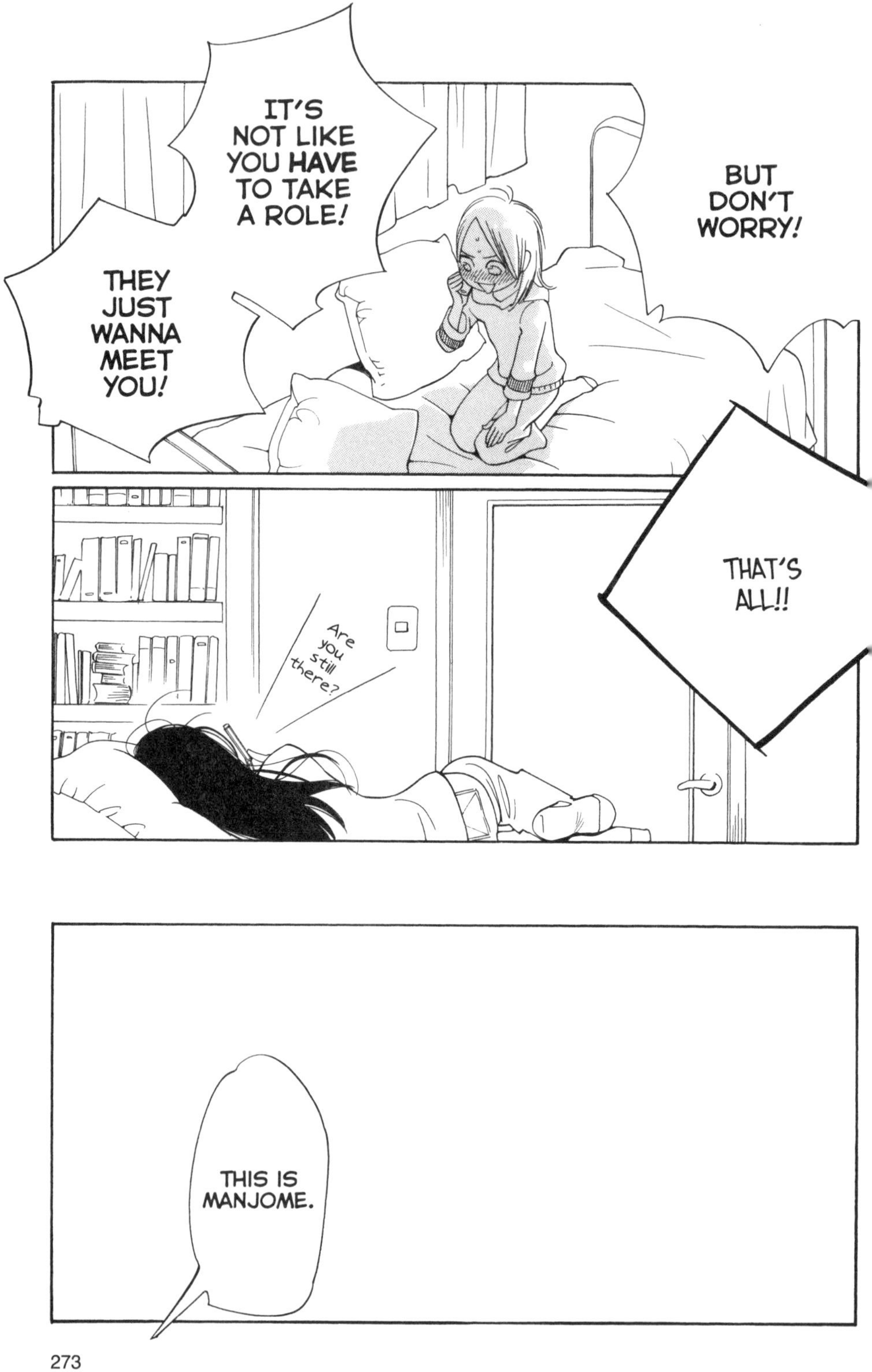
BUT DON'T WORRY!
IT'S NOT LIKE YOU HAVE TO TAKE A ROLE!
THEY JUST WANNA MEET YOU!
THAT'S ALL!!
Are you still there?
THIS IS MANJOME.

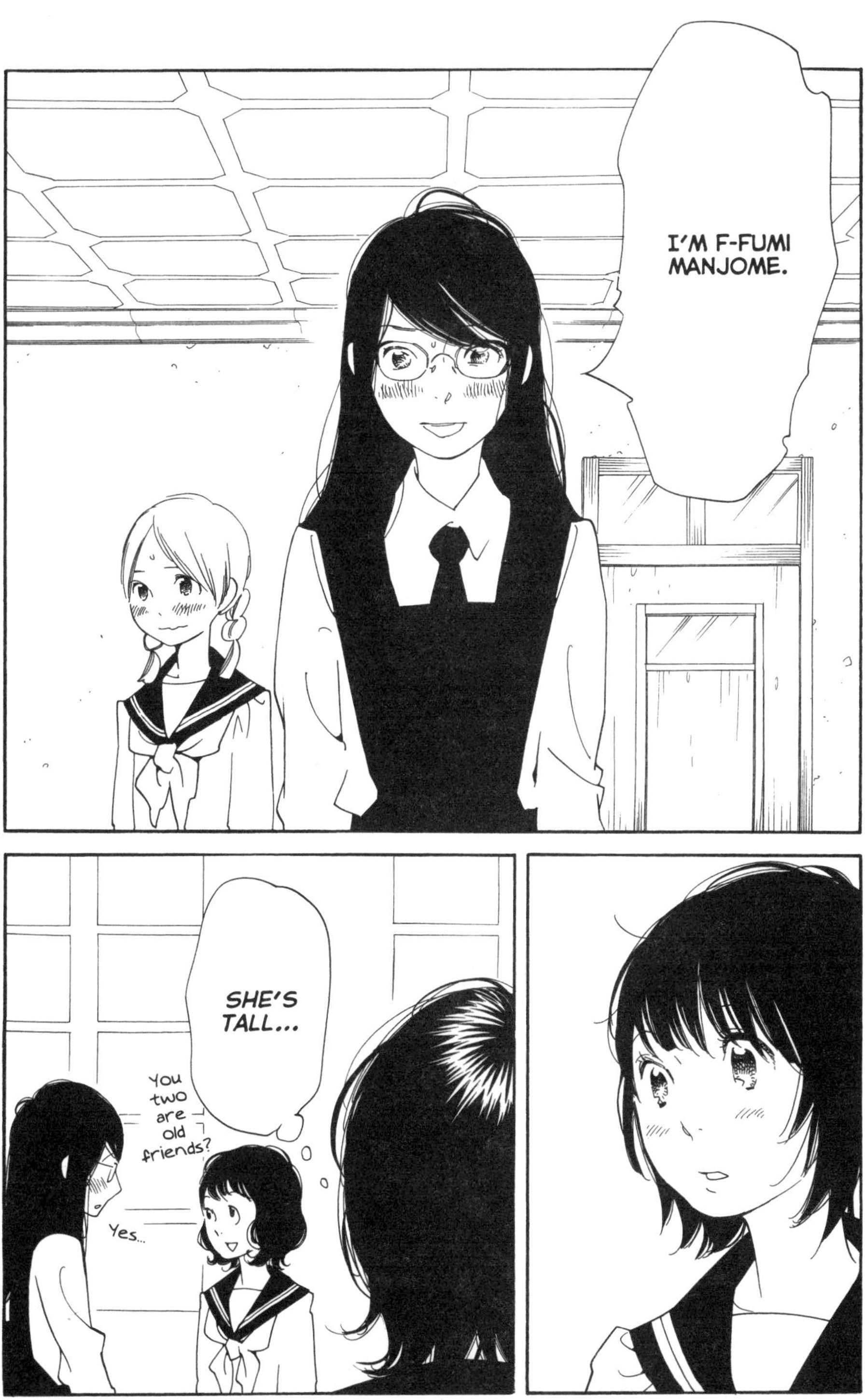
I'M F-FUMI MANJOME.
SHE'S TALL...
You two are old friends?
Yes...

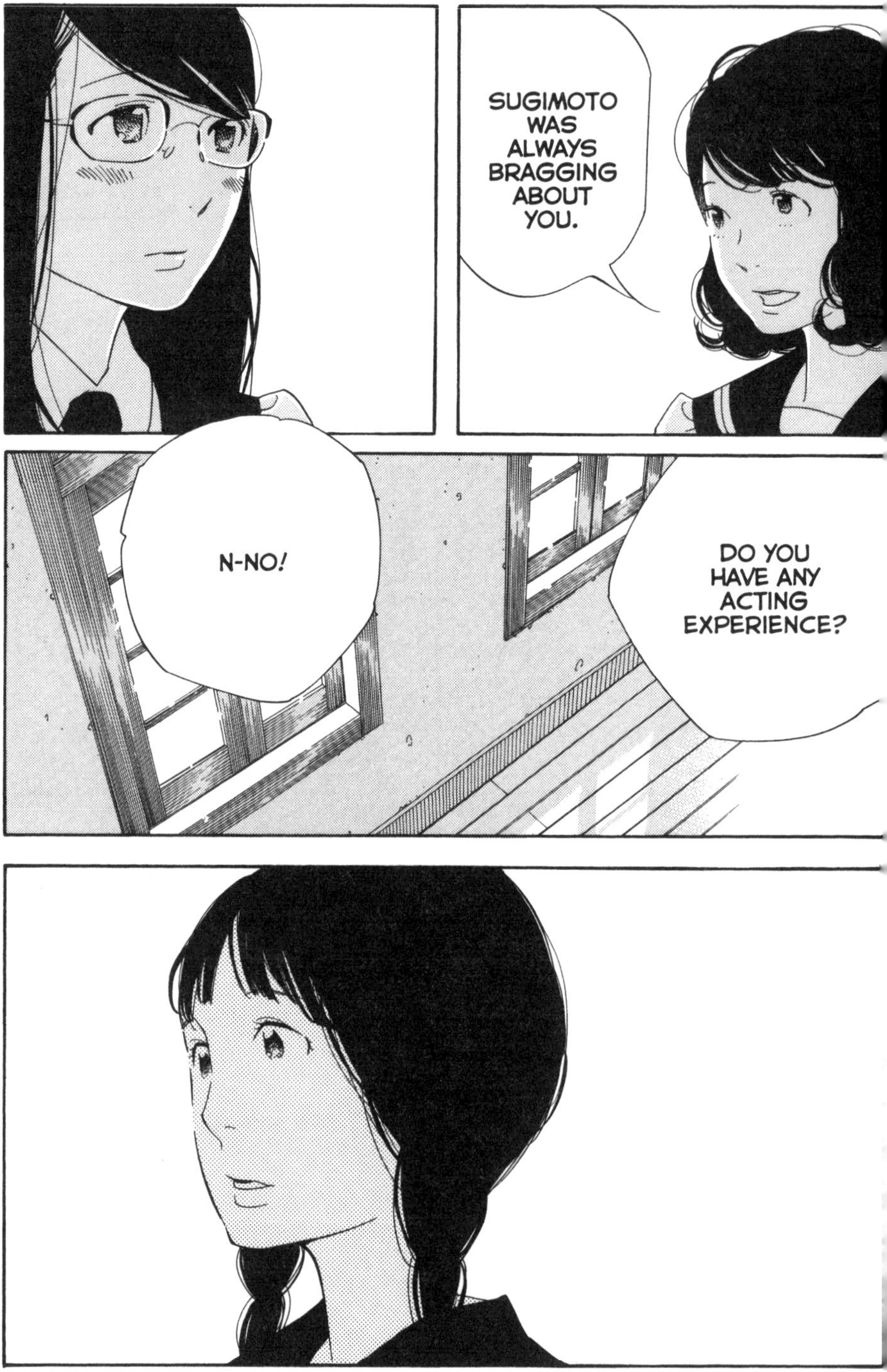
SUGIMOTO WAS ALWAYS BRAGGING ABOUT YOU.
DO YOU HAVE ANY ACTING EXPERIENCE?
N-NO!

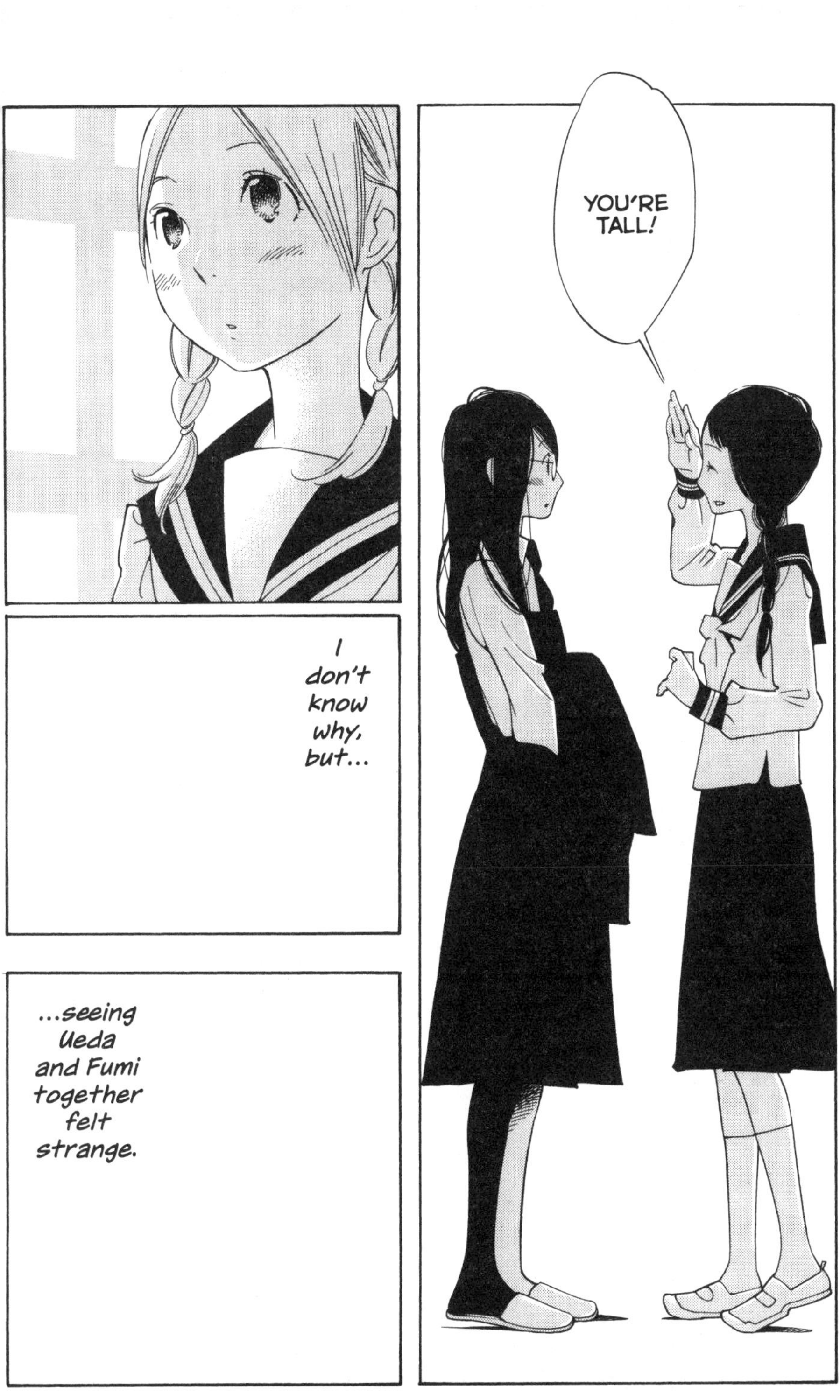
YOU'RE TALL!
I don't know why, but...
...seeing Ueda and Fumi together felt strange.

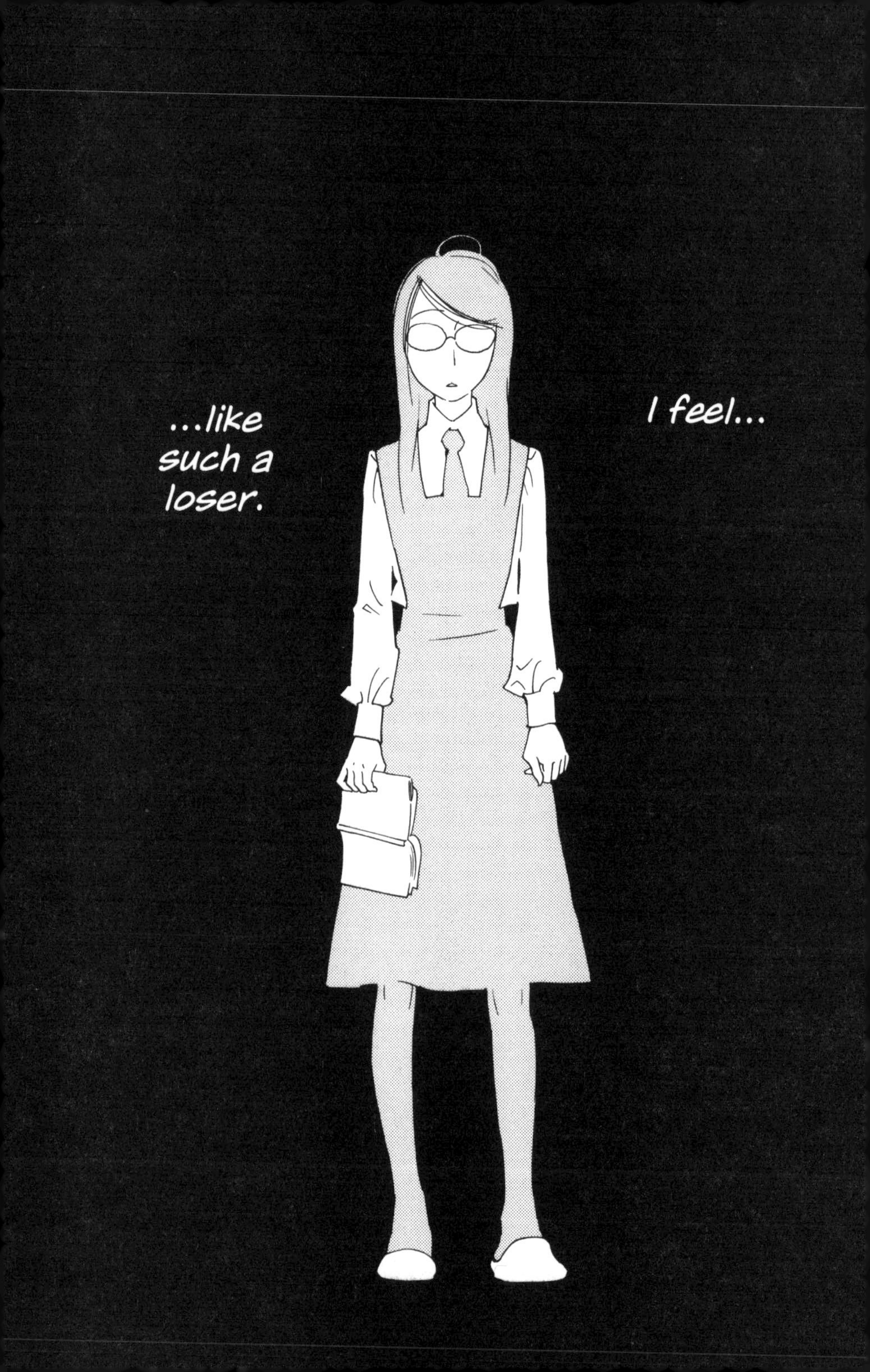
I feel...
...like such a loser.

Sweet Blue Flowers

#23 Rokumeikan, Part 3

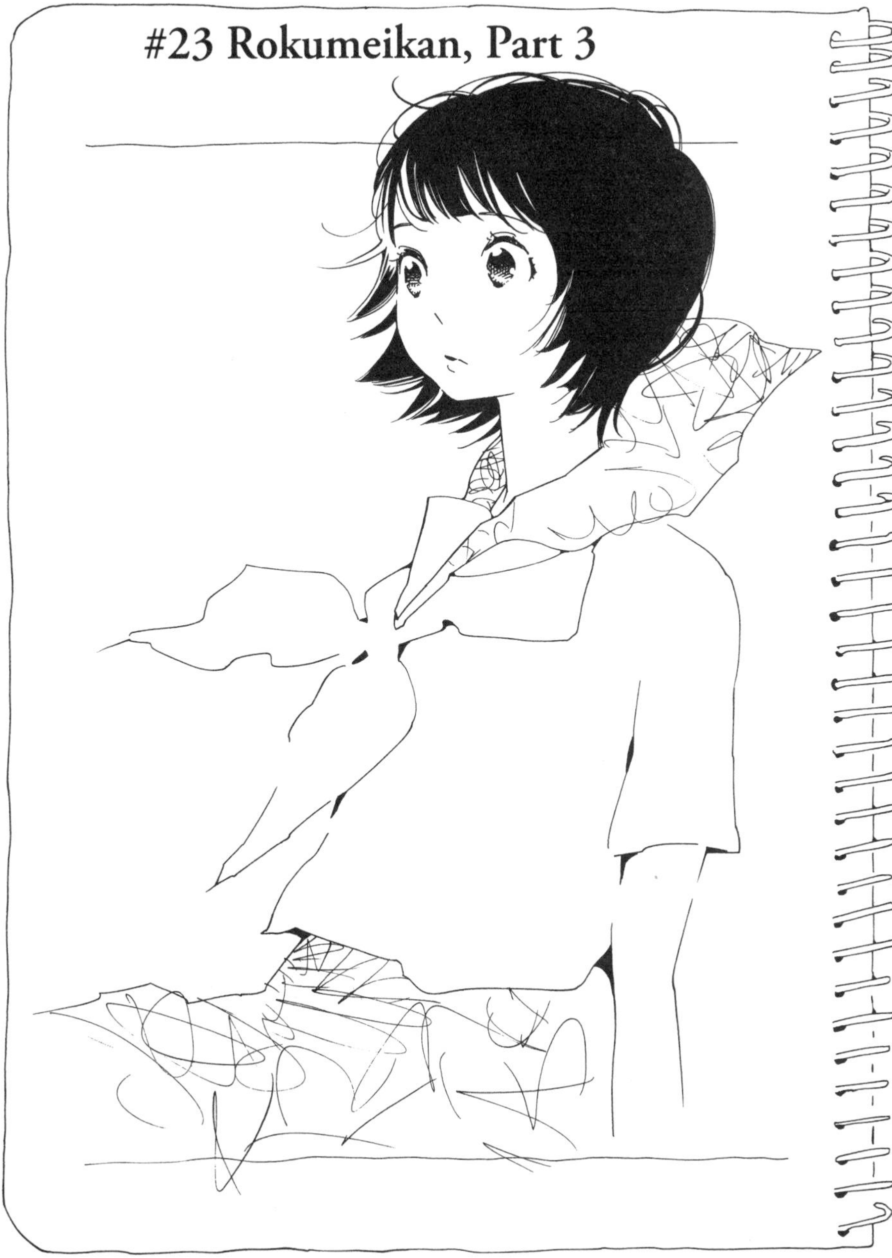

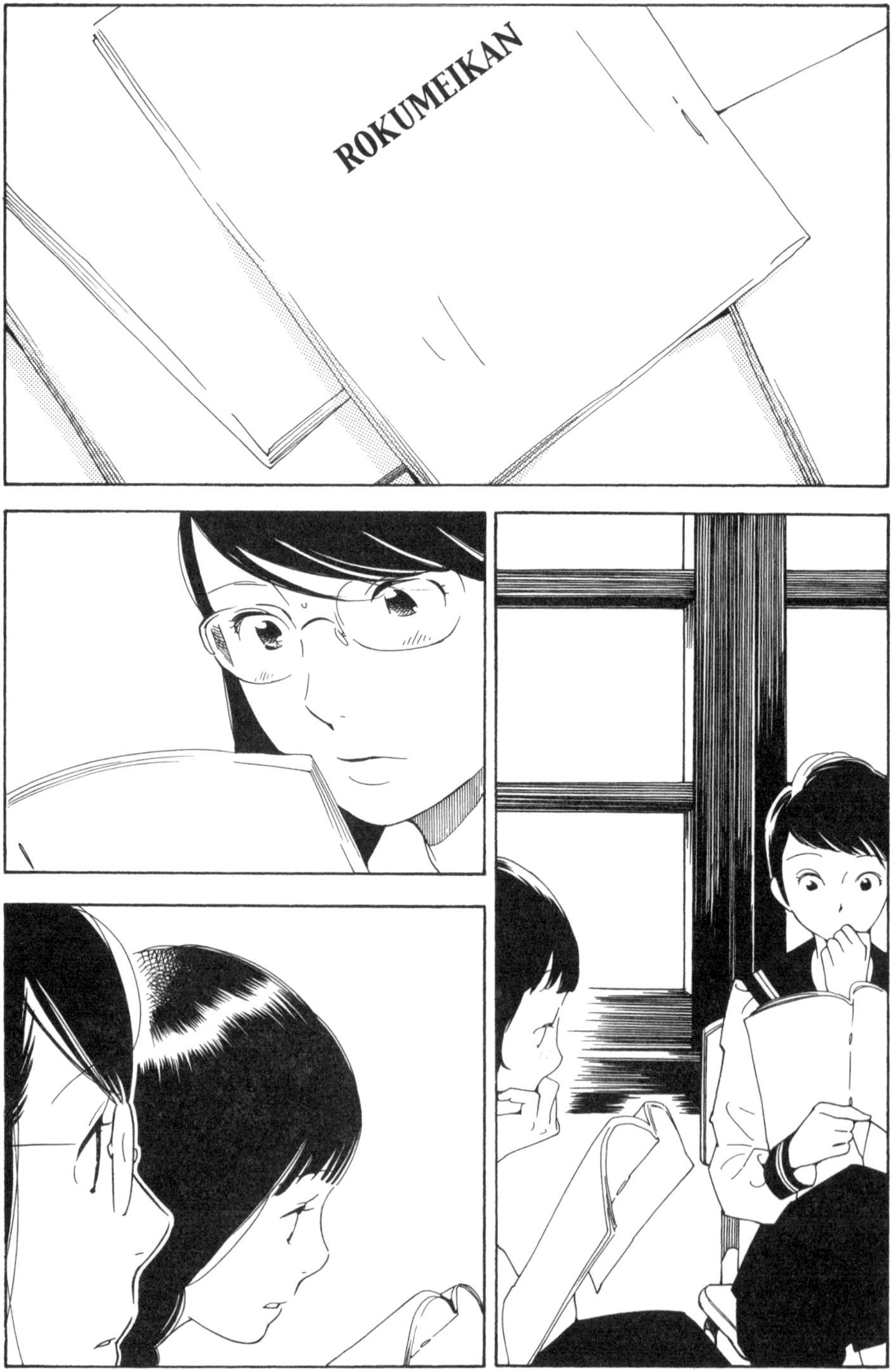
ROKUMEIKAN

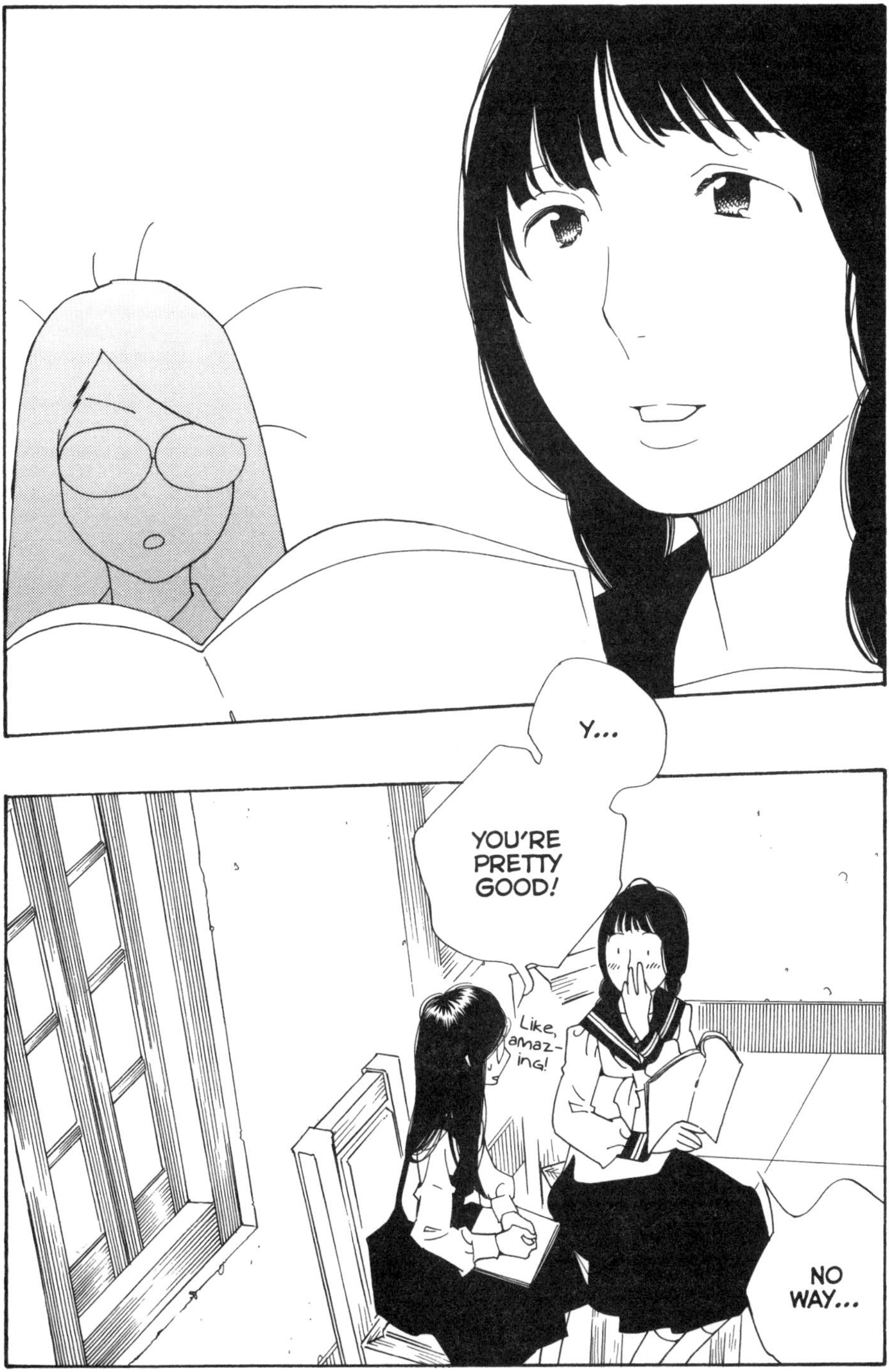
Y...
YOU'RE PRETTY GOOD!
Like, amaz-ing!
NO WAY...

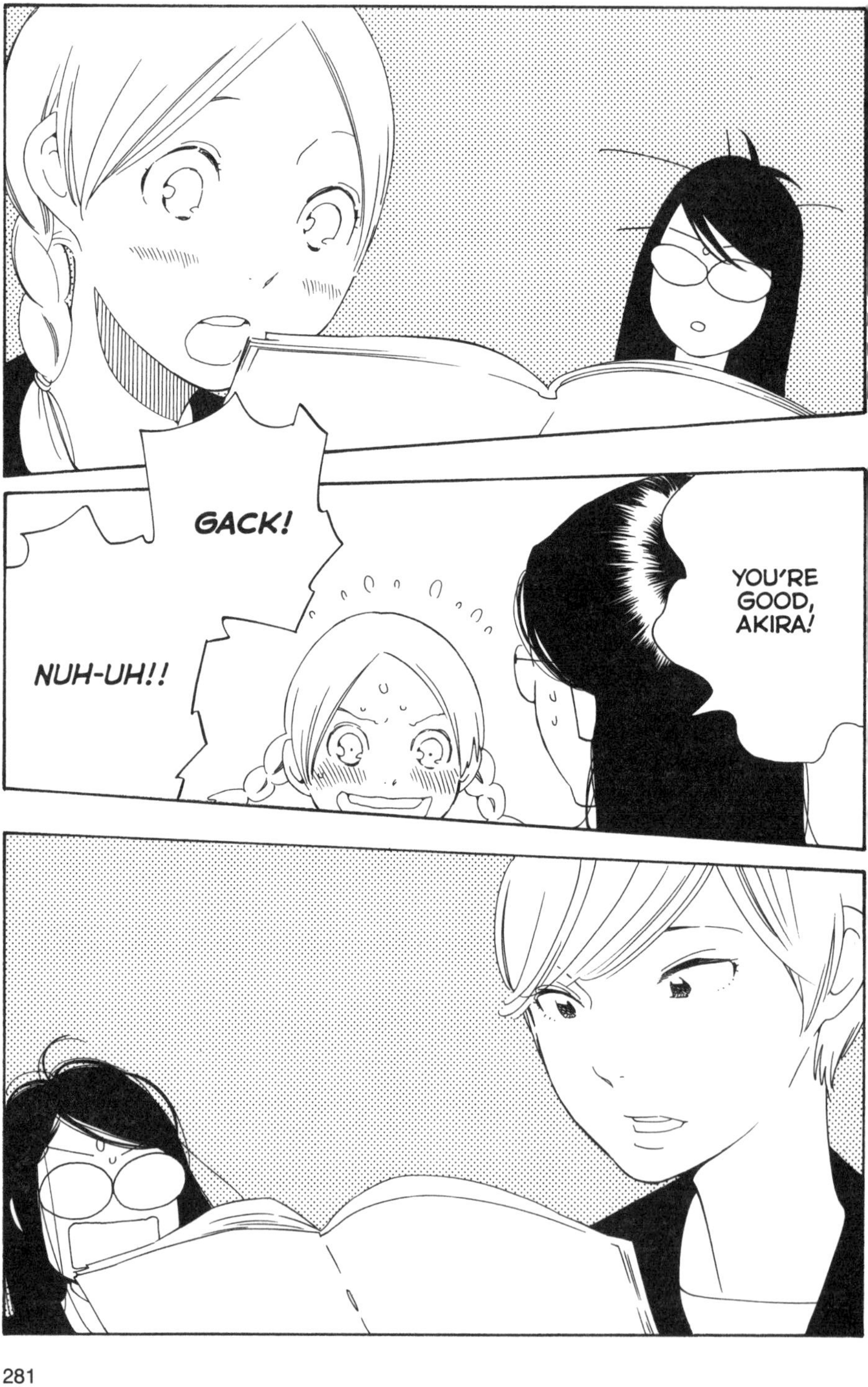
YOU'RE GOOD, AKIRA!
GACK!
NUH-UH!!

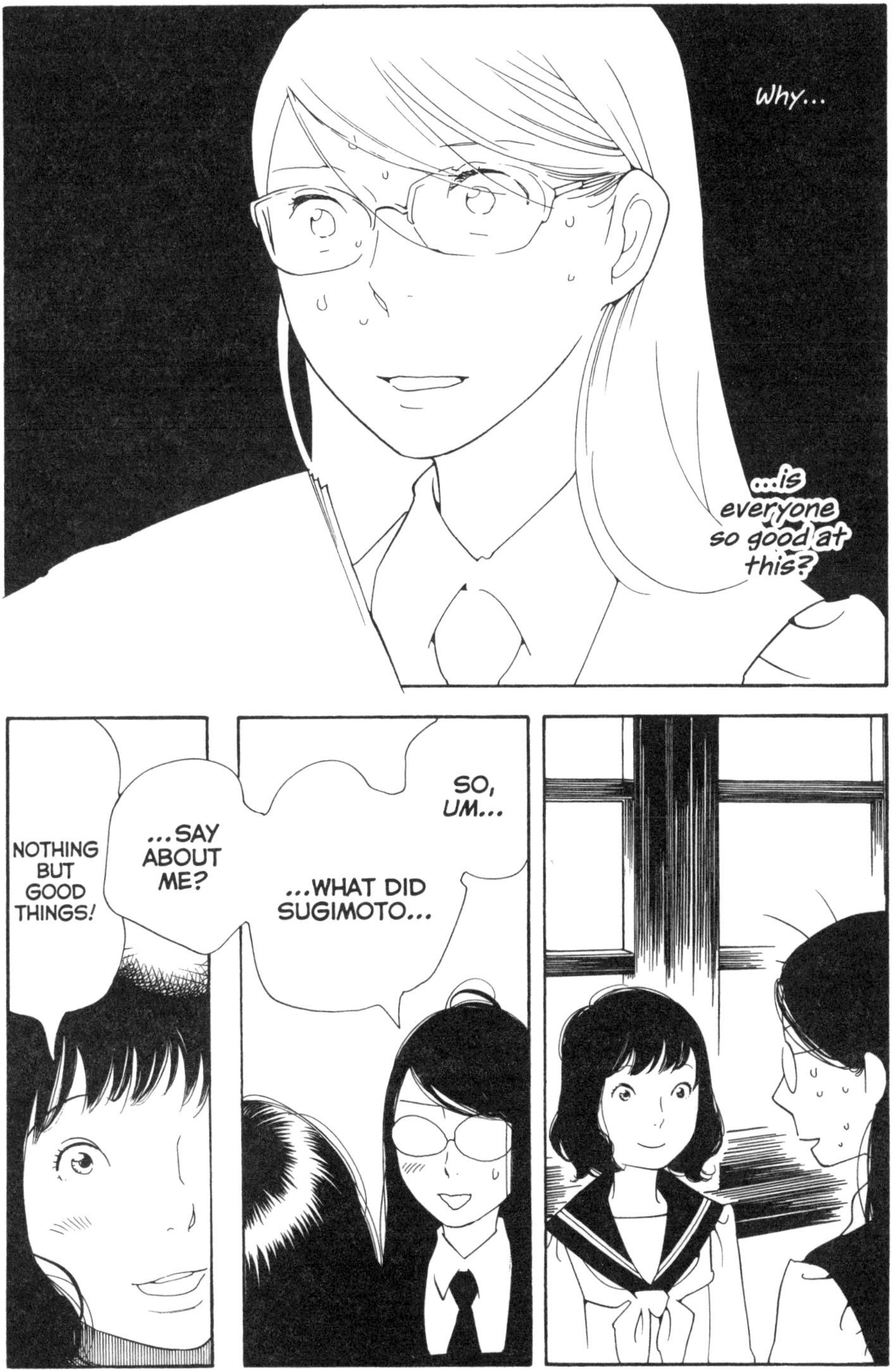
Why...
...is everyone so good at this?
SO, UM...
...WHAT DID SUGIMOTO...
...SAY ABOUT ME?
NOTHING BUT GOOD THINGS!

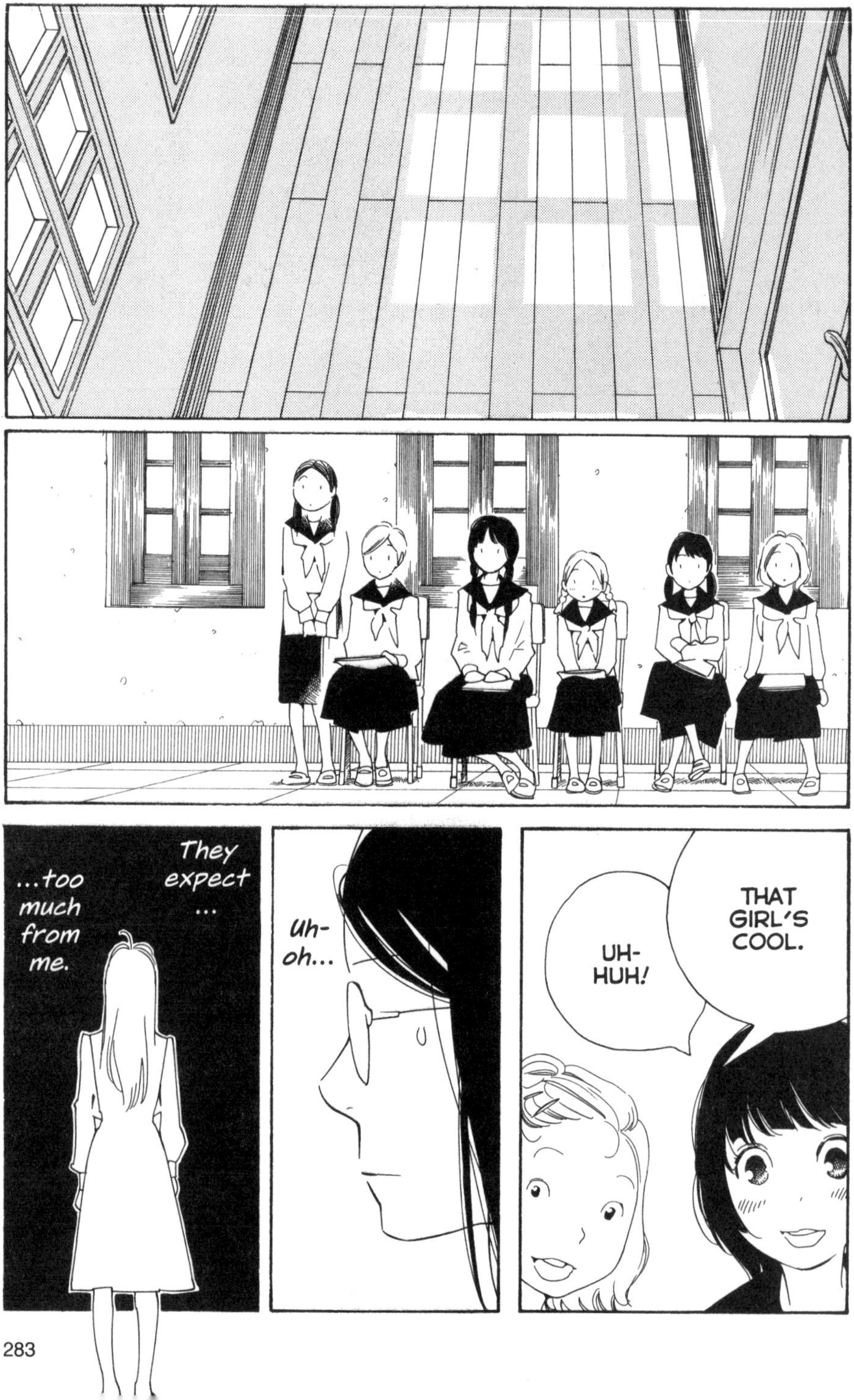
THAT GIRL'S COOL.
UH-HUH!
Uh-oh...
They expect ...
...too much from me.

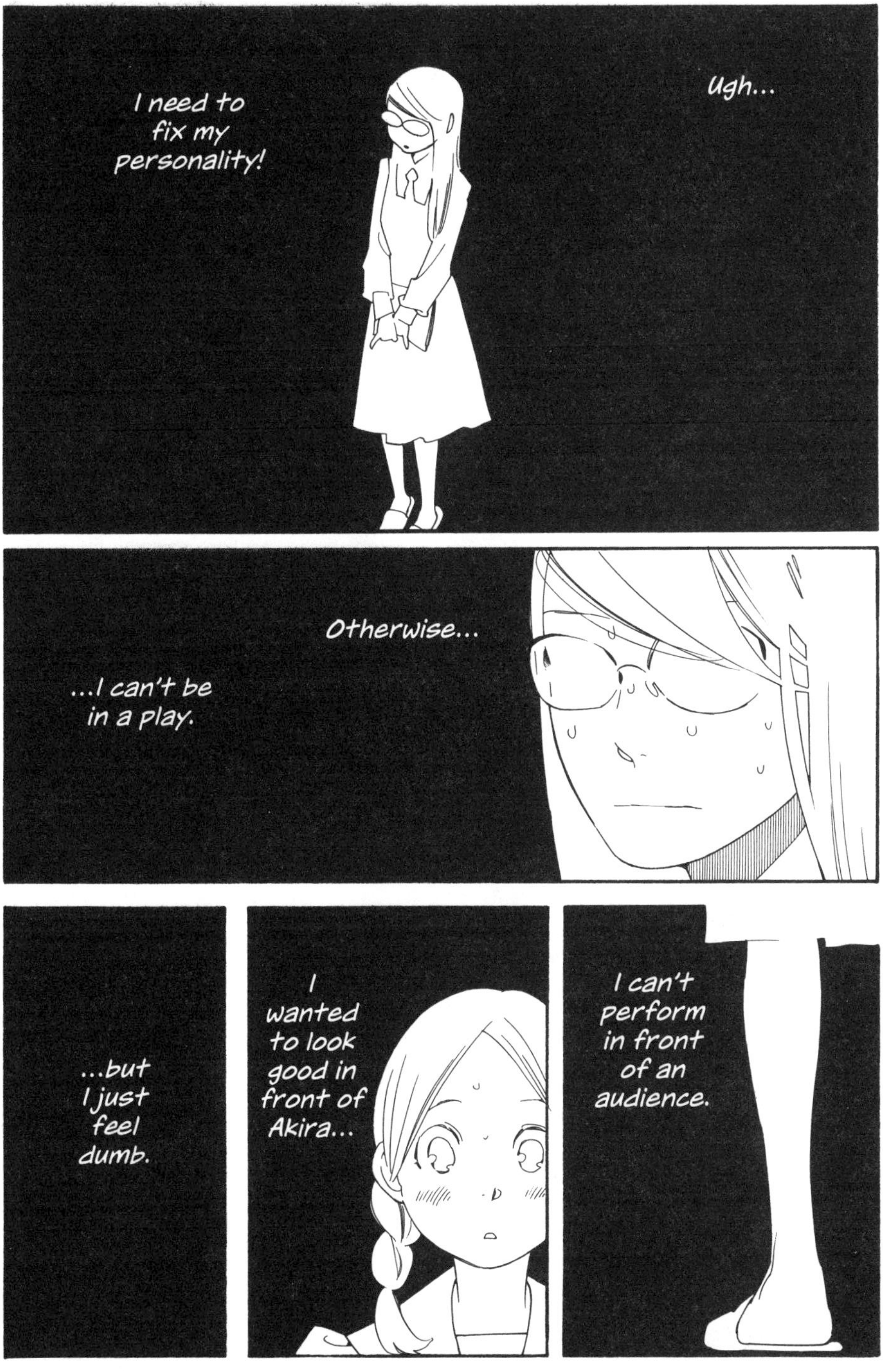
Ugh...
I need to fix my personality!
Otherwise...
...I can't be in a play.
I can't perform in front of an audience.
I wanted to look good in front of Akira...
...but I just feel dumb.

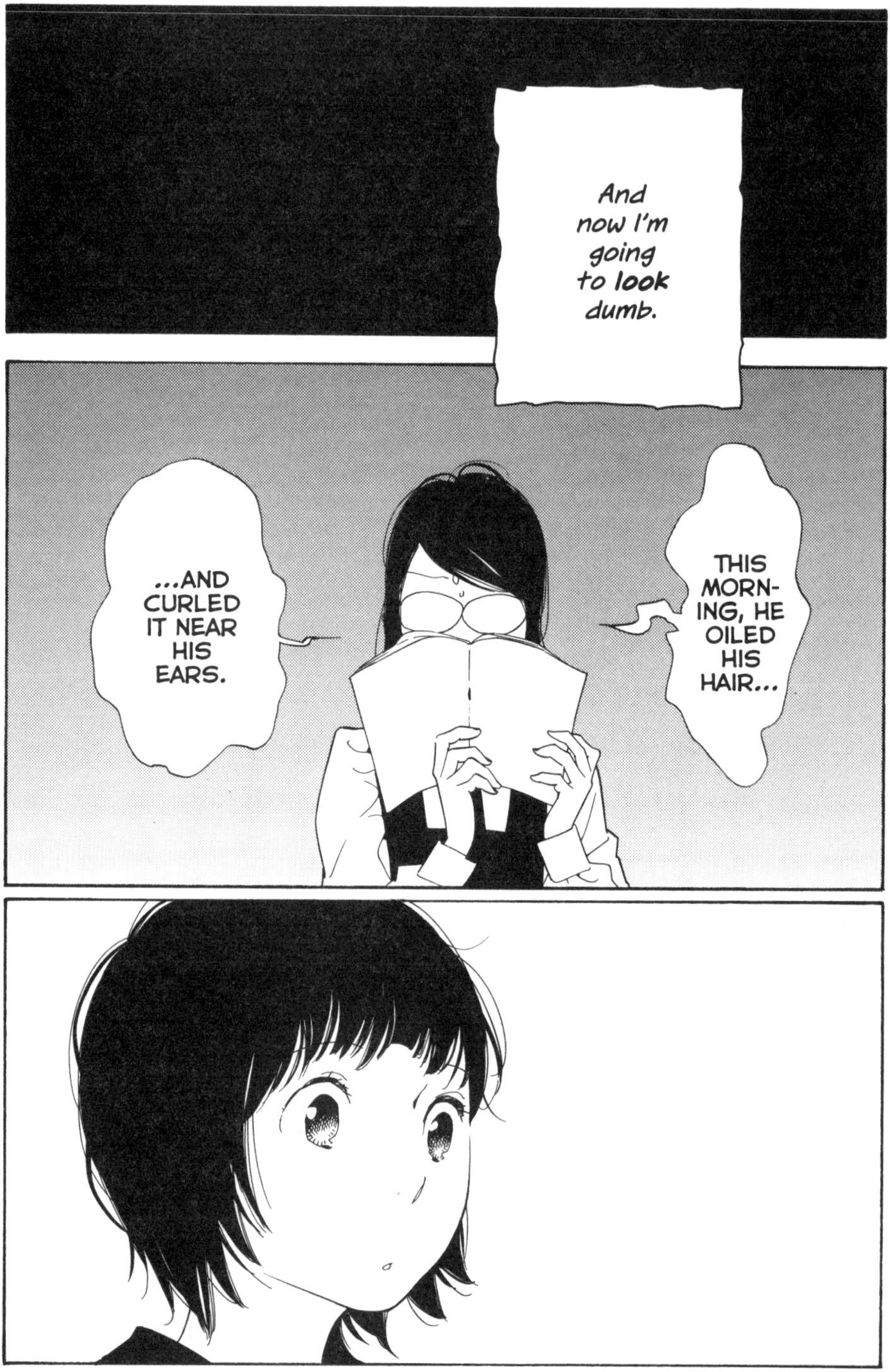
And now I'm going to look dumb.
THIS MORNING, HE OILED HIS HAIR...
...AND CURLED IT NEAR HIS EARS.

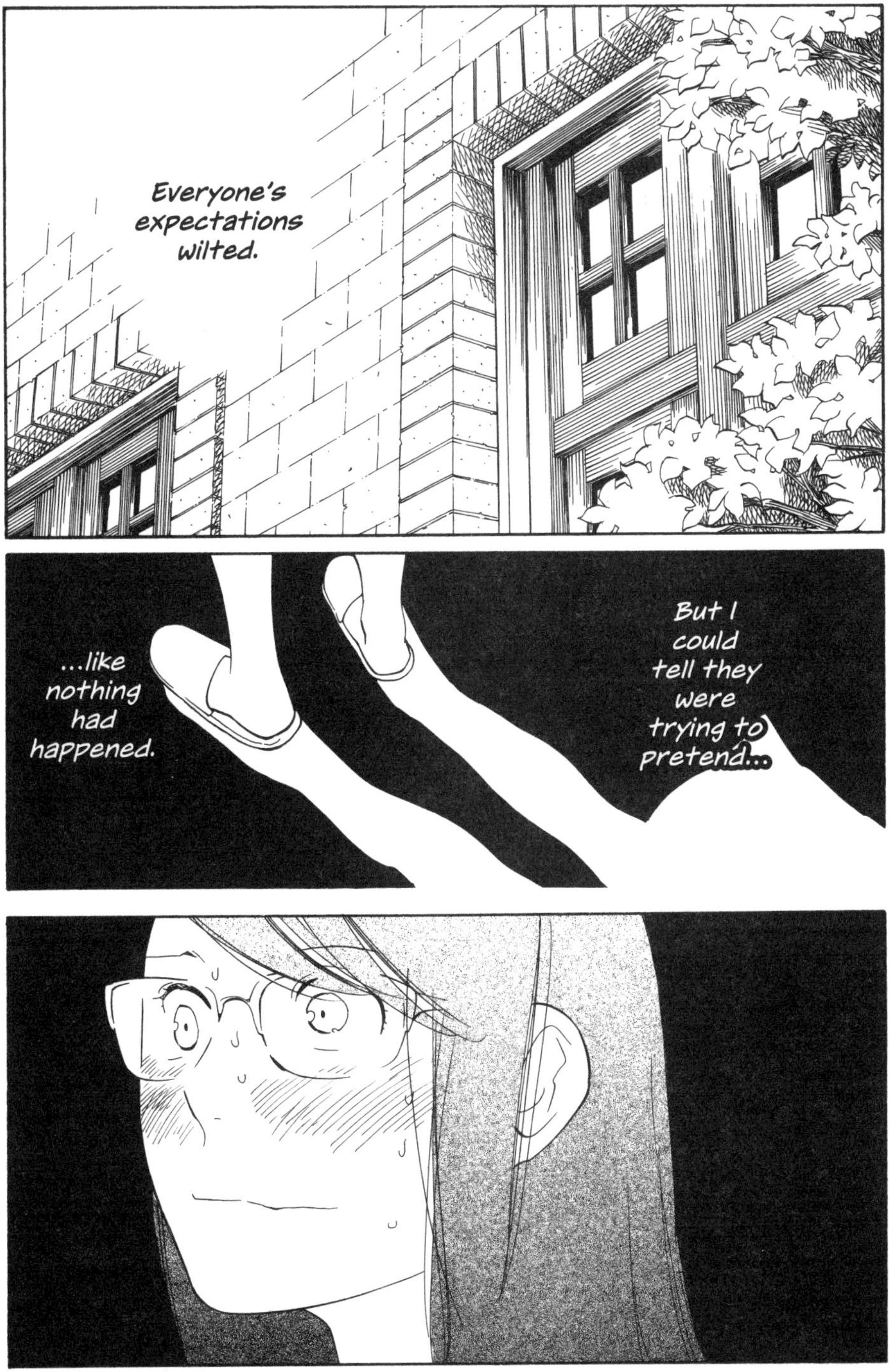
Everyone's expectations wilted.
But I could tell they were trying to pretend...
...like nothing had happened.

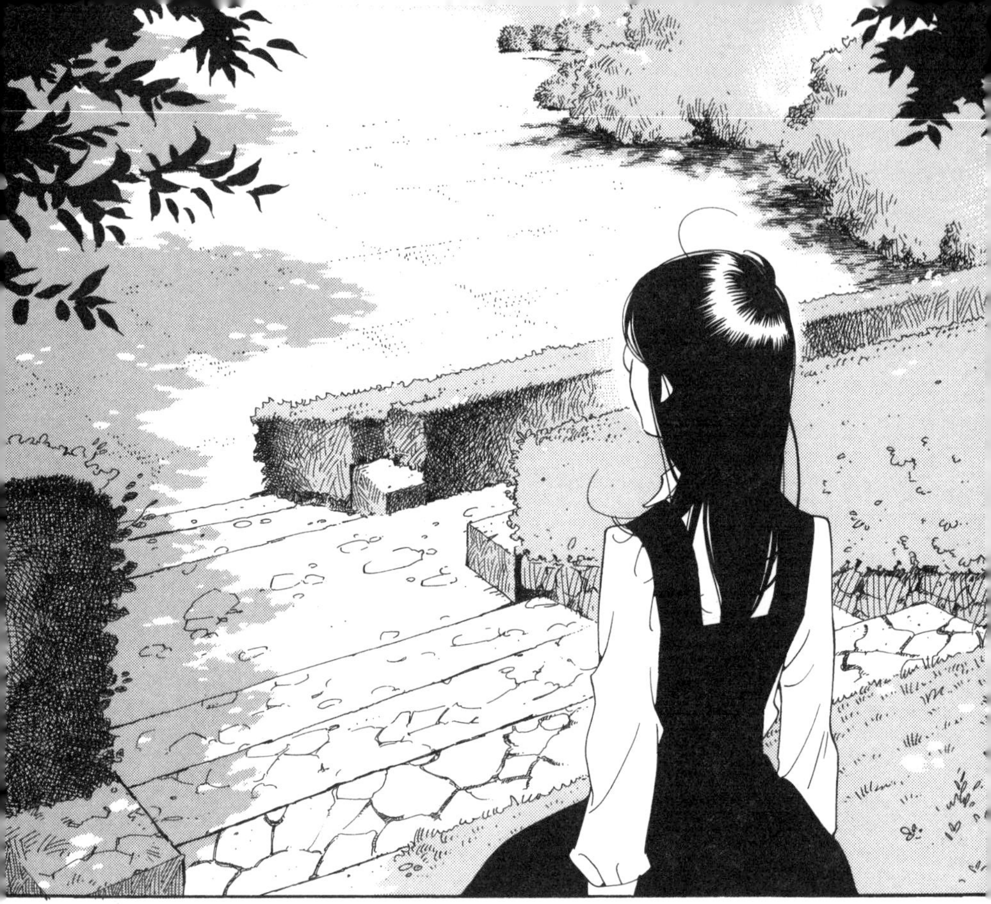

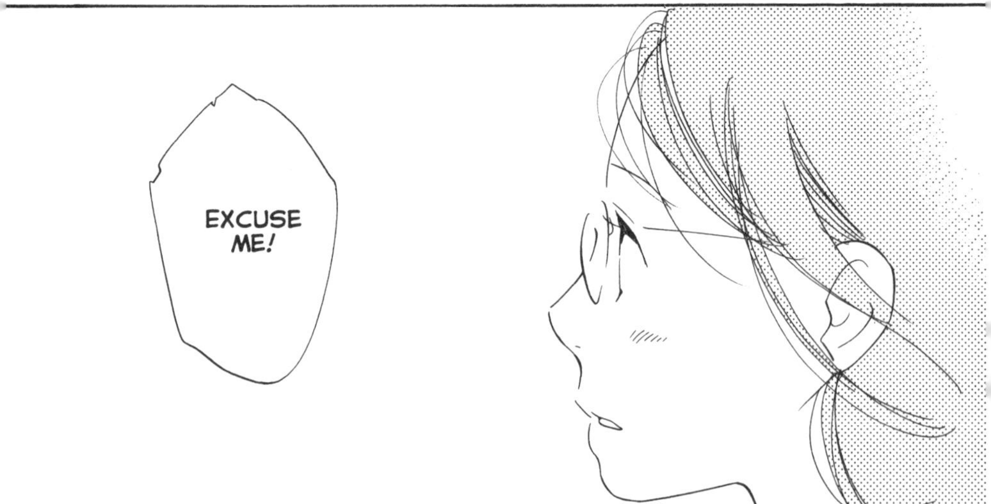
EXCUSE ME!

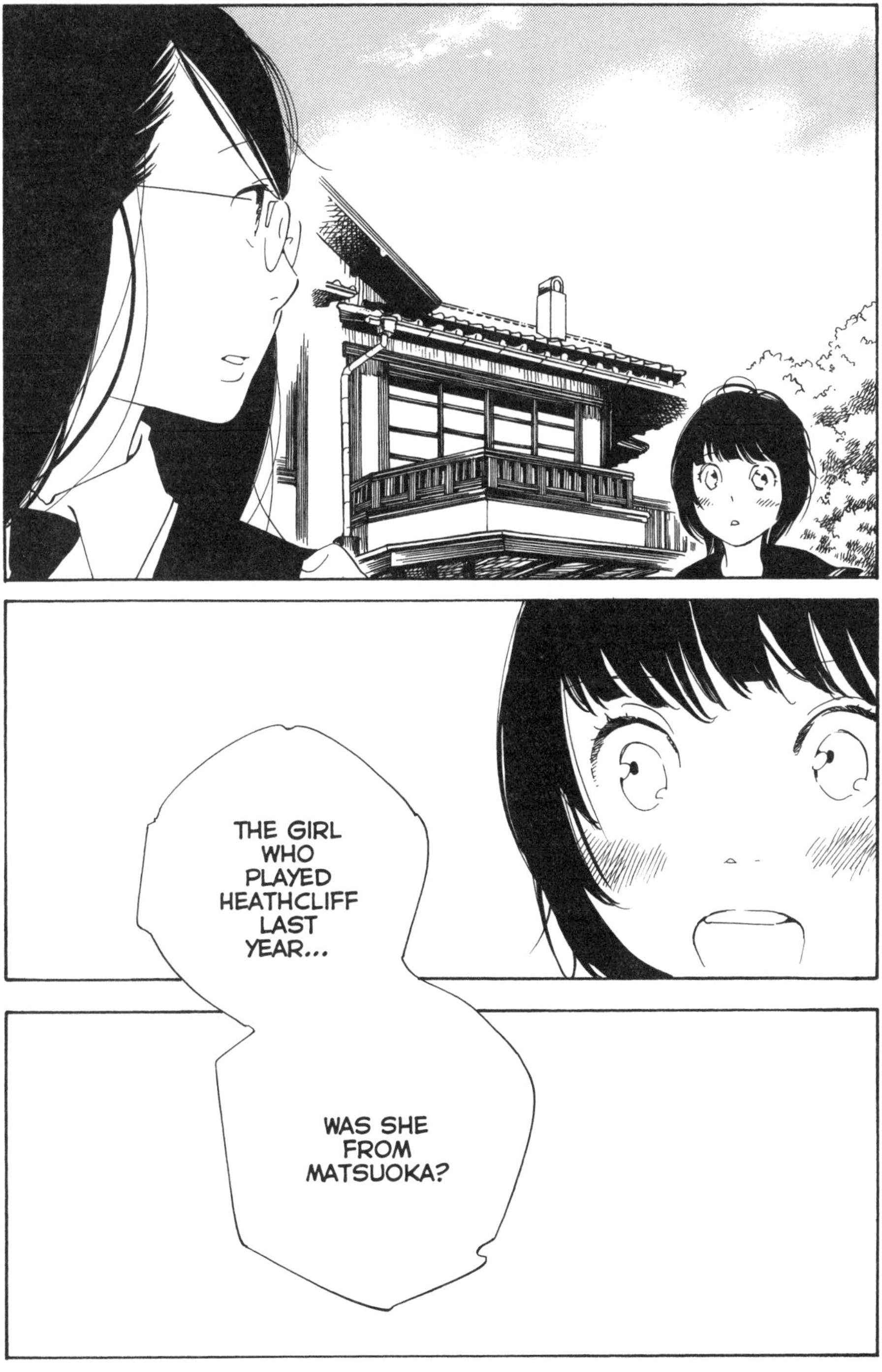
THE GIRL WHO PLAYED HEATHCLIFF LAST YEAR...
WAS SHE FROM MATSUOKA?

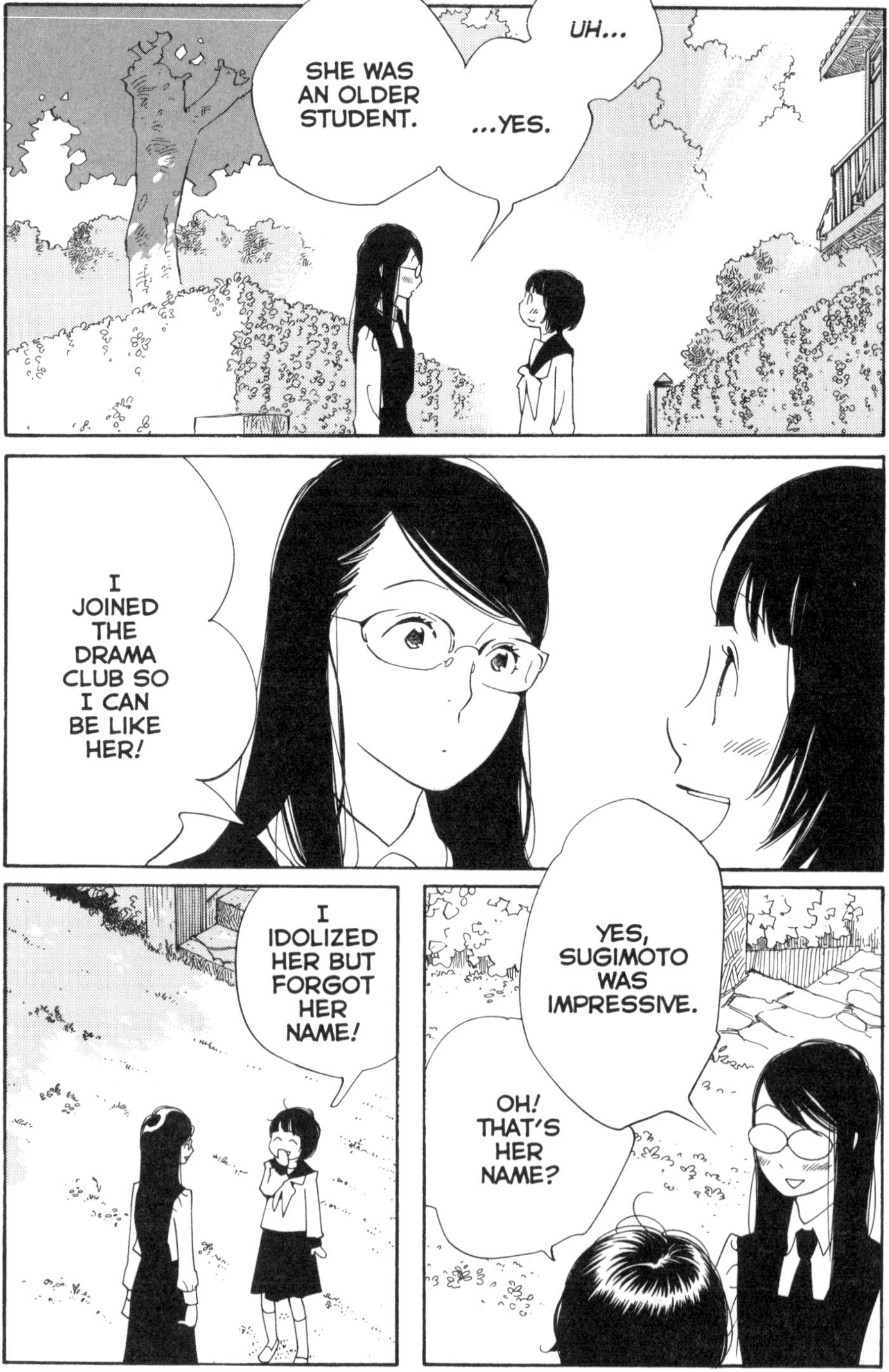
UH...
...YES.
SHE WAS AN OLDER STUDENT.
I JOINED THE DRAMA CLUB SO I CAN BE LIKE HER!
YES, SUGIMOTO WAS IMPRESSIVE.
OH! THAT'S HER NAME?
I IDOLIZED HER BUT FORGOT HER NAME!

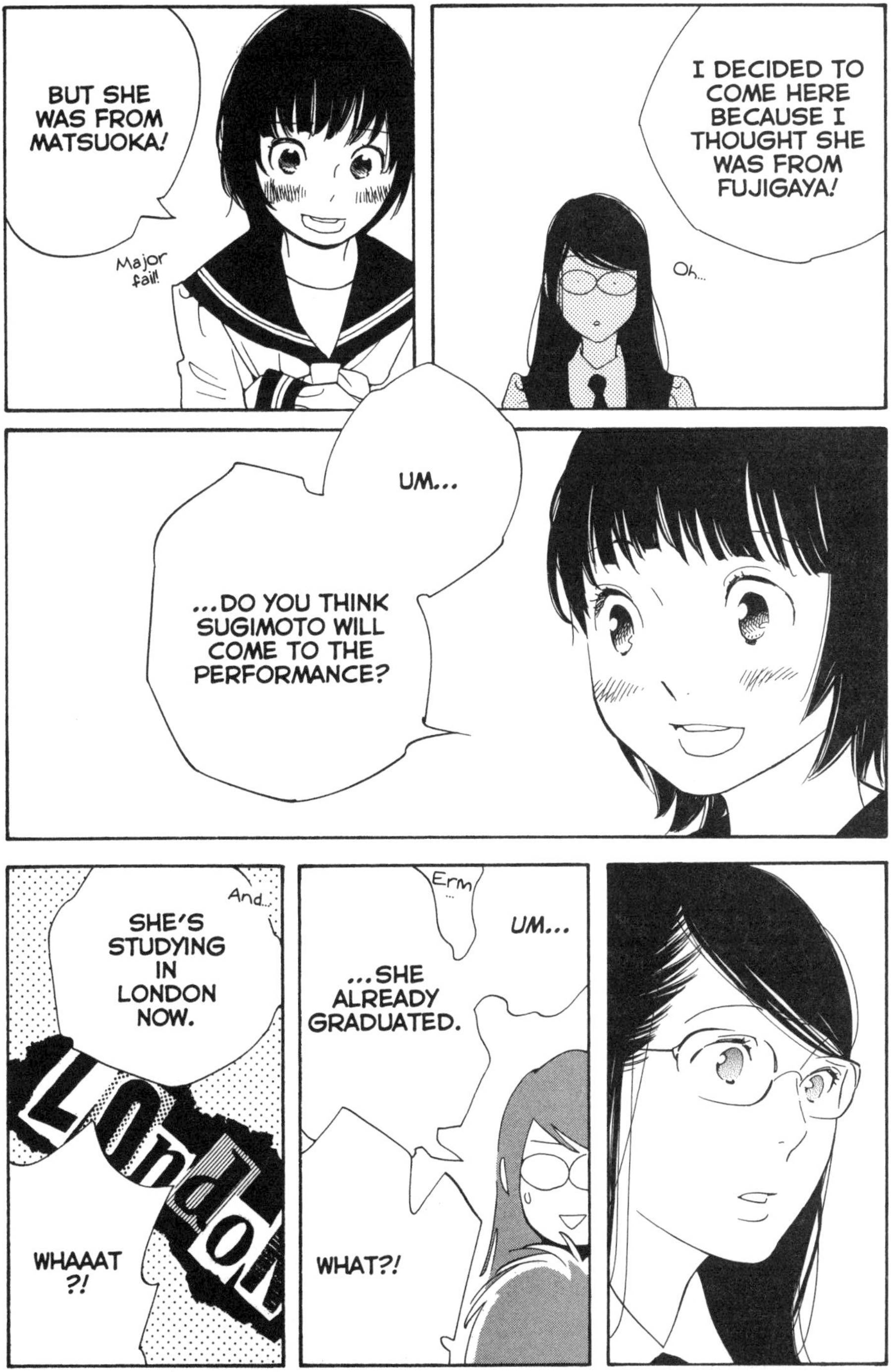
I DECIDED TO COME HERE BECAUSE I THOUGHT SHE WAS FROM FUJIGAYA!
Oh...
BUT SHE WAS FROM MATSUOKA!
Major fail!
UM...
...DO YOU THINK SUGIMOTO WILL COME TO THE PERFORMANCE?
Erm...
UM...
...SHE ALREADY GRADUATED.
WHAT?!
And...
SHE'S STUDYING IN LONDON NOW.
London
WHAAAT?!

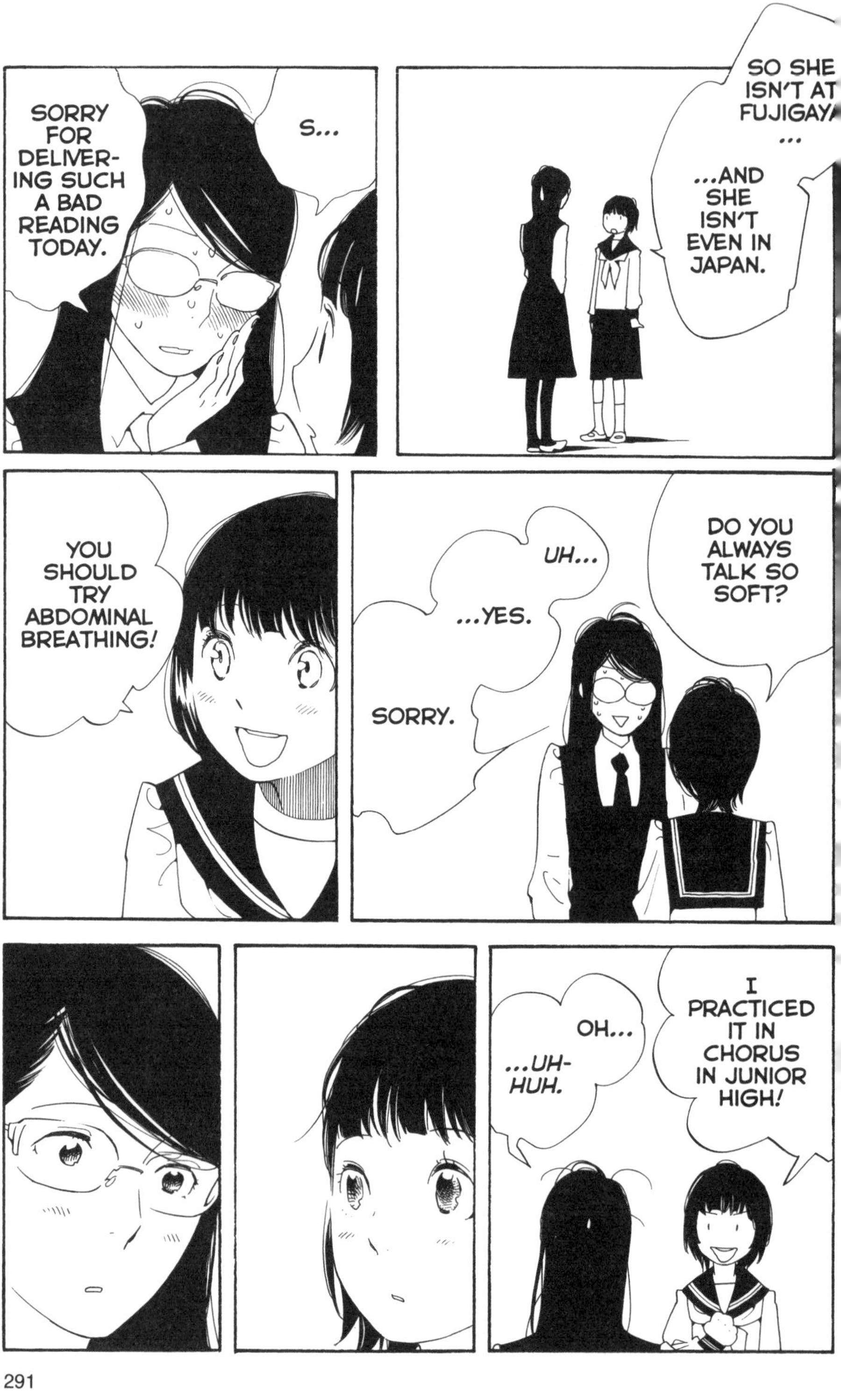
SO SHE ISN'T AT FUJIGAYA ...
...AND SHE ISN'T EVEN IN JAPAN.
S...
SORRY FOR DELIVERING SUCH A BAD READING TODAY.
DO YOU ALWAYS TALK SO SOFT?
UH...
...YES.
SORRY.
YOU SHOULD TRY ABDOMINAL BREATHING!
I PRACTICED IT IN CHORUS IN JUNIOR HIGH!
OH...
...UH-HUH.

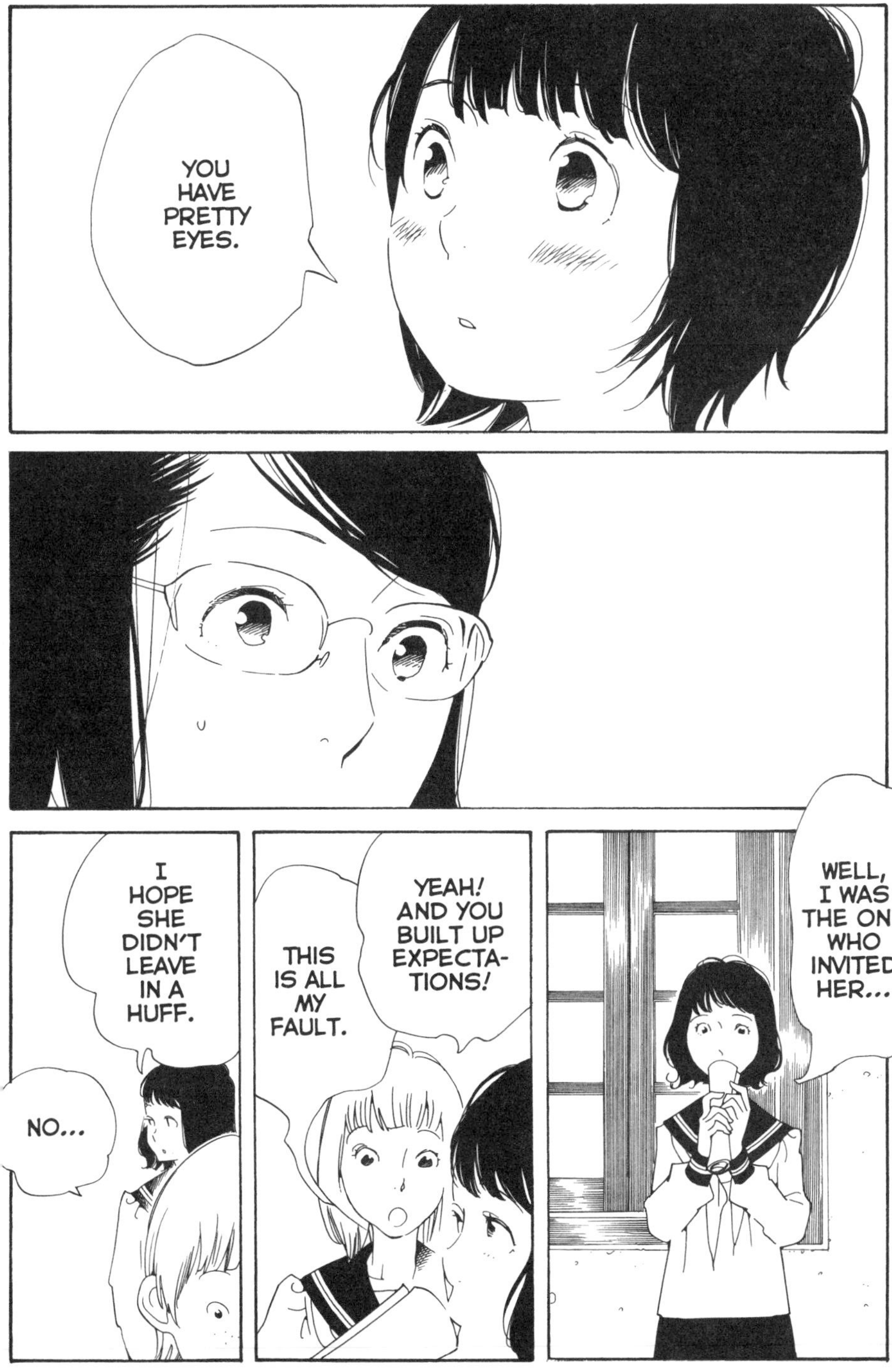
YOU HAVE PRETTY EYES.
WELL, I WAS THE ONE WHO INVITED HER...
YEAH! AND YOU BUILT UP EXPECTATIONS!
THIS IS ALL MY FAULT.
I HOPE SHE DIDN'T LEAVE IN A HUFF.
NO...

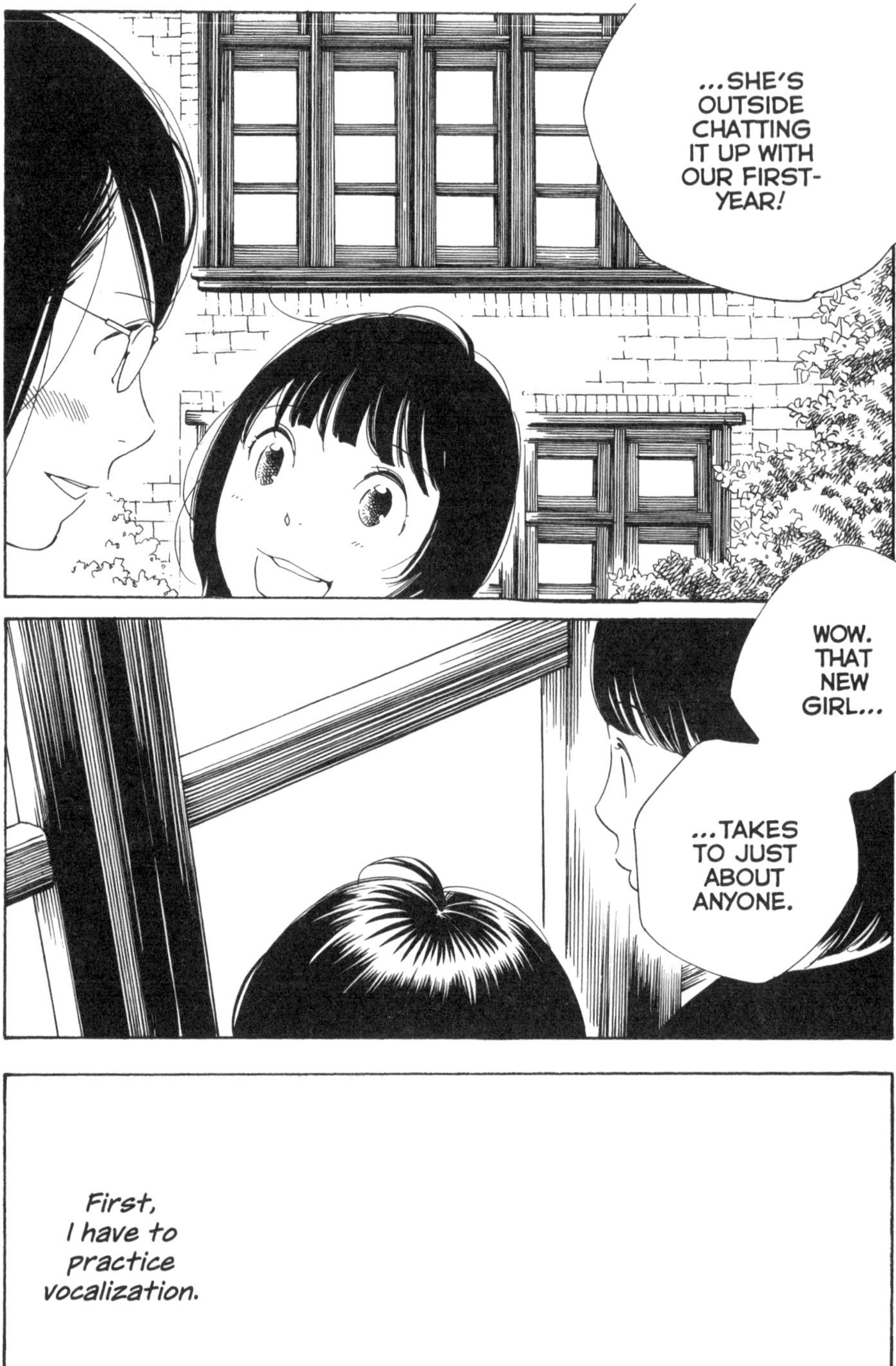
...SHE'S OUTSIDE CHATTING IT UP WITH OUR FIRST-YEAR!
WOW. THAT NEW GIRL...
...TAKES TO JUST ABOUT ANYONE.
First, I have to practice vocalization.

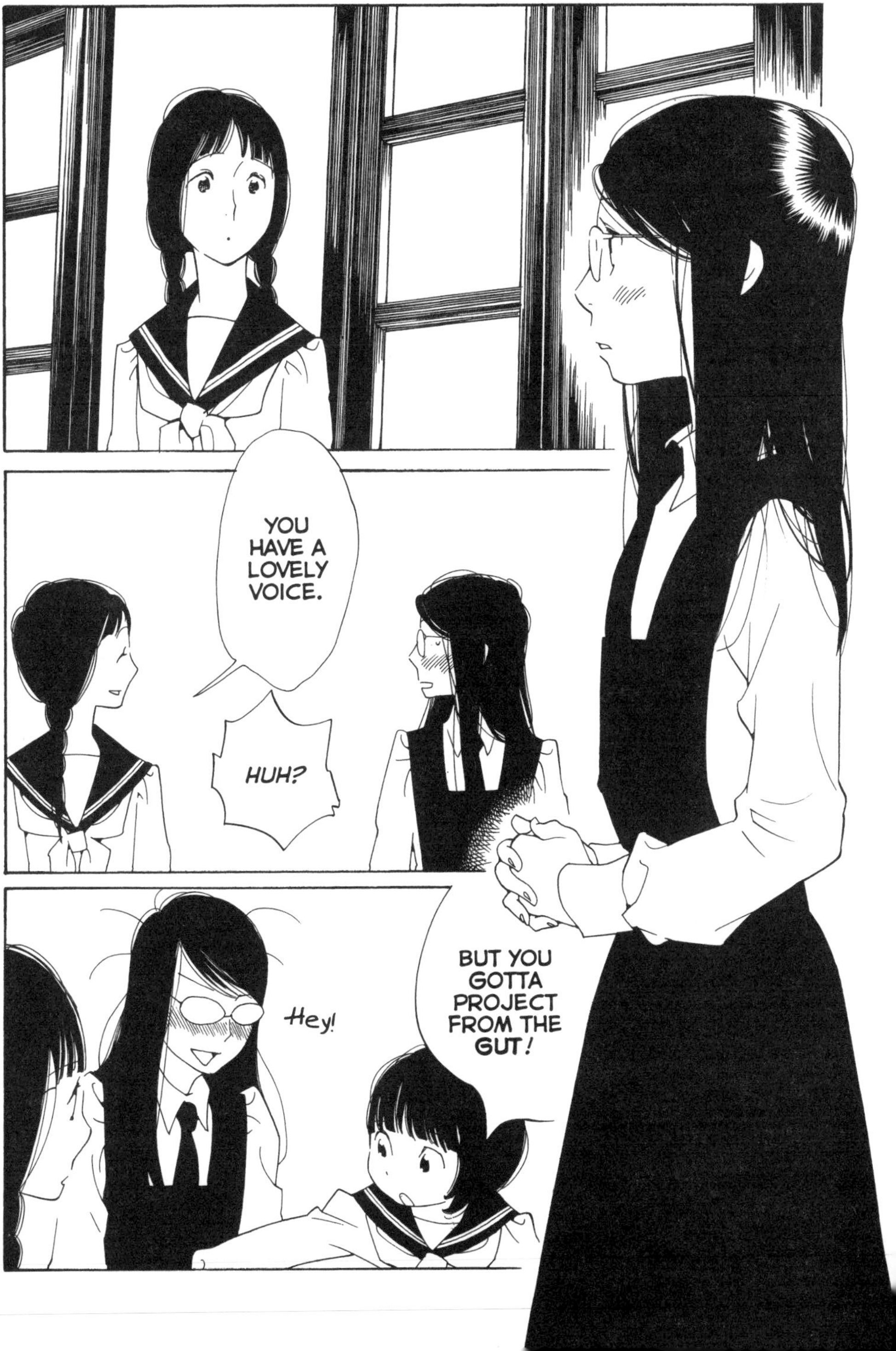
YOU HAVE A LOVELY VOICE.
HUH?
BUT YOU GOTTA PROJECT FROM THE GUT!
Hey!

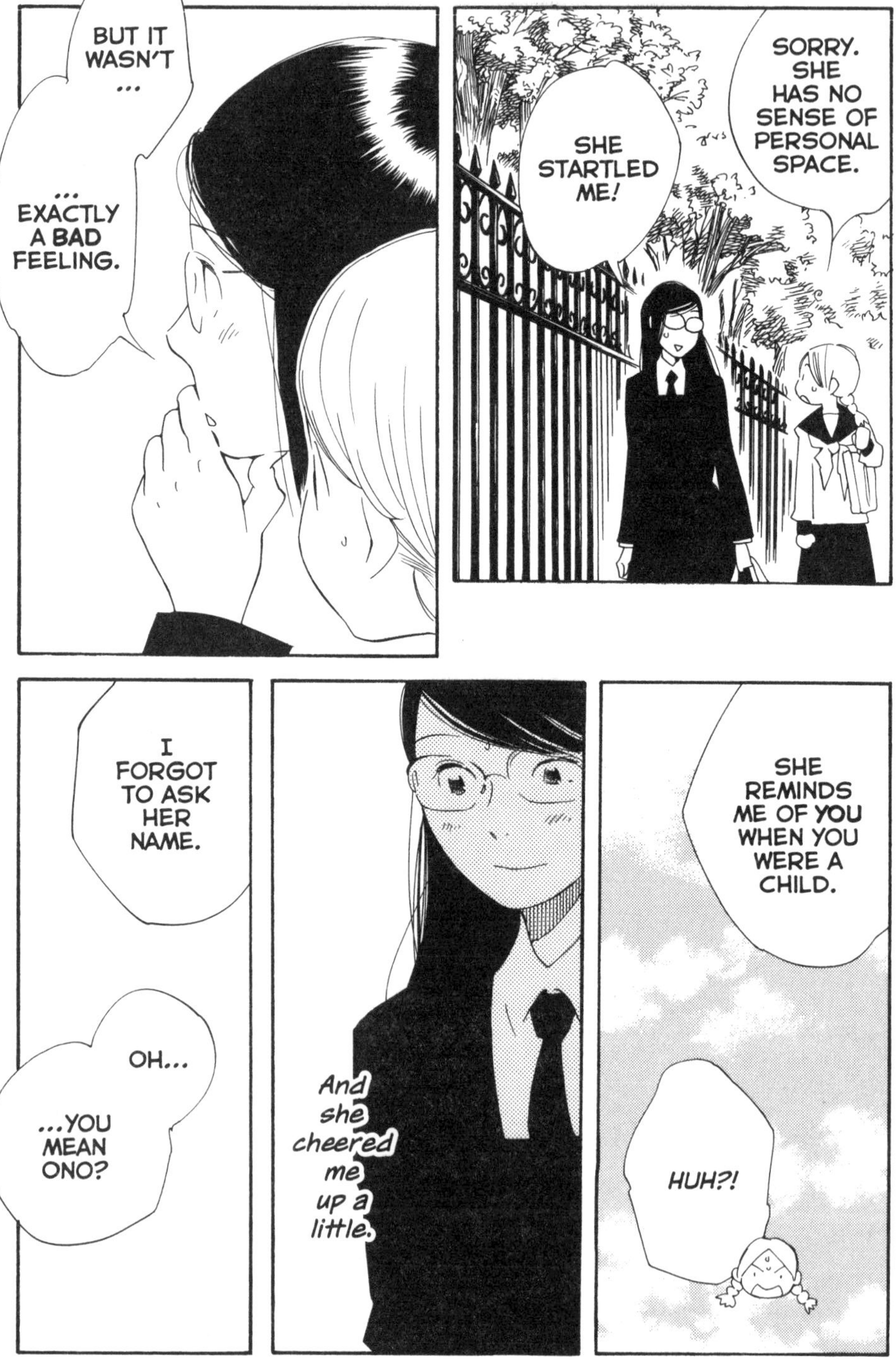
SORRY. SHE HAS NO SENSE OF PERSONAL SPACE.
SHE STARTLED ME!
BUT IT WASN'T ...
... EXACTLY A BAD FEELING.
SHE REMINDS ME OF YOU WHEN YOU WERE A CHILD.
HUH?!
And she cheered me up a little.
I FORGOT TO ASK HER NAME.
OH...
...YOU MEAN ONO?

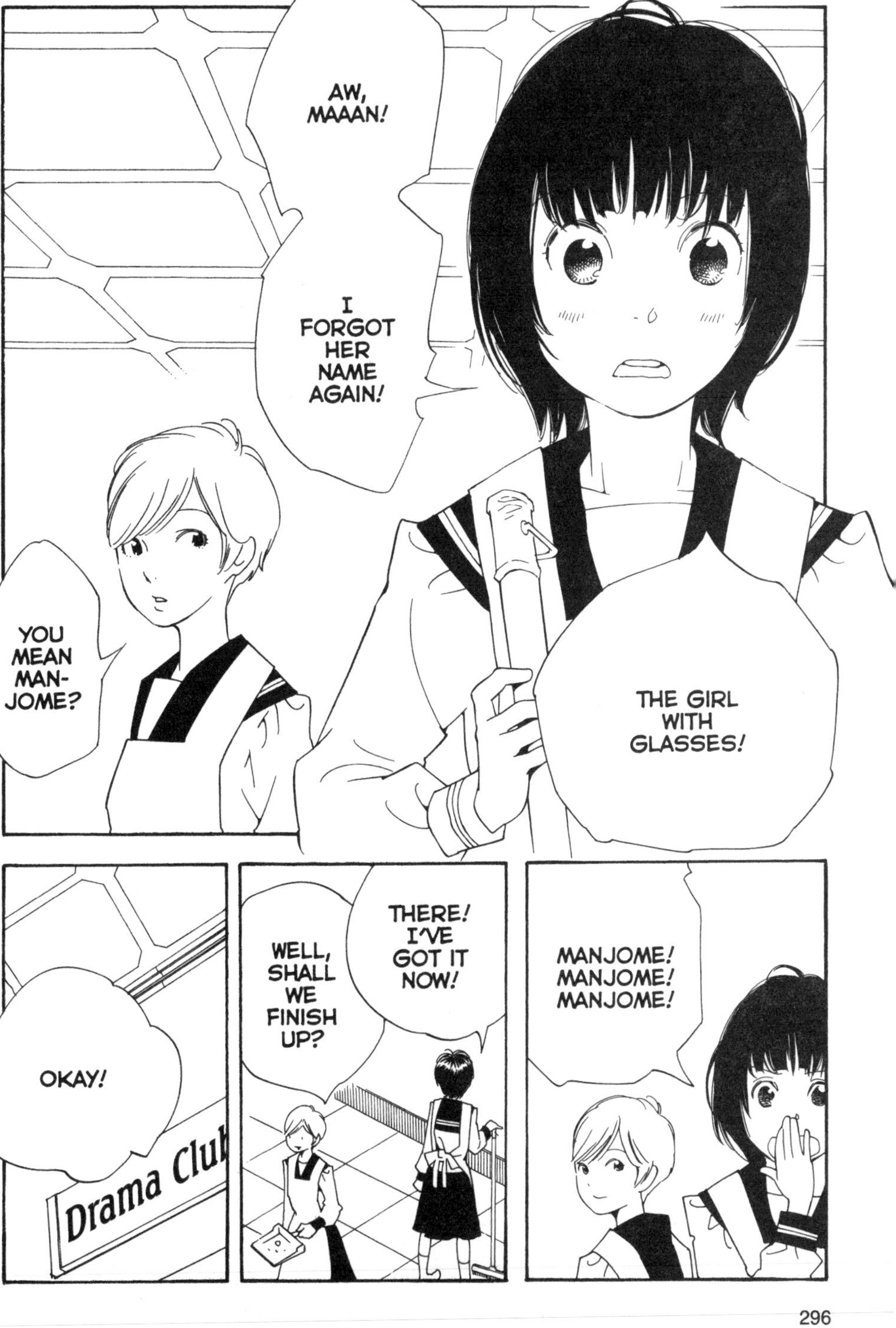
AW, MAAAN!
I FORGOT HER NAME AGAIN!
THE GIRL WITH GLASSES!
YOU MEAN MAN-JOME?
MANJOME! MANJOME! MANJOME!
THERE! I'VE GOT IT NOW!
WELL, SHALL WE FINISH UP?
OKAY!
Drama Club

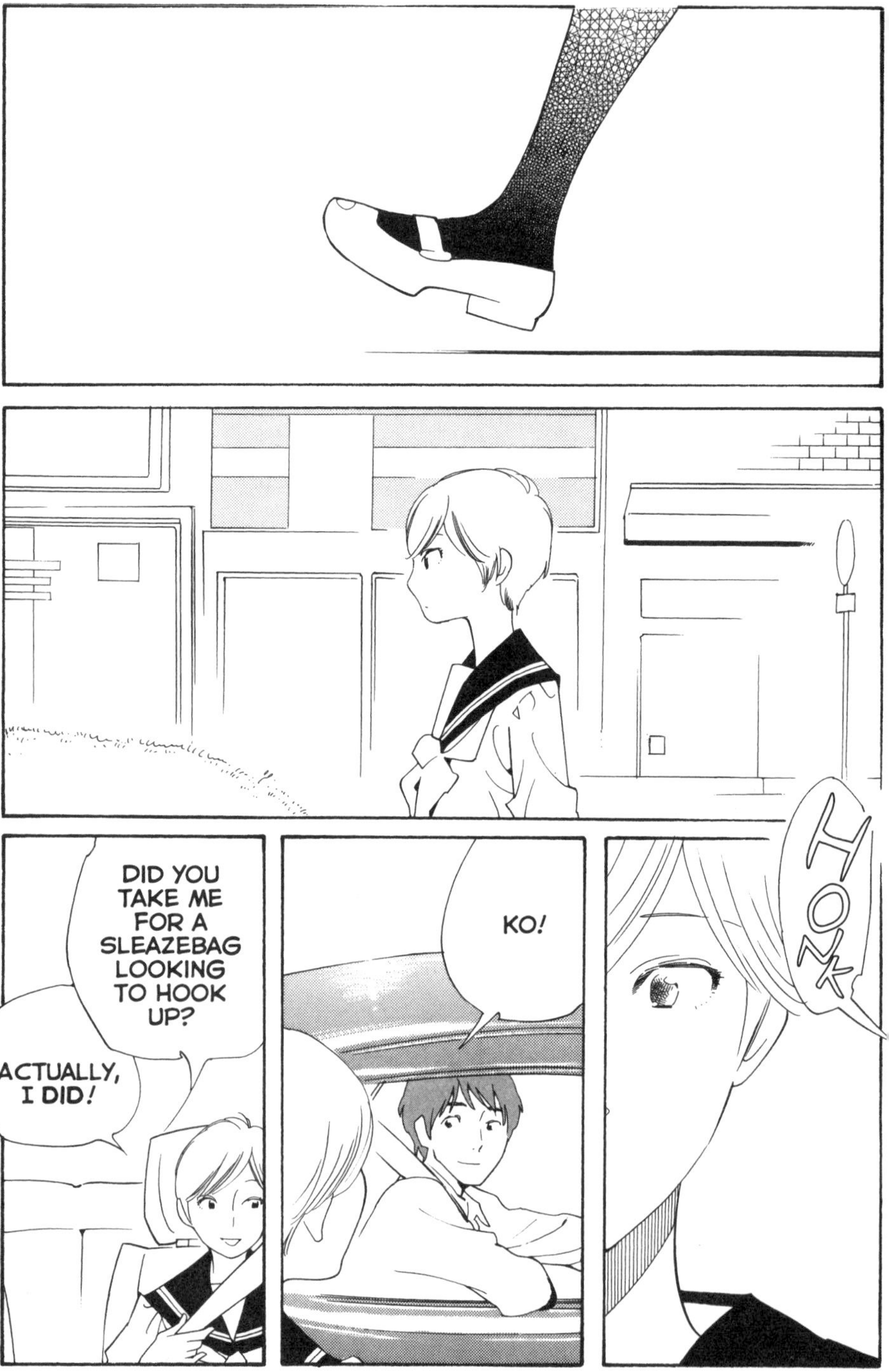
HONK
KO!
DID YOU TAKE ME FOR A SLEAZEBAG LOOKING TO HOOK UP?
ACTUALLY, I DID!

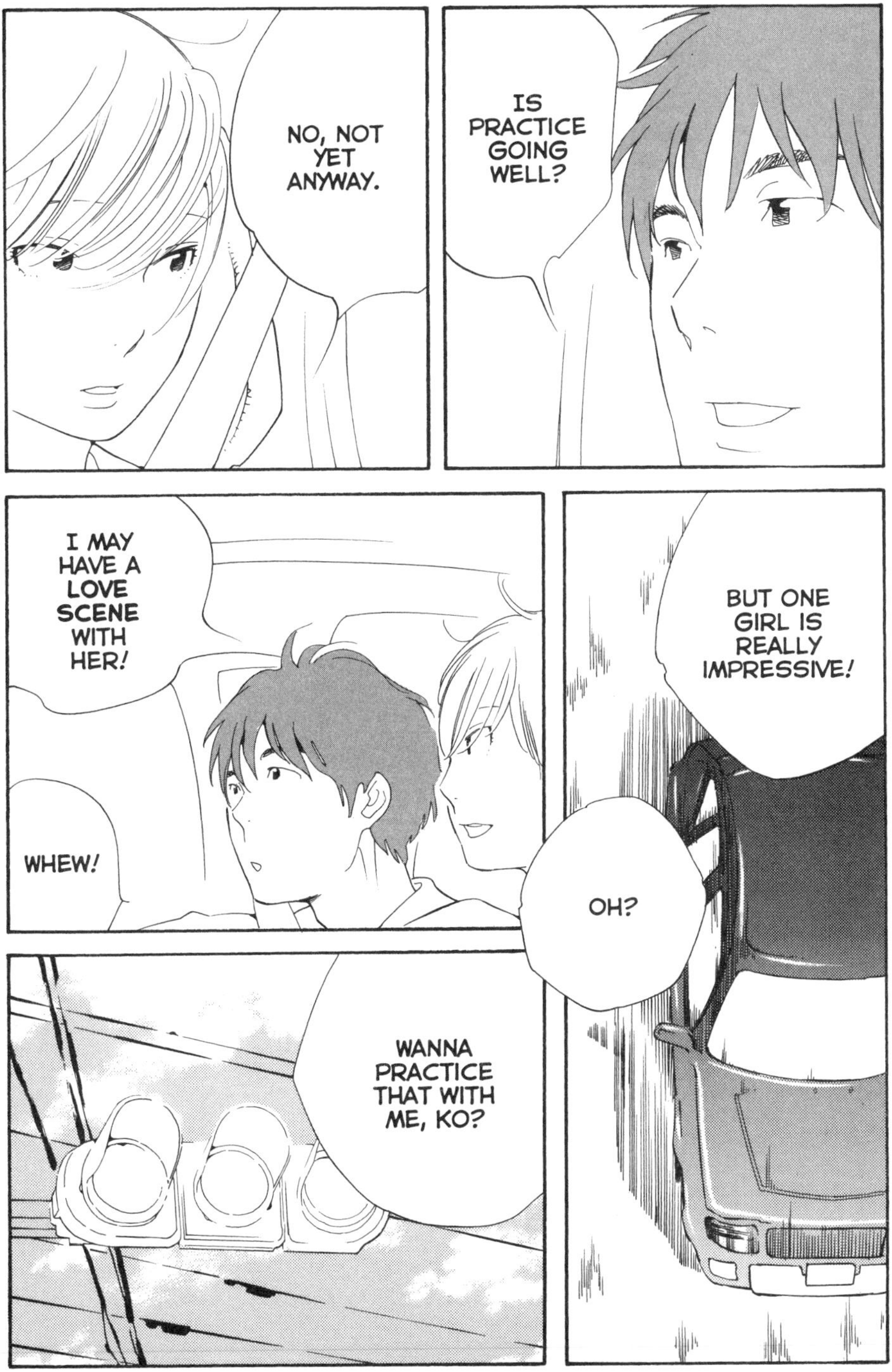
IS PRACTICE GOING WELL?
NO, NOT YET ANYWAY.
BUT ONE GIRL IS REALLY IMPRESSIVE!
OH?
I MAY HAVE A LOVE SCENE WITH HER!
WHEW!
WANNA PRACTICE THAT WITH ME, KO?

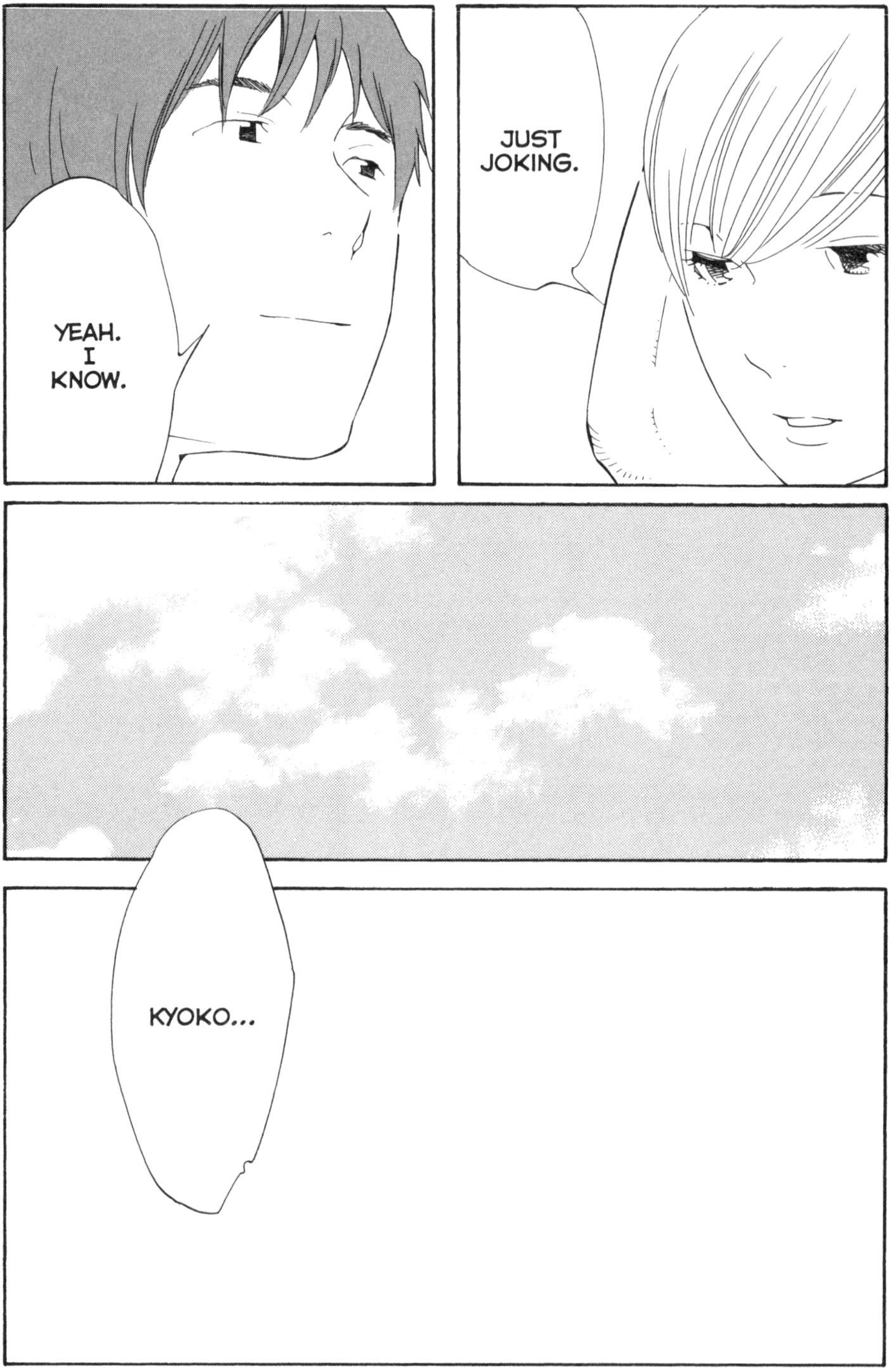
JUST JOKING.
YEAH. I KNOW.
KYOKO...

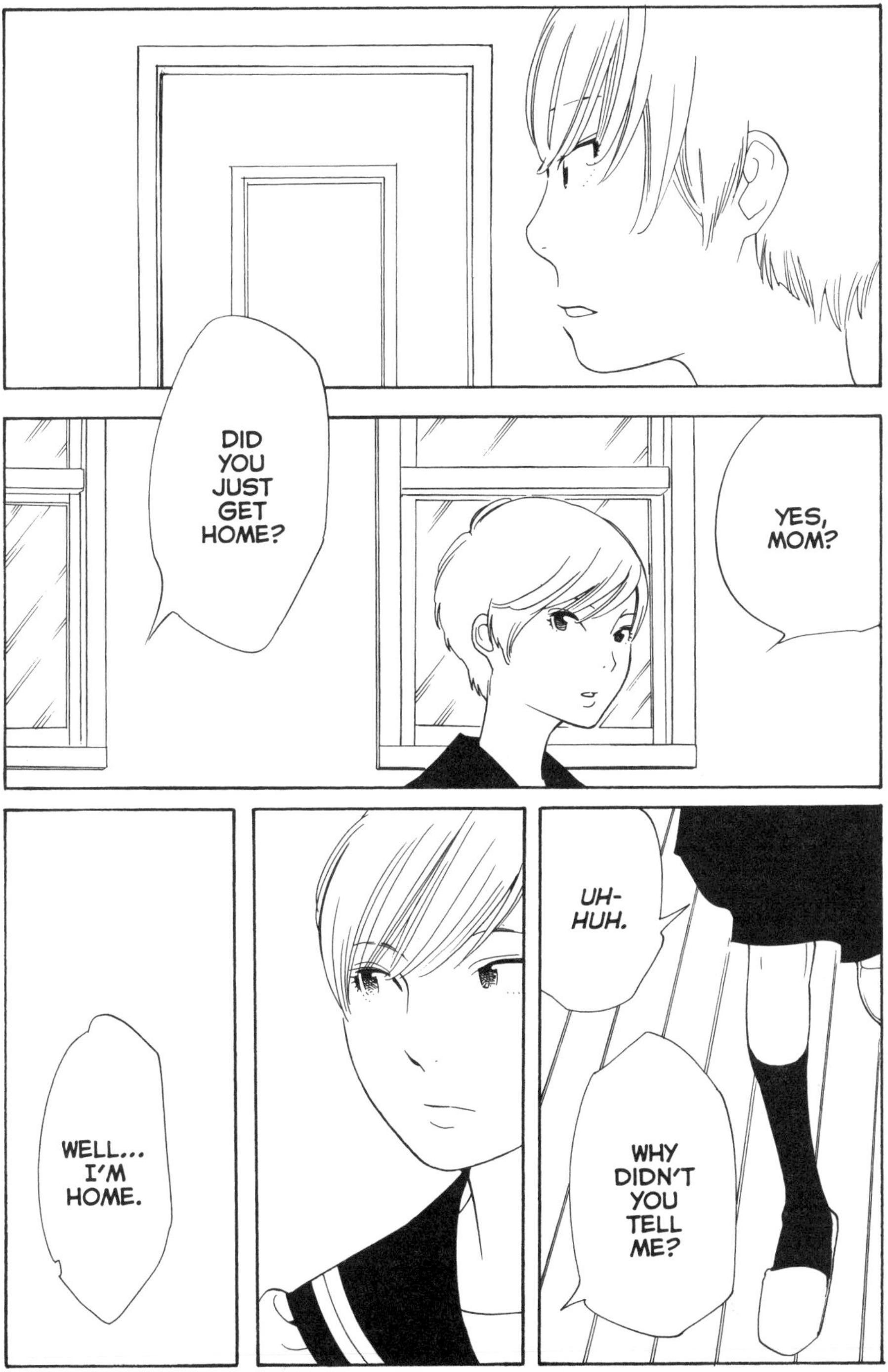
YES, MOM?
DID YOU JUST GET HOME?
UH-HUH.
WHY DIDN'T YOU TELL ME?
WELL... I'M HOME.

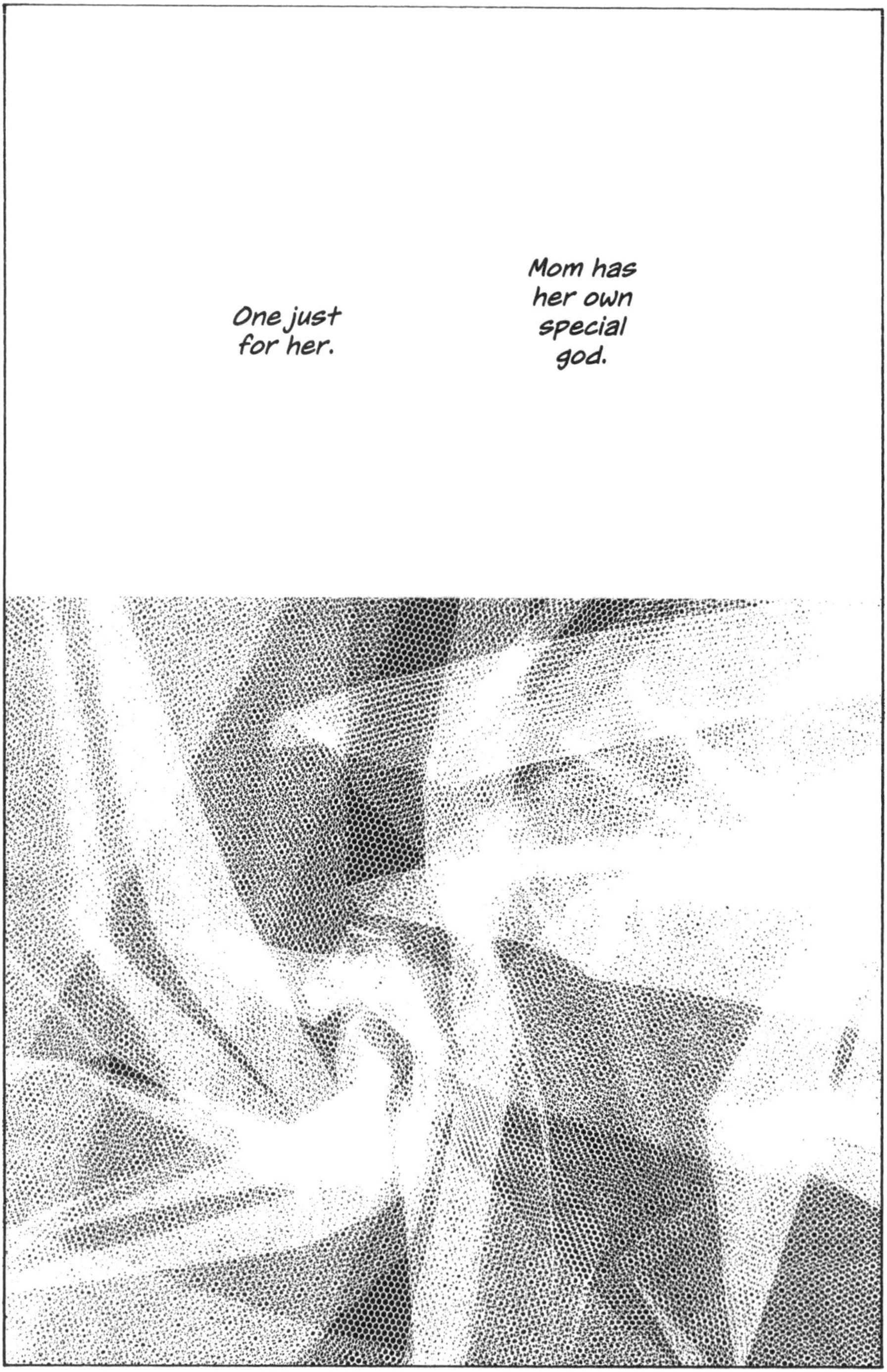
Mom has her own special god.
One just for her.

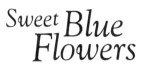

Sweet Blue Flowers

#24 Rokumeikan, Part 4

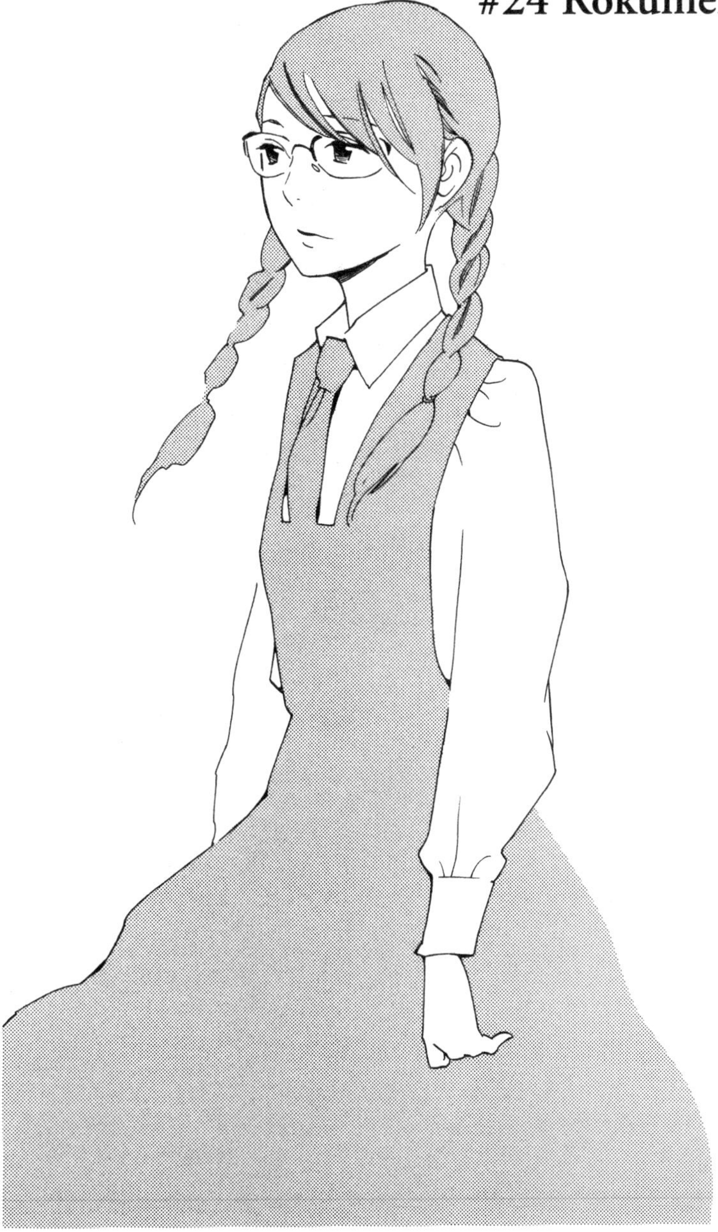

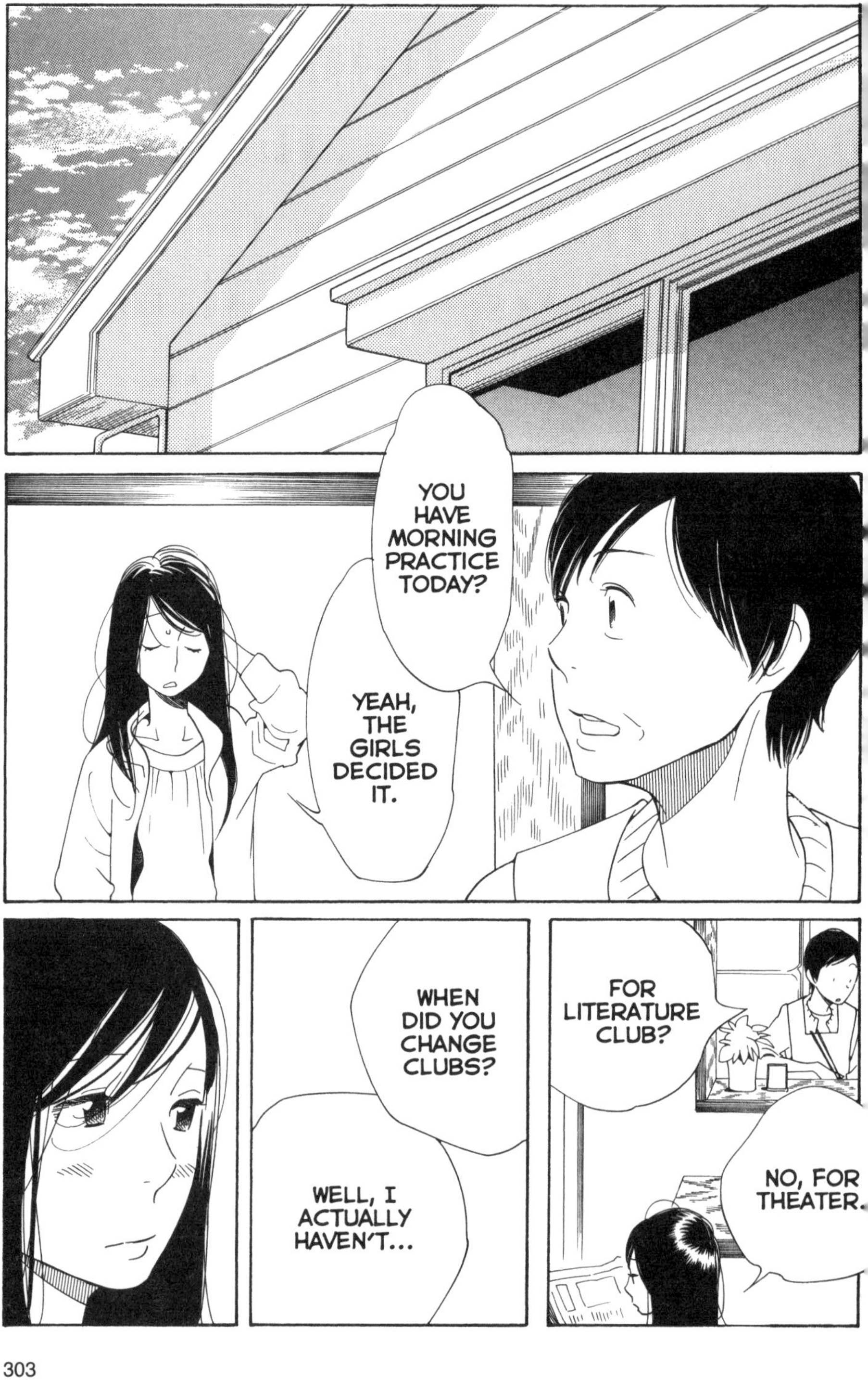
YOU HAVE MORNING PRACTICE TODAY?
YEAH, THE GIRLS DECIDED IT.
FOR LITERATURE CLUB?
NO, FOR THEATER.
WHEN DID YOU CHANGE CLUBS?
WELL, I ACTUALLY HAVEN'T...

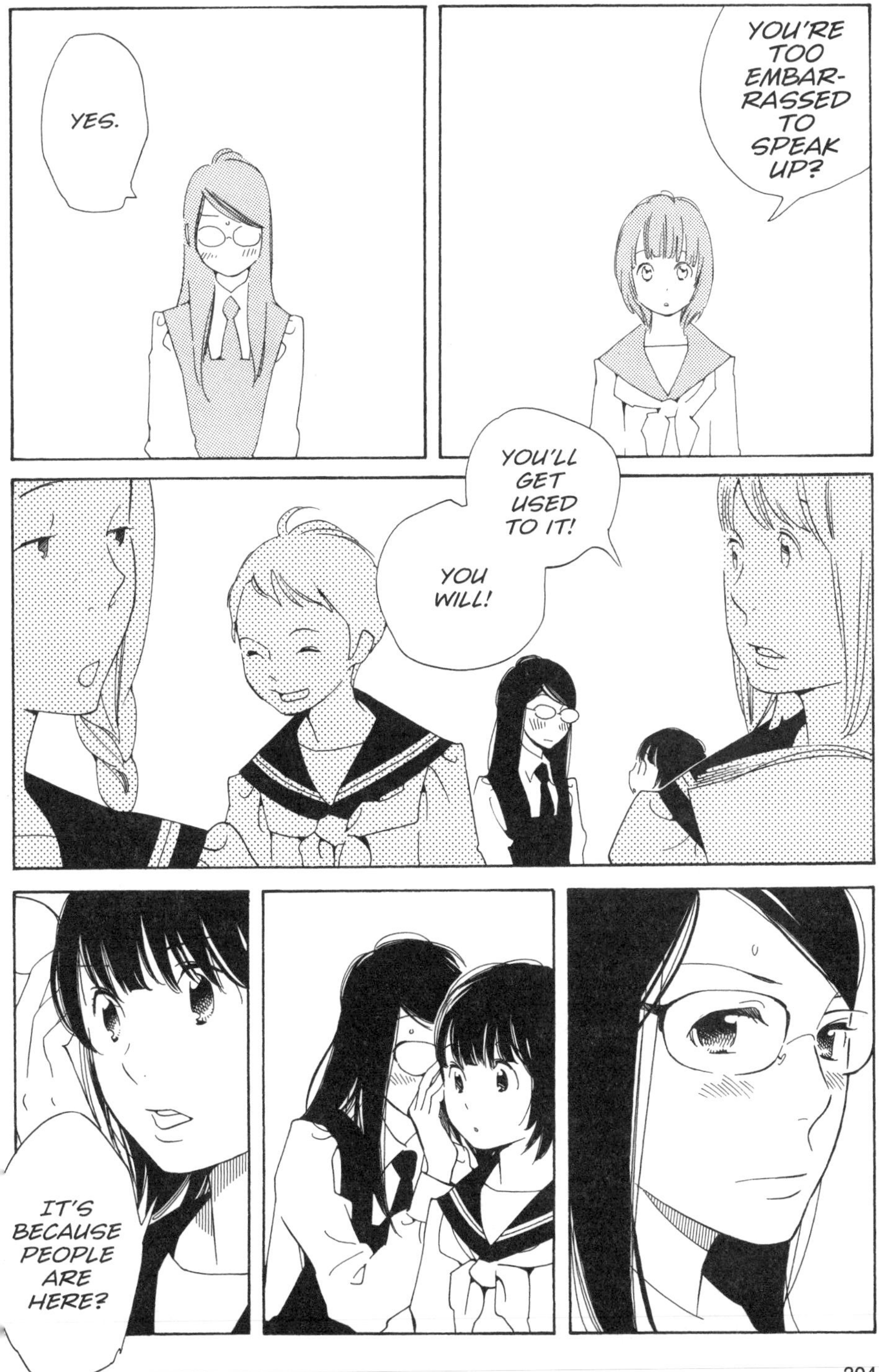
YOU'RE TOO EMBAR-RASSED TO SPEAK UP?
YES.
YOU'LL GET USED TO IT!
YOU WILL!
IT'S BECAUSE PEOPLE ARE HERE?

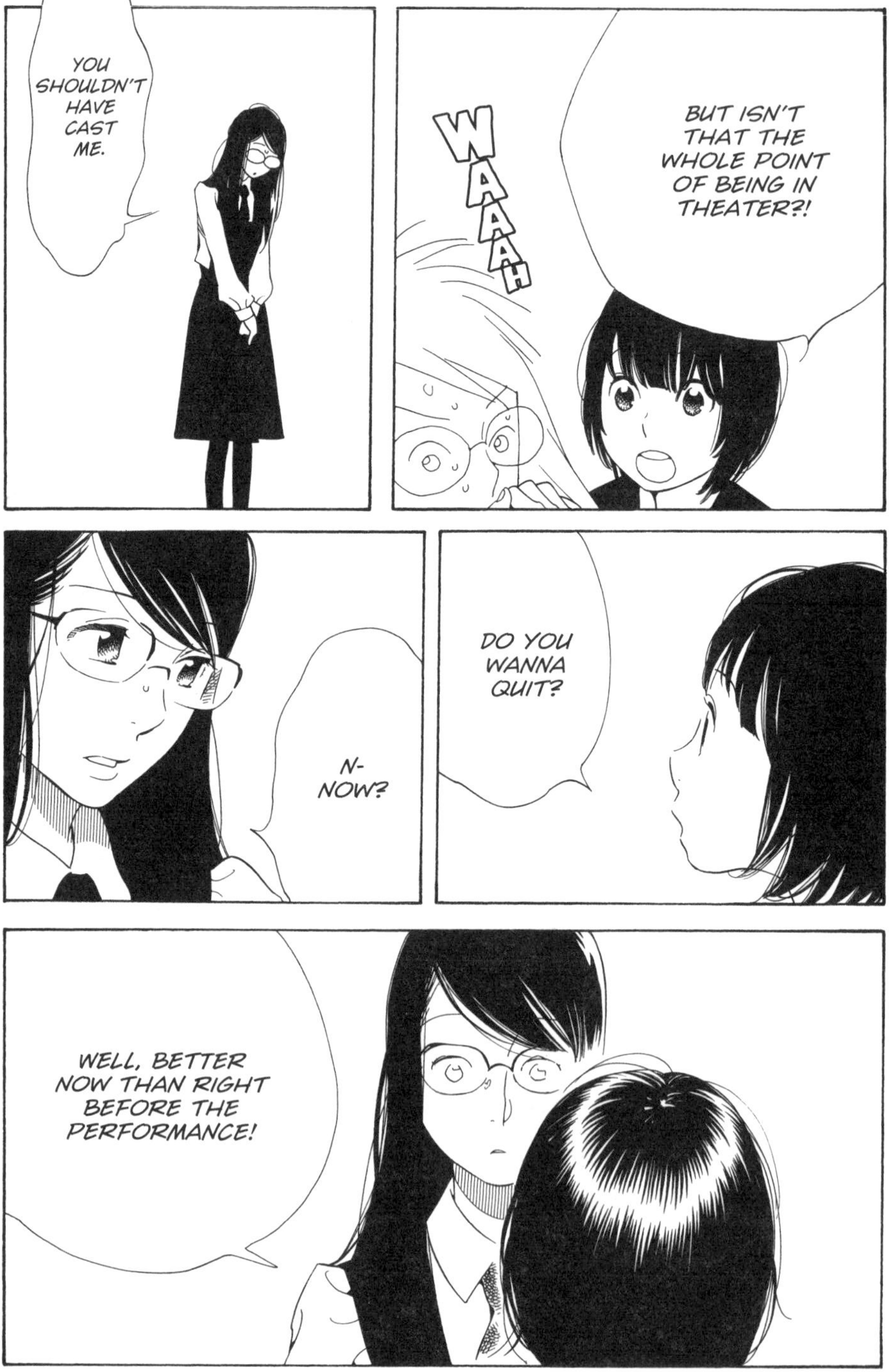
BUT ISN'T THAT THE WHOLE POINT OF BEING IN THEATER?!
WAAAAH
YOU SHOULDN'T HAVE CAST ME.
DO YOU WANNA QUIT?
N-NOW?
WELL, BETTER NOW THAN RIGHT BEFORE THE PERFORMANCE!

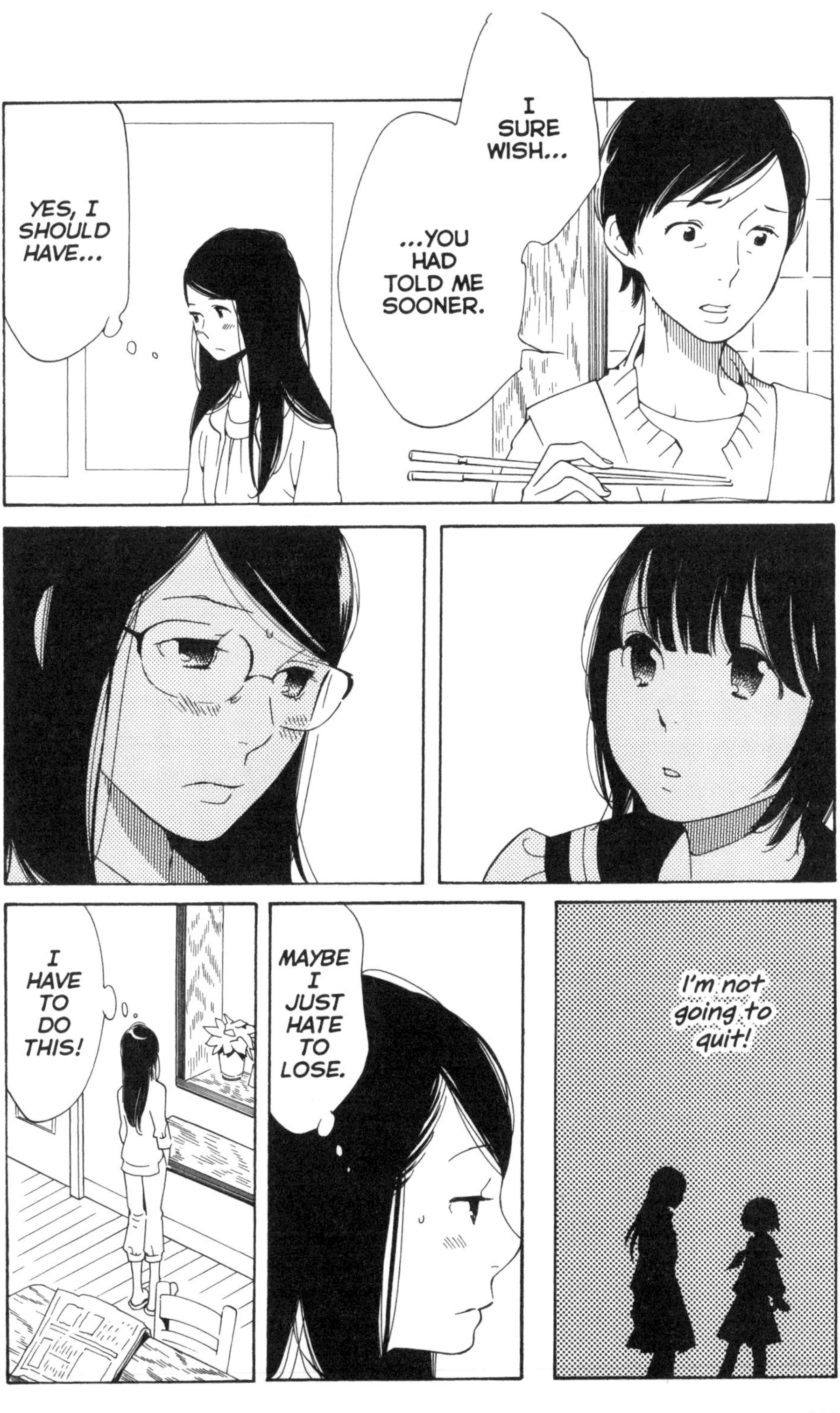
I SURE WISH...
...YOU HAD TOLD ME SOONER.
YES, I SHOULD HAVE...
I'm not going to quit!
MAYBE I JUST HATE TO LOSE.
I HAVE TO DO THIS!

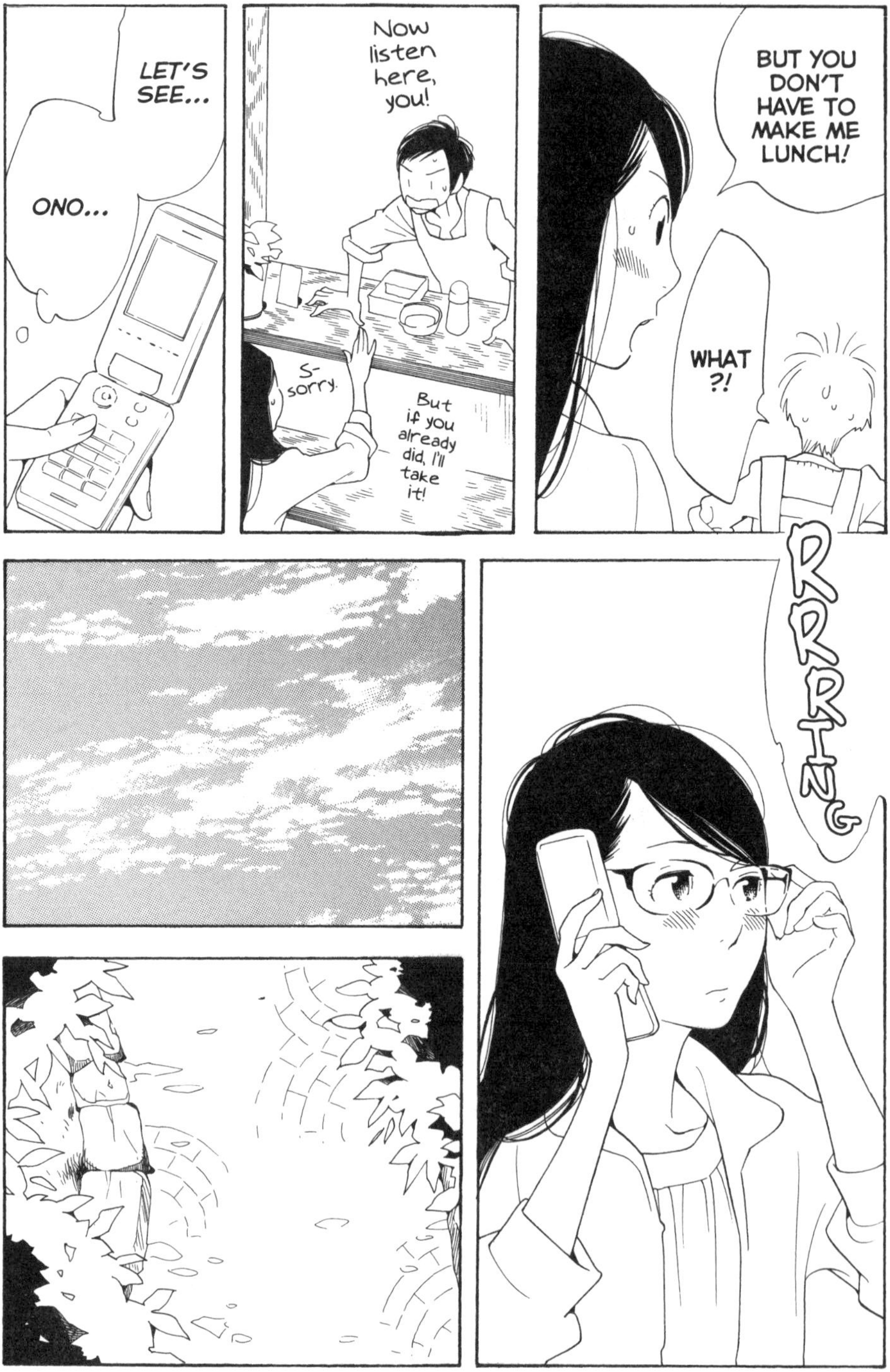

BUT YOU DON'T HAVE TO MAKE ME LUNCH!
WHAT?!
Now listen here, you!
S-sorry.
But if you already did, I'll take it!
LET'S SEE...
ONO...
RRRING

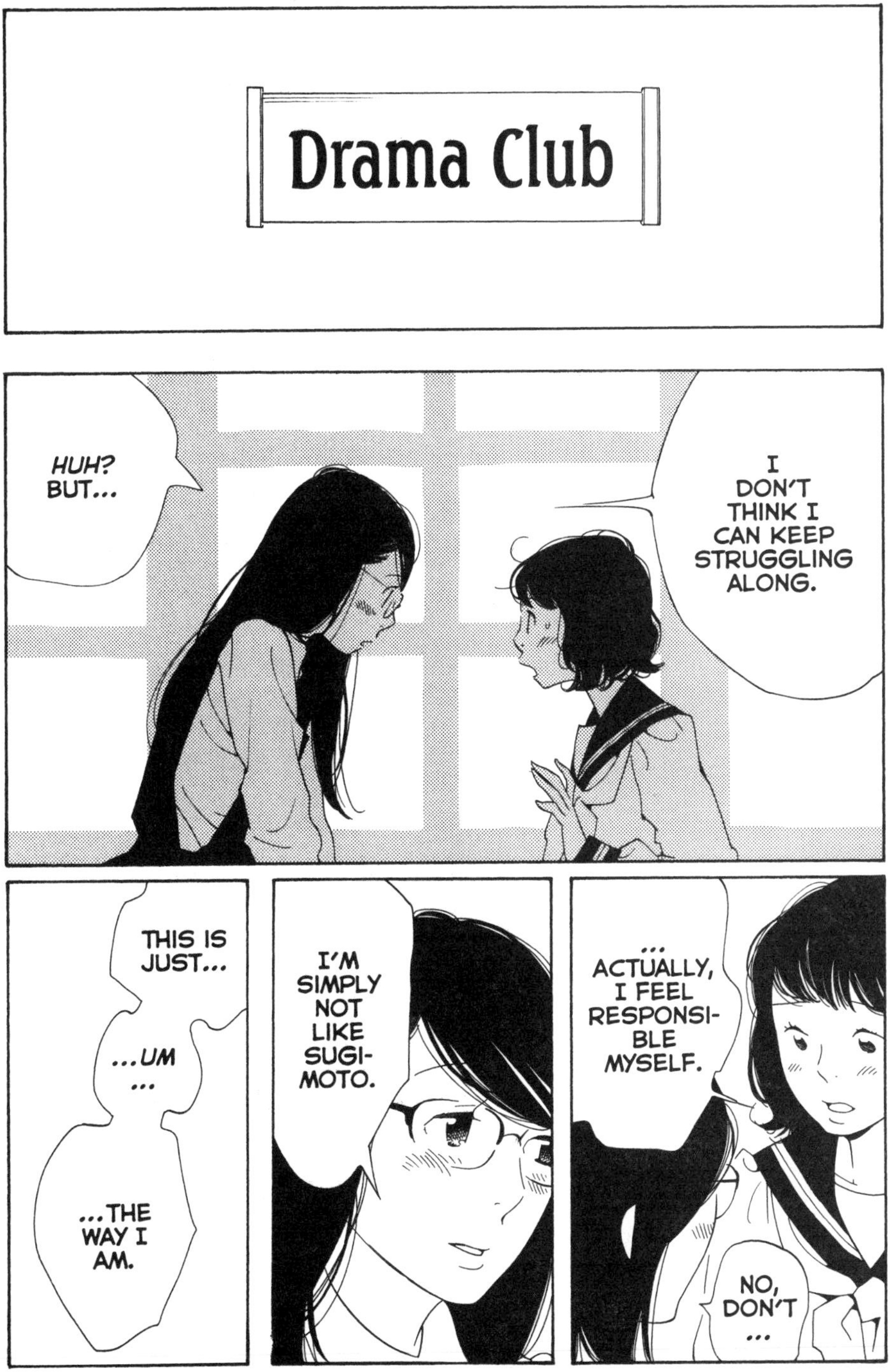
Drama Club
I DON'T THINK I CAN KEEP STRUGGLING ALONG.
HUH? BUT...
... ACTUALLY, I FEEL RESPONSIBLE MYSELF.
NO, DON'T ...
I'M SIMPLY NOT LIKE SUGIMOTO.
THIS IS JUST...
...UM ...
...THE WAY I AM.

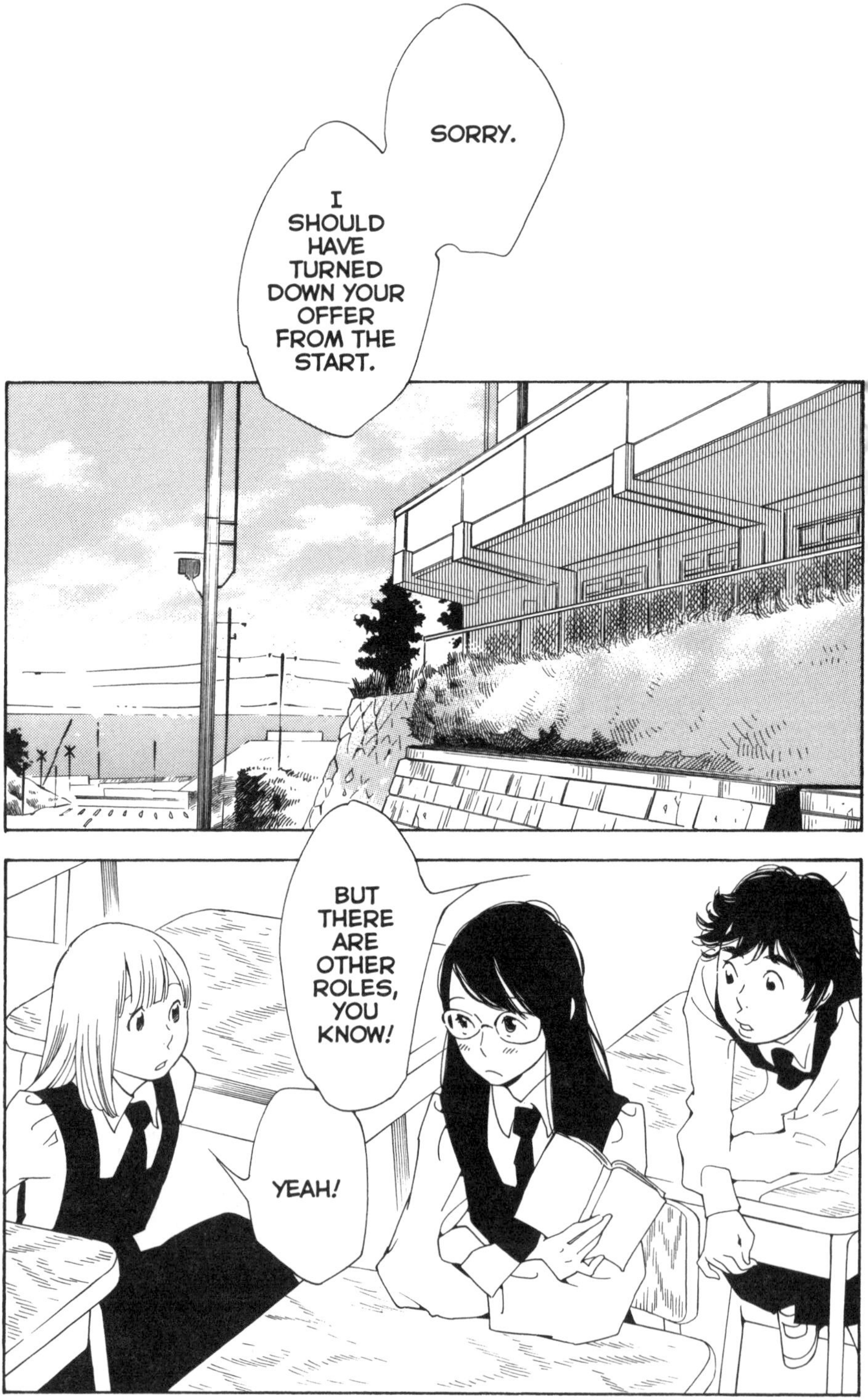
SORRY.
I SHOULD HAVE TURNED DOWN YOUR OFFER FROM THE START.
BUT THERE ARE OTHER ROLES, YOU KNOW!
YEAH!

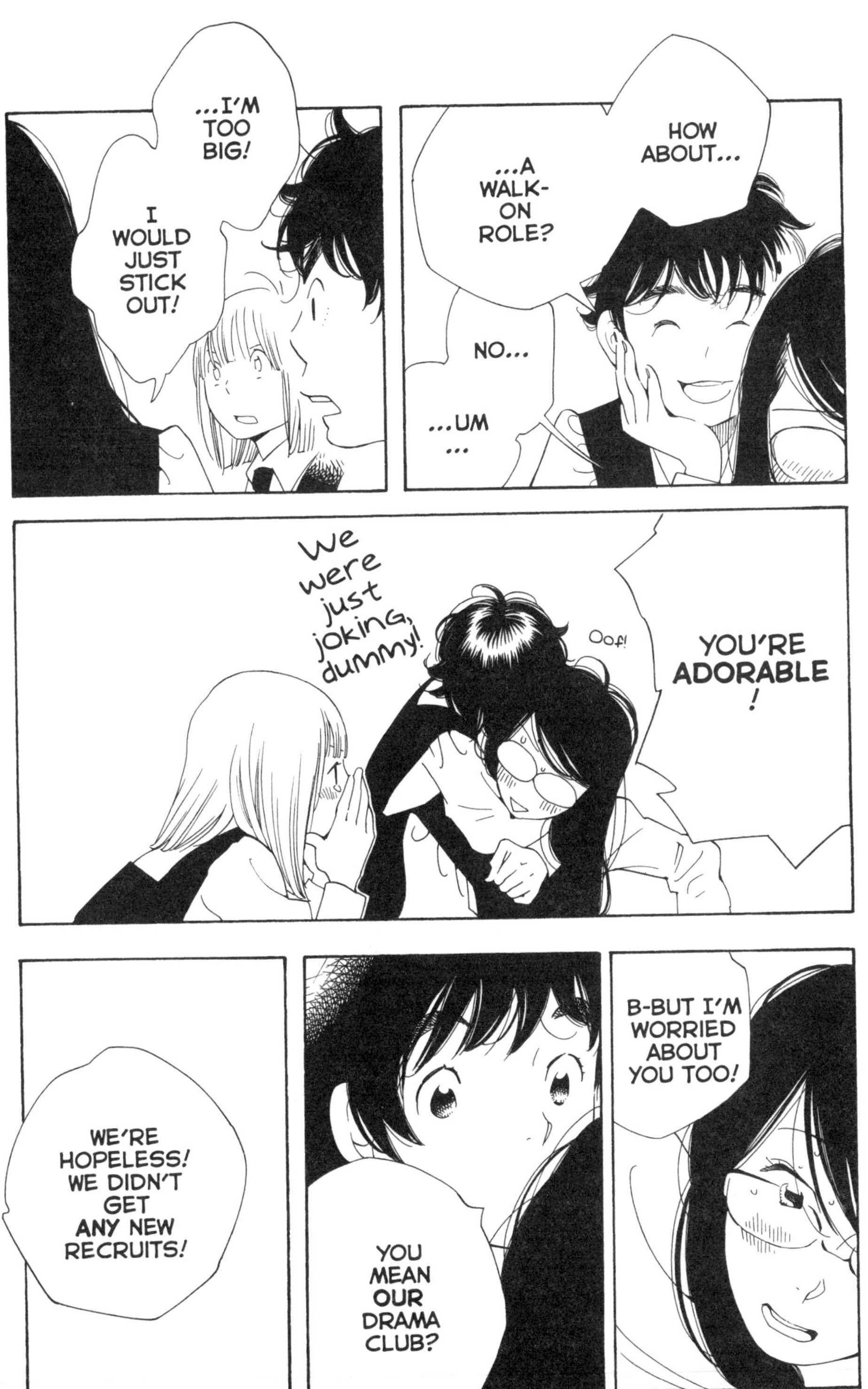
HOW ABOUT...
...A WALK-ON ROLE?
NO...
...UM ...
...I'M TOO BIG!
I WOULD JUST STICK OUT!
YOU'RE ADORABLE!
Oof!
We were just joking, dummy!
B-BUT I'M WORRIED ABOUT YOU TOO!
YOU MEAN OUR DRAMA CLUB?
WE'RE HOPELESS! WE DIDN'T GET ANY NEW RECRUITS!

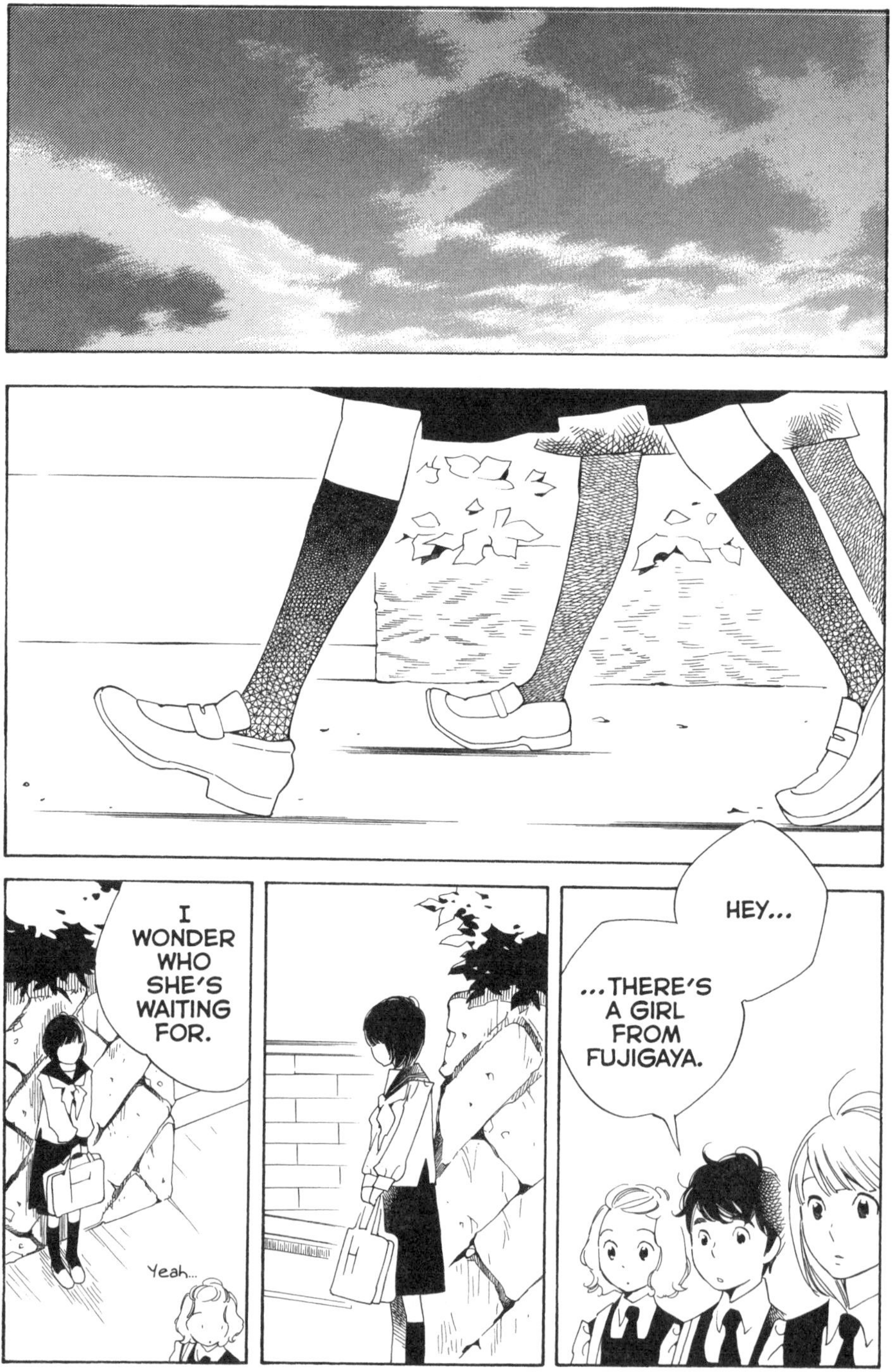
HEY...
...THERE'S A GIRL FROM FUJIGAYA.
I WONDER WHO SHE'S WAITING FOR.
Yeah...

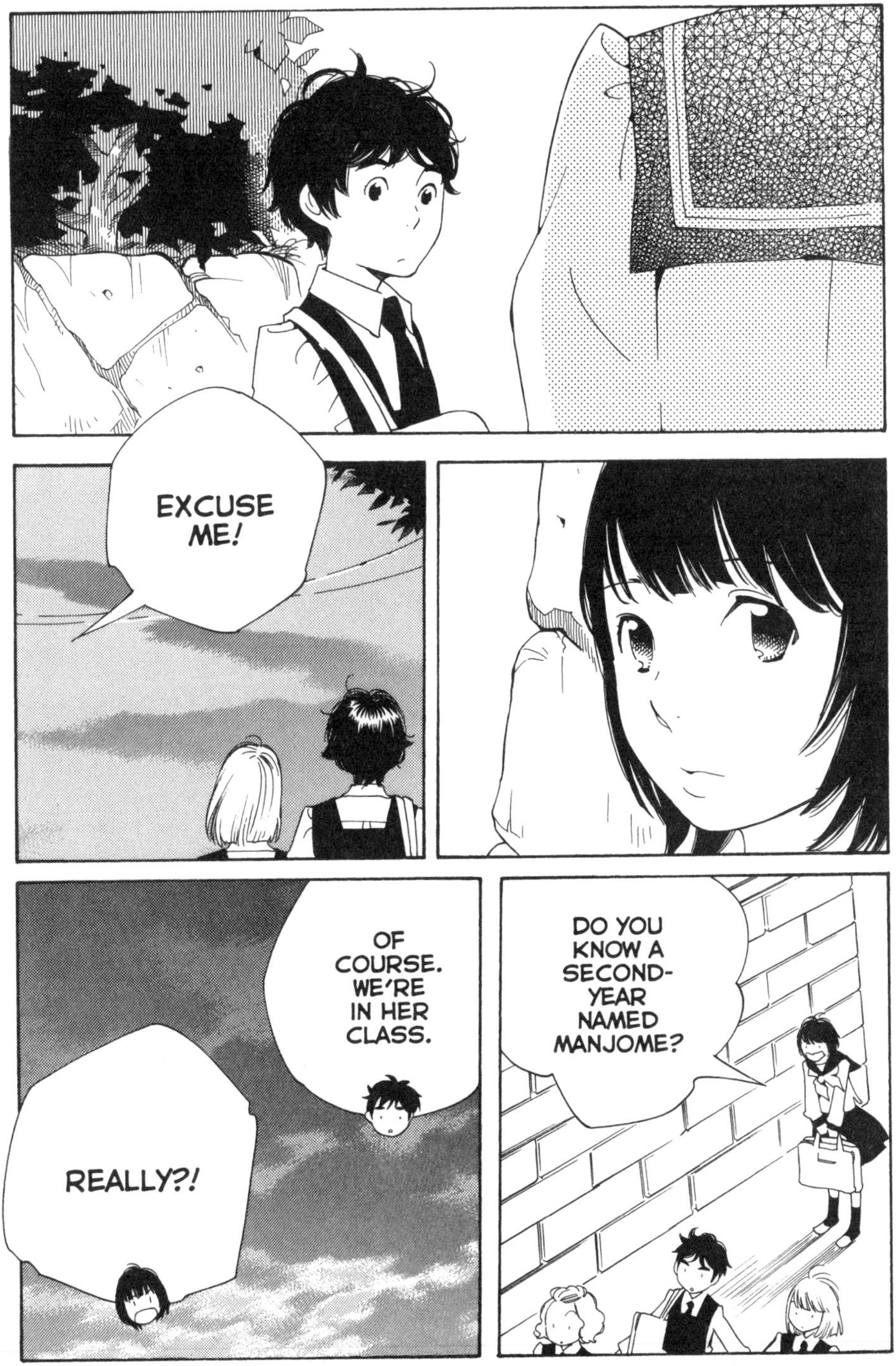
EXCUSE ME!
DO YOU KNOW A SECOND-YEAR NAMED MANJOME?
OF COURSE. WE'RE IN HER CLASS.
REALLY?!

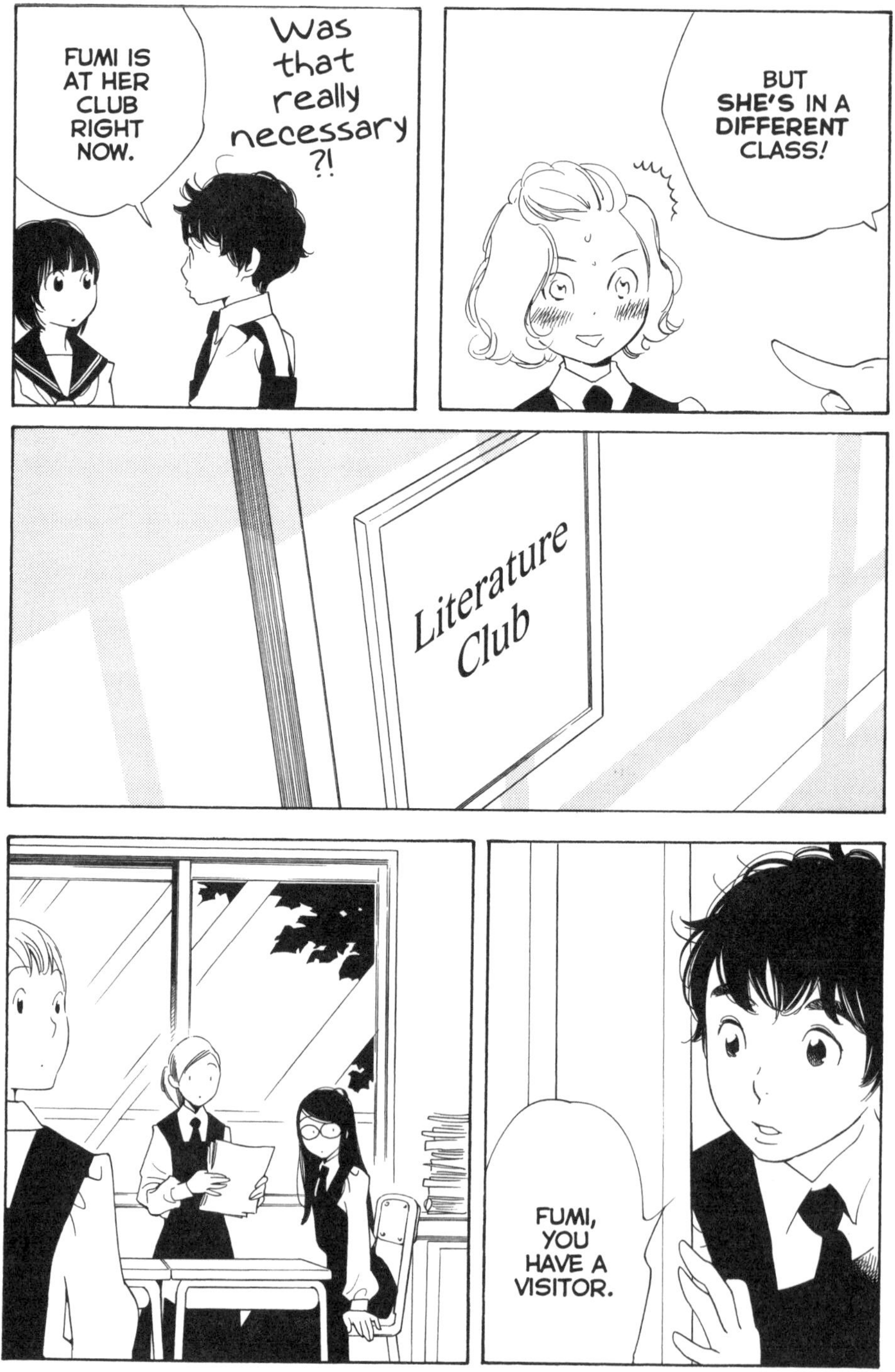
BUT SHE'S IN A DIFFERENT CLASS!
Was that really necessary?!
FUMI IS AT HER CLUB RIGHT NOW.
Literature Club
FUMI, YOU HAVE A VISITOR.

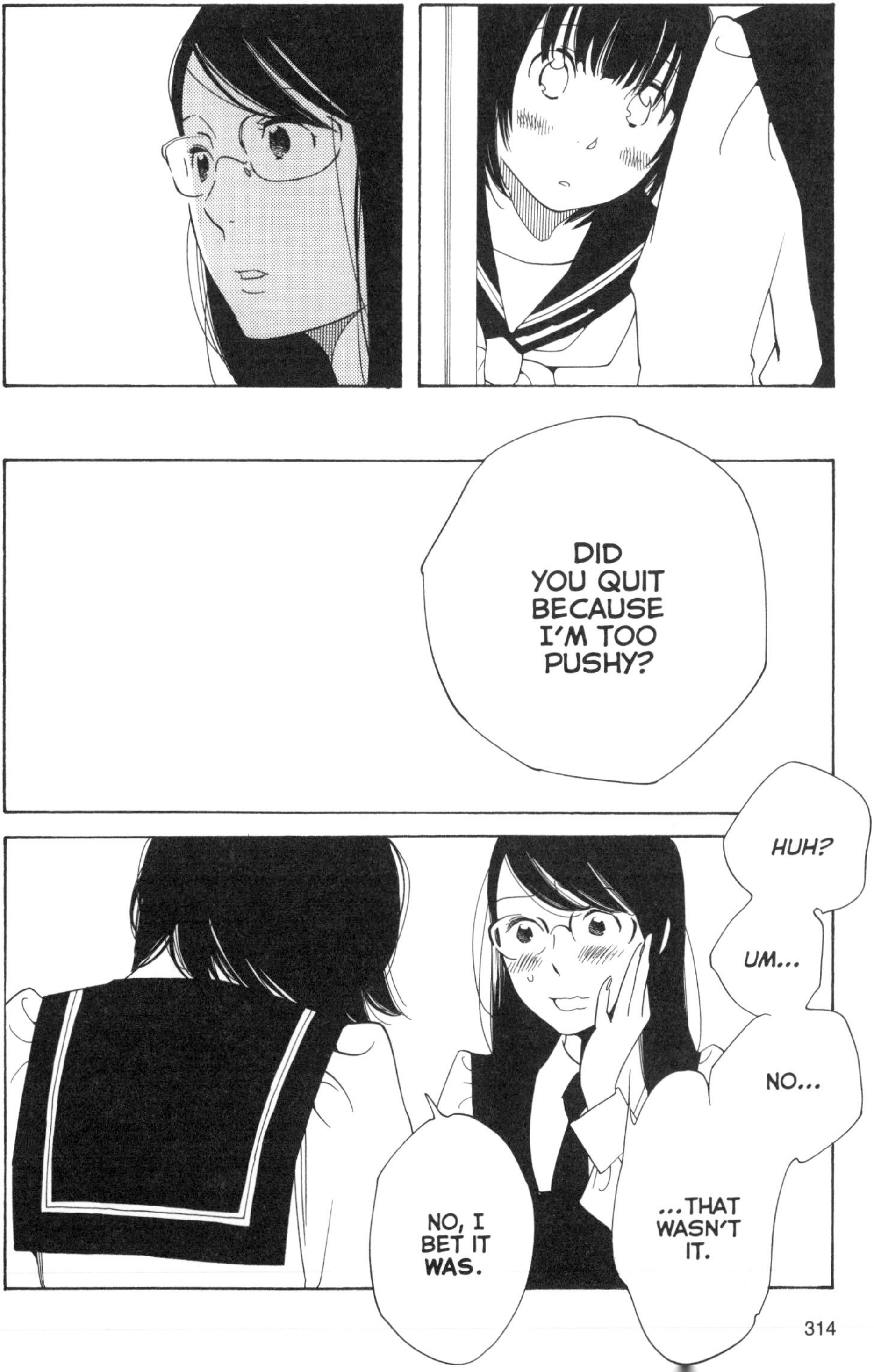
DID YOU QUIT BECAUSE I'M TOO PUSHY?
HUH?
UM...
NO...
...THAT WASN'T IT.
NO, I BET IT WAS.

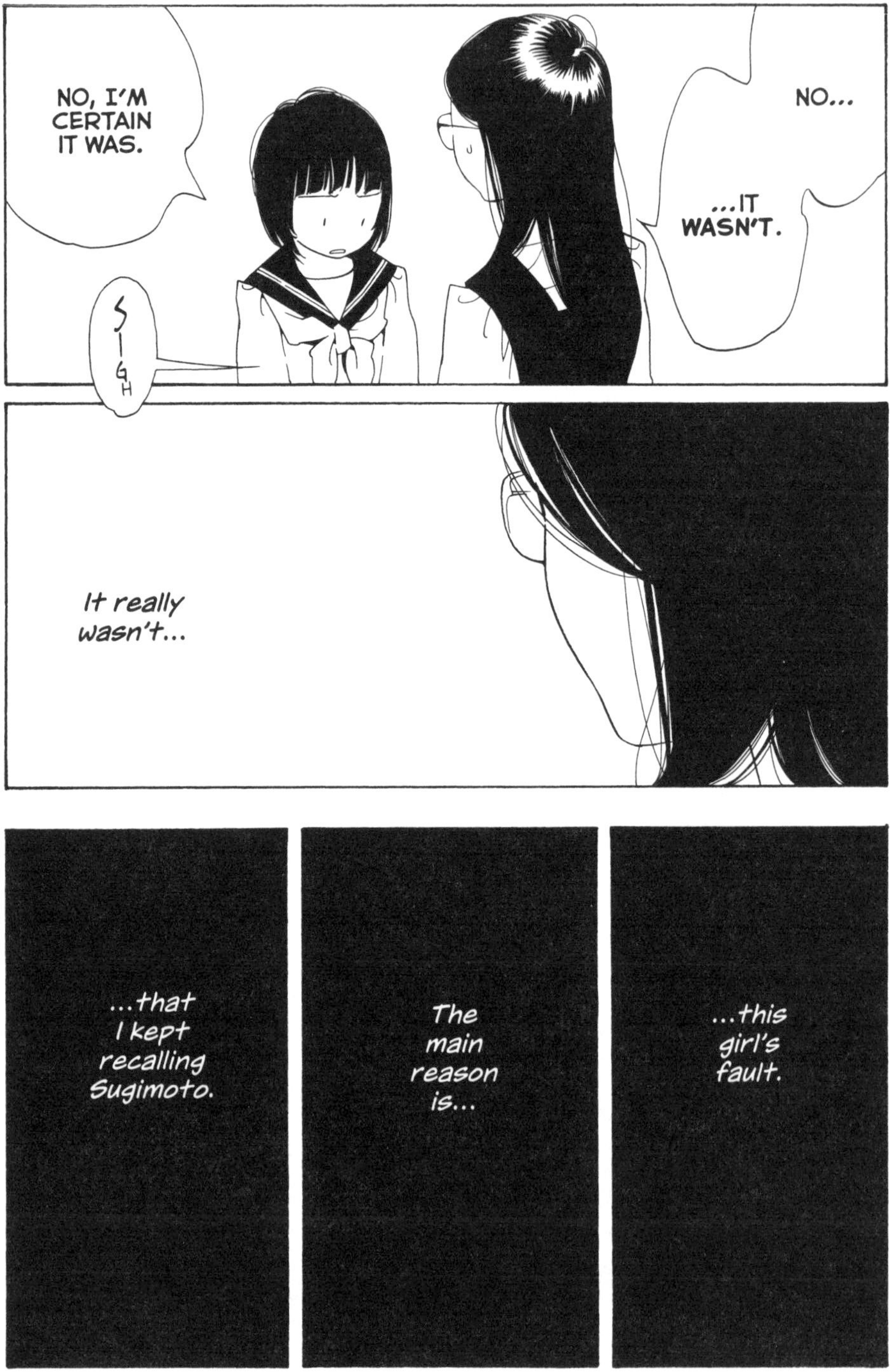
NO...
...IT WASN'T.
NO, I'M CERTAIN IT WAS.
SIGH
It really wasn't...
...this girl's fault.
The main reason is...
...that I kept recalling Sugimoto.

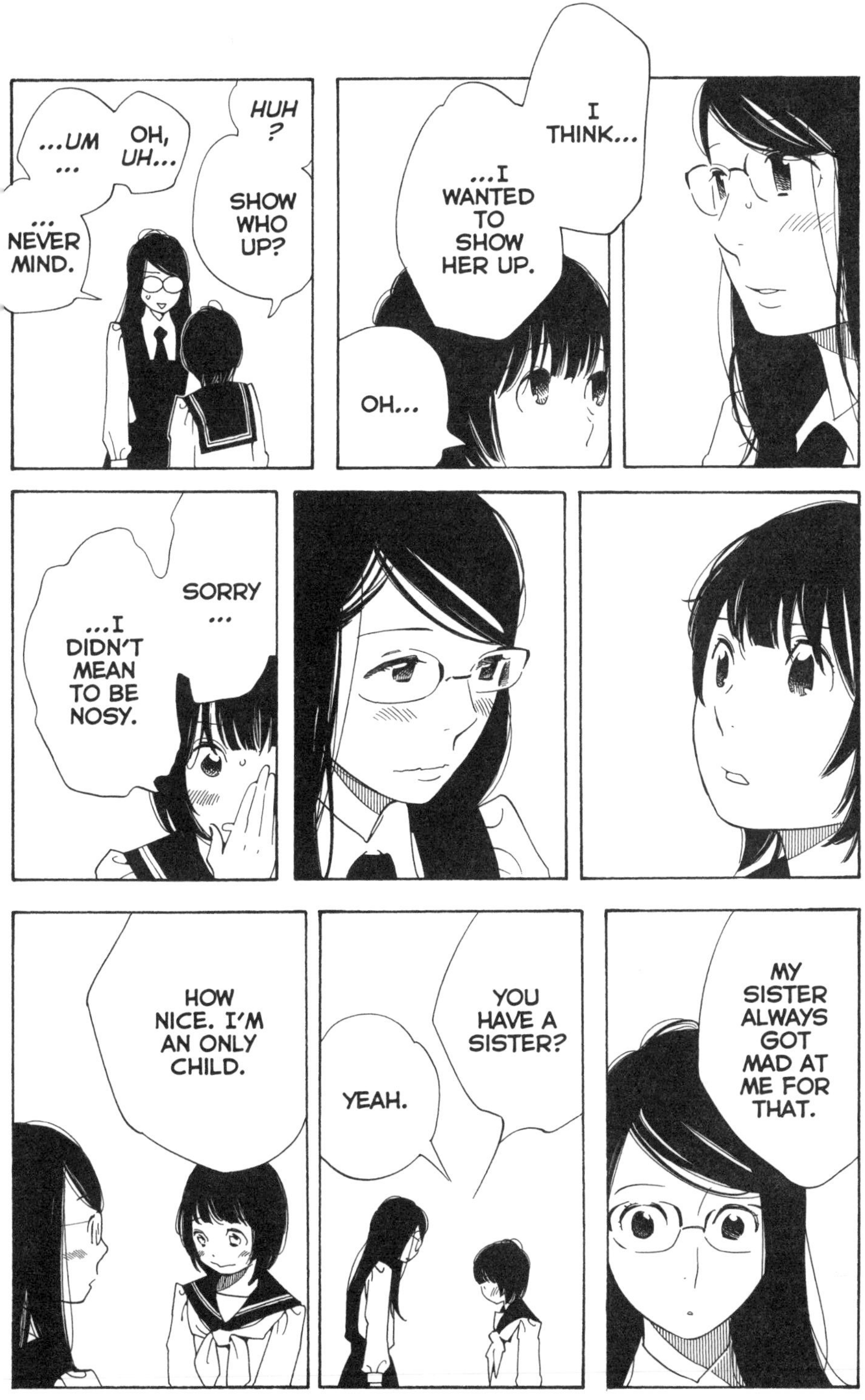
I THINK...
...I WANTED TO SHOW HER UP.
OH...
HUH?
SHOW WHO UP?
OH, UH...
...UM...
...NEVER MIND.
SORRY...
...I DIDN'T MEAN TO BE NOSY.
MY SISTER ALWAYS GOT MAD AT ME FOR THAT.
YOU HAVE A SISTER?
YEAH.
HOW NICE. I'M AN ONLY CHILD.

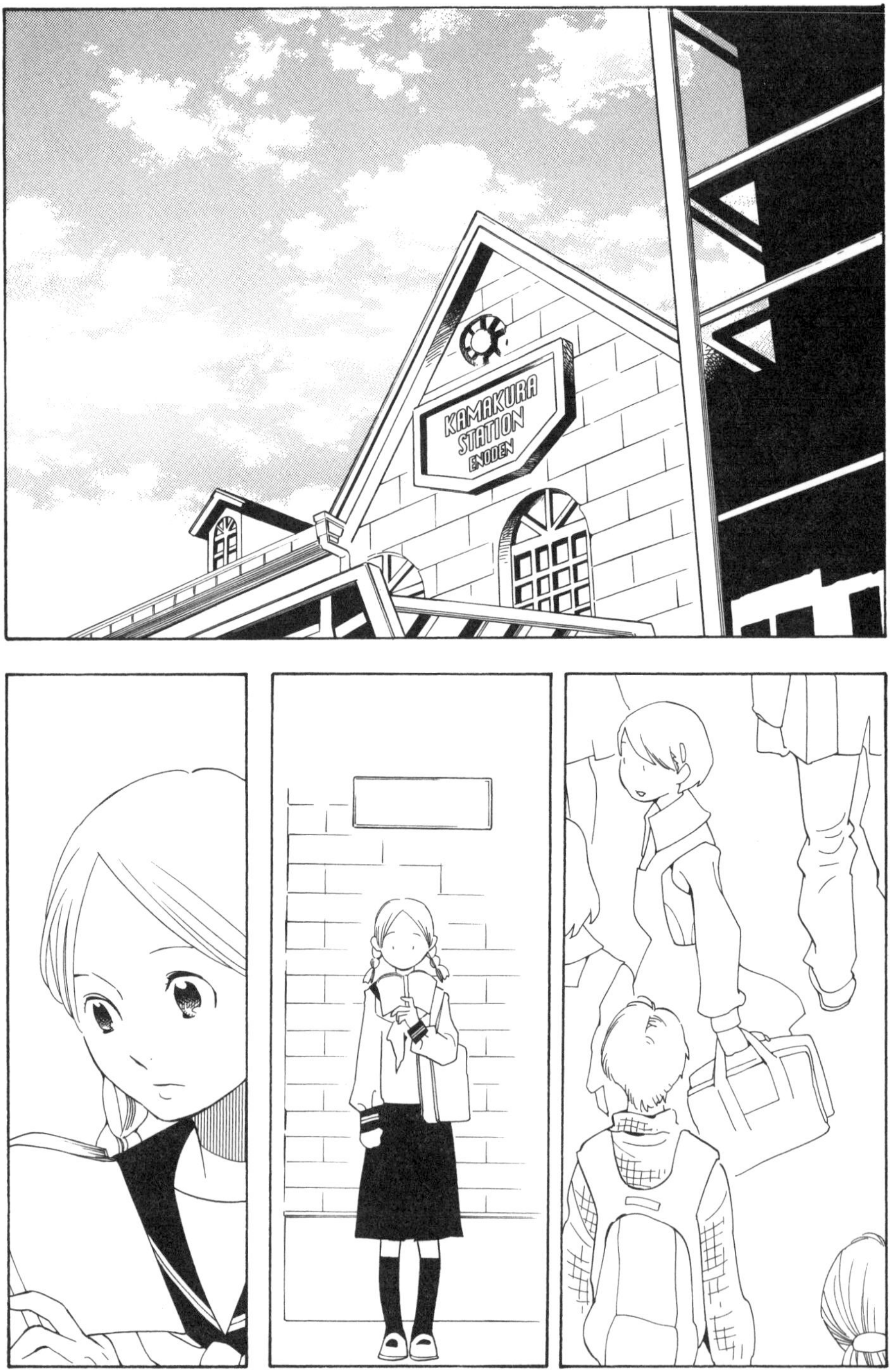
KAMAKURA STATION
ENODEN

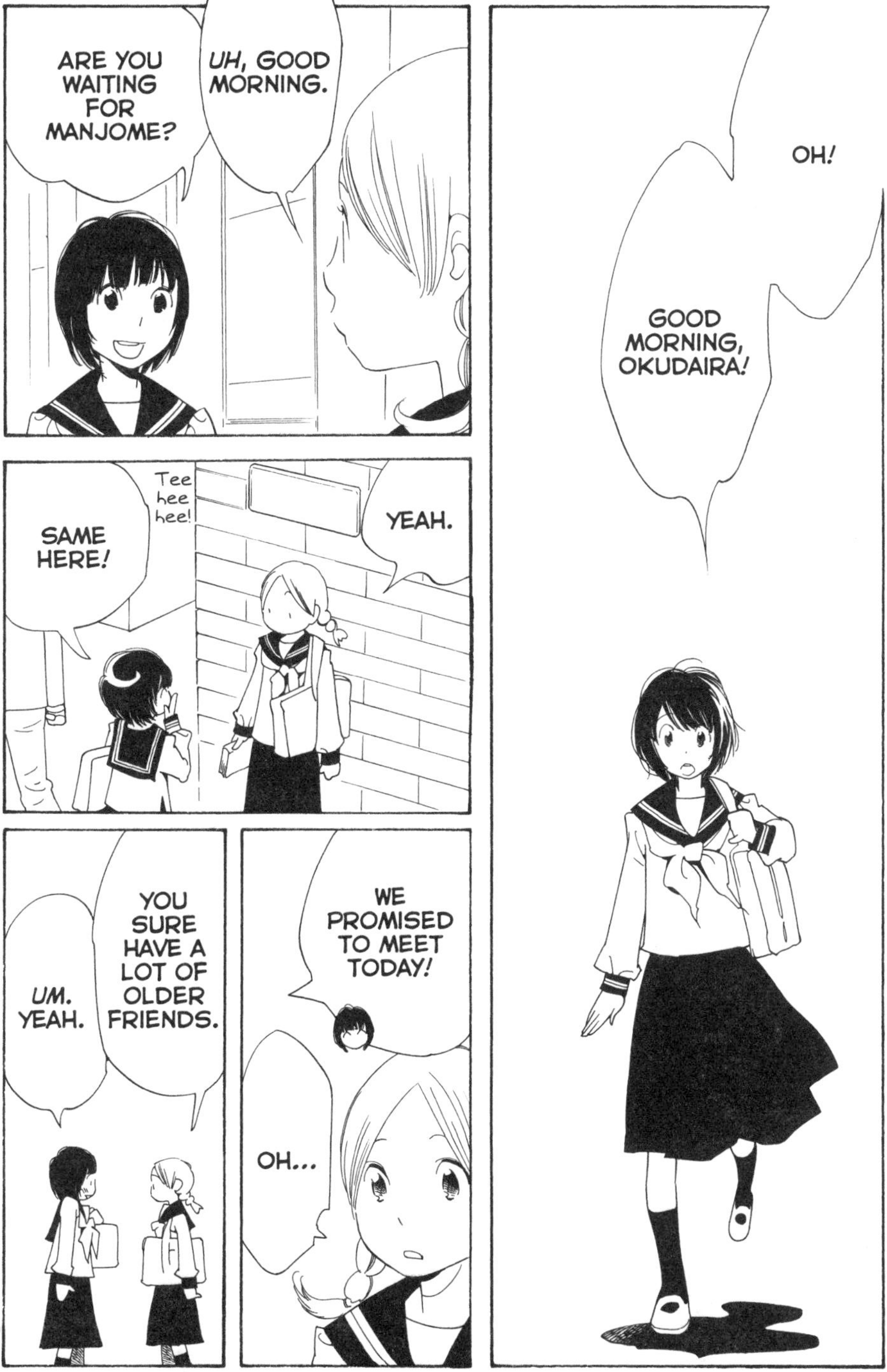
OH!
GOOD MORNING, OKUDAIRA!
UH, GOOD MORNING.
ARE YOU WAITING FOR MANJOME?
YEAH.
Tee hee hee!
SAME HERE!
WE PROMISED TO MEET TODAY!
OH...
YOU SURE HAVE A LOT OF OLDER FRIENDS.
UM. YEAH.

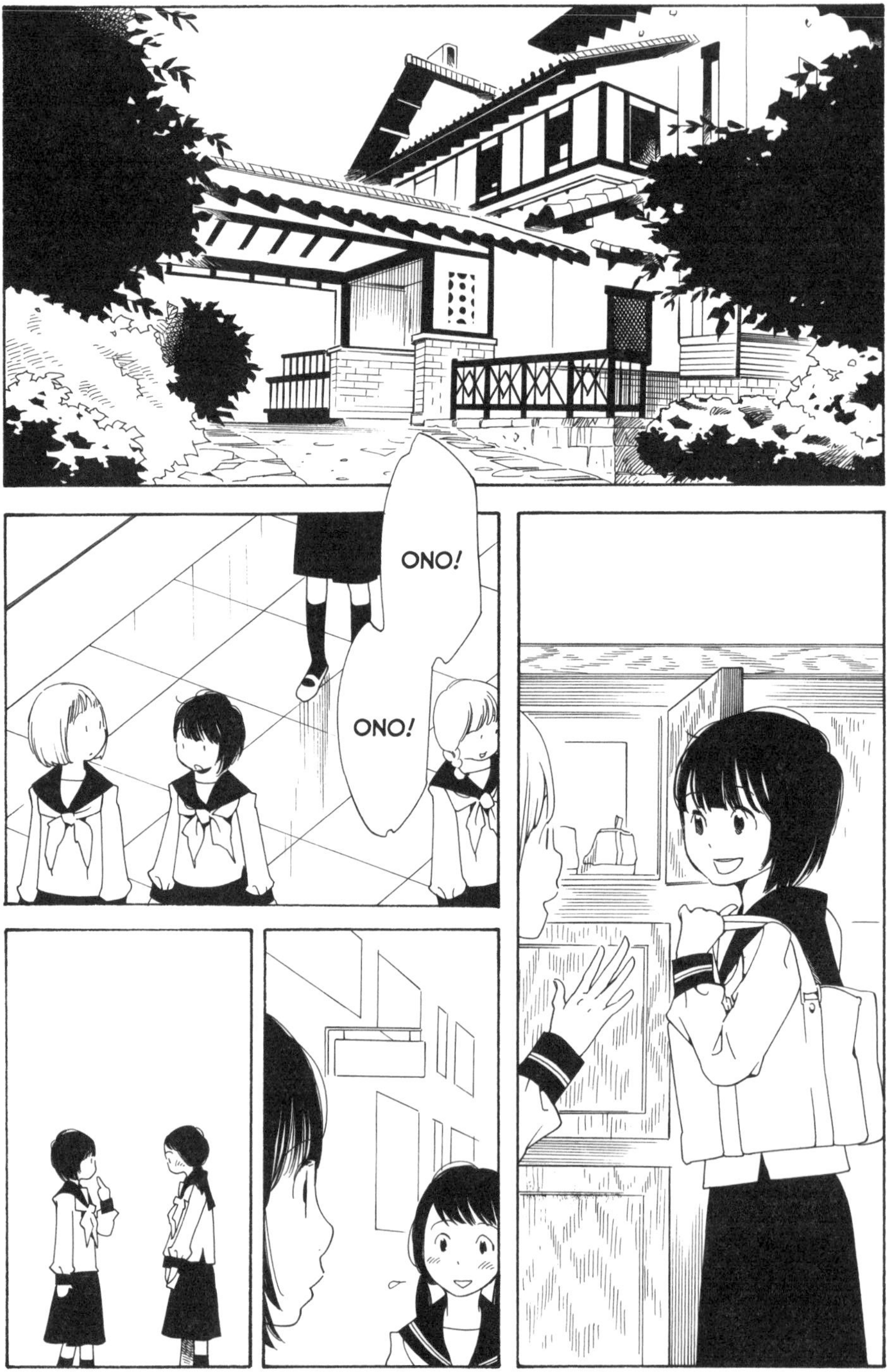
ONO!
ONO!

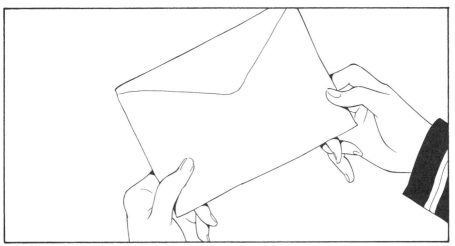

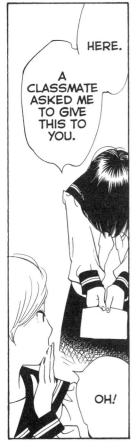

HERE.

A CLASSMATE ASKED ME TO GIVE THIS TO YOU.

OH!

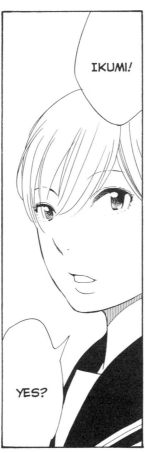

IKUMI!

YES?

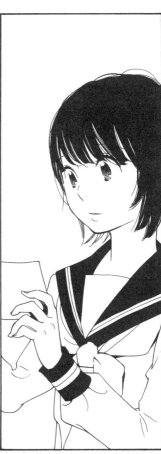

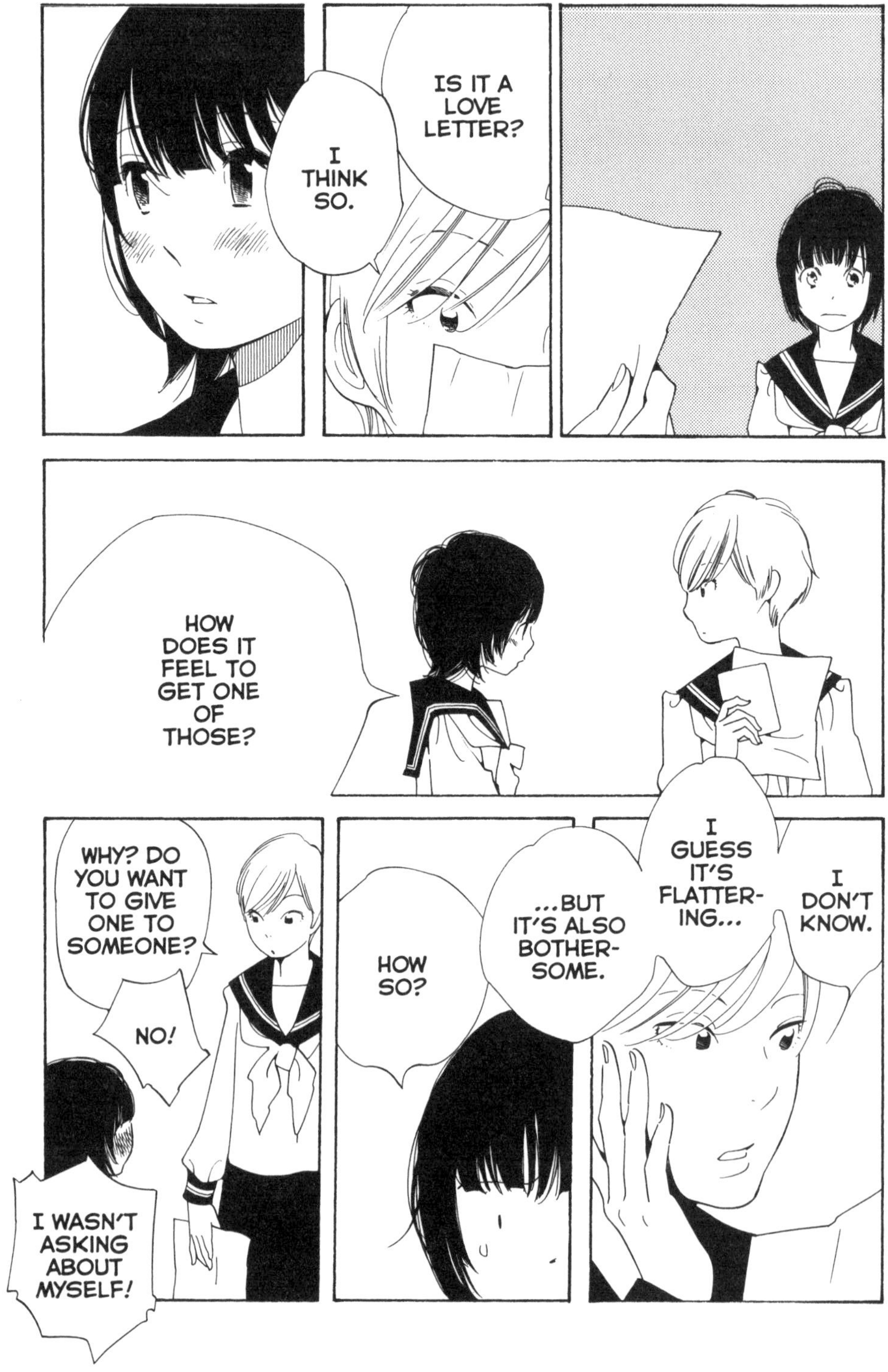
IS IT A LOVE LETTER?
I THINK SO.
HOW DOES IT FEEL TO GET ONE OF THOSE?
I DON'T KNOW.
I GUESS IT'S FLATTER-ING...
...BUT IT'S ALSO BOTHER-SOME.
HOW SO?
WHY? DO YOU WANT TO GIVE ONE TO SOMEONE?
NO!
I WASN'T ASKING ABOUT MYSELF!

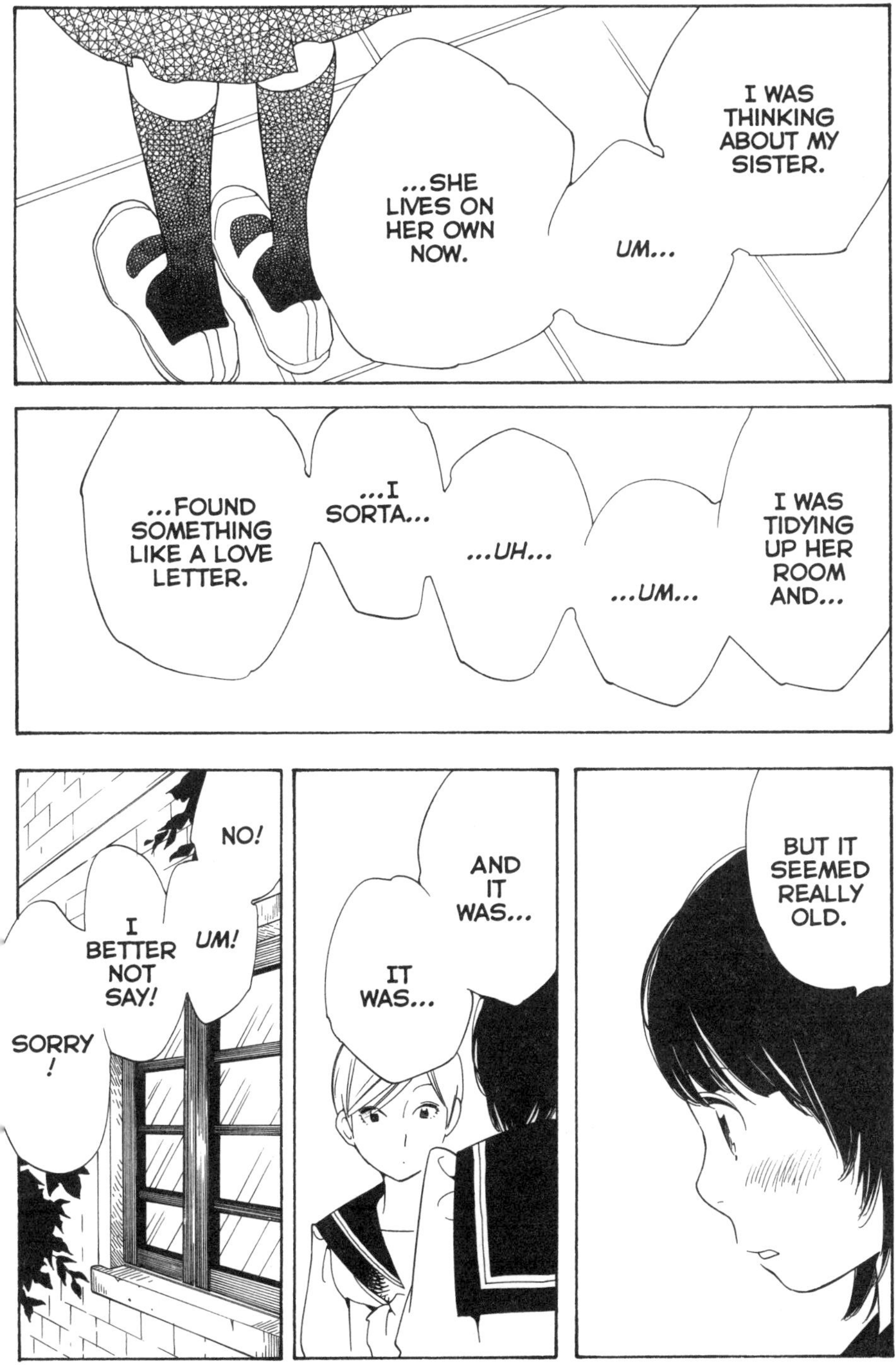
I WAS THINKING ABOUT MY SISTER.
UM...
...SHE LIVES ON HER OWN NOW.
I WAS TIDYING UP HER ROOM AND...
...UM...
...UH...
...I SORTA...
...FOUND SOMETHING LIKE A LOVE LETTER.
BUT IT SEEMED REALLY OLD.
AND IT WAS...
IT WAS...
NO!
UM!
I BETTER NOT SAY!
SORRY!

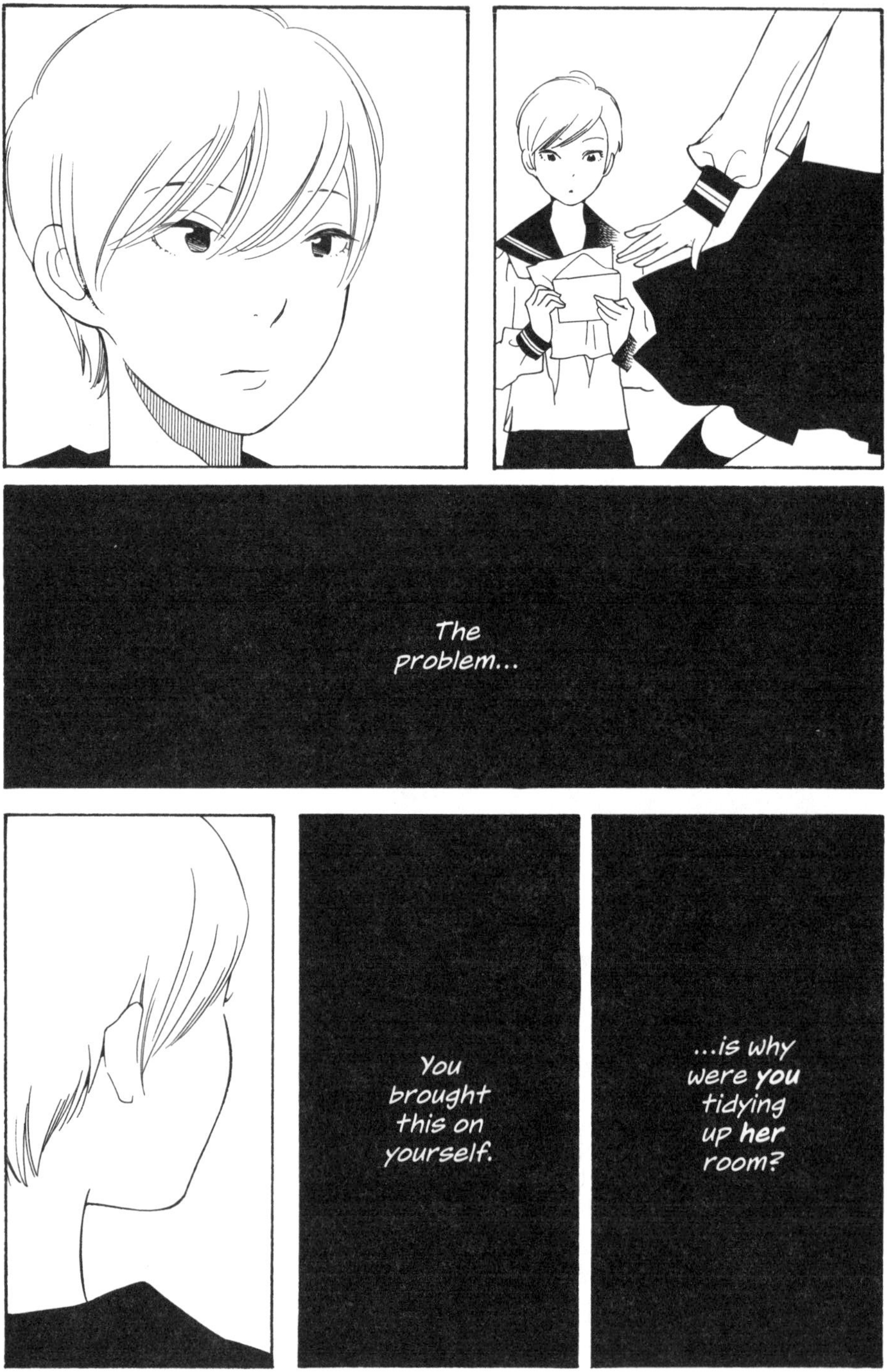
The problem...
...is why were you tidying up her room?
You brought this on yourself.

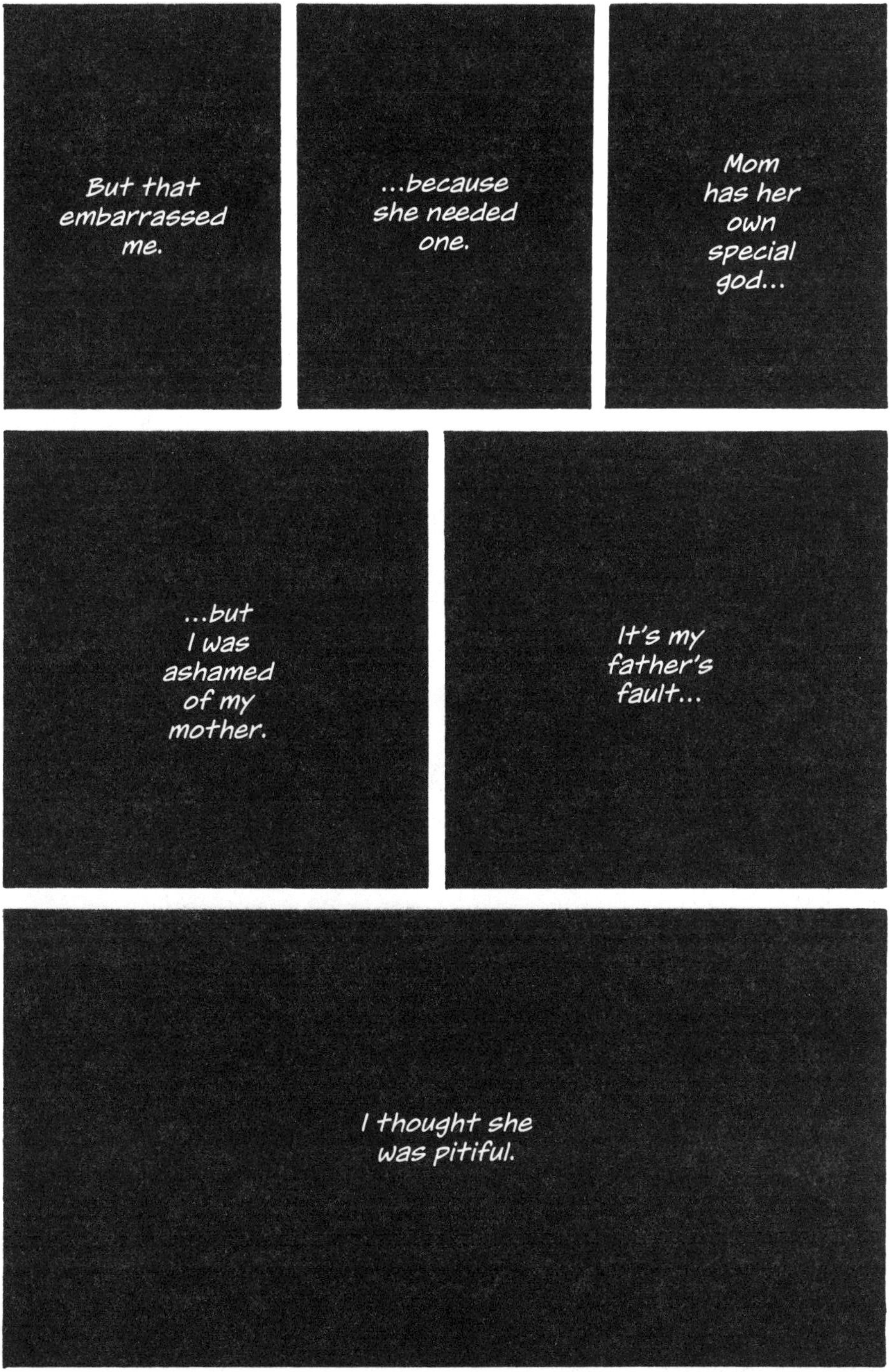
Mom has her own special god...
...because she needed one.
But that embarrassed me.
It's my father's fault...
...but I was ashamed of my mother.
I thought she was pitiful.

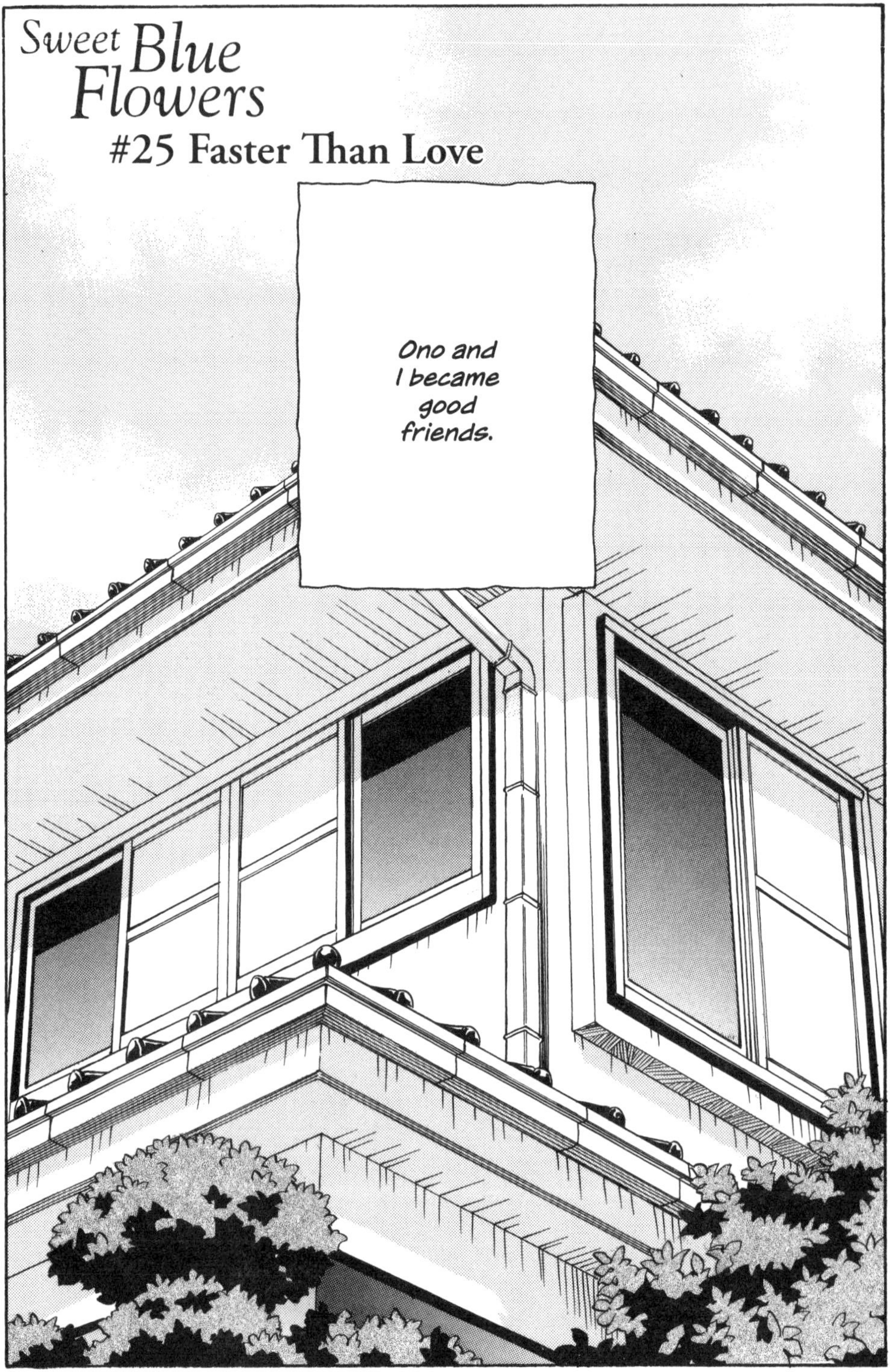
Sweet Blue Flowers
#25 Faster Than Love
Ono and I became good friends.

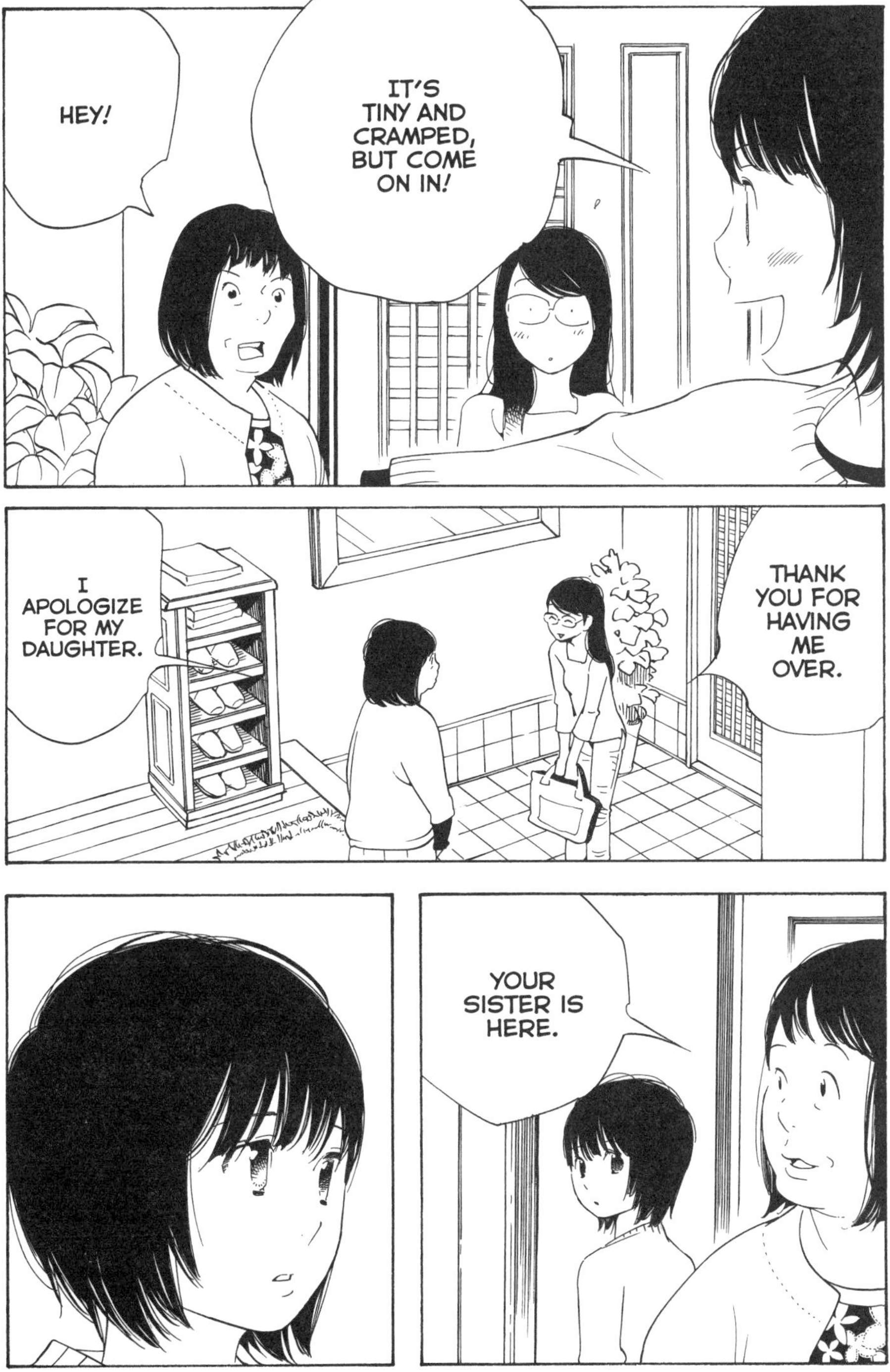
IT'S TINY AND CRAMPED, BUT COME ON IN!
HEY!
THANK YOU FOR HAVING ME OVER.
I APOLOGIZE FOR MY DAUGHTER.
YOUR SISTER IS HERE.

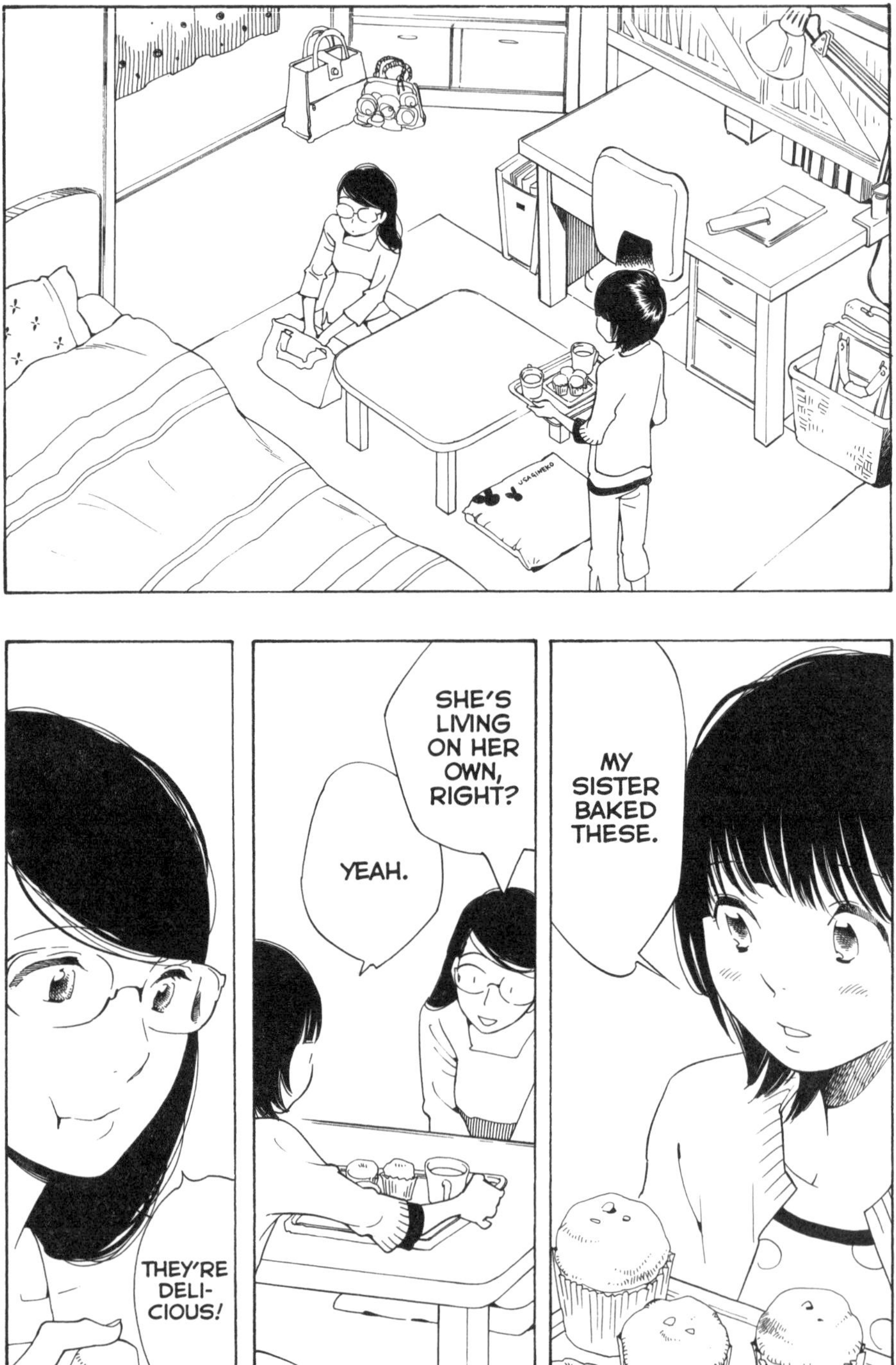
USAGINEKO
MY SISTER BAKED THESE.
SHE'S LIVING ON HER OWN, RIGHT?
YEAH.
THEY'RE DELI- CIOUS!

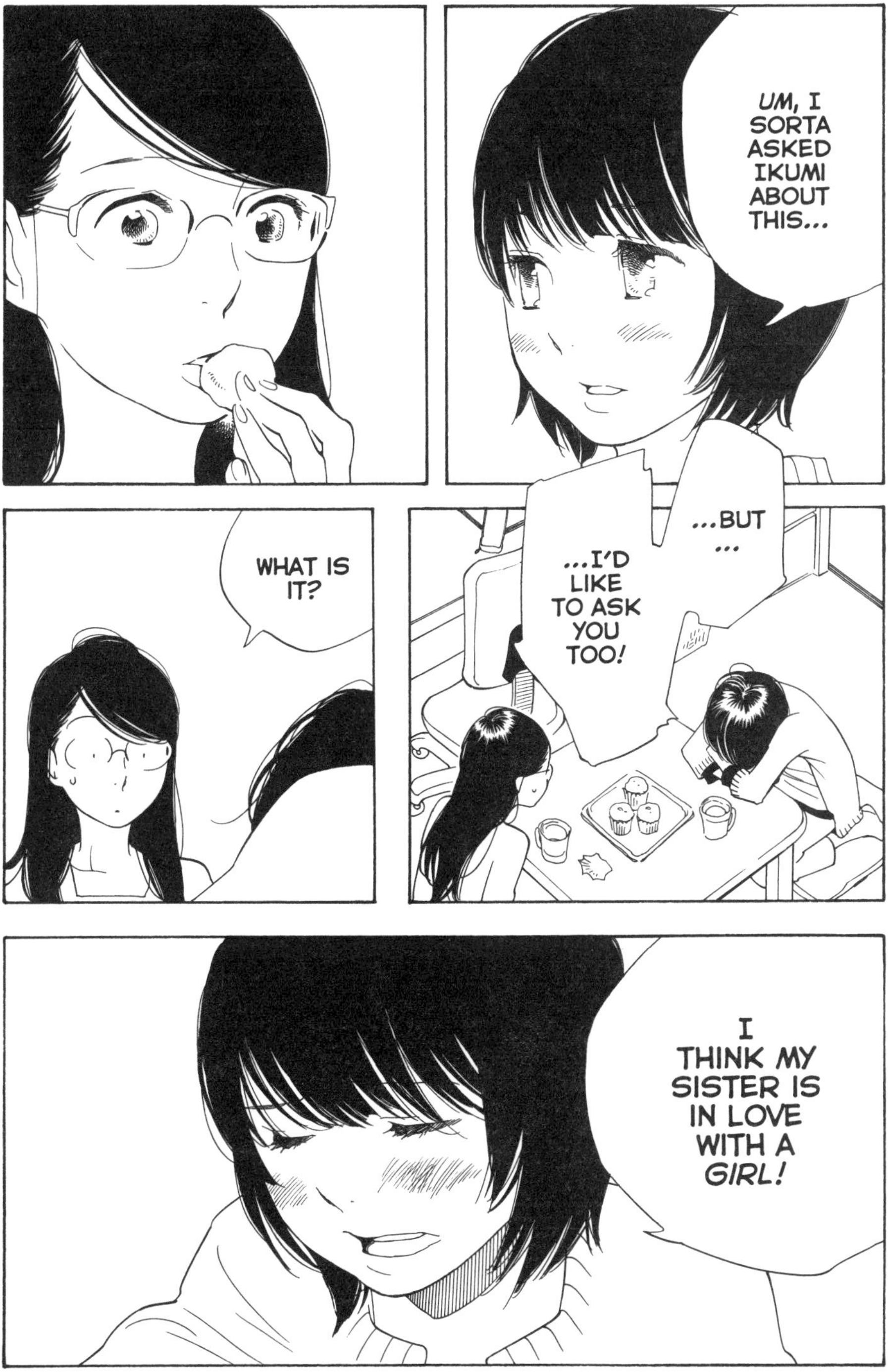
UM, I SORTA ASKED IKUMI ABOUT THIS...
...BUT ...
...I'D LIKE TO ASK YOU TOO!
WHAT IS IT?
I THINK MY SISTER IS IN LOVE WITH A GIRL!

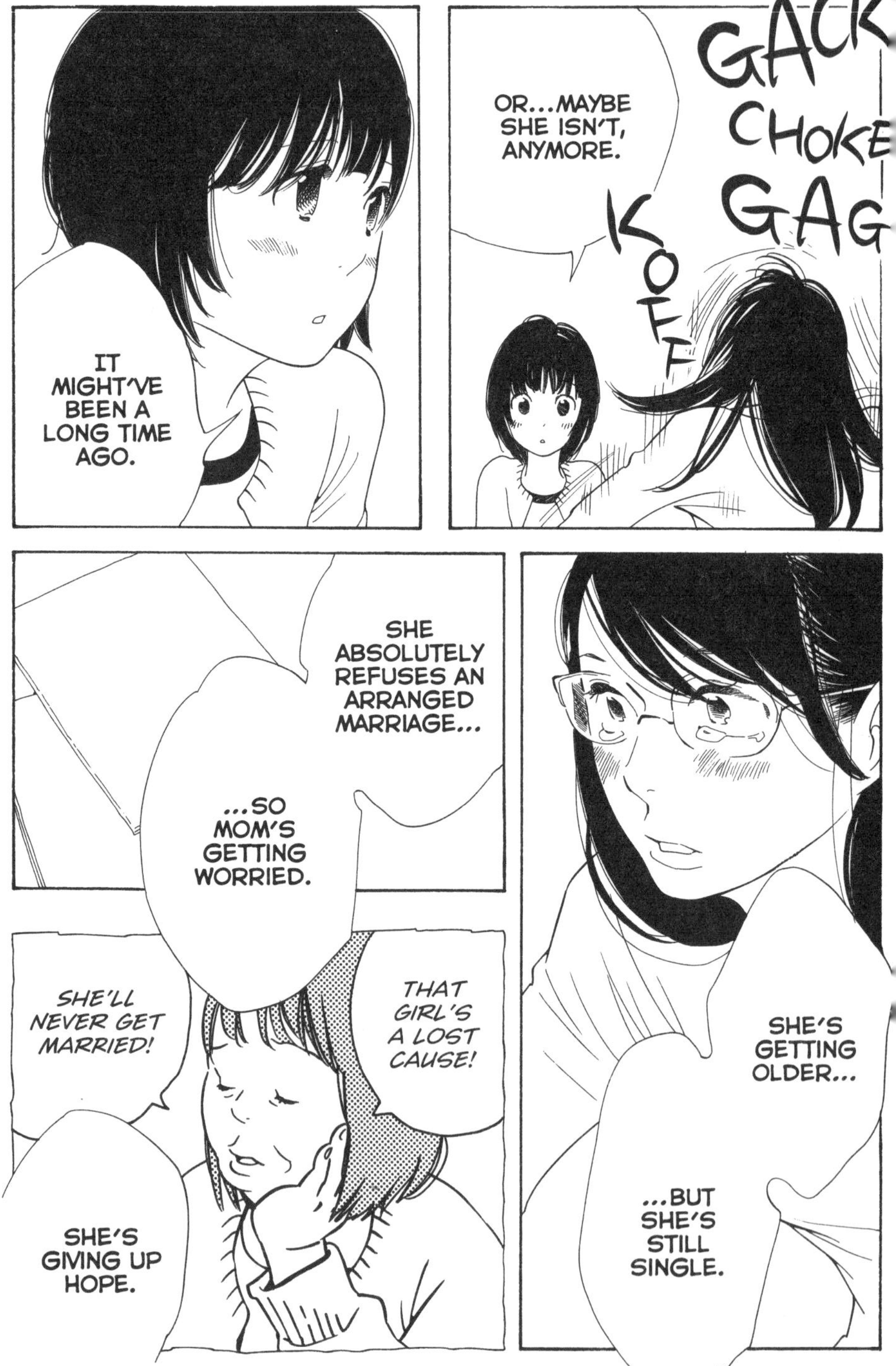
OR...MAYBE SHE ISN'T, ANYMORE.
GACK
CHOKE
GAG
KOFF
IT MIGHT'VE BEEN A LONG TIME AGO.
SHE'S GETTING OLDER...
...BUT SHE'S STILL SINGLE.
SHE ABSOLUTELY REFUSES AN ARRANGED MARRIAGE...
...SO MOM'S GETTING WORRIED.
THAT GIRL'S A LOST CAUSE!
SHE'LL NEVER GET MARRIED!
SHE'S GIVING UP HOPE.

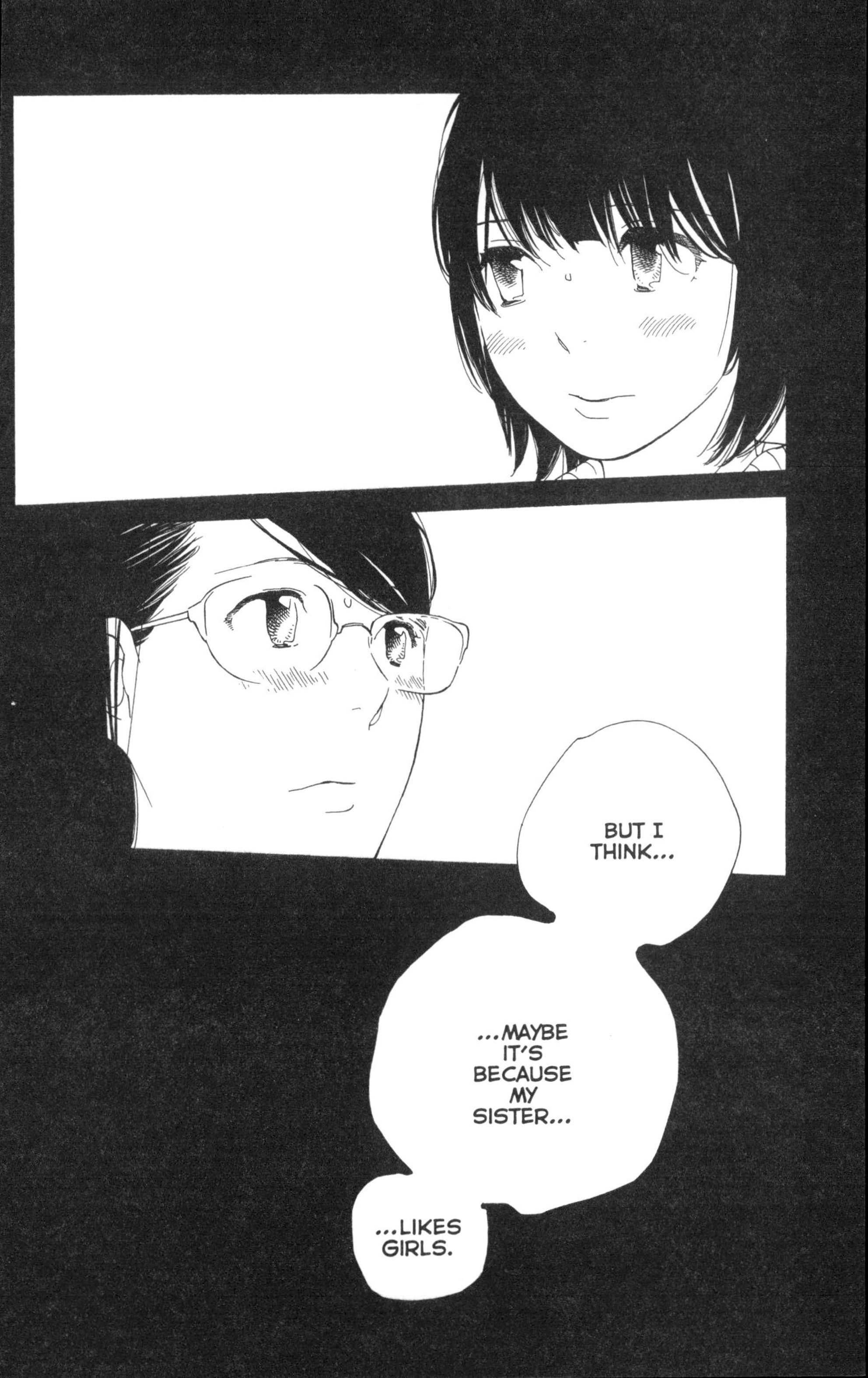
BUT I THINK...
...MAYBE IT'S BECAUSE MY SISTER...
...LIKES GIRLS.

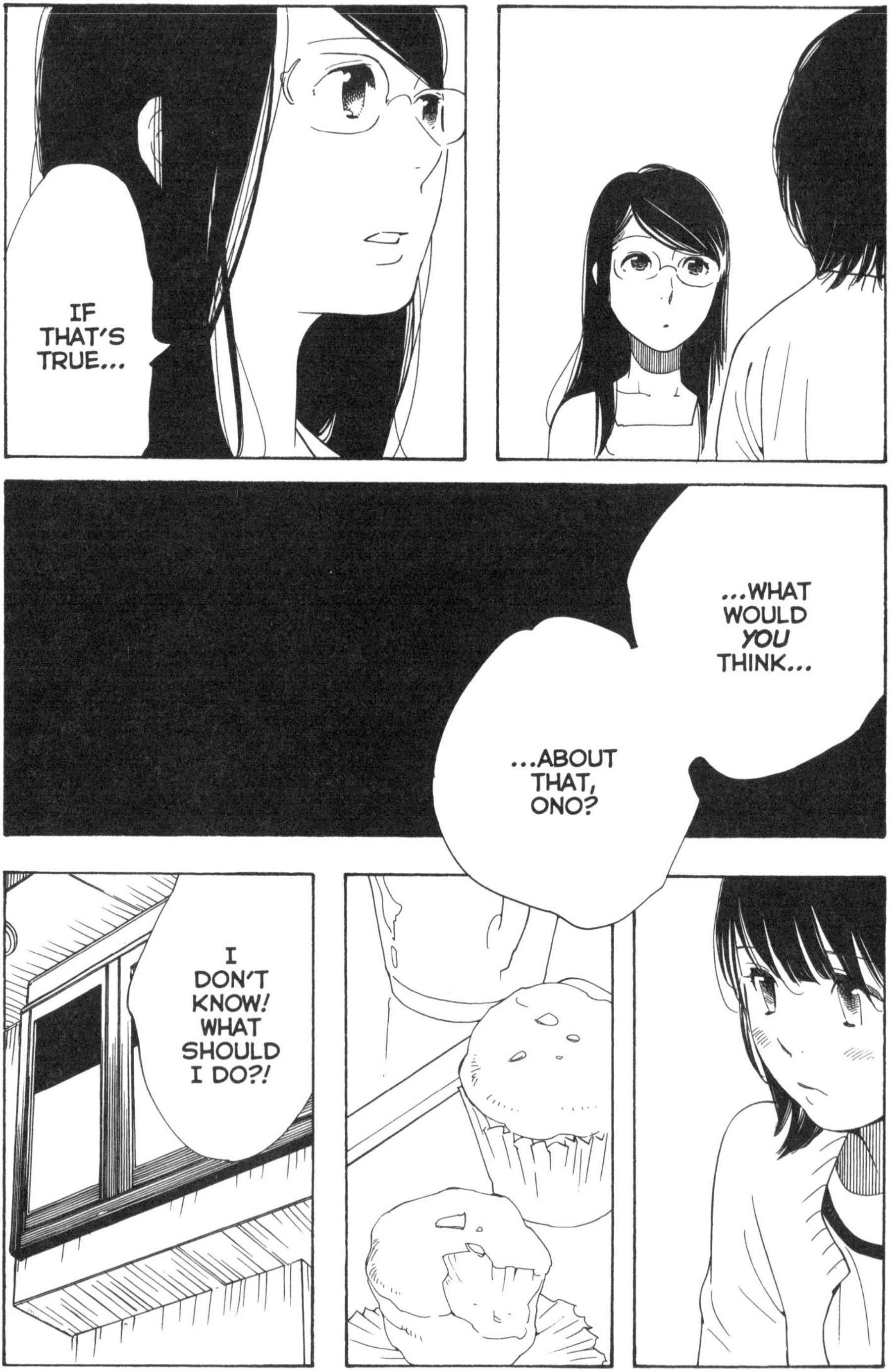
IF THAT'S TRUE...
...WHAT WOULD *YOU* THINK...
...ABOUT THAT, ONO?
I DON'T KNOW! WHAT SHOULD I DO?!

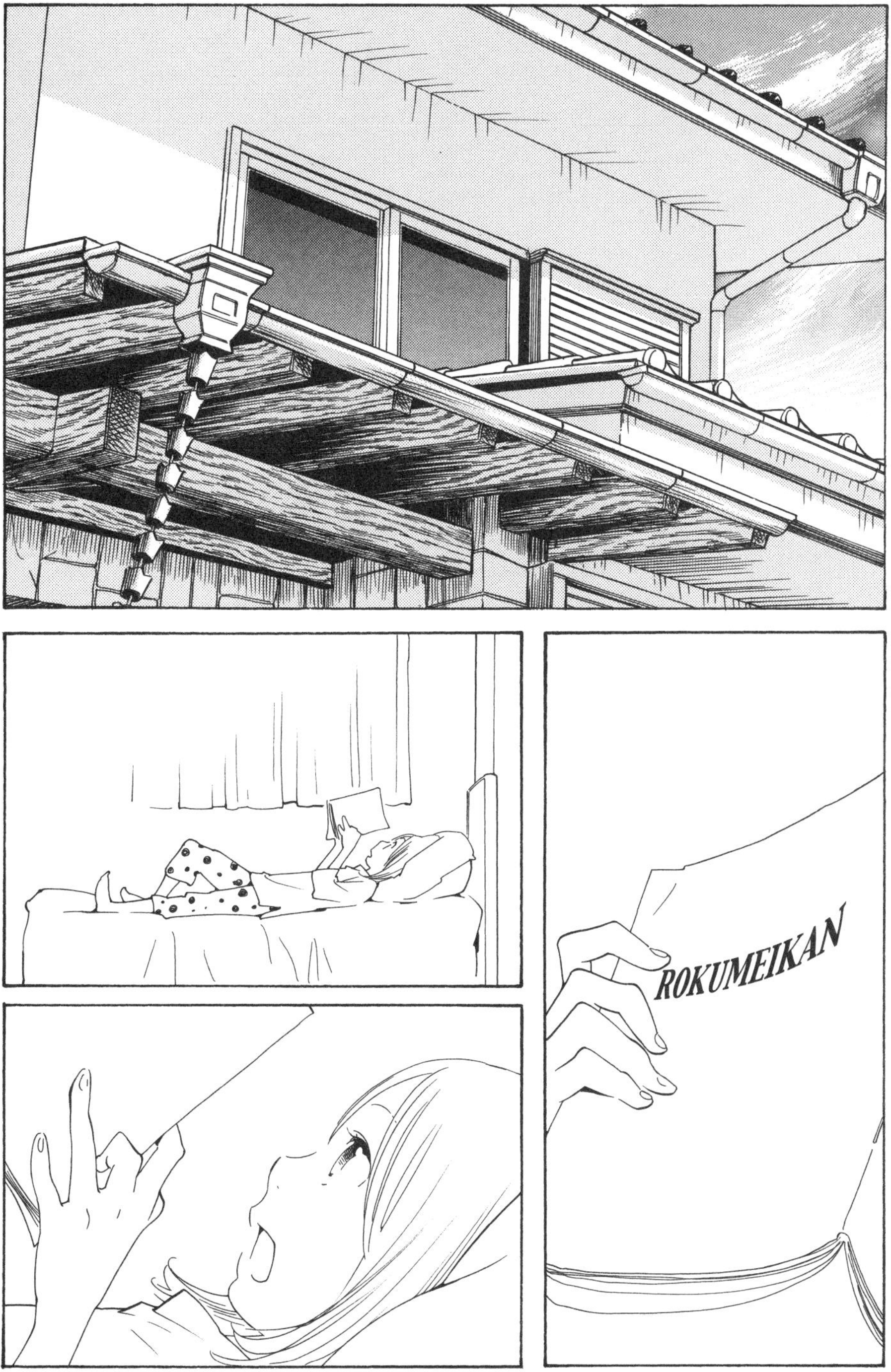
ROKUMEIKAN

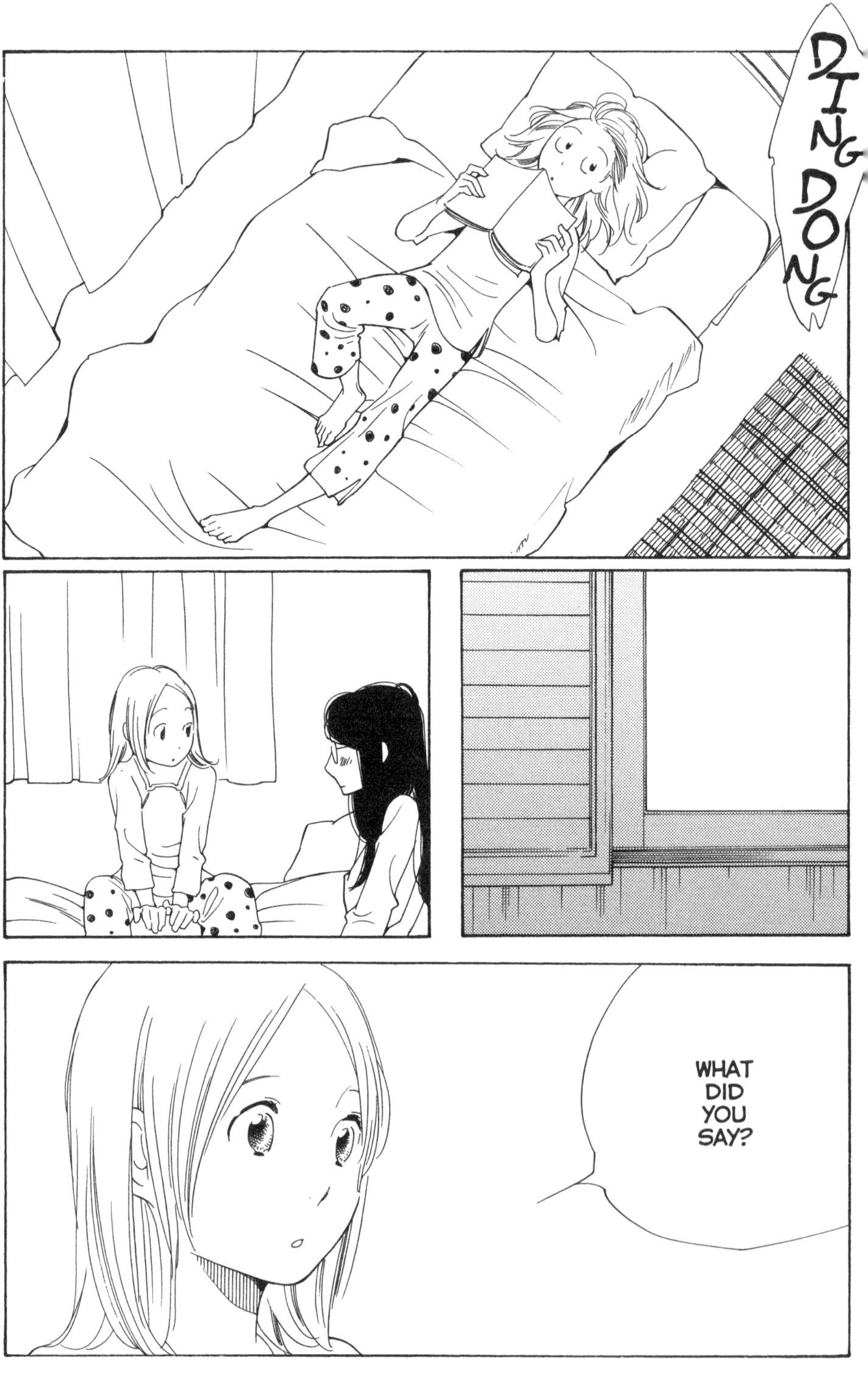
DING DONG
WHAT DID YOU SAY?

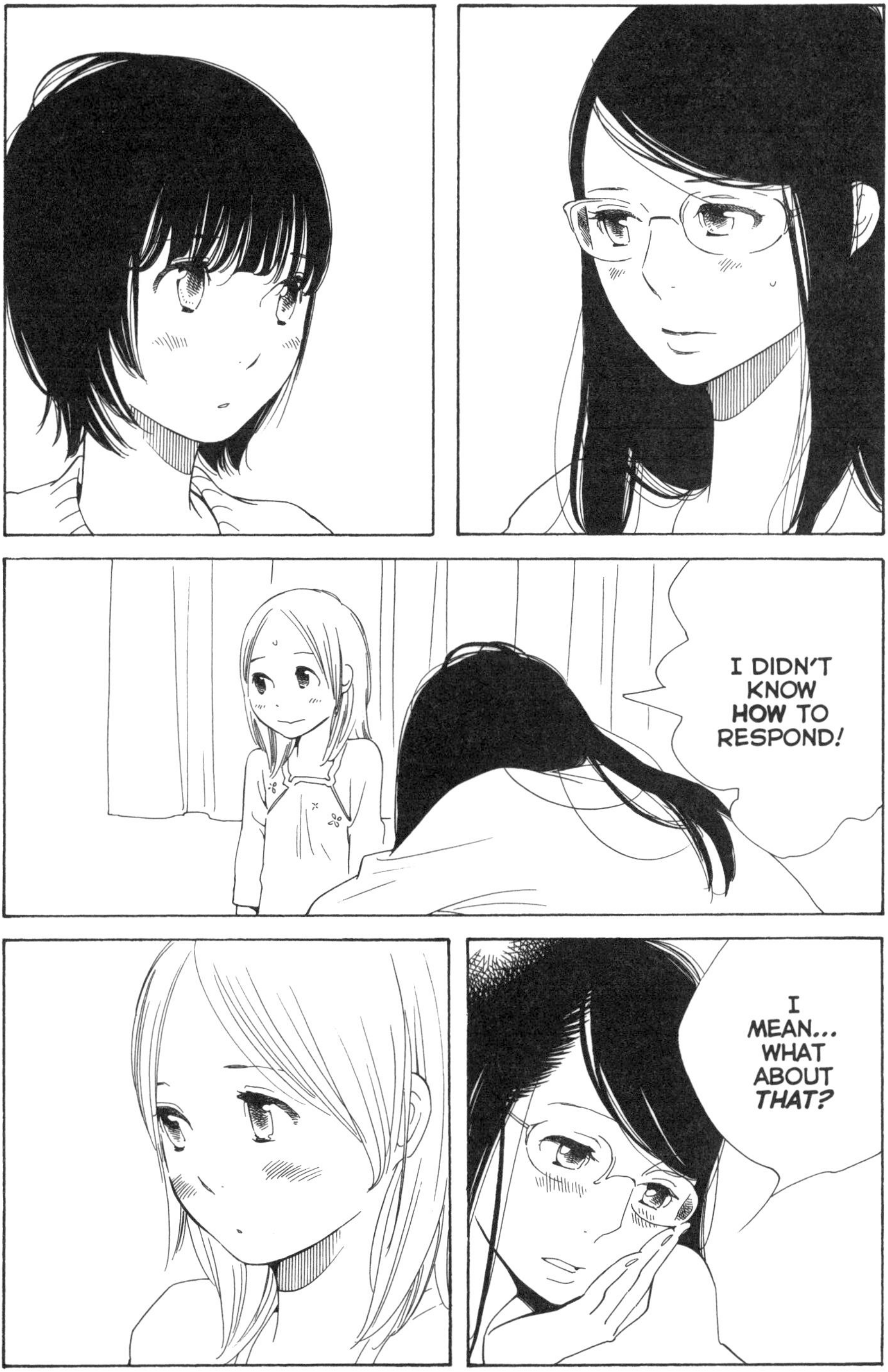
I DIDN'T KNOW HOW TO RESPOND!
I MEAN... WHAT ABOUT THAT?

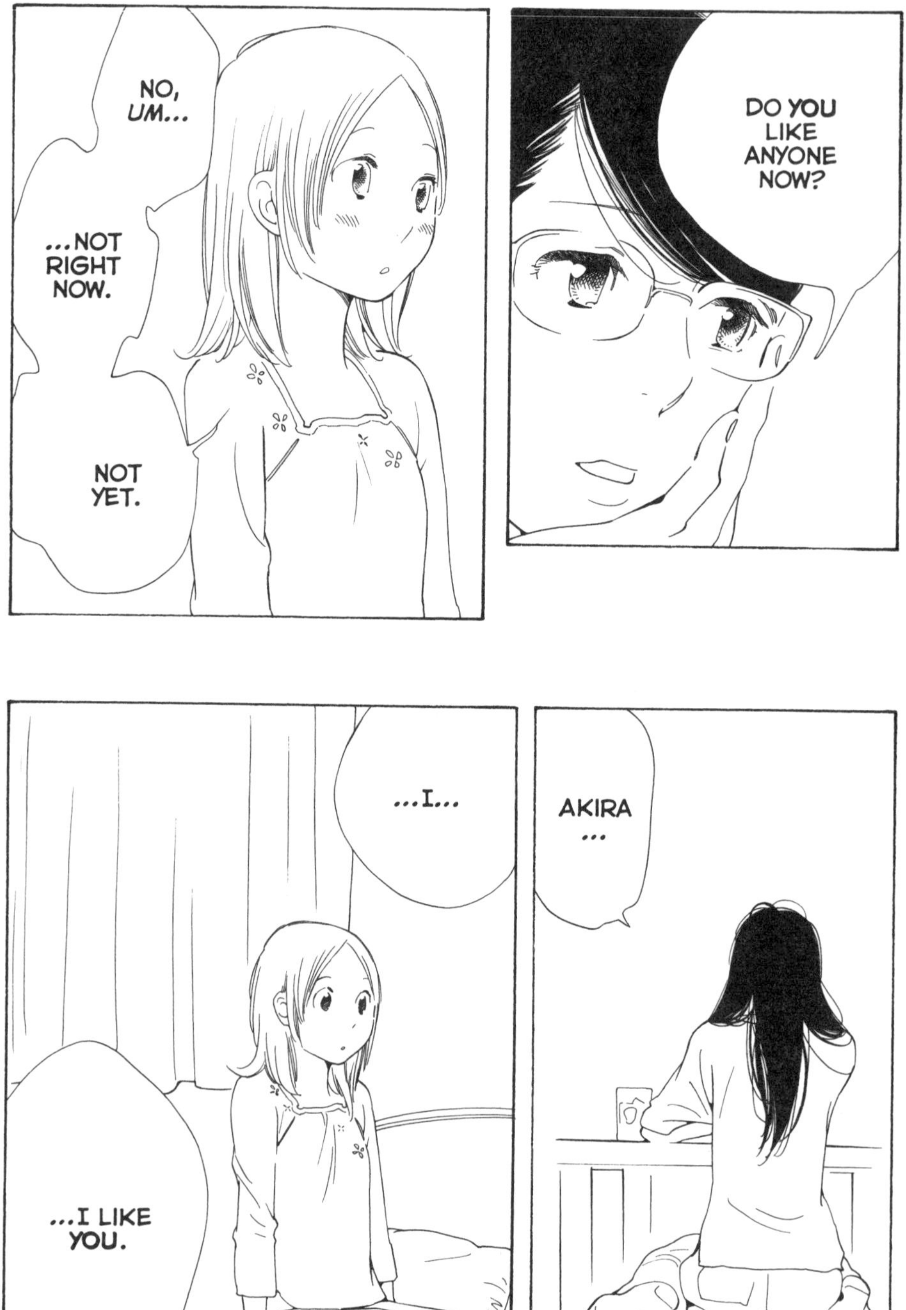
DO YOU LIKE ANYONE NOW?
NO, UM...
...NOT RIGHT NOW.
NOT YET.
AKIRA ...
...I...
...I LIKE YOU.

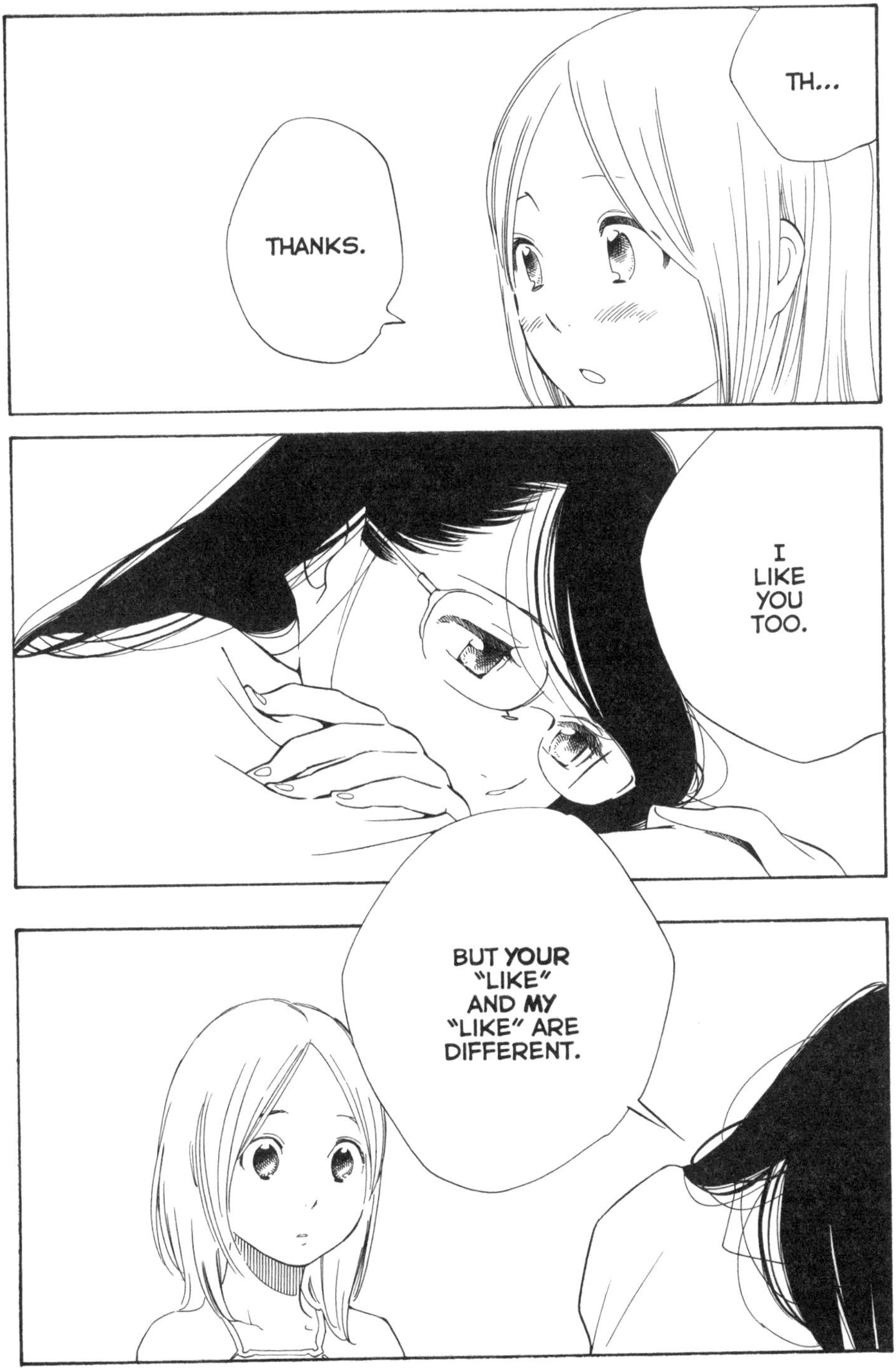
TH...
THANKS.
I LIKE YOU TOO.
BUT YOUR "LIKE" AND MY "LIKE" ARE DIFFERENT.

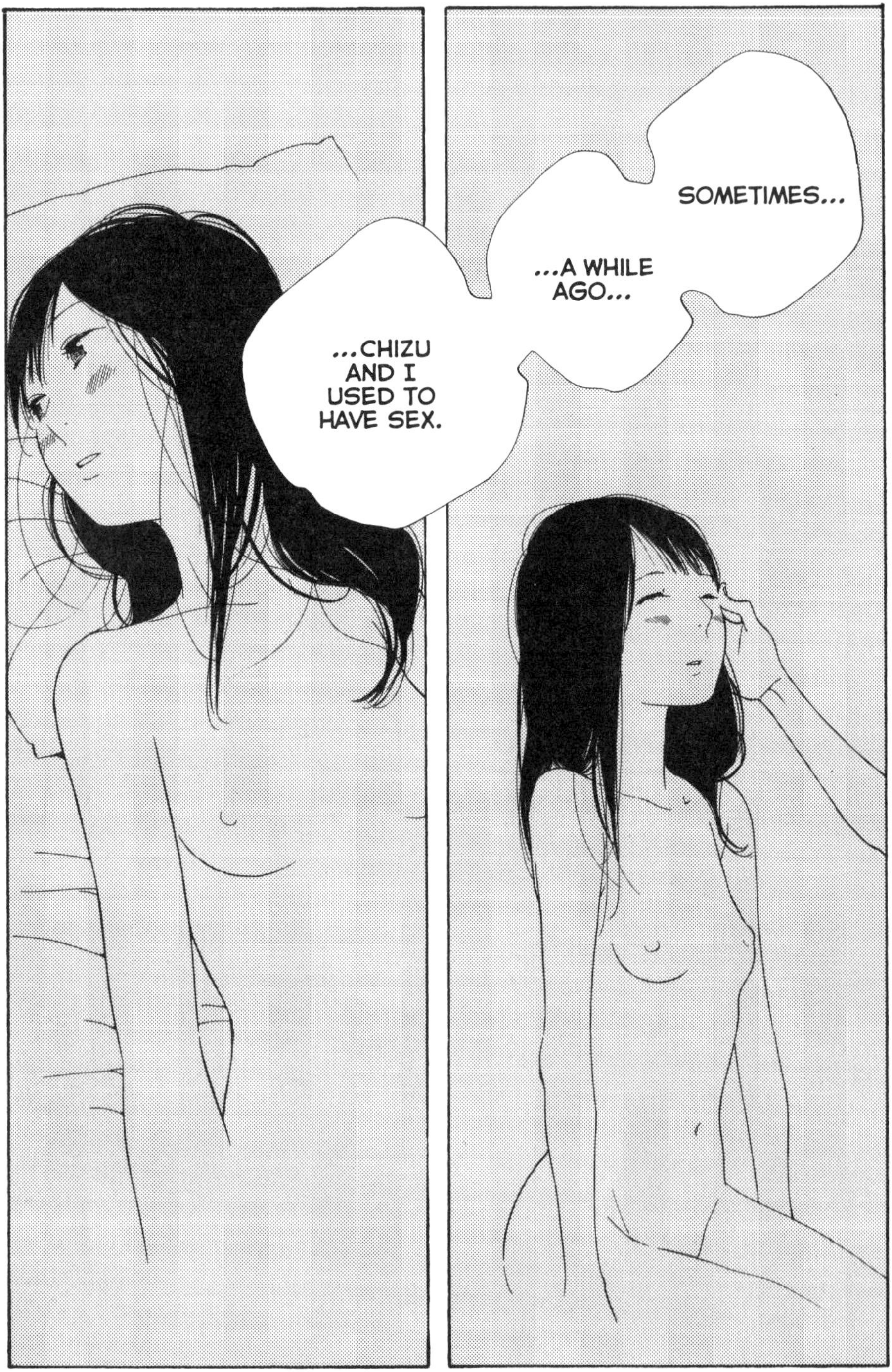
SOMETIMES...
...A WHILE AGO...
...CHIZU AND I USED TO HAVE SEX.

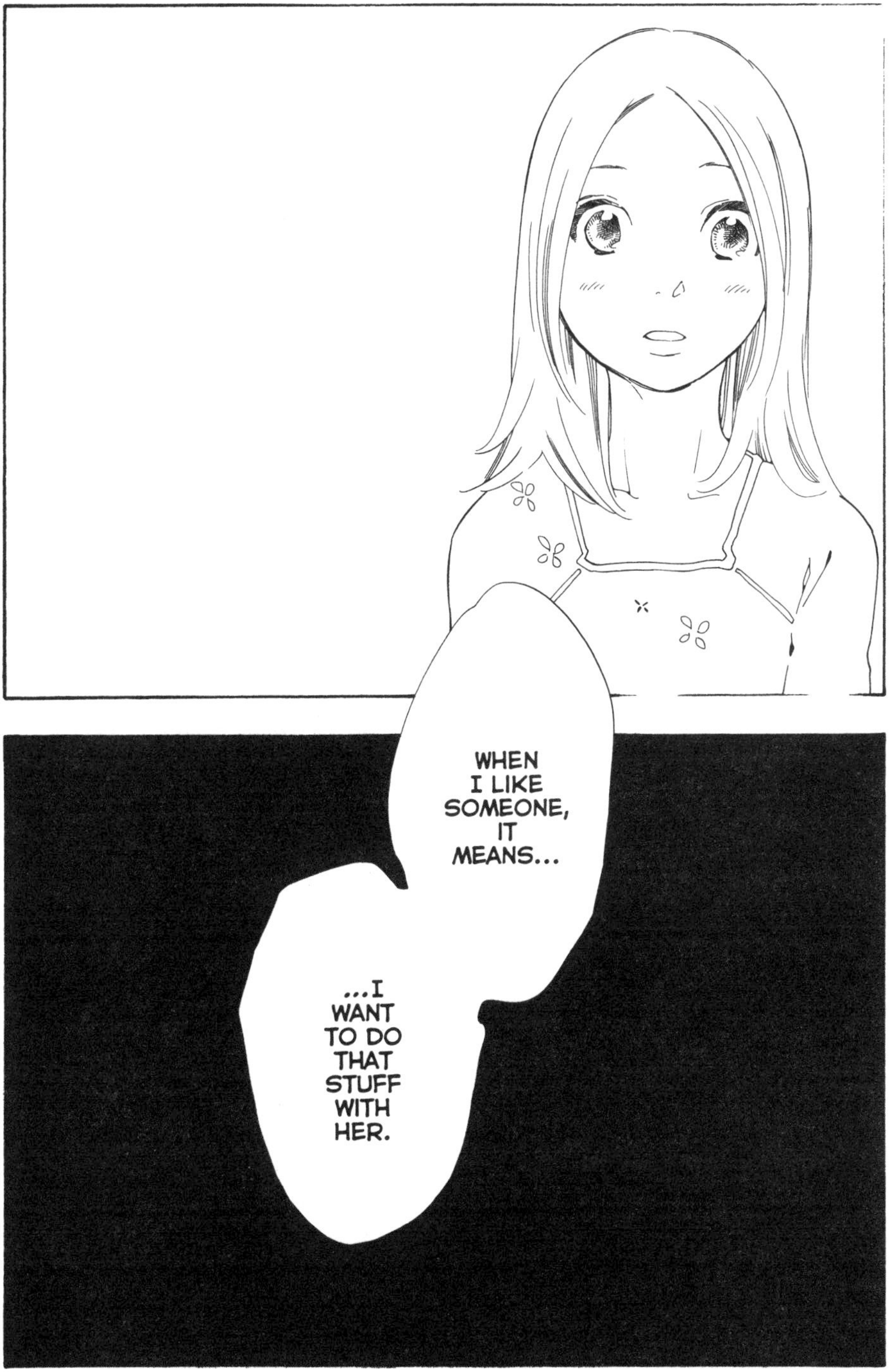
WHEN I LIKE SOMEONE, IT MEANS...
...I WANT TO DO THAT STUFF WITH HER.

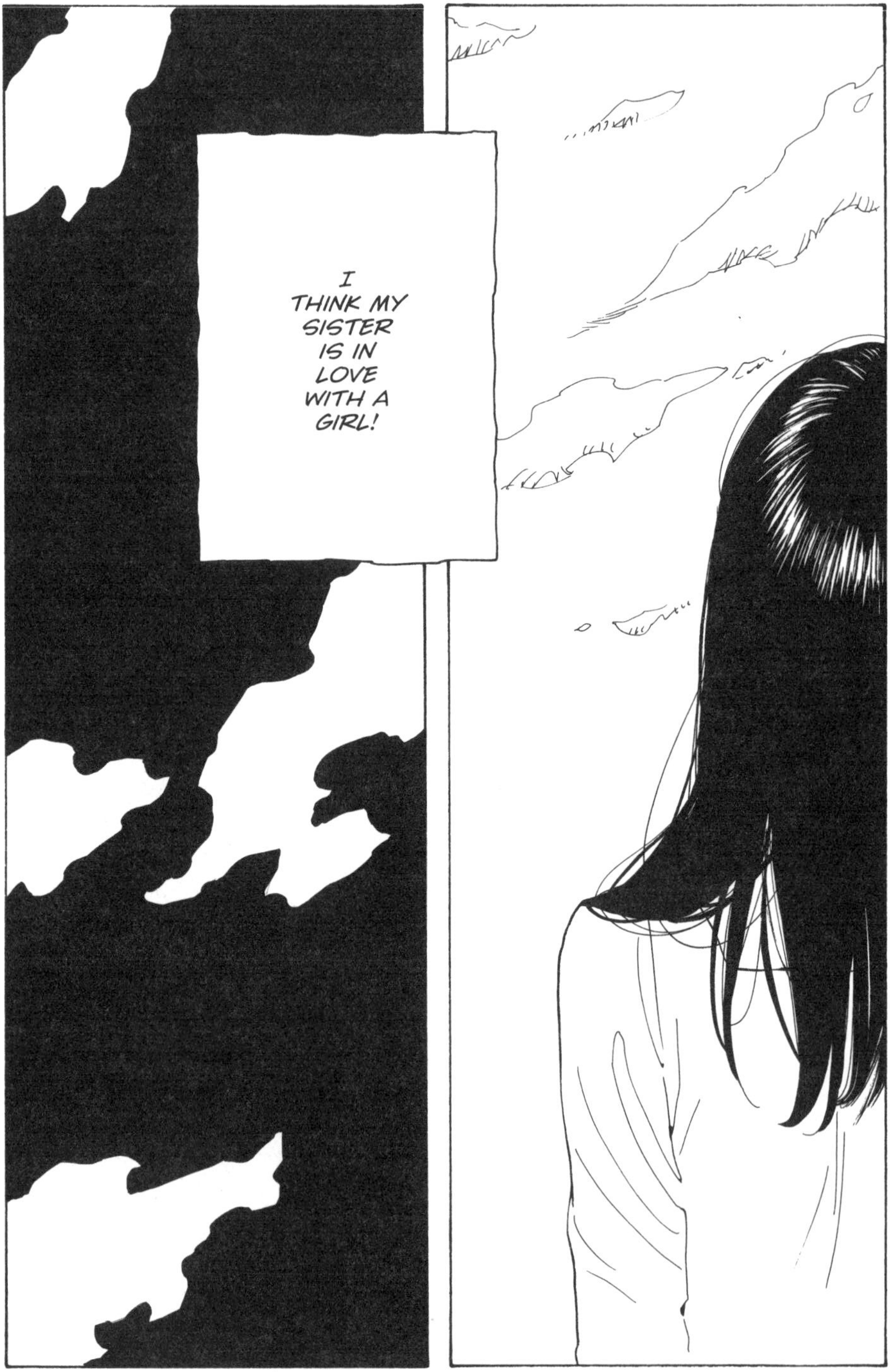
I THINK MY SISTER IS IN LOVE WITH A GIRL!

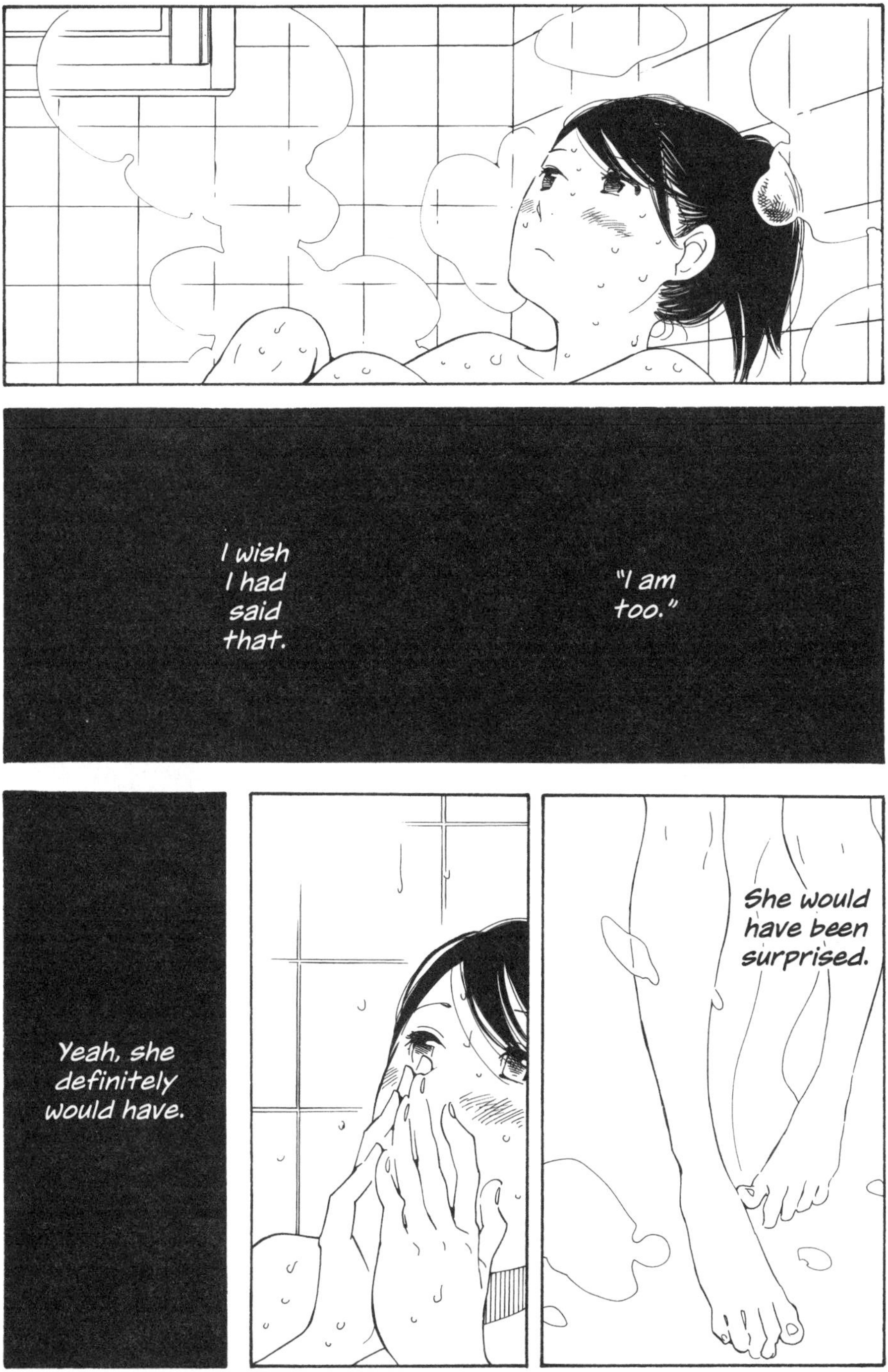
"I am too."
I wish I had said that.
She would have been surprised.
Yeah, she definitely would have.

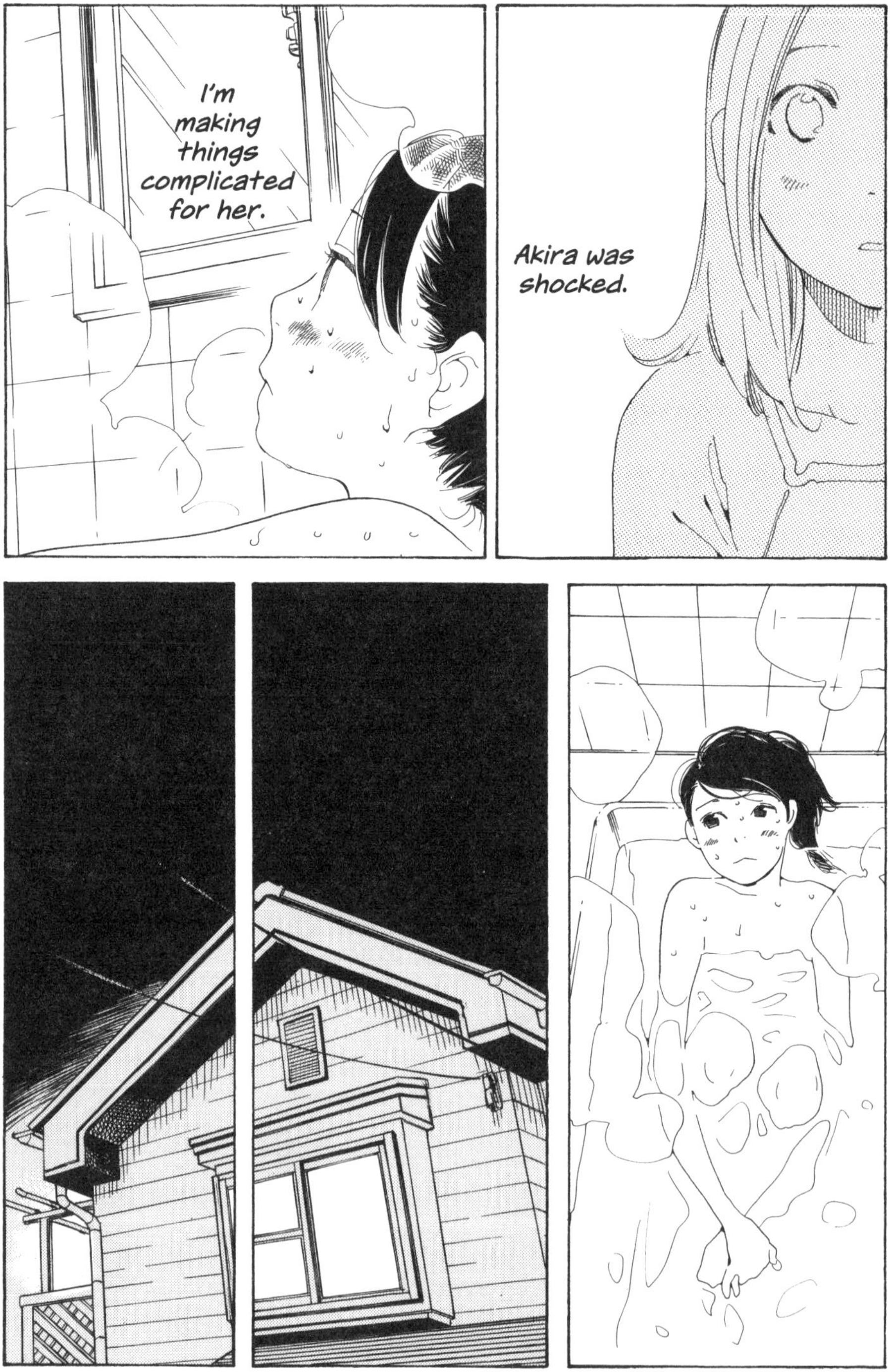
Akira was shocked.
I'm making things complicated for her.

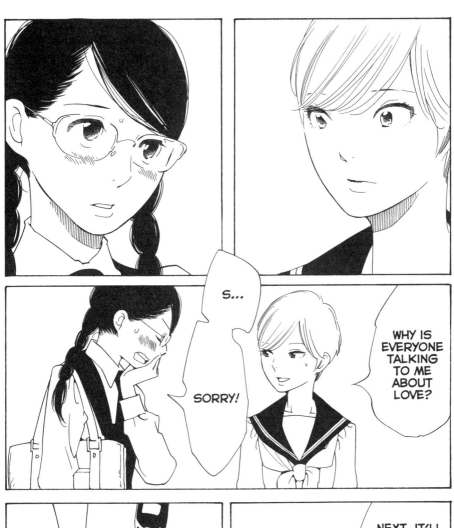

S...

SORRY!

WHY IS EVERYONE TALKING TO ME ABOUT LOVE?

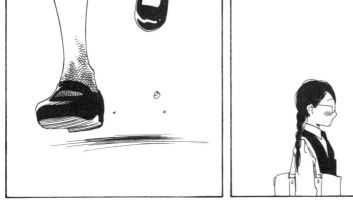

NEXT, IT'LL PROBABLY BE OKUDAIRA!

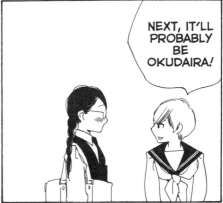

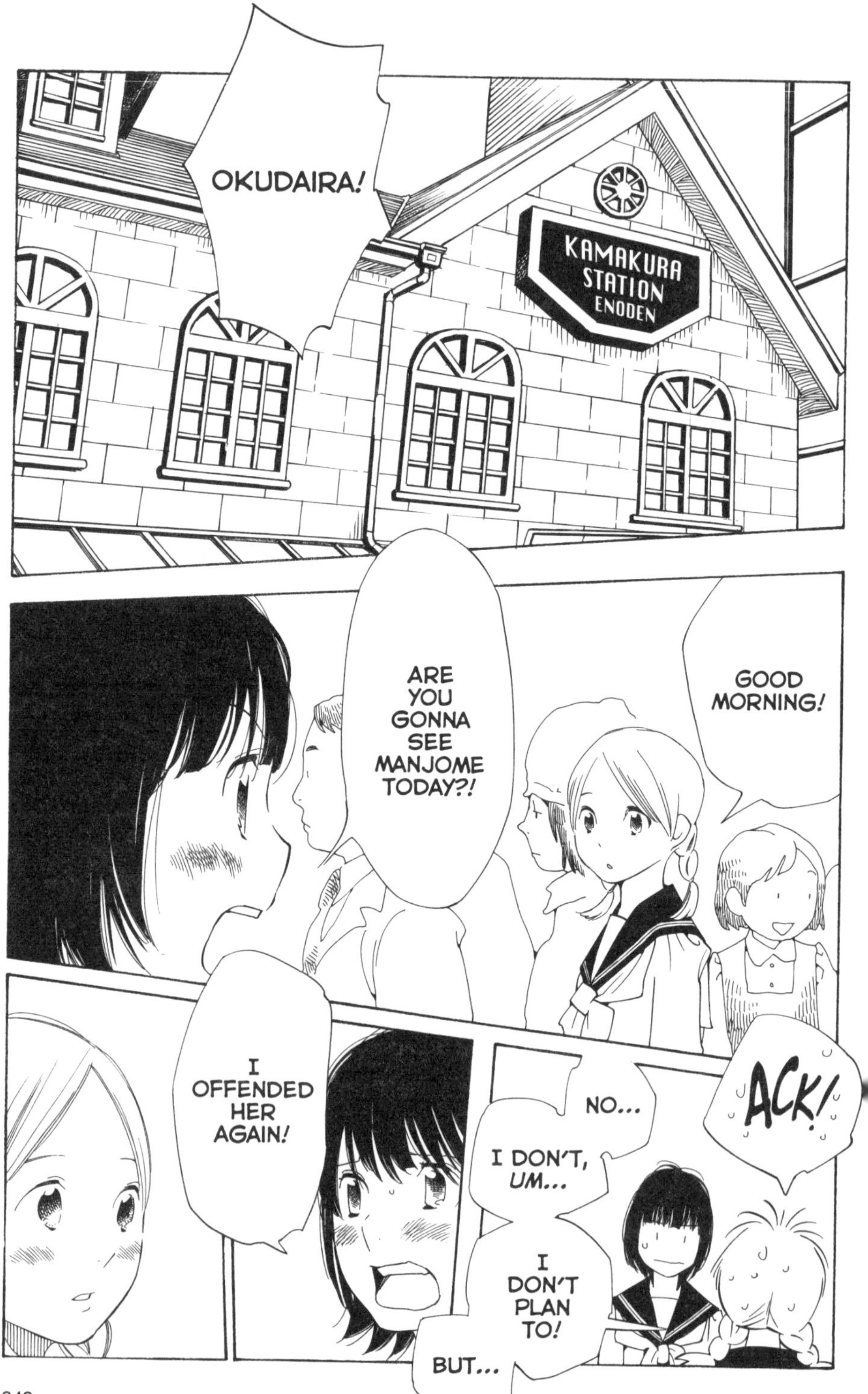
OKUDAIRA!
KAMAKURA STATION ENODEN
GOOD MORNING!
ARE YOU GONNA SEE MANJOME TODAY?!
ACK!
NO...
I DON'T, UM...
I DON'T PLAN TO!
BUT...
I OFFENDED HER AGAIN!

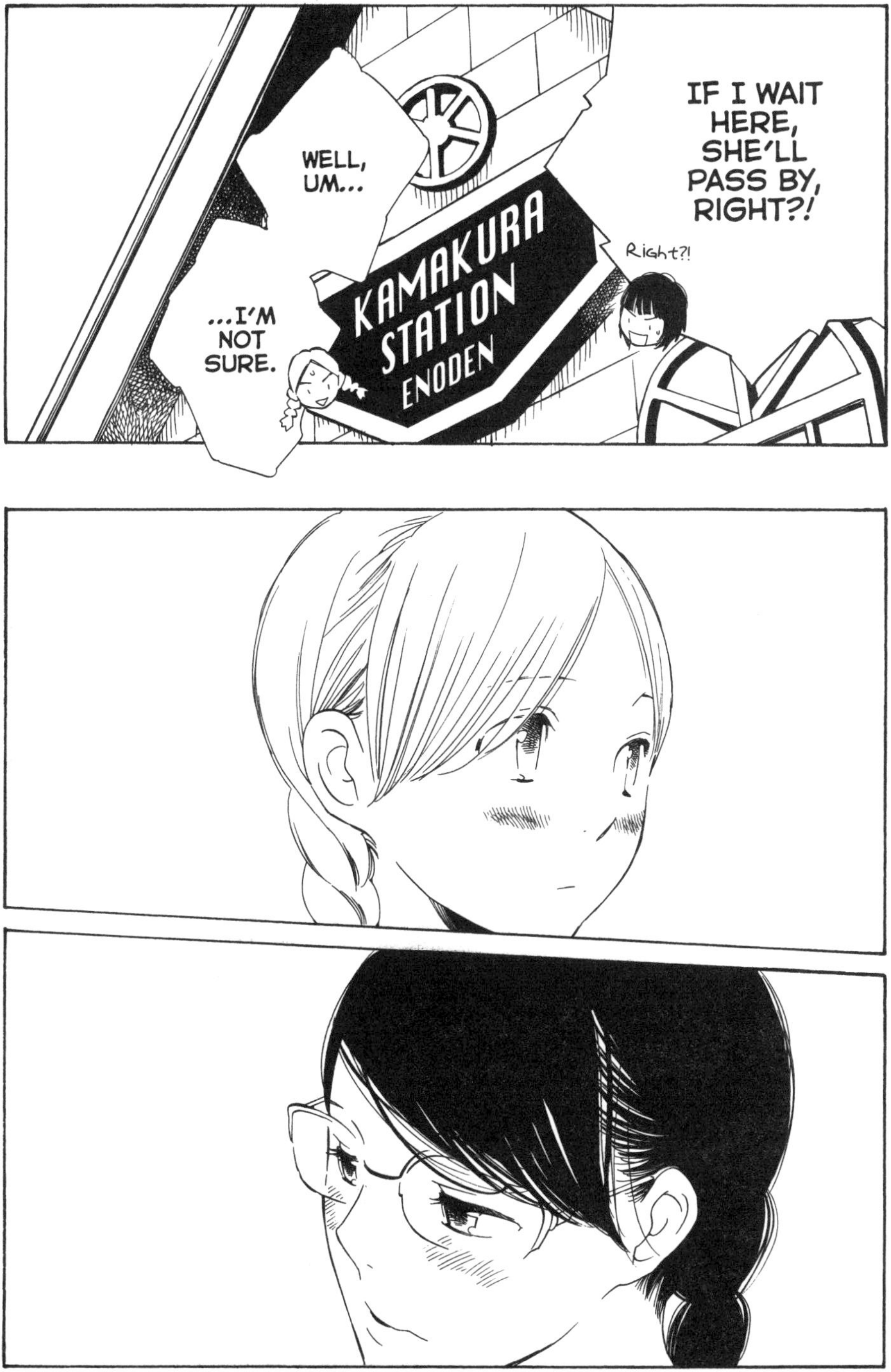
IF I WAIT HERE, SHE'LL PASS BY, RIGHT?!
Right?!
KAMAKURA STATION
ENODEN
WELL, UM...
...I'M NOT SURE.

Sweet **Blue**
Flowers

LITTLE WOMEN

Shinako and Kaoruko

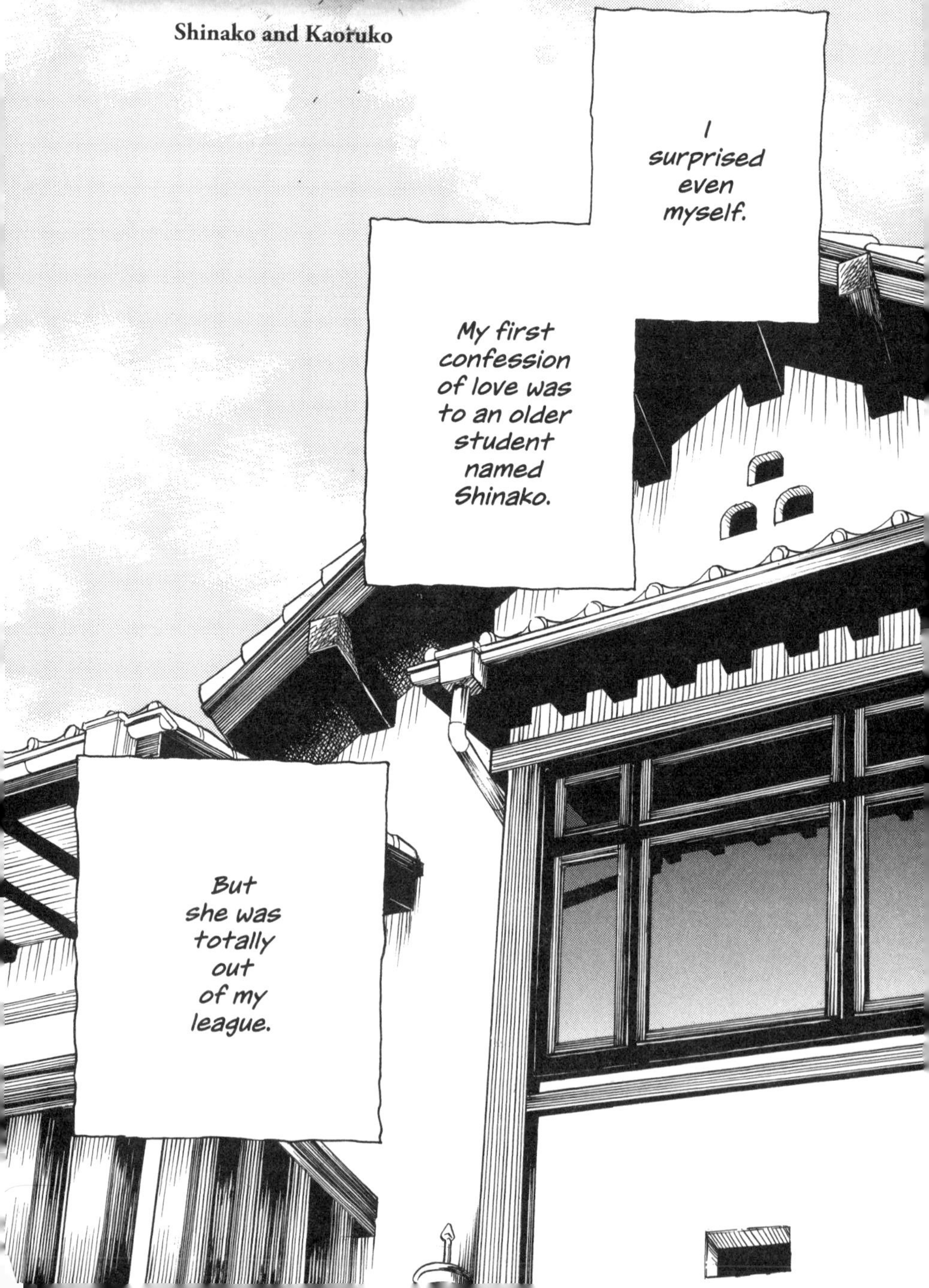
I surprised even myself.
My first confession of love was to an older student named Shinako.
But she was totally out of my league.

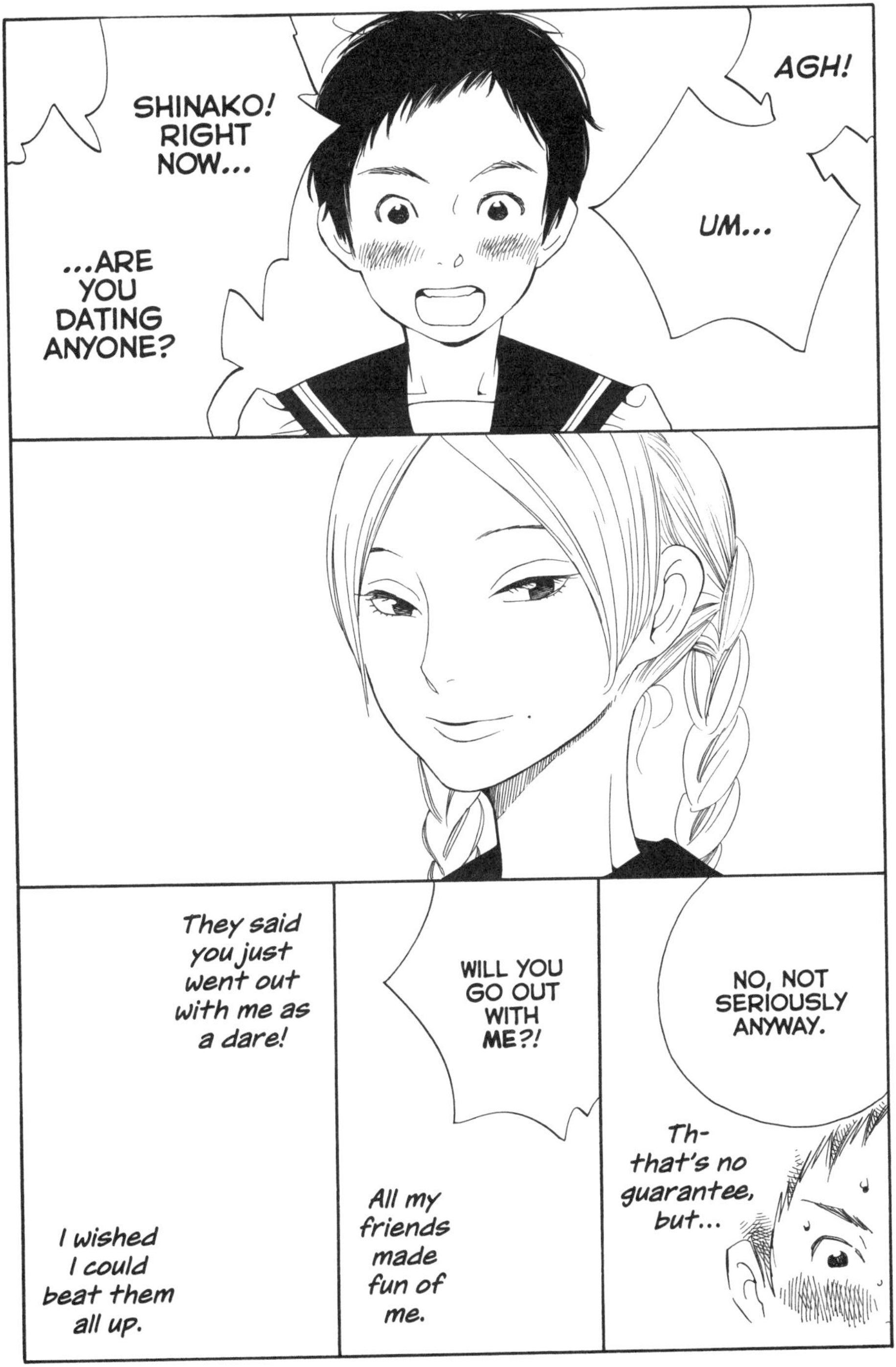
AGH!
UM...
SHINAKO! RIGHT NOW...
...ARE YOU DATING ANYONE?
NO, NOT SERIOUSLY ANYWAY.
Th- that's no guarantee, but...
WILL YOU GO OUT WITH ME?!
All my friends made fun of me.
They said you just went out with me as a dare!
I wished I could beat them all up.

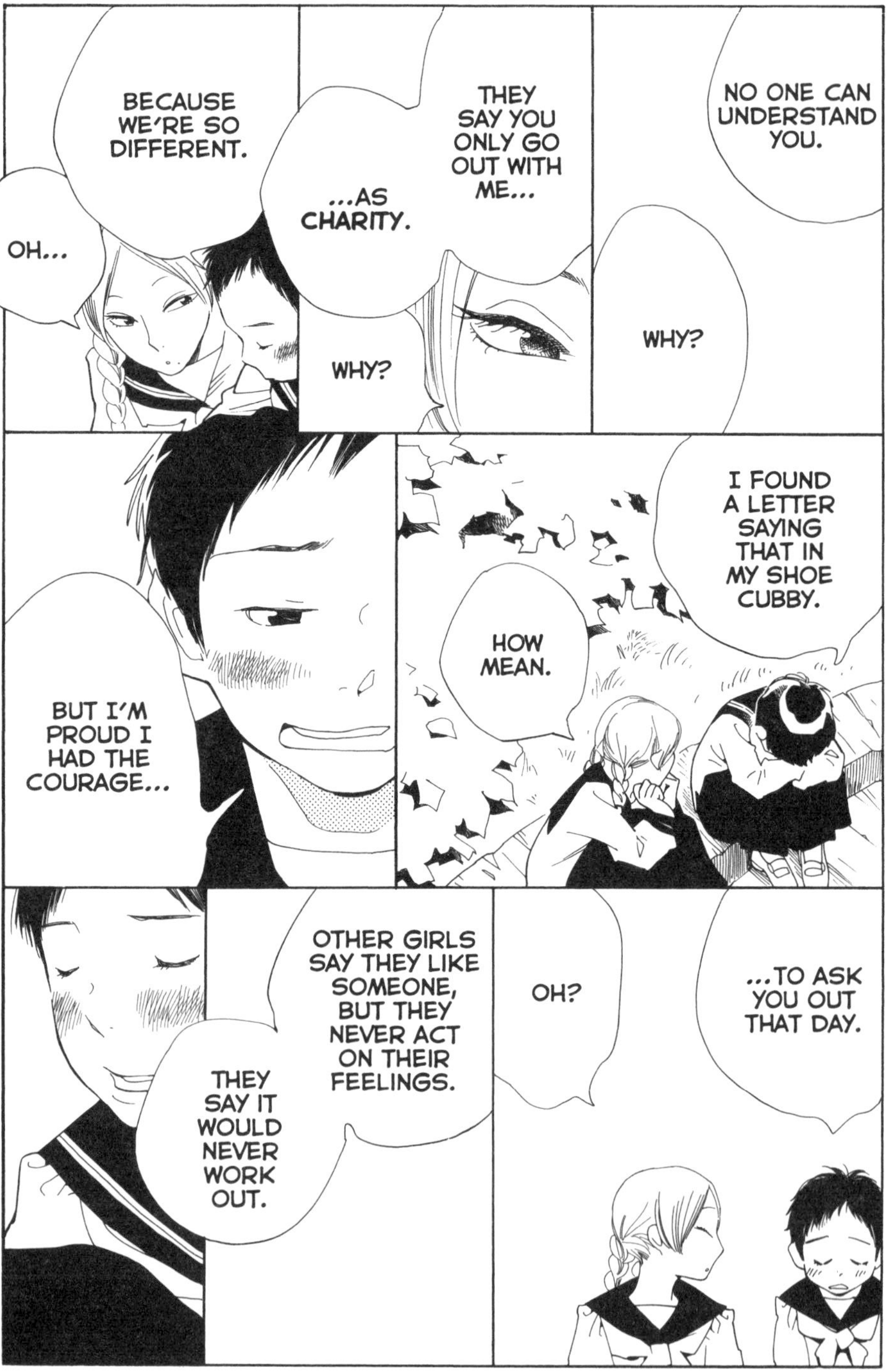
NO ONE CAN UNDERSTAND YOU.
WHY?
THEY SAY YOU ONLY GO OUT WITH ME...
...AS CHARITY.
WHY?
BECAUSE WE'RE SO DIFFERENT.
OH...
I FOUND A LETTER SAYING THAT IN MY SHOE CUBBY.
HOW MEAN.
BUT I'M PROUD I HAD THE COURAGE...
...TO ASK YOU OUT THAT DAY.
OH?
OTHER GIRLS SAY THEY LIKE SOMEONE, BUT THEY NEVER ACT ON THEIR FEELINGS.
THEY SAY IT WOULD NEVER WORK OUT.

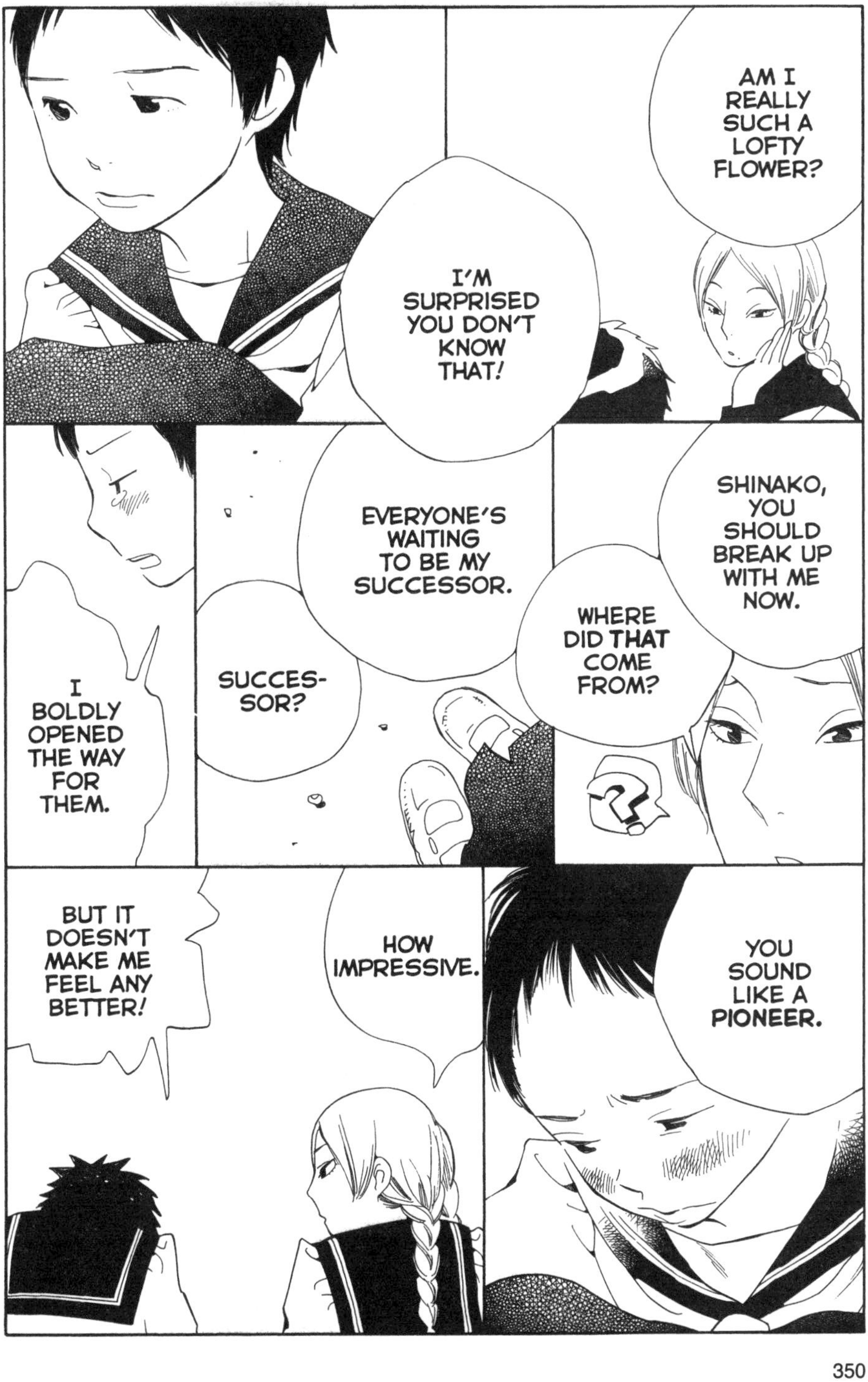
AM I REALLY SUCH A LOFTY FLOWER?
I'M SURPRISED YOU DON'T KNOW THAT!
SHINAKO, YOU SHOULD BREAK UP WITH ME NOW.
WHERE DID THAT COME FROM?
?
EVERYONE'S WAITING TO BE MY SUCCESSOR.
SUCCES- SOR?
I BOLDLY OPENED THE WAY FOR THEM.
YOU SOUND LIKE A PIONEER.
HOW IMPRESSIVE.
BUT IT DOESN'T MAKE ME FEEL ANY BETTER!

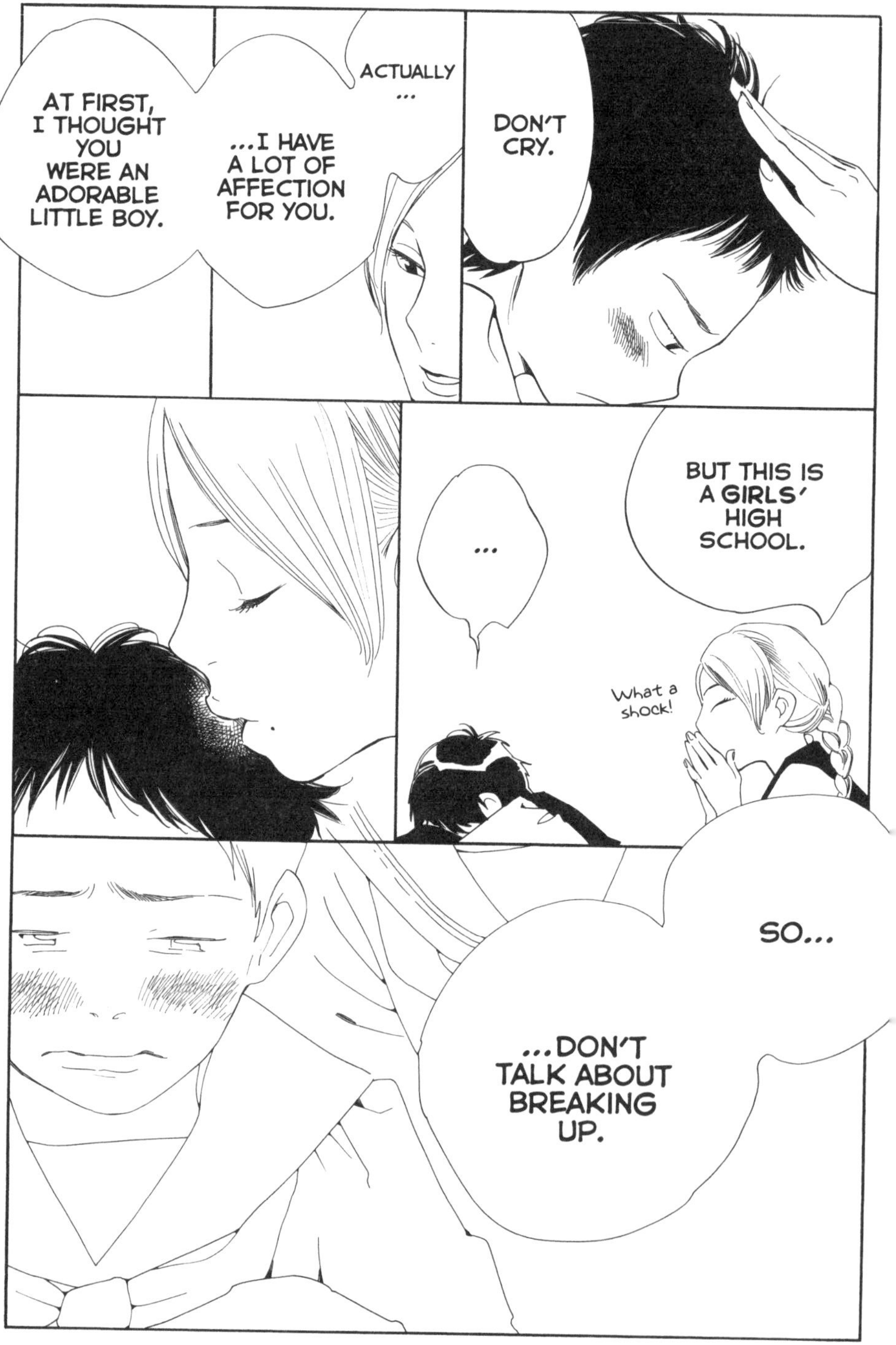
DON'T CRY.
ACTUALLY ...
...I HAVE A LOT OF AFFECTION FOR YOU.
AT FIRST, I THOUGHT YOU WERE AN ADORABLE LITTLE BOY.
BUT THIS IS A GIRLS' HIGH SCHOOL.
...
What a shock!
SO...
...DON'T TALK ABOUT BREAKING UP.

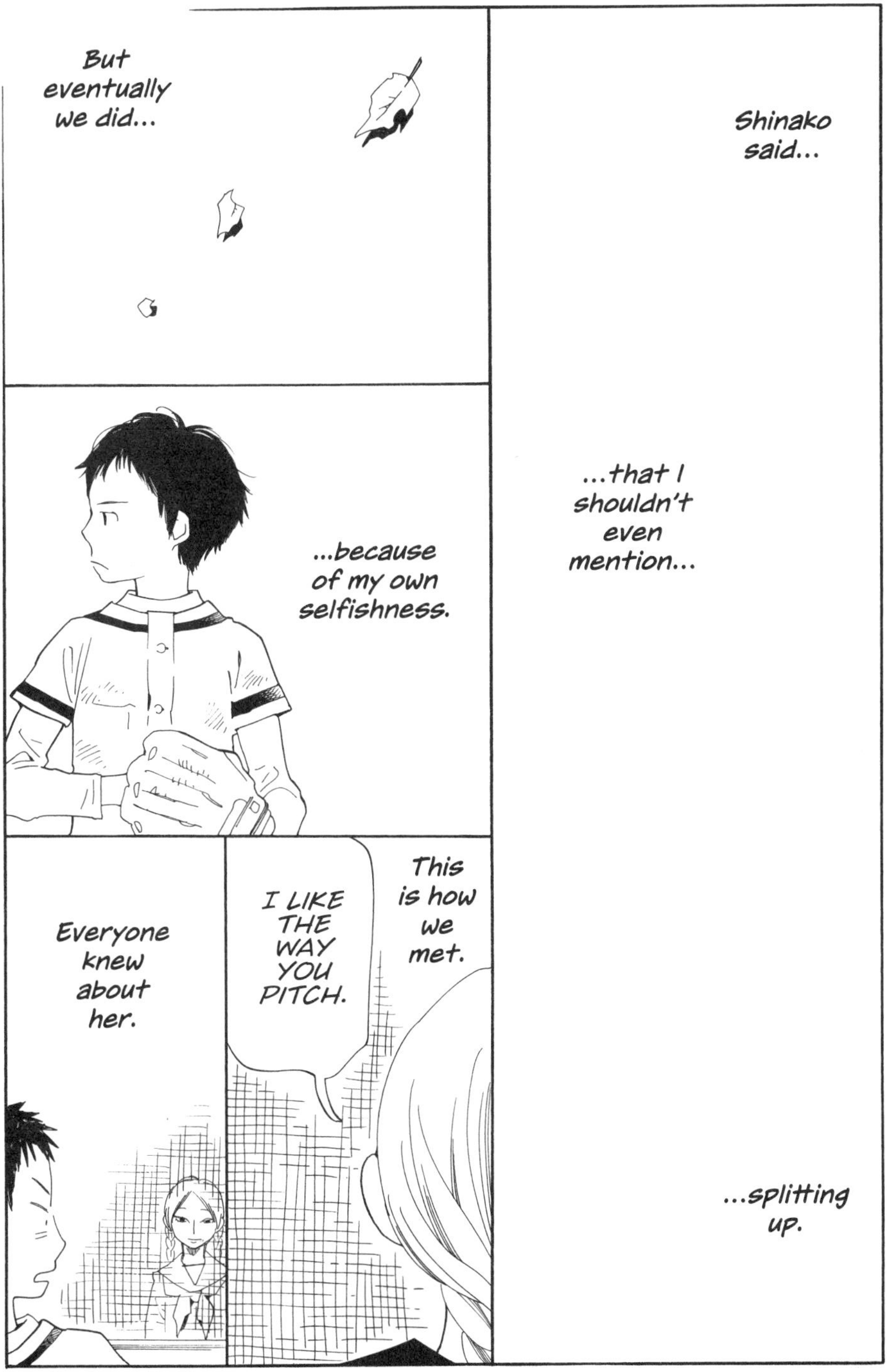
Shinako said...
...that I shouldn't even mention...
...splitting up.
But eventually we did...
...because of my own selfishness.
This is how we met.
I LIKE THE WAY YOU PITCH.
Everyone knew about her.

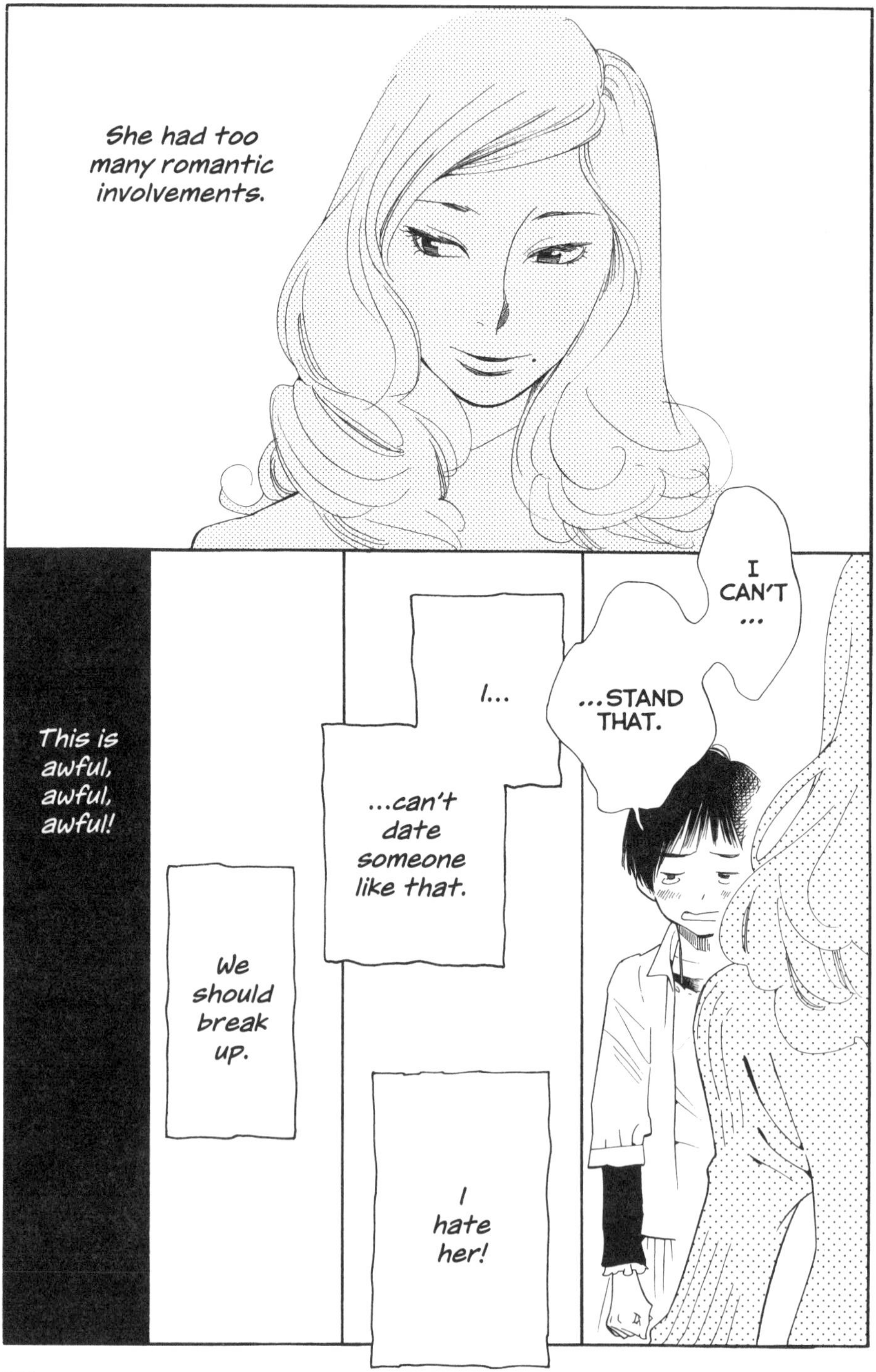
She had too many romantic involvements.
I CAN'T ...
...STAND THAT.
I...
...can't date someone like that.
I hate her!
We should break up.
This is awful, awful, awful!

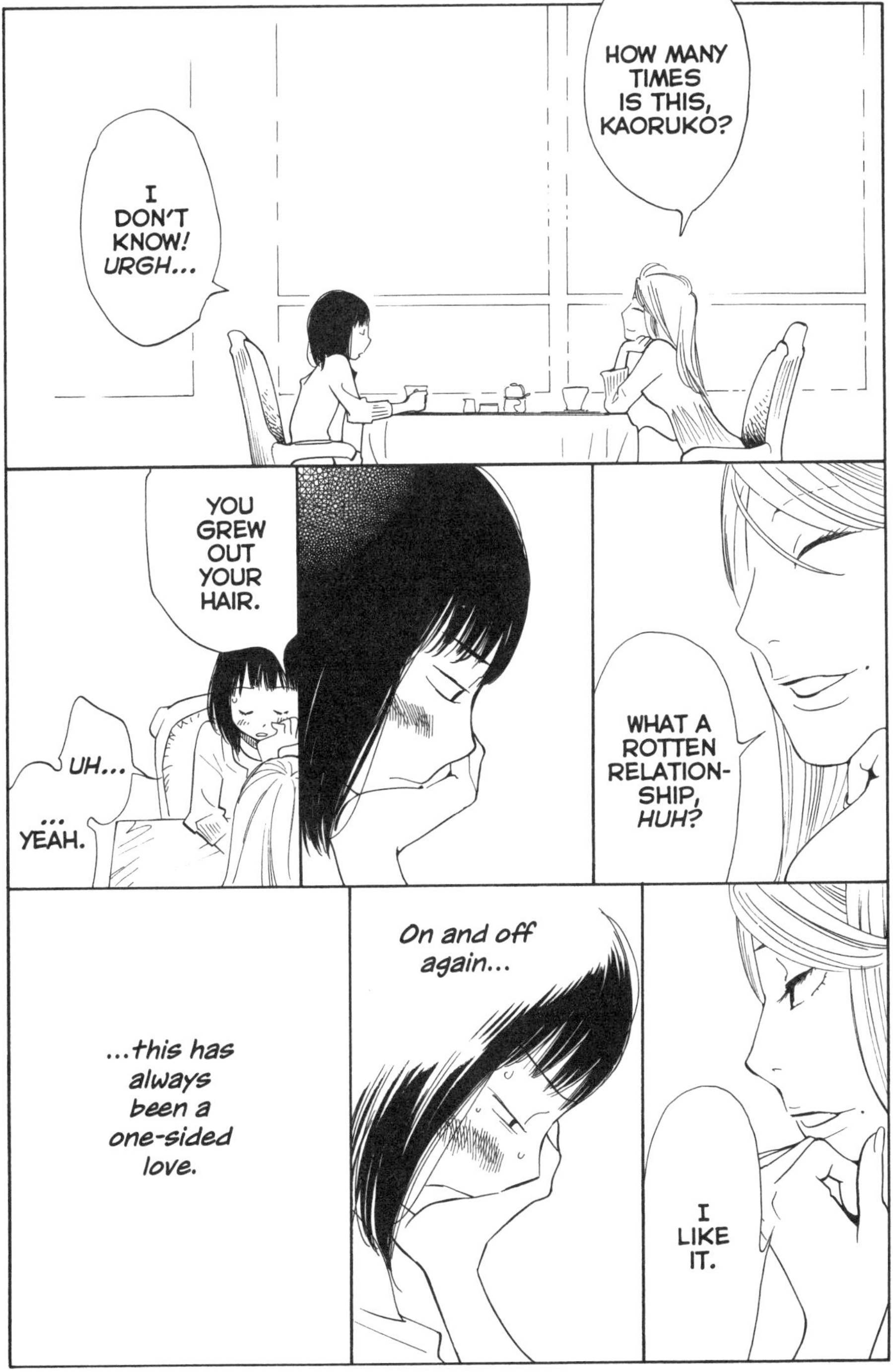
HOW MANY TIMES IS THIS, KAORUKO?
I DON'T KNOW! URGH...
WHAT A ROTTEN RELATION-SHIP, HUH?
YOU GREW OUT YOUR HAIR.
UH...
...YEAH.
I LIKE IT.
On and off again...
...this has always been a one-sided love.

The End

Afterword

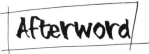

Thank you for reading Sweet Blue Flowers part4. I'm Takako Shimura.

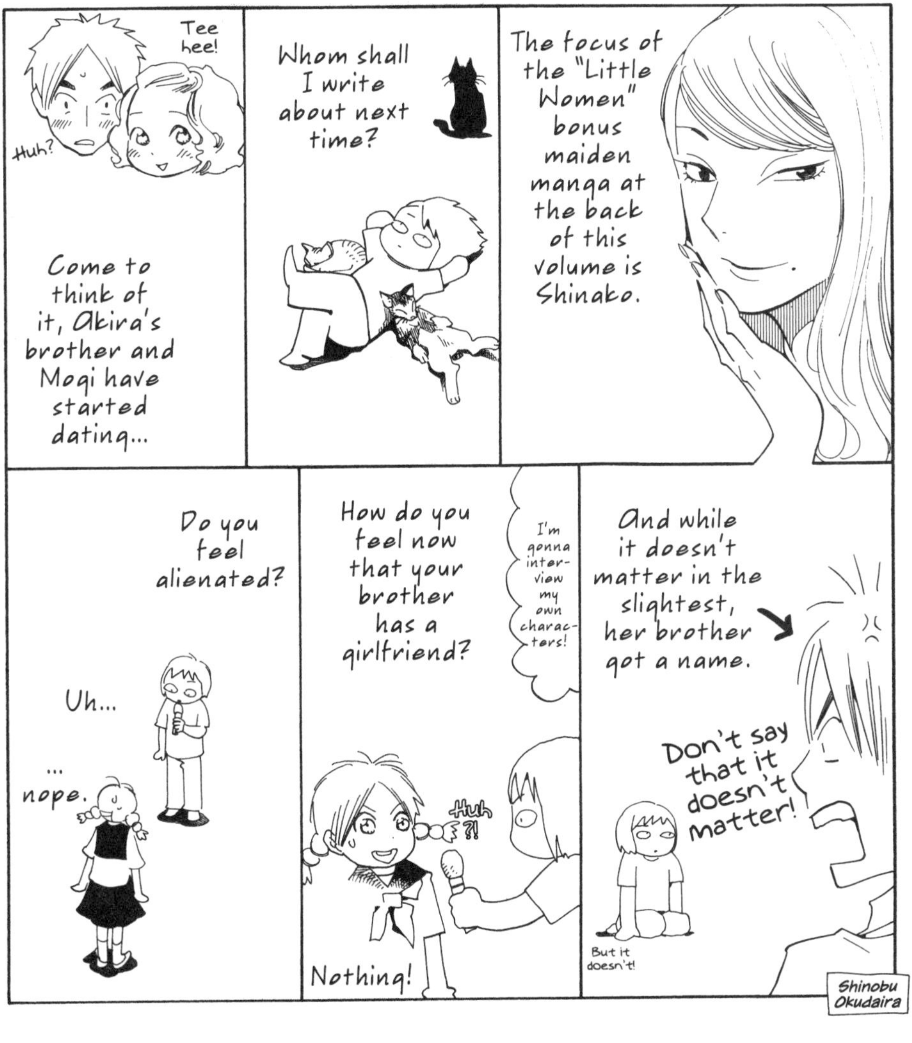

The focus of the "Little Women" bonus maiden manga at the back of this volume is Shinako.
Whom shall I write about next time?
Tee hee!
Huh?
Come to think of it, Akira's brother and Moqi have started dating...
And while it doesn't matter in the slightest, her brother got a name.
Don't say that it doesn't matter!
But it doesn't!
I'm gonna interview my own characters!
How do you feel now that your brother has a girlfriend?
Huh ?!
Nothing!
Do you feel alienated?
Uh...
... nope.
Shinobu Okudaira

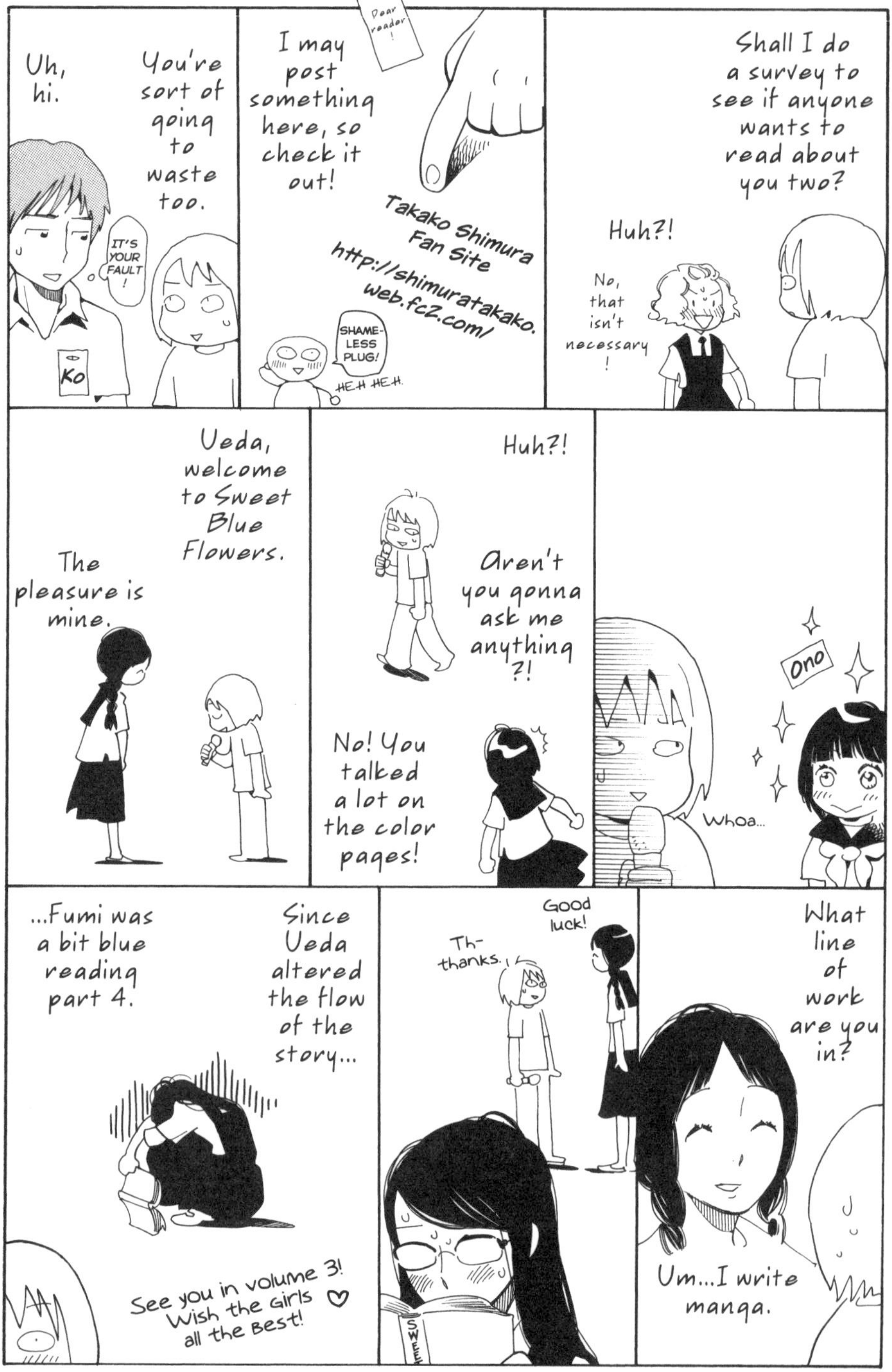
Shall I do a survey to see if anyone wants to read about you two?
Huh?!
No, that isn't necessary!
Dear reader!
I may post something here, so check it out!
Takako Shimura Fan Site
http://shimuratakako.web.fc2.com/
SHAME-LESS PLUG!
HEH HEH.
You're sort of going to waste too.
Uh, hi.
IT'S YOUR FAULT!
KO
Ono
Whoa...
Huh?!
Aren't you gonna ask me anything?!
No! You talked a lot on the color pages!
Ueda, welcome to Sweet Blue Flowers.
The pleasure is mine.
What line of work are you in?
Um...I write manga.
Good luck!
Th-thanks.
Since Ueda altered the flow of the story...
...Fumi was a bit blue reading part 4.
See you in volume 3! Wish the Girls all the Best! ♡

The End

End Notes

Page 33, panel 5: Woman in the Cracks
Known as *Sukima-Onna* (Gap Woman) in Japanese, she is
a figure in various ghost stories who attacks her victims by
appearing out of cracks and other narrow openings.

Page 117, panel 2: Shirasu
Whitebait or immature fish.

Page 183: Place name
There is a bus stop in Gifu Prefecture that uses the same kanji
as Ryoko Ueda but is pronounced differently.

Page 210: Tsujigahana
The title of a movie that refers to a method of fabric dyeing.

Page 229: Rokumeikan
A 1956 play by Yukio Mishima named after the building
commissioned to house foreign guests during the Meiji era.

Page 233, panel 1: Meiji 19
The year 1886.

Page 349, panel 4: Shoe cubby
Every student has a cupboard or box for putting her outdoor
shoes in when entering the building.

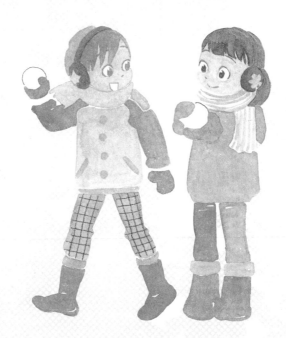

SWEET BLUE FLOWERS
VOL. 2
VIZ Signature Edition

Story & Art by
Takako Shimura

Translation & Adaptation/John Werry
Touch-Up Art & Lettering/Monalisa De Asis
Design/Yukiko Whitley
Editor/Pancha Diaz

AOI HANA
© Takako Shimura 2008, 2009
All rights reserved.
First published in Japan in 2008, 2009 by Ohta Publishing Co., Tokyo
English translation rights arranged with Ohta Publishing Co.
through Tuttle-Mori Agency, Inc., Tokyo

The stories, characters and incidents mentioned in this publication are
entirely fictional.

Printed in Canada

Published by VIZ Media, LLC
P.O. Box 77010
San Francisco, CA 94107

10 9 8 7 6 5 4 3 2 1
First printing, December 2017

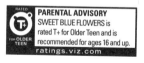
VIZ SIGNATURE
vizsignature.com

viz.com

This is the last page. *Sweet Blue Flowers*
has been printed in the original Japanese
format to preserve the orientation
of the original artwork.

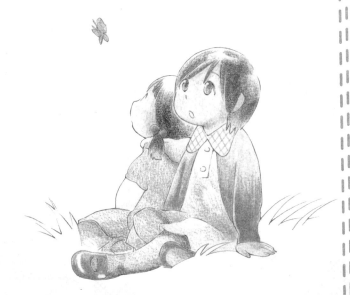